Rwanda

the Bradt Travel Guide

Philip Briggs
with Janice Booth

edition
5

www.bradtguides.cc

Bradt Travel Guides Ltd, UK
The Globe Pequot Press Inc, USA

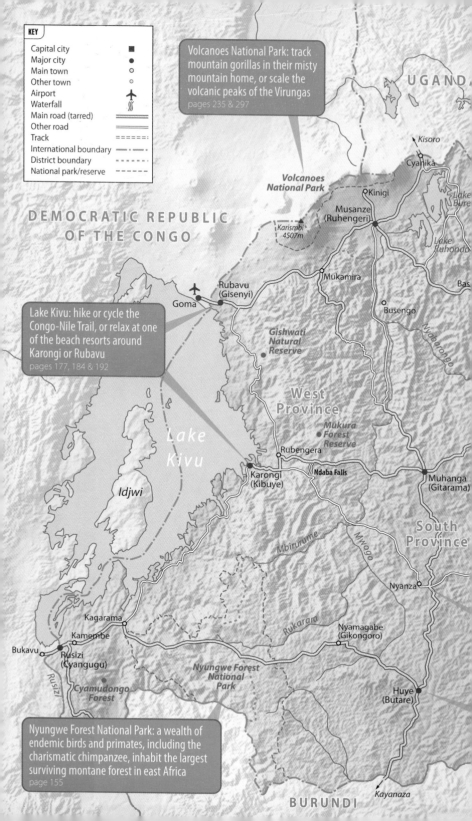

KEY

Capital city	■
Major city	●
Main town	○
Other town	○
Airport	✈
Waterfall	〰
Main road (tarred)	═══
Other road	───
Track	=====
International boundary	─·─·─
District boundary	······
National park/reserve	-----

Volcanoes National Park: track mountain gorillas in their misty mountain home, or scale the volcanic peaks of the Virungas
pages 235 & 297

UGAND

Kisoro

Cyanika

Volcanoes National Park

Kinigi

Musanze (Ruhengeri)

Lake Bure

Lake Ruhondo

Karisimbi 4507m

DEMOCRATIC REPUBLIC OF THE CONGO

Mukamira

Rubavu (Gisenyi)

Goma

Busengo

Bas

Lake Kivu: hike or cycle the Congo-Nile Trail, or relax at one of the beach resorts around Karongi or Rubavu
pages 177, 184 & 192

Gishwati Natural Reserve

Nyabarongo

West Province

Lake Kivu

Mukura Forest Reserve

Idjwi

Rubengera

Ndaba Falls

Muhanga (Gitarama)

Karongi (Kibuye)

Mbirurume

Mwogo

South Province

Nyanza

Rukarara

Kagarama

Kamembe

Nyamagabe (Gikongoro)

Bukavu

Rusizi (Cyangugu)

Rusizi

Cyamudongo Forest

Nyungwe Forest National Park

Huye (Butare)

Nyungwe Forest National Park: a wealth of endemic birds and primates, including the charismatic chimpanzee, inhabit the largest surviving montane forest in east Africa
page 155

Kayanaza

BURUNDI

Kigali Genocide Memorial: this sobering museum and memorial marks the site of one of the largest massacres that took place during the 1994 genocide
page 113

Akagera National Park: Rwanda's only savannah reserve; home to elephant, buffalo, hippo and numerous antelope and bird species
page 273

Ntungamo

Kabale

Nyagatare

Gabiro

Gicumbi
(Byumba)

North
rovince

*East
Province*

Akagera
National
Park

TANZANIA

Lake
Ihema

Gakenke

Kigali

Lake Muhazi

Kayonza

KIGALI

Rwamagana

Kabarondo

Ngoma
(Kibungo)

Cyasemakamba

*East
Province*

Nyamata

Nyabarongo

Akanyaru

Akagera

Nyakarambi

Kirundo

Lake
Rweru

Rusumo

Nyakanazi

TANZANIA

Nyanza: the hilltop Rukali Palace Museum marks the site of the old Mwami's (King's) palace
page 137

National Museum of Rwanda: the top cultural site in Rwanda's second city, Huye, provides a rich insight into traditional cultures
page 148

N

Bradt

0   25km
0   25 miles

Rwanda
Don't
miss...

Gorilla tracking
Tracking mountain gorillas in the Virungas is a peerless wildlife experience, and one of Africa's indisputable travel highlights
(AZ) page 244–51

Arts and handicrafts
Weaving is one of the specialities of Rwanda — baskets, mats and pots are crafted with traditional patterns. Pictured here, a group of women from the Muhanga area
(AZ) page 30

Hiking on dormant volcanoes
Hike through atmospheric hagenia woodland to reach the summit of Mount Bisoke, where you will be rewarded with stunning views of the crater lake
(AZ) page 256

***Intore* dancing**
Dance is as instinctive as music in Rwanda and its roots stretch back through the centuries. Pictured, *Intore* dancers in Ruhengeri
(AZ) pages 29–30

Forest and savanna wildlife
Akagera National Park is home to an abundance of wildlife and retains a genuine off-the-beaten-track character
(AZ) pages 273–89

Rwanda in colour

left   The hike up to the mountain gorilla's preferred habitat of bamboo forest involves a combination of steep slopes, dense vegetation and high altitude
(AZ) pages 235–57

below   The scenery around Lake Burera is enhanced by the outlines of the Virunga Mountains that provided the stunning backdrop to *Gorillas in the Mist*
(AZ) pages 223 & 297–302

right   Often a baby gorilla will put on a chest-beating display as tourists walk past it, safe in the knowledge that they'll accept its dominance (AZ) pages 244–51

below   Consisting of six extinct and three active volcanoes, Volcanoes National Park is home to over half of the world's population of mountain gorilla (AZ) pages 235–57

below right   Staring into the eyes of an adult mountain gorilla (*Gorilla beringei beringei*) is, for most visitors, a deeply humbling experience (SF) pages 244–51

PARC NATIONAL DES VOLCANS

RWANDA

above Running along the Congolese border for 90km, the stunning Lake Kivu has long served as a popular weekend getaway for residents of this otherwise landlocked country (AZ) pages 177–210

left The *amato* is a distinctive boat used on Lake Kivu, comprising three dugouts bound together (AZ) pages 184

below Home to spectacular old colonial buildings, bustling markets and a lakeside beach, Rubavu is the perfect town to explore at your own pace (AZ) page 192–210

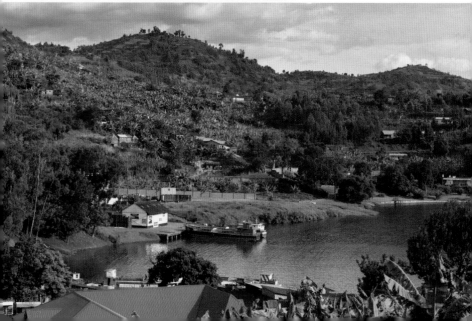

AUTHOR

Philip Briggs has been exploring the highways, byways and backwaters of Africa since 1986, when he spent several months backpacking on a shoestring from Nairobi to Cape Town. In 1991, he wrote the Bradt guide to South Africa, the first such guidebook to be published internationally after the release of Nelson Mandela. Over the rest of the 1990s, Philip wrote a series of pioneering Bradt guides to destinations that were then – and in some cases still are – otherwise practically uncharted by the travel publishing industry. These included the first
dedicated guidebooks to Tanzania, Uganda, Ethiopia, Malawi, Mozambique, Ghana and Rwanda (co-authored with Janice Booth), all now in their 4th–6th editions. More recently, he has written the first guidebook to Somaliland, published in 2012. Philip has visited more than two dozen African countries in total and written about most of them for specialist travel and wildlife magazines, including *Africa Birds & Birding, Africa Geographic, BBC Wildlife, Travel Africa* and *Wanderlust*. He still spends at least four months on the road every year, usually accompanied by his wife, the travel photographer Ariadne Van Zandbergen, and spends the rest of his time battering away at a keyboard in the sleepy village of Bergville, in the uKhahlamba-Drakensberg region of South Africa.

CONTRIBUTORS

Janice Booth's career has included stage management, archaeology, writing, selling haberdashery in Harrods, compiling puzzle magazines, editing Bradt guides and travelling. Since initiating and co-authoring the first edition of this guide she has lectured and written about Rwanda and led tours there. Apart from various sections of boxed text she is responsible for the history sections, from ancient legends to the present day, and talks more about the guide on page VI.

Camilla Gore caught the travel bug in 2006 during a backpacking trip to Sri Lanka and since then she has been travelling whenever possible. She has just returned to the UK following an 18-month UNICEF education placement in Rwanda where, apart from training teachers, she took long motorbike rides through the mountains, climbed volcanoes and danced the night away in Kigali. She enjoys writing her blog, trying to improve her French and getting lost in various European cities. This is her first journey into guidebook writing.

PUBLISHER'S FOREWORD   *Hilary Bradt*

The other day I came across a letter I had published in the *Sunday Times* in 1978. I championed the idea of tourism as a solution to the slaughter of Rwanda's gorillas by poachers. 'Sensibly run, with international help if necessary, the park could offer tourists the wonderful sight of gorillas in the wild.' My visit to the Parc des Volcans in 1977 in quest of gorillas had been met with 'indifference and corruption'.

How much has changed! Now Rwanda not only leads the field in the conservation and appreciation of mountain gorillas, but the whole infrastructure of the country has been transformed. And it is now considered one of the least corrupt in Africa. This remains *the* guidebook to the country and I am happy that it continues in the hands of the original authors whose enthusiasm for Rwanda is shared by all visitors.

Fifth edition December 2012   First published 2001

Bradt Travel Guides Ltd
IDC House, The Vale, Chalfont St Peter, Bucks SL9 9RZ, England
www.bradtguides.com

Printed edition published in the USA by The Globe Pequot Press Inc, PO Box 480, Guilford, Connecticut 06437-0480

Text copyright © 2012 Philip Briggs
Maps copyright © 2012 Bradt Travel Guides Ltd
Illustrations copyright © 2012 Individual photographers
Project Manager: Greg Dickinson

The author and publisher have made every effort to ensure the accuracy of the information in this book at the time of going to press. However, they cannot accept any responsibility for any loss, injury or inconvenience resulting from the use of information contained in this guide.

ISBN-13: 978 1 84162 418 1
e-ISBN: 978 1 84162 744 1 (e-pub)
e-ISBN: 978 1 84162 645 1 (mobi)
British Library Cataloguing in Publication Data
A catalogue record for this book is available from the British Library

Photographs Elspeth Beidas & Matthew Coates (EB/MC); FLPA: Wayne Hutchinson (WH/FLPA), Frans Lanting (FL/FLPA), Cyril Ruoso/Minden Pictures (CR/MP/FLPA); Stuart Forster (SF); Eric Lafforgue (EL); Shutterstock: Goran Bogicevic (GB/S), Willem Tims (WT/S); Ariadne Van Zandbergen (AZ)
Front cover Mountain gorilla (*Gorilla beringei beringei*) (AZ)
Back cover Lake Burera (AZ), *Intore* dancer (EL)
Title page Batwa man (EL), Elephant, Akagera National Park (AZ), Orchid, Gisakura (EB/MC)

Maps David McCutcheon FBCart.S. Colour map relief base by Nick Rowland FGRS

Typeset from the authors' disc by Wakewing, High Wycombe
Production managed by Jellyfish Print Solutions; printed in India

Acknowledgements

PHILIP BRIGGS AND ARIADNE VAN ZANDBERGEN The successful research of this fifth edition is largely thanks to the generous support of the following tourist-related individuals and institutions: Rica Rwigamba and Philibert Ndandali of the RDB; Praveen Moman and Vanessa Townsend of Volcanoes Safaris; Danny Bizimana and Theogene Murekezi of Bizidanny Tours; and Michael Otieno, Jackie Tumuhairwe, Gaelle Munongo and Anna Bah of Rwandair.

For various editorial contributions, updates and fact checking, thanks firstly to Camilla Gore for her sterling work updating the Kigali chapter, and also in no particular order to Stella Martin, Geri Skeens, Cai Tjeenk Willink, Sarah Bendelow, Sarah Hall, Kathryn Nadeau, Devon Kuntzman, Tom Tofield, Phil Vernon, Nick McClure, David Brown, Sam Boarer, Jamila Hamood, Deruta De Ruta, Ali Stanger-Leathes, Eleanor Dunkels, Pauline Quinn, Charlotte Phillips, Wil Resing and the many readers of earlier editions whose updates are posted and acknowledged on our update website, http://updates.bradtguides.com/rwanda.

We remain indebted to the late Florence Nkera, who made sure our introduction to Rwanda in 2000 was such a positive experience, and to co-author Janice Booth for her hard work on earlier editions of this guide and committed 'behind the scenes' involvement in this one.

RWANDA UPDATES WEBSITE AND FEEDBACK REQUEST

For the latest travel news about Rwanda, please visit the new interactive Bradt Rwanda update website: http://updates.bradtguides.com/rwanda.

Administered by *Rwanda* author Philip Briggs, this website will supplement the printed Bradt guidebook, providing a forum whereby the latest travel news can be publicised online with immediate effect.

This update website is a free service for readers of Bradt's *Rwanda* – and for anybody else who cares to drop by and browse – but its success will depend greatly on the input of those selfsame readers, whose collective experience of Rwanda's tourist attractions and facilities will always be broader and more divergent than those of any individual author.

So if you have any comments, queries, grumbles, insights, news or other feedback, you're invited to post them directly on the website, or to email them to Philip at e philari@hixnet.co.za. You can also now 'like' Bradt's *Rwanda* guidebook at www.facebook.com/BradtRwanda.

Contents

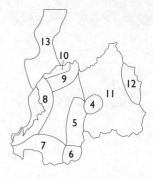

LIST OF MAPS

AUTHOR STORY   *Janice Booth*

This should really be Philip's story, as the guide is now his, but he's allowing me to reminisce a little about how it all started. When I first went to Rwanda, in February 2000, I had no thought whatever of writing a travel guide. I was hoping to track down news of a Rwandan friend and his family; we'd been in touch for many years but since the 1994 genocide his letters had ceased. I assumed he was dead, and didn't expect to enjoy my visit. The media were portraying a grim, damaged, inhospitable place, still volatile and dangerous.

In fact, as I jolted along twisty, pot-holed cross-country roads in battered public transport, I was captivated. Stunningly beautiful landscapes unfolded at every turn. People were still deeply traumatised and grieving, but friendly. I felt completely safe, and even visited the mountain gorillas. From Kigali I faxed Hilary Bradt and convinced her that a guidebook was essential. Luckily Philip was available to co-author it – and you're now holding the fifth edition.

There's no doubt how much it helped Rwanda as the country struggled to recover. Before the genocide, tourism had been an important source of foreign exchange, and regaining this income was vital. The guide's existence reassured travellers and tour operators that the country was now safe and accessible. It was also read by aid workers, diplomats, investors – and even Rwandans, newly arrived from exile abroad.

Tourists came back, in increasing numbers. Each time I or Philip returned to prepare a new edition, we saw more hotels, restaurants, newly surfaced roads and other facilities. Tourism is now the top earner of foreign exchange. But – how much impact has this had on villagers at grass-roots level? Have the 'small people', away from the tourist areas, benefited from this influx of dollars, sterling and euros? Did our guidebook's usefulness extend to them too? To find out, I made a 'study visit' to Rwanda in 2009.

Visiting remote hamlets deep in the green, hilly countryside, I saw the answers to my questions. From the fees paid by tourists visiting the national parks, around 5% is used to finance small-scale development in the surrounding areas: water-tanks, classrooms, bridges, beekeeping, brick-making, market gardening, livestock, and dozens of other practical projects at the heart of rural life. Visitors are thus helping to fund activities they may never see, but which are a life-line for local people beyond the tourist routes. It's exactly the result I had hoped for.

My friend had indeed died in the genocide, as had his wife, child, brother, sister, father, cousins and more. That's how it was in Rwanda then. But I found other members of his family who'd survived and have since rebuilt their lives; they're doing well and we're in regular touch. I'm so proud of their friendship. Their bright, confident children are part of the new, post-genocide generation that will carry Rwanda forward into the future. It is an astonishing – and humbling – country. I feel so privileged to have been involved.

Introduction

Is there any other wildlife encounter to match tracking mountain gorillas through the thin moist air of Rwanda's Virunga Mountains? Ascending first through fertile volcanic slopes dense with cultivation, one crosses the boundary into Volcanoes National Park, to follow a narrow footpath into a hushed montane forest composed of impenetrable bamboo skyscrapers, broadleaved herbaceous shrubs and fragrant hagenia stands. This is nature in the raw: the muddy forest floor scattered with elephant and buffalo spoor while birds and monkeys chatter overhead and spiteful nettles lie waiting in the margins.

Deep in the misty forest, you finally come upon your quarry. It might be a young female attempting to climb a liana, soft black coat comically fluffed-up as it demonstrates the arboreal incompetence of this most sedentary of apes. Or perhaps a barrel-headed silverback, no taller than an average human, but thrice as bulky, delicately shredding a succulent stick of bamboo as it sits peaceably on the forest floor. Or a curious mother, taking two paces forward then raising its head in your direction to stare questioningly into your eyes, as if seeking a connection. Or maybe a young male putting on a chest-beating display for your benefit, safe in the knowledge that this naked ape won't challenge its dominance. No two gorilla encounters can be exactly the same but, as anybody who has looked into the liquid brown eyes of a wild mountain gorilla will confirm, it is always an awesome experience – inspirational, emotional, and profoundly satisfying.

Rwanda is the world's premier gorilla-tracking destination. It was here, on the southern slopes of the Virungas, that the late Dian Fossey studied gorilla behaviour for almost 20 years, and on these very same bamboo-covered slopes that the acclaimed movie *Gorillas in the Mist* was shot in 1988. At that time, Rwanda was entrenched as *the* place to see mountain gorillas, and tourism had become its third main source of foreign revenue. All else being equal, that should have been the start of Rwanda's emergence as a truly great ecotourism destination. Instead, the country was destabilised by a protracted civil war that started in 1990 and four years later reached its horrific climax: the 1994 genocide that claimed the lives of one-eighth of its population, and forced almost twice as many to flee into wretched makeshift refugee camps in Tanzania, Uganda or the Congo.

In the restless eyes of the international mass media, the likes of Rwanda are deemed newsworthy only when disaster strikes. The moment things calm down, cameras and correspondents shift their attention to the next breaking crisis. And so it was that, once the genocide had been quelled by the Rwanda Patriotic Front after barely 100 days, interest faded and the world largely ignored the country as it embarked on its long and arduous road to normalisation – miraculously, a path from which it has barely deviated in 18 years. For a long while, like Uganda after Idi Amin or Ethiopia after the 1985 famine, it remained known to most outsiders only for the genocide. Today, with its energetic programmes of recovery and reconstruction, it is widely considered to be among the most economically buoyant and politically enlightened African countries.

Few could travel through Rwanda and not be cognisant of the terrible events of 1994. Indeed, almost every town and village houses a genocide memorial paying respect to the massacred, whilst also highlighting the survivors' determination that such atrocities should be neither forgotten nor repeated. However, for potential visitors it is more important to dwell on the future and the capacity of tourism to stimulate economic growth and nurture political stability.

Some figures. In 1999, when Volcanoes National Park reopened for gorilla tracking, it attracted fewer than 2,000 visitors, most of them backpacking or on overland trucks making a pit-stop visit from Uganda. By contrast, in 2011 an estimated 666,000 tourists visited Rwanda and tourism is now the country's largest source of foreign revenue, contributing more than US$200 million to the annual GDP and providing direct or indirect employment to over 350,000 people.

So if you've ever dreamed of tracking gorillas on the same misty slopes once trodden by Dian Fossey or Sigourney Weaver, go to Rwanda. And while you're about it, don't forget that there is much to see there besides gorillas. The mountain-ringed inland sea that is Lake Kivu; the immense Nyungwe Forest National Park with its chimpanzees, monkeys and rare birds; the wild savanna of Akagera National Park – and, perhaps above all, the endless succession of steep cultivated mountains that have justifiably earned Rwanda the soubriquets 'Land of a Thousand Hills' and 'The Switzerland of Africa'. It's a wonderful place to visit.

Part One

GENERAL INFORMATION

GEOGRAPHY

Land area 26,340 km^2 (less than half that of Scotland)
Location 120km south of the Equator
Capital Kigali
Rainfall Annual average 900–1,600mm; rainy seasons March–May and October–December
Average temperature 24.6–27.6°C; hottest August and September
Altitude From 1,000 to 4,500m above sea level; highest point is Mt Karisimbi (4,507m)
Terrain Mostly grassy uplands and hills; relief is mountainous with altitude declining from west to east
Vegetation Ranges from dense equatorial forest in the northwest to tropical savanna in the east
Land use 47% cropland, 22% forest, 18% pasture, 13% other
Natural resources Some tin, gold and natural gas
Main exports Coffee and tea
National parks Volcanoes (northwest); Nyungwe (southwest); Akagera (east)

HUMAN STATISTICS

Population 11.7 million (2012 estimate)
Life expectancy at birth 55 years
Religion Roman Catholic (majority), Protestant, Muslim, traditional
Official languages Kinyarwanda, English, French. Swahili is also widely spoken.
Education Primary, secondary, technical/vocational, higher/university
GDP per capita US$1,350 (2011 estimate)

POLITICS/ADMINISTRATION

Government Multi-party democracy dominated by the RPF, which won 93% of the vote in the 2010 presidential election
Ruling Party Rwanda Patriotic Front (RPF)
President Paul Kagame
Prime Minister Pierre Habumuremyi
National flag Blue, yellow and green, with a sun in the top right-hand corner
Administrative divisions 4 *intara* (provinces) plus Kigali City, subdivided into 30 *uturere* (districts; singular *akarere*) and 416 *imirenge* (sectors, singular *umurenge*)

PRACTICAL DETAILS

Time GMT + 2 hours
Currency Rwandan franc
Main health risk Malaria
Electricity 230/240 volts at 50Hz
International telephone country code 250
Airport Kigali International Airport
Nearest seaports Mombasa (1,760km); Dar es Salaam (1,528km)

1

Background Information

Rwanda is a land-locked country in Central Africa. Also known as the 'Land of a Thousand Hills', Rwanda has five volcanoes, 23 lakes and numerous rivers. The country lies 1,270km west of the Indian Ocean and 2,000km east of the Atlantic – literally in the heart of Africa.

GEOGRAPHY

Rwanda's mountainous topography is a product of its position on the eastern rim of the Albertine Rift Valley, a western arm of the Great Rift Valley which cuts through Africa from the Red Sea to Mozambique. The country's largest freshwater body, Lake Kivu, which forms the border with the Democratic Republic of the Congo (DRC), is effectively a large sump hemmed in by the Rift Valley walls, while its highest peaks – in the volcanic Virunga chain – are geologically modern (and in some cases still active) products of the same tectonic process that started forming the Rift Valley 20 million years ago. The Rift Valley escarpment running through western Rwanda also serves as a watershed between Africa's two largest drainage systems: the Nile and the Congo.

Western and central Rwanda are characterised by a seemingly endless vista of steep mountains, interspersed with several substantial lakes whose irregular shape follows the mountains that surround them. Much of this part of the country lies at elevations of between 1,500 and 2,500m. Only in the far east of the country, along the Tanzania border, do the steep mountains give way to the lower-lying, flatter terrain of the Lake Victoria Basin. The dominant geographical feature of this part of the country is the Kagera River and associated network of swamps and small lakes running along the Tanzania border, eventually to flow into Lake Victoria, making it the most remote source of the world's longest river, the Nile (see box *The Riddle of The Nile*, pages 4–5). Much of this ecosystem is protected within Akagera National Park.

NATURAL HISTORY AND CONSERVATION

VEGETATION In prehistoric times, as much as a third of what is now Rwanda was covered in montane rainforest, with the remainder of the highlands supporting open grassland. Since the advent of Iron-Age technology and agriculture some 2,000 years ago, much of Rwanda's natural vegetation has been replaced by agriculture, a process that has accelerated dramatically in the last 100 years. The only large stand of forest left in Rwanda today is Nyungwe, in the southwest, though several other small relic forest patches are dotted around the country, notably Gishwati and Mukura Forests. Patches of true forest still occur on the Virungas, though most of the natural vegetation on this range consists of bamboo forest and open moorland.

The first European to see Lake Victoria was John Hanning Speke, who marched from Tabora to the site of present-day Mwanza in 1858 following his joint 'discovery' of Lake Tanganyika with Richard Burton the previous year. Speke named the lake for Queen Victoria, but prior to that Arab slave traders called it Ukerewe (still the name of its largest island). It is unclear what name was in local use, since the only one used by Speke is Nyanza, which simply means lake.

A major goal of the Burton-Speke expedition had been to solve the great geographical enigma of the age, the source of the White Nile. Speke, based on his brief glimpse of the southeast corner of Lake Victoria, somewhat whimsically proclaimed his 'discovery' to be the answer to that riddle. Burton, with a comparable lack of compelling evidence, was convinced that the great river flowed out of Lake Tanganyika. The dispute between the former travelling companions erupted bitterly on their return to Britain, where Burton – the more persuasive writer and respected traveller – gained the backing of the scientific establishment.

Over 1862–3, Speke and Captain James Grant returned to Lake Victoria, hoping to prove Speke's theory correct. They looped inland around the western shore of the lake, arriving at the court of King Mutesa of Buganda, then continued east to the site of present-day Jinja, where a substantial river flowed out of the lake after tumbling over a cataract that Speke named Ripon Falls. From here, the two explorers headed north, sporadically crossing paths with the river until they reached Lake Albert, then following the Nile to Khartoum and Cairo. Speke's declaration that 'The Nile is settled' met with mixed support back home. Burton and other sceptics pointed out that Speke had bypassed the entire western shore of his purported great lake, had visited only a couple of points on the northern shore, and had not attempted to explore the east. Nor, for that matter, had he followed the course of the Nile in its entirety. Speke, claimed his detractors, had seen several different lakes and different stretches of river, connected only in his own deluded mind. The sceptics had a point, but Speke had nevertheless gathered sufficient geographical evidence to render his claim highly plausible. His notion of one great lake, far from being mere whimsy, was backed by anecdotal information gathered from local sources along the way.

Matters were scheduled to reach a head on 16 September 1864, when an eagerly awaited debate between Burton and Speke – in the words of the former, 'what silly tongues called the "Nile Duel"' – was due to take place at the Royal Geographic Society (RGS). And reach a head they did, but in circumstances more tragic than anybody could have anticipated. On the afternoon of the debate, Speke went out shooting with a cousin, only to stumble while crossing a wall and in the process discharging a barrel of his shotgun into his heart. The subsequent inquest recorded a verdict of accidental death, but it has often been suggested – purely on the basis of the curious timing – that Speke deliberately took his life rather than face up to Burton in public. Burton, who had seen Speke less than three hours earlier, was by all accounts deeply troubled by Speke's death, and years later he was quoted as stating 'the uncharitable [say] that I shot him' – an accusation that seems to have been aired only in Burton's imagination.

Speke was dead, but the 'Nile debate' would keep kicking for several years. In 1864, Sir Stanley and Lady Baker became the first Europeans to reach Lake Albert and nearby Murchison Falls in present-day Uganda. The Bakers, much to the delight of the anti-Speke lobby, were convinced that this newly named lake was a source of the Nile, though they openly admitted it might not be the only one. Following the Bakers' announcement, Burton put forward a revised theory, namely that the most remote source of the Nile was the Rusizi River, which he believed flowed out of the northern head of Lake Tanganyika and emptied into Lake Albert.

In 1865, the RGS followed up on Burton's theory by sending Dr David Livingstone to Lake Tanganyika. Livingstone, however, was of the opinion that the Nile's source lay further south than Burton supposed, and so he struck out towards the lake along a previously unexplored route. Leaving from Mikindani in the far south of present-day Tanzania, Livingstone followed the Rovuma River inland, continuing westward to the southern tip of Lake Tanganyika. From there, he ranged southward into present-day Zambia, where he came across a new candidate for the source of the Nile: the swampy Lake Bangweulu and its major outlet the Lualaba River. It was only after his famous meeting with Henry Stanley at Ujiji, in November 1871, that Livingstone (in the company of Stanley) visited the north of Lake Tanganyika and Burton's cherished Rusizi River, which, it transpired, flowed into the lake. Burton, nevertheless, still regarded Lake Tanganyika as the most likely source of the Nile, while Livingstone was convinced that the answer lay with the Lualaba River. In August 1872, Livingstone headed back to the Lake Bangweulu region, where he fell ill and died six months later, the great question still unanswered.

In August 1874, ten years after Speke's death, Stanley embarked on a three-year expedition every bit as remarkable and arduous as those undertaken by his predecessors, yet one whose significance is often overlooked. Partly, this is because Stanley cuts such an unsympathetic figure, the grim caricature of the murderous pre-colonial White Man blasting and blustering his way through territories where Burton, Speke and Livingstone had relied largely on diplomacy. It is also the case, however, that Stanley set out with no intention of seeking headline-making fresh discoveries. Instead, he determined to test methodically the theories advocated by Speke, Burton and Livingstone about the Nile's source. First, Stanley sailed around the circumference of Lake Victoria, establishing that it was indeed as vast as Speke had claimed (and, incidentally, crossing the so-called 'Alexandra Nile' (Kagera River) into what is now Akagera National Park, where he camped on the shore of Lake Ihema). Stanley's next step was to circumnavigate Lake Tanganyika, which, contrary to Burton's long-held theories, clearly boasted no outlet sufficiently large to be the source of the Nile. Finally, and most remarkably, Stanley took a boat along Livingstone's Lualaba River to its confluence with an even larger river, which he followed for months with no idea as to where he might end up.

When, exactly 999 days after he left Zanzibar, Stanley emerged at the Congo mouth, the shortlist of plausible theories relating to the source of the Nile had been reduced to one. Clearly, the Nile did flow out of Lake Victoria at Ripon Falls, before entering and exiting Lake Albert at its northern tip to start its long course through the sands of the Sahara. Stanley's achievement in putting to rest decades of speculation about how the main rivers and lakes of East Africa linked together is estimable indeed. He was nevertheless generous enough to concede that: 'Speke now has the full glory of having discovered the largest inland sea on the continent of Africa, also its principal affluent as well as its outlet. I must also give him credit for having understood the geography of the countries we travelled through far better than any of us who so persistently opposed his hypothesis'.

Outside of Nyungwe (now designated a national park) and the Virungas, practically no montane grassland is left in Rwanda; the highlands are instead dominated by the terraced agriculture that gives the Rwandan countryside much of its distinctive character. The far east of Rwanda supports an altogether different vegetation: the characteristic African 'bush', a mosaic of savanna woodland and grassland dominated by thorny acacia trees.

FAUNA Rwanda naturally supports a widely varied fauna, but the rapid human population growth in recent decades, with its by-products of habitat loss and poaching, has resulted in the extirpation of most large mammal species outside of a few designated conservation areas. Rwanda today has three national parks - Volcanoes, Akagera and Nyungwe - along with a few smaller forest reserves (of which Gishwati is earmarked for future national park status). Each of the three established national parks protects a very different ecosystem and combination of large mammals, for which reason greater detail on the fauna of each reserve is given under the appropriate regional section. Broadly speaking, however, Akagera supports a typical savanna fauna dominated by a variety of antelope, other grazers such as zebra, buffalo and giraffe, the aquatic hippopotamus, and plains predators such as lion, leopard and spotted hyena.

Nyungwe and Volcanoes national parks probably supported a similar range of large mammals 500 years ago. Today, however, their faunas differ greatly, mostly as a result of extensive deforestation on the lower slopes of the Virungas. The volcanoes today support bamboo specialists such as golden monkey and mountain gorilla, as well as relict populations of habitat-tolerant species such as buffalo and elephant. The latter two species are extinct in Nyungwe (buffalo were hunted out 25 years ago, while no elephant spoor has been detected since the last known carcass was found in late 1999), but this vast forest still supports one of Africa's richest varieties of forest specialists, ranging from 13 types of primate to golden cat, duiker and giant forest hog. Despite the retreat of most large mammals into reserves, Rwanda remains a rewarding destination for game viewing: the Volcanoes Park is the best place in the world to track mountain gorillas, while Nyungwe offers visitors a good chance of seeing chimpanzees and 400-strong troops of Angola colobus monkeys – the largest arboreal primate troops in Africa today.

Rwanda is a wonderful destination for birdwatchers, with an incredible 700 species recorded in an area smaller than Belgium and half the size of Scotland. Greater detail is supplied in regional chapters, but prime birdwatching destinations include Nyungwe (310 species including numerous forest rarities and 27 Albertine Rift endemics) and Akagera (480 species of savanna bird, raptor and water bird). Almost anywhere in the country can, however, prove rewarding to birders: an hour in the garden of one of the capital's larger hotels is likely to throw up a variety of colourful robin-chats, weavers, finches, flycatchers and sunbirds.

HISTORY

EARLIEST TIMES Even back in the **ice age**, Rwanda was showing its typically green and fertile face; a part of the Nyungwe Forest remained uncovered by ice, so that animal and plant life could survive there. Excavations undertaken from the 1940s onwards identified several **early Iron-Age** sites in Rwanda and neighbouring Burundi, yielding fragments of typical 'dimpled' pottery (see *Africa in the Iron Age*, Roland Oliver & Brian M Fagan, Cambridge University Press, 1975). At Nyirankuba in what is now South Province, a site of **late Stone-Age** occupation (without pottery) underlay a later occupation level containing both pottery and iron slag. Iron-smelting furnaces at two other sites in southern Rwanda (Ndora and Cyamakusa) gave radio-carbon datings of around AD200–300. Oliver & Fagan describe these furnaces as being some 5ft in diameter, built of wedge-shaped bricks. Other sites in the area of Rwanda, Burundi and Kivu show late Stone-Age occupation sites underlying early Iron-Age occupation. The early Iron-Age pottery was later succeeded by a different and coarser type, apparently made by newcomers from the north who were cattle raisers – but archaeological investigation in Rwanda has been sparse, and there must be much still awaiting discovery. Some artefacts are displayed in the National Museum in Huye (formerly named Butare).

Rwanda's earliest inhabitants were pygmoid **hunter-gatherers**, ancestors of the *Twa* (the name means, roughly, 'indigenous hunter-gatherers'), who still form part of the population today and are still known for their skill as potters. Gradually – the dates are uncertain, but probably before about 700BC – they were joined by Bantu-speaking **farmers**, who were spreading throughout Central Africa seeking good land on which to settle. Fertile Rwanda was a promising site. The arrival of these incomers, known as *Hutus*, was bad news for the Twa; now a minority, they saw some of their traditional hunting grounds cleared to make way for farming, and retreated further into the forests. Then Iron-Age technology developed tools – such as hoes – which enabled the farmers to grow more crops than were needed for subsistence and thus to trade.

Next came the **cattle raisers**, taller and lankier people than either the pygmoid Twa or the sturdy farmers, who may have come from either the north or the northeast. With only oral tradition to guide us, there's no hard historic evidence for the timing of their arrival – some say before the 10th century AD, others after the 14th. Gradually, whether by conquest or by natural assimilation, a hierarchy emerged in which the cattle raisers (known as *Tutsis*, meaning 'owners of cattle') were superior to the farmers and a master–client relationship known as *ubuhake* developed. Then most of Rwanda was a monarchy ruled by a Tutsi king or *Mwami* – although there remained outlying areas where the farming groups did not accept his authority.

Note The three groups are more correctly called Batwa, Bahutu and Batutsi, while individuals are a Mutwa, a Muhutu and a Mututsi. However, we have opted for the forms Twa, Hutu and Tutsi because outside Rwanda they are commonly used. The plural of Mwami (sometimes spelt Mwaami) is Bami. The language spoken by all three groups is Kinyarwanda.

THE KINGDOMS OF RWANDA Rwanda has a rich oral history, which was maintained primarily by members of the Rwandan royal court. According to this history the founder of Rwanda's ruling dynasty, Abanyiginya, was not born naturally like other humans, but was born from an earthenware jar of milk. The grandmother of Rwandans lived in heaven with Nkuba (thunder) who was given the secret of creating life. He made a small man out of clay, coated him with his saliva, and placed him in a wooden jar filled with milk and the heart of a slaughtered bull. The jar was constantly refilled with fresh milk. At the end of nine months the man took on the image of Sabizeze. When Sabizeze learned of his origin, he was angry that his mother had revealed the secret and decided to leave heaven and come to earth. He brought with him his sister Nyampundu, his brother Mututsi, and a couple of Batwa. Sabizeze was welcomed by Kabeja who was of the Abazigaba clan and king of the region (in the present-day Akagera National Park). Sabizeze then had a son named Gihanga who was to found the Kingdom of Rwanda. A Rwandan historian,

Alexis Kagame, estimates that Gihanga ruled as King of Rwanda in the late 10th or early 11th century.

Before the arrival of Europeans, Rwandans believed they were the centre of the world, with the grandest monarchy, the greatest power and the highest civilisation. Their king or mwami was the supreme authority and was magically identified with Rwanda. There was a strong belief that if the ruling monarch was not the true king, the people of Rwanda would be in danger. The well-being of Rwanda was directly linked to the health of the king. When he grew old, Rwanda's prosperity was compromised. Only when the ageing ruler died and a new, stronger king was enthroned did the country re-stabilise.

The centralised control by the king was balanced by a very powerful queen mother and a group of dynastic ritualists: the *abiiru*. Queen mothers could never come from the same family clan as the king and rotated among four different family clans. The abiiru, who were also drawn from four different clans, could reverse the king's decisions if they conflicted with the magical Esoteric Code, protected and interpreted by the abiiru. They also governed the selection and installation of a new king. Any member of the abiiru who forgot any part of his assigned portion of the Esoteric Code was punished severely. Members of the abiiru and other custodians of state secrets who revealed the secrets of the royal court were forced to drink *igihango*, a mixture containing a magical power to kill traitors or anyone who failed in his duty. While the king could order the death of a disloyal member of the abiiru, he was required to replace the traitor with a member from the same family clan.

Rwanda's dynastic drums, which could be made only by members of one family clan from very specific trees with magical elements, had the same dignity as the king. The genitals of the enemies of Rwanda killed by the king hung from the drum. The capture of a dynastic drum from an enemy country normally signified annexation, with the group whose drum was stolen losing all faith in itself. This tradition is shared among all Bantu-speaking peoples in Africa. When Rwanda's royal drum Rwoga was lost to a neighbouring kingdom by King Ndahiro II Cyaamatare in the late 15th century, Rwanda was devastated. Rwoga was eventually replaced by Karinga, the last dynastic drum, when King Ruganzu II Ndori regained Rwanda's pride through his military exploits. The fate of Karinga is unknown. It is reported to have survived the colonial period, but disappeared soon after Rwanda's independence.

The origin of the division between Tutsis and Hutus is still being debated, but oral history portrays a feudal society with one group, the Tutsis or cattle herders, occupying a superior status within the social and political structure, and the other group, the Hutus or peasant farmers, serving as the serfs or clients of a Tutsi chief. The hunter-gatherer Twa were potters and had various functions at the royal court – for example, as dancers and music makers.

The complex system known as *ubuhake* provided for protection by the superior partner in exchange for services from the inferior: ubuhake agreements were made either between two Tutsis, or between a Tutsi and a Hutu. While ubuhake was a voluntary and revocable private contract between two individuals, with subjects able to switch loyalty from one chief to another, a peasant could not easily survive without a patron. Cattle could be acquired through ubuhake as well as by purchase, fighting in a war, or marriage. A Hutu who acquired enough cattle could thus become a Tutsi and might take a Tutsi wife, while a Tutsi who lost his herds or otherwise fell on hard times might become a Hutu and marry accordingly. A patron had no authority over a client who had gained cattle, whether Hutu, Tutsi or Twa. Whereas Hutus and Tutsis could and did sometimes switch status, a Twa seldom became a Tutsi or Hutu. In the rare instances when this did occur, it would be because the king rewarded a Twa for some act of bravery by granting him the status of a Tutsi. He would then be given a Tutsi wife and a political post within the royal court. Meanwhile the three groups spoke the same language (Kinyarwanda, a language in the Bantu group), lived within the same culture and shared the same recent history.

Rwandan nobles were experts in cattle breeding and an entire category of poetry was devoted to the praises of famous cows. Cattle were bred for their beauty, rather than utility. Between AD1000 and 1450, herders in the Great Lakes region invented no fewer than 19 words for the colourful patterns of their animals' hides. As elsewhere in Africa, cattle were closely associated with wealth and status.

AD1000–1894 Whatever the exact timespan may have been, Rwanda (or the larger part of it) was ruled over by a sequence of Tutsi monarchs, each with his various political skirmishes, battles and conquests. Oral tradition shows us a colourful bunch of characters: for example, Ndahiro II Cyaamatare who catastrophically lost the royal drum; Mibambwe II who organised a system of milk distribution to the poor, ordering his chiefs to provide jugs of milk three times a day; and Yuhi III Mazimpaka, the only king to compose poetry – and to go mad. From the 17th century onwards the rulers seem to have become more organised and ambitious, using their armies to subjugate fringe areas. The royal palace was by then at Nyanza – and can still be seen, carefully reconstructed, today.

The Mwami was an absolute monarch, deeply revered and seen to embody Rwanda physically. The hierarchy beneath him was complex and tight-knit, with different categories of chief in charge of different aspects of administration. His power covered most of Rwanda, although some Hutu enclaves in the north, northwest and southwest of the country clung to their independence until the 20th century. The country was divided into a pyramid of administrative areas: in ascending order of size, from base to apex, these were the immediate neighbourhood, the hill, the district and the province. (These are echoed in today's administrative pyramid of Commune, Sector, District and Province.) And through this intricate structure ran the practice and spirit of ubuhake, the master–client relationship in which an inferior receives help and protection in return for services and allegiance to a superior.

Beneath the mwami, power was exercised by various chiefs, each with specific responsibilities: *land chiefs* (responsible for land allocation, agriculture and agricultural taxation), *cattle chiefs* (stock-raising and associated taxes), *army chiefs* (security) and so on. While Hutus might take charge at neighbourhood level, most of the power at higher administrative levels was in the hands of Tutsis.

Since our only source of information about these early days is oral tradition, which by its nature favours the holders of power, we cannot be certain to what extent the power structure was accepted by those lower down the ladder, to what extent they resented it and to what extent they were exploited by it. But, whether harsh, benevolent or exploitative (or possibly all three), it survived, and is what the Europeans found when they entered this previously unknown country.

Rwanda had remained untouched by events unfolding elsewhere in Africa. Tucked away in the centre of the continent, the tiny kingdom was ignored by slave traders; consequently Rwanda is one of the few African countries that never sold its people, or its enemies, into slavery. There is no record of Arab traders or Asian merchants, numerous in other parts of East and Central Africa, having penetrated its borders, with the result that no written language was introduced and oral tradition remained the norm until the very end of the 19th century.

THE DISCOVERY OF THE MOUNTAIN GORILLA

The mountain gorilla was first discovered on 17 October 1902, on the ridges of the Virunga Mountains, by German explorer Captain Robert von Beringe, then aged 37. Captain von Beringe, together with a physician, Dr Engeland, Corporal Ehrhardt, 20 Askaris, a machine gun and necessary porters set off from Usumbura on August 19 1902 to visit the Sultan Msinga of Rwanda and then proceed north to reach a 'row of volcanoes'. The purpose of the trip was to visit the German outposts in what was then German East Africa in order to keep in touch with local chiefs and to confirm good relations, while strengthening the influence and power of the German Government in these regions. On arriving at the volcanoes, an attempt was made to climb Mount Sabinyo.

Captain von Beringe's report of the expedition (below) is adapted from *In the Heart of Africa* by Duke Adolphus Frederick of Mecklenburg (Cassell, 1910).

From October 16th to 18th, senior physician Dr. Engeland and I together with only a few Askaris and the absolutely necessary baggage attempted to climb the so far unknown Kirunga ya Sabyinyo which, according to my estimation, must have a height of 3,300 metres. At the end of the first day we camped on a plateau at a height of 2,500 metres; the natives climbed up to our campsite to generously supply us with food. We left our camp on October 17th taking with us a tent, eight loads of water, five Askaris and porters as necessary.

After four and a half hours of tracking we reached a height of 3,100 metres and tracked through bamboo forest; although using elephant trails for most of the way, we encountered much undergrowth which had to be cut before we could pass... After two hours we reached a stony area with vegetation consisting mainly of blackberry and blueberry bushes. Step by step we noticed the vegetation becoming poorer and poorer, the ascent became steeper and steeper, and climbing became more difficult – for the last one and a quarter hours we climbed only over rock. After covering the ground with moss we collected, we erected our tent on a ridge at a height of 3,100 metres. The ridge was extremely narrow so that the pegs of the tent had to be secured in the abyss. The Askaris and the porters found shelter in rock caverns, which provided protection against the biting cold wind.

From our campsite we were able to watch a herd of big, black monkeys which tried to climb the crest of the volcano. We succeeded in killing two of these animals, and with a rumbling noise of falling rocks they tumbled into a ravine, which had its opening in a north-easterly direction. After five hours of strenuous work we succeeded in retrieving one of these animals using a rope. It was a big, human-like male monkey of one and a half metres in height and a weight of more than 200 pounds. His chest had no hair, and his hands and feet were of enormous size. Unfortunately I was unable to determine its type; because of its size, it could not very well be a chimpanzee or a gorilla, and in any case the presence of gorillas had not been established in the area around the lakes.

On the journey back to Usumbura, the skin and one of the hands of the animal that von Beringe collected were taken by a hyena but the rest (including the skull) finally reached the Zoological Museum in Berlin. It was classified as a new form of gorilla and named *Gorilla beringei* in honour of the Captain. Later it was considered to be a subspecies and renamed *Gorilla gorilla beringei*.

The Kingdom of Rwanda was isolationist and closed to foreigners (also to many Africans) until the 1890s. The famous American explorer, Henry Stanley, attempted to enter several times and did penetrate as far as Lake Ihema in 1874, but was then forced to retreat under arrow attack. Trade with neighbouring countries was extremely limited and Rwanda had no monetary system.

GERMAN EAST AFRICA Unlike most African states, Rwanda and Burundi were not given artificial borders by their colonisers – they had both been established kingdoms for many centuries. At the Berlin Conference of 1885, they – under the name of Ruanda-Urundi – were assigned to Germany as a part of German East Africa, although at that stage no European had officially set foot there. The first to do so formally was the German Count Gustav Adolf von Götzen on May 4 1894 (an Austrian, Oscar Baumann, had previously entered privately from Burundi in 1892 and spent several days in the south of the country). Von Götzen entered Rwanda by the Rusumo Falls in the southeast and crossed the country to reach the eastern shore of Lake Kivu. En route he stopped off at Nyanza where he met the mwami, King Rwabugiri – apparently causing consternation among the watching nobles when he, a mere mortal, shook the sovereign by the hand. They feared that such an affront might cause disaster for the kingdom. At this stage the mwami had no idea that his country had officially been under German control for the past nine years.

Von Götzen subsequently became Governor of German East Africa, into which Ruanda-Urundi was formally absorbed in 1898; the same year that the mountain gorilla was first recorded by a European (see box opposite). At this time the kingdom was larger, stretching as far as Lake Edward in the north and beyond Lake Kivu in the west; it was reduced to its present area at the Conference of Brussels in 1910.

The Germans were surprised to find that their new colony was a highly organised country, with tight, effective power structures and administrative divisions. They left these in place and ruled through them, believing that support for the traditional chiefs would render them and their henchmen loyal to Germany. Meanwhile various religious missions, Roman Catholic at first and then Protestant, began setting up bases in Ruanda-Urundi and establishing schools, farms and medical centres. In 1907 the colonisers opened a 'School for the Sons of Chiefs' in Nyanza, as well as providing military training.

Allowing for the blurring caused by intermarriage and the switching of status between Tutsi and Hutu, the power structures encountered by the colonisers were linked – and this proved to be a matter of great anthropological fascination – to three very visibly different groups of inhabitants: the tall, lanky Tutsi chiefs and nobles; the shorter, stockier Hutu farmers (who formed the majority); and the very much smaller Twa. The Duke of Mecklenburg, visiting the country in 1907, noted:

> The population is divided into three classes – the Watussi, the Wahutu, and a pygmy tribe, the Batwa, who dwell chiefly in the bamboo forests of Bugoie, the swamps of Lake Bolero, and on the island of Kwidschwi on Lake Kiwu.
>
> The Watussi are a tall, well-made people. Heights of 1.80, 2.00 and even 2.20 metres are of quite common occurrence, yet the perfect proportion of their bodies is in no wise detracted from… The primitive inhabitants are the Wahutu, an agricultural Bantu tribe, who look after the digging and tilling and agricultural economy of the country in general. They are a medium-sized type of people…Ruanda is certainly the most interesting country in the German East African Protectorate – in fact in all Central Africa – chiefly on account of its ethnographical and geographical position. Its interest is further increased by the fact that it is one of the last negro kingdoms

governed autocratically by a sovereign sultan, for German supremacy is only recognised to a very limited extent. Added to this, it is a land flowing with milk and honey, where the breeding of cattle and bee-culture flourish, and the cultivated soil bears rich crops of fruit. A hilly country, thickly populated, full of beautiful scenery, and possessing a climate incomparably fresh and healthy; a land of great fertility, with watercourses which might be termed perennial streams; a land which offers the brightest of prospects to the white settler.

In 1911–12 the Germans joined with the Tutsi monarchy to subjugate some independent Hutu principalities in the north of the country which had not previously been dominated. Their inhabitants, who had always been proud of their independence, resisted vigorously, overrunning much of what is now Northern Province before they were defeated and brought under the mwami's control. Their resentment and deep sense of grievance were to endure for the next half-century.

Germany had little time to make its mark in the colonies; in 1916 Belgium invaded Ruanda-Urundi and occupied the territories until the end of World War I; Belgium was subsequently officially entrusted with their administration under a League of Nations mandate in 1919, to be confirmed in 1923.

THE BELGIAN ERA In its adjoining colony of the Congo, Belgium had full control, but for Ruanda-Urundi it remained responsible first to the League of Nations and then (after 1945) to the United Nations Organisation. Annual reports had to be submitted and no important changes could be made without agreement from above. Despite these constraints, and despite the fact that Ruanda-Urundi had far less potential wealth than the Congo, Belgium took its charge seriously, and by the time of independence some 40 years later its material achievements (in terms of increased production; public services such as roads, schools, training centres, hospitals and dispensaries; and buildings and administrative infrastructures) were considerable. In terms of human beings it did far less well, as later events demonstrated.

Priorities Rwanda had always been subject to periodic famines, to such an extent that some were named and absorbed into history as milestones of time: such-and-such a child was born 'just after the *Ruyaga* famine' (1897), or a man died 'just before the *Kimwaramwara* famine' (1906). Most had climatic origins, but some which occurred around the time of the Belgian takeover (in 1916/17 and 1917/18) could also be blamed on World War I, as precious foodstuffs were shipped overseas to feed the troops. At the same time the new Belgian authorities commented that the local chiefs made little attempt to prevent the famines recurring, or to get emergency relief to the worst-hit areas. They therefore set about implementing a strict overall food strategy to make supplies less precarious.

The peasant farmers were first of all encouraged (by field workers) to maximise their production using traditional methods. They were then given help to improve their existing techniques, for example by using higher-yielding varieties of their normal crops. From 1924 the cultivation of food crops was made compulsory, including foreign species such as manioc and sweet potatoes. Next the distribution channels were upgraded, with a new road network and the development of markets and co-operatives. Storage facilities were set up; high-grade seed was distributed; the use of manure and fertiliser was promoted; the problem of erosion (caused by overuse of vulnerable land) was tackled; farmers were required to set aside a small emergency hoard of beans, peas or cereals each year; and various new types of stock breeding were initiated. Factories and processing plants were built. Finally, the farmers were encouraged to grow crops (especially coffee) for export, so that they could earn cash with which to buy extra food in times of hardship.

These measures – not easily implemented, because of the farmers' understandable initial resentment and resistance to change – proved more or less successful, helped by a regulated but controversial and sometimes harsh policy of forced labour (*uburetwa*), avoidance of which could incur severe punishment. Famine did recur in 1942–44 and resulted in thousands of deaths, but this could be blamed partly on the appropriation of manpower and the lack of efficient machinery caused by World War II. By the time of independence, large areas of farmland had been better protected against erosion and per-hectare crop yields had risen substantially. The scale of the anti-erosion terracing on the hillsides was massive: first horizontal ditches were dug, following the contours; then directly below these, hedges were planted. Water running down the slope of the hillside was trapped by the ditch, and then seeped through it to irrigate the hedge on the lower side; while the roots of the hedge contributed by securing the soil and strengthening first the ditch and then the hillside. By 1960, mainly in Rwanda but also to some extent in Burundi, around 570,000km of these protective barriers had been installed, benefiting some 750,000ha of land. However, because much of the work had been carried out under *uburetwa*, local people tended to see it as a colonial intrusion rather than a useful acquisition; after independence, except on the land of a few enlightened farmers, maintenance lapsed, hedges were destroyed and ditches crumbled. Fifty years later, an extensive scheme of terracing is under way once more and demonstrating its agricultural value.

Agricultural research was also important. The Belgian *Institut National pour l'Etude Agronomique du Congo Belge* (INEAC), although based mainly in the Congo, ran a large Agricultural Research Station in Rubona, as well as the Rwerere Experimental Station (working on food and industrial crops, cropping trials and animal husbandry) and the Karama Planning Centre, focused mainly on animal husbandry, pasture research and crop yields .

Alongside the extensive public, educational, physical and administrative provisions, the agricultural programmes and improvements were probably colonisation's most helpful input to Rwanda. Its contribution to the relationship between the country's long-term inhabitants was unfortunately far less positive.

Power structures Like the Germans before them, the Belgians decided to retain and use the existing power structures, but unlike their predecessors they then proceeded to undermine the authority of the mwami and his chiefs and to forbid some of their traditional practices, introducing their own Belgian experts and administrators at every level. This interference did not make for easy collaboration. In any case the mwami in power at the time of Belgian accession, Mwami Musinga, was hostile to colonisation and also resented the missionaries, since their innovations undermined the established order and worked against the subjugation of Hutus. In 1931 he was forced by the Belgians to abdicate in favour of his son, the more amenable and Westernised Mwami Mutara Rudahigwa. Until well into the 1950s, although the traditional structures keeping them in a subservient position were somewhat weakened, the Hutus still got a bad deal and remained 'second-class citizens' in almost all respects. So both Hutus and Tutsis – and indeed the minority Twas too, because they received virtually no recognition or privilege – reacted to colonisation with varying degrees of grievance.

Education The Germans had established a few government schools in Rwanda and the Belgians followed suit, but the main source of education was always the Church. In the 1930s, the Catholic Bishop Léon Classé, who had arrived in Rwanda almost 30 years earlier as a priest and worked his way up through the hierarchy, entered into an agreement with the Belgian administration by which the Catholic Church took over full responsibility for the educational system. He may not have been entirely without financial motive, since the government then subsidised the church to the tune of 47 francs per pupil and 600 francs per qualified teacher.

The Church broadened its curriculum to cover more secular subjects such as agronomy, medicine and administration; however, the main beneficiaries of the increased educational possibilities were still largely Tutsis, although Hutus were not entirely neglected and many attended primary school. Some did make good use of the limited educational openings available to them but could not easily progress beyond a certain level. Of those who trained in the Catholic seminaries (which they could enter more easily than secular educational institutions) some went on to become priests, while others switched back to secular careers. Less than one-fifth of the students attending the Groupe Scolaire in Astrida (later known as Butare and still later as Huye) from 1945 to 1957 – and emerging as agronomists, doctors, vets and administrators – were Hutus. The School for the Sons of Chiefs originally opened by the Germans in Nyanza had a minimum height requirement which effectively reserved it for Tutsis.

In 1955, there were some 2,400 schools of various types and levels (the majority were primary) in Rwanda, with around 215,000 pupils. Of the 5,500-odd teachers, over 5,000 were Rwandan.

Categorisation Size mattered. Like the Germans before them, the Belgians were intrigued by the sharply differing physical characteristics of their colony's inhabitants, and enthusiastically measured, recorded, compared and commented on the facial and bodily proportions of Rwanda's three indigenous groups. For the more timid of the Rwandans, this 'attack' with callipers, measuring tapes, scales and other paraphernalia proved a fearsome ordeal. So man dehumanises his brothers...

Most tellingly, in the early 1930s the Belgians embarked on a census to identify all indigenous inhabitants, on the basis of these physical characteristics, as either Hutu, Tutsi or Twa, and in 1935 issued them with identity cards on which these categories ('ethnic groups' or, in French, '*ethnies*', although the accuracy of this term is debatable) were recorded. If, even after strenuous measuring, someone's *ethnie* was not immediately clear, having been blurred by intermarriage or a change of status, those who were reasonably wealthy and/or had more than ten cattle were generally recorded as Tutsis. Identity cards – and the habit of classification they engendered – were still in use at the time of the genocide in 1994, providing an extra pointer (if one were needed) as to who should or should not die. Today there is a tendency to blame these divisive cards directly for the genocide, but the reality was more complex: power, personalities, demographic differences and pre-colonial history also played their parts. It is worth remembering that under Belgian rule Rwanda and Burundi were one country – Ruanda-Urundi – and subject to the same laws, yet they followed different paths after independence.

In 1945 the United Nations Organisation was created, with its charter promising the colonised peoples of the world justice, protection and freedom. Formerly a League of Nations mandate, Ruanda-Urundi now became a UN Trust Territory and Belgium was responsible to the UN's trusteeship council, which was to preside over all colonies' transition to independence. In 1948 a UN mission visited Ruanda-

Urundi, and its report was critical of the administration, particularly regarding the inferior status of the Hutus and Twa by comparison with the Tutsis. All too often, compulsory labour was harshly enforced, and the educational system remained heavily biased in favour of Tutsis, although many priests and missions were starting to veer more towards the Hutus.

At the same time, the observers were surprised by the completeness and intricacy of the social and political hierarchy which, if used properly, would offer a sound framework for democratic development. All the necessary command structures were in place, but badly oriented.

Subsequent visits gave rise to similarly critical reports. The Belgians introduced elections at local and administrative levels – which Tutsis won, except in the far north where resentment still smouldered after the 1912 defeat. Throughout Africa, colonies were becoming restless and the scent of independence was in the air, but in Ruanda-Urundi far too little preparation had yet been made, in terms of both political awareness and practical training. Nothing was ready.

THE RUN-UP TO INDEPENDENCE From about 1950, as the numbers of educated Hutus increased, the Hutu voice grew stronger. Hutu leaders such as Grégoire Kayibanda began to demand recognition for the majority. In 1954 the system of *ubuhake* was officially abolished, although in reality it lingered for a few more years. In 1957 the Superior Council of Rwanda (which had a huge Tutsi majority) called for independence preparations to be speeded up.

In 1956, Mwami Rudahigwa had called for total independence and an end to Belgian occupation. Just before another UN visit in 1957, a *Hutu Manifesto* drawn up by a group of Hutu intellectuals was presented to the Vice Governor General, Jean-Paul Harroy. It challenged the whole structure of Rwanda's administration, called for political power to be placed in the hands of the Hutu majority, pointed out injustices and inequalities, and proposed solutions. Little official action was taken.

The Catholic Church, now pro-Hutu, encouraged Grégoire Kayibanda and his associates to form political parties: APROSOMA (*Association pour la Promotion Sociale des Masses*) was openly sectarian, championing Hutu interests strongly, while RADER (*Rassemblement Démocratique Rwandais*) was more moderate. Whereas Tutsis, comfortably in a position of power, were calling for immediate independence without any changes to the system, Hutus wanted change first (to a more democratic system, recognising the fact that they were the majority) and then independence. For whatever reasons and after whatever deliberations, Belgium, having supported the powerful Tutsi minority throughout colonisation, now switched its allegiance to the Hutu majority, ostensibly in the name of fairness and democracy.

The wind of independence was blowing strongly in colonial Africa. More political parties sprang up. UNAR (*Union Nationale Rwandaise*) was formed by the proponents of immediate independence under the Rwandan monarchy, while PARMEHUTU (*Parti du Mouvement de l'Emancipation Hutu*) was established under the guidance of the Catholic Church by those favouring delayed independence. MSM (*Mouvement Social Muhutu*) was created by Grégoire Kayibanda to support Hutu interests, while UNAR (above) was a pro-monarchy and anti-Belgium party.

In July 1959 the Mwami Rudahigwa died in hospital, in circumstances that may or may not have been suspicious. Rumours of Belgian involvement were rife and tension grew. He was succeeded by one of his brothers. There were arrests and some sporadic small-scale violence – which erupted on a larger scale on 1 November, when a Hutu sub-chief belonging to PARMEHUTU was attacked and beaten in Gitarama (now Muhanga) by young members of UNAR. Within 24 hours, highly organised Hutu gangs were out on the streets of towns and villages throughout the country, burning, looting and killing. Then Tutsis began to retaliate. Within about a fortnight things were calm again – around 300 had died, and 1,231 (919 Tutsis and 312 Hutus) were arrested by the Belgian authorities. The country was placed under military rule headed by the Belgian Colonel Guy Logiest, who quickly began replacing Tutsi chiefs with Hutus. He was strongly pro-Hutu, claiming to be righting the injustices of colonisation, and played a virtually unconcealed part in anti-Tutsi attacks.

It is worth remembering that this was the first organised violence between the two groups, and it happened little more than 40 years ago. Those who speak of a long-drawn-out feud originating before colonisation are mistaken. But the revolution had begun, Tutsis started to flee the country in large numbers, and outbursts of violence continued.

PARMEHUTU won hastily manipulated elections in 1960. Belgium, the reins of power slipping rapidly from its grasp, organised a referendum on the monarchy under the auspices of the United Nations. In January 1961, Rwanda's elected local administrators were called to a public meeting in Gitarama, Grégoire Kayibanda's birthplace. They and a massed crowd of some 25,000 declared Rwanda a republic – and the United Nations had little option but to accept this ultimatum. However, the 1960 elections were not recognised by the UN so more were held in September 1961, under UN supervision. Again they were won by PARMEHUTU, with Grégoire Kayibanda at its head. Later that year, some 150 Tutsis were killed in the Astrida area, 5,000 homes were burned and 22,000 people were displaced. In July 1962 Rwanda's independence was finally confirmed with Kayibanda as its new president, heading a republican government. Astrida, so named in 1935 after Queen Astrid of Belgium, reverted to its local name Butare. Violence against Tutsis continued; by now about 135,000 had fled as refugees to neighbouring countries and the number was growing. Among those who left in 1960 was a three-year-old child named Paul Kagame, of whom much more would be heard later.

It is true that Belgium emerged from the fiasco with little credit. But it is equally true that, even without colonisation, some kind of revolution would inevitably have occurred sooner or later, for the tightly stratified hierarchy of the 19th century could not have held firm indefinitely against the pressures, promises and potentials of the modern world.

The trend today in Rwanda is to hold the colonisers – through their behaviour during colonisation – responsible for the eventual genocide. Indeed, without colonisation the explosion might well, as a Rwandan friend said to me, 'have happened differently', and perhaps after something as inexplicable as a genocide there is a need to apportion blame as part of the recovery process. But to claim – as is also the trend today – that before the arrival of the Europeans all was peace and harmony may simply reflect the fact that oral tradition tends to favour those in power.

1962–1994 The situation became yet more tangled and yet more sensitive. Since this is a guidebook rather than a historical treatise, readers who want a fuller picture than is given below will find several good sources in *Appendix 3*, pages 311–13. John Reader's *Africa* (Penguin, 1998) is particularly recommended, as is Gérard Prunier's *The Rwanda Crisis – History of a Genocide* (Hurst, 1998). They (among others) have been used as sources in this chapter.

Once in power, the government sought to reinforce its supremacy. 'Quotas' were introduced, giving the Tutsis (who were a minority of about 9% of the population) a right to only 9% of school places, 9% of jobs in the workforce and so on. Small groups of Tutsi exiles in neighbouring countries made sporadic commando-style raids into Rwanda, leading to severe reprisals. In late 1963, up to 10,000 Tutsis were killed. The pattern of violence continued.

In 1964 the Fabian Society (London) published a report entitled *Massacre in Rwanda*, commenting on events since 1959. Also – chillingly, in view of what happened 30 years later – a report entitled *Attempted Genocide in Rwanda* appeared in the March 1964 issue of *The World Today* (vol 20, no 3).

In 1965 Kayibanda was re-elected president and Juvenal Habyarimana was appointed Minister of Defence. In 1969 Kayibanda was again re-elected and PARMEHUTU was renamed the MDR (*Mouvement Démocratique Républicain*). But Kayibanda's regime was becoming increasingly dictatorial and corrupt. The 'quotas' and other 'cleansing' measures began to be enforced so rigidly that even Hutus became uneasy. In 1973, ostensibly to quell violence following a purge of Tutsis from virtually all educational establishments, Major General Juvenal Habyarimana toppled Grégoire Kayibanda in a military coup.

In 1975, a single party, the MRND (*Mouvement Révolutionnaire et National pour le Développement*), was formed. For a while, there were signs of improvement, although this tends to be forgotten in the light of subsequent events. Despite initial optimism and a period of relative stability, however, the regime eventually proved little better than its predecessor. Some educational reforms were undertaken, with the object of 'Rwandanisation' – revaluing Kinyarwanda and Rwandan culture. Habyarimana was reconfirmed as president in 1978, 1983 and 1988 – unsurprisingly, since he was the only candidate. The Hutu–Tutsi conflict was to some extent replaced by conflict between Hutus from the south and those from the north (Habyarimana was a northerner, so was accused of favouring 'his own'). Meanwhile, in the international sphere, rising oil prices and falling commodity prices were bringing the country's economy close to collapse and, among all but the privileged elite, dissatisfaction grew.

In 1979 a group of Rwandan exiles in Uganda established the RRWF (Rwandan Refugee Welfare Foundation) which in 1980 became RANU (Rwandan Alliance for National Unity), whose name explains its aim. In 1981, in Uganda, one Yoweri Museveni, later to become Uganda's president, started a guerrilla war against the oppressive regime of Dr Milton Obote – among his men were two Rwandan refugees, Paul Kagame and Fred Rwigyema. Obote was hostile to the Rwandan refugees in Uganda and political youth groups were encouraged to attack them and their property. As a result of such attacks in 1982–83, there was massive displacement of the refugees in southern Uganda and large numbers tried (or were forced) to return to Rwanda. The Rwandan government quickly closed its borders with Uganda and confined those who had already entered to a small and inhospitable area in the north, where many of the young and the old died of hunger and disease.

In 1986, in Uganda, Yoweri Museveni's National Resistance Army (which contained a number of Rwandan refugees) overthrew Obote, and Museveni assumed power. In 1987 RANU was renamed the RPF (Rwandan Patriotic Front), and was supported not only by exiled Tutsis but also by a few prominent Hutus opposed to Habyarimana's regime.

In 1987/8, a military coup in Burundi and consequent ethnic tensions caused a wave of Burundian refugees to flood into Rwanda. In 1989 the price of coffee, Rwanda's main export, collapsed, causing severe economic problems. Censorship rules were flouted, new politically oriented publications emerged and reports of corruption and mismanagement appeared openly. In July 1990, under pressure from Western aid donors, Habyarimana conceded the principle of multi-party democracy and agreed to allow free debate on the country's future. In practice, little changed.

Then, on 1 October 1990, the RPF (led by Major General Fred Rwigyema), invaded the northeast of Rwanda from Uganda, with the stated objective of ending the political stalemate once and for all and restoring democracy. French, German and Zairean troops were called in to support the Rwandan national army and the incursion was soon suppressed; but the government now took the RPF threat seriously. Habyarimana enlarged the Rwandan army from around 5,000 in 1990 to about 24,000 in 1991 and 35,000 in 1993. Various overseas countries (France, South Africa, the US) provided arms. Additionally, the 1990 RPF invasion was followed by severe reprisals: thousands of Tutsi and southern Hutu were arrested and held in prison for some months. Several were tried and sentenced to death but the sentences were not carried out, although, as one of those arrested later wrote, 'many died of the hunger and the beatings'. Sporadic unrest continued throughout the country.

Political solutions were sought, both nationally and internationally, with several Western countries now involved. In November 1990 Habyarimana agreed to the introduction of multi-partyism and the abolition of 'ethnic' identity cards, but nothing was implemented. The Rwandan army began to train and arm civilian militias known as *interahamwe* ('those who stand together'). It was later estimated that up to 2,000 Rwandans (Tutsis or anti-government Hutus) were killed by their government between October 1990 and December 1992.

The RPF – now led by Major Paul Kagame, since the charismatic Rwigyema had died in the October 1990 invasion – continued its guerrilla raids, striking at targets countrywide. By the end of 1992 it had expanded to a force of almost 12,000 and was growing rapidly. Its stated aim was always to bring democracy to Rwanda rather than to claim supremacy. Meanwhile, French troops were supporting the government forces. In the face of increasing violence, international pressure was applied more strongly and the Arusha Agreement (so named because it was drawn up in Arusha, Tanzania) committed Habyarimana to a number of reforms, including the establishment of the rule of law, political power-sharing, the repatriation and resettlement of refugees, and the integration of the armed forces to include the RPF. A 70-member Transitional National Assembly was to be established. The Agreement was signed in August 1993 and should have been implemented within 37 days, overseen by a United Nations force. But the process, unpalatable to both Tutsi and Hutu hardliners, stalled. Hostilities deepened. Radio stations poured forth inflammatory propaganda. Rwanda's *Radio-Télévision Libre des Mille Collines*, in particular, insistently and viciously identified Tutsis as 'the enemy', in dehumanising and vilifying terms. Scattered outbursts of violence rumbled on.

On 21 October, the Hutu president of neighbouring Burundi, Melchior Ndadaye, elected only a few months previously, was killed in a military coup, fuelling ethnic tensions in Rwanda. The UN began sending UNAMIR (UN Assistance Mission for Rwanda) forces to the country. Politics were deadlocked. A sense of impending danger grew and, by March 1994, vulnerable (or well-informed) citizens were starting to evacuate their families from Kigali.

On 6 April 1994, a plane carrying Rwanda's President Habyarimana and Burundi's new President Cyprien Ntaryamira was shot down by rocket fire near Kigali airport. Both men died. The source of the attack has never been confirmed. Within hours, the killing began.

THE GENOCIDE It had been well planned, over a long period. Roadblocks were quickly erected and the army and *interahamwe* went into action, on a rampage of death, torture, looting and destruction. Tutsis and moderate Hutus were targeted. Weapons of every sort were used, from slick, military arms to rustic machetes. Orders were passed briskly downward from *préfecture* to *commune* to *secteur* to *cellule* – and the gist of every order was: 'These are the enemy. Kill.'

A painfully detailed account, which includes many eyewitness testimonies and brings home the full horror of the slaughter, is given in the 1,200 pages of *Rwanda – Death, Despair and Defiance* (African Rights, London, 1995). In *A People Betrayed*, L R Melvern analyses the political and international background (Zed Books,

THE 'GENOCIDE AGAINST THE TUTSI'   *Janice Booth*

Until relatively recently, the events of 1994 were spoken of in Rwanda as 'the Genocide' without further definition. Now you will often hear the phrase 'the Genocide against the Tutsi'; this new clarification is because, despite the overwhelming physical proof to the contrary, a scattering of former *génocidaires* and their supporters maintain either that it was not genocide but rather a civil war; or that a 'double genocide' occurred, with Hutu *en masse* targeted also; or that it was simply a spontaneous uprising of Rwandans angry at their President's death.

The prolonged and systematic campaigns of anti-Tutsi vilification carried out in the Rwandan media and elsewhere well before April 1994 powerfully contradict these claims, as does reading the many carefully researched books on the subject and visiting the genocide memorials in Rwanda. Linda Melvern, author of (among others) *A People Betrayed: the Role of the West in Rwanda's Genocide*, speaking at a high-level conference in Stockholm in April 2012, explained that the denials, as with the Holocaust, had started directly after the massacres began. 'The final stage of genocide is denial, where evidence is destroyed, investigations are blocked, and the death toll is manipulated. With the Holocaust, the first deniers were the Nazis themselves. The pattern was repeated with the Genocide in Rwanda.'

This is not to say that, during the 100 days of bloodshed, Hutus in Rwanda – both innocent and guilty – did not die: some refused to slaughter their Tutsi neighbours and so lost their own lives; some killers met resistance from those they attacked; some were victims of the surprisingly few reprisal killings which did patchily occur. Later, many who had fled to the DRC succumbed to the sickness and hardships of the refugee camps, and *interahamwe* hiding in and around the camps were pursued. But the scale of non-military Hutu deaths was only a very tiny proportion of the Tutsi death toll and suffering.

There were many acts of heroism among those of the Hutu villagers who had no heart for genocide. Some hid Tutsi neighbours in their homes while the fighting raged across the countryside, knowing that discovery meant certain death; or sent the killers on false trails. Others, despite the danger to themselves, looked after Tutsi children who were orphaned or separated from their parents. Some refused to kill when ordered, so they or their families were slaughtered. Local officials, ostensibly transporting Tutsis to their deaths, in fact took them to safety: and paid the penalty. A group of schoolgirls were ordered to divide themselves into Tutsi and Hutu, with the implication that the Tutsis would die; they refused, saying they were all Rwandans, so all died together. Amid the terror and carnage there was much unsung courage, and these village heroes were equally victims of the 'Genocide against the Tutsi'.

London & New York, 2000), as does Gérard Prunier in *The Rwanda Crisis* (see *Appendix 2*). A condensed overview of events is given below.

In three months, up to a million people were killed, violently and cruelly. Barely a family was untouched. The international media suddenly found Rwanda newsworthy. Chilling images filled our TV screens and the scale of the massacre was too great for many of us to grasp. Amid the immensity came tiny tales of heroism: of villagers who flatly disobeyed the order to kill or who actively protected their Tutsi neighbours, at great (often fatal) risk to their own lives. But these glimpses of humanity were engulfed and lost in the great, surging tide of slaughter that spread across the country.

On 8 April, just two days after the plane crash, the Rwandan Patriotic Front (RPF) launched a major offensive to end the genocide. As they advanced from Uganda, they rescued and liberated Tutsis still hiding in terror from the killers. Meanwhile, however, a new Hutu government, based on the MRND and supporting parties, was formed in Kigali and later shifted to Gitarama.

The United Nations' UNAMIR force was around 2,500 strong at the time. They watched helplessly, technically unable to intervene as this would breach their 'monitoring' mandate. After the murder of ten Belgian soldiers the force was cut to 250. On 30 April the UN Security Council spent eight hours discussing the Rwandan crisis – without ever using the word 'genocide'. Had this term been used, they would have been legally obliged to 'prevent and punish' the perpetrators. Meanwhile tens of thousands of refugees were fleeing the country. In May the UN agreed to send 6,800 troops and police to Rwanda to defend civilians, but implementation was delayed by arguments over who would cover costs and provide equipment. The RPF army had taken control of Kigali airport and Kanombe barracks and was gaining ground elsewhere. In June, France announced that it would deploy 2,500 peacekeeping troops to Rwanda (*Opération Turquoise*) until the UN force arrived. These created a controversial 'safe zone' in the southwest.

On 4 July the RPF captured Kigali and set up an interim government. The remnants of the Hutu government fled to Zaire, followed by a further tide of

AFTER THE GENOCIDE...

A report produced in July 2000 by the Statistics Department of Rwanda's Ministry of Finance and Economic Planning concluded that the horrors of the 1994 genocide had left large segments of the population with severe mental health problems that could not in fact be expressed in statistics. Many people had lost family members, and/or had witnessed, experienced (or participated in) massacres or rapes. A National Trauma Survey by UNICEF in 1995, quoted in the same report, estimated the percentages of children affected by the genocide as follows:

* 99.9% witnessed violence
* 79.6% experienced death in the family
* 69.5% witnessed someone being killed or injured
* 61.5% were threatened with death
* 90.6% believed they would die
* 57.7% witnessed killings or injuries with machete
* 31.4% witnessed rape or sexual assault
* 87.5% saw dead bodies or parts of bodies

refugees. The RPF continued its advance westward and northward. Many thousands of refugees streamed into the French 'safe zone' and still more headed towards Zaire, cramming into makeshift camps on the inhospitable terrain around Goma. The humanitarian crisis was acute, later to be exacerbated by disease and a cholera outbreak which claimed tens of thousands of lives.

On 18 July 1994, the RPF announced that the war had been won, declared a ceasefire, established a broad-based Government of National Unity and named Pasteur Bizimungu as president. Faustin Twagiramungu was appointed prime minister. The following day, the new president and prime minister were sworn in, and RPF commander Major General Paul Kagame was appointed defence minister and vice president. By the end of July, the UN Security Council had reached a final agreement about sending an international force to Rwanda. By the end of August *Opération Turquoise* was terminated and UN forces had replaced the French. Internationally, it had now been accepted that a 'genocide' had indeed taken place – and it was over. At sites of the worst massacres, memorials now commemorate the dead and remind the world that such an atrocity must never, never be allowed to occur again.

THE AFTERMATH The 70-member Transitional National Assembly provided for in the Arusha Agreement of 1993 finally became operational in December 1994. In November 1994, the UN Security Commission set up the International Criminal Tribunal for Rwanda (ICTR), whose brief is to prosecute those who were guilty, between 1 January and 31 December 1994, of genocide and other violations of international humanitarian law; by the end of 1996 suspects were being brought to trial.

Sporadic bursts of violence were to continue for a further three years or so, with killings on both sides, as tensions in and around refugee settlements persisted and hardline Hutus who had fled across the border mounted guerrilla raids. But the RPF army and the new government remained in control. UN forces left the country in March 1996. Refugees returned home, in massive numbers. Problems of insecurity posed by former Rwanda government forces and *interahamwe* troops caused Rwanda to become militarily involved with the Democratic Republic of the Congo (DRC).

In 1999, local elections were held at sector and cellule level, and the Lusaka Agreement, to end the war in the DRC, was signed.

In March 2000, President Pasteur Bizimungu resigned and in April Major General Paul Kagame was sworn in as the fifth president of Rwanda, exactly four decades after his flight as a three-year-old refugee.

In July 2000, the Organisation of African Unity (OAU) recommended that the international community should make payments to the government and people of Rwanda in reparation for the genocide. Later the same year, the Rwandan government launched a census to determine the true and total number of genocide victims – irrespective of whether they were Hutus, Tutsis, Twa or foreigners.

In June 2002, with some 115,000 genocide suspects still in gaol after eight years and the country's regular courts unable to clear the backlog, the *Gacaca* Judicial System was launched. Gacaca (pronounced Ga-cha-cha, with a hard g) means 'grass', and was based on the traditional form of Rwandan justice where villagers used to gather together on a patch of grass to resolve conflicts between families, with heads of household acting as judges. See *Gacaca* box on page 22.

In the first half of 2003, around 30,000 genocide suspects were released from prison and, after a spell of 're-education', returned to their villages, in an amnesty aimed at those who were aged 14–18 at the time of the genocide, the old and sick, those accused of lesser crimes and those who had already been in gaol for longer than the sentence they would have received. Subsequent releases over several years returned tens of thousands more prisoners to their home villages. Solving one problem (prison overcrowding) risked creating another, as survivors – many of them still suffering either physically or mentally – found themselves once again

GACACA

The traditional system of 'Gacaca' courts was revived in Rwanda in 2002, in order to clear the prisons of the very large number of genocide suspects still awaiting trial. It was estimated that the regular justice system, lacking adequate facilities and qualified personnel, could take almost 100 years to clear the backlog, whereas Gacaca offered a faster solution. Around 160,000 local judges, both men and women, were elected by and from their local communities in 2001, and in 2002 were given brief training in such subjects as law, conflict resolution and judicial ethics. They received no salaries but were entitled to free schooling and medical fees for their families. Throughout Rwanda up to 11,000 Gacaca courts were established, each with a panel of 19 judges, and requiring the presence of at least 15 judges and 100 witnesses to be valid.

First, the courts identified victims of the genocide. Then, suspects were identified and categorised, according to the extent of their crime. They attended courts in their home areas, where local witnesses spoke for or against them. Suspects who confessed fully and pled guilty usually received lighter sentences, as did those who agreed to community service in atonement for their crimes. The courts were authorised to try, and then to sentence, anyone suspected of carrying out (or being an accomplice to) killing, serious assault or property crimes during the genocide. The more serious 'Category 1' suspects, those who allegedly organised, instigated, led or played a particularly zealous part in the violence, initially continued to be tried and sentenced in the formal judicial system; from 2009, some were transferred to the Gacaca courts. The Gacaca courts could not impose the death penalty (which was anyway abolished in Rwanda in 2007), nor could they try army personnel.

For the witnesses and families of the victims, confronting the *génocidaires* and re-living the events of 1994 could be both traumatic and cathartic. And while nobody claimed that the Gacaca courts were a perfect solution, many felt they were the best option under the circumstances – if nothing else, offering a very visible form of justice in which the villagers had a voice. Observers monitored their progress and overall they seemed to be uncorrupt, although instances of witness intimidation, and of people giving false evidence to settle personal scores, were occasionally noted.

It was originally hoped that the Gacaca courts would complete their task by the end of 2007. This proved to be optimistic: the massive size of their caseload forced the deadline to be extended several times. For all their efforts, it is thought that up to 10,000 suspects died in prison before they could be tried. The courts finally closed down in June 2012; they had judged an astonishing total of 1.95 million cases, with convictions resulting in about 65%. Any cases that remained unheard or unresolved were passed to primary courts or community mediators depending on their category.

living close to the alleged *génocidaires*, and it's a tribute to the extraordinary strength, courage and forbearance of Rwanda's village communities that the situation has so far proved manageable.

In June 2003, Rwanda's new Constitution was signed, marking the end of the transition period that followed the genocide and replacing various documents referred to as the Fundamental Law. The presidential elections held – entirely peacefully – in August 2003 saw Paul Kagame returned as president for a term of seven years, with 3,544,777 votes or 95.05% of the total. Parliamentary elections followed in September 2003 in which women took 48.8% of the seats, making Rwanda the country with the highest number of women in its parliament at the time. This statistic partly reflects a belief that women would never allow the sort of mass killing that has occurred in the past, and many others hold high positions in both state and private institutions.

Rwanda has qualified for debt relief under the Highly Indebted Poor Countries Initiative and had economic reform and development programmes supported by the IMF, the World Bank, the African Development Bank and the EU Mission in Rwanda. Huge amounts of foreign aid have been provided – and the fact that these grants have been ongoing since the genocide demonstrates international satisfaction about how the money is used. Donors (of which the UK is among the largest) renew their contracts. In 2011, Rwanda and Tanzania were the only two countries out of 78 worldwide to receive an 'A' rating from the Organization for Economic Cooperation and Development (OECD) for using aid effectively. The economy keeps growing, and more children are attending school than at any other time in the country's history. In October 2011 a World Bank survey named Rwanda as the fourth least corrupt African country, beaten only by Mauritius, Cape Verde and Botswana, and the 2012 World Bank '*Doing Business*' Report named it as the third easiest African country in which to do business, after Mauritius and South Africa.

Rwanda's international links have strengthened steadily. In 2006 it was accepted into the East African Community, and in November 2009 it became the 54th member of the Commonwealth, in which it and Mozambique are the only two member countries to have had no British colonial connections. For several years a contingent from the Rwandan army has played an active part in the peace-keeping force in Sudan's troubled Darfur region, and in 2011 some of its members began work on a school in Turba village there, with support from the local community. The school, now fully equipped, was handed over to the village in 2012; it can accommodate more than 500 students. A contingent of Rwandan police officers, sent to Haiti after its disastrous earthquake, has introduced *Umuganda* (see page 56) among the local people as a very practical and personal way of repairing the damage, and in 2012 a group of Rwandans living in Germany introduced *Umuganda* in two cities with projects to help the homeless and needy.

The country's second round of democratic parliamentary elections was held in September 2008, with the RPF under Kagame gaining 79% of the vote, whilst the remainder was divided between the minority Social Democratic and Liberal Parties. By law, at least a third of parliamentary representatives must be female, but in 2008 a remarkable 45 of the 80 seats were won by women. Rwanda is now one of only two countries in the world whose parliament contains fewer males than females (the other being Andorra; the UK and USA both have fewer than 20%).

In August 2010, the country held its second presidential election. The RPF once again dominated, with Kagame winning 93% of the vote, while his closest rival, Jean Damascene Ntawukuriryayo of the Social Democratic Party, took a mere 5.15%. The election was conducted peacefully, but some opposition and human rights groups claimed the result was tainted by intimidation and lack of credible competition. Certainly, the two months prior to the election were marked by violent attacks on critics and opponents of Kagame, among them the attempted assassination of Lt-Gen Faustin Nyamwasa in Johannesburg, the shooting of the outspoken journalist Jean-Leonard Rugambage, and the murder and partial beheading of André Kagwa Rwisereka, a founder and Vice President of the Democratic Green Party. Were the RPF responsible? Or opponents hoping to cast suspicion on them? Or personal vendettas? In these days of mafia-style killings and political skullduggery worldwide, it's anyone's guess.

A guiding principle of current government strategy in Rwanda is *Vision 2020*, a progressive and consultative set of policies that aim to transform the country's economy to that of a middle-income country. Vision 2020 also places strong emphasis on gender equality, anti-corruption, sustainable management of natural resources, technological progress centred on the IT field, private sector-led economic and infrastructural development, and regional economic integration. An important development in this regard is the recent laying of Fibre Optic cables throughout the country, which has made Rwanda a regional leader in internet technology.

The pro-poor targets set when Vision 2020 was first implemented seemed ambitious at the time: the reduction of poverty from 60% of the population to 25%, the increase of the per-capita income to US$900, raising life expectancy to 65 years, and literacy to 90%. However, by 2012 poverty had already reduced to around 45% and per-capita income had increased to around $540 (from $212 in 2001), so the targets could be attainable. Of course, on the political front, the country still has its tensions, the government inevitably has its critics, and there's still too wide a gap between the 'haves' and the 'have-nots' – indeed, many Rwandans still live in economic conditions that are far from ideal.

But considering the size and resources of Rwanda, considering what happened there in 1994, and considering the inherent problems faced by almost all countries in sub-Saharan Africa, even without the aftermath of a genocide, the achievements of the past 18 years have been amazing, and based on a huge amount of energy, courage, goodwill and sheer hard work. Progress has been dramatic and durable. Rwanda today is a vibrant and forward-looking country, well able to cope with the demands and technologies of the 21st century.

PEOPLE

Rwanda today probably contains inhabitants raised in a greater number of countries than most other African nations, as long-term exiles returned after the genocide from Uganda, Kenya, Tanzania, Burundi, Europe, the USA and more. But of course Rwanda is their origin and their home.

Following the disruptive ethnic clashes of the post-colonial years, which culminated in the 1994 genocide, the currently accepted line is to stress Rwandan unity: the fact that before the arrival of the colonisers Rwandans were living together on the same hills, speaking the same language and practising the same culture.

In fact, matters may not be quite so clear-cut and the insistence on 'same-ness' should not be carried to the extent of concealing historical individuality. But there's no doubt that the people of Rwanda in general are committed to overcoming any awkward or damaging differences. One genocide survivor wrote: 'Before the genocide, Hutus and Tutsis lived together. I remember we used to play with Hutu children and share everything. There were even intermarriages. The only time when we felt discriminated against was when a place at school, or a job, was given to a Hutu, even if there was a Tutsi more qualified for it. But this was no reason for hatred between the two groups.'

Of course individual attitudes may vary from place to place and person to person. Inevitably differences persist in some areas; sadly these have led to a few instances of bullying in schools, which are being firmly tackled. However, the energetic – and courageous – efforts at reconciliation and peaceful coexistence are visible nationwide, extending from the top down to rural groups and individuals.

LANGUAGE

The local language is Kinyarwanda, but almost all Rwandans speak a little of at least one international language. In rural areas, this is most likely to be KiSwahili, a coastal Bantu language with strong Arabic influences which, thanks largely to the 19th-century slave caravans, has come to serve as the lingua franca of East Africa. Most educated Rwandans who were brought up within the country also speak passable to fluent French, but may not speak English. By contrast, many returned long-term exiles were educated in Uganda, Kenya or Tanzania or another Anglophone territory, and don't know any French, but do speak fluent English.

The upshot of this is that French speakers will have no difficulty getting by in the towns, and should always be able to find somebody who can speak French in rural areas. English speakers will get by almost as easily in Kigali and other large towns, but less so in rural areas. Travellers who know some Swahili will also find this very useful, particularly in rural areas. The potential for chaos is, of course, immense: in Musanze/Ruhengeri, I regularly tried my faltering Swahili in a bar or hotel to no avail, followed up on this in my even more limited French, only to have the person I was addressing ask me whether perhaps I spoke English?

In 2008, the government controversially replaced French with English as the main language of education from primary school onwards. This move was intended to help Rwanda integrate into the (Anglophone) East Africa Community, and in the long term it will no doubt result in the spread of English at the expense of French. However, critics complain that the transition was unworkably abrupt, since many experienced teachers (not to mention their pupils) are less than conversant in English, making it almost impossible for them to pursue the official curriculum in any language other than Kinyarwanda. In 2011/12, English-speaking teachers have been brought in from Kenya and Uganda to help out.

The national language, spoken by everyone, remains Kinyarwanda, and for the sake of friendliness and courtesy you should try to take on board a few words. At the very least aim for *yégo* (yes), *oya* (no), *murakozé* (thank you), *muraho* (hello, good

WHAT THE 'ELL...? *Janice Booth*

The transposition of r and l can be tongue-twisting as well as confusing. I have friends named Hilary and Florence – in Rwanda aka Hiraly and Frolence. The multiple mwamis or kings of Rwanda – les rois – can be called les lois (the laws); while the queen (la reine) can sound like la laine (the wool!). In a recent letter, a young girl asked me to 'play' for her – which, unmusical as I am, would be difficult. She meant 'pray'. And New Year greetings wished me the 'fun and floric of the festive season'. Fortunately I've never heard the transposition applied to gorilla.

Rwanda's new flag, coat of arms and national anthem were launched on 31 December 2001, to replace the old ones designed in 1962, at a time when Rwanda was shaken by internal conflicts and bad governance.

The old flag contained red, symbolising the blood shed for independence, but in today's peaceful Rwanda this is seen as inappropriate. The new flag is blue, yellow and green: blue to signify peace and tranquillity; yellow to signify wealth as the country strives for economic growth; green to symbolise agriculture, productivity and prosperity. There is a sun in the top right-hand corner, against a blue background, representing new hope for the country and its people. The flag was designed by Alphonse Kirimobenecyo, a Rwandan artist and engineer.

The coat of arms consists of a green ring with a knot tied at the upper end, representing industrial development through hard work. Inscriptions read Repubulika Y'U Rwanda and the national motto Ubumwe, Umurimo, Gukunda Igihugu (Unity, Work, Patriotism). Other features are the sun, sorghum and coffee, a basket, a cog wheel – and two shields, representing defence of national sovereignty and integrity and justice.

The national anthem, Rwanda Nziza, has four verses and highlights heroism, the Rwandan culture and the people's patriotism. The words are by Faustin Murigo of Karubanda prison in South Province. The music is by Captain Jean-Bosco Hashkaimana of the army brass band.

morning/afternoon), *bitesé?* (how are you?) and *byiza* (good). For me, an essential phrase in any language is 'What's your name?', to be used on children; their faces light up and they start to take you seriously! Then point to yourself and say your own name, and the introduction is complete. In Kinyarwanda it's easy – *Witwandé?* The above words are written phonetically – the value of consonants may change a bit in different parts of the country; for example 'b' may sometimes sound more like 'v' or 'w'. If you're linguistically ambitious, turn to the more comprehensive vocabulary in *Appendix 1* on page 303.

PLACE NAMES In Kinyarwanda, as in most African languages, place names are more or less phonetic, so that the town of Base, for instance, is pronounced *Bahsay*. But the transcription of place names in Rwanda displays some other quirks that I've not encountered anywhere, namely the occasional pronunciation of 'g' as 'j' (Kinigi, for instance, is pronounced *Kiniji*), and of an initial 'k' as 'ch' and 'cy' as 'sh'(Kigali = Chigali, Cyangugu = Shangugu). Further complication is created by the African tendency to treat 'r' and 'l' as interchangeable, and the local custom of distinguishing certain towns from the synonymous region by adding the French word *ville* to the end of the town's name. Hence, when you hear a bus conductor yelling *Chigari-ville* at the top of his voice, he is in fact referring to the city of Kigali!

The names of nine main towns were changed in 2006; for details see *Chapter 2*, pages 38–9.

RELIGION

The Christian religions are a powerful force in Rwanda today, as witnessed by the great number of active churches throughout the country. According to statistics released in 2006, Roman Catholicism leads the field with 57% adherence (hence Pope John Paul II's visit to Rwanda in 1990), followed by 26% for Protestantism, and 11% for Seventh Day Adventism. There is a small (less than 5%) Muslim population, leaving only 2% of the population claiming no religious affiliation or following traditional beliefs.

TRADITIONAL RELIGION AND BELIEFS Rwandans traditionally believe in a supreme being called *Imana*. While Imana's actions influence the whole world, Rwanda is his home where he comes to spend the night. Individuals hold informal ceremonies imploring Imana's blessing. There is a tradition that, before retiring, a woman may leave a pitcher of water for Imana in the hope he will make her fertile.

Since words can have a magical impact, the name of Imana is often used when naming children, also in words of comfort, warnings against complacency, blessings, salutations, and during rites associated with marriage and death. Oaths take the form of 'May Imana give me a stroke', or 'May I be killed by Imana'. In instances when a long-desired child is born, people say to the new mother, 'Imana has removed your shame.' Tales of Imana granting magical gifts to humans, who then lose these gifts through greed and disloyalty, are common.

There is a special creative act of Imana at the beginning of each person's life. Impregnation in itself would not be sufficient to produce a new human being. This is why the young wife, at evening, leaves a few drops of water in a jar. Imana, as a potter, needs some water to shape the clay into a child in her womb. Then after birth, Imana decides what life is to be for that individual: happy or unhappy. If, later on, a man is miserable, poverty-stricken or in bad health, it is said that he was created by Ruremakwaci, a name given to Imana when he does not create very successfully, when 'he is tired', or, for some inscrutable reason, decides that a certain destiny will be unhappy.

Rwandans traditionally believe that a life force exists in all men and animals. In animals this invisible soul disappears when the creature dies, but in humans it is transformed into *bazimu*, spirits of the dead who live in *Ikuzimu*, the underworld or the world below the soil. While the deceased kings of Rwanda constitute a kind of governing body in the underworld, there are no social distinctions. Life is neither pleasant nor unhappy. The bazimu continue the individuality of living persons and have the same names. Though non-material, they are localised by their activity. They do not drink, eat, or mate but their existence in other respects is similar to that in the world of the living. Bazimu return to the world, often to places where they used to live. Some may stay permanently in the hut where their descendants live or in the small huts made for them in the enclosure around the dwelling. Bazimu are generally bad. They bring misfortune, sickness, crop failure and cattle epidemics because they envy the living the cherished things they had to leave behind. Their power, actuated by the male spirits, or grandfathers, extends only over their own clan. The living members of a family must consult a diviner to discover the reason for the ancestor's anger. Respect to bazimu is shown principally by joining a secret cult group.

The cult of Ryangombe

Ryangombe is said to be the chief of the *imandwa*, Rwandans who are initiated into the cult of Ryangombe. According to Rwandan legend, he was a great warrior who was accidentally killed by a buffalo during a hunting party. To share their hero's fate, his friends threw themselves on the bull's horns. Imana gave Ryangombe and his followers a special place, the Karisimbi volcano in the Virunga volcano chain, where they have a notably more agreeable afterlife than the other bazimu. The cult of Ryangombe became an important force of social cohesion, with Tutsi, Hutu and Twa being initiated into it. Ryangombe is propitiated by the *babandwa*, a politico-religious fraternity, who perform rituals, chants and dances in his honour. They meet only once a year, during July, at which time initiation takes place. During their festival the members of the fraternity paint themselves and decorate the spirit huts. A member of the group appears as the personification of the spirit of Ryangombe, carrying his sacred spear. After a ritual is performed, all members purify themselves at the stream. While involvement in the cult is not common today, Rwandans can recall when their grandfathers or fathers participated in the Ryangombe festival and a popular Rwandan song recounts Ryangombe's exploits as a warrior and lover. Also see box *Ryangombe and the Buhanga Forest* on page 225.

EDUCATION *Updated for the 5th edition by Charlotte Phillips*

More children are attending school in Rwanda today than at any time in the country's history. Although access to schools is very high, the issue of quality education remains, and a number of international organisations are working with the Government of Rwanda to ensure that children, once in school, are learning appropriate things.

The Government of Rwanda has put in place free education for the first nine years (primary and lower secondary school) and is currently working to increase free education to 12 years – however, some of the poorest parents do find it difficult to fund costs such as uniforms. A number of local and international charities are offering support with this. In addition to state schools, there are many Church schools that follow the national curriculum and are also fee free. There are also some (paying) private schools; in general, their quality is lower than that of state schools. English is the language of instruction from the third year of primary school – before that, it is Kinyarwanda, with English taught as a subject. French is also offered as an option in secondary schools. Before 2009, French was the language of instruction, so the change to English has meant that many teachers need significant training in English.

Better-quality training for teachers in pedagogy, and for school head teachers and district and sector education officers in school leadership, will really help to support the improved quality of education in Rwanda. Organisations such as VSO (*www.vsointernational.org; vso.org.uk*), UNICEF (*www.unicef.org*) and VVOB (*http://www.vvob.be*) are working on these areas. In addition, the US Government is investing $25 million in Rwanda's education sector over the next five years, to support improved literacy and numeracy in the early years of primary education; while the UK government will invest around £55 million over the same period to support improved quality of education across the whole sector. Two areas which have been identified as needing further attention are education for children with special educational needs; and early childhood education.

In October 2008, Rwanda became the eighth country to sign up to the 'One laptop per child' scheme (*http://laptop.org*), with the aim of providing internet access to all of its 2.3 million schoolchildren. Although there have been reports of teachers and students finding it difficult to study the curriculum as well as learning computer skills, the initiative should transform classroom learning and expand the children's horizons over the longer term.

A further noticeable change over the past few years is that far more girls are now attending primary school and continuing to secondary education (see page 225). The Rwanda chapter of the Forum for African Women Educationalists (*www. fawerwa.org.rw*) strongly supports this trend and runs two girls' schools as well as working with schools throughout the country.

Further education is also well catered for. Apart from the long-established National University in Huye/Butare, the Kigali Institute of Science and Technology (KIST), the Kigali Free University (Université Libre) and the Kigali Institute of Education (KIE), there are colleges and training schools throughout the country, several of which have opened or re-opened since the genocide. In some cases distance learning via the internet is possible, enabling students to study in their spare time while holding down a job and just attending the institute in order to sit exams.

CULTURE

LITERATURE A written language was not introduced until the Europeans arrived in Rwanda at the end of the 19th century, so there is no great tradition of written literature. However, there is a wealth of oral literature in the form of myths, folk stories, legends, poetry and proverbs. These have passed on not only stories but also moral values and historical traditions from generation to generation. Before (and to some extent after) the arrival of the Europeans, the Mwami's court was a centre for training young nobles in various art forms, particularly the composition and performance of songs and poems dedicated to valour in warfare and the magnificence of their cattle.

The historian Alexis Kagame wrote extensively about oral poetry and recorded many poems in both Kinyarwanda and French. A display in the National Museum of Rwanda in Huye/Butare (see pages 148–9) gives an idea of the intricacy of some poetic structures.

MUSIC Music is of great importance to all Rwandans, with variations of style and subject among the three groups. Traditionally, Tutsi songs praised excellence and valour; Hutu songs were lighter, sometimes humorous and linked to social occasions; Twa songs related more directly to aspects of their original occupation, hunting. During the time of the monarchy, the court was dominated musically by the royal drummers, and drumming is still of great artistic importance.

A full drum ensemble typically consists of either seven or nine drums. The smallest of these, sometimes called the soprano, which is often (but not invariably) played by the director of the orchestra, sets the rhythm for each tune and is backed up by some or all of the following drums: a tenor, a harmonist alto, two baritones, two bass and two double bass. The other widely used musical instrument is the *lulunga*, an eight-stringed instrument somewhat resembling a harp. It is most often played solo, perhaps as the background to singing or dancing, but may also be used to provide a melodic interlude and/or as a counterpoint to drums.

DANCE Dance is as instinctive as music in Rwanda and its roots stretch back through the centuries. As with music, there are variations of style and subject among the three groups. Best known today are the *Intore* dancers, who perform both nationally and internationally. At the time of the monarchy and for centuries before colonisation, the Intore dancers at the royal court were selected young men who had received a privileged education and choreographic training in order to entertain their masters and to perform at special functions. The name intore means 'best', signifying that only the best of them were chosen for this honour.

Traditionally their performances consisted mainly of warlike dances, such as the *ikuma* (lance), *umeheto* (bow) and *ingabo* (shield), in which they carried authentic weapons. In the 20th century dummy weapons were substituted, the dances were given more peaceful names and rhythm and movement (rather than warfare) became their main feature. The Intore dancers were divided into two groups. The first group, the *indashyikirwa* or 'unsurpassables', were all Tutsi. The second, the *ishyaka* or 'those who challenge by effort', were Twa led by a Tutsi. A description nearly three-quarters of a century old leads us through a performance:

> In the opening movement, the group of Twa advances with measured step. The musicians also are Twa. The dancers form a square or line up in double file. They perform the opening sequence and then a dance representing 'safety'. Next they stand at ease, chanting the exploits of real or imaginary Rwandan heroes. Then come movements representing 'tattooing', 'stability', 'the incomparable' and 'the most difficult case'. At this point the Tutsi dancers leap into the arena, armed, to mingle with the Twa and demonstrate that they deserve the name of 'unsurpassables'. The names of some of their dances translate into English as 'that which puts an end to all discussion', 'the crested crane', 'the exit dance' and 'thanks'.
>
> The costume worn by the Tutsi dancers consists of either a short floral skirt or a leopard skin wound around their legs. Crossed straps decorated with coloured beads are generally worn across the chest. On their heads they wear a fringe of white colobus monkey fur. Depending on the theme of the dance and the region they may carry a bow, a spear or a stick decorated with a long tail of raffia. Around their ankles they wear bells, the sound of which adds to the rhythm of the dance.

The Intore dancers perform regularly today and it's a dramatic spectacle. You may come across them in Kigali, Nyanza, Huye/Butare – or abroad, on one of their tours. Ask at the Tourist Office in Kigali (see page 86) for details of any scheduled performances. The Twa dancers are mainly in the Rubavu/Gisenyi area: ask at the Tourist Office or see *Chapter 8*, page 198.

HANDICRAFTS As in other countries, most genuinely traditional handicrafts have a practical use or are decorated forms of everyday objects. An object which gives purely visual pleasure and is unrelated to any function has probably evolved for the tourist market – although it is none the worse for that. In Rwanda the weaving (of bowls, mats, baskets, storage containers, etc) from various natural fibres is particularly fine. The quality of wood-carving is variable, but at best it's excellent. Pottery made by the Twa community is plain but strong and its uncluttered style is attractive. For handicrafts in Kigali, see *Chapter 4*, pages 107–8.

SPORT
Football *Chris Frean and Philip Briggs*

Sport is a passion in Rwanda. Volleyball, rugby, swimming, cricket, tennis, golf and even karate are all there, and developing. But the most popular, as throughout most of Africa, is football, whose supporters include President Kagame.

A few years ago, the future of Rwandan football looked very exciting, with the national side the Amavubi (which translates as 'wasps') qualifying ahead of Uganda and Ghana for the African Nations Cup, and APR reaching the Semi Finals of the African Cup Winners' Cup. Since then, unfortunately, Rwandan football has had limited cause for celebration.

The Amavubi finished last in their qualifying group for the Nations Cup and World Cup (one group for both) in 2006, with the only result of note being a 1–1 home draw to Nigeria. The Wasps fared better in the preliminary rounds of the 2008 Africa National Cup, coming third in their group of four, with two wins in six matches (including a 4–0 home drubbing of Liberia), but still failed to qualify.

They started strongly in the 2010 qualifiers for the Africa Nations Cup, winning three out of four matches in the first round, but failed to quality when finishing last in a strong qualifying group below Egypt, Algeria and Zambia. Rwanda fared even worse in the 2012 qualifiers, conceding 15 goals during the course of losing four out of six fixtures in a relatively weak pool.

Rwanda has enjoyed greater recent success in the CECAFA Cup, which involves 11 East African nations. True, its solitary championship win came way back in 1998, but Rwanda has emerged as runner-up five times since 2003 (strangely, on every odd-numbered year), and also taken third place three times since 2001. Despite this, it now stands at a lowly 105 in the FIFA World Rankings.

Domestically, the Primus National Soccer League (sponsored by the eponymous brewer, whose products are of course on sale at the National Stadium) is a popular

THE BATWA OF RWANDA   *Elaine Gardner*

The Batwa are a Pygmy people, comprising Rwanda's third 'ethnic' group – today numbering around 22–25,000. That they are indigenous Rwandans is surprisingly little known; even the recent film *A Hundred Days* mentioned only two groups in Rwanda's cultural diversity. The Batwa are, both today and historically, Rwanda's favourite exponents of a particularly distinctive dance. In olden times, they were dancers and potters at the Royal court.

They lived originally as hunter-gatherers in the high mountain forests around Central Africa's Great Lakes. As the forests were felled and national parks established, the Batwa evolved another lifestyle, as potters, using the clay found in the marshes that lie between Rwanda's many hills. They left the forests with virtually no material possessions – and they process the clay with none. They use their feet to trample it into malleability and then their hands to shape cooking pots, stoves, decorative vases, traditional lamps, candle-holders and charming little replicas of local animals, from cattle to gorillas. The pots are fired without kilns, largely in a hollow in the ground, by burning grasses and natural debris, and sealed with earth.

Because of their pygmy origins the Batwa have suffered extreme prejudice over the years; they are socially and economically marginalised and extremely poor. Only 28% of Batwa children attend primary school (and far fewer start secondary school) compared with 88% in the population as a whole. Only 1.6% Batwa have enough land to feed their families. Most survive by begging, working on the land of others in return for food, or carrying loads. An estimated 30% of the Batwa population, as against 14% of the population overall, was lost during the 1994 genocide. So, income-generating schemes are vital – which is where the pottery and dance come into their own.

The UK-based charity, Forest Peoples' Project (*www.forestpeoples. org*), works in Rwanda in partnership with CAURWA (Communauté des Autochtones Rwandais or Community of Indigenous Peoples in Rwanda), which FPP has supported since 1995. In December 2001, the UK Community Fund awarded FPP a three-year grant to start a Pottery Commercialisation Project with the Batwa potters. You can see some of the results if you visit the 'Dancing Pots' villages around Rubavu/Gisenyi. Items on sale include many traditional designs plus a new range of mugs, bowls, vases and pen pots, as well as terrace stoves for chilly Rwandan evenings; and you can arrange to attend performances of the lively and inventive Batwa dances.

and hotly contested competition. It has been dominated in recent years by Kigali's APR FC (supported by the President, who sometimes attends home matches), which topped the league 12 out of 17 times since 1995. Other successful clubs include Nyanza's Rayon Sport, which took four of the remaining titles, and the 2008 champions ATRACO club (sponsored/owned by the ATRACO transport company). For details of how to attend a football match in Kigali, see *Chapter 4*, page 104.

Women's rugby Rwanda made history in February 2005 when the inaugural East African international women's rugby match was held against Uganda in the floodlit Amahoro Stadium. A return match was held in Kampala in December of the same year. Unfortunately, Rwanda was thrashed in both matches. However, despite having no dedicated rugby pitches in the country, there's huge enthusiasm nationwide and progress is being made. Rwanda was one of eight teams participating in the inaugural women's tournament staged by the Confederation of African Rugby (*www.carugby.com*) in Kampala in 2009. Young people in Rwanda (both girls and boys) are increasingly being coached and enabled to play; the UK-registered charity Friends of Rwandan Rugby (*www.friendsofrwandanrugby.org.uk*; see page 60) is strongly involved in this, running an annual Rugby Development Tour to recruit and train new players, and teams from across the country meet regularly at tournaments.

Cricket Occasional and very small-scale cricket was played in Rwanda before the genocide, but the game didn't really catch on until after 1994. Among the thousands of Rwandans who returned home from exile in countries such as Kenya, Uganda and Tanzania, many had grown up playing it, and in 1999 some of them founded the **Rwanda Cricket Association** (RCA). In 2003 Rwanda became an Affiliate Member of the International Cricket Council. The Kigali 'Oval' was – and still is – the rather bumpy sports field of the Kicukiro Secondary School; to everyone's delight Brian Lara played a brief three-ball innings there in 2009 when visiting Rwanda.

In any post-conflict country, sport is an important therapy and unifier. Almost 5,000 Rwandans have now taken up the game, and cricket is played competitively at international, club and school levels. A club league, three club tournaments, a schools competition and a university competition make up the 11-month formal cricketing calendar. In addition, thousands of young Rwandans, both male and female, play cricket in orphanages, primary and secondary schools and universities. The Rwandan boys' and girls' teams compete well within the East and Central African region. Visitors with cricketing prowess are welcome to join in.

In 2011 the **Rwanda Cricket Stadium Foundation** (RSCF; *www.rscf.co.uk*) was formed. (Its website is the source of much of this information.) Run by both Rwandan and British members, it is fundraising energetically in order to provide the country's first dedicated national cricket ground, which will give the game the facilities it deserves. Cricket is well rooted in the country now, and looks set to develop as fast as means allow. (Also see *Chapter 4*, page 106.)

2

Practical Information

WHEN TO VISIT

Rwanda can be visited at any time of year. The long dry season, June to September, is the best time for tracking gorillas in the Volcanoes National Park and for hiking in Nyungwe Forest, since the ground should be dry underfoot and the odds of being drenched are minimal. This should not be a major consideration for any reasonably fit and agile travellers unless they are planning to hike to Virunga peaks such as Bisoke or Karisimbi, in which case the rainy season is best avoided. The dry season is also the best time to travel on dirt roads, and when the risk of malaria is lowest.

There are two annual rainy seasons. The big rains run from mid-February to early June, and the small rains from mid-September to mid-December. Rainfall, especially over the mountains, can be heavy during these two periods – particularly from March to May, although it is still perfectly feasible to travel at these times of year, and, for those visiting at short notice, it is far easier to obtain a gorilla permit at the last minute.

As for the two dry seasons, the major one lasts from June to September and the shorter from December to February. However, the climate is not uniform throughout the country: it is generally dryer in the east than in the west and north. On occasion, the volcanoes of the north may be capped by snow, and evenings in Kigali can call for a sweater – as do days anywhere in the highlands should you happen to hit a cold snap! Nevertheless, every season is good for swimming and tanning on the banks of Lake Kivu.

An advantage of travelling during the rainy season is that the scenery is greener, and the sky less hazy (at least when it isn't overcast), a factor that will be of particular significance to photographers. The wet season is also the best time to track chimps in Nyungwe (in the dry season they may wander further off in search of scarce food), while the months of November to March will hold the greatest appeal for birders, as resident birds are supplemented by flocks of Palaearctic migrants.

TOURIST INFORMATION AND SERVICES

The **Rwanda Development Board** (RDB; \ *0252 580388;* e *reservation@ rwandatourism.com; www.rwandatourism.com*) doubles as both tourist office and national parks authority. It operates two offices in Kigali, one at its headquarters in a high-rise on the junction of Boulevard de l'Umuganda and the Nyarutarama Road, and the other in the airport arrivals hall; it also has offices in Rubavu/Gisenyi, Kinigi (the headquarters to Volcanoes National Park) and at Nyungwe National Park. These all stock a fair range of booklets and maps, and the offices in Kigali and Gisenyi can issue permits for gorilla tracking and certain other activities in the national parks (see box, *Booking a gorilla permit*, page 52). Regular updates are posted on our website http://updates.bradtguides.com/rwanda.

TOUR OPERATORS

All those listed below will arrange gorilla visits plus international travel. Most offer both scheduled tours and tailor-made trips. More will start to cover the rest of Rwanda during the life of this guide. The many operators in neighbouring countries (Uganda etc) are deliberately not all listed, because readers in those countries are less likely to need them. Tour operators based in Rwanda are listed in the chapter on Kigali (see pages 87–8).

UK *(national code +44)*

Aim 4 Africa Ltd ☎0114 255 2533; e enquiries@ aim4africa.com; www.aim4africa.com

Aardvark Safaris ☎01980 849160; e mail@ aardvarksafaris.com; www.aardvarksafaris.co.uk

Abercrombie & Kent ☎0845 485 1681; e info@ abercrombiekent.co.uk; www.abercrombiekent. co.uk

Absolute Africa ☎020 8742 0226; e absaf@ absoluteafrica.com; www.absoluteafrica.com. Overland truck & camping safaris.

Africa Travel Centre ☎0845 450 1541; e info@ africatravel.co.uk; www.africatravel.co.uk

Exodus ☎(020 8675 5550; e sales@exodus.co.uk; www.exodus.co.uk

Expert Africa ☎020 8232 9777; e info@ expertafrica.com; www.expertafrica.com

Footprint Adventures ☎01522 804929; e sales@footprint-adventures.co.uk; www. footprint-adventures.co.uk

Imagine Africa ☎020 7622 5114; e info@ imagineafrica.co.uk; www.imagineafrica.co.uk

Naturetrek ☎01962 733051; e info@naturetrek. co.uk; www.naturetrek.co.uk

Rainbow Tours ☎020 7226 1250; e info@ rainbowtours.co.uk; www.rainbowtours.co.uk

Reef & Rainforest Tours ☎01803 866965; e mail@reefandrainforest.co.uk; www. reefandrainforest.co.uk

Steppes Travel ☎01285 880980; e enquiries@ steppestravel.co.uk; www.steppestravel.co.uk

Terra Incognita Ecotours ☎0800 098 8454; e info@ecotours.com; www.ecotours.com

Tribes Travel ☎01728 685971; e bradt@tribes. co.uk; www.tribes.co.uk

Vintage Africa Ltd UK office: ☎01451 850803; e vintagelon@vintageafrica.com; www. vintageafrica.com

Volcanoes Safaris UK office: ☎0870 870 8480; e salesuk@volcanoessafaris.com; www. volcanoessafaris.com (offices in UK, USA, Uganda & Rwanda – also see details on page 87)

Wildlife Worldwide ☎0845 130 6982; e sales@ wildlifeworldwide.com; www.wildlifeworldwide. com

World Primate Safaris ☎01273 691642; e sales@worldprimatesafaris.com; www. worldprimatesafaris.com

Zambezi Safari & Travel Company ☎01548 830059; e info@zambezi.co.uk; www.zambezi. co.uk

USA *(national code +1)*

Aardvark Safaris ☎888 776 0888 (toll free); e info@aardvarksafaris.com; www.aardvarksafaris. com

Africa Adventure Company ☎800 882 9453 (toll free US & Canada); e safari@africanadventure. com; www.africa-adventure.com

Expert Africa ☎800 242 2434 (toll free); e info@ expertafrica.com; www.expertafrica.com.

Ker & Downey ☎281 371 2500, (toll free US & Canada) 800 423 4236; e info@kerdowney.com; www.kerdowney.com

Steppes Travel ☎855 352 7606 (toll free); e enquiry@steppestravel.co.uk; www. steppestravel.co.uk

Terra Incognita Ecotours ☎855 326 8687; e info@ecotours.com; www.ecotours.com

Volcanoes Safaris ☎866 599 2737 (toll free); e salesus@volcanoessafaris.com; www. volcanoessafaris.com

AFRICA

Uganda *(national code +256)*

Adventure Trails Ltd ☎031 226 1930; f 0392 842044; e info@gorilla-safari.com; www.gorilla-safari.com

Magic Safaris ☎717 342 926; e info@magic-safaris.com; www.magic-safaris.com

The Far Horizons ☎312 264 894; e info@ thefarhorizons.com; www.thefarhorizons.com

Volcanoes Safaris ☎414 346464; e salesug@ volcanoessafaris.com; www.volcanoessafaris.com

South Africa *(national code +27)*
Wild Frontiers ☎72 927 7529; e wildfront@
icon.co.za; www.wildfrontiers.com

XA! nini African Wildlife Safaris ☎21 434
7184; e limar@iafrica.com; www.xasafaris.com

RED TAPE

Check well in advance that you have a valid **passport**, and that it won't expire within six months of the date you intend to leave Rwanda. Should your passport be lost or stolen, it will generally be easier to get a replacement if you travel with a photocopy of the important pages.

Bilateral agreements currently allow nationals of the following countries to visit Rwanda without a **visa** for a period of up to 90 days: Burundi, Canada, Democratic Republic of Congo (DRC), Germany, Hong Kong, Ireland, Kenya, Mauritius, Singapore, South Africa, Sweden, Tanzania, Uganda, UK and USA. This might change, however, so check at the website below before you travel.

Visas are required by all other visitors and cost up to US$60, depending on the place of issue. They can no longer be bought upon arrival. Either arrange yours through the nearest Rwandan consulate, or apply online at www.migration.gov.rw (click on 'public forms' then 'single entry visa'). So far as we can ascertain, the visa issued online is valid for 15 days only, but can be extended for up to 90 days after you arrive. For further details contact the Directorate General of Immigration and Emigration in Rwanda (m *078 8152222/8899971*; e *visa@migration.gov.rw*).

If there is any possibility that you'll want to drive or hire a vehicle while you're in the country, do organise an **international driving licence** (via one of the main motoring associations in a country in which you're licensed to drive), which you may be asked to produce together with your original licence. You may be asked at borders for an **international health certificate** showing you've had a **yellow-fever shot**.

For security reasons, it's advisable to detail all your important information in one file that you can forward to the email address you use when travelling, and also print and distribute through your luggage. The sort of things you want to include are travel insurance policy details and 24-hour emergency contact number, passport number, details of relatives or friends to be contacted in an emergency, bank and credit card details, camera and lens serial numbers, etc. It's also handy to carry a photo of your suitcase or other luggage, to save trying to describe it if it's misplaced by an airline.

EMBASSIES AND CONSULATES

RWANDAN EMBASSIES AND CONSULATES ABROAD

🅔 **Belgium** 1 Av des Fleurs, 1150 Brussels; ☎(+32) 02 761 9420; www.ambarwanda.be

🅔 **Burundi** 24 Av de la RDC, Bujumbura; ☎(+257) 22228755; e ambuja@minaffet.gov.rw; www.burundi.embassy.gov.rw

🅔 **Canada** 121 Sherwood Dr, K1Y 3V1; ☎(+1613) 569 5420/4; e ambaottawa@minaffet. gov.rw; www.canada.embassy.gov.rw

🅔 **China** Hsieu Shaouei Bei Yie, Beijing; ☎(+86 10 65322193; e ambabeijing@minaffet.gov.rw; www.china.embassy.gov.rw

🅔 **Ethiopia** Africa Av, H 17k-20 No 001, PO Box 5618 Addis Ababa; ☎(+251) 661 0300; e ambaddis@minaffet.gov.rw; www.ethiopia. embassy.gov.rw

🅔 **Germany** Jägerstrasse 67-69, 10117 Berlin; ☎+49 (0) 30 209 165 90; e info@rwanda-botschaft.de; www.rwanda-botschaft.de

India B 112 Neet Bash, New Delhi 110016; ☎(+91) 11 51661604; e ambadelhi@minaffet.gov.rw

🅔 **Kenya** Gigiri, Limuru Rd, Nairobi; ☎+254 20 7121321/2; m +254 722 207844;

e rwanemba@wananchi.com; www.kenya.
embassy.gov.rw

🄴 **South Africa**   983 Schoeman St, Arcadia,
Pretoria; ☎+27 12 342 6536; www.southafrica.
embassy.gov.rw

🄴 **Switzerland**   Rue de la Serviette 93, CH-1202
Geneva; ☎(+41) 22 919 1000; e ambageneve@
minaffet.gov.rw; http://switzerland.embassy.gov.rw

🄴 **Tanzania**   32 Ali Hassan Mwinyi Rd, PO Box
2918 Dar es Salaam; ☎(+255) 22 2701394;
e ambadsm@minaffet.gov.rw; www.tanzania.
embassy.gov.rw

🄴 **Uganda**   2 Nakayima Rd, PO Box 2446
Kampala; ☎(+256) 41 256 0414;
e ambakampala@minaffet.gov.rw; www.uganda.
embassy.gov.rw

🄴 **UK**   120–122 Seymour Pl, London W1H 1NR;
☎(+44) 020 7224 9832; e uk@ambarwanda.org.
uk; www.rwandahc.org

🄴 **USA**   1714 New Hampshire Av NW, Washington,
DC 20009; ☎(+1) 202 232 2882;
e info@rwandaembassy.org; www.
rwandaembassy.org

FOREIGN REPRESENTATION IN RWANDA   Foreign embassies and consulates in
Kigali are given below.

🄴 **Belgium**   Rue de Nyarugenge, Kigali;
☎0252 575551–3; e kigali@diplobel.be; www.
diplomatie.be/kigali

🄴 **Burundi**   4 Rue Ntaruka, Kigali ☎0252
517529/575512

🄴 **Canada**   1534 Rue Akagera, Kigali ☎0252
573210; e kgali@international.gc.ca; www.
embassy-canada.com/rwanda-kigali.html

🄴 **China**   44 Bd de la Révolution, Kigali; ☎0252
570843/5; e chinaemb_rw@mfa.gov.cn; http://
rw.china-embassy.org/eng/

🄴 **France**   Rue Nyarugenge, Kigali; ☎0252
551800; www.ambafrance-lc.org

🄴 **Germany**   10 Av Paul VI, Kiyovu, Kigali; ☎0252
575141; www.kigali.diplo.de

🄴 **Netherlands**   Bd de Kacyiru; ☎0252 584711;
e kig@minbuza.nl; www.rwanda.nlembassy.org

🄴 **Russian Federation**   19 Av de l'Armée, Kigali;
☎0252 575286; e ambruss@rwanda1.com; www.
rwanda.mid.ru

🄴 **South Africa**   1370 Bd de l'Umuganda, Kigali;
☎0252 551300; e kigali.admin@foreign.gov.za;
www.dirco.gov.za

🄴 **Switzerland**   38 Bd de la Révolution, BP 1257
Kigali; ☎0252 575534; www.eda.admin.ch/kigali

🄴 **Tanzania**   15 Av Paul VI; ☎0252 505400;
e teanzarep@rwanda1.com

🄴 **Uganda**   Plot 9, Av de l'Akagera, ☎0252
576854; e ugaemb@rwanda1.com; www.
ugandaembassy.rw

🄴 **United Kingdom**   Bd de l'Umuganda;
☎0252 556000; e BHC.kigali@fco.gov.uk; www.
ukinrwanda.fco.gov.uk

🄴 **USA**   2756 Av de la Gendarmerie, Kacyiru,
Kigali; ☎0252 596400; e consularkigali@state.gov;
http://rwanda.usembassy.gov

GETTING THERE AND AWAY

BY AIR   The national airline **Rwandair Express** (☎ *078 8177000*; e *info@rwandair.
com or reservations@rwandair.com*; *www.rwandair.com*) flies directly between
Kigali and Brussels (Belgium), Entebbe (Uganda), Johannesburg (South Africa),
Nairobi (Kenya), Bujumbura (Burundi), Dar es Salaam, Mwanza and Kilimanjaro
(Tanzania), Addis Ababa (Ethiopia), Brazzaville (Republic of the Congo), Libreville
(Gabon), Lagos (Nigeria) and Dubai. It has a reservations office in the Union Trade
Centre in central Kigali, as well as in all the countries to which it flies (see website
for contact details), and bookings can also be made online.

Other operators that fly directly to Kigali include **Kenya Airways** (*www.kenya-
airways.com*), **Brussels Airlines** (*www.brusselsairlines.com*), **Ethiopian Airways**
(*www.flyethiopian.com*), and **South African Airways** (*www.flysaa.com*). All of these
carriers operate a good network of intra- and intercontinental flights – travellers
coming from the Americas and Australasia will do best to aim for Johannesburg or

Nairobi, while those from Europe are best off flying via Brussels, Nairobi and Addis Ababa. For those tagging a visit to Rwanda on to a safari in northern Tanzania, it is worth knowing that **Coastal Aviation** (*www.coastal.cc*) operates a flight between Kigali and Arusha, Manyara or the Serengeti by inducement.

Kibale International Airport lies less than 10km from central Kigali, and taxis are available to/from the city centre (see *Chapter 4*, page 82), though it's possible that the existing airport will be replaced by the planned Bugesera International Airport about 40km south of the city during the lifespan of this edition. The departure tax that used to be payable at the airport is now included in your ticket – but check when you book, in case this changes again.

Remember to confirm your return flight at least three days in advance, via an airline office or travel agent in Kigali. Unless you do this, there is – at least with some airlines – a serious risk of being 'bumped' at the last minute, or of finding that the schedule changed unexpectedly and your flight left early.

Air tickets A number of travel companies are good sources of cut-price tickets, as well as offering various other services. London is the best place for cheap fares, hence the bias of the list below! It isn't exhaustive but should give you a start. As shown on their websites, most of the companies listed also have offices in other countries.

UK (London)

Africa Travel Centre New Premier Hse, 3rd Flr, 150 Southampton Row, Bloomsbury, London WC1B 5AL; ✆0845 450 1520; e info@africatravel.co.uk; www.africatravel.co.uk

Flight Centre ✆(booking) 0870 499 0040; www. flightcentre.com. Flight Centre has several offices in London & elsewhere in UK. It offers cut-price airfares & insurance services. Also in Australia, New Zealand, South Africa & USA.

STA Travel ✆0871 230 0040; e enquiries@ statravel.co.uk; web (very comprehensive): www. statravel.co.uk. Has 65 branches in UK & over 450 worldwide.

Trailfinders 194 Kensington High St, London W8 7RG (one-stop travel shop); ✆020 7938 3939; web (very comprehensive): www.trailfinders.com. Also in Ireland, Australia, etc.

WEXAS 45–49 Brompton Rd, Knightsbridge, London SW3 1DE; ✆0845 643 6568; www.wexas. com. There is an annual subscription to WEXAS (*for current details:* ✆*020 7581 8768;* e *mship@wexas. com*) but membership gives access to a whole range of useful services (good rates for hotels & airport parking, use of airport lounges, travel insurance, visas…) as well as an excellent travel magazine, *Traveller*.

OVERLAND Four countries border Rwanda: Burundi to the south, the Democratic Republic of the Congo (DRC) to the west, Uganda to the north and Tanzania to the east. Assuming peaceful conditions, frontier formalities aren't too much of a hassle – but nor are they standardised. Most frontier offices used to open at 08.00 and close at 17.00 or 18.00, but the Gatuna border post with Uganda and main border posts with the DRC now operate 24 hours a day, and others are likely to follow suit. See page 34 for details of which nationalities don't require visas; for others, a visa must be bought in advance, either in your home country or a neighbouring state. Don't count on official exchange facilities being available; there are likely to be 'black-market' money-changers around, but you should decide in advance what rate you're prepared to accept.

At the time of writing, there are still buses running between Kigali and Bujumbura in Burundi and bus travel is reckoned to be safe. However, historically it's a volatile area, and the situation could change at any time. The most reliable option is the Kampala Coach (*Gayo House, opposite the Nyabugogo taxi park;* m *(Rwanda) 078*

2

In January 2006, the federal map of Rwanda was redrawn to merge the 12 former provinces, namely Butare, Byumba, Cyangugu, Gikongoro, Gisenyi, Gitarama, Kibungo, Kibuye, Kigali Rural, Kigali City, Ruhengeri and Umutara, into the larger and more neutrally named North, South, East, West and Kigali Provinces. The creation of these new provinces (*intari* in Kinyarwanda) was designed to have several benefits, among them the increased decentralisation of government, the blurring of old provincial ethnic distinctions, and the dissociation of the present-day administration with names that retained associations with the genocide.

At the same time, each province was divided up into several new administrative districts (*akarere*), and where the main municipality (*umujyi*) in that new district shared its name with one of the old provinces, it was decided that, with the notable exception of Kigali, both the district and town would be given a new name, generally one that commemorated a nearby geographic landmark. So the town of Butare, formerly capital of Butare Province, was renamed Huye (after Mount Huye), as was the new district of which it was capital, while Ruhengeri, former capital of the eponymous province, became Musanze (after the Musanze Caves). And so on, and so on… as listed below:

Old name	New name	Old name	New name
Butare	Huye	Gitarama	Muhanga
Byumba	Gicumbi	Kibungo	Ngoma
Cyangugu	Rusizi	Kibuye	Karongi
Gikongoro	Nyamagabe	Ruhengeri	Musanze
Gisenyi	Rubavu		

8616348; (Burundi) +257 7935 4629; e info@kampalacoach.com or kampalacoach@ yahoo.com; www.kampalacoach.com), which runs a daily coach service between Bujumbura, Kigali and Kampala in either direction. Many other vehicles cover the route, including cheaper but less reliable minibus-taxis.

Despite the ongoing unrest in the DRC, it is normally safe to travel in the immediate Rwanda border area, which includes the Congolese border towns of Goma and Bukavu, though you're strongly advised to check the current situation first as this can change. Regular minibus services run between Kigali and Rubavu/ Gisenyi (for Goma) and Rusizi/Cyangugu (for Bukavu). On both sides of each border there is accommodation reasonably close by – in the case of Rusizi and Rubavu, only a few minutes away, but further for Bukavu. From Goma, it is also currently possible to visit Virunga National park (see *Chapter 13*, page 291). Travelling further into the DRC remains highly risky.

Crossing to and from Uganda is simple. Direct buses and minibus-taxis connect Kampala and Kigali, taking around 12 hours if you do the trip in one leg. Among the better companies are the Kampala Coach (see contact details above) and Jaguar Executive Coaches (\ (Uganda) 041 4251855; m (Rwanda) 078 8640796/8703591), both of which charge around Rfr6,000 one-way. Kampala Coach also has connections on to Nairobi and Dar es Salaam. There is a limited number of local minibus-taxis along the roughly 50km road between Kisoro in southwest Uganda and Musanze/Ruhengeri in northwest Rwanda (an hour's trip, not allowing for changing vehicles and other delays at the Cyanika border post, which might add another hour to the journey). It is also easy to travel by

Straightforward enough so far, but in practice the transition of names has been a slow and inconsistent process, one that has posed a dilemma to the authors of the guidebook for all subsequent editions. When the fourth edition was researched, most minibus-taxis, for instance, still used the old name, but that has changed completely over subsequent years. By contrast, maps and other references from outside the country still stick almost exclusively to the old name, while most recent publications within Rwanda use the new name (though the RDB map of the Congo-Nile Trail, launched as recently as November 2011, still uses the old names).

Whatever the official situation, our guiding principle for this guidebook has to be pragmatism. For the fourth edition we decided to stick with the established town name, on the basis that they remained in wider use within the country, and were almost ubiquitous outside it, whether you are looking at maps, Google results, tourist brochures, or whatever. For this edition, we have decided to use the new names throughout; though to make this transition easier and more accessible we have regularly included 'reminders', in the form of the new name followed by the old as in Huye/Butare or Musanze/Ruhengeri. It is not the most elegant solution, but it does have the advantage of being easy to use and foolproof. And looking ahead, it is to be hoped that by the time of sixth edition the old name can be dispensed with entirely.

To add to the confusion, it's possible that street names in Kigali and some other towns will change during the life of this edition, perhaps to an alphabetical/numerical system. However, if you need to ask directions, you'll find that Rwandans tend to orient themselves according to landmarks rather than street names, and the old names will be remembered for some time.

minibus-taxi between Kabale, the largest town in southwest Uganda, and Kigali, though once again you might have to change vehicles at the border – this trip should take about five hours in total. Entering from Uganda in your own vehicle is relatively hassle-free.

Crossing between Rwanda and Tanzania is something of a slog, due to the poor state of roads and lack of large towns in northwest Tanzania. The Rusumo border post lies about 160km from Kigali, roughly a four-hour trip by minibus-taxi, with the possibility of staying the night *en route* at the town of Ngoma, 60km from the border. Or there is a restaurant with basic accommodation at Rusumo itself, on the Rwandan side (page 272). The closest Tanzanian town to the border is Ngara, which is connected to Rusumo by occasional minibus-taxis taking about six hours, and has a few small guesthouses. From Ngara, daily buses to Mwanza on Lake Victoria take 12–18 hours depending on the condition of the road. Mwanza is a large port with a full range of accommodation and other facilities, including thrice-weekly rail links to Dar es Salaam on the coast and daily buses to Arusha in northeast Tanzania. A rail link between Rwanda and Tanzania is planned, but don't count on it being up and running in the near future.

SAFETY

THEFT So far as tourists need be concerned, Rwanda is among the most crime-free of African countries. Kigali is a very safe city, even at night, though it would probably be courting trouble to stumble around dark alleys with all your valuables on your person. Be aware, too, that this sort of thing can change very quickly: all too often, as tourism volumes increase, so too does opportunistic and petty crime.

The following security hints are applicable anywhere in Africa:

- Most casual thieves operate in busy markets and bus stations. Keep a close watch on your possessions in such places, and avoid having valuables or large amounts of money loose in your daypack or pocket.
- Keep all your valuables and the bulk of your money in a hidden money belt. Never show this money belt in public. Keep any spare cash you need elsewhere on your person – a button-up pocket on the front of the shirt is a good place as money cannot be snatched from it without the thief coming into your view. It is also advisable to keep a small amount of hard currency (ideally cash) hidden in your luggage in case you lose your money belt.
- Where the choice exists between carrying valuables on your person or leaving them in a locked room I would favour the latter option (thefts from locked hotel rooms are relatively rare in Africa). Obviously you should use your judgement on this and be sure the room is absolutely secure. Bear in mind that some travellers' cheque companies will not refund cheques which were stolen from a room.
- Leave any jewellery of financial or sentimental value at home.

USEFUL CONTACT
Police ☎08311117 or 112

OTHER HAZARDS People new to exotic travel often worry about tropical diseases, but it is accidents which are most likely to carry you off. Road travel isn't as dangerous in Rwanda as in some other African countries but still accidents aren't uncommon, and the number of vehicles is increasing; so be aware and do what you can to reduce risks. For example, try to travel during daylight hours and refuse to be driven by anyone who is drunk. Always heed local advice about where you should (or should not) travel, or about areas where you should take particular care. At the

DRIVING INTO RWANDA   *John Osman*

When you bring your vehicle into Rwanda you need to buy a Carte d'Entrée. It's not expensive, but police checkpoints often ask to see this slip of paper, so don't lose it!

Compulsory vehicle insurance is also available at the border, just after you go through Rwandan customs. You may be approached by an insurance salesman even while you're still going through the customs registration for the car, but we preferred to go to one of the official offices set up in that area rather than to deal with a guy on the street. The insurance process is quick and easy. Minimum coverage is for three days, then one week, and so on. Again it is not prohibitively expensive. The procedure is all carried out in English, in case anyone is worried about having to cope in French.

Police at checkpoints on Rwandan roads may ask to see if you have a fire extinguisher and triangles (which you're supposed to set up on the road to warn of an accident) in your car. Luckily we'd been warned of this beforehand, so we'd bought a little Russian-made fire extinguisher in Kampala for around US$6 and a pair of triangles for about US$10. The police were perfectly satisfied with that.

time of writing, Rwanda is a relatively safe country – but, sadly, it has been seen elsewhere that an increase in tourism can lead to an increase in opportunistic crime. Be as sensible in Rwanda as (I hope!) you would be in any other strange country about carrying your cash discreetly and not flaunting jewellery, and (particularly in towns) about where you walk after dark. Also be sensible in hotels and guesthouses: don't leave tempting items too readily accessible.

HASSLES
Overcharging and bargaining
Tourists may sometimes need to bargain over prices, but this need is often exaggerated. Hotels, restaurants and supermarkets generally charge fixed prices, and deliberate overcharging is so rare that it's not worth challenging a price unless it is blatantly ridiculous. In other situations – mostly markets or in the street – you're bound to be asked a higher price than the vendor will expect, and a certain degree of bargaining is considered normal. It is, however, important to keep this in perspective.

Minibus conductors may occasionally ask tourists for higher fares than normal. The way to counter this is to watch what other people are paying, or to ask a fellow passenger what the fare should be. The main instance where bargaining is essential is when buying handicrafts or curios. However, the fact that a curio seller is open to negotiation does not mean that he or she was initially trying to rip you off. Vendors will generally quote a starting-price knowing full well that you are going to bargain it down – they'd probably be startled if you didn't – and it is not necessary to respond aggressively. It is impossible to say what size of reduction you should expect (some people say that you should offer half the asking price and be prepared to settle at around two-thirds, but my experience is that curio sellers are far more whimsical than such advice allows for). The sensible approach is to ask the price of similar items at a few different stalls before you actually contemplate buying anything.

In fruit and vegetable markets and stalls, bargaining is often the norm, even between Africans, and the healthiest approach to this sort of haggling is to view it as an enjoyable part of the travel experience. There will normally be an accepted price-band for any particular commodity. To find out what it is, listen to what other people pay (it helps if you know some Kinyarwanda) and try a few stalls – a ludicrously inflated price will drop the moment you walk away. When buying fruit and vegetables, a good way to feel out the situation is to ask for a bulk discount or a few extra items thrown in. And bear in mind that the reason why somebody is reluctant to bargain may be that they asked a fair price in the first place.

Above all, don't lose your sense of proportion. No matter how poor you may feel, it is your choice to travel on a tight budget. Most Rwandans are much poorer than you will ever be, and they do not have the luxury of choosing to travel. If you find yourself quibbling with an old lady selling a few piles of fruit by the roadside, stand back and look at the bigger picture. There is nothing wrong with occasionally erring on the side of generosity.

Begging
To anyone who knows Africa it should come as no surprise to see beggars on the streets; the surprise, in view of Rwanda's recent past, is that they aren't more numerous. Nor are they often aggressive. For a charity (one of several) helping Kigali's street kids, see rYico on page 62. The maimed, handicapped and very old tell an obvious story. I can't advise you what to do about them. It's true that if you give to one you risk being surrounded by a dozen – but sometimes it's hard to walk on by. Rwandans themselves often recommend that you give something; they and the country's budget have little enough to spare. If you don't believe in

giving cash, see *Becoming involved*, pages 60–3, which lists some charities where your money will be well used.

Bribery and bureaucracy For all you read about the subject, bribery is not the problem to travellers in Africa that it is often made out to be. Those who are most often asked for bribes are people with private transport; but this seldom happens in Rwanda. Visit the DRC, however, and it may become more of an issue.

There is a tendency to portray African bureaucrats as difficult and inefficient in their dealings with tourists. As a rule, this reputation says more about Western prejudices than it does about Africa. A big determining factor in the response you receive from officials, will be your own attitude. If you walk into every official encounter with an aggressive, paranoid approach, you are quite likely to kindle the

NOTES FOR DISABLED TRAVELLERS   *Gordon Rattray*

Renowned as the 'Land of a Thousand Hills', Rwanda might sound like one to avoid if mobility is an issue for you. Furthermore, the country's tourism industry is relatively new and there are few provisions foreseen for the local disabled population. Despite all that, my advice is to go, making sure your itinerary is not rushed and being prepared to compromise to some degree. Africans are usually delighted to offer help and are often, through necessity, experts in improvisation.

ACCOMMODATION In general, it is not easy to find disabled-friendly accommodation. Only top-of-the-range hotels and lodges have 'accessible' rooms while budget guesthouses and campsites are more basic. Occasionally (more by accident than through design) bathrooms are step-free and spacious, but they usually contain standard fittings only.

TRANSPORT
By road Most tour companies use 4x4s and minibuses, which are higher than normal cars and therefore might make entry more difficult. Similarly, buses and minibuses have no facilities for wheelchairs, and getting off and on can be a hectic affair. Drivers, guides and fellow passengers are usually prepared to assist but they are not trained in this skill so you must thoroughly explain your needs and stay in control of the situation.

By air If you need assistance then let the airline know in advance and arrive early for your departure. During the flight, anyone who uses a pressure-relieving wheelchair cushion should consider using it instead of or on top of the fitted seat cushion. There is no guarantee that aisle chairs will be present at airports in Rwanda, so expect to be manhandled if you cannot transfer unaided.

ACTIVITIES Gorilla tracking is literally a stumble in the jungle, even for able-bodied people. You don't need to be super-fit, but check with your tour operator if you think your disability may exclude you. I have heard of non-ambulant people being physically carried, though this would obviously require extra planning and payment. Museums and other public places rarely have disability access but are unlikely to be completely inaccessible.

feeling held by many Africans that Europeans are arrogant and offhand in their dealings with other races. Instead, try to be friendly and patient, and remember that the person to whom you are talking does not speak English (or French) as a first language and may thus have difficulty understanding you. Treat people with respect rather than disdain, in Rwanda as elsewhere, and they'll tend to treat you in the same way.

WHAT TO TAKE

In 1907, when the Duke of Mecklenburg set off on an expedition through Rwanda with a group of scientific researchers, he carried (or rather his team of bearers carried) numerous cases of soap, candles, rope and cigars, as well as such items as

HEALTH AND INSURANCE Rwandan hospitals and pharmacies are often basic so, if possible, take all essential medication and equipment with you. It is advisable to pack this in your hand luggage during flights in case your main bags don't arrive immediately. Doctors will know about 'everyday' illnesses, but you must understand and be able to explain your own particular medical requirements. It can also be hot; if this is a problem for you then try to book accommodation and vehicles with fans or air-conditioning, and a plant-spray bottle can be a useful cooling aid.

Travel insurance can be purchased from Age Concern (0800 169 2700; www. ageconcern.org.uk), who have no upper age limit, and Free Spirit (0845 230 5000; www.free-spirit.com), who cater for people with pre-existing medical conditions. Most insurance companies will insure disabled travellers, but it is essential that they are made aware of your disability.

SECURITY For anyone following the usual security precautions (see page 39) the chances of robbery are greatly reduced. In fact, as a disabled person I personally feel more 'noticed', and therefore a less attractive target for thieves. But the opposite may also apply, so do stay aware of where your bags are and who is around you, especially during car transfers and similar activities.

SPECIALIST OPERATORS There are currently no disability-specialised operators running trips to Rwanda. Having said that, most travel companies will listen to your needs and try to create an itinerary suitable for you.

FURTHER INFORMATION
Books Bradt Travel Guides' *Access Africa – Safaris for People with Limited Mobility* doesn't deal with Rwanda specifically but is packed with useful advice and resources for disabled adventure travellers.

Online
www.able-travel.com A regularly updated website with both worldwide and country-specific info
www.globalaccessnews.com A searchable database of disability travel information
www.rollingrains.com A searchable website advocating disability travel
www.youreable.com A UK-based general resource for disability information, with an active forum
www.apparelyzed.com A site dedicated to spinal injury, but containing information that other disabilities will also find useful. It also hosts a hugely popular forum.

salt, wire, beads and woollen blankets to barter with the natives. You could probably cut down on this a little.

In fact Rwanda is a relatively well-stocked little country, in terms of clothing, toiletries, stationery, batteries and so forth. Unless you have particularly exotic tastes (or your schedule is too crowded to allow you time for shopping), you should be able to find most of the everyday items a traveller needs, even if the brands are unfamiliar. Obviously you should bring a supply of any personal

WOMEN TRAVELLERS *Janice Booth*

As a lone female traveller, I have experienced far less hassle and anxiety in Rwanda during my several visits than I have in many other countries. I travelled all over the country by public transport feeling completely safe. There was a refreshing absence of 'smart Alecs' trying to engage me in dubious conversation.

In one town, a young man (Congolese, as it turned out) overheard me asking directions to the guesthouse and spontaneously walked with me, chatting occasionally, to make sure I found it safely. Then he shook my hand and went off. Another day I gave my driver, who had had a long hard morning, Rfr2,000 to go and buy a good lunch, and he spontaneously handed me Rfr1,000 change when he returned. Once I left my unlockable duffel bag with a smiling girl in a small wooden drinks kiosk near a minibus stop while I explored a village; when I returned to collect it, it had been stowed safely in a corner and the girl's baby was gurgling happily on top. I felt a kind of 'sisterhood', particularly with village women – if I smiled it was always reciprocated, although often shyly, and I always asked a woman first if I needed help or directions.

In Kigali I've spent a lot of time walking both in and outside the city centre and never felt threatened, although there are some poorer areas which (and a Rwandan woman friend agrees with me) become scarier after dark. This applies to men too, of course, but women are generally seen – rightly or wrongly! – as a target less likely to put up resistance. The rule here is to take the same sensible precautions you'd take in any capital city, and then relax.

As a matter of courtesy, watch what the local women wear and don't expose parts of yourself that they leave covered, particularly in village areas. In business areas people are smartly dressed; I've been glad of bringing a skirt and some crumple-free tops. Be sensitive to the fact that people here have suffered a great deal; if someone is reluctant to talk or to answer questions, don't push it. Remember that in shops it's polite to give some kind of greeting like 'good morning' or 'hello' (in whatever language) before asking for what you want.

You may not be as fortunate as I've been. Nor do I suggest that you drop your guard and behave over-confidently. There can be bad apples in any barrel. Would-be Lotharios exist in any country and they tend to home in on female travellers. In fact, one night in Kigali a strange man did knock on my bedroom door at 11pm, but it turned out that he needed money to take a sick street kid to hospital (yes, honestly!).

I place Rwanda very high on the list of relatively hassle-free countries where good manners, honesty and trust are the order of the day – and of course this should be a two-way process.

medication (and some extra, in case your return home is delayed); as well as enough sunscreen. Otherwise, unless you plan to go way off the beaten track (or you need camping/trekking gear, which is in shorter supply), don't feel that you must fill your bag up with a lot of semi-useful items 'just in case'. Buying things locally helps Rwanda's economy!

The comments below apply as much to any neighbouring African countries you may pass through or visit as they do to Rwanda.

CARRYING YOUR LUGGAGE If you are unlikely to carry your luggage for any significant distance, a conventional suitcase is fine. Make sure it is tough and durable, and seals well, so that its contents survive bumpy drives and boisterous baggage handlers at airports. Travellers with a lot of valuable items should use a bag that can be padlocked easily. Of course it can still be slashed open, but that would be highly unusual in Rwanda – you are more likely to encounter casual theft to which a padlock would be a real deterrent.

On public transport, a durable backpack is the most practical solution, ideally with several pockets. A small daypack will be useful for gorilla tracking and other walks, and to stow any breakable goods on your lap during long drives – anything like an MP3 player or camera will suffer heavily from vibrations on rutted roads.

CLOTHES Try to keep your clothes to a minimum, especially if you are travelling with everything on your back. Bear in mind that you can easily and cheaply replace worn items in markets. The minimum is one or possibly two pairs of trousers and/or skirts, one pair of shorts, three shirts or T-shirts, one light sweater or similar, one heavy sweater or similar, a waterproof jacket during the rainy season, enough socks and underwear to last five to seven days, one solid pair of shoes or hiking boots for walking, and one pair of sandals, flip-flops or other light shoes.

It's widely held that jeans are not ideal for African travel, since they are bulky to carry, hot to wear and take ages to dry. In their favour, however, jeans do have the advantages of durability and comfort, and of hiding the dust and dirt that tend to accumulate during public transport rides – and they are excellent for gorilla tracking and other forest walks. A good alternative is light cotton trousers, which dry more quickly and weigh less, but try to avoid light colours, as they show dirt more easily. Skirts are best made of a light natural fabric such as cotton. T-shirts are lighter and less bulky than proper shirts, though the top pocket of a shirt (particularly if it buttons up) is a good place to carry spending money in markets and bus stations, since it's easier to keep an eye on than a trouser pocket. A couple of sweaters or sweatshirts will be necessary in places such as Nyungwe, which get chilly at night. Remember that mosquitoes and tsetse flies in some areas show a liking for dark blue.

Socks and underwear *must* be made from natural fabrics. Bear in mind that re-using sweaty undergarments will encourage fungal infections such as athlete's foot, as well as prickly heat in the groin region. Socks and underpants are light and compact enough to make it worth bringing a week's supply. As for footwear, only if you're a serious off-road hiker should you consider genuine hiking boots, since they are very heavy whether on your feet or in your pack. A good pair of walking shoes, preferably leather with good ankle support, is a good compromise. For gorilla-tracking, old gardening gloves can be handy when you're grabbing for handholds in thorny vegetation.

Another factor in selecting your travel wardrobe is local sensibilities. In Rwanda, which is predominantly Christian, this isn't the concern it would be in several other parts of Africa, but modest dress is nevertheless recommended. For women, the ideal garment is a knee-length skirt, though long trousers – while unconventional in rural Rwanda – are unlikely to give offence. For men, shorts are fine, but it is considered more respectable to wear trousers. Walking around in a public place without a shirt is unacceptable.

OTHER USEFUL ITEMS Many backpackers, even those with no intention of camping, carry a **sleeping bag** as a fallback for rooms with dirty bedding. A **padlock** is useful if you have a pack that is lockable. Combination locks are reputedly easier to pick than conventional padlocks, but potential thieves in Rwanda will have far less experience with them.

If you're interested in natural history, a pair of compact binoculars is very useful, and it needn't be much heavier or bulkier than a pack of cards. Binoculars are essential if you want to get a good look at birds, or to watch distant mammals in game reserves. For most purposes, 7x21 compact binoculars will be fine, though some might prefer 7x35 traditional binoculars for their larger field of vision. Serious birdwatchers will find a 10x magnification more useful.

Your toilet bag should at the very minimum include **soap** (secured in a plastic bag or soap holder unless you enjoy a soapy toothbrush!), **shampoo**, **toothbrush** and **toothpaste**. This sort of stuff is easy to replace as you go along, so there's no need to bring family-sized packs. Men will probably want a **razor**. Women should carry enough **tampons** and/or **sanitary pads** to see them through at least one heavy period, since these items may not always be immediately available. Nobody should forget to bring a **towel**, or to keep handy a roll of **loo paper**, which although widely available at shops and kiosks cannot always be relied upon to be present where it's most urgently needed.

You should carry a small **medical kit**, the contents of which are discussed in the chapter on health, as are **mosquito nets**. For those who wear **glasses**, it's worth bringing a spare pair, though in an emergency a new pair can be made up cheaply and quickly in most Rwandan towns, provided that you have your prescription available. If you wear **contact lenses**, be aware that the various fluids are not readily available in Rwanda, and, since many people find the intense sun and dust irritate their eyes, you might consider reverting to glasses.

Other essentials include a **torch (flashlight)**, a **penknife** and a compact **alarm clock** for those early morning starts. Some travellers carry **games** – most commonly a pack of cards, less often chess, draughts or travel Scrabble. A lot of washbasins in Rwanda lack **plugs**, so one of those 'universal' rubber plugs that fit all sizes of plughole can be useful.

MONEY

The unit of currency is the **Rwandan franc** (Rfr), which comes in Rfr5,000, 2,000, 1,000 and 500 notes and Rfr100, 50, 20, 10, 5 and 1 coins. The August 2012 exchange rate was around Rfr600 to the US dollar, Rfr900 to the euro and Rfr830 to the British pound, depending on whether the transaction involved cash or travellers' cheques, and where it took place. Most local services are best paid in local currency, but there are exceptions, such as gorilla-tracking fees and some upmarket hotels, which require payment in US dollars or another hard currency. Throughout this guide, prices are quoted in local currency except where the institution in question quotes rates in another currency such as US dollars or euros, in which case we follow their lead. Prices are correct for 2012, but will almost certainly be subject to inflation during the lifespan of this edition.

ORGANISING YOUR FINANCES Normally there are three ways of carrying money: hard cash, travellers' cheques and credit/debit cards. However, travellers' cheques are of little to no practical use in Rwanda, and the only card worth carrying is Visa.

There are ATMs where international Visa cards can be used to draw local currency at several branches of the Bank of Kigali and EcoBank in Kigali, as well as at the same banks in most other large towns. Even so, if the electricity is down, or the computers or server are offline, then this service will be temporarily unavailable. As things stand, you cannot draw money from an ATM with any other type of card. However, MasterCard can be used to draw cash at the Access Bank in Kigali (and sometimes also in Musanze/Ruhengeri and Rubavu/Gisenyi), but you need to do this over the counter, which can be time consuming and may involve a double currency conversion.

It is possible to pay bills with credit cards at certain upmarket hotels in Kigali and other main tourist centres, but not elsewhere. If you are relying on using a card, then it's best to check what cards your hotel accepts when you make your booking. Worth noting here too that the RDB head office in Kigali now accepts Visa but not MasterCard – see box *Booking a gorilla permit* on page 52.

That leaves cash. The US dollar is the most widely accepted foreign currency, but all main currencies should be exchangeable in Kigali, whether in banks or in official or private forex bureaux. If you do bring US dollars, be aware that US$100 and US$50 bills attract a significantly better rate than smaller-denomination bills, and few if any institutions will accept notes issued before 2006, or that are torn or marked in any way. After the US dollar, the euro and pound sterling are the most widely recognised currencies in Kigali, with the advantage that there are no problems related to changing older notes. Away from Kigali, US dollars cash is the only foreign currency easily exchangeable outside of banks.

This is a changing situation. And if you don't want to carry too much cash, or your budgeting has fallen apart and you need to be bailed out, there are Western Union facilities all over the place. This isn't cheap – the cost depends on the amount being transferred – but it's quick and secure. Any Rwandan francs left over at the end of your trip can be changed back into dollars, euros or whatever by banks, forex bureaux or money-changers.

FOREIGN EXCHANGE All Rwandan banks have branches in Kigali and there's at least one bank in each other main town, but these generally deal in cash only and rates tend to be poorer than in the capital. There are also several private bureaux de change (known locally as forex bureaux) in Kigali, which generally offer slightly better rates than banks against cash (especially if you bargain), not to mention a quicker service, but don't handle travellers' cheques. Banking hours are approximately 08.00–12.00 and 14.00–17.00 Monday–Friday (some banks stay open longer), and 08.00–12.00 Saturday. Private forex bureaux keep slightly longer hours than banks. Both are closed on Sundays and public holidays.

There are private forex bureaux in several other large towns, particularly those that lie close to a border crossing (eg: Musanze/Ruhengeri, Rubavu/Gisenyi and Rusizi/Cyangugu) and they are usually as efficient as their counterparts in Kigali.

BUDGETING

Any budget will depend so greatly on how and where you travel that it is almost impossible to give sensible advice in a general travel guide. As a rule, readers who are travelling at the middle to upper end of the price range will have pre-booked most of their trip, which means that they will have a good idea of what the holiday will cost them before they set foot in the country. Pre-booked packages do vary in terms of what is included in the price, and you are advised to check the exact conditions in advance, but generally the price quoted will cover everything but drinks, tips and perhaps some meals.

For budget travellers, Rwanda is no longer one of the cheaper countries in Africa. Genuine budget accommodation is thin on the ground; in many towns it can be difficult to find a basic room for much under US$15 and you'll often need to spend two or three times that amount for something less basic. Throughout the country, a soft drink in a local bar or shop will cost you less than US$0.50 and a 700ml beer slightly more than US$1, but these things cost a lot more in a hotel or restaurant that caters primarily to Westerners. Outside of Kigali, a simple meal in a local restaurant might cost around US$3–4, a main course in a restaurant catering more to Western palates seldom costs less than US$8, while snacks such as brochette and chips fall

CHANGING MONEY AT BORDERS

The black markets that once thrived in East Africa were killed off some years ago, but you might still need to exchange money on the street at some international borders, so that you have enough local currency to pay for transport to the next town, for a room when you get there, and – should you expect to arrive outside banking hours or over the weekend – to cover other expenses until the next banking day. As a rule you won't get the greatest rate of exchange at any border, which is fair enough, considering that moneychangers, like banks, profit by offering different rates of exchange in either direction. So there's no sense in exchanging significantly more money than you'll require before you reach a bank or forex bureau. The only exception is when you have a surfeit of cash from the country you're leaving and no intention of returning there – the border may be the last place you can unload it.

Many private moneychangers are incidental con artists, so be prepared. Check the exchange rate in advance and calculate roughly what sum of local currency you should expect. Put whatever bills you intend to change in a pocket discrete from your main stash of foreign currency before you arrive at the border. And don't stress too much if you are offered a slightly lower rate than might be expected, since pushing too hard for a good rate carries the risk of weeding out the honest guys so you end up dealing with a con artist. And be wary of a quick-talking moneychanger trying to exploit the mind-boggling decimal shifts involved in many African currency transactions.

Should you be surrounded by a mob of yelling moneychangers, pick any one of them and tell him that you will only discuss rates when his pals back off. Having agreed a rate, insist on taking the money and counting it before you hand over, or expose the location of, your own money. Should the amount be incorrect, it is almost certainly phase one of an elaborate con trick, so safest to hand it back and refuse to have anything further to do with that person. Alternatively, if you do decide to continue, then re-count the money after it is handed back to you and keep doing so until you have the correct amount counted in your hand – some crooked moneychangers possess such sleight of hand they can seemingly add notes to a wad right in front of your eyes while actually removing a far greater number of notes. Only when you are sure you have the right amount should you hand over your money.

somewhere in between. Public transport is cheap – typically about US$1.50–US$2 per 50km – and distances are relatively small. Taking the above figures into account, the most scrupulous budget travellers should bank on spending around US$30 daily (a bit less for couples, as accommodation costs less per person than for single travellers) and more like US$75–100 if you plan on staying in moderate hotels and eating in proper restaurants. This doesn't include expensive one-off activities such as gorilla tracking or visiting other national parks.

GETTING AROUND

BY AIR Rwandair Express (see page 64) operates several flights weekly between Kigali and Kamembe (for Rusizi/Cyangugu) and Rubavu/Gisenyi. There are no other scheduled domestic flights.

SELF-DRIVE Several travel agencies in Kigali rent out saloons and 4x4s, with or without drivers. For their contact details see pages 87–8. Further up-to-date listings are given in the tourism section of the Rwanda website www.rwandatourism.com. Rates vary according to whether you'll be driving outside Kigali, and whether fuel is included. A 4x4 can cost from US$120 to US$200 per day including driver, depending on its type/size. If the deal excludes fuel, bear in mind that this is not cheap – more than US$1.50 per litre – and that most 4x4s have a heavy consumption.

If you rent a self-drive vehicle, be aware that Rwanda follows the continental and American custom of driving on the right side of the road. Check the vehicle over carefully and ask to take it for a test drive. Even if you're not knowledgeable about the working of engines, a few minutes on the road should be sufficient to establish whether it has any seriously disturbing creaks, rattles or other noises. Check the condition of the tyres and that there is at least one spare tyre, better two, both in a condition to be used should the need present itself. Ask to be shown the wheel spanner and jack, check that all parts of the latter are present, and ensure that the licence is valid for the duration of your trip. Ask also to be shown filling points for oil, water and petrol and check that all the keys do what they are supposed to do. Once on the road, check oil and water regularly in the early stages of the trip to ensure that there are no existing leaks. See also the *Driving into Rwanda* box, page 40, for further survival tips.

Most trunk roads in Rwanda are surfaced and in reasonable condition, including the main road from Kigali to Rusizi/Cyangugu via Huye/Butare; to Rubavu/Gisenyi and Kinigi via Musanze/Ruhengeri; to Rusumo via Ngoma/Kibungo; to Karongi/Kibuye via Muhanga/Gitarama; and to the Uganda border via Gicumbi/Byumba or Umutara. Roads are generally good but there are still some pot-holed sections along most routes which, together with the winding terrain and the tendency for Rwandans to drive at breakneck speeds and overtake on sharp or blind corners, necessitate a more cautious approach than one might take at home.

The unsurfaced roads most likely to be used by tourists include the long stretch running parallel to Lake Kivu between Rubavu/Gisenyi, Karongi/Kibuye and Rusizi/Cyangugu, the approach roads to Akagera National Park (and roads within the park), and the roads around Lakes Burera and Ruhondo. All of these are in variable condition, and should be passable in a saloon car when dry, though a 4x4 would certainly be preferable. Do bear in mind that unsurfaced roads tend to vary seasonally, with conditions most difficult during the rains and least so towards the end of the dry season. Even within this generalisation, an isolated downpour can do major damage to a road that was in perfectly good nick a day earlier, while the

APPROXIMATE DISTANCES BETWEEN MAIN TOWNS

In kilometres

	Kigali	Huye	Gicumbi	Muhanga	Ngoma	Karongi	Rubavu	Nyamagabe	Musanze	Rusizi
Kigali		125	60	50	105	125	175	145	120	240
Huye/Butare	125		185	85	175	150	210	29	165	120
Gicumbi/Byumba	60	185		105	160	180	175	210	105	185
Muhanga/Gitarama	50	85	105		150	75	130	100	85	175
Ngoma/Kibungo	105	175	160	150		225	275	250	230	325
Karongi/Kibuye	125	150	180	75	225		85	160	130	105
Rubavu/Gisenyi	175	210	175	130	275	85		225	60	190
Nyamagabe/Gikongoro	145	29	210	100	250	160	225		190	100
Musanze/Ruhengeri	120	165	105	85	230	130	60	190		235
Rusizi/Cyangugu	240	120	185	175	325	105	190	100	235	

arrival of a grader can transform a pot-holed 4x4 track into one navigable by any saloon car.

The main hazard on Rwandan roads, aside from unexpected pot-holes, is the road-hog mentality of most drivers. Minibus-taxis in particular regularly overtake on blind corners, and speed limits (60–80km/h) are universally ignored except when enforced by road conditions. On all routes, be alert to banana-laden cyclists swaying from the verge, and livestock and pedestrians wandering blithely into the middle of the road. Putting one's foot to the floor and hooting like a maniac is the customary Rwandan approach to driving through crowded areas; driving rather more defensively than you would at home is the safer one!

A peculiarly African road hazard – one frequently taken to unnecessary extremes in Rwanda – is the giant sleeping policeman, which might be signposted in advance, might be painted in black-and-white strips, or might simply rear up without warning like a 30cm-tall macadamised wave. It's to be assumed that the odd stray bump will exist on any stretch of road that passes through a town or village, so slow down at any looming hint of urbanisation.

Rwandans, like many Africans, display an inexplicable aversion to switching on their headlights except in genuine darkness – switch them on at any other time and every passing vehicle will blink its lights back at you in bemusement. In rainy, misty or twilight conditions, it would be optimistic to think that you'll be alerted to oncoming traffic by headlights, or for that matter to expect the more demented element among Rwandan drivers to avoid overtaking or speeding simply because they cannot see more than 10m ahead. It's best to avoid driving at night, since a significant proportion of vehicles lack functional headlights, whilst others go around with their lights permanently on blinding full beam!

MOUNTAIN BIKING OR CYCLING The relatively short distances between tourist centres and the consistently attractive scenery should make Rwanda ideal for travelling by mountain bike. These cannot easily be bought locally, so you would have to bring one with you (some airlines are more flexible than others about carrying bicycles; you should discuss this with them in advance). More and more Rwandans are using cycles now, and if you ask around you should be able to find some for hire – but check the brakes carefully and carry a repair kit. Minibuses will allow you to take your bike on the roof, though expect to be charged extra for this. Minor roads vary in condition, but in the dry season you're unlikely to encounter any problems. Several of the more off-the-beaten-track destinations mentioned in this book would be particularly attractive to cyclists. The best contact for bicycle tours, particularly in the Lake Kivu region, is Rwanda Adventures in Rubavu/ Gisenyi (see page 198). They offer guided and unguided tours, and also sell reliable new and used bicycles tailored to Rwandan conditions.

HITCHING This is an option on main roads, but you should expect to pay for lifts offered by Rwandans. Some minor roads have little traffic so you could face a long wait.

PUBLIC TRANSPORT
Boat and rail There are no rail services in Rwanda (although a rail link with Tanzania has been under discussion for some time), nor is there at present a public ferry service on Lake Kivu, although private links operate between Rusizi/Cyangugu, Karongi/Kibuye, Rubavu/Gisenyi and Goma. It's possible to rent local dugouts for short excursions on the lake. Motor boats are also available for hire at Karongi, Rusizi and Rubavu. Small boats can be used to get around the smaller lakes, such as Burera and Ruhondo, by making an informal arrangement with the boat owner.

Road The main mode of road transport is shared **minibuses**, generally known as taxis (and referred to in this book as minibus-taxis to distinguish them from cabs). These connect all major centres (and most minor ones) and leave from the town's minibus station (*gare taxi/minibus*) when they are full. No smoking inside is the rule, as it is on all public transport. Departures continue throughout the day but it's best not to wait until too late, in case the last one proves to be full. Fares generally work out at around Rfr1,000 (US$1) per 50km. More precise fares for specific routes are given throughout this book, but do note that they are subject to regular inflation and occasional deflation as a result of fluctuations in the oil price and to a lesser extent the US dollar exchange rate. Travel times along main surfaced roads typically average about 50km/h, with frequent pauses to drop off passengers balanced against driving that verges on the manic between the stops.

If you're carrying luggage, either keep it on your lap (if it's small enough) or else ask for it to be stuffed in at the back or put on the roof. If you have anything fragile, keep it with you. Overloading is not the problem it is in many African countries, nor are tourists routinely overcharged, though the latter does happen from time to time, so check the fare with other passengers if it feels too high. Fares are collected just before you alight rather than when you board; you'll see other passengers getting their money ready as their destinations approach. If you're not sure of the fare, ask another passenger.

There are also several private companies running regular express services to fixed timetables with bookable seats between Kigali and other main towns. These start and finish at the company's offices rather than at the public minibus stations. The price is generally much the same as for public minibuses. Details appear under the relevant towns in *Part Two*.

BOOKING A GORILLA PERMIT

The one thing that almost all tourists to Rwanda want to do is track gorillas in Volcanoes National Park, and it is no longer the case that you can just pitch up in Kigali and be almost certain of obtaining a permit for the next day, or failing that, the day after. Particularly during the peak season of June to September, and again over the Christmas and New Year holiday period, it is now often the case that all 64 gorilla permits available daily are booked up months in advance for several days running – a scenario that is likely to become increasingly normal as greater volumes of tourists visit Rwanda.

What this means is that any visitors with a tight schedule should book their permits as far in advance as possible. If a tour operator arranges your trip, they will also arrange your gorilla permit and will normally include it in the cost of the trip (or specify it as an extra). But if you are travelling independently, you will need to arrange it yourself. There are two approaches to doing this. The first is to get a reliable local tour operator to act as a go-between and buy the permit on your behalf, which can save a lot of hassle, though the operator will add a small (and deserved) service charge to the normal cost of US$750.

The alternative is to book directly through the RDB (see page 86 for contact details), which is normally a fairly straightforward procedure, though the booking office has a reputation for ignoring email queries, so better perhaps to phone. In order to secure the booking, you may be required to transfer a deposit (around US$100 per permit) a month prior to your tracking date, with the outstanding balance to be paid upon your arrival in Kigali. The best way to pay this is in US dollars cash, but RDB accepts cash in most other hard currencies (including sterling and euro) calculated at the official US$ bank rate for the day. Visa cards can also be used to pay for your gorilla permit at the booking office in Kigali or Rubavu/Gisenyi, though a small levy may be added. Or you can transfer the full amount upfront, and save yourself the hassle of paying in Rwanda. It is possible to book (and if you like pay for) any other activities and park entrance fees associated with Volcanoes National Park at the same time. If you are prepared to take the risk, it does remain possible to pitch up at the RDB office in Kigali until 17.00 on the day before you want to track, and – assuming availability – to buy a permit on the spot. And if you are coming from across the Uganda border and want to skip Kigali altogether, you can also buy a permit at the RDB office in Rubavu/Gisenyi or the Volcanoes National Park headquarters at Kinigi the day before you want to track. There is of course no guarantee that a permit will be available at such short notice, particularly at busy times when there may already be a waiting list, but the odds are reasonable in the main rainy season of March to May.

Two-wheeled taxis In and around minibus-taxi stations you may find 'taxis' in the form of motorbikes (motos) or bicycles. They're handy for short distances – but be aware that your travel insurance may not cover you for accidents when on either of them. Agree a price beforehand, and check with a passer-by if it seems excessive. If you've got a heavy bag, a comfortable alternative is to stick it on the saddle of the bicycle and walk alongside. Commercial moto drivers and passengers are obliged by law to wear helmets, and drivers always carry one for passengers – though the chin straps are often not very secure.

Taxis In larger towns you may find normal taxis – identifiable by a yellow or orange stripe round the side – known as *taxi-voitures* to distinguish them from taxi-minibuses. Agree a price in advance and haggle if it seems extortionate. Fares in Kigali are fixed according to distance.

ACCOMMODATION

Accommodation options in Rwanda range from five-star international hotels to dingy local guesthouses, and prices vary accordingly. The main concentration of high-quality accommodation is in Kigali, but there are also facilities to international standards in and around Volcanoes, Nyungwe and Akagera National Parks and the Lake Kivu resorts of Karongi/Kibuye and Rubavu/Gisenyi. Elsewhere, there are usually mid range hotels geared to local businesspeople as much as to tourists, and cheaper local guesthouses favoured by genuine budget travellers.

Most accommodation establishments are recognisably signposted as a hotel, *logement*, guesthouse or similar, but some local places are signposted as *Amacumbi* (pronounced 'amachoombi') – which literally means 'Place with rooms' in Kinyarwanda. Note, too, that in the Swahili language – not indigenous to Rwanda but more widely spoken by locals than any other exotic tongue – a *hoteli* is a restaurant, which can create confusion when asking a non-French speaker for a hotel.

All accommodation listings in this guidebook are placed in one of five categories: exclusive/luxury, upmarket, moderate, budget, and shoestring. The purpose of this categorisation is twofold: to break up long hotel listings that span a wide price range, and to help readers isolate the range of hotels that will best suit their budget and taste. The application of categories is not rigid. Aside from an inevitable element of subjectivity, it is based as much on the feel of a hotel as its rates (which are quoted anyway) and placement is also sometimes influenced by the standard of other accommodation options in the same location.

EXCLUSIVE/LUXURY This category embraces a handful of international four- and five-star luxury hotels, as well as a few select smaller lodges and resorts notable less for their luxury than for offering a genuinely exclusive experience. Rates are typically upwards of US$300 for a double, but many cost twice as much as that. This is the category to look at if you want the best and/or most characterful accommodation and have few financial restrictions.

UPMARKET This category includes most Western-style hotels, lodges and resorts that cater mainly to international tourist or business travellers but lack the special something that might elevate them into the luxury or exclusive category. Hotels in this range would typically be accorded a two- to three-star ranking elsewhere, and they offer smart en-suite accommodation with a good selection of facilities. Rates are typically around US$120–250 for a double, dependent on quality and location. Most package tours and privately booked safaris use accommodation in this range.

MODERATE In Rwanda, as in many African countries, there is often a wide gap in price and standard between the cheapest hotels geared primarily towards tourists and the best hotels geared primarily towards local and budget travellers. For this reason, the moderate bracket is rather more nebulous than other accommodation categories, essentially consisting of hotels which, for one or other reason, couldn't really be classified as upmarket, but are also a notch or two above the budget category in terms of price and/or quality. Expect unpretentious en-suite accommodation with hot water and possibly television, a decent restaurant and some English-speaking staff. Prices for moderate city and beach hotels are generally in the US$50–100 range. This is the category to look at if you are travelling privately on a limited or low budget and expect a reasonably high but not luxurious standard of accommodation.

BUDGET Hotels in this category are aimed largely at the local market and definitely don't approach international standards, but are still reasonably clean and comfortable, and a definite cut above the basic guesthouses that proliferate in most towns. More often than not, a decent restaurant is attached, there are English-speaking staff, and rooms have en-suite facilities with running cold or possibly hot water, and netting. Expect to pay around US$25–50 for a double, less away from major tourist centres. This is the category to look at if you are on a limited budget, but want to avoid total squalor!

SHOESTRING This is the very bottom end of the market, usually small local guesthouses with simple rooms and common showers and toilets. Running the gamut from pleasantly clean to decidedly squalid, hotels in the category typically cost around US$10–20 for a room. It is the category for those to whom keeping down costs is the main imperative.

CAMPING Few formal campsites exist in Rwanda. Some hotels will permit camping in the gardens, but at little saving over the price of a budget room. There are campsites at the Volcanoes and Akagera national parks and in Nyungwe Forest. At Nyungwe, the campsite is far more attractively located than the resthouse for travellers without a vehicle. A tent may also come in handy for travellers backpacking or cycling through relatively non-touristed rural areas, where you are strongly advised to ask permission of the local village official before setting up camp.

EATING AND DRINKING

EATING OUT Kigali boasts a good range of restaurants representing international cuisines such as Indian, Italian, Chinese and French. In most other towns, a couple of hotels or restaurants serve uncomplicated Western meals – chicken, fish or steak with chips or rice. Possibly as a result of the Belgian influence, restaurant standards seem to be far higher than in most East African countries, and Rwandan chips are among the best on the continent. Servings tend to be dauntingly large, and prices very reasonable – around Rfr1,500–2,500 (US$3–4) for a *mélange* (mixed plate) at local eateries and Rfr4,000–8,000 (US$6–12) for a main course at a smarter restaurant.

Buffet or self-service meals are also on offer, often at very inexpensive rates, and are said to originate from a period in the 1980s when the government decreed that civil servants should have shorter lunch breaks. As a result, enterprising restaurants dreamed up this way of enabling them to eat faster. Smarter restaurants, especially in Kigali, may be closed or take a while to rustle up food outside of normal mealtimes.

Wherever you travel, local restaurants serve Rwandan favourites such as goat kebabs (brochettes), grilled or fried tilapia (a type of lake fish), bean or meat stews. These are normally eaten with one of a few staples: *ugali* (a stiff porridge made with maize meal), *matoke* (cooking banana/plantain), *chapatti* (flat bread), and boiled potatoes (as in Uganda, these are somewhat mysteriously referred to as Irish potatoes) – not to mention rice and the ubiquitous chips.

Unless you have an insatiable appetite for greasy omelettes or stale *mandazi* (deep-fried dough balls not dissimilar to doughnuts), breakfast outside of Kigali (where good French bread and croissants are available) or the larger hotels can be a problematic meal. One area in which Rwanda is definitely influenced more by its anglophone neighbours than by its former coloniser is baking: in common with the rest of East Africa, the bread is almost always sweetish and goes stale quickly. In such cases a bunch of bananas, supplemented by other fresh fruit, is about the best breakfast option: cheap, nutritious and filling.

COOKING FOR YOURSELF The alternative to eating at restaurants is to put together your own meals at markets and supermarkets. The variety of foodstuffs you can buy varies from season to season and from town to town, but in most major centres you can rely on finding a supermarket that stocks frozen meat, a few tinned goods, biscuits, pasta, rice and chocolate bars. If you're that way inclined, and will be staying in hotels rather than camping, bring a small electric immersion heater for use in your bedroom (sockets take standard continental two-pin plugs), plus some teabags or instant coffee, so you can supplement your picnic with a hot drink.

Fruit and vegetables are best bought at markets, where they are very cheap. Potatoes, sweet potatoes, onions, tomatoes, bananas, sugar cane, avocados, paw-paws, mangoes, coconuts, oranges and pineapples are seasonally available in most towns.

For hikers, about the only dehydrated meals available are packet soups. If you have specialised requirements, you're best doing your shopping in Kigali, where a wider selection of goods (cheese, local yoghurt…) is available in the supermarkets; there are also a handful of excellent bakeries, with mouth-watering goodies hot from the oven.

DRINKS Brand-name soft drinks such as Pepsi, Coca-Cola and Fanta are widely available, and cheap by international standards. Tap water is debatably safe to drink in Kigali, although the smell of chlorine may put you off; bottled mineral water is widely available if you sensibly prefer not to take the risk. Locally bottled fruit juice (passion fruit, orange, pineapple…) isn't bad and comes in concentrated versions too.

The most widely drunk hot beverage is tea (*icyayi* in Kinyarwanda, sometimes also referred to by the Swahili name *chai*). In rural areas, the ingredients are often boiled together in a pot: a sticky, sweet, milky concoction that is sometime referred to as African tea, and that definitely falls into the category of acquired tastes. Most Westernised restaurants serve tea as we know it, but if you want to be certain, specify that you want black tea. The milk served separately with it is almost always powdered, but of a type that dissolves well and doesn't taste too bad. Coffee is one of Rwanda's main cash crops, but you'd hardly know it judging by the insipid slop that passes for coffee in some restaurants and hotels – though this is starting to change for the better as something akin to café culture has taken hold in Kigali. You're on safe if unexciting ground with instant coffee (ask for Nescafé).

The most popular alcoholic drink is beer, brewed locally near Rubavu. The cheaper of the two local brands is Primus, which comes in 700ml bottles which cost around Rfr800–1,200 in local bars and as much as Rfr3,000 in Kigali's swankiest hotels. The most popular alternative is Mutzig, which tastes little different, costs about 30% more and comes in 700ml or 350ml bottles.

South African and French wines are sold at outrageously inflated prices in a few upmarket bars and restaurants. Far more sensibly priced are the boxes of Spanish or Italian wine sold in some supermarkets. If you want to check out your capacity

2

for locally brewed banana wine (also called *urwagwa*) before ordering it with a meal, most supermarkets and some small grocers/snack bars have bottles on sale. It comes in many varieties – some have honey added, and I've heard of a kind made in the northeast that contains hibiscus flowers. There's also a banana liqueur.

As for the harder stuff, *waragi*, a millet-based clear alcohol from Uganda, is available everywhere; either knock it back neat or mix it as you would gin. (In its undistilled form it could strip away a few layers of skin!) The illegal Rwandan firewater, *kanyanga*, is also available widely: treat with care.

PUBLIC HOLIDAYS AND EVENTS

In addition to the following fixed public holidays, Rwanda recognises Good Friday and Eid-el-Fitr (end of Ramadan).

1 January	New Year's Day
1 February	Heroes' Day
7 April	Genocide Memorial Day
1 May	Labour Day
1 July	Independence Day
4 July	Liberation Day
15 August	Assumption Day
1 October	Patriots' Day
25 December	Christmas Day
26 December	Boxing Day

The week around Genocide Memorial Day is an official week of mourning during which commemorative ceremonies are held and some activities may be reduced.

Two public events may draw crowds large enough to affect the availability of accommodation in some areas: the International Peace Marathon and Fun Run held annually in and around Kigali in May (see *www.kigalimarathon.com* and page 109), and the Kwita Izina Gorilla Naming Ceremony and cycle race held near the Volcanoes National Park in June (details from the Tourist Board and on page 240).

The last Saturday of any given month is Umuganda (Public Cleaning) Day. Between 08.00 and 11.00 there is a countrywide ban on road traffic, as the whole country embarks on communal work for the public good. This can consist of anything from local street-cleaning to road repairs, tree planting, land clearance and building homes for genocide survivors – and can result in sizable portions of the workforce being too busy to attend to travellers! Tourists are welcome to join in too. Generally, tour operators' vehicles are permitted to carry on as normal, but it is worth checking with your tour operator. If you need to be at the airport to catch a flight, a passport and valid travel ticket should be enough to secure dispensation in a taxi.

SHOPPING

All basic requirements (toiletries, stationery, batteries and so forth) are available in Kigali, and, away from the capital, most towns of any size have a pharmacy as well as a reasonable supermarket or general store. In Kigali, the pharmacy in Boulevard de la Révolution is open 24 hours, as is the superb Nakumatt Supermarket in the gleaming new Union Trade Centre.

For handicrafts you've a very wide range – wood-carvings, weaving, pottery, baskets, clay statues, beadwork, jewellery, masks, musical instruments, banana-leaf products, batik – see *Handicrafts* in *Chapter 4,* pages 107–8, and *Chapter 6*, pages 147, for more details. CDs or cassettes of Rwandan music make good gifts, as does local honey: buy it in a market and decant it into a screw-top soft-drinks bottle for travelling. (Some countries prohibit the import of foodstuffs, so check local regulations before you take any home.) Some markets stock candles made of local beeswax. Locally made wines, spirits and liqueurs are heavier to carry but generally appreciated! For traditional musical instruments, you need a well-informed local advisor to help you to pick the best and most authentic.

Women can buy lengths of brightly dyed fabric in the market and have street dressmakers make up a garment on the spot; men can similarly kit themselves out with hand-tailored shirts. And just browsing in any large street market will give you dozens more ideas…

MEDIA AND COMMUNICATIONS

NEWSPAPERS AND MAGAZINES The main English-language newspaper is the daily *New Times* (*www.newtimes.co.rw*) which provides reasonably balanced coverage with a pro-government slant. Imported dailies and weeklies from Uganda and Kenya are also available on the streets of Kigali and Huye/Butare. A very limited range of international papers can be bought at the kiosks of upmarket hotels such as the Mille Collines in Kigali. News magazines such as *Time* and *Newsweek* are available from street vendors and some bookshops. The Ikirezi bookshop in Remera has a good stock, and also sells them at the airport.

INTERNET, EMAIL AND FAX The electronic communications age has fast gained a foothold in Rwanda, and it has become an regional leader in internet services following the recent completion of a high-capacity national fibre-optic cable network worth us$50 million. Outside of Kigali, local servers tend to be slower, and some smaller towns have no public internet facilities at all. Most hotels in the moderate and higher brackets have email facilities.

TELEPHONE Rwanda's telephone system is reasonably efficient, though mobile providers tend to be more reliable than land lines. From overseas, it is definitely one of the easier African countries to get through to first time. The international code is 250. Because of the small size of the country, and limited number of phones, no area codes are in use. In 2009 the old six-digit land lines were extended to 10 digits. Numbers in this book have been modified to reflect these changes, but in case we missed any, or you come across old numbers elsewhere, just add the prefix 0252.

In Kigali, international phone calls can be made from the central post office in Avenue de la Paix and from various other shops and kiosks in the city. For calls within Rwanda the street kiosks and shops with public phones work well – calls are metered and you pay when you've finished, so there's no fussing with coins or tokens. Some of these can handle international calls too. To make an international call out of Rwanda, dial 000 then the country code, area code and local number.

Cell phones (mobiles) have caught on in a big way in Rwanda. The main provider is MTN, with around three million subscribers, and this is definitely the best option for travellers due its wide national network. The alternative is Tigo, with about one million subscribers. Cell-phone numbers are recognisable as ten-digit numbers starting with 078 (MTN) or 072 (Tigo). Mobile-phone owners from overseas can buy a local SIM card giving them a local number using the local satellite network for next to nothing. International text messages and phone calls are also surprisingly cheap from local mobile phones, and phones with internet access also usually work with local SIM cards, though it is advisable to get one of the many MTN and Tigo service centres dotted around the country to set this up.

The ubiquity and relative efficiency of mobile phones means that many hotels and other organisations in Rwanda no longer bother with landlines. Unfortunately, when it comes to hotels, this means that contact telephone details tend to change more regularly than is the case with fixed lines. For this reason we have included both numbers where they exist – the mobile will usually be easier to get through to, but there's a far greater chance a landline will still be in place in two or three years' time. Readers are welcome to alert us to any such changes by posting on our website http://updates.bradtguides.com/rwanda.

PHOTOGRAPHIC TIPS
Ariadne Van Zandbergen

EQUIPMENT Although with some thought and an eye for composition you can take reasonable photos with a 'point and shoot' camera, you need an SLR camera with one or more lenses if you are at all serious about photography. The most important component in a digital SLR is the sensor. There are two types of sensor: DX and FX. The FX is a full size sensor identical to the old film size (36mm). The DX sensor is half size and produces less quality. Your choice of lenses will be determined whether you have a DX or FX sensor in your camera as the DX sensor introduces a 0.5x multiplication to the focal length. So a 300mm lens becomes in effect a 450mm lens. FX ('full frame') sensors are the future, so I will further refer to focal lengths appropriate to the FX sensor.

Always buy the best lens you can afford. Fixed fast lenses are ideal, but very costly. Zoom lenses make it easier to change composition without changing lenses the whole time. If you carry only one lens a 24–70mm or similar zoom should be ideal. For a second lens, a lightweight 80–200mm or 70–300mm or similar will be excellent for candid shots and varying your composition. Wildlife photography will be very frustrating if you don't have at least a 300mm lens. For a small loss of quality, teleconverters are a cheap and compact way to increase magnification: a 300mm lens with a 1.4x converter becomes 420mm, and with a 2x it becomes 600mm. NB: 1.4x and 2x teleconverters reduce the speed of your lens by 1.4 and 2 stops respectively.

The resolution of digital cameras is improving the whole time. For ordinary prints a 6-megapixel camera is fine. For better results and the possibility to enlarge images, and for professional reproduction, higher resolution is available up to 21 megapixels.

It is important to have enough memory space. The number of pictures you can fit on a card depends on the quality you choose. You should calculate how many pictures you can fit on a card and either take enough cards or take a storage drive on to which you can download the card's content. Taking a laptop gives the advantage that you can see your pictures properly at the end of each day and edit and delete rejects. If you don't want the extra bulk and weight you can buy a storage device which can read memory cards. These come in different capacities.

Keep in mind that digital camera batteries, computers and other storage devices need charging. Make sure you have all the chargers, cables, converters with you. Most hotels/lodges have charging points, but it will be best to enquire about this in advance. When camping you might have to rely on charging your equipment from the car battery.

POST Post from Rwanda is cheap and fairly reliable, but can be slow. Yellow post-buses with *Iposita* on the side shuttle mail around Rwanda. Letterboxes outside post offices have a variety of appellations – sometimes *Boîte aux Lettres*, sometimes (eg: in Huye) *Box of Letters* and sometimes (a Belgian/Flemish relic in Karongi) *Brievenbus*.

RADIO AND TELEVISION The BBC World Service comes across loud and clear, on different frequencies according to the time of day. Local radio stations broadcast in Kinyarwanda, French, English and Swahili. TV is largely piped in from elsewhere, notably by the South African company DSTV, whose bouquet of channels includes CNN, Sky, BBC News et al. For football fans, the Supersport Channel operated by the DSTV shows most international and English Premiership matches and can be seen at bars all around the country.

DUST AND HEAT Dust and heat are often a problem. Keep your equipment in a sealed bag, and avoid exposing equipment to the sun when possible. Digital cameras are prone to collecting dust particles on the sensor which results in spots on the image. The dirt mostly enters the camera when changing lenses, so you should be careful when doing this. To some extent photos can be 'cleaned' up afterwards in Photoshop, but this is time-consuming. You can have your camera sensor professionally cleaned, or you can do this yourself with special brushes and swabs made for this purpose, but note that touching the sensor might cause damage and should only be done with the greatest care.

LIGHT The most striking outdoor photographs are often taken during the hour or two of 'golden light' after dawn and before sunset. Shooting in low light may enforce the use of very low shutter speeds, in which case a tripod/beanbag will be required to avoid camera shake. The most advanced digital SLRs have very little loss of quality on higher ISO settings, which allows you to shoot at lower light conditions. It is still recommended not to increase the ISO higher than necessary.

With careful handling, side lighting and back lighting can produce some stunning effects, especially in soft light and at sunrise or sunset. Generally, however, it is best to shoot with the sun behind you. When photographing animals or people in the harsh midday sun, images taken in light but even shade are likely to look nicer than those taken in direct sunlight or patchy shade, since the latter conditions create too much contrast.

PROTOCOL In some countries, it is unacceptable to photograph local people without permission, and many people will refuse to pose or will ask for a donation. In such circumstances, don't try to sneak photographs as you might get yourself into trouble. Even the most willing subject will often pose stiffly when a camera is pointed at them; relax them by making a joke, and take a few shots in quick succession to improve the odds of capturing a natural pose.

Ariadne Van Zandbergen is a professional travel and wildlife photographer specialised in Africa. She runs 'The Africa Image Library'. For photo requests, visit the website www.africaimagelibrary.com or contact her direct on e ariadne@hixnet. co.za

CULTURAL ETIQUETTE

As in most African countries, Rwandans tend to be tolerant of Westerners' ways and won't easily take offence at mildly inappropriate behaviour. All the same, it is a relatively conservative and by-and-large highly religious society, and visitors should bear in mind that certain behaviours are very unacceptable. This would include public affection between members of the opposite sex (even if they are married), overt drunkenness, skimpy attire (particularly for women), proclamations of atheism, and in some circles smoking. In conversation, extended greetings are normal, and it is considered rude to ask somebody directions or ask for something in a shop or restaurant without first greeting the person and asking after their health. Probably the biggest social gaffe you could make in Rwanda, however, is insensitive probing into matters of ethnicity or perceived ethnicity – in the aftermath of the genocide people understandably avoid referring to themselves or others as Hutu and Tutsi, and it would be wise for visitors to follow suit.

BECOMING INVOLVED   *Janice Booth*

You may leave Rwanda without a backward glance, or you may find that it has affected you more than you realised. It's an amazing country. Many visitors feel that they want to remain – or become more – involved in its people and development. Most of the large mainstream charities have activities there, but below we're listing, alphabetically, a handful of the many smaller ones for whom even one new supporter can make a difference. All describe their work and give contact details on their websites. New ones are appearing all the time: ask around when you're in Rwanda, do an internet search, or check out any listed on www.stuffyourrucksack.com (see box opposite). Also see the **Forest People's Project** (*Batwa of Rwanda* box, page 31), **Cards from Africa**, the **Centre Cesar** and the **Meg Foundation** (all in *Chapter 4*, pages 116–17), the **Imbabazi Orphanage** (pages 207–8 and 209–10) and the **Ubushobozi Foundation** (page 222). **Gorilla conservation** organisations are listed in *Chapter 10*, pages 238–9.

ENGALYNX (*www.ukvbuilder.co.uk/sites/engalynx*) Based in Essex, this is a small UK-registered charity that was set up in 1998 to help post-genocide Rwanda rebuild. Since then, it has sent to Rwanda not only funds but also computers, tools, clothes, shoes, sewing machines, hairdressing equipment, photocopiers and even bicycles. Every penny counts! It has given microscopes to students, goats to child-headed families, and equipment to schools and hospitals. It has supported training schemes for widows, orphans and young diabetics, and is currently building a village maternity unit in East Province.

FRIENDS OF RWANDAN RUGBY (*www.friendsofrwandanrugby.org.uk*) This may seem an unusual choice of charity, but sport is what binds people – particularly young people – together, which is vital in post-genocide Rwanda. FORR is a UK-registered charity supporting school and community participation in rugby, providing coaching and encouraging young people (girls as well as boys) to play. It started in 2001 when a VSO volunteer English teacher discovered that the kids in her village had no knowledge of the game, so she got them started using one ball and some old socks filled with sand as markers. The passion grew, and spread. Now many rural schools and communities around the country are involved and there is huge enthusiasm to learn. FORR runs an Annual Rugby Development Tour during which it trains and includes new schools and clubs. Matches become social events as teams from different areas meet. Rugby-minded tourists are welcome to join in a game and offer a bit of coaching, or to donate some old balls, provide some kit, or just make a donation to the work.

HELP A RWANDAN PERSON (*www.harpcharity.org.uk*) Established by UK and Rwandan co-founders in 2007, the UK-registered charity **HARP** works towards the Rwandan government's Millennium Development Goals and Rwanda Vision 2020, helping those most in need to become self-reliant. Projects are on a small and manageable scale. Outreach education is provided in health, hygiene and sanitation, together with formal education and skills training for children and adults, including adult literacy. A livestock-rearing project (chickens, rabbits and goats) is planned. Other activities assist orphans, the elderly and those with HIV/AIDS; and provide sources of safe, clean drinking water to rural schools.

RWANDA UNITED KINGDOM GOODWILL ORGANISATION (*www.rugo.org*) Registered as a UK charity in 1999, **RUGO** is one of the stalwarts among Rwanda's supporters. It has been instrumental in building and equipping two vocational training institutions and a community centre; provided specialist hospital beds, mattresses, wheelchairs, zimmer frames etc for use by Kigali Health Institute in a polyclinic; provided and channelled donations of computers and books for the National University of Rwanda and other educational establishments; supported centres such as Kigali Junior Academy, Kigali Parents' School, Village of Hope (part of the Rwanda Women's Network), Village d'Orphelins in Karongi and Uyisenga N'Imanzi (which supports child-headed households); and given practical, long-term help to so many of Rwanda's neediest individuals and communities.

One of the consequences of the genocide was that most of Rwanda's artisans with skills were lost, so RUGO's vocational training centres have been particularly valuable, both in rebuilding the country's skills base and in enabling disadvantaged young people who have missed out on secondary school to make a living for themselves and their families. For example, the Vocational School in Nyamata (in Bugesera, a remote and previously undeveloped area badly affected by the genocide – see pages 119–23) has courses including masonry and construction, carpentry, plumbing and appropriate technology, information technology, and tailoring. At the Amizero Vocational Training Centre in Kayonza, near Akagera, many students come from disadvantaged backgrounds: among them are genocide survivors, demobilised soldiers, released prisoners or members of extremely poor families.

2

STUFF YOUR RUCKSACK – AND MAKE A DIFFERENCE

Before you set off for Rwanda, do check the website www.stuffyourrucksack. com. It was set up by TV's Kate Humble, and enables travellers to give direct help to small charities, schools or other organisations in whatever country they are visiting. All of those listed on the site under Rwanda specify their requirements and will welcome your gifts – for example they may need school or sports equipment, or handicrafts materials, or small items of clothing: all things that can easily be 'stuffed in a rucksack' before departure. Their contact details are given, so you can get in touch beforehand and arrange to deliver your items; the organisation thus gets exactly what it needs, and you have the chance to meet local people and see how and where your gifts will be used.

In Rwanda darkness falls at 6pm and lasts 12 hours. For rural villagers, it's hard to work or study in the evening, and venturing outside in the pitch black can be hazardous. After funding reconstruction projects in Rwanda since 1999, RUGO (*www.rugo.org*; see page 61) has turned its attention to the small rural village of Karambi, in Nyamata sector: a remote and neglected area, which suffered badly during the genocide.

In 2011/12 RUGO raised £25,000 for equipment to provide solar power to Karambi's 110 homes: a solar panel for each house to power a fixed light inside, also to charge a portable lantern and the all-important mobile phone. These are small, plain, tin-roofed houses made of mud bricks, like those in a child's drawing, with a small shuttered opening on either side of the wooden front door.

Four ladies – 'grannies' – were chosen by the villagers to jet off to India for training in the assembly and installation of solar equipment. For unsophisticated rural women – Claudine, Cecile, Odette and Dative, aged 47 to 50 – this was a huge and frightening undertaking but they were determined to succeed. Their travel to India was supported by the Indian Government and they spent six months at the Barefoot College in Tilonia, a small village in the desert region of Rajasthan. Bunker Roy, founder of the Barefoot College, is collaborating with RUGO on the project, as is the Rwanda Women's Network.

After some early adaptation difficulties they settled in, supporting each other, and worked hard at their studies: it was a point of pride to prove that

RUGO's current project is perhaps its most innovative: four grandmothers from a remote rural village, none of whom had studied beyond primary school, have just spent six months at India's Barefoot College in Rajasthan (*www.barefootcollege.org*), training in the assembly, installation and maintenance of solar power systems. Now back home, full of enthusiasm, they are currently applying their new knowledge and abilities to setting their village electrically alight. See box *RUGO's Solar Grannies*, above.

In the UK, RUGO issues newsletters giving information about Rwanda, organises annual genocide memorial services, and holds social events to promote Rwandan culture and fundraising events to finance its work. All of its staff are unpaid volunteers; its income is dependent on members' subscriptions, donations and fundraising. The more it receives, the more it can do. Full details of how to support – and join – RUGO and share its activities are on its website.

RWANDAN YOUTH INFORMATION COMMUNITY ORGANISATION (*www.rYico. org*)

Both a UK-registered charity and a locally registered Rwandan NGO based in Kigali, **rYico** works to support and empower vulnerable young people in Rwanda. In the UK it holds events to increase social and cultural understanding about Rwanda and to fundraise for its activities; for example in July 2012 it mounted an interactive multimedia exhibition *Keeping Memories: the Rwandan Community in the UK*, combining audio, text, photos and paintings to commemorate the Rwandan past and celebrate its future. This is part of a two-year project (of the same name) for which rYico has been awarded a grant from the Heritage Lottery Fund.

In Rwanda, rYico established its **Centre Marembo** (e *marembo@ryico.org*) in Kigali in 2005. This youth centre provides a space for young people of all ages to meet, discover the services and benefits available to them, access training and education, and obtain help in building or rebuilding their lives. Vocational they were worthy of the opportunity. Training alongside them were women from other countries and they used sign language to communicate, learning to build solar lanterns and assemble the various components of the solar power systems. Tourism wasn't neglected; they were taken to local sights and even visited the Taj Mahal. They swapped their traditional village clothes for tunics and trousers and learned to climb ladders and milk cows (culturally taboo for women in Rwanda). In the end they adapted so well that friends meeting them at Kigali airport on their return hardly recognised them in their t-shirts and baseball caps!

Excited by their training and their new roles, the grannies are already demonstrating their ability. Construction of a workshop to house the solar equipment has been delayed, because the current rainy season makes the locally fired bricks too soft and wet to handle; but in the meantime they have electrified two pilot houses, so that the villagers can see their training has paid off and understand what the scheme will provide. By the time you read this, the solar-electrification of Karambi should be complete, with all of its small homes gleaming like glow-worms in the dark Rwandan night.

RUGO intends to repeat this project in other Rwandan villages. Bunker Roy, Barefoot College and the Indian Government have promised continued support, and certainly the country has no shortage of determined and conscientious women to act as 'solar grannies'!

training courses are held, and items made by students in the handicrafts courses can be bought there or in the UK via rYico's online shop (*www.Shop4Rwanda.com*). Accommodation can be provided for the homeless, and there's a weekly drop-in service for street-kids where they can wash, have a square meal and talk to non-judgemental staff. In 2012, rYico received a grant from Comic Relief to develop a transit refuge home there for girls and women, the first such in Rwanda.

Centre Marembo is also the ideal place to drop off any unwanted possessions when you're returning home – that t-shirt you won't need again, left-over toiletries or medicines, notebooks you didn't use… etc. They operate on a shoestring budget, so everything is valuable. For how to visit the Centre, see *Chapter 4*, page 117.

INVESTING IN RWANDA

The ultimate involvement in Rwanda is to invest in one of the many opportunities that the country's rapid development has created. The Rwanda Development Board (*www.rdb.rw*; e *ipd@rdb.rw*; \ (*+250) 0252 585179*) can provide full information, including the generous incentives and concessions available. The mechanisms are straightforward and investor-friendly, with a minimum of red tape.

Openings exist in many sectors; for example food processing (tea, coffee, fruit, vegetables…), financial services, ICT, mining, tourism and hospitality, solar installations, medical services, construction and transport. It's an Aladdin's cave of opportunity. And remember that the 2012 World Bank '*Doing Business*' Report named Rwanda as the third easiest African country in which to do business, after Mauritius and South Africa.

3

Health

with Dr Felicity Nicholson

Rwanda itself isn't a particularly unhealthy country for tourists and you'll never be far from some kind of medical help. The main towns have hospitals (for anything serious you'll be more comfortable in Kigali) and all towns of any size have a pharmacy, although the range of medicines on sale may be limited. In Kigali, the pharmacy in Boulevard de la Révolution is open 24 hours.

Away from Kigali, district hospitals and health centres are spread countrywide. A health centre generally has around five nurses, supported by a doctor and community health workers. In rural areas traditional medicine is also widely used. The ratios of about 1,300 inhabitants per nurse and 16,000 per doctor are high; however, in July 2012 former US president Bill Clinton announced a seven-year programme, supported by the medical faculties of 13 US universities, to train up existing medical personnel so that they in turn can train effectively. The growing private sector has more than 310 clinics and dispensaries. The incidence of HIV/AIDS is hard to estimate accurately but seems at last to be falling, thanks to preventive measures and the wider availability of antiretroviral drugs.

The most serious health threat to travellers in Rwanda is malaria. Akagera National Park and other low-lying parts of the east qualify as high risk malarial areas, especially in the rainy season. The risk exists but is far lower in highland areas such as Kigali, Butare, Nyungwe National Park, the Virunga Mountains and foothills, and the Lake Kivu region. Nevertheless, all visitors to Rwanda should take preventative measures against malaria, and be alert to potential symptoms both during their trip and after they return home.

Other less common but genuine health threats include the usual array of sanitation-related diseases – cholera, giardia, dysentery, typhoid etc – associated with the tropics (though these seem to affect visitors to Africa less than they do travellers in Asia), and bilharzia, which can only be caught by swimming in freshwater habitats inhabited by the snail that carries the disease.

If you do get ill in Rwanda, bear in mind that the most likely culprit – as in most parts of the world – will be the common cold, flu or travellers' diarrhoea, none of which normally constitute a serious health threat. However, travellers with overt cold- or flu-like symptoms might not be allowed to track gorillas or chimpanzees, both of which are susceptible to infectious airborne human diseases and may lack our resistance.

BEFORE YOU GO

IMMUNISATIONS Preparations to ensure a healthy trip to Rwanda require checks on your immunisation status: it is wise to be up to date on tetanus, polio and diphtheria (now given as an all-in-one vaccine, Revaxis, that lasts for ten years), and hepatitis A.

Immunisations against meningococcus and rabies may also be recommended. Proof of vaccination against yellow fever is needed for entry into Rwanda for all travellers over one year of age, regardless of where you are coming from. If the vaccine is not suitable for you, discuss your options with a travel-health expert; if you decide to visit Rwanda regardless, obtain an exemption certificate from your GP or a travel clinic, and try to avoid the day-biting mosquitoes that spread the disease (see *Insect bites* on page 70). Immunisation against cholera may also be recommended for Rwanda.

Hepatitis A vaccine (Havrix Monodose or Avaxim) comprises two injections given about a year apart. The course costs around £100, but in the UK may be available on the NHS; it protects for 25 years and can be administered even close to the time of departure. Hepatitis B vaccination should be considered for longer trips (two months or more) or for those working with children or in situations where contact with blood is likely. Three injections are needed for the best protection and can be given over a three-week period for those aged 16 or older if time is short. Longer schedules give more sustained protection and are therefore preferred if time allows and must be used for those under 16. Hepatitis A vaccine can also be given as a combination with hepatitis B as 'Twinrix', though two doses are needed at least seven days apart to be effective for the hepatitis A component, and three doses are needed for the hepatitis B. Again, this schedule can only be used by those aged 16 or over.

The newer injectable typhoid vaccines (eg: Typhim Vi) last for three years and are about 85% effective. Oral capsules (Vivotif) may also be available for those aged six and over. A dose of three capsules over five days lasts for approximately three years but may be less effective than the injectable forms. They should be encouraged unless the traveller is leaving within a few days for a trip of a week or less, when the vaccine would not be effective in time. Meningitis vaccine containing strains A, C, W and Y is recommended for all travellers, especially for trips of more than four weeks (see *Meningitis*, page 74). Vaccinations for rabies are ideally advised for everyone, but are especially important for travellers visiting more remote areas, especially if you are more than 24 hours from medical help and definitely if you will be working with animals (see *Rabies*, page 74).

Experts differ over whether a BCG vaccination against tuberculosis (TB) is useful in adults: discuss this with your travel clinic.

In addition to the various vaccinations recommended above, it is important that travellers should be properly protected against malaria. For detailed advice, see below. Ideally you should visit your own doctor or a specialist travel clinic (see opposite) to discuss your requirements, if possible at least eight weeks before you plan to travel.

MALARIA PREVENTION Malaria is probably the greatest health risk to travellers in Rwanda, although it is less prevalent there than in some other African countries. There is no vaccine against malaria, but using prophylactic drugs and preventing mosquito bites will considerably reduce the risk of contracting it. Seek professional advice to ascertain the preferred anti-malarial drugs for Rwanda at the time you travel. If mefloquine (Lariam) is suggested, start this 2½ weeks (three doses) before departure to check that it suits you; stop it immediately if it seems to cause depression or anxiety, visual or hearing disturbances, severe headaches, fits or changes in heart rhythm. Side effects such as nightmares or dizziness are not medical reasons for stopping unless they are sufficiently debilitating or annoying. Anyone who has been treated for depression or psychiatric problems, who has diabetes controlled by oral therapy or who is epileptic (or has suffered fits in the past) or has a close blood relative who is epileptic, should probably avoid mefloquine.

In the past doctors were nervous about prescribing mefloquine to pregnant women, but experience has shown that it is relatively safe and certainly safer than the risk of malaria. That said, there are other issues, so if you are travelling to Rwanda whilst pregnant, seek expert advice before departure.

Malarone (proguanil and atovaquone) is as effective as mefloquine. It has the advantage of having few side effects and need only be continued for one week after returning. However, it is expensive and because of this tends to be reserved for shorter trips. Malarone may not be suitable for everybody, so advice should be taken from a doctor. It can safely be used for up to a year though the cost may be prohibitive, and a paediatric form of tablet for children weighing 11kg or more is also available, prescribed on a weight basis.

Another alternative is the antibiotic doxycycline (100mg daily). Like Malarone it can be started one day before arrival. Unlike mefloquine, it may also be used by travellers with epilepsy, although certain anti-epileptic medication may make it less effective. In perhaps 1–3% of people there is the possibility of allergic skin reactions developing in sunlight; the drug should be stopped if this happens. Women using the oral contraceptive should use an additional method of protection for the first four weeks when using doxycycline. It is also unsuitable in pregnancy or for children under 12 years.

Chloroquine and proguanil are no longer thought to be effective enough for Rwanda but may be considered as a last resort if nothing else is deemed suitable.

All tablets should be taken with or after the evening meal, washed down with plenty of fluid and, with the exception of Malarone (see above), continued for four weeks after leaving.

In addition to prophylactic drugs, there is a case for carrying a treatment for malaria, in case you develop malarial symptoms when medical assistance is unavailable. The longer you are spending in Africa, the more the case for this strengthens, and it would certainly be recommended to anybody undertaking a long overland trip, or volunteering or working in a remote area, or who travels in Africa regularly. Whatever you decide, you should seek up-to-date advice to find out the most appropriate medication.

There is no malaria transmission above 3,000m; at intermediate altitudes (1,800–3,000m) the risk exists but is low. In addition to taking anti-malarial medicines, it is important to avoid mosquito bites between dusk and dawn, which is when the anopheles (malaria-carrying) mosquito is most active. Pack a **DEET-based insect repellent** (ideally containing 50–55% DEET), such as one of the Repel range, and take either a **permethrin-impregnated bednet** or a **permethrin spray** so that you can treat bednets in hotels. Permethrin treatment makes even very tatty nets protective and mosquitoes are also unable to bite through the impregnated net when you roll against it. Putting on socks and long clothes (including long-sleeved shirts or blouses) at dusk reduces the risk of bites and the amount of repellent needed. Be aware, however, that malaria mosquitoes usually hunt at ankle level and their bite can penetrate through socks, so apply repellent to your feet and ankles whether or not you wear socks. Travel clinics usually sell a good range of nets, treatment kits and repellents. See *Insect bites* on page 70 for more information on how to avoid mosquito bites.

TRAVEL CLINICS AND HEALTH INFORMATION A full list of current travel clinic websites worldwide is available on www.istm.org. For other journey preparation information, consult www.nathnac.org/ds/map_world.aspx. Information about various medications may be found on www.netdoctor.co.uk/travel.

3

LONG-HAUL FLIGHTS, CLOTS AND DVT

Any prolonged immobility including travel by land or air can result in deep vein thrombosis (DVT) with the risk of embolus to the lungs. Certain factors can increase the risk and these include:

- Previous clot or close relative with a history
- People over 40 but > risk over 80 years
- Recent major operation or varicose veins surgery
- Cancer
- Stroke
- Heart disease
- Obesity
- Pregnancy
- Hormone therapy
- Heavy smokers
- Severe varicose veins
- People who are very tall (over 6ft/1.8m) or short (under 5ft/1.5m)

A deep vein thrombosis (DVT) causes painful swelling and redness of the calf or sometimes the thigh. It is only dangerous if a clot travels to the lungs (pulmonary embolus). Symptoms of a pulmonary embolus (PE) include chest pain, shortness of breath, and sometimes coughing up small amounts of blood and commonly start three to ten days after a long flight. Anyone who thinks that they might have a DVT needs to see a doctor immediately.

PREVENTION OF DVT
- Keep mobile before and during the flight; move around every couple of hours
- Drink plenty of fluids during the flight
- Avoid taking sleeping pills and excessive tea, coffee and alcohol
- Consider wearing flight socks or support stockings (see *www.legshealth. com*)

If you think you are at increased risk of a clot, ask your doctor if it is safe to travel.

TRAVEL INSURANCE Before you travel, make sure that you have adequate medical insurance – choose a policy with comprehensive cover for hospitalisation as well as for repatriation in an emergency. Nowadays the range of cover available is very wide – choose whatever suits your method of travel. Be aware, if you plan to use cycles or motorbike taxis in Rwanda, that not all policies cover you for this form of transport. Remember to take all the details with you, particularly your policy number and the telephone number that you have to contact in the event of a claim.

PERSONAL FIRST-AID KIT A minimal kit contains:
- A good drying antiseptic, eg: iodine or potassium permanganate (don't take antiseptic cream)
- A few small dressings (Band-Aids)
- Suncream

- Insect repellent; anti-malarial tablets including treatment for those going to remote places; impregnated bed-net or permethrin spray
- Aspirin or paracetamol
- Antifungal cream (eg: Canesten)
- Ciprofloxacin or norfloxacin, for severe diarrhoea
- Tinidazole for giardia or amoebic dysentery (see below for regime)
- Antibiotic eye drops, for sore, 'gritty', stuck-together eyes (conjunctivitis)
- A pair of fine pointed tweezers (to remove hairy caterpillar hairs, thorns, splinters, coral, etc)
- Alcohol-based hand rub or bar of soap in plastic box
- Condoms or femidoms
- A digital thermometer

ON THE GROUND

COMMON MEDICAL PROBLEMS

Travellers' diarrhoea At least half of those travelling to the tropics/developing world will experience a bout of travellers' diarrhoea during their trip; the newer you are to exotic travel, the more likely you will be to suffer. By taking precautions against travellers' diarrhoea you will also avoid typhoid, cholera, hepatitis, dysentery, worms, etc.

From food Travellers' diarrhoea and the other faecal-oral diseases come from getting other peoples' faeces in your mouth. This most often happens from cooks not washing their hands after a trip to the toilet, but even if the restaurant cook

TREATING TRAVELLERS' DIARRHOEA

It is dehydration which makes you feel awful during a bout of diarrhoea and the most important part of treatment is drinking lots of clear fluids. Sachets of oral rehydration salts give the perfect biochemical mix to replace all that is pouring out of your bottom but they do not taste nice. Any dilute mixture of sugar and salt in water will do you good, so if you like Coke or orange squash, drink that with a three-finger pinch of salt added to each glass. Otherwise make a solution of a four-finger scoop of sugar with a three-finger pinch of salt in a glass of water. Or add eight level teaspoons of sugar (18g) and one level teaspoon of salt (3g) to one litre (five cups) of safe water. A squeeze of lemon or orange juice improves the taste and adds potassium, which is also lost during a bout of diarrhoea. Drink two large glasses after every bowel action, and more if you are thirsty. If you are not eating, then you need to drink three litres a day plus the equivalent of whatever is pouring into the toilet. If you feel like eating, take a bland, high-carbohydrate diet. Heavy, greasy foods will probably give you cramps.

If the diarrhoea is bad, or you are passing blood or slime, or you have a fever, you will probably need antibiotics in addition to fluid replacement. A three-day course of Ciprofloxacin 500mg twice daily (or Norfloxacin) is appropriate treatment for dysentery and bad diarrhoea. If the diarrhoea is greasy and bulky and is accompanied by 'eggy' burps, the likely cause is giardia. This is best treated with Tinidazole (2g in one dose repeated seven days later if symptoms persist).

does not understand basic hygiene you will be safe if your food has been properly cooked and arrives piping hot. The maxim to remind you what you can safely eat is:

PEEL IT, BOIL IT, COOK IT OR FORGET IT.

This means that fruit you have washed and peeled yourself, and hot foods, should be safe, but raw foods, cold cooked foods, salads, fruit salads prepared by others, ice cream and ice are all risky, as are foods kept lukewarm in restaurant or hotel buffets. Self-service or buffet meals are popular in Rwanda, so try to eat these when the food is hot and freshly cooked – for example a late buffet lunch eaten in the mid-afternoon will have been sitting around a long while. If you do get travellers' diarrhoea, see box on page 69 for treatment.

From water It is also possible to get sick from drinking contaminated water, so try to drink from safe sources. You must assume that tap water is risky wherever you are in Rwanda. To make risky water safe it should be brought to the boil (even at altitude it only needs to be brought to the boil), passed through a good bacteriological filter or purified with iodine; chlorine tablets (eg: Puritabs) are also adequate although theoretically less effective, and they taste nastier. Micropur tablets are tasteless but take at least two hours to become effective. If you buy bottled water (which is widely available in Rwanda) make sure the seal is intact. Iodine is not recommended in pregnancy so you should ask a doctor what you should do.

Insect bites The prevalence of malaria in parts of Rwanda means it is crucial to avoid mosquito bites between dusk and dawn, paying particular attention to your ankles, since malaria-carrying mosquitoes often hunt at ground level. As the sun is setting, don long clothes and socks, and apply repellent to your ankles (under or over your socks) and to any other exposed flesh. Ideally, sleep under a permethrin-treated bednet or in an air-conditioned room. If that is not possible, burning a mosquito coil or mat will hugely reduce mosquito activity, as will putting on a fan (mosquitoes dislike turbulent air). In areas where mosquitoes seem common, it is advisable to close all windows at night, or any time you have the lights on, to prevent them from infiltrating the room from outside.

Many budget hotels make no effort to control mosquito numbers, so rooms are often infested. If you suspect this to be the case, spray the room with a suitable aerosol insecticide before you go out for dinner, paying special attention to the dark corners where they rest up by day (under the bed or behind curtains or cupboards) and any en suite bathroom. If you didn't bring an aerosol room spray with you, you should be able to buy one at larger supermarkets in most towns.

By day it is wise to wear long, loose (preferably 100% cotton) clothes if you are pushing through scrubby country; this will deter ticks as well as tsetse flies and day-biting Aedes mosquitoes which may spread dengue and yellow fever. Tsetse flies hurt when they bite and are attracted to the colour blue; locals will know where they are a problem and where they transmit sleeping sickness (see page 74).

Minute pestilential biting blackflies spread river blindness in some parts of Africa between 19°N and 17°S; the disease is caught close to fast-flowing rivers since flies breed there and the larvae live in rapids. The flies bite during the day but long trousers tucked into socks will help keep them off. Citronella-based natural repellents do not work against them.

Tumbu flies or *putsi* are a problem in hot and humid areas of eastern, western and southern Africa. The adult fly lays her eggs on the soil or on drying laundry;

Malaria usually begins with a fever, the first symptoms of which are often a general flu-like feeling of slight disorientation in the head or weakness in the legs. You may then feel cold, shivery, shaky and very sweaty. Headache, feeling sick and vomiting are common with malaria and you are also likely to experience muscle aches. The cycle of fever and sweating is repeated at intervals from daily, to alternate days to around three days with a fever-free period between. Some people develop jaundice (yellowing of the eyes and or skin). However, it is not necessary for all these symptoms to be present before suspecting malaria. The only consistent symptom is a fever of 38° C or more which lasts for more than a few hours.

While you are away, assume that any high fever lasting more than a few hours is malaria, regardless of other symptoms. Although the progression of malaria is variable and unpredictable, early diagnosis and treatment will greatly increase the likelihood it doesn't develop into a life-threatening condition, so seek medical help as soon as possible, or – if this is not possible – be prepared to self-diagnose and medicate. Remember that the symptoms of malaria may develop anything from seven days after entering a malarious area up to one year after leaving, so if symptoms appear after your return home tell a doctor immediately and mention that you have been in a malarious area.

when the eggs come in contact with human flesh (when you put on clothes or lie on a bed) they hatch and bury themselves under the skin. Here they form a crop of 'boils' each of which hatches a grub after about eight days, when the inflammation will settle down. In putsi areas either dry your clothes and sheets within a screened house, or dry them in direct sunshine until they are crisp, or iron them.

Jiggers or sandfleas are another kind of flesh-feaster. They latch on if you walk barefoot in contaminated places, and set up home under the skin of the foot, usually at the side of a toenail where they cause a painful, boil-like swelling. These need picking out by a local expert; if the distended flea bursts during eviction the wound should be dowsed in spirit, alcohol or kerosene, otherwise more jiggers will infest you.

Skin infections Any mosquito bite or small nick in the skin provides an opportunity for bacteria to foil the body's usually excellent defences; it will surprise many travellers how quickly skin infections start in warm humid climates and it is essential to clean and cover even the slightest wound. Creams are not as effective as a good drying antiseptic such as dilute iodine, potassium permanganate (a few crystals in half a cup of water), or crystal (or gentian) violet. One of these should be available in most towns. If the wound starts to throb, or becomes red and the redness starts to spread, or the wound oozes, and especially if you develop a fever, antibiotics will probably be needed: flucloxacillin (250mg four times a day) or cloxacillin (500mg four times a day). For those allergic to penicillin, erythromycin (500mg twice a day) for five days should help. See a doctor if the symptoms do not start to improve in 48 hours.

Fungal infections also get a hold easily in hot moist climates, so wear 100% cotton socks and underwear and shower frequently. An itchy rash in the groin or flaking between the toes is likely to be a fungal infection. This needs treatment with

Health ON THE GROUND

3

African ticks are not the prolific disease transmitters they are in the Americas, but they may occasionally spread disease. Lyme disease, which can have unpleasant after-effects, has now been recorded in Africa, and tick-bite fever also occurs. The latter is a mild, flu-like illness, but still worth avoiding. If you get the tick off whole and promptly, the chances of disease transmission are reduced to a minimum.

Manoeuvre your finger and thumb so that you can pinch the tick's mouthparts, as close to your skin as possible, and slowly and steadily pull away at right angles to your skin. This often hurts. Jerking or twisting will increase the chances of damaging the tick which in turn increases the chances of disease transmission, as well as leaving the mouthparts behind.

Once the tick is off, dowse the little wound with alcohol (local spirit, whisky or similar is excellent) or iodine. An area of spreading redness around the bite site, or a rash or fever coming on a few days or more after the bite, should stimulate a trip to a doctor.

an antifungal cream such as Canesten (clotrimazole); if this is not available try Whitfield's ointment (compound enzoic acid ointment) or crystal violet (although this will turn you purple!).

Prickly heat   A fine pimply rash on the torso is likely to be heat rash; cool showers, dabbing (not rubbing) dry, and talc will help; if it's bad you may need to check into an air-conditioned hotel room for a while. Slowing down to a relaxed schedule, wearing only loose, baggy 100% cotton clothes and sleeping naked under a fan reduce the problem.

Sun damage   Give some thought to packing suncream. The incidence of skin cancer is rocketing as Caucasians are travelling more and spending more time exposing themselves to the sun. Keep out of the sun during the middle of the day and, if you must expose yourself to the sun, build up gradually from 20 minutes per day. Be especially careful of exposure in the middle of the day and of sun reflected off water, and wear a T-shirt and lots of waterproof suncream (at least SPF20) when swimming. Sun exposure ages the skin, makes people prematurely wrinkly and increases the risk of skin cancer. Cover up with long, loose clothes and wear a hat when you can. The glare and the dust can be hard on the eyes, too, so bring UV-protecting sunglasses and, perhaps, a soothing eyebath.

Sexual risks   Travel is a time when we may enjoy sexual adventures, especially when alcohol reduces inhibitions. Remember the risks of sexually transmitted infection are high, whether you sleep with fellow travellers or with locals. More than half of HIV infections in British heterosexuals are acquired abroad and AIDS is a serious problem in Rwanda. Use condoms or femidoms, preferably bearing the British kite mark and ideally bought before travel. If you notice any genital ulcers or discharge get treatment promptly.

OTHER DISEASES
Bilharzia or schistosomiasis *with thanks to Dr Vaughan Southgate of the Natural History Museum, London, and Dr Dick Stockley, The Surgery, Kampala*

Bilharzia or schistosomiasis is a disease that commonly afflicts the rural poor of the tropics. Two types exist in sub-Saharan Africa – Schistosoma mansoni and Schistosoma haematobium. It is an unpleasant problem that is worth avoiding, though can be treated if you do get it. This parasite is common in almost all water sources in Rwanda – even places advertised as 'bilharzia-free', such as Lake Kivu. The most risky shores will be close to places where infected people use water, wash clothes, etc.

It is easier to understand how to diagnose it, treat it and prevent it if you know a little about the life cycle. Contaminated faeces are washed into the lake, the eggs hatch and the larva infects certain species of snail. The snails then produce about 10,000 cercariae a day for the rest of their lives. The parasites can digest their way through your skin when you wade, or bathe in infested fresh water.

Winds disperse the snails and cercariae. The snails in particular can drift a long way, especially on windblown weed, so nowhere is really safe. However, deep water and running water are safer, while shallow water presents the greatest risk. The cercariae penetrate intact skin, and find their way to the liver. There male and female meet and spend the rest of their lives in permanent copulation. No wonder you feel tired! Most finish up in the wall of the lower bowel, but others can get lost and can cause damage to many different organs. *Schistosoma haematobium* goes mostly to the bladder.

Although the adults do not cause any harm in themselves, after about 4–6 weeks they start to lay eggs, which cause an intense but usually ineffective immune reaction, including fever, cough, abdominal pain, and a fleeting, itching rash called 'safari itch'. The absence of early symptoms does not necessarily mean there is no infection. Later symptoms can be more localised and more severe, but the general symptoms settle down fairly quickly and eventually you are just tired. 'Tired all the time' is one of the most common symptoms among expats in Africa, and bilharzia, giardia, amoeba and intestinal yeast are the most common culprits.

Although bilharzia is difficult to diagnose, it can be tested at specialist travel clinics. Ideally tests need to be done at least six weeks after likely exposure and will determine whether you need treatment. Fortunately it is easy to treat at present.

Avoiding bilharzia

* If you are bathing, swimming, paddling or wading in fresh water which you think may carry a bilharzia risk, try to get out of the water within ten minutes
* Avoid bathing or paddling on shores within 200m of villages or places where people use the water a great deal, especially reedy shores or where there is lots of water weed.
* Dry off thoroughly with a towel; rub vigorously.
* If your bathing water comes from a risky source try to ensure that the water is taken from the lake in the early morning and stored snail-free; otherwise it should be filtered or Dettol or Cresol should be added.
* Bathing early in the morning is safer than bathing in the last half of the day.
* Cover yourself with DEET insect repellent before swimming: it may offer some protection.

Dengue fever This mosquito-borne disease resembles malaria but there is no prophylactic available to deal with it. The mosquitoes which carry this virus bite during the daytime, so it is worth applying repellent if you see them around. Symptoms include strong headaches, rashes and excruciating joint and muscle pains with high fever. Dengue fever lasts for only a week or so and is not usually fatal if you have not previously been infected. Complete rest and paracetamol are the usual treatment. Plenty of fluids also help. Some patients are given an intravenous drip to keep them from dehydrating. Dengue may be a serious illness particularly with repeated infections so it is best to avoid it in the first place.

Ebola Visitors to Africa often express concern about this deadly, very contagious and highly publicised disease. However, Ebola has never been diagnosed in Rwanda, and while outbreaks have occurred in neighbouring Uganda and Congo, these were highly localised and occurred some distance from the Rwandan border. In the unlikely event of an outbreak, protective measures will be taken and you should follow whatever local advice is given. Even in Rwanda, it is probably advisable to avoid entering bat caves following a recent isolated fatality caused by transmission of the similar but equally rare Marburg virus in one such cave in Uganda.

Meningitis This is a particularly nasty disease as it can kill within hours of the first symptoms appearing. The telltale symptoms are a combination of a blinding headache (light sensitivity), a blotchy rash and a high fever. Immunisation with the newer tetravalent vaccine ACWY protects against the most serious bacterial form of meningitis and is usually recommended for longer-stay trips to Rwanda or if you are working closely with the local population – in particular with children. A single injection gives good protection for three years. Other forms of meningitis exist (usually viral) but there are no vaccines for these. Local papers normally report outbreaks. If you show symptoms go to a doctor immediately.

Sleeping sickness African trypanosomiasis, or sleeping sickness, is a parasitic infection transmitted by the tsetse fly. There are two sub-species; one predominates in East Africa and usually causes an acute infection, whereas the other predominates in Central and West Africa and causes a slower progressive, chronic infection. In Rwanda, tsetse flies are more or less confined to low-lying Akagera National Park, and at the time of writing no sleeping sickness has been recorded in the country for longer than a decade. However, if you cross into the Democratic Republic of the Congo (DRC), be aware that over 500 new cases were recorded there in 2010 (the most recent statistics available), so take extra care in parts of the country where tsetse flies are present (see *Insect bites* on page 70).

Other sanitary diseases Travellers in Rwanda are at risk of suffering from a bout of the usual array of sanitation-related diseases – cholera, giardia, dysentery, typhoid, worms, etc – associated with the tropics. Preventative measures are the same as those for travellers' diarrhoea (see *Travellers' diarrhoea* on page 69).

ANIMALS

RABIES Rabies can be carried by all mammals (beware the village dogs and small monkeys in the parks) and is passed on to man through a bite, scratch or a lick of an open wound. You must always assume any animal is rabid, and seek medical help as soon as possible. Meanwhile scrub the wound with soap under a running tap or while pouring water from a jug. Find a reasonably clear-looking source of water (but at this stage the quality of the water is not important), then pour on a strong iodine or alcohol solution of gin, whisky or rum. This helps stop the rabies virus entering the body and will guard against wound infections, including tetanus.

Pre-exposure vaccinations for rabies are ideally advised for everyone, but are particularly important if you intend to have contact with animals and/or are likely to be more than 24 hours away from medical help. Ideally three doses should be taken over a minimum of 21 days as this will change and simplify the treatment course. Contrary to popular belief these vaccinations are relatively painless.

If you are bitten, scratched or licked over an open wound by a sick animal, then post-exposure prophylaxis should be given as soon as possible, though it is never too late to seek help, as the incubation period for rabies can be very long. Those who have not been immunised will need a full course of injections and in most cases the first dose of vaccine is given with a weight-determined injection of rabies immunoglobulin (RIG). This is expensive (around US$800) and may be very hard to come by, but if you have had the full course of pre-exposure vaccination then it is not needed. This is a good reason to vaccinate travellers before they go if they have time.

And remember that, if you do develop rabies, mortality is virtually 100% and death from rabies is probably one of the worst ways to go.

SNAKEBITE Snakes rarely attack unless provoked and bites to travellers are unusual. You are less likely to get bitten if you wear stout shoes and long trousers when in the bush. Most snakes are harmless and even venomous species will only dispense venom in about half of their bites. If bitten, then, you are unlikely to have received venom; keeping this fact in mind may help you to stay calm. Many so-called first-aid techniques do more harm than good: cutting into the wound is harmful; tourniquets are dangerous; suction and electrical inactivation devices do not work. The only treatment is antivenom. In case of a bite which you fear may have been from a venomous snake:

- Try to keep calm – it is likely that no venom has been dispensed.
- Prevent movement of the bitten limb by applying a splint.
- Keep the bitten limb BELOW heart height to slow the spread of any venom.
- If you have a crepe bandage, bind up as much of the bitten limb as you can, but release the bandage every half hour.
- Evacuate to a hospital which has antivenom. At the time of writing this is only known to be available in Kampala. Many centres have an Indian antivenom that does not include the most common biting snakes in Rwanda

And remember:

- NEVER give aspirin; you may offer paracetamol, which is safe.
- NEVER cut or suck the wound.
- DO NOT apply ice packs.
- DO NOT apply potassium permanganate.

If the offending snake can be captured without risk of someone else being bitten, take it to show to the doctor – but beware, since even a decapitated head is able to dispense venom in a reflex bite.

USEFUL CONTACTS IN KIGALI

+ **King Faisal** (or Faycal) ☎0252 582421/585397; emergency ☎0252 588888; e faisal@rwanda1.com; www.kfh.rw

+ **Central Hospital of the University of Kigali** ☎0252 575406/575555; e chuck.hospital@ chuckigali.org; www.chk.org.rw

✚ **Faith Clinic** ✎0252 570296   ✚ **Central Kigali Polyclinic** ✎0252 576377
✚ **Plateau Polyclinic** ✎0252 578767; **m** 078   ✚ **Polyfam** ✎0252 573477
8301630; **e** pcp@rwanda1.com

For emergency dental treatment, contact the **Adventist Dental Clinic** (✎ *0252 582431*), while optometric services are available at **Eye Care Optical** (**m** *078 8867121;* **e** *eyecareoptical.rwanda@yahoo.com*). For further medical listings, see www.theeye.co.rw.

Part Two

THE GUIDE

4

Kigali

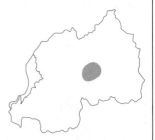

The low-key but attractive Rwandan capital city of Kigali stands in the centre of the country, where it straggles over several hills and valleys, spanning altitudes of around 1,300m to 1,600m. The city was founded in 1907 at a location chosen by Dr Richard Kandt, who built an administrative residence close to the present-day Gakinjiro Market. Two years later, 20 houses were built close to the present-day prison (one of which has been restored as a natural history museum) on the eastern slopes of Nyarugenge Hill, which now forms the commercial city centre.

Kigali remained a small and isolated colonial outpost until 1916, when Belgium ousted Ruanda-Urundi's German colonisers. Under Belgian rule, Kigali retained an important administrative role, but urban growth was very slow and confined mainly to Nyarugenge. Indeed, when Rwanda gained independence in 1962, the population of Kigali stood at no more than 6,000. When Ruanda-Urundi (the capital of which was Usumbura, now Bujumbura) split into Rwanda and Burundi, the strongest contender to become Rwanda's new capital seemed to be Butare (now named Huye), which had been the more important administrative centre during colonisation.

However, Kigali's central position and good road links to the rest of the country won out. As a result, while Huye has avoided capital-city brashness and remains relatively calm, Kigali has grown dramatically, with a population that reached 965,398 by 2009 and is likely to have already passed the one-million mark. The commercial city centre is still on Nyarugenge Hill, while the government and administrative quarter is further east on Kacyiru Hill. Between and around these elevated twin centres, empty spaces on the hillsides are filling with new housing, and pollution in the valleys (from the increasing volume of traffic) could soon be a problem.

The centre of Kigali is bustling, colourful and noisy, but (for an African city) surprisingly clean and safe (indeed, in 2008, Kigali was effectively pronounced the cleanest city on the continent, when it became the first African urban centre to be presented with the Habitat Scroll of Honour award, an annual award launched by the UN Human Settlements Programme in 1989). However it is undergoing rapid development and change, with shiny new shopping malls and office buildings springing up all over the city centre; most recently, the construction of a huge city hall has begun with an estimated cost of US$12.9bn. It remains to be seen if Kigali's green credentials survive all this development.

Kigali's occupants, from smart-suited businesspeople to scruffy kids hawking newspapers or pirated cassettes, go purposefully about their activities, only lessening tempo briefly in the middle of the day. Occasional traffic lights, roundabouts, a strictly enforced one-way road system and a cacophony of car horns manage (more or less) to regulate the traffic, although it's heavy and congested at peak times.

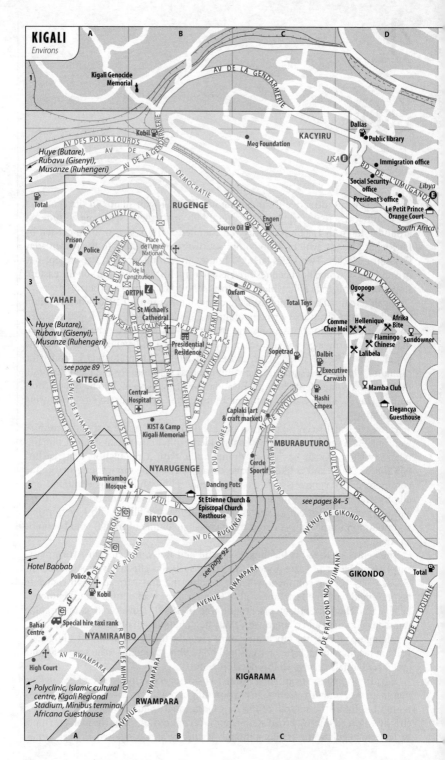

KIGALI
Environs

Kigali Genocide Memorial

AV DE LA GENDARMERIE

Kobil

AV DES POIDS LOURDS

Huye (Butare), Rubavu (Gisenyi), Musanze (Ruhengeri)

AV DE LA GENDARMERIE

AV DE LA DEMOCRATIE

Meg Foundation

KACYIRU

Dallas
Public library

USA

Immigration office

BD DE L'UMUGANDA

Libya

Social Security office
President's office

Le Petit Prince
Orange Court

South Africa

RUGENGE

AV DES POIDS LOURDS

Engen
Source Oil

Total

AV DE LA JUSTICE

Prison
Police

Place de l'Unité National

Place de la Constitution

ORTPN

St Michael's Cathedral

CYAHAFI

R DU COMMERCE
R DE BULERA
R DU LAC BULERA
R DES MILLE COLLINES
R DE LA PAIX

AV DES GDS LACS

AV DE LA JUSTICE

AV DE DEPUTE KAMUZINZI

Huye (Butare), Rubavu (Gisenyi), Musanze (Ruhengeri)

see page 89

GITEGA

AVENUE DE MONT KIGALI

AVENUE DE NYAKABANDA

AVENUE DE LA JUSTICE

Central Hospital

KIST & Camp Kigali Memorial

Presidential Residence

AVENUE PAUL VI

R DEPUTE KAYURU

R DU PROGRES

Oxfam

BD DE L'OUA

Total Toys

Comme Chez Moi

Hellenique

Afrika Bite

Flamingo Chinese

Lalibela

Ogopogo

Sundowner

AV DU LAC MUHAZI

Sopetrad

Dalbit

Executive Carwash

Mamba Club

Elegancya Guesthouse

Hashi Empex

AV DE KIYOVU

AV DE YAKAGERA

Caplaki (art & craft market)

NYARUGENGE

Nyamirambo Mosque

AV PAUL VI

Dancing Pots

Cercle Sportif

MBURABUTURO

BOULEVARD DE L'OUA

see pages 84–5

St Etienne Church & Episcopal Church Resthouse

BIRYOGO

AV DE RUGUNGA

AVENUE DE GIKONDO

AVENUE DE LA NYABARONGO

Hotel Baobab

Police

Kobil

AV DE RUGUNGA

see page 92

AVENUE RWAMPARA

GIKONDO

Total

AV DE FRAIPOND NDAGIJIMANA

R DE LA DOUANE

Bahai Centre

Special hire taxi rank

NYAMIRAMBO

AV RWAMPARA

High Court

AVENUE DE LES MIHINDI

AVENUE RWAMPARA

KIGARAMA

Polyclinic, Islamic cultural centre, Kigali Regional Stadium, Minibus terminal, Africana Guesthouse

RWAMPARA

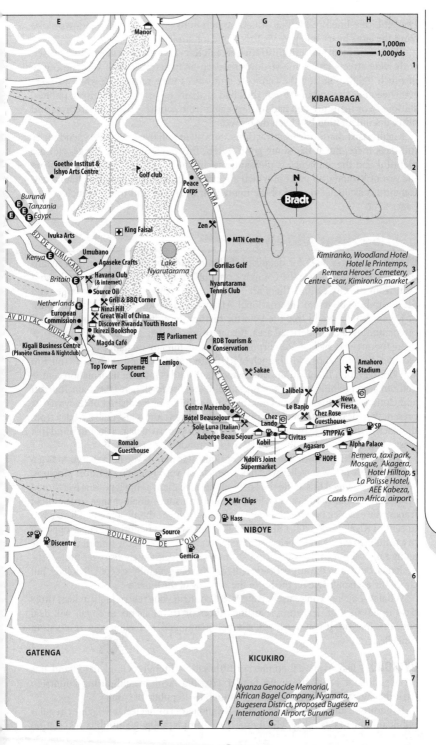

Manor

KIBAGABAGA

0 ——— 1,000m
0 ——— 1,000yds

1

2

Goethe Institut &
Ishyo Arts Centre

Golf club

NYARUTARAMA

Peace
Corps

Bradt

N

Burundi
Tanzania
Egypt

Ivuka Arts

King Faisal

Zen

Kenya

Umubano

MTN Centre

Kimiranko, Woodland Hotel
Hotel le Printemps,
Remera Heroes' Cemetery,
Centre Cesar, Kimironko market

3

Agaseke Crafts

Lake
Nyarutarama

Gorillas Golf

Britain

Havana Club
(& internet)

Source Oil

Nyarutarama
Tennis Club

BD DE L'UMUGANDA

Netherlands

Grill & BBQ Corner

European
Commission

Ninzi Hill
Great Wall of China

Sports View

AV DU LAC

Discover Rwanda Youth Hostel

MUHAZI

Ikirezi Bookshop

Parliament

Amahoro
Stadium

Kigali Business Centre
(Planète Cinema & Nightclub)

Magda Café

RDB Tourism &
Conservation

4

Top Tower

Supreme
Court

Lemigo

BD DE L'UMUGANDA

Sakae

Lalibela

Le Banjo

New
Fiesta

Centre Marembo

Chez
Lando

Chez Rose
Guesthouse

Hôtel Beausejour

Sole Luna (Italian)

Civitas

STIPPAG

SP

Auberge Beau Séjour

Kobil

Agasaro

Alpha Palace

Romalo
Guesthouse

Ndoli's Joint
Supermarket

HOPE

Remera, taxi park,
Mosque, Akagera,
Hotel Hilltop,
La Palisse Hotel,
AEE Kabeza,
Cards from Africa, airport

5

Mr Chips

Hass

NIBOYE

SP

Discentre

BOULEVARD DE L'OUA

Source

Gemica

Kigali

4

6

GATENGA

KICUKIRO

7

Nyanza Genocide Memorial,
African Bagel Company, Nyamata,
Bugesera District, proposed Bugesera
International Airport, Burundi

81

Peaceful, tree-lined residential streets stretch outwards and generally downwards from the city's heart, and give visitors scope for strolling.

The government and administrative area in Kacyiru quarter is newer and quieter, with wide streets and some striking modern architecture. Kigali was the centre of much fighting during the genocide and offices were ransacked; when workers returned after the end of the war they had virtually no usable typewriters, phones, stationery or furniture and had to start again from scratch. Also files, archives and other documentation had been destroyed.

Kigali hasn't many tourist attractions and you're unlikely to want to spend many full days there, but it has some good hotels, the services (shops, banks, etc) are plentiful and the ambience is pleasant, making it an excellent base for exploring the rest of Rwanda, all parts of which are easily reached by road in less than a day. Car-hire is available via one of the many tour operators and travel agencies – see pages 87–8.

GETTING THERE AND AWAY

BY AIR See pages 36–7 for details of flights to and from Rwanda – which means to and from Kigali, since the country's only international airport is situated about 5km from the city centre. There are firm plans to replace this with the larger and more modern Bugesera International Airport near Nyamata, about 40km south of Kigali, which would free the land for further development and bring jobs and opportunities to an underused area. the latest news is that it is due to open in 2015.

In the arrivals hall of the airport you'll find foreign exchange and telephone facilities, various shops and a branch of RDB (Rwanda Development Board) Tourism and Conservation Reservation Office which is Rwanda's tourism information centre. You can get a preliminary stock of maps, guides and so forth here (the main Tourism and Conservation Reservation Office is in the administrative district of Kacyiru). At present there is no pestering from porters – there aren't any – just grab a trolley from the stack in the baggage reclaim area and deal with your own bags. (Bear in mind that plastic bags are banned in Rwanda; stick to more solid alternatives.)

To get into Kigali town you've three options. (Or four, if you're prepared to beg a lift from some fellow traveller who has a vehicle.) If your hotel does airport pick-ups, you'll have arranged this at the time of booking; give them a ring if no-one has turned up to collect you. If you've very little luggage and some small change in Rwandan francs, you can pick up a minibus-taxi in the road outside the airport and it'll take you to central Kigali for Rfr200. Otherwise take a *taxi-voiture* (a normal taxi, as opposed to a minibus-taxi). Agree a price with the driver in advance. At the time of writing the going rate is about Rfr10,000 or US$20, but rates do legitimately rise over time. If the exchange bureau in the airport is closed, taxi-drivers generally accept US dollars, but check the exchange rate on the list in the window of the bureau.

Whatever airline you've used, you MUST confirm your return flight at least three days in advance of departure – airline offices or travel agents in Kigali will deal with this for you. If you don't, you risk being 'bumped' or having your reservation cancelled.

BY ROAD Kigali is a well-connected little city – literally. Good roads and bus services link it to all the main border crossings with neighbouring countries: Uganda, Tanzania, Burundi and the Democratic Republic of Congo.

In addition, almost all towns within Rwanda are connected to Kigali by regular public minibus-taxis, all of which now leave from Nyabugogo minibus-taxi station (*gare routière* Nyabugogo), 2km from the city centre along the Byumba Road. Minibus-taxis from the city centre to Nyabugogo station leave from Av de la Justice [89 A3]. Or you can take a taxi-voiture. Nyabugogo is a huge taxi park and the minibuses are lined up in ranks, some signposted with destinations, others not – if in doubt, just ask someone and you'll be shown where to wait.

The minibuses leave as soon as they've a full complement of passengers – and that does mean *full* as in can of sardines – but everyone gets a seat and there's a non-smoking policy on board. In addition to the minibus taxis there are many private companies that operate regular express bus services from Nyabugogo to all the major towns in Rwanda. These buses are much faster, reliable and more comfortable. They leave at scheduled times regardless of the number of passengers on board, but they are invariably full as they are a popular and relatively convenient way to get around, so you may have to wait until there is a bus with seats available.

While you're waiting for your minibus to leave, vendors of all sorts will be trying to catch your eye and sell you something – including bottled drinks and fruit, as well as fresh bread and cakes. You can even buy hard-boiled eggs, and season them from the salt and pepper pots conveniently provided! If you want something more substantial to eat before you leave, the **Amahoro restaurant** behind the International and Stella Express bus stands is clean, cheerful and serves hearty plates of African buffet food for Rfr1,500.Recently the private bus companies have specialised in serving different geographical areas of the country. These times and prices are correct at the time of writing, but may change during the lifetime of this edition. For going to the east of the country, **Stella** operates services to Rwamagana, Rfr1,200, every 30 mins, and Ngoma/Kibungo, Rfr2,000, every 30 mins. **International** operates an hourly service to Rusumo on the Tanzanian border, Rfr3,000, and Kahana (Tanzania) Rwf 7,500 once daily departing at 05.45.

For going to the south of Rwanda, **Volcano** operates regular services to Muhanga/ Gitarama, Rfr1,000, every 15 mins; Nyanza, Rfr1,800, every 30 min; Huye/Butare, Rfr2,600, every 30 mins; and Nyamagabe/Gikongoro, Rfr3200, every 30 mins. **Horizon** also operates a reliable and regular service to Muhanga/Gitarama, Rfr1,000, every 15 mins; and Huye/Butare, Rfr2,600, every 30 mins.

For going to the north and west, **Virunga** (m *250 788 43 19 60; www. virungatravel.com/express*) operates services to Gicumbi/Byumba, Rfr1,100, every 45 mins; Musanze/Ruhengeri, Rfr1,800, every 30 mins; and Rubavu/Gisenyi, Rfr3,100, every 30 mins.

Belvadere (m *078 08565081;* e *karefely@yahoo.fr*), is another good, reliable company that operates services to Musanze/Ruhengeri, Rfr1,800, every 30 mins; Rubavu/Giseny, Rfr3,100, every 30 mins. Belvadere also operates a service to Bujumbura in Burundi, Rfr11,000 return; and to Nyagatare in the far east of the country near Uganda, Rfr3,000, every 30 mins.

For travel to Kampala in Uganda, **Kampala Coach** operates 2 services a day from Nyabugogo, departing at 05.45 and 18.00, Rfr10,000 at the time of writing.

GETTING AROUND

The centre of Kigali – for shopping, banks, airline offices, tour operators, etc – is tiny; once you're there, you'll never be far from what you're looking for. It's based around two streets, Boulevard de la Révolution and Avenue de la Paix, and the various roads branching off them. However, if you ask directions you'll soon become aware that people don't go much on street names, rather on well-known landmarks. The **Union**

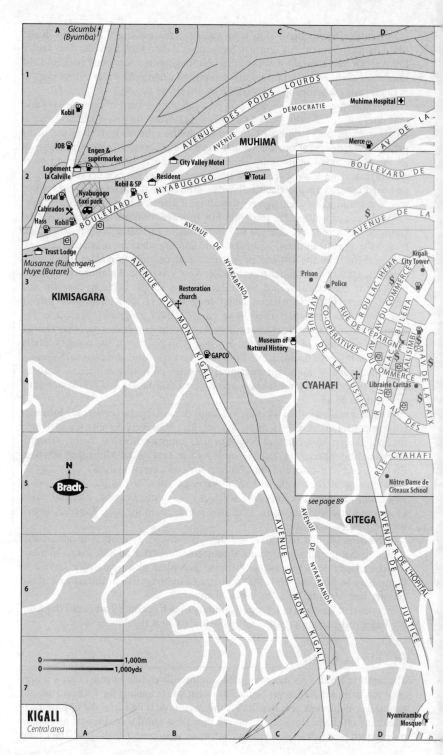

KIGALI
Central area

see page 89

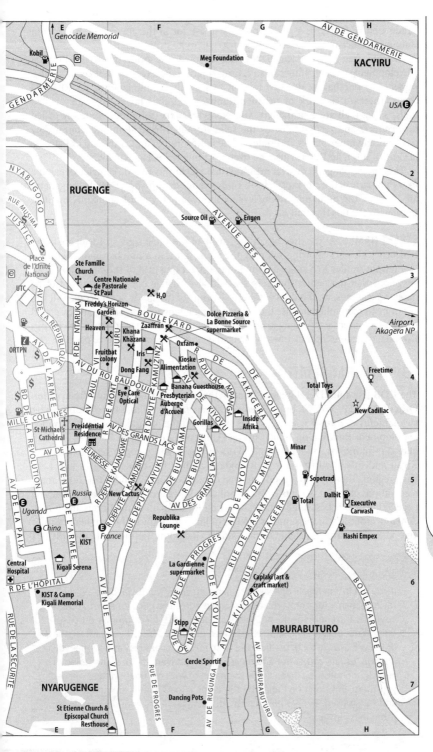

Kigali GETTING AROUND

4

Trade Centre (UTC) is a good landmark to ask for in the city centre. It is within walking distance of most places and all taxi and moto drivers know it.

A good free map of Kigali city can be obtained from the RDB (Rwanda Development Board) Tourism and Conservation Reservation Office. It is also possible to purchase a detailed foldout map of the whole country for Rfr8,500 there. There's a network of urban **minibuses** (minibus-taxis, commonly called taxis) serving all areas of the city, and plenty of **taxis** (saloons, commonly called *taxi-voitures* and recognisable by the yellow/orange stripe along the side) – they park, among other places, in Boulevard de la Révolution and at the top of Place de la Constitution, and also cruise the streets waiting to be flagged down.

There is no longer a central **minibus-taxi station** in Kigali. Vehicles departing for other parts of the city mostly leave from Avenue de la Justice. Despite the general air of chaos, there's an underlying level of sanity and, if you ask someone, you'll be pointed to the bus that you need.

STREET NAMES At the time of writing, many of the street signs in Kigali are being replaced with ones showing not only the name but also a number-and-letter code (somewhat similar to a zip code) linking the street to a grid of the city. It had been suggested that the names themselves would also change but this seems not to be happening at present. If it does within the lifetime of this guide, local people will still continue to remember and use the old names for a long while – and in any case tend to orient themselves according to popular landmarks rather than roads. (Elsewhere in Rwanda, the names of nine towns were changed in 2006; for details see pages 38–9.)

TOURIST INFORMATION

The **RDB (Rwanda Development Board) Tourism and Conservation Reservation Office** (☏ *0252 576514 or 573396;* e *reservation@rwandatourism.com; www. rwandatourism.com or www.rdb.rw*) is situated on the ground floor of the Rwanda Development Building on Boulevard de l'Umuganda [81 F4] in Kacyiru. The staff here can inform you about current events in Kigali, and you can get a free map of Kigali and other tourist areas in Rwanda including the national parks and Lake Kivu region. There is also a good selection of books about Rwanda. This is the main reservations office for permits to track gorillas in Volcanoes National Park (details on page 52), which is best done before you set off for the park as the tickets are in high demand, especially in the summer months of July and August. The staff here can also give advice on travel to neighbouring countries including Tanzania and the DRC.

MOTO-ING AROUND   *Caroline Pomeroy*

If you get lost in Kigali, or it starts to rain, you will never be far from a moto – the local name for a motorbike taxi. Always agree the price for a moto ride in advance, and check the helmet – they are often good for decorative purposes only, as the buckles and straps are broken or far too loose. If you protest, the driver will usually try tp readjust the strap for you, or as likely as not offer you his own, usually rather hot and greasy…! Most drivers speak a smattering of French or English, so if you know the name of your destination they will get you there. But don't be fooled by the maps – road names are non-existent and rarely used. People navigate by buildings and local landmarks, so try using these instead.

An excellent source of information on Kigali for visitors and expatriates alike is the website *www.livinginkigali.com*. It has a guide to living in different areas of the city, restaurant reviews, a calendar of events and a forum to post questions. Another good source of information is *The Eye* (m *078 8496897/8570353;* e *theeye@theeye. co.rw; www.theeye.co.rw*), a quarterly magazine distributed for free at several outlets in Kigali; it includes (as does its website) extensive listings of hotels, restaurants, shops and other facilities. Last, but hopefully not least, check out the updates, or contribute your own, on our website http://updates.bradtguides.com/rwanda.

TOUR OPERATORS

All of the operators listed below can organise day excursions or longer safaris, as well as vehicle hire, accommodation, airport transfers, gorilla-tracking permits, and so forth. All have some English-speaking staff. In addition there are several more travel agents, who can deal with national and international travel but don't necessarily obtain gorilla permits (which are issued byhe RDB Tourism and Conservation Reservation Office). The two below offer particularly varied services.

Volcanoes Safaris [89 D5] Hotel des Mille Collines; `0252 502452, 576530; m 078 8302069; e salesrw@volcanoessafaris.com; www. volcanoessafaris.com. A recommended first stop, this well-established company is widely regarded as the leading tour company in Rwanda, & it is also specialised in Uganda (& included under international operators on pages 34–5). It can arrange gorilla trips (including fly-in visits) as well as tours to most other corners of the country, & its Virunga Lodge near Volcanoes National Park is one of the most beautifully located & best run in Rwanda.

Bizidanny Tours & Safaris [89 B5] Cnr Av du Commerce/Lac Bulera; m 078 8501461; e infobizidanny@yahoo.fr; www.bizidanny.com & http://bizidanny.over-blog.com. Praised by several readers of previous editions, this small operator offers relatively budget-friendly tailor-made trips. As well as all the standard trips he also offers visits to schools, orphanages, women's cooperatives, local development projects, etc.

Other established operators include:

Abacus Rwanda Safaris Hotel des Mille Collines, Annex Kigali; `+256 414 232 657 (Uganda); e info@ rwanda-safari.com; www.rwanda-safari.com
Amber Expeditions PO Box 3090; `0280 306090; e info@amberexpeditions.com; www. amberexpeditions.com
Concord/Magic Safaris Rwanda Chadel Building, Bd des Mille Collines; `078 8433499; e rwoperations@magic-safaris.com; www.magic-safaris.com
International Tours & Travel SORAS building, Bd de la Révolution; `078 8461913; e itt@ rwanda1.com; www.itt.co.rw
Intore Expeditions `078 8353736; e info@ intoreexpeditions.com; www.intoreexpeditions.com
Primate Safaris Av de la Paix; `078 8300495; e primatesafaris@rwanda1.com; www. primatesafaris-rwanda.com

Rwanda Eco-tours RUMA Building, Av de la Paix; `0252 500331; m 078 8352009/ 078 8301080; e info@rwandaecotours.com; www.rwandaecotours.com
The Far Horizons `0252 580752; e info@ thefarhorizons.com; www.thefarhorizons.com
Thousand Hills Expeditions 1000 Av de l'Akanyaru, Kiyovu; `078 830100/078 8300430; e info@thousandhillsexpeditions.com; www. thousandhillsexpeditions.com
Wildlife Tours – Rwanda Opp Banque Populaire du Kimironko; m 078 8357052; e info@ wildlifetours-rwanda.com; www.wildlifetours-rwanda.com

There are several more around the city offering various levels of service, and new ones are opening. Check the current position on www.rwandatourism.com. We can't list them all – so by all means try some out, and tell us about them for the next edition! Also, away from Kigali, see Green Hill Eco-Tours and Rwandan Adventures (*Chapter 8*, page 198) and Amahoro Tours (*Chapter 9*, page 219.)

WHERE TO STAY

Virtually all of the Kigali hotels in the 'Luxury' to 'Middle' categories can arrange airport pick-ups – just ask (and check the cost, if any) at the time of booking. Unless otherwise specified, bedrooms in all of the Kigali hotels listed here have en-suite facilities with either bath or shower. Hotels in Remera suburb are closer to the airport than are those in the centre.

LUXURY (*over $200 double*) Kigali is served by four city hotels that conform to international standards at every level. These hotels tend to be bland and somewhat impersonal, and they cater mainly to business travellers, however they offer an excellent range of facilities. In terms of quality of service and facilities, the **Serena** is undoubtedly the pick – indeed, it's still the only hotel that conforms to international 5-star standards – and it is priced accordingly. However the **Gorillas Golf Hotel** in the upmarket suburb of Nyarutarama and the more established **Umubano Hotel** are more conveniently located for the administrative district of Kacyiru and also have excellent facilities and very good-quality rooms. The recently renovated **Hotel des Mille Collines** made famous by the film *Hotel Rwanda* is something of a Kigali institution and a worthy place to stay right in the heart of the city.

Kigali Serena Hotel [85 E6] (104 rooms) 0252 597100; m 078 8184500; e reservations@serena.co.rw; www.serenahotels.com. This top-notch 5-star hotel opened as the InterContinental in 2003 on the site of the former Diplomates, & was bought & renamed by the Kenya-based Serena Group in 2007. It lies on the tree-lined Bd de la Révolution, a flat 10min stroll from the city centre. The large carpeted rooms are the best on offer in Kigali, & come with king-size beds, DSTV, Wi-Fi, mini-bar, tea/coffee-making facilities, safe, hairdryer, combined tub/shower, & 24hr room service. Other facilities include a 550-seat conference centre, gym, spa, several boutiques, top-class cuisine at 2 restaurants & 24hr business services. The compact green grounds are centred on a large swimming pool & the relaxed poolside Sokon Café. Credit cards are accepted. *US$273/364 sgl/dbl; US$295/395 superior; US$400 upwards for suites; all rates inc a superb buffet b/fast.*

Gorillas Golf Hotel [81 G3] (18 rooms) m 0788174000; e reservation@gorillashotels.com; www.gorillashotels.com. This new hotel which is part of the Gorillas chain is situated in the peaceful, upmarket suburb of Nyarutarama, between the airport & the city centre. It boasts excellent views of the city & golf course & the staff appear to be

very friendly, professional & attentive. The hotel has very good facilities including a sauna, gym, massage parlour, bar, 100-seat conference centre & a swimming pool with a sweeping panoramic view. Rooms are smart, spacious & well maintained with DSTV, Wi-Fi, mini bar, shower & tub, safe, tea/coffee-making facilities. The hotel restaurant serves upmarket French & continental cuisine, although a snack menu is also available. The hotel is a short walk from the MTN centre & some good restaurants. *US$250/280 sgl/dbl, US$300/330 deluxe, US$400 upwards for suites; discounts possible for stays longer than 7 days.*

Hotel des Mille Collines [89 D5] (112 rooms) 0252 576530/3; f 0252 576541; e millecollines@millecollines.net; www.millecollines.net. This Kigali institution was founded in 1973 & gained more recent international fame as the subject of the film *Hotel Rwanda* although the film was not made there. Despite its convenient location, a 5min moderately sloping walk from the city centre, it lies in attractive grounds that offer some enjoyable urban birdwatching, dominated by a large swimming pool & a massive fig tree that looks as if it's been there since time began, but is only 40-odd years old. The rooms have recently been renovated & updated to four-star standards with smart new

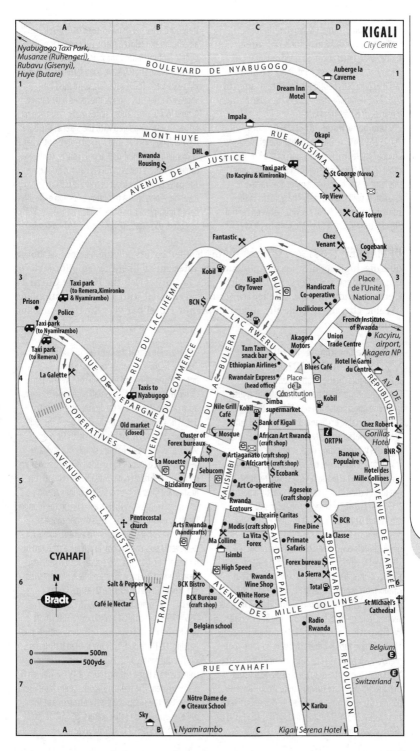

Nyabugogo Taxi Park,
Musanze (Ruhengeri),
Rubavu (Gisenyi),
Huye (Butare)

BOULEVARD DE NYABUGOGO

MONT HUYE

RUE MUSIMA

Auberge la
Caverne

Dream Inn
Motel

Impala

Okapi

Rwanda
Housing

DHL

AVENUE DE LA JUSTICE

Taxi park
(to Kacyiru & Kimironko)

St George (forex)

Top View

Café Torero

Fantastic

Chez
Venant

Cogebank

KABUYE

Kobil

Kigali
City Tower

Handicraft
Co-operative

Place
de l'Unité
National

Taxi park
(to Remera,Kimironko
& Nyamirambo)

Prison

Police

BCN

SP

Jucilicious

RUE DU LAC IHEMA

Taxi park
(to Nyamirambo)

Taxi park
(to Remera)

LAC RWERU

Akagera
Motors

French Institute
of Rwanda

Kacyiru,
airport,
Akagera NP

La Galette

RUE DE L'EPARGNE

RUE DE LA BULERA

Tam Tam
snack bar

Ethiopian Airlines

Union
Trade Centre

Hotel le Garni
du Centre

CO-OPERATIVES

AVENUE DU COMMERCE

Taxis to
Nyabugogo

Rwandair Express
(head office)

Blues Café

Place
de la
Constitution

Kobil

AV DE LA RÉPUBLIQUE

AVENUE DE LA JUSTICE

Old market
(closed)

RUE DE LA

Nile Grill
Café

Kobil

Simba
supermarket

Cluster of
Forex bureaux

Mosque

African Art Rwanda
(craft shop)

Bank of Kigali

Chez Robert

Gorillas
Hotel

La Mouette

Ibuhoro

Artiaganato (craft shop)

ORTPN

BNR

KALISIMBI

Sebucom

Africarte (craft shop)

Banque
Populaire

Bizidanny Tours

Ecobank

Hotel des
Mille Collines

Art Co-operative

Ageseke
(craft shop)

Pentecostal
church

Rwanda
Ecotours

Librairie Caritas

BCR

CYAHAFI

Arts Rwanda
(handicrafts)

Modis (craft shop)

Fine Dine

La Classe

AVENUE DE L'ARMÉE

Ma Colline

La Vita
Forex

Primate
Safaris

N

Isimbi

Forex bureau

AV DE LA PAIX

High Speed

La Sierra

Salt & Pepper

BCK Bistro

Rwanda
Wine Shop

White Horse

Total

BOULEVARD

TRAVAIL

Café le Nectar

BCK Bureau
(craft shop)

AVENUE DES MILLE COLLINES

St Michael's
Cathedral

Belgian school

Radio
Rwanda

Belgium

DE LA RÉVOLUTION

Switzerland

RUE CYAHAFI

Nôtre Dame de
Citeaux School

Sky

Karibu

Nyamirambo

Kigali Serena Hotel

0 ——— 500m
0 ——— 500yds

Bradt

bathroom suites, carpets & furniture. In-room facilities include DSTV, mini-bar & Wi-Fi access, & safe, & the hotel also has a good restaurant, a pricey bar, a tennis court, conference & business facilities & various boutiques. Credit cards accepted. *US$229/249 sgl/dbl, suites US$391 upwards including an excellent buffet breakfast.*

🏠 **Umubano Hotel** [81 E3] (100 rooms) 📞0252 593500; e info@umubanohotel.rw; www. umubanohotel.rw. Formerly part of the Novotel chain (& still frequently referred to by that name), this large 4-star hotel has a quiet & attractive location in well tended leafy 4ha gardens in the administrative quarter of Kacyiru, between central Kigali & the airport, & linked to both by plenty of transport, whether minibus-taxis or *taxi-voitures*. It's an efficient but relaxed place, very popular with local people for functions, & the personnel are friendly. The rooms are large & have good facilities, including king-size beds, DSTV, safe, fan, combined tub/shower & mini-bar, though the faded blue carpets & tired looking bathroom suites make them appear rather shabby compared with the Serena. The hotel has banking facilities, also a good restaurant & bar, swimming pool, mini-golf, tennis courts, conference facilities, fitness centre, Wi-Fi & various boutiques. The patisserie in the foyer serves the best coffee in Rwanda, along with a tempting selection of freshly baked mini-pizzas, pastries & filled baguettes. Visa accepted. *US$180/220 sgl/dbl; US$220–260 suite.*

UPMARKET (*US$130–180 double*) This header covers a wide variety of hotels offering high-quality accommodation at rates more likely to be affordable to non-business travellers. It's difficult to pick favourites, but the **Hotel le Garni du Centre** stands out as a smaller owner-managed hotel with a useful location and likeable character, while the suburban **Manor Hotel** has very smart rooms and good facilities.

🏠 **Banana Guesthouse** [85 F4] (8 rooms) 📞0252 500154; m 078 8826777/075 8826777; e fbananaguesthouse@yahoo.com; www. bananaboutiquehotel.net. This small but stylish boutique guesthouse opened in Sept 2008 & offers very comfortable accommodation in small but nicely decorated en-suite rooms with terracotta tiles, DSTV, fan, writing desk & dbl beds. The restaurant is no longer open to the general public but meals can be made for guests on request. Its got lots of character, but it's not exactly a bargain. *US$130–150 dbl, depending on room size.*

🏠 **Hotel Gorillas** [85 G4] (31 rooms) 📞0252 501717/8; m 078 8300473; e reservation@ gorillashotels.com; www.gorillashotels.com. This calm & efficient hotel, about 1km east of the city centre, has small & somewhat dated but comfortable rooms & one of Kigali's most highly rated continental restaurants, with indoor & outdoor seating, & large draft beer on tap. Facilities include Wi-Fi access in the restaurant & TV in all rooms, some of which have tubs & others showers, so state your preference if you have one. The downhill walk to the hotel from the centre of town is manageable but the upward walk into town is quite steep; however plenty of taxi-voitures ply the route & minibus-taxis run nearby. *US$90/110 standard sgl/dbl, US$120/140 deluxe rooms, inc b/fast.*

🏠 **Hotel le Garni du Centre** [89 D4] (11 rooms) 📞0252 572654; e garni@rwanda1.com; hotelgarnikigalirwanda@gmail.com; www.garni. co.rw. This commendable small hotel, tucked away down a side street near the better-known Hotel des Mille Collines, is an unqualified gem. The quiet, comfortable rooms, which come with TV, free Wi-Fi, phone & mini-bar, are simply but stylishly decorated, & overlook the garden & small swimming pool. Lunch & dinner are available by request; the Restaurant Chez Robert & Mille Collines are only a few mins' walk away. There's a log fire in the lounge for chilly evenings, & the Swiss owner-manager – who lives on the premises – is very obliging. It's deservedly popular so book in advance (this can be done online). *US$140/180 sgl/dbl for 1 night, inc a superb buffet b/fast, with discounts for longer stays.*

🏠 **Hotel le Petit Prince Orange Court** [80 D2] (14 rooms) 📞0252 580181; m 078 8861479; e oracourts@yahoo.com. This smart newish hotel in Kacyiru has sgl rooms with ¾ bed, netting, DSTV, fridge, balcony & tiled bathrooms, similar dbl rooms with king-size beds, & immense suites with a large sitting room, 2 TVs, a kitchen & a dining area. The ordinary rooms seem indifferent value, but the suites are pretty attractive at the price, especially for self-caterers. *US$80/120 sgl/dbl room; US$120/140 sgl/dbl suite.*

🏠 **Lemigo Hotel** [81 F4] (97 rooms) ☎078 4040924; e info@lemigohotel.com; www. lemigohotel.com. Located on the edge of Kacyiru near several international organisations & somewhat bland & impersonal, nevertheless this hotel has very good facilities & everything you would need for a comfortable stay in Kigali. It has a swimming pool & spa/gym, conference centre, bar & restaurant. Rooms have large TVs with DSTV, Wi-Fi, safe, hairdryer & AC. *US$160/185 sgl/dbl for a standard room, US$270 upwards for suites.*

🏠 **The Manor Hotel** [81 F1] (23 rooms) ☎072 7690030; m 078 6654435; e info@ themanorrwanda.com; www.themanorrwanda. com. Located off the Nyarutarama road down a cobbled street, this hotel has a lovely swimming pool with views across the city & Chinese, Indian, Italian & Irish restaurants within the hotel grounds. Rooms are smart, carpeted & have big balconies, DSTV, mini bar, Wi-Fi, tea/coffee-making facilities, & very well maintained bathrooms with tub & shower. There is also a bakery & boutique shops. Expats from the local community sometimes come for the day to use the swimming pool & other facilities which gives the hotel a livelier atmosphere at weekends. Service is friendly & professional if a little slow at times. *US$150/195 sgl/dbl; upwards of U$200 for deluxe & executive rooms.*

🏠 **Stipp Hotel Kiyovu** [85 F6] (50 rooms) ☎0252 587301; m 078 8305682; e management@stipphotelrwanda.com; www. stipphotelrwanda.com. This large newish hotel has a suburban setting about 2km east of the city centre & excellent facilities including a large swimming pool, continental restaurant with an Italian- & French-influenced menu, health & fitness centre with gym, sauna & massage, & Wi-Fi & DSTV in all rooms. The carpeted rooms are spacious & smartly decorated, with en-suite combined tub/shower, & suites have AC, sofa & safe. It's very smart but a bit soulless. Visa, MasterCard & Amex accepted. *Rfr84,800/90,100 sgl/dbl B&B; Rfr106,000 dbl suite.*

🏠 **Top Tower Hotel** [81 E4] (48 rooms) ☎0252 553100/ 078 8301225; e info@toptowerhotel.com; www.toptowerhotel.com. This 8-storey hotel in Kacyiru has made its name locally as the site of Kigali's first casino, which is on the 2nd floor & opens 20.00–05.00 daily. It also aspires to be one of the city's leading upmarket hotels, & the accommodation certainly impresses, consisting of spacious well-lit carpeted en-suite rooms with twin or king-size beds, large flat screen DSTV, writing desk, & combined tub/shower, as well as larger suites with a sitting area. It's also well placed for nightlife, with its in-house casino & bar with a view, & proximity to the lively Kigali Business Centre. That said, it suffers from something of a character deficit, lacks any outdoor seating or garden worth talking about, & the asking price seems steep for what it is. *US$150/170 sgl/dbl B&B; US$220–270 suite.*

MODERATE (*US$60–120 double*) Cheaper and generally of lower quality than the upmarket options listed above, hotels listed in the moderate category mostly still cater routinely to bona fide tourists. That said, it's difficult to draw a clear qualitative line between some hotels listed as upmarket and the best of those in the moderate bracket, so we've settled on a cut-off price of US$120 for a standard double, which means that the best hotels in the moderate category – strikingly, **Inside Afrika**, **La Palisse** and the **Iris Guesthouse** – represent some of the best value in town.

🏠 **Alpha Palace Hotel** [81 H5] (38 rooms) m 078 8304947; e alphapalace@ymail.com; www.alphapalacerw.com. Situated in Remera, about 1km from the airport & 4km from the centre of town, this is a comfortable, modern hotel with a swimming pool, a 24hr restaurant with French, African & oriental cuisine, a snack-bar for grills, & a nightclub on Fri/Sat. The tiled rooms are very comfortable & spacious, & come with king-size beds, DSTV, balcony & en-suite bath & shower. *US$70/90 sgl/dbl or US$150 suite, inc continental b/fast.*

🏠 **Civitas Hotel** [81 G5] (23 rooms) ☎078 8887823; e info@civitasrwanda.com; www. civitashotelrwanda.com. This new hotel on the airport road opposite Chez Lando has smart, spacious & clean rooms with TV, en-suite bathrooms with tub & shower, minibar & Wi-Fi. Also offers special packages for stays of above 1 month. Good restaurant with an outside patio area which has become popular with local people. *Fair value at US$70/80 sgl/dbl.*

4

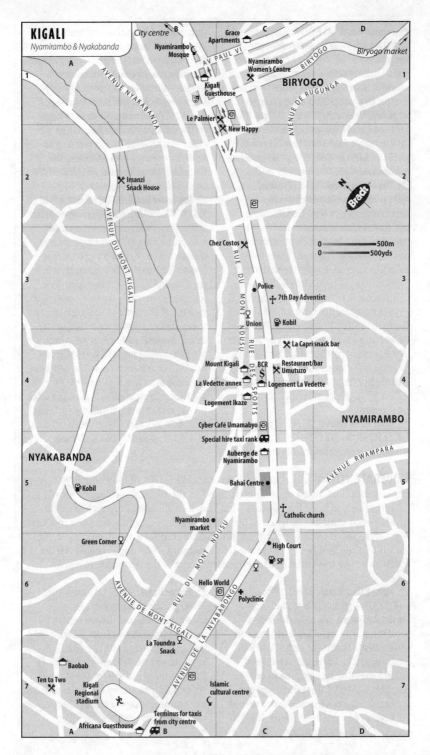

KIGALI
Nyamirambo & Nyakabanda

City centre

Grace
Apartments

Nyamirambo
Mosque

AV PAUL VI

Nyamirambo
Women's Centre

BIRYOGO

BIRYOGO market

Kigali
Guesthouse

AVENUE DE RUGUNGA

AVENUE NYAKABANDA

Le Palmier

New Happy

Imanzi
Snack House

AVENUE DU MONT KIGALI

N

Bradt

Chez Costos

RUE DU MONT NDUSU

0   500m
0   500yds

Police

7th Day Adventist

Union

Kobil

La Capri snack bar

Mount Kigali

BCR

Restaurant/bar
Umutuzo

RUE DES SPORTS

La Vedette annex

Logement La Vedette

Logement Ikaze

NYAMIRAMBO

Cyber Café Umamabyo

Special hire taxi rank

Auberge de
Nyamirambo

AVENUE RWAMPARA

NYAKABANDA

Bahai Centre

Kobil

Catholic church

Nyamirambo
market

RUE DU MONT NDUSU

Green Corner

High Court

SP

AVENUE DE MONT KIGALI

Hello World

Polyclinic

AVENUE DE LA NYABARONGO

La Toundra
Snack

Baobab

Ten to Two

Islamic
cultural centre

Kigali
Regional
stadium

Terminus for taxis
from city centre

Africana Guesthouse

A   B   C   D

🛏 **Elegancya Guesthouse** [80 D4] (13 rooms) m 078 4666483/077 2695399; e stefenomute@ yahoo.com; www.elegancya.com. Situated in a quiet residential street in Kimihurura, this friendly little guesthouse is within walking distance of all the restaurants & nightspots in Kimihurura, & a short moto ride from the city centre. It has smart rooms with Wi-Fi, DSTV, large wardrobes, phone & en-suite shower. There are also a couple of spacious suites which have a lounge area & a tub as well as a shower. There is a small restaurant at the guesthouse & several other restaurants nearby. *US 70/80 sgl/dbl, suites US 100–120 including breakfast, discounts available for stays of longer than 3 days.*

🛏 **Hotel Beausejour** [81 G4] (28 rooms) 0252 580760/072 5158116; e info@beausejourhotel.rw; www.beausejourhotel.rw. Not to be confused with the nearby & similarly named Auberge Beau Séjour, this hotel is located next to the Sole Luna restaurant on the airport road. Open since 2009, it has very smart & well-maintained rooms with great views overlooking the city. The rooms have DSTV, a fan, Wi-Fi, fridge & en-suites with hot shower & tub. It has a good restaurant too which serves weekly culinary themes & African speciality foods. The hotel runs a free airport shuttle service & the staff seem helpful & friendly. *At US$90/120 sgl/dbl it is a little overpriced but the rates do include breakfast.*

🛏 **Hotel Chez Lando** [81 G5] (82 rooms) 0252 582050; e info@chezlando.com; www. chezlando.com. Founded in the 1980s, this well-established family hotel lies in green grounds just off the main road through the suburb of Remera, an easy taxi or minibus-taxi ride from town. The spacious rooms have satellite TV, international direct dialling, Wi-Fi, private balcony, & en-suite tub & shower. The indoor La Fringale restaurant does a good buffet b/fast but can be slow & cheerless for other meals; for these the outdoor, downstairs restaurant is brisker & livelier. Several good restaurants & shops lie within easy walking distance of the hotel, as does a fast internet café & a sauna/massage centre. *US$60/70 sgl/dbl in the old building; US$90/120 in the new extension; US$100/130 bungalow.*

🛏 **Hotel le Printemps** [81 H3] (20 rooms) 0252 582142; m 078 8307133; e agrimak@ rwanda1.com; www.leprintempshotel.com. Set in pleasant gardens opposite Kimironko Taxi Park, this small suburban hotel offers a variety of spotlessly

clean accommodation, ranging from tiled singles with ¾ bed, TV, phone & en-suite hot shower to larger suites & apartments. Facilities include an internet café, Wi-Fi & restaurant. *Acceptable value at Rfr20,000/35,000 sgl/dbl without a sitting room, Rfr25,000/29,000 sgl/dbl with sitting room to Rfr70,800 for an apartment.*

🛏 **Hotel Okapi** [89 D2] (39 rooms) 0252 571667; m 078 8359877; e okapihotel@hotmail. com; www.okapi.co.rw. This 5-storey hotel on Rue Musima (between Bd de Nyabugogo & Av de la Justice) is a popular central choice in this price range, & convenient for public transport. While there is a slightly confusing array of different room categories, it is worth paying extra for one of the comfortable tiled rooms in the main building, which have queen-size or twin beds, netting, fridge, DSTV & en-suite combination tub/shower, as their cheaper & gloomier counterparts in the downstairs annexe represent truly poor value for money. The restaurant offers a decent selection of Indian, Rwandan & continental dishes in the Rfr2,000–4,000 range, & vegetarians are well catered for. It also has a panoramic view across the Kigali landscape. *US$70/90 in the main building; US$50/70 in the annexe.*

🛏 **Impala Hotel** [89 C2] (20 rooms) 078 8304866/072 8300144; e impalahotelrw@yahoo. fr. Situated a few doors down from the Okapi, this 3-storey place opened in 2007 & can be recognised by the garish statues of gazelles (rather than impalas) that adorn the front parking. The tiled rooms have king-size or twin beds, DSTV, phone, en-suite hot shower & a nice little balcony offering great views on the non-street side. There is free computer usage at reception & Wi-Fi for those with laptops. *Nothing special, but conveniently central & decent value at US$70/90 sgl/dbl or US$150 suite.*

🛏 **Inside Afrika Boutique Hotel** [85 G4] (9 rooms) 0252 578950; m 078 3599370/ 8503698; e info@inside-afrika.com; www.inside-afrika.com. Situated on Rue du Lac Mpanga around the corner from the Gorillas Hotel, this attractive new boutique hotel has large rooms with stylish contemporary ethnic décor, king-size or twin beds with net, flatscreen satellite TV, & en-suite hot showers. Although it has no restaurant, there are several good eateries within easy walking distance. Facilities include free Wi-Fi throughout, a tempting swimming pool, & a good breakfast. *US$115/135 dbl/twin B&B.*

🛏 **Iris Guesthouse** [85 F4] (19 rooms) 📞 0252 501172/81; 📱 072 8501181; 📧 iris@rwanda1.com. Situated in Rue Député Kajangwe downhill from the city centre, this well-managed guesthouse has been popular with NGO workers & other regular visitors to Kigali since it opened in 2001, & as a result it is often full, so try to book in advance. It stands in pleasant grounds in a shady street away from the traffic, & the neat rooms all come with dbl or twin bed with netting, phone, DSTV, private terrace with seating, & en-suite hot tub. You can eat indoors or al fresco at the attached restaurant, which serves a varied selection of grills, sandwiches, salads & pasta dishes in the Rfr2,000–6,000 range. Wi-Fi is available at Rfr3,000 per day. *Rfr45,000/55,000 sgl/dbl; Rfr90,000 2-bedroom apt; all rates B&B.*

🛏 **La Palisse Hotel** [81 H5] (71 rooms) 📱 078 8305505; 📧 palisseho@yahoo.fr; www.hotel-lapalisse.com. Situated 2km from the airport along the Akagera Rd, the new La Palisse is the least urban hotel in Kigali, set in sprawling wooded grounds that harbour a varied birdlife, as well as a swimming pool, children's playground, & outdoor bar & barbecue. The best accommodation is in spacious standalone rondawels (round huts), with king-size or twin beds with net, DSTV, mini-bar, writing desk, phone & en-suite shower. The cheaper standard rooms in the main 4-storey building are similar but smaller & less outdoorsy. *Exceptional value at US$60/70 standard sgl/dbl, US$80 twin, US$60/70 sgl/dbl bungalow, US$100 suite.*

🛏 **Ninzi Hill Hotel** [81 E3] (15 rooms) 📞 0252 587711–4; 📧 ninzihill@yahoo.fr. Set in the administrative quarter of Kacyiru not far from the Umubano Hotel, this is a quiet, comfortable place well away from city bustle, & it has a pleasantly laidback feel, although it is a little bland. The spacious tiled rooms are very comfortable, with queen-size bed, DSTV & balcony, & those at the back overlook gardens & greenery. There's a good mid-price restaurant, & the more interesting Kigali Great Wall of China restaurant is very close by. It's only a 10min walk to the Kigali Business Centre which has some shops & services. *US$70/90 sgl/dbl or US$120 semi-suite.*

🛏 **Romalo Guesthouse** [81 F5] (10 rooms) 📱 078 8301353/078 8421208; 📧 sylvia@romaloltd.com; www.romaloltd.com. Tucked away in the sloping backstreets below the Parliament Buildings, this small family-run guesthouse is a little isolated so only really convenient for those with private transport. Set in a large 2-storey house with a wide balcony overlooking a green compound, the large, clean, tiled rooms come with king-size or twin beds, fridge, TV & en-suite hot shower. *It seems quite good value at Rfr25,000/40,000 sgl/dbl.*

🛏 **Woodland Hotel** [81 H3] (26 rooms) 📱 078 6542166; 📧 whkigali@gmail.com; www.woodlandhotelkigali.com. Also situated in Kimironko, this likeable hotel under new management in 2012 lies in large grassy gardens dotted with plastic tables & benches. The bright & spacious en-suite rooms have queen-size or twin beds, DSTV & combined tub/shower; there is free internet access & Wi-Fi & a restaurant serving European & African cuisine. *Rfr35,000/40,000 sgl/dbl B&B w/day rate; Rfr20,000,25,000 sgl/dbl w/end rate; suite Rfr70,000 for the entire week representing very good value.*

BUDGET The hotels listed below are more basic and in some cases a little seedy by comparison with those placed in higher brackets, but they will meet the requirements of reasonably undemanding cost-conscious travellers. The most popular choice with backpackers is the new **Discover Rwanda Youth Hostel**. Other good options include the central **Dream Inn Motel** and **Hotel Isimbi**, and the suburban **Hotel Baobab** and **Hotel Hilltop**, while **Grace Apartments** is worth a look for those seeking affordable longer-term accommodation.

🛏 **AEE Kabeza** [81 H5] (18 rooms) 📱 078 8744011. This large & bright pastoral centre is located in Remera, close to the airport, down a side road signposted 'AEE street'. It has basic but clean & cheerful rooms with nets, towels & a desk. The shared bathrooms have showers & flush toilets, & some have hot water. The staff are always friendly & helpful & although it is a religious institution there is no curfew. The guesthouse has spacious gardens & sitting areas for guests to meet in, & there is also a conference room & free Wi-Fi available. Although it is a distance from the city centre, it is a 10min walk from Remera bus park where buses go very frequently to all parts of the city. *At Rfr10,500/15, 000 sgl/dbl it is a very good option for those wanting an inexpensive place to stay near the airport.*

🏠 **Auberge Beau Séjour** [81 G5] (19 rooms) 📞078 830323; e beausejourhotel@yahoo.com. This homely lodge lies just off the main road to the airport & has a good reputation locally. The rooms are very pleasant, & come with TV & hot bath. Dinner is served by request. The owner supervises personally & takes a pride in the place – there are thoughtful touches like drinking-water in the bedrooms, & all rooms lead out to the well-cared-for garden. *Rfr22,000/24,000 sgl/dbl with a shared bathroom; Rfr27,000/30,000 sgl/dbl en-suite, B&B.*

🏠 **Auberge la Caverne** [89 D1] (20 rooms) m 078 8754110; e aubecav@yahoo.fr. This long-serving lodge receives mixed reports from travellers, but there's no doubt it is about the most affordable option in central Kigali. Spacious & mostly en-suite rooms with hot water are set away from the traffic around a central courtyard in Bd de Nyabugogo. There is also an apartment that sleeps up to 6 people which is good value if you are travelling in a group. Back windows have a good view out over the valley. The restaurant does a standard range of meals. It's a steepish but short walk up into the town centre, but the hotel lies along the main road used by minibus-taxis to/from the intercity Nyabugogo Taxi Park. *Rfr12,000/15,000 sgl/dbl; Rfr20,000 en-suite dbl with TV; Rfr40,000 apartment.*

🏠 **City Valley Motel** [84 B2] (19 rooms) m 078 3050775. Situated on Av des Poids Lourds a few hundred metres from Nyabugogo Taxi Park, this is a pleasant hotel with a decent-looking garden bar & restaurant attached, as well as a nightclub. The location, on a road used by heavy trucks, is potentially noisy, so best to ask for a room facing away from the traffic. The large rooms all have fan, net, TV & a balcony. *Rfr12,000 dbl using common showers; Rfr20,000 en-suite with hot water.*

🏠 **Discover Rwanda Youth Hostel** [81 E4] (7 rooms, 4 dorms) m 078 2265679; e info@ hostelkigali.com; www.hostelkigali.com or www.aegistrust.org. This welcome addition to the accommodation scene in Rwanda finally provides budget travellers with a genuinely relaxed focal point from which to explore the city & the rest of the country. Conveniently situated in Kacyiru behind the conspicuous Great Wall Of China Restaurant, it is close to the RDB office, &

numerous shops & restaurants. Facilities include a sociable balcony with comfortable seating overlooking a large green garden, Wi-Fi, common hot showers, regular movie nights (usually Fri) & affordable evening meals by advance order. The hostel is operated by the Aegis Trust (see *Kigali Genocide Memorial* page 113) & all proceeds go towards its Peace-building Education Programme for genocide survivors. *US$15/17 pp 4/8-bed dorm; US$25/40 sgl/twin; US$10pp camping. All rates include a good breakfast.*

🏠 **Dream Inn Motel** [89 D1] (17 rooms) 📞0252 503988/502477; e dreaminn7@yahoo.fr. This smart hotel opposite the venerable Auberge la Caverne is arguably the pick of the budget options. The tiled rooms & dorms are clean, comfortable & modern-looking, with nets, TV, Wi-Fi & fridge, & there are internet facilities on the ground floor, along with a good-value restaurant & bar. It's also very central, within walking distance of several restaurants, & plenty of public transport passes right by the door. Recommended. *US$30/40 sgl/ dbl; US$60 suite; b/fast inc .*

🏠 **Grace Apartments** [92 C1] (60 rooms) m 0788501107; e grace.apartments@yahoo.fr; www.grace-apartment.com. This 4-storey building a block east of Nyamirambo Mosque looks run down & closed when you approach it but that said, if the aura of abandonment doesn't put you off, the en-suite rooms with dbl bed, net, TV & phone are fair value at the daily rate. For those seeking no-frills longer-term accommodation, the monthly rate looks to be a genuine bargain. Best to get one of the apartments with a kitchen as the rate is the same as for apartments without one. There's no restaurant but it's well placed for eating out. *US$$30 per night; US$$200 per month.*

🏠 **Hotel Baobab** [92 A7] (9 rooms) 📞0252 575633; e baobab@inbox.rw. This great place is full of character but some distance from the city centre, down in Nyakabanda suburb in the southwest near Mount Kigali & the Stade Régional de Kigali. If you have your own transport (or don't mind taking taxis), do consider it. The area is peaceful, with widespread views across the valley & to Mount Kigali, & the possibility of quite rural walks. The restaurant (mostly outdoor) has a good reputation locally. Rooms are en-suite with hot water, phone & TV. *Rfr20,000 dbl; b/fast not inc.*

🏠 **Hotel Hilltop** [81 H5] (38 rooms) m 078 8622522/8541409; e hilltopcountryclub@yahoo.fr.

Conveniently located about 1km from the airport alongside the main road towards the city centre, this unpretentious & reasonably priced hotel lies in large green grounds with a good garden bar & restaurant. The rooms are simple but clean, with nets, DSTV, phone, lockable wardrobe & en-suite hot shower, & sgl (¾ bed), dbl & twin are all available. *At Rfr18,000/23,000 sgl/dbl B&B it is a good-value option for staying close to the airport.*

🏠 **Hotel Isimbi** [89 C6] (20 rooms) ✆078 6090557; e isimbi@hotmail.com or isimbi@ rwanda1.com; www.hotelisimbi.co.rw. The most central hotel in this range, situated on Rue Kalisimbi just a few mins' walk from Av de la Paix, this is an efficient, clean, business-type hotel. The unpretentious en-suite rooms with hot water are very good value (the back ones are quietest), & there's a non-smoking snack-bar & restaurant for main meals (up to around Rfr5,000), as well as room service. *US$30/35 sgl/dbl exc b/fast.*

🏠 **Mount Kigali Hotel** [92 C4] (20 rooms) m 078 5746312/072 8840420; e mountkigali@ gmail.com or cite.rwanda@yahoo.fr; www. mountkigalihotel.com. Situated in the lively suburb of Nyamirambo, south of the city centre, this 3-storey hotel has comfortable accommodation in the form of singles (1 dbl bed) & doubles (2 ¾ beds). There are 4 categories of room ranging from basic twins with nets & shared bathrooms to rooms with DSTV & en-suite shower.

A restaurant & sauna/massage are attached. *Basic rooms Rfr12,000/15,000 sgl/dbl; the more luxurious superior rooms Rfr21,000/26,000 sgl/dbl.*

🏠 **Presbyterian Auberge d'Accueil** [85 F4] (30 rooms) ✆0252 578915; e eprauberge@ yahoo.fr. Close to the Gorillas Hotel, a 10min walk downhill from the city centre, this church hostel is a clean, relaxing place with cheerful rooms, a good-value dining room, & a computer room offering free internet access to residents. It can get busy with church guests so book in advance. Good monthly rates are available. *Rfr20,000/30,000 sgl/ dbl B&B.*

🏠 **Sky Hotel** [89 B7] (25 rooms) ✆0252 503882; e skyhotel2020@yahoo.fr; www. skyhotelrw.net. This multi-storey hotel on Av de la Justice at the southern edge of the city centre has comfortable albeit rather tired-looking en-suite rooms with TV, queen-size bed, balcony, hot water, 24hr internet access, & a lovely view over the valley from the back. The room rates are very reasonable, as is the restaurant, & there's an affordable nightclub at w/ends, as well as a few other bars & restaurants within 5mins' walk, & plenty of public transport running straight past the door, otherwise it is quite a long & steep walk to the city centre. However, it can also be very noisy when the nightclub is on song, & readers have expressed some concerns about security. *US$30/40 sgl/dbl B&B; Rfr40,000 suite.*

SHOESTRING (*below US$20 double*) The lodgings listed below are all on the basic side, with rooms using common showers or cold water only – or both! Most cater primarily to the local market, though they are also suitable for backpackers and other travellers on a rock bottom budget. Unusually for an African capital, there are very few real cheapies in the city centre. Instead, they're mostly clustered south of the city centre in the lively and characterful quarters of Nyamirambo and Nyakabanda, between Nyamirambo Mosque [92 B1] and the Kigali Regional Stadium [92 B7]. Probably the best choices in this category are the **Kigali Guest House**, and for single travellers, **Auberge de Nyamirambo**, which has the added advantage of being close to a cluster of similarly-priced options you could fall back on if it's full. To reach Nyamirambo and Nyakabanda on foot from the city centre, continue walking southwards (downhill) from the Sky Hotel [89 B7] for about 15 minutes. Alternatively, a steady stream of minibus-taxis runs towards the stadium from the city centre (you can pick them up in front of the Sky Hotel or Kigali Prison), charging Rfr100 per person and passing within 100m of most of the listed hotels.

🏠 **Auberge de Nyamirambo** [92 C5] (9 rooms) m 078 8612311/078 8683831; e auberge.nyamirambo@yahoo.fr. This homely

2-storey lodge is one of the best-value options in Kigali for those wanting a single room, The Auberge has clean en-suite rooms & a convenient location on the main road out of town towards the Islamic Centre. Six rooms are in the main building, some en-suite & some using common showers, & the other 3, all en-suite, are in a little street-side annexe. The rooms in the annexe are marginally nicer but look slightly less secure, as you don't have to pass through reception to reach them. There's no in-house restaurant or bar, but there are 2 decent options within 500 metres. There's a good internet café next door. Note that now there are no double rooms available so the following prices are for single rooms. *Rfr8,000 full en-suite, Rfr7,000 sink & shower but shared toilet, Rfr4,000 shared bathroom facilities.*

🏠 **Centre National de Pastorale St Paul**
[85 E3] m 078 3191589. Situated alongside the Eglise Saint-Famille about 200m east of the Place de l'Unité Nationale, this is the most central shoestring option in Kigali, offering basic accommodation in twin rooms with nets, electricity, a desk, towels & soap. The shared showers sometimes have hot water & the pretty gardens are very relaxing to sit in. Although it is a religious institution, people staying here can come home any time in the night. Most of the staff speak French or Kinyarwanda only & there have been reports that the reservation system can be unreliable. *Rfr8,000 twin with shared facilities, Rfr16,000 en-suite twin.*

🏠 **Episcopal Church Resthouse** [80 B5] (13 rooms) m 078 8847592. Part of the St Etienne Church on Av Paul VI in Biryogo (aka Bilyogo) district some 500m east of Nyamirambo Mosque, this church guesthouse is not that convenient, though the clean but rundown rooms with nets are fair value. Inexpensive meals are available. *Rfr7,000 twin B&B or Rfr2,500 per dorm bed exc b/fast.*

🏠 **Kigali Guest House** [92 B1] (16 rooms)
☎ 078 8499506/078 8512776; e kigaliguesth@ yahoo.com. Situated a block past the mosque on a one-way stretch of Av de la Justice, this is a good-value hotel, offering accommodation in small en-suite rooms with cold water, phone & TV. There's no restaurant or bar, so it's pretty quiet – if you can ignore the passing traffic & early morning mosque calls! There are plenty of other eateries & bars in the area. Minibus-taxis from central Kigali stop right opposite – ask for 'Chez Mayaka' or the mosque. *Rfr7,000/9,000/10,000 sgl/dbl/twin.*

🏠 **Logement Ikaze** [92 C4] (8 rooms)
☎ 078 8431659. The least inviting of the lodges in Nyamirambo, this place has spacious rooms, but the overall feel is rather dingy & some rooms are in quite a bad state of disrepair. *Rfr7,000 for all rooms.*

🏠 **Logement La Vedette** [92 C4] (14 rooms)
☎ 078 8429985/078 3072077. Situated around the corner from the Auberge de Nyamirambo, this unpretentious guesthouse, which now incorporates the former Home St Bernard, has comfortable large rooms, some en-suite, others with sinks & clean common showers – nothing special but fine at the price. *Rfr5,000–8,000 depending on room type & sgl/dbl occupancy.*

🏠 **Nyamirambo Women's Centre** [92 C1] (2 rooms) m 078 2111860/078 5002302; e nwcoffice.kigali@gmail.com; www.nwc-kigali. org. Part of a self-help women's centre near Biryogo market that hosts the This is Africa day tours (see page 112), this offers accommodation in 2 en-suite dbl rooms & has a wireless internet connection. *US$10 (or US$12 B&B). FB also offered.*

✕ WHERE TO EAT AND DRINK

For this section we remain indebted to André Verbruggen, the author of *Guide André: my 100 best Restaurants in Kigali*, last updated in 2008, who lived and worked in Kigali for well over a decade and contributed much of the content of this section for the third edition of this guidebook. What follows is a cross-section of the city's better eateries in various price categories, aimed mainly at short-term visitors, and organised according to suburb rather than price, with the top few picks for each area generally listed first. Most hotels offer acceptable food so, if you prefer to eat wherever you're staying, you won't necessarily miss out.

CITY CENTRE The city centre boasts an excellent selection of cafés, snack bars and coffee shops, and restaurants serving more traditional fare. For a coffee, snack or filled baguette, **La Galette** is still arguably the best place in the city centre though the somewhat pricier **Blues and Bourbon Café** provides it with some trendier competition. The city centre is a also great place to join Kigali's office workers at lunchtime and try the traditional Rwandan buffet, otherwise known as a *mélange*. **Fantastic Restaurant** stands out for the size of its buffet and great downtown atmosphere. Formal restaurants are thin on the ground; the best options are in the upmarket **Serena** and **Mille Collines** hotels, but both are very pricey and there's a far more interesting selection of dedicated eateries within easy walking distance in Kiyovu, the suburb sloping eastward from the city centre.

✗ **Blues Café** [89 D4] m 078 8323666; e bluescafe@gmail.com; ⊕ 07.00–20.00 daily. Situated next to the Union Trade Centre, this trendy little coffee shop has Wi-Fi access & an adjoining internet café. The coffee, as is so often the case in Rwanda, can be disappointing, but it also serves a selection of sandwiches & salads for around Rfr2,000 & light meals for Rfr3,500.

✗ **Café Bourbon** [89 D4] 0252 505307; ⊕ 08.00–19.00 daily. This popular coffee chain has branches in the Union Trade Centre, the Kigali City Tower, the MTN centre & Kigali International airport. The coffee is pretty good (though it doesn't beat the coffee shop in the lobby of the Umubano Hotel) & a fair selection of snacks & sandwiches are available, mostly around Rfr2,000–3,000. It has free Wi-Fi access.

✗ **Chez Venant** [89 D3] ⊕ daily from lunchtime until late. This is an agreeable & inexpensive local drinking hole with outdoor seating on Av de la Justice.

✗ **Diplomat Restaurant** [85 E6] 0252 597100. This highly rated restaurant in the Serena Hotel serves a good selection of mostly continental-style dishes at similar prices to the above. It has been closed for renovations but should have been reopened by the time you read this.

✗ **Fantastic Restaurant** [89 C3] m 078 8767036/078 5833605 e fantasticrwanda@yahoo.com; ⊕ 07.00–11.00 for b/fast, 10.00–18.00 for the buffet. Opposite the new Kigali City Tower, this restaurant has quickly become a Kigali institution because it serves the biggest & best Rwandan buffet in town & for a very reasonable Rfr1,800. The African music & chatter of lots of locals enjoying some time out from work gives it a bustling, jovial atmosphere. The restaurant is on the 2nd floor, above a block of shops, which gives you a great view of one Kigali's busiest streets so it is an ideal place to watch city life & soak up the vibe of downtown Kigali.

✗ **Juicilicious** [89 D3] m 072 2731862; ⊕ 09.00–22.00 e juicilicious.rwanda@gmail.com. Centrally located by the Cooperative for Trade & Promotion in Rwanda handicraft market & on the same road as the UTC , this laid-back juice bar is a good place to retreat from the heat & pick up refreshing juices, fruit & vegetable cocktails or milkshakes at Rfr1,500–3,000. Juices include tree tomato & papaya while the vegetable cocktails range from cleansing to anti-ageing!

✗ **Karibu Restaurant** [89 C7] m 078 8528900; ⊕ 08.00–late. At the edge of the city centre on Av de la Paix, this is a shady place to stop for a cool drink or snack if you're in central Kigali, & it also has a convenient & varied lunchtime buffet for Rfr2,500; this is deservedly popular, so try to get there before 13.00 when it tends to fill up with business people.

✗ **La Classe** [89 D6] 072 8303118; m 078 8308018; ⊕ 07.00–24.00. This centrally located restaurant opposite the BCR bank is another good place to try a lunchtime buffet, for the price of Rfr2,500 including a soft drink. If you want to try something else they also serve a range of sandwiches, pizzas & snacks. The restaurant has a pleasant covered courtyard area to sit in & service seems pretty swift.

✗ **La Galette** [89 A4] 0252 575434; ⊕ 07.30–19.30 Mon-Sat, 07.30–14.30 Sun. To combine sustenance with shopping, try the snack-bar attached to this excellent supermarket at the bottom of Rue du Marché just after it turns sharply to join Rue de l'Epargne. This is a popular meeting place for ex-pats & aid workers, & there are notice boards listing various items (cars, dogs, homes, motorbikes, TVs, garden hoses…) wanted or for sale. The supermarket stocks a good selection of fresh & imported groceries; the snack-bar serves fresh filled baguettes for Rfr700–850, salads in the Rfr1,200–2,400 range, light meals for Rfr2,000–3,000 & draft beer, as well as pastries (including croissants) & good coffee – b/fast nirvana!

✗ **La Sierra** [89 D6] 0252 575486; ⊕ from 07.30. Founded in 1968, this is a more low-key & central equivalent to La Galette, combining a good supermarket with a pleasant although somewhat characterless terrace snack-bar on Bd de la Révolution. At other times, burgers, sandwiches & light meals are mostly in the Rfr1,200–2,500 range; it also serves samosas, burritos, pancakes & waffles, & is a good spot for b/fast. Somewhat pricier is the Indian-influenced lunchtime buffet, which costs Rfr5,000 & runs over 12.00–14.30.

✕ **Le Palmier** [92 C1] One of several good local eateries dotted along the one-way roads around Nyamirambo Mosque, & also worth trying should you be staying in this area, are the **New Happy Restaurant** & **Chez Costos**, both of which serve buffets & meals for around Rfr1,500.

✕ **Panorama Restaurant** [89 D5] ✆0252 576530; ⏰ 06.00–10.30 (b/fast) & 19.00–23.00 (dinner). On the top floor of the Hotel des Mille Collines, this exclusive place has an appropriately panoramic view over the city, & background music is supplied by a pianist & saxophonist. Official dinners & banquets are held here & there are regular 'themed evenings'. The 'suggestion of the day' plus dessert is around Rfr10,000 but it's easy to spend more. The wine list is comprehensive.

✕ **Simba Café** [89 C4] ⏰ 07.00–11.00. This efficient, busy & conveniently located café

attached to the **Simba supermarket** is a great place to pick up a quick lunch or snack & provides some welcome respite from shopping on Kigali's busy streets. Service is swift & the food is filling & tasty. The menu includes a range of burgers, snacks & light meals for Rfr2,000–3,000.

✕ **Ten To Two** [92 A7] Although this restaurant is not particularly close to the city centre as it is on the edge of Nyamirambo district on the same road as **Hotel Baobab**, the fish served here has come highly recommended by other travellers. There is a lovely terrace to sit on & it is a great place to go for an evening meal especially if you are staying in Nyamirambo district or you have your own transport.

✕ **White Horse Pizzeria** [89 C6] ✆0750 260964; e whitehorsepizzeria@gmail.com; ⏰ 08.00–late. Situated opposite the Belgian school on Rue des Mille Collines, this restaurant has a quiet outdoor garden to sit in & serves a big selection of pizzas & pasta dishes for Rfr4,000–6,000. Later in the evening the places doubles as a small nightclub; see the nightlife section (page 102) for more details.

KIYOVU This leafy suburb on the eastern verge of the city centre is blessed with a fine selection of top-quality restaurants, a fortunate situation given that many of the city's most popular tourist hotels also lie in the area. Coming from the city centre, the closest restaurant is the rather unremarkable Chez Robert, but if you are prepared to walk a bit further – or to take a taxi – top recommendations are **Heaven Restaurant** and **Republika Lounge** for ambience, **Khana Khäzana** and **Dong Fang** for exotic variety, and **Dolce** and **Iris** for affordability.

✕ **Dong Fang Chinese Restaurant** [85 F4] m 078 8307168; ⏰ 11.00–22.00 daily. This pleasant garden restaurant is about 10mins' walk from the city centre, a couple of gates down from the Iris Guesthouse. The superb & inexpensive soups are a meal in themselves, while the pick of the other dishes are the sizzler plates of meat or chicken. Main dishes are Rfr4,000–5,000, soups are cheaper.

✕ **Heaven Restaurant & Bar** [85 F4] m 078 8486581; e heavenrwanda@gmail.com; www.heavenrwanda.com; ⏰ 17.00–23.00 daily. This popular restaurant in Kiyovu consists of a massive wooden deck scattered with wooden tables & chairs, set below a cane roof & offering good views over suburban Kigali. The main restaurant has a pleasant al fresco ambience & delicious continental

fusion cusine in the Rwf 6,000–8,000 range which uses 95% local Rwandan ingredients. There is also a new bar menu with chappatis, burgers & other light meals for Rfr2,000–3,500 . The restaurant shows recent adult movies at 19.30 on Sat nights. It costs Rwf 2,500 for entrance to the movie evening plus popcorn & Rwf 7,000 for a movie & a buffet. Check the website for special events.

✕ **Iris Restaurant** [85 F4] ✆0252 501172; ⏰ 07.00–21.00 daily. Situated in the same part of town as the Indian Khäzana, the terrace restaurant at this popular guesthouse has a giddying choice of (mainly) continental dishes & grills. The superb pasta dishes are mostly around Rfr3,000, while salads & sandwiches cost Rfr2,000–3,500 & more substantial meat & fish dishes are in the Rfr4,500–6,000 range.

4

✗ **Khana Khäzana Restaurant** [85 F4]
m 078 8772087; **e** khazanarwanda@yahoo.com;
⏰ 12.00–15.00 & 18.00–23.00 daily. This
superb & popular Indian restaurant is situated on
Kajangwe Av, a 10min walk downhill from the
Mille Collines & the city centre. Most main courses
are in the Rfr5,000–7,000 range & the Indian
bread is excellent. A new branch of the Khana
Khazana Restaurant has also just opened inside the
Kigali City Tower.

✗ **Kioske Alimentation** [85 F4] Situated
opposite the Banana Guesthouse, this welcoming
but no-frills local drinking hole serves the
cheapest drinks in Kiyovu – around Rfr800 for a
large Primus, which is a third of the price charged
by most of the restaurants & hotels in this posh
suburb.

✗ **New Cactus Restaurant** [85 F5] ☎0252
572572; **m** 078 8678798; ⏰ 12.00–14.00 &
18.00–22.30 daily. Situated in Rue Député Kayuku
(near the Hotel Gorillas) this is a super place,
particularly for pizza-lovers – it's very welcoming,
with a pleasant outdoor terrace giving a beautiful
view over Kigali, good food (French cuisine as well
as pizzas), & free Wi-Fi access. Steak & fish main
dishes up to Rfr7,000. There's also a take-away
pizza service – phone beforehand & it'll be ready
for you to collect.

✗ **Republika Lounge** [85 F6] ☎0252 504051;
m 078 8303030; ⏰ 17.00–late Mon–Sat. Tucked
away along a dirt side road branching downhill
from Av des Grand Lacs about 15mins' walk
from the city centre, this good-looking eatery
boasts earthy adobe architecture that makes it
blissfully cool inside on a humid day. The funky
décor contrasts attractively with the more stolid
appearance of most other Kigali restaurants, &

there's a large wooden deck with views across
to a eucalyptus-clad hill. Reliably busy even on
weekday nights, it serves a selection of grills &
brochettes in the Rfr4,000–6,000 range. There's a
good handicraft shop under the restaurant.

✗ **Restaurant Chez Robert** [89 D4] ☎0252
501305; ⏰ for lunch & dinner daily. Situated on
Av de la République, on the eastern border of the
city centre opposite Hotel des Mille Collines, this is
easily distinguished by the 2 elephantine statues
marking its walk-in entrance (the drive-in entrance
is actually a block east, on Rue de Ntaruka). It
serves a good selection of continental dishes for
around Rfr8,000, & brochettes, pasta & other light
meals from Rfr4,000 upwards. You can eat indoors
or in a large garden with several niches.

✗ **Restaurant Le Dos Argenté** [85 G4] ☎0252
501717; ⏰ 07.00–22.00 (bar stays open late). On
the ground floor of the Hotel Gorillas, this smaller
restaurant – whose name translates as silverback
– is a member of the *Chaîne des Rôtisseurs* &
the food usually lives up to its reputation. Main
dishes (French cuisine) go up to around Rfr10,000,
desserts to Rfr4,000. There's indoor & outdoor
seating, draft beer, & a good wine list. Service is
relaxed.

✗ **Zaaffran Indian Restaurant** [85 F4]
m 078 3042504. Located on Rue de l'Akagera
near La Bonne Source supermarket, this restaurant
serves Indian cuisine that is flavoursome &
good quality for around Rrf 4,000–6,000. The
Rwandan waiters clad in Indian costume give
the restaurant an interesting multicultural twist
& the décor is suitably bright & cheerful. The
naan bread is delicious & they have some good
vegetarian options on the menu, including paneer
& vegetable-based curries.

KIMIHURURA A variety of new restaurants has mushroomed in this sedate
residential suburb to the east of Kiyovu, but many are quite difficult to find and
somewhat isolated unless you have a private vehicle or take a taxi. There are no
duds listed below, but the lunchtime buffet at **Afrika Bite** stands out for those
wanting to sample Rwandan food at its finest,

✗ **Afrika Bite** [80 D3] **m** 078 8685184/078
8503888; ⏰ 12.00–15.00 daily except Sun &
18.00–22.30 daily except Wed & Sun. Widely
regarded as the city's leading purveyor of Rwandan
cuisine, this homely restaurant on a side road in
Kimihurura has indoor & outdoor garden seating &
oodles of character. Aside from a legendary buffet

costing Rfr3,000, it serves a good selection of à la
carte dishes in the Rfr2,500–3,500 range in the
evening.

✗ **Flamingo Chinese Restaurant** [80 D4]
☎0252 501944; **m** 078 8300333; ⏰ lunch &
dinner Mon–Sat. Generally rated as the best
Chinese in Kigali, but also perhaps the priciest,

this veteran restaurant is now installed in a suburban property in Kimihurura, diagonally opposite Afrika Bite. Mains are in the Rfr5,000–7,000 range.

✕ **Lalibela** [80 D4] m 078 8505293/078 8355579; ⏰ 12.00–15.00, 18.00–23.00 daily. This Ethiopian restaurant now located near Ogopogo Restaurant & Wine bar serves traditional Ethiopian fare including *injera*, big, flat savoury pancakes, & spicy *wat* stews. Mains cost Rfr4,000–5,000 & there is also a very good buffet for Rfr5,000.

✕ **Ogopogo Restaurant & Wine Bar** [80 D3] ☎078 864064/078 849595; ⏰ 11.00–late. On the site where Papyrus nightclub used to be, Ogopogo is a café, restaurant & wine bar rolled into one. It

serves a decent range of pasta, pizza & continental cuisine in the Rfr3,000–5,000 range. The café area has a good selection of bread, pastries & cakes & it is open until late.

✕ **Restaurant Hellenique** [80 D3] m 078 8512342; ⏰ 12.00–14.30 &17.00–21.00, closed Sun. This is tucked away in a residential part of Kimihurura not far from the Cadillac Club, in the valley between Kiyovu & Kacyiru – taxi-drivers will know it & it's signposted. The food is Greek/International with some unusual dishes & a good wine list, the ambience is relaxed & there's a pleasant terrace. Service is attentive but may be slow. Government VIPs & ambassadors come here. Mains around Rfr5,000 upwards.

KACYIRU AND REMERA This area of the city has a developing restaurant scene ranging from the tasty fast food of **Mr Chips** and **New Fiesta** to the upmarket cuisine at the poolside **Côté Jardin** at the Umubano Hotel. Elsewhere, **Sole Luna** and the **Kigali Great Wall of China Restaurant** serve good Italian and Chinese respectively, while the restaurant in **Civitas Hotel** serves some of the best brochettes in Kigali.

✕ **Civitas Restaurant** [81 G5] m 078 8887823; ⏰ 06.30–24.00. Located on the ground floor of the Civitas Hotel, this restaurant has a good selection of mains including steaks, spaghetti dishes & arguably the tastiest brochettes in Kigali. The restaurant has a very pleasant leafy outdoor patio area where you can watch the chef grilling brochettes on the open barbecue.

✕ **Côté Jardin Restaurant** [81 E3] ☎0252 593500; ⏰ 07.00–22.00 daily. The poolside restaurant at the Umubano Hotel has a good & varied midday & evening buffet (sizzling main dishes, salads, calorific desserts...) as well as the type of general menu you'd expect from a hotel of this standard & special menus for functions or celebrations. Service is attentive & the atmosphere is relaxed. It's deservedly one of Kigali's most popular meeting places, & the coffee shop in the lobby of the same hotel is truly excellent.

✕ **Great Wall of China Restaurant** [81 E3] m 078 8503111; ⏰ lunch & dinner. Around the corner from the Discover Rwanda Youth Hostel & within walking distance of the Umubano, this popular Chinese restaurant is friendly & has a great atmosphere in the evening when it is lit up by lots of red Chinese lanterns. The food is good value & the sizzling hotplates are especially good.

✕ **Grill & BBQ Corner** [81 E3] ☎0788 826195/0782369053; ⏰10.00–22.00 Sun–

Thu, 10.00–17.00 Fri & 18.00–22.00 Sat. This newish restaurant, tucked away around the corner from the Ninzi Hill Hotel, has indoor & outdoor seating, serves a huge variety of Western, Asian & African dishes, & has facilities for online ordering & delivery.

✕ **Magda Café** [81 E4] Situated in the back of the same building as Shokola Lite, this café serves tasty croissants, pastries & hot sandwiches, & has become popular with the lunchtime office crowd. Snacks & pastries are Rfr700–1,000, while sandwiches are around Rfr4,000.

✕ **Mr Chips** [81 G5] ⏰ 09.00–21.30. This newly opened bright red kiosk located in Remera near the Sonatubes roundabout, opposite the sign for Remera church, serves some of the best fast food in Kigali & is already very popular. Its menu includes authentic American-style cheeseburgers, fish & chips & pork sandwiches accompanied by onion rings & garlic mayonnaise, priced at Rfr2,000–3,000. The secluded outside balcony is filled with rustic picnic-style benches where you can enjoy the food while peeking at the life going past on one of the busiest streets in Kigali.

✕ **New Fiesta** [81 H4] ⏰ 07.30–21.00. This bright, cosmopolitan little restaurant located close to the Chez Lando hotel has excellent, speedy service & it has become deservedly very popular amongst Kigali's office workers & expats

4

who want a quick & tasty lunch or breakfast. The chicken & Greek salads are delicious, as are the hot sandwiches. Mains cost around Rwf 2,000–3,000. Next door to the restaurant is a small shop selling freshly baked La Galette bread, pastries, snacks & samosas & other essentials.

✕ **Ndoli's Joint Supermarket** [81 G5] If you are staying in this area of town, this handy supermarket sells most things you could need including snacks, bread, drinks including spirits & wine & it also has a forex bureau.

✕ **Shokola Lite** [81 E3] ⏱ 09.00–22.00. This new café next to the Kigali Great Wall of China restaurant & above the Ikirezi bookshop has a laid-back, cool vibe with lots of comfortable sofas, a small library & free Wi-Fi. The menu has a middle-eastern flavour & includes hummus, harira soup & lemon & herb grilled chicken.

✕ **Sole Luna** [81 G4] ☎ 0252 583062; www. soleluna-rw.com; ⏱ 12.00–24.00. Slightly cheaper than most upmarket eateries in Kigali, out along the airport road at the edge of Remera, this long-serving Italian restaurant has a good range of pizzas & pasta, well presented – & a beautiful view over the city from its terraces. Service is friendly & reasonably brisk.

NYARUTARAMA This small upmarket suburb of Kigali between Remera and Kacyiru has some expensive but nonetheless very good restaurants. **Zen** tops the list for its delicious Thai fusion cuisine, while simple but stylish **Sakae** is a good place for a plate of Japanese sushi. **The Manor Hotel** is also home to a range of restaurants of which **Marco's Italian Restaurant** and **O'Connell's Bar and Roof Terrace** are the best.

✕ **Marco's Italian Restaurant** [81 F1] Located inside the Manor Hotel in Nyarutarama, this Italian restaurant has a particularly delicious selection of vegetarian dishes for Rfr5,000–6,000 including roasted pumpkin & pine nut ravioli with parmesan & goats cheese, red onion & basil risotto, along with roasted meat & steaks for Rfr8,000–9,000.

✕ **O'Connell's Bar & Roof Terrace** [81 F1] This Irish themed bar also found inside in the Manor hotel serves pu-style food such as club sandwiches, fishcakes, burgers & chicken wings for around Rfr5,000. It also has a good range of whiskies & a pleasant panoramic view of the city.

✕ **Sakae Japanese Restaurant** [81 G4] 📱 078 4578435/078 4577738; e sakaeres@gmail.com; ⏱ 12.00–15.00, 18.00–22.30. This simple, elegant restaurant can be found down a side street signposted from the beginning of the main Nyarutarama road. It serves the best Japanese food in Kigali & it has an impressive range of sushi including sushi set menus & roll sushi. A la carte sushi isRfr1500–4000 & set menus with many different types of sushi are Rfr8000–15,000. There is also a good selection of Korean & Japanese noodle dishes.

✕ **Zen** [81 G3] ☎ 078 2588593; ⏱ 12.00–15.00, 18.00–23.30. Located on the main Nyarutarama road, a short distance from the MTN centre, this smart & tranquil restaurant serves an enticing range of oriental cuisine including Thai curries & soups & Chinese dim sum dumplings. Mains cost around Rfr7,000. Rather strangely, the dining area is hidden through a parking lot & around the back of a building, so don't be put off when you look through the gates & fail to see the restaurant.

NIGHTLIFE

For a capital city, Kigali isn't over-rich in nightclubs and discos. The biggest and best known is the **New Cadillac** [85 H4] (☎ *0252 511622*) in Kimihurura, of which there are two parts: one for VIPs and the smart set and one for more relaxed and younger people. The VIP part, which charges a rather steep entrance fee, consists of a good Thai restaurant, piano bar, live band and disco, and opens 11.00–15.00 and 18.00–24.00 Tuesday to Sunday. Drinks aren't exorbitant. If a group of visitors wants traditional music or dancers, this can be arranged. For young people, the New Cadillac Night Club functions Wednesday to Sunday, 21.00 to dawn.

Smaller than the New Cadillac but the same price is the smart **Planète Club** [81 E4] (m *078 8683043*) in the Kigali Business Centre. The **Sky Hotel** [89 B7] has a nightclub, and the **Alpha Palace Hotel** [81 H5] has one on Fridays/Saturdays.

If you want to dance the night away in a less formal atmosphere, the **White Horse Restaurant and Pizzeria** [89 C6] in the city centre has a dance-floor and disco at weekends and sometimes has live music on Friday and Saturday nights. Out in Kimihurura, **Sundowners Bar** [80 D4] is the latest nightspot on the scene. Entrance is free, and on Fri/Sat nights there are DJs spinning tunes until the small hours.

A popular out-of-town drinking hole is the **Green Corner Bar** [92 B6], a lofty outdoor set-up in Nyakabanda offering cheap chilled beers and great views towards Mount Kigali. In Kiyovu, trendier drinking spots include **Republika Lounge** [85 F6] and **Heaven** [85 F4], while the more down-to-earth **Kioske Alimentation** [85 F4] opposite the Banana Guesthouse is a great place to enjoy a few cheap beers in company with local Rwandans. In the city centre, **La Mouette** [89 B5] (✆ *078 8514365/8421450*) on Rue du Lac Bulera has occasional live music at weekends.

If you want to try something a bit different, the **Mamba Club** [80 D4] in Kimihurura (🕐 *12.00–late;* ✆ *078 2208824*) has a fun vibe at the weekends with very reasonably priced cocktails and a 5-lane bowling alley, table tennis, volleyball net and swimming pool. Burgers and snacks are also available for Rfr2,000–4,000. Another relaxed place to have a drink in Kimihurura is **Ogopogo Restaurant and Wine Bar** [80 D3] (🕐 *11.00–late;* ✆ *078 864064/078 849595*) on the site where Papyrus club used to be. Also, there is a pastry and coffee shop in the same building which is open late.

ARTS AND ENTERTAINMENT

CINEMA The **cinema** opposite the Kigali Guest House [92 B1] in Nyamirambo shows somewhat dated Western films as well as screening live international and Premiership football fixtures. There are plans to build a cinema on the top floor of the new **Kigali City Tower**, although it looks as if it will take some time before it is completed.

FESTIVALS The **KigaliUP!** Rwandan music festival (*www.kigaliup.com*), first held on 10 September 2011 at Kimihurura roundabout in downtown Kigali, is set to become an annual event. The inaugural festival featured two stages showcasing the best of Rwandan and East African music. The festival is spearheaded by Planet Folk, a Canadian NGO (e *cmurigande@rogers.ca*), and it is possible to help with the festival as a volunteer. For the last couple of years, the **Mutzig Beer Festival** has been held in October at Juru Park on the outskirts of the city, with a stage featuring live music.

MUSIC AND DANCE Performances of traditional dancing and music take place from time to time in various venues around the city – these are publicised on local radio and in the local press. The RDB Tourism and Reservation Office should also have a list. One worth trying is the **RwaMakondera** (Rwandan Horns) Children's Dance Troupe, which was formed by **Ivuka Arts Studios** [81 E3] (see page 108); this was founded by Collin Sekajugo to provide skills, income and a sense of belonging to orphans and other children from disadvantaged backgrounds.

The **Centre Culturel d'Echanges Franco-Rwandaises** [89 D4] near the Hotel des Mille Collines is now closed but is in the process of being reinvented as the **French Institute of Rwanda (IFR)** (*www.ambafrance-rw.org*). The IFR has begun to hold cultural events again, often in collaboration with the German **Goethe-Institut**, at various locations in Kigali. Recent performers have included Ugandan singer Maurice Kirya who won the Radio France International music award and the

4

acclaimed Cameroonian opera singer Jacques-Greg Belobo. The best place to find out about these events is in the **Goethe-Institut Liaison Office** in the **Ishyo Arts Centre** [81 E2] (*http://ishyo.wordpress.com*), in Kacyiru.

In addition to this, the website www.livinginkigali.com has a monthly calendar that lists events in Kigali including events held by the Goethe-Institut, concerts and live music, karyoke, salsa dancing classes and movie nights.

LIBRARIES The new **Kigali Public Library** [80 D2] (⏲ *08.00–17.00; www. kigalilibrary.org*) is at last open: see box opposite. By the time you read this, the opening hours may extend further into the evening. Building and equipping this library has been a big financial struggle but it is already being well used; if you have leftover books in good condition at the end of your visit, do consider donating them.

SPORT

Kigali caters for both golfers and cricketers! For **cricket**, see the box on page 106. The 18-hole **Nyarutarama Golf Club** [81 F2] (m *078 8524619;* e *info@ rwanda-direct.com   www.rwanda-direct.com/rwanda-golf*) is in an attractively green corner of northeastern Kigali and non-members are welcome to play for a reasonable fee. Nearby is the **Nyarutarama Tennis Club** [81 F3] (☏ *0252 587009;* e *cnorw@rwanda1.com*). The more central **Cercle Sportif** [85 G7] in Lower Kiyovu has facilities for tennis, table tennis, basketball, volleyball, badminton, darts, swimming, etc. Also check out the current **football** fixtures – enthusiast Chris Frean explains how:

> Going to a football match in Kigali is simple as long as you know that it's on.
> Matches generally take place at the Amahoro Stadium on Sunday afternoons at 4pm, sometimes preceded by each side's reserves' match on the same pitch. Fixtures are generally advertised in the New Times during the week beforehand. It is, however, pretty simple to find out if something is about to happen at Amahoro. Just go up to Kisimenti crossroads – the one by Chez Lando – and check the activity. If you see matatus with fans, and police on the crossroads holding up ordinary traffic for dignitaries, then something is on. Domestically the Kigali teams APR, Atraco and Rayon dominate. You can tell by the colours who is playing. Black and white means APR; blue and white Rayon; green and white Kiyovu.
>
> Inside the ground, you shouldn't expect anything like a programme or team info; although with the Rwanda Premier League now sponsored by the brewer Primus, you can actually buy a drink in the ground. For the World Cup qualifiers, tents were set up outside the stands, and a barbeque too.
>
> International match tickets are easy enough to come by too, and priced towards the local market, so not expensive, especially for the terraces. Just go up to the main Amahoro stadium in the hours before kick-off. But beware: you're not allowed to take a mobile phone into the main stand for an international. For one Angola match, I had to submit to a metal detector and was told my phone was not allowed. This, the police later told me, was because people might use phones in the ground to contact hooligans outside and cause problems. However, this policy is only in place when the President is likely to attend a match.

There's more on football (and rugby) in *Chapter 1*, pages 30–2.

Recently a few large shopping centres have opened in Kigali including the **Union Trade Centre (UTC)**, the **Kigali City Tower** and **Simba** supermarket. The **Union Trade Centre** [89 D4] dominates the eastern side of Boulevard de la Révolution between Place de l'Unité Nationale and Place de la Constitution. The centrepiece of this two-storey mall is an immense 24-hour branch of the Kenyan Nakumatt supermarket chain, by far the best stocked shop of its type in Kigali (urban legend has it that more than one expatriate wept for joy outside when it opened, a story which, even if untrue, demonstrates the supermarket's impact on resident shoppers). In addition to a wide range of imported goods and electrical and other household items, the supermarket has an excellent bakery (freshly baked bread, croissants and

KIGALI PUBLIC LIBRARY   *Janice Booth*

In 1999, the Rotary Club of Kigali-Virunga decided to build a public library, its first major project as a chartered Rotary Club, to counter the serious shortage of books in Rwanda and the consequent lack of a culture of reading. Also, a key path to ending violence and preventing another genocide is to make knowledge and ideas – from books – freely available to all Rwandans of all ages, regardless of social and economic status.

It was no daydream! The embryonic library received generous financial support both from overseas and from local Rwandan companies. It was supported by the American Friends of the Kigali Public Library (AFKPL) – via whom the international literary association, PEN, pledged US$45,000 in April 2002. The Government of Rwanda pledged US$500,000 of which US$100,000 was released in July 2003. Secondhand Book Sales (a 'first' for Kigali) were among various events held to raise funds.

In 2002, a young Rwandan boy named Sam called into the office of the Chairman of the Kigali Public Library Project – who initially thought he had come to ask for school fees, a common practice among Rwanda's youth who struggle every year to find the necessary amount. However, what Sam wanted was to donate 200 Rwandan francs (less than 50 US cents, but for him a large sum). He'd discovered the project through one of the book sales, and wanted to contribute in order to make sure the library would be completed.

Construction work started on the foundations in 2002, but later stalled through lack of funds. However, by 2009 the Kigali Public Library campaign had received donations and pledges of approximately US$2 million from individuals, businesses and corporations, foundations, governments, and intergovernmental organisations, and money continued to trickle in. Finally, in 2012, the brand-new library opened its doors. It contains a children's and teenagers' section, an African and Rwandan reader section, reference sections, study and reading areas, an internet café and a rooftop coffee shop. Now that it's open it can better assess local needs and adapt itself to meet them; for example business people and workers who are not free during the day have asked for its opening hours to be extended into the evening. It is also providing books to outlying schools.

Young Sam has had a 10-year wait to see the result of his donation, but surely he will approve!

Kigali SHOPPING

4

other pastries) and meat-and-cheese counter. Sometimes referred to as the Nakumatt Centre, the UTC also hosts several fast-food outlets, a Bourbon Café for fresh coffee and light meals, an efficient forex bureau, a fast internet café, an MTN shop, the Rwandair Express booking office, several boutique shops, and a

CRICKET IN RWANDA

Although the country only really seems to have shifted to a pro-English bent since 1994, cricket has been played for several years in Rwanda. In Butare, the University boys, under Professor Singh, had been playing for quite some time before then. There was a match on a volcanic field in Rubavu/Gisenyi in the 1990s, which finally received appropriate recognition in *Wisden Cricketers' Almanack 2004*. Further reports have been recorded in the *Cricket Round the World* sections of *Wisden*.

By 2003 the RCA managed to get the ground at the Ecole Technique Officielle in the Kicukiro district of Kigali into a good enough condition for regular matches. The ground is basically the school's sports field, so is not exclusive to the Rwanda Cricket Association. Games are subject to regular interruptions, some of the more unusual having been unannounced athletics meetings and the 2004 filming of the BBC feature film *Shooting Dogs*.

Early attempts to bring in kit proved a headache, as Lillywhites has yet to open a branch in Kigali. The Rwanda Revenue Authority, anxious to squeeze whatever they could from persons perceived to have money to burn, decided that a rubber matting pitch supplied free of charge by the ICC was in fact a carpet, and should be subject to duty. Months of wrangling and negotiation failed to convince them. We could only assume a member of RRA staff wanted it to carpet her home.

After achieving ICC membership, Rwanda came 7th in the African Affiliates Championships in 2004 and in 2006 came 6th in Division Three of the African region of the ICC World Cricket League. In 2009, the RCA entered an U13 team in a regional ICC tournament in Uganda. In the event the team could not travel, but it's the desire that matters. Also in 2009, international cricket icon Brian Lara played a brief three-ball innings at Kicukiro 'Oval', as part of a one-day visit to Rwanda.

In 2011 the Rwanda Cricket Stadium Foundation (www.rcsf.co.uk) was formed, run by both British and Rwandan members, and is fundraising energetically to provide Rwanda's first dedicated national cricket ground. See page 32.

Most excitingly, in February 2012, Rwanda won the ICC Africa Division 3 title in Ghana, beating Seychelles, Lesotho, Morocco, Gambia, Cameroon, Mali and St Helena. This secured it a place in the Division 2 qualifier for the 2012 ICC Twenty20 World Cup, where unfortunately it finished bottom of the nine-team league, winning just one of its eight matches, against Malawi.

Nationwide, around 5,000 Rwandans have now taken up the game, and cricket continues to flourish in Kigali. Matches of 40 overs a side are played on Sundays almost throughout the year, several tournaments have been held, and the national side participates in International Cricket Council competitions. Pitch availability, early sunsets, the superiority of ball over bat and the weather all combine to mean that 20/20 has often been the best format – long before it caught on elsewhere.

branch of Access Bank where you can draw currency against a Visa or MasterCard. The public toilets here are very clean and a nominal fee is charged to use them.

The newly opened **Kigali City Tower** [89 C3] also has a branch of Nakomatt supermarket of a similar size to the store in the UTC. In addition, the Kigali City Tower has a branch of Bourbon Café which has a spacious terraced area overlooking Kigali's busy shopping streets. There is also Mr Price, a large shop selling new Western-style clothing and homewares, an authorised Apple dealer and an electrical store, as well as fast food restaurants. Lots of boutique shops are opening and there are plans to build a cinema on the top floor.

Simba supermarket, nearish the UTC, also stocks a large range of goods including Western clothing and shoes, household items and electrical goods. It has good bakery, butchery and grocery sections, and it also has a very good café where you can pick up a quick lunch or snack (see restaurant section on page 97). Otherwise, most of the shops that are of interest to tourists lie within a rough rectangle formed by Boulevard de la Révolution, Avenue du Commerce, Avenue des Mille Collines and Rue de l'Epargne. In **Boulevard de la Révolution**, south of the UTC, the large Banque Commerciale du Rwanda (BRC) is on the eastern side [89 D5], almost on Place de l'Indépendance (where the fountain is). Looking across the road from the bank you have, among other small shops/offices, the Agaseke handicrafts kiosk [89 D5], a small supermarket, internet facilities, a 24-hour pharmacy, an MTN phone shop, the Sierra Café and Supermarket [89 D6], and a filling station [89 D6].

Turn right at the petrol station into Avenue des Mille Collines, then right again into **Avenue de la Paix**. On the opposite side of Avenue de la Paix before it reaches Avenue du Commerce [89 C6] you have (not necessarily in order) a florist, an excellent wine shop , a forex bureau, various clothing and stationery shops, phone/internet facilities, and a few tour operators and travel agents.

The first road running west from here is **Avenue du Commerce**, where the Librairie Caritas bookshop [89 C5] stands a little way down on the left. The next junction is with **Rue de l'Epargne** [89 C5], where you'll find a good internet café, and a cluster of excellent handicraft shops, including Africarte and Artiaganato. Another block down Rue de l'Epargne you'll find Kigali's main cluster of forex bureaux [89 B5], most of which will change cash in any hard currency. Further west is the central market [89 B4], which has been closed for redevelopment for several years now, and La Galette [89 A4], which hosts the city's best delicatessen and butchery, as well as a great café serving fresh coffee, filled baguettes and light meals – a good place to refuel after a morning's shopping.

The biggest suburban mall in Kigali is the **MTN Centre** [81 G3] on the Nyarutarama Road about 1km north of its junction with Boulevard de l'Umuganda. Though not as well equipped as the UTC, it has a good bookshop, a butcher and delicatessen affiliated to La Galette in the city centre (and of a similar quality), a branch of Bourbon Café, an MTN Shop, and a sports bar.

Be aware that plastic bags have been banned in Rwanda since 2005, following a city clean-up in which almost a million old bags or remnants were discovered. This ban is strictly enforced, so it's best to carry your own (non-plastic!) shopping bag if you plan to make many purchases.

HANDICRAFTS AND ART A wide range of handicrafts are sold in Kigali and there's great scope for browsing.

The most centrally located handicrafts market is the **Cooperative for Trade and Promotion of Rwanda** [89 D3] (m *078 8453720*); located just down the hill from the UTC, inside a gate next to the Juicilicious café. Open seven days a week during normal business hours, this covered craft market sells a fine range of traditional Rwandan earrings and paper bead necklaces, batik paintings, wood carvings and colourful woven bowls. You can bargain prices down a little, but due to the close proximity to the city centre it is difficult to get big reductions.

The biggest craft market in town is the **Caplaki handicrafts co-operative** [85 G6] (✆ *078 8568596;* e *gerardmuhizi@yahoo.fr*), also near the Cercle Sportif. As part of the recent Kigali clean-up, the clutter of craft stalls and pavement vendors in the city centre (for example along the edge of Avenue de l'Armée) had to move. A group of about 35 craftspeople approached the Kigali City Council asking for a piece of land where they could relocate. In line with the government's policy of encouraging small-scale income-generating projects, land was allocated. The craftspeople contributed by building the 30-odd wooden huts and stalls.

The complex isn't too far from the city centre, on the Gikondo/Nyenyeri minibus-taxi route. There's parking space inside and outside for a few cars. The stallholders, men and women of all ages, between them sell a huge variety of goods. Carvings, weaving, sculpture, batik, pottery, metalwork, semi-precious stones, palm-fibre items, musical instruments, leather, fabrics, toys, stationery, small furniture, novelties … there's every chance you'll find it at Caplaki. You can visit as part of the Kigali City Tour (see page 112), catch a minibus-taxi or take a taxi-voiture.

Founded by Collin Sekajugo, **Ivuka Arts** [81 E3] (m *078 8620560;* e *ivukaartskigali@yahoo.com or info@ivukaarts.com; www.ivukaarts.com*) provides a workshop and showcase for more than a dozen up-and-coming Rwandan artists whose innovative work typically blends tradition and contemporary styles. *Ivuka* is the Kinyarwanda word for birth. The workshop is tucked away behind the Umubano Hotel and visitors are welcome.

Weaving is one of the specialities of Rwanda – baskets, mats, hangings and pots appear in a variety of shapes and sizes, with carefully interwoven traditional patterns. They are sold by some street vendors, and there's a good selection (including woven hammocks) in the craft shop called **ASAR** [89 C5] (*Association des Artistes Rwandais; Rue Karesimbi, BP 939 Kigali;* ✆ *0252 571139*). This excellent little shop combines the work of several craft-making co-ops; some items are very touristy but others are traditional and all make good gifts. As well as the weaving there are carvings, musical instruments, pottery, beadwork, palm-leaf crafts (including decorated notepaper and cards) and even stuffed toys. Prices are marked, so you needn't worry about bargaining – but a reduction for quantity would be legitimate.

Amahoro ava Hejuru (✆ *0788 869 295; www.amaniafrica.org*) is a peace-building women's sewing cooperative, whose goal is to provide sustainable income generation to women. They make a variety of high-quality fabric items such as purses, backpacks, laptop bags, aprons, place mats, quilts and children's toys. If you have two or three days they can make any custom item you like, from clothing to draperies. The cooperative is located in Gikondo; look for their blue gate and sign on the left of the road about 100 metres uphill from the roundabout, or call the manager Grace on m 078 8751878 for directions.

You'll also find street vendors selling most kinds of small handicrafts – carvings, jewellery, woven baskets, masks, musical instruments, notepaper and postcards decorated with palm fibres – and so on.

BOOKSHOPS Two good bookshops in Kigali, both of them stocking a wide range of books on the history and culture of Rwanda, the background to the genocide and an assortment of other relevant themes, are the Librairie Caritas [89 C5] (✆ *0252 574295/576503;* e *librcar@rwanda1.com; www.caritasrwanda.org*) in Rue du Commerce just downhill from its junction with Avenue de la Paix, and the Ikirezi Bookshop [81 E4] (📞 *0252 571314;* m *078 8560358;* e *info@ikirezi.biz; www. ikirezi.biz*) on Boulevard de l'Umuganda in Kacyiru, next to the Kigali Great Wall of China restaurant. The Ikirezi, which sometimes holds book signings and other events, is open 09.00–12.30 and 14.00–18.00 (closes at 13.00 on Saturday) as well as 10.30–13.00 on Sunday; while Caritas keeps normal shop hours, but is closed on Saturday afternoon and Sunday. Also, the branch of Nakomatt in the **Kigali City Tower** stocks a good range of fiction and non-fiction books in English, including books with an African theme.The RDB tourism and conservation office in Kacyiru has a good selection of books relating to Rwanda.

MARKETS In all market areas, take care – crowds are popular with pickpockets and opportunistic thieves, and instances of crime, though far from common, have been reported. Also be tactful about taking photos; for every dozen people who don't object to being in a picture, there'll be someone who does. Respect their privacy.

INTERNATIONAL PEACE MARATHON

This colourful and energetic event is an initiative of the European Federation of Soroptimists (*www.soroptimisteurope.org*), aimed at giving people from other countries the chance to run shoulder to shoulder with Rwandans in the name of peace. After long and careful preparations by the Soroptimists and Rwanda's Ministry of Youth, Sports and Culture, the first International Peace Marathon took place in Kigali on 15 May 2005. On that bright, hot Sunday morning, 2,000 runners from 20 different nations flocked into the Amahoro Stadium. Among them were 500 children, who set off with the less athletic participants on the accompanying 5km Fun Run.

Ever since that day the Kigali Peace Marathon has become a popular annual event attracting participants from the USA, UK, Italy, France, Finland, Belgium, Germany, Austria, Netherlands, Greece, Luxembourg, Malta, Morocco, Kenya, Ethiopia and other African countries. There are many children selected to take part in the fun run from schools all over Rwanda. Many are from underprivileged backgrounds, and the Soroptimists have raised funds to provide each with a commemorative T-shirt, a contribution to his/her school fees for a year, and a backpack with some school equipment. The Ministry of Sport looks after their transport and accommodation.

At the Peace Marathon held in May 2012, Kenyans swept up the honours, winning the men's and women's sections of both the marathon and the half marathon. Over 930 runners took part. There is a great atmosphere of good humour, energy and enthusiasm on the streets of Kigali on marathon day, but.as you might expect in the 'Land of a Thousand Hills', the marathon itself is inevitably, hilly! And Kigali's altitude of 1,500m can cause breathlessness among some runners from lower countries. If you choose to take part, bring plenty of water, and remember that you may need more breaks because of the altitude and heat .

Check out the details on www.kigalimarathon.com. You have to register to take part before the event and you must go to get your race number from the Amahoro stadium in Kigali at least three days beforehand. And start training now…

Kimironko market is a short bus journey from the city centre or Remera and is one of the main markets in the city. You can get a bus there from either Av de la Justice (Rfr200) or the blue taxi sign opposite Chez Lando (Rfr100). There is a dazzling array of goods for sale from fresh fruits and vegetables to shoes and handbags, household items, clothes and kitchen equipment. You can chose from a huge selection of colourful fabrics and visit one of the many tailors who will measure you up and make it into whatever you want in a few days. There is also a section which sells the cheapest handicrafts in the city, if you are prepared to bargain!

The frenetic market across the road from the Nyabugogo bus station is also worth a visit. Located at the bottom of Rue du Lac Hago it's like a human kaleidoscope – a changing, shifting mass of colours and noise. A few minutes being jostled by these brisk crowds, determinedly going about their own business, may be enough for you – but it's a typical and non-touristy experience which it would be a pity to miss completely. See the walk *To Nyabugogo market* on page 118.

TOURISM AND LOCALLY MADE CRAFTS   *Patrick S*

The prospects for tourism in Rwanda lie mainly in the safe haven offered to the remaining mountain gorillas in our Volcanoes National Park, other various flora and fauna in the Akagera National Park and Nyungwe Forest, and physical features like the volcanoes on our border with the DRC, the Rusumo Falls in southern Rwanda, etc.

But the Rwandan people also have an important part to play. Among other talents, we are skilled at carving, sculpture and weaving. Most of this is done by the ordinary Rwandan. Weaving is particular to women and girls while wood-carving is done mostly by men.

Most importantly, the work is created according to various themes: mother nature, beauty, achievement and virtues such as valour etc, as well as everyday scenes. A woman carrying a baby on her back, a pot of milk on her head and a bundle of firewood under her arm is a common sight around here. An old man sitting on a traditional stool with a long straw dipped in a pot is also familiar.

However, it is sad when in some cases such talent is wasted through poor sales, bad storage and poor preservation. Many pieces are sold on roadsides where they gather so much dust, washed away by rains, that even an occasional tourist who passes by can hardly notice their beauty!

A lot can be done to keep this heritage alive through publicity abroad: Rwandan embassies setting up sales-points for such goods, modest though they may be, and interested individuals taking it upon themselves to sell Rwandan handicrafts for the good of it. But most of all, local government can help by giving assistance to these craftspeople and tourists can help by purchasing their products.

The price of such items is quite small and affordable. The Caplaki centre near the Cercle Sportif in Kigali is one place to find them on display. Even at the Kigali International Airport there is a stall, and another near the Rwanda Revenue Authority offices. Also independent vendors display and sell their wares in the street.

Come and buy 'at your eye's pleasure'! And help to promote traditional craftsmanship in Rwanda as you explore the beauties of our Republic of a Thousand Hills.

KIGALI FOR CHILDREN While Kigali isn't overly rich in things for little ones to do, there are a few places where they can go to play. Next to New Cadillac Nightclub, a new children's play area has opened called **Total Toys** (☉ *08.30–19.00*). For an entrance fee of Rfr2,000 per child you can let them loose on a variety of play equipment including a bouncy castle, swings, trampolines, slides, roundabouts and carousels. About 15km east of Kigali on the road towards Rwamagana is **Bambino Supercity**, with a swimming pool, gardens and some play equipment for children. Also many hotels in Kigali including the Hotel des Mille Collines, Hotel Umubano and La Palisse have swimming pools which the general public can use for a small fee.

OTHER PRACTICALITIES

COMMUNICATIONS The main **post office** at the top of Boulevard de Nyabugogo in the city centre has a counter for international phone calls and an efficient fax office. If you want someone to send a fax to you there, the number is (+250) 252 51 40 91. There's also a philatelic counter. Two former post offices, in Avenue de la Paix and near the Kigali Business Centre, have both closed.

Internet Cyber cafés are springing up fast and you'll see them all over the city. One hour online typically costs around Rfr400–600, with faster facilities such as the excellent Blues Café [89 D4] next to the UTC generally charging slightly higher rates. The main hotels (and some smaller ones) also offer internet access, but usually at an inflated cost. Public business facilities generally close on Sundays.

Telephone You can find **public telephones** in shops and kiosks all over Kigali – they are metered, so you pay when you've finished and don't need handfuls of small change. Calls to mobile phones from these are more expensive than those to normal phones, although calls from mobile to mobile are cheaper. Rwanda is now said to have one of the most modern telephone systems in East Africa.

You can buy a local SIM card to convert most imported **mobiles** for use in Rwanda; these cost around Rfr1,000 from any MTN (Mobile Telephone Networks) shop – there's one in the UTC [89 D4] and another in Boulevard de la Révolution near the Sierra Restaurant [89 D6], and various others around the city. If you need voicemail and international texting, check that your card includes this; some don't. Then it's a pay-as-you-go system: you buy cards in denominations of Rfr500 upwards to top up the balance in your account. You can also buy a plug-in modem for your laptop from MTN shops which will give you internet access. It uses the same pay-as-you-go airtime system as the phone network.

MEDICAL FACILITIES The largest hospitals are:

✚ **King Faisal** (or Faycal) [81 F3] ☎0252 582421/585397; emergency ☎0252 588888; e faisal@rwanda1.com; www.kfh.rw

✚ **Central Hospital of the University of Kigali** [85 E6] ☎0252 575406/575555; e chuck. hospital@chuckigali.org; www.chk.org.rw

Clinics and laboratories include:

✚ **Faith Clinic** ☎0252 570296
✚ **Plateau Polyclinic** ☎0252 578767; m 078 8301630; e pcp@rwanda1.com

✚ **Central Kigali Polyclinic** ☎0252 576377
✚ **Polyfam** ☎0252 573477

4

For emergency dental treatment, contact the Adventist Dental Clinic (\ *0252 582431*), while optometric services are available at Eye Care Optical [85 F4] (m *078 8867121;* e *eyecareoptical.rwanda@yahoo.com*). For further medical listings, see www.theeye.co.rw.

MONEY Assuming you arrive with hard-currency cash (ideally, US dollars, euros or UK pounds sterling), the easiest option is to change at a private **bureaux de change** (known locally as **forex bureaux**), whch are scattered around the city centre. These are mostly clustered along the east end of Rue de l'Epargne, and have current exchange rates chalked up on blackboards outside. You might want to shop around a bit, and bargain, if you're changing large amounts, and you should keep your wits about you. If the touts that hang out here seem intimidating, there is also an efficient forex bureau nearby in Avenue de la Paix as well as on the top floor of the Union Trade Centre (UTC) [89 D4]. There are counters in most hotels and banks, and at Kigali International Airport. Forex bureaux offer a significantly lower rate of exchange for US dollar bills smaller than US$50, and the same applies to low-denomination bills in other currencies. US dollars printed before 2003 are unlikely to be accepted.

Travellers' cheques are practically useless in Kigali. The Banque Commerciale du Rwanda (BCR) in Boulevard de la Révolution [89 D5] may change up to US$200 worth per day, but this is a tedious procedure and you may be required to produce proof of purchase. The Banque Continentale Africaine Rwanda (BACAR) has a **Moneygram** service and the BCR a **Western Union** service via which funds can be transferred quickly from abroad. In fact Western Union has hit Rwanda in a big way – there are several other offices in Kigali, and at least one in each of the other main towns, but bear in mind that these transfers attract a hefty charge.

It is now possible to draw local currency from **ATMs** (auto-tellers) in Kigali. You can use an international Visa debit card at ATMs at the **Bank of Kigali** (\ *0252 593100,* e *bk@bk.rw*) This e-mail address is being protected from spambots. You need JavaScript enabled to view it and **Ecobank** (\ *250 5035808* e *contact@ ecobank.com*). However be aware that from time to time they stop working or run out of cash so it is advisable to bring some hard currency that can be changed as well as your Visa card. In the writer's experience, the ATM at the main branch of the Bank of Kigali in Avenue de la Paix is fairly reliable. The only way that money can be drawn against a MasterCard is by a manual transaction at the Access Bank (⊕ *08.00–18.00 Mon–Fri, 09.00–16.00 Sat*) in the UTC [89 D4]. You can draw up to US$1,500 daily, and the transaction attracts a commission of 3%.

WHAT TO SEE AND DO

For a capital city, Kigali doesn't offer a great deal in terms of buildings, museums and historical/cultural sites, but it is a pleasant place for strolling and people-watching. If you want to see the best of the city in an organised manner, this can be arranged through the RDB Tourism and Conservation Reservation Office [81 F4] (contact details on page 33), which runs **guided bus tours** of Kigali from Monday to Saturday at US$20 per person (minimum four persons). The tour takes in several places covered below, including the Museum of Natural History, Nyamirambo (the oldest quarter of Kigali), Caplaki Handicrafts Co-operative, Gisozi Genocide Memorial and the Heroes' Cemetery, as well as the Parliament Building and Kigali Institute of Science and Technology.

For those more interested in day-to-day African life than in landmarks, a **'This is Africa' experience** is offered by the Nyamirambo Women's Centre (m *078 211*

1860; e *nwcoffice.kigali@gmail.com; www.nwc-kigali.org*; see page 97). It introduces visitors to the vibrant culture of contemporary urban Rwanda in Nyamirambo, the city's oldest and arguably most multi-cultural suburb. The women of Nyamirambo take visitors to a local hair salon and tailor, as well as the Muslim quarter and market, and finally a private home for a cooking lesson and traditional lunch. Rates range from US$60 to US$80 per person, depending on group size (minimum two), 70% of which goes straight to the community.

Note that it is forbidden to take photos near Kigali Prison, which lies on Avenue de la Justice opposite Rue de l'Epargne.

MEMORIALS
Kigali Genocide Memorial [80 B1] (*www.kigalimemorialcentre.org*; m *078 8307666*; e *office@aegistrust.org*) This dignified memorial has been constructed in Gisozi, the burial site of over 250,000 people killed in a three-month period during Rwanda's 1994 genocide. It opened fully for the tenth anniversary of the genocide in April 2004. You can see it across the valley – a large, white, modern building with terraces in front – on the right as you go downhill on Boulevard de Nyabugogo. To drive there is easy as it's in sight for much of the way – take a right turn halfway down Boulevard de Nyabugogo, continue downwards into the valley, and when you're a little way past the memorial take a left turn across the valley, then (at a T-junction) go sharp left along a short dirt road and you'll come to the gate.

Importantly, the memorial centre is not just a mass grave and exhibition. At the request of Kigali City Council, it was created – and is managed today – by the UK-based Aegis Trust (a non-sectarian, non-governmental genocide prevention organisation; *www.aegistrust.org*). Aegis operates a Rebuilding Lives programme to help widows and orphans of the genocide, and a peace-building education programme (hosted at the Memorial) educating a new generation about the dangers of prejudice and helping to establish trust between the children of survivors and perpetrators.

The memorial centre is now also home to the Genocide Archive of Rwanda, which is open to the public. The purpose of the archive centre is to illuminate genocidal ideologies and their impact. The archive collection includes photographs, official documents and geographical data.

Entry is free but contributions are very much welcomed because the centre relies on proceeds for the upkeep of the mass graves and the exhibitions. Recently it has developed an audio tour which costs US$15. The audio tour is currently available in English, French, Dutch and German. Italian and Spanish versions are coming soon. It is comprehensive, and is particularly helpful for understanding the outside exhibits such as the gardens and mass graves. There is also a bookshop that sells a good selection of films, music and books on the theme of genocide and prevention. Further to this, a café has recently opened on the site selling a good range of snacks, sandwiches and drinks (serving premium Rwandan coffee), and proceeds from this also go towards the upkeep of the museum and its educational outreach work.

To maximise accessibility – particularly for those whose loved ones are buried here – there is no charge for entry to the Kigali Genocide Memorial. However, its operation – and Aegis's programmes in Rwanda – are entirely dependent on donations and revenue from Aegis Social Enterprises (including services provided both on site and at the Discover Rwanda Youth Hostel – see page 95), so visitors are invited to make a donation of at least $15 if choosing not to spend money on any of the Centre's services or facilities.

See also the boxed text *Responses to the Kigali Genocide Memorial* on page 115.

Nyanza Genocide Memorial [81 G7] (*www.kigalimemorialcentre.org/old/centre/ other/nyanza.html*) In April 2009, this stark memorial overlooking the new Bugesera Road in the suburb of Kicukiro was the site of the official Genocide Memorial Day ceremony on the 15th anniversary of the Rwandan genocide. An estimated 10,000 victims of the genocide are buried in mass graves here, covered in large slabs of concrete. Many of these victims were Tutsis who, when the killing started, took refuge in the Ecole Technique Officielle (ETO), which fell under the protection of Belgian troops from the United Nations Assistance Mission for Rwanda (UNAMIR). Tragically, UNAMIR withdrew the Belgians from Rwanda, and the Interahamwe descended on the ETO to massacre the thousands of refugees gathered there. Started in 2008, a museum at the site will document the massacre at the ETO, and chart the abandonment of Rwanda by the International Community. The site is now open to the public but is still under construction. To get there, get a bus to Kicukiro and stay on until you reach the main bus park. Then look for ETO; it's on the main road not far from the bus park.

Remera Heroes' Cemetery [81 H3] Situated on Kimironko Road a few hundred metres past Amahoro Stadium, Heroes' Cemetery is another site associated with the 1994 genocide. Three graves here are of particular significance. The first is the grave of **Fred Gisa Rwigyema**, the co-founder and leader of the RPF, who was killed in battle on 2 October 1990 during a failed invasion of Rwanda. The second is the grave of **Agathe Uwilingiyimana**, the first (and thus far only) female prime minister of Rwanda, who was less than a year into her term when she was assassinated by the Interahamwe on 7 April 1994, within hours of the plane crash that killed President Habyarimana. The third is the **Tomb of the Unknown Soldier**, whose anonymous occupant symbolises all those who died in the civil war.

Camp Kigali Memorial [85 E6] Now the Kigali Institute of Science and Technology (KIST), Camp Kigali is where ten Belgian UNAMIR peacekeepers, deployed to guard the house of Prime Minister Agathe Uwilingiyimana, were executed brutally by the Presidential Guard on the first day of the genocide. The former military camp now hosts a memorial and small museum that still bears the scars of grenade shrapnel. In the garden, ten stone obelisks have been erected, each with the initials of one of the soldiers carved into the base, and horizontal slashes indicating his age.

For memorials outside Kigali, see *Ntarama and Nyamata genocide memorials* on page 121.

MUSEUMS
State House Museum (e *info@museum.gov.rw; www.museum.gov.rw*) The whitewashed state house situated about 4km from Kigali international airport was the home of the former Rwandan president Juvenal Habyarimana until his death in 1994, and it was then occupied by his successor, President Pasteur Bizimungu, until 2000. The aim of the museum is to educate people about Rwandan culture in general, but more specifically the events leading up to the Rwandan Genocide.

On the ground floor of the state house, there are information boards describing various everyday aspects of Rwandan culture from jewellery and hairstyling to traditional dress from the early 1900s. The rest of the house has been left largely unchanged since it was last occupied in 2000, including the threadbare sofa rumoured to be the place where Habyarimana's wife, Agathe, was sitting at the moment her husband's plane was shot down on 6 April 1994. While showing us around the property, our enthusiastic and knowledgeable guide talked us through some of the decisions made by the Habyarimanas during their 20-year stay in the state house and how these decisions contributed to the Rwandan genocide.

Outside, in the extensive grounds of the museum, lie the remains of the plane crash that killed Habyarimana. Looking at the scattered remains of the plane is a poignant and sobering experience, and serves as a powerful reminder of how Rwanda fell apart during the events of April 1994. The museum and its grounds are still being developed. There are plans for a cafeteria and gift shop, and a small zoological park. The museum is well worth a visit for those who seek a better understanding of the events leading up to the 1994 genocide. The Rfr3,000 entrance fee includes an English- or French-speaking guide. There is also a café on site.

Museum of Natural History [84 C4] (m *078 4577776; www.museum.gov.rw; ⏱ 08.00–17.00 daily*). Standing alongside a small dirt road leading west from Avenue de la Justice, this new museum is set in Kandt House, which was built by Richard Kandt in 1907, restored with German aid over 2004–05, and opened as a museum in 2007. Effectively the founder of Kigali, Kandt embarked on his first journey to

RESPONSES TO THE KIGALI GENOCIDE MEMORIAL

'You are the stone on which we will build a Rwanda without conflict.'
Bernard Makuza, Rwandan Prime Minister, 2004.

'Since my own visit to Rwanda's genocide memorial site, I have been talking to many colleagues in the United Nations.... Anyone who goes there cannot come out without crying, without being very humble about how the international community failed to react to this.'
Ban Ki-moon, UN Secretary-General, speaking at the UN Headquarters in New York at the launch of the Aegis Trust/UN exhibition 'Lessons from Rwanda', 30 April 2007.

'Finally, a beautiful and profound memorial.'
Alain Destexhe, Senator, Belgium.

'I want to thank the local government and the Aegis Trust and all the people who've worked on this. This is in some ways the most moving memorial of its kind I've ever seen, simply for the power and simplicity of it.... it faithfully, honestly, painfully presents the truth of the Rwandan genocide. It is a profoundly important contribution to the ability of this country to go on with its life, and it's an important contribution to the recent history of the world that no-one can afford to forget. We are all in debt to everyone who had anything to do with the creation of this magnificent museum, and I urge those of you who can to see it and to support it.'
Former US President Bill Clinton at the Kigali Memorial Centre, Rwanda.

'Before our colleagues visited the Memorial, there were some students who had lost their parents or siblings during the genocide and who had the feeling that someone who prevented your parents from living is your enemy; but now, we have learnt and things changed.'
Student response to Aegis Rwanda's genocide education programme.

Rwanda in 1897 in search of the most remote source of the Nile, and he was appointed first Resident Governor of Rwanda upon his return in 1907. An ardent naturalist, he was the first westerner to visit Nyungwe Forest, and he also discovered several plant and animal species, among them the localised golden monkey.

Kandt House, probably the oldest in Kigali, is a moderately interesting example of German colonial architecture, set in pretty gardens with a lovely view over the valleys. Unfortunately, however, its contents fall into the 'mildly diverting' rather than 'must see' category, with captions in German and Kinyarwanda only (no French or English), and there are no plans to change this anytime soon. However you can get an English-speaking guide to give you a tour which is included in the

COMMUNITY PROJECTS TO VISIT IN KIGALI   *Camilla Gore*

In the past few years, a number of individuals and NGOs (Non-Governmental Organisations) have been seeking to help Rwandans, particularly young orphans, under-privileged children and abandoned or widowed women, to develop their skills and lift themselves out of poverty and into education and a better future. The places mentioned in this box all work towards empowering Rwandans to learn and use new skills and they invest profits back into local communities in Kigali. All are very welcoming towards visitors and show the many positive changes that are happening across the city. Other travellers have reported that visiting one of these projects is a particularly powerful experience after going to the Gisozi genocide memorial centre.

AFRICAN BAGEL COMPANY (ABC) [81 G7] (❘ *078 8408308; e africanbagelco@yahoo. com; ⊕ 09.00–14.00*) Robin Smith and her husband Rich started this business a few years ago to help local young people and women get into employment and education and off the streets. Tucked away on a little street on the left up the hill past Kicukiro market (and signposted from the main road), this café serves mouth-watering bagels, donuts and chocolate chip cookies. Other than the owners and a few volunteers, all of the staff are local Rwandan people. Some of the delicious bagel options include the hot pizza bagel, bagel chips with hummus or barbeque sauce and bagels with vegetables and cream cheese; on Saturdays, donuts are cooked outside on a traditional charcoal stove. You can also buy handicrafts from local disabled artisans at the café.

CENTRE CESAR [81 H3] (*www.ubuntuedmonton.org/en; ⊕ Mon–Fri daytime*) Centre Cesar began in 2005 to assist widows in the Kimironko area of Kigali. The women learned how to make handicrafts at the centre and profits were re-invested to provide the women and their children with services and facilities, including a lovely little pre-school. If you visit the centre you can see the women making beautiful and intricate beaded handicrafts and you can visit the pre-school where you will receive a warm welcome from lots of friendly little faces. You can buy handicrafts from the centre and there is also a sewing shop where you can get items made for you. To get to the centre go to Kimironko market and turn left down a dirt road, following the signs, or alternatively hop on a moto and ask for Centre Cesar.

CARDS FROM AFRICA [81 H5] (m *078 8658158; www.cardsfromafrica.com; ⊕ 09.00–15.00 Mon–Fri*) These beautiful, textured paper cards are made by young people entrance fee. Most interesting, in this writer's opinion, is a collection of monochrome photographs of the settlement on Nyarugenge Hill in the early days of Kigali, but other displays cover minerals, hydrology, fossils, wildlife and volcanism in Rwanda. Also present is a motley collection of stuffed animals and mounted butterflies from the various national parks, and (rather bizarrely) a collection of plastic toy dinosaurs. Whether the sum of these rather meagre parts justifies an entrance fee of Rfr6,000 (or Rfr5,000 for residents) is very questionable. However, perhaps the best reason to visit the museum is for the excellent view of Kigali from the terrace at the back of the building. This is an ideal place to take photos of the city and there is no extra charge for using your camera.

in the Kigali area who have lost both of their parents. The young people are trained to make the cards, and the work provides them with an income for supporting their families or getting an education. If you visit their workshop in Kigali near the airpor, you can take a guided tour and see the card-making process from making the paper pulp to assembling the cards. To get to Cards from Africa by public transport, go to the Remera crossroads and stand so you are on the road opposite the bus park with the MTN shop on your left. Walk a short way down the road until you see a blue taxi sign and get a bus to Kabeza town. Stay on the bus for about 10 minutes until you reach its terminus. Walk a couple of hundred yards down the road and you should see Cards from Africa just down the hill on your left.

THE MEG FOUNDATION [85 F1] (m *078 3206154;* e *info@kinambaproject.org.uk;* ⏱ *8.00–17.00 Mon–Fri*) The Meg Foundation was founded by former VSO volunteer Meg Fletcher in 2007 to provide educational opportunities for under-privileged children in the Kinamba area of Kigali, a small area tucked behind the US Embassy. Visitors are most welcome. In the mornings, visitors can join the nursery children in their daily activities including, singing, reading, painting and playing games. In the afternoons, the foundation runs an after-school club for primary children who attend local government schools. The foundation also provides literacy and skills training for local women and their handicrafts can be bought at the site. There are also sometimes longer-term volunteering opportunities available. To get to the centre, ask for a moto or taxi to Kinamba Jehova and the foundation is opposite; or turn left at the roundabout by the US Embassy, then take the first right cobbled road and walk for 1km until you see the blue-and-white building on the left.

CENTRE MAREMBO [81 G4] (m *078 8505355/072 2505353;* e *centremarembo@gmail.com; www.rYico.org;* ⏱ *Mon–Fri daytime*) Centre Marembo provides vulnerable young people, especially street children and former street children, with much-needed youth services. They have a drop-in centre and dormitory for the youth, and they also help with vocational skills training including mechanics, moto driving and sewing. They also provide education to the young people and others at local secondary schools on reproductive health and HIV/AIDs prevention. The staff are welcoming and keen to show you around and you can also buy handicrafts made by the youth here. The centre is located on the road behind the Sole Luna restaurant, opposite the Beausejour hotel. Also see pages 62–3.

NYARUTARAMA LAKE [81 F3] Situated at the south end of the Kigali Golf Club, in the valley between Nyarutarama and Kacyiru Hills, this small artificial lake and surrounding patchwork of exotic and indigenous woodland offers the best nature walk and birdwatching opportunity within Kigali city limits. The open water and its margins frequently support a variety of ducks, pelicans, herons and egrets, along with black crake, African jacana and pied and malachite kingfisher. The handsome long-crested eagle also appears to be resident, and the rank grasslands around the lake host widow birds, weavers, waxbills and seedeaters such as African citril.

The lake can be approached from two directions, either by following a rough dirt road downhill from King Faisal Hospital (a short way northeast of the Umubano Hotel), or by following Nyarutarama Road north from the junction with Boulevard de l'Umuganda, then taking the first major intersection left and continuing northwards past the Nyarutarama Tennis Club for about 1.5km. These two main roads are connected by a vehicle-width track that runs through the woodland south of the lake, a promising area for barbets, cuckoos and other acacia-associated species.

STROLLING ROUND KIGALI If you don't mind the unavoidable hills, Kigali offers some good strolls. There are plenty of places where you can stop for a snack or a drink if you need to cool off. Two walks which could each fill up a morning, depending on how often you stop on the way, are given below; but just look at a map of the whole city and you'll see that there are plenty more.

To the mosque and Nyamirambo district

One way of getting to the big mosque in the Muslim quarter is to walk southwards along Avenue de la Justice, with views out across the valley to your right; the mosque is at the junction where Rue de la Sécurité joins from the left [80 A5]. Continue for a few minutes and you're in a lively, busy district (Nyamirambo) of small streets and colourful little local shops. The atmosphere has a touch of London's Soho about it. This is said to be the part of the present-day city where people first settled, long ago. There's a lot of small-scale activity going on here, and small bar/cafés where you can stop for a drink.

To return to the centre, you can either catch a minibus-taxi (they serve Avenue de la Justice; look out for the yellow signs indicating bus stops) or flag down a taxi. (A short stretch of Avenue de la Justice is one-way and minibuses only travel outward from the centre; to get one going back you'll need to be in the two-way part.) Or else retrace your steps towards the mosque and look out for Avenue Paul VI on your right – follow this upwards and it'll bring you on to the area covered by the map on page 92. Or – be adventurous and find your own variations!

To Nyabugogo market

This takes you through an area of many small shops and market stalls, finishing at the busy market opposite Nyabugogo minibus-taxi stand [84 A2]. If you can cope with seething crowds and a lot of jostling, try it (but don't take photos without the permission of the subjects).

Walk down Rue de l'Epargne or along Avenue de la Justice until you come to the prison [89 A3]. As you face it from the road, the first road beside it to your right, turning off at a sharp angle, is Rue du Mont Huye, an unsurfaced road running downhill. Take this and follow it – you'll pass homes, small shops, an enclosed market area off it to your right, and then you arrive at the bottom – and the lively Nyabugogo market. Just look at the variety of people here – you'll see so many different bone structures, shades of colour, styles of clothing…

If you cross over into the minibus-taxi station (which is a 'market area' all of its own, with vendors offering everything from leather shoes and hi-fi equipment to – improbably – plastic hair curlers and freshly baked bread) you can get a minibus-taxi back to the central minibus station or else take a taxi-voiture; they park just by the main gate. Or turn right up the main road as you leave the market; this upward hill is Boulevard de Nyabugogo and will take you back to Place de l'Unité Nationale and the centre of town.

EXCURSIONS FURTHER AFIELD

Rwanda is such a small country that almost any of the towns and other attractions covered in this guidebook make for a feasible day or overnight trip from the capital. This is certainly true for **Huye** (formerly Butare) and the National Museum of Rwanda (*Chapter 6*), as well as the former royal capital of **Nyanza** along the same road (*Chapter 5*), though it would be a push to squeeze both sites into a one-day outing from Kigali. If you were to go to Huye by public minibus-taxi, you could ask to be dropped at the museum, and walk from there to the town centre to catch a minibus back. If you leave early and check the return times, you should be able to visit the attractive little lakeside town of **Karongi** (formerly Kibuye, *Chapter 8*) as a round trip from Kigali.

Of the national parks, **Akagera** (*Chapter 12*) can technically be visited from Kigali in a day, but you'll need your own transport, a very early start, and would get a lot more from the exercise by overnighting in or near the park. The mountain gorillas in **Volcanoes National Park** (*Chapter 10*) can also be visited as a day trip from Kigali, but you'd need a very early start (before 05.00) in a private vehicle to reach the park headquarters by the check-in time of 07.00. **Nyungwe** (*Chapter 7*) really is too far away for a day trip, but it could be visited as an overnight trip, though two nights would be more realistic.

The following suggestions are closer to Kigali.

BUGESERA DISTRICT The relatively hot and low-lying part of Rwanda running directly south from Kigali to the Burundi border now forms the administrative district of Bugesera, which is centred upon the town of Nyamata, some 35km south of the capital. Bugesera was severely affected by the genocide. At least 80% of the local Tutsi population was killed (actual numbers are unknown), and many of the victims were thrown into the Nyabarongo River, eventually to wash up on the Uganda shore of Lake Victoria. Two of the most brutal massacres in Bugesera are commemorated at the genocide memorials at Ntarama and Nyamata (see overleaf).

Although Bugesera receives a relatively low rainfall and is prone to periodic droughts, its dominant geographic feature is the Nyabarongo River, the country's longest, a tributary of the Akagera that rises in Nyungwe and feeds a wetland area comprising at least a dozen lakes and several large areas of swampland. Listed as one of Rwanda's seven Important Bird Areas, these vast wetlands are of special interest for waterbirds, including localised papyrus-associated species such as papyrus gonolek, Carruthers cisticola, white-winged scrub-warbler, papyrus yellow warbler, northern brown-throated weaver, papyrus canary and possibly even shoebill. In addition to boasting immense potential for birding tourism, several of the lakes also host hippos and crocodiles (indeed, wild elephants still roamed the area until 1975, when the last 26 elephants were rounded up and transported to Akagera National Park).

Until recently, road access to Bugesera was poor, and few tourists visited the area. But this has changed following the construction of an excellent surfaced road from Kigali to the Burundi border in 2008, and the area is likely to gain greater prominence as and when the proposed Bugesera International Airport opens outside Nyamata to replace the current international airport in Kigali, a switch

WALKING AND CYCLING AROUND KIGALI   *Caroline Pomeroy*

Sprawling over numerous hills and valleys, with roads that wind crazily around and across the contours, Kigali can be a confusing city to navigate. Just when you think you know where you are going, your destination appears on the horizon in another direction! However, it's a fairly compact city and, assuming that you aren't put off by the idea of steep slopes, over-friendly children and changeable weather, walking is a fantastic way to get about. If you have just arrived, don't forget that Kigali lies at an altitude of around 1,600m, so take it easy on the hills!

Although the geography of the city is confusing, you can nearly always spot a landmark to help you find your way to your destination. Many buildings offer great views across Kigali, so if you plan to explore on foot you will do well to start by getting to grips with the geography, map in hand, from one of these: the panoramic top-floor bar of the Top Towers Hotel in Kacyiru; Bourbon Café in the MTN building, Nyarutarama; the upper floors of the Bank of Kigali; the terrace of the Museum of Natural History; and Bourbon Café in the UTC. If you don't have a map, there's a good one on the foyer wall of the Umubano Hotel.

As well as walking as a means of getting about town, there are plenty of good hikes on the hills which ring the city. These offer spectacular views and can be surprisingly peaceful away from the constant calls of 'muzungu'. You could start your walk by taking a minibus taxi from the centre of town – these are very cheap and are all labelled with their eventual destination.

At 1,850m, Mount Kigali is the highest peak around the city, and it can be climbed from Nyamirambo. Catch a minibus-taxi as far as the terminus opposite the stadium, then keep walking along the main cobbled road until it eventually peters out to dirt. There are many routes up the mountain – follow your nose or ask locals to direct you. At the top, there's a path along a wooded ridge, with very few people about. Beware that as you head north, you will encounter a military camp and be asked to turn back.

The hills above Gikondo and Kicukiro can be reached by taking a taxi to Gikondo 'Stade'. Get off at the last stop, and then keep walking uphill. When you reach the ridge, veering left will bring you to Park Juru, a laid-back outdoor restaurant with pleasant gardens and views over the city. There are numerous roads and tracks all over this ridge, many with spectacular views in all directions. One leads to Kicukiro, where you can find transport back to the city centre.

While the heat, the hills and the traffic mean that cycling in Kigali is not for the faint-hearted, it can be an exhilarating and rewarding experience. Heading out of town in any direction will soon lead you to a huge network of dirt tracks and paths, offering a great insight into rural Rwandan life. A good direction to start is to the east and south of the city (head for Kibagabaga, Kimironko, Remera, Kicukiro or the airport, and keep going) where the terrain is a little flatter. Mercator Assistance (m *078 8306830/078 8512630; www. mercatorassistance.rw*) rents out bikes and arranges guided cycling tours.

Anecdotes collected by the first Europeans to visit northwest Rwanda suggest that Mount Muhabura's perfect cone, topped today by a small crater lake, still glowed at night as recently as the early 19th century (AZ) page 252–3

left A girl from the Cyamudungo Forest carrying wood on her head (EL) page 174–5

below Traditional potters at work at the Gatagara Pottery, a workshop piled with bowls, teacups, vases and other ceramic wares (AZ) page 134

bottom Tea and coffee are the most important export crops for Rwanda. Here, tea-pickers in Byumba (AZ) page 260–1

above   A colourful shop in Nyamirambo, Kigali's oldest and arguably most multicultural suburb (EL) page 118

right   The Maraba Coffee Co-operative, based in Huye, has excelled in international taste tests (WH/FLPA) pages 150–2

below   On the road from Musanze to Muhanga, and at an altitude of 1,760m, Ngororero is host to a large multi-level market (AZ) page 213

above left Rwanda's last savanna elephant herds (*Loxodonta africana*) inhabit the lake hinterland of Akagera National Park (AZ) pages 6 & 273–89

above right Common and widespread in Rwanda, chameleons are arguably the most intriguing of African reptiles. Pictured, a rudis chameleon (*Trioceros rudis*) (EB/MC) pages 164–5

below The impala (*Aepyceros melampus*) is common in the woodland around and between the lakes of Akagera National Park (GB/S) pages 278–9

right Maasai giraffe (_Giraffa camelopardalis_) were first introduced to Akagera from Kenya in 1986; the original herd of two males and four females has now multiplied to a population of around 80 (WT/S) pages 6 & 273–89

below Hippo (_Hippopotamus amphibious_) are present in impressive numbers in Akagera National Park; some lakes support several hundred (AZ) pages 6 & 277

bottom Akagera is the only place in Rwanda where zebra (_Equus quagga_) still roam in the wild (GB/S) pages 6 & 273–89

above   The chimpanzee (*Pan troglodytes*), which occurs in Nyungwe Forest National Park, is man's closest genetic relative (FL/FLPA) pages 160–1

top left   Tracking golden monkeys (*Cercopithecus kandti*), which are more or less endemic to the Virungas, is a popular activity in Volcanoes National Park (AZ) pages 162–3 & 235–8

above left   The olive baboon (*Papio anubis*) is the most visible primate in Akagera National Park (EB/MC) pages 163 & 277

left   The Ruwenzori colobus (*Colobus angolensis Ruwenzori*) is a gregarious monkey found in Nyungwe (AZ) page 162

below   Extending 1,015km² over the mountainous southwest of Rwanda, Nyungwe Forest National Park is a remarkably rich centre of biodiversity (AZ) pages 155–75

above   The grey crowned crane (*Balearica regulorum*) is usually associated with marshes and moist grassland (AZ) page 262

above right   Montane double-collared sunbird (*Nectarinia ludovicensis*) (CR/MP/FLPA) pages 6 & 226—7

right   The lakes of Akagera support a prodigious number of fish eagles (*Haliaeetus vocifer*) (AZ) page 280

below   Open-bill storks (*Anastomus lamelligerus*) forage in the shallows of Lake Hago (AZ) pages 168 & 288

above A wall at the Kigali Genocide Memorial displaying photographs of some of the victims of the 1994 killings (EL) pages 18–24 & 113

left The bullet-holed walls of Camp Kigali, now a memorial to the ten Belgian peacekeepers executed in the 1994 genocide (EL) pages 18–24 & 114

below The ancient royal palace has been carefully reconstructed at the Rukali Palace Museum in Nyanza (AZ) pages 137–8 currently scheduled for 2015. Already, two attractive hotels have opened on the shores of Lakes Rumira and Mirayi, to the east of Nyamata, a promising start for future tourist development in this underrated part of Rwanda.

All distances below are given from the traffic circle nicknamed 'Sonatubes' on OAU Road.

Nyabarongo Bridge (⊕ S 2°03.261, E 30°05.243)
The nippy new bridge that spans the Nyabarongo River 12.5km south of Sonatubes forms the northern boundary of Bugesera. It also offers a superb viewpoint over the river and associated patches of papyrus swamp and acacia woodland, which it fringes for about 1km to form probably the best birding spot in the immediate vicinity of Kigali (only 15 minutes' drive away). You might easily record a few dozen species in the space of two hours with an early-morning start – among the more interesting species we picked up were pink-backed pelican, common moorhen, African jacana, three types of weaver, marsh flycatcher and black-headed gonolek – and it looks like good potential territory for the eagerly sought papyrus gonolek.

Nyamata and Ntarama genocide memorials *Co-written with Rachel J Strohm*
The Catholic Church at **Nyamata**, about 26km from 'Sonatubes' in Kigali, was the scene of a horrific massacre during the genocide. Many people from the town and surrounding areas took refuge in the church, thinking that they were safe there. But on 10 April 1994, members of the Interahamwe and army attacked the church compound and killed the 10,000 people who had gathered there. Today, the victims' clothing and personal belongings are piled up on every single pew in the church, and the altar has a machete on it, as well as a rosary in a glass box, which is said to have been blessed by John Paul II and given to the memorial a few years ago. Two underground crypts hold the bodies of 41,000 people who died in the church massacre and elsewhere in Nyamata. Visitors can enter both of the crypts with a guide, though many will prefer not to be underground in an unlit chamber with skulls piled on four layers of shelves all around them. The remains of genocide victims are still being exhumed around the country today, and on most days there's a bag or two of bones in a corner of the church right next to the door (under the wall where babies were smashed to death), waiting to be added to the piles in the crypts. The guides who work at the site all lost family members in the attacks there.

There is another genocide memorial at **Ntarama**, about 1km down a right-hand fork that branches off the Nyamata road at Kuri Arete 21km outside Kigali. As was the case at Nyamata, people fled to the church here seeking safety. A sign outside the gate records that around 5,000 victims died there. The church interior is now piled with the clothes of victims, similar to Nyamata, although it's even eerier because a good deal of the clothing is hanging from the rafters near the doorways. Two sets of large metal shelves, at the front and back of the church, hold the skeletons and personal belongings (ID cards, jewellery, toys, etc) of a number of victims from the site. Outside, a memorial garden is slowly being created, with all the flowers now planted and a wall of names being inscribed whenever they find money to do it. The single guide at Ntarama now is English-speaking.

Both memorials are grim, and go some way to conveying the appalling scale of the tragedy. There's no charge for entry to the sites and the guides do a difficult job with dignity. A donation is requested (a few thousand Rwandan francs or US$5–10 would be appropriate), as the memorials are almost entirely dependent on such contributions for their basic operations and salaries. Further information is available at www.museum.gov.rw.

4

Getting there and away It is easy to visit either site, or both, as a day trip from Kigali. Now that the road is paved, the drive takes about 30 minutes. For visitors who didn't rent a car or don't wish to hire a private taxi at a cost of about Rfr25,000 for the round trip, minibus-taxis bound for Nyamata leave from the Kicukiro stand in Kigali every hour on the hour. Easier still, Sotra Tours has very nice buses that leave for Nyamata every half hour from their station on Rue Mont Kabuye in central Kigali. The trip costs Rfr500 one way, and buses stop directly in central Nyamata. The memorial at Ntarama is 1.8km from the main road, along a feeder road signposted a few hundred metres south of the town centre. The easiest way to get to Ntarama from Nyamata is by moto-taxi.

 Where to stay A large hotel is currently under construction outside Nyamata, on the Kigali side of town. There are also a couple of adequate hotels in the town centre.

☗ **Heaven Motel** (7 rooms) m 078 8483208; e heavenmotel2011@gmail.com. This is a quite modern hotel with rooms set around a large courtyard bar & restaurant 100m from the main road. The clean rooms have a double bed, & en-suite cold showers. *Rfr15,000 dbl.*

☗ **Peace Motel** (18 rooms) m 078 8568607. This basic place on the left side of the main road coming from Kigali is attached to an internet café & the best restaurant in town. *Rfr5,000/7,500 sgl/ dbl, or Rfr15,000 for a VIP room with ¾ bed.*

Gashora and environs

The small and rather nondescript town of Gashora lies at the heart of the Nyabarongo Wetlands, where it is flanked by Lake Rumira to the north and Lake Mirayi to the south. The La Palisse Hotel, 2km from the town centre, is a superb location in its own right, set on the reed-lined shore of Lake Rumira, and it also forms the ideal base for exploring the surrounding wetlands. This one hotel aside, the area is poorly developed for tourism, but the possibilities are boundless. Plenty of local footpaths surround Lake Rumira itself, and it's also possible to walk to Lake Mirayi, which lies about 1km north of the town centre.

Further afield, follow the Kibungo road out of Gashora for about 2km, and you'll find yourself on an elevated causeway running through the dense papyrus swamp that divides the two lakes – potentially a superb spot for papyrus endemics. Once roadworks along the 65km to Kibungo are complete, it would be possible to follow this road in its entirety, passing through several areas of swamp and within eyeshot of a trio of lakes: Birara, Mugesera and Sake.

Further south, Rweru (also known as Rugweru) is the largest lake in the Nyabarongo Wetlands, extending over some 100km², of which four-fifths lies within Burundi. A shallow sump set at an altitude of around 1,350m, it is nowhere more than 4m deep, and much of its marshy shoreline is difficult to access. A motorable track to the Rwandan part of the lakeshore branches left from the surfaced road to the Burundi border about 57km south of Kigali (and 3km before the border post). It's a rather circuitous 18km drive, and after 7km you need to turn right (downhill) in a small trading centre called Mayuboro. You reach the lakeshore at a village called Nyiragiseke, where it is easy enough to arrange to be taken out in a local dugout, and there's even a motorboat available if you can supply the fuel.

Getting there and away The town lies 53km from Kigali along a dirt side-road to the left signposted 48km along the surfaced road to the Burundi border (the junction is at ⊕ S 2°15.081, E 30°12.861). The drive shouldn't take longer than 45 minutes in a private vehicle, though you might want to stop at the Nyabarongo

Bridge and Nyamata on the way. A regular minibus-taxi service from Kigali to Gashora is operated by Rugali Travel Agency and costs around Rfr1,000. From the town, you can get a motorbike taxi or walk the 2km to La Palisse.

You can drive via Gashora and Sake to Ngoma/Kibungo on fairly good, and picturesque, unsealed road. If coming the other way – from Ngoma/Kibungo to Kigali – don't be put off by the sign saying a bridge is closed. They fixed the bridge ages ago but forgot to remove the sign!

Where to stay

La Palisse Hotel & Clubhouse (52 rooms) m 078 8306111; e palisseho@yahoo.fr; www. lapalissehotel.com; ✪ S 2°11.805, E 30°14.414. This lovely resort on the south shore of Lake Rumira is one of the most attractive spots to stay near Kigali, & its popularity is likely to soar as & when the international airport relocates to Bugesera. (Don't confuse it with La Palisse Hotel 2km from the current airport, listed on page 94.) Spread across large green gardens rattling with birdlife, the comfortable tiled rooms have king-size or twin beds with netting, satellite TV, fridge, wardrobes & a large en-suite bathroom with shower & tub. There are also larger suites designed in the shape of a traditional royal palace. A lakeside restaurant with indoor & outdoor seating serves

a varied selection of mains in the Rfr4,000–5,000 range. But the setting is the real attraction here: the lake supports hippos, crocs & a varied birdlife, including the magnificent African fish eagle & an array of colourful weavers & bishops. *US$60/70 sgl/dbl B&B; US$100 suite.*

Mirayi Lake Hotel (10 rooms) m 078 8307454/8785898; ✪ S 2°13.652 E 30°15.323. Reached via a 6.5km road that branches southeast from the junction for Gashora, this low-key new lodge on the south shore of Lake Mirayi offers accommodation in clean tiled cottages with dbl bed, en-suite hot shower, net & balcony. There is a restaurant & a beach with a jetty, but it feels a little neglected. *Rfr20,000 dbl.*

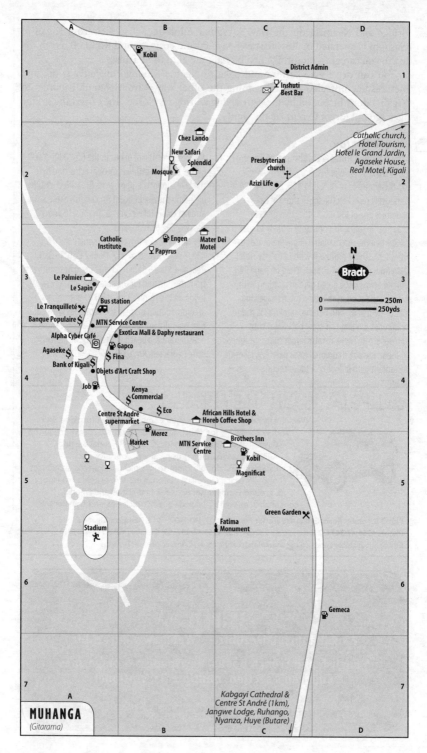

MUHANGA
(Gitarama)

A B C D

Kobil
District Admin
Inshuti
Best Bar
Catholic church,
Hotel Tourism,
Hotel le Grand Jardin,
Agaseke House,
Real Motel, Kigali
Chez Lando
New Safari
Splendid
Mosque
Presbyterian
church
Azizi Life
Catholic
Institute
Engen
Papyrus
Mater Dei
Motel
Le Palmier
Le Sapin
Bus station
N
Bradt
0 ——— 250m
0 ——— 250yds
Le Tranquilleté
Banque Populaire
MTN Service Centre
Alpha Cyber Café
Exotica Mall & Daphy restaurant
Agaseke
Gapco
Bank of Kigali
Fina
Objets d'Art Craft Shop
Job
Kenya
Commercial
Eco
Centre St André
supermarket
African Hills Hotel &
Horeb Coffee Shop
Merez
Market
MTN Service
Centre
Brothers Inn
Kobil
Magnificat
Stadium
Green Garden
Fatima
Monument
Gemeca
Kabgayi Cathedral &
Centre St André (1km),
Jangwe Lodge, Ruhango,
Nyanza, Huye (Butare)

1
2
3
4
5
6
7

124

5

The Road to Huye (Butare)

The surfaced 136km road between Kigali and Huye (formerly Butare) can usually be covered in about two hours, partly depending on how often you get stuck behind trucks on the steeper slopes, and how aggressively your driver attempts to overtake such obstacles. The largest town *en route*, Muhanga, sprawls alongside the main road for several kilometres either side of the junction westward to Karongi. Nearby tourist attractions include the Kabgayi Cathedral and associated museum on the outskirts of Muhanga, as well as the former royal compound at Nyanza, which lies about halfway between Muhanga and Huye, and is now a museum. Any of these sites can be visited as a day trip out of Kigali or *en route* to Huye.

For details of town name changes (Huye, Muhanga, Karongi etc) see box, *New provinces and town names*, on pages 38–9.

MUHANGA (GITARAMA)

The scattered capital of Muhanga District, often still referred to by its pre-2006 name Gitarama, comes across as an improbable contender for the honour of second-largest town in Rwanda. And yet that is exactly what it is, with a population of 85,000 in the 2002 census now likely to have passed the 100,000 mark. Thanks to its strategic location at the junction of the roads running southward to Huye and westward to Lake Kivu, Muhanga is passed through by a great many tourists, but explored by few. And, with the exception of the cathedral and associated museum at nearby Kabgayi (more details on page 130), there really is very little to do or see in this workaday town, though the everyday hustle and bustle of ordinary Rwandans going about their lives can be a change from more intensive tourism.

Despite its unassuming appearance, Muhanga has often been involved in Rwanda's recent history. It is famous as the location of the historic gathering on 28 January 1961 at which the people first declared Rwanda a republic, and it was the probable starting point for the violence that led to the imposition of martial law under Colonel Guy Logiest in November 1959. It was also was the birthplace of Rwanda's first president Grégoire Kayibanda, whose modest tomb now stands in the town centre alongside a disused open-air auditorium built during his rule. On 12 April 1994, it replaced Kigali as the seat of the Provisional Government that presided over the genocide, prior to its capture by the RDF on 13 June 1994.

If you do opt to explore Muhanga, you'll find a Bank of Kigali almost opposite the main taxi-minibus park in the town centre [124 A3], together with a handful of small shops and bar/restaurants. The post office [124 C1] is about 1km away: turn right as you leave the minibus stand and keep straight on; you'll come to it on the left just after the Rwanda Revenue Authority. There are motorbike-taxis at the minibus stand.

Over recent years, the town has experienced a tangible drift in development from its old town centre to the recently built main Kigali–Huye road, which is lined with tall modern buildings, including several new hotels and the Exotica Mall [124 A4], which houses a restaurant, pharmacy, supermarket, sauna/massage centre, and nightclub. Also on the main road, further in the direction of Kigali, the main tourist focus in Muhanga is Azizi Life, a committed fair-wage handicraft exporter that runs a worthwhile craft shop and also offers popular full-day village visits: see page 130.

GETTING THERE AND AWAY Muhanga lies about 50km south of Kigali, a drive that shouldn't take longer than an hour except in very heavy traffic. Regular minibus-taxis connect the centrally located taxi park [124 C3] to Kigali (Rfr1,000), Karongi/Kibuye (Rfr2,000), Huye (Rfr1,500) and smaller towns *en route*.

WHERE TO STAY

Upmarket Muhanga now boasts quite a few hotels with upmarket aspirations, but none of them quite fits the bill and some feel less than fully functional as things stand. The one option that does conform to upmarket standards is Jangwe Lodge, which lies about 8km out of town near Shyogwe.

Jangwe Lodge [124 C7] (6 rooms) m 078 5066081/8216829; e georges.kamanayo@gmail.com or lydie.becart@gmail.com. This beautiful peaceful retreat makes an excellent weekend getaway from Kigali, with its attractive location amidst green rolling hills, good Belgian food, & the only swimming pool in this part of the country. To get there follow the Huye Road out of Muhanga for 2km, then take the dirt road signposted for Shyogwe to the left. It is about 6km from the turn-off to the lodge, passing through Shyogwe about halfway. Booking is recommended, whether you want to stay or just to pop in for a meal. *Rfr25,000 pp inc b/fast & swimming.*

Moderate

African Hills Hotel [124 B4] (25 rooms) m 078 8534179; e africanhillshotel@yahoo.fr. This new high-rise hotel stands almost opposite Brothers Inn & is ostensibly similar in price & standard, but has an unfinished & semi-abandoned feel. The large carpeted rooms have dbl beds with en-suite hot showers, & there is free Wi-Fi in the restaurant-bar. *Overpriced at Rfr15,000/25,000 sgl/dbl.*

Brothers Inn [124 C5] (22 rooms) m 078 8562217/072 7152136; e brothersinn2010@gmail.com. This new hotel has the smartest rooms on offer in Muhanga, spacious with clean tiled floors & hot water, the only drawback being that they are a little dark & gloomy. Standard rooms have a double bed, but it's arguably worth paying extra for a VIP room, which comes with a king-size bed, net, & combined tub-shower. There is an appealing outdoor bar too. *Rfr12,000/20,000 sgl/dbl, Rfr25,000 suite.*

Chez Lando [124 B2] (12 rooms) m 078 5001674. Set in large grounds along the same road as the Splendid Hotel, this is another hotel that suffers from a rather unfinished atmosphere. The large tiled rooms with dbl bed, net, TV & en-suite shower are rather gloomy but otherwise adequate. *Rfr20,000 dbl.*

Real Motel [124 D2] (7 rooms) m 078 8403424/8610354; e realmotel@gmail.com. This small hotel stands in neat gardens alongside the main Kigali road about 4km from the town centre. There are 3 large rooms with hot tub & shower, TV, built-in cupboard, balcony & dbl bed with netting, & 4 smaller twins & dbls using shared showers. A ground-floor bar & restaurant serves a typical selection of snacks & meals in the Rfr1,200–3,000 range. *Rfr20,000 B&B; Rfr12,000–15,000 sharing facilities.*

Splendid Hotel [124 B2] (16 rooms) 0252 562344; m 078 8301894; e splendidhotel@yahoo.fr. The best-value & most appealing option in this range is this well-managed 3-storey hotel, which has a quiet but central location around the corner from the mosque & cultural centre. The rooms with hot shower are clean, spacious & comfortable (though you might want to test the mattress for sagginess),

Budget

🏠 **Centre St André** [124 C7] (89 rooms) 📞0252 562812/562450; **m** 078 8421378; **e** saintandrekabgayi@yahoo.fr; ⊕ S 02°05.896, E 029°45.147, 1,867m. Situated alongside Kabgayi Cathedral about 3km south of central Muhanga & some 200m or so off the Huye road, this large & reasonably priced church-run guesthouse is undoubtedly the best place to stay in the area, assuming that you don't mind the non-central location. Rooms range from basic dbls using common showers to comfortable mini-suites, while facilities include a restaurant, bar (serving beer as well as soft drinks), internet café, & well-equipped business centre. *Rfr5,000/8,000 sgl/dbl using common showers; Rfr12,000 dbl; Rfr20,000*

Shoestring

🏠 **Le Palmier** [124 A3] (5 rooms) **m** 078 842 0632; ⊕ S 02°04.788, E 029°45.123, 1,884m. This adequate but potentially noisy local lodging is conveniently located opposite the main taxi park. The clean spacious rooms are centred around a pleasant courtyard, shaded by the namesake palm tree, & basic meals & drinks are served. *Dbl with common shower Rfr6,000; dbl Rfr10,000.*

& there's a ground-floor bar & 1st-floor restaurant serving excellent steak & other dishes at around Rfr3,000. *Rooms Rfr12,000–18,000.*

mini-suite, b/fast an additional Rfr1,500 pp, other meals Rfr3,000.

🏠 **Le Grand Jardin** [124 D2] (7 rooms) **m** 078 8627080. This new hotel along the road towards Kigali is nothing special, but seems decent value in its range. *Rooms with queen-size bed & cold shower Rfr10,000–12,000.*

🏠 **Mater Dei Motel** [124 B3] (8 rooms) **m** 078 8463006/4925492. The best central option in its range is this clean lodge set in a quiet garden only 100m from the bus station. A pleasant terrace bar & restaurant is attached. *Large tiled dbls with king-size bed & en-suite hot tub Rfr15,000; smaller en-suite dbls Rfr13,000; & dbls using common shower Rfr10,000.*

🏠 **Tourism Bar & Hotel** [124 D2] (7 rooms) **m** 078 869 0836; ⊕ S 02°04.551, E 029°46.1679, 1,880m. Situated about 3km from the town centre alongside the main road to Kigali, this is a pleasant, peaceful place with large but rundown rooms & concrete-dominated grounds. There's a bar but no restaurant, though it does serve evening meals by request. *Rooms with net & hot water Rfr5,000–7,000.*

❌ **WHERE TO EAT AND DRINK** Most of the hotels offer meals of a sort, with the **Splendid Hotel** undoubtedly the best option for meat dishes, assuming you don't mind a bit of a wait. Other options include the following :

❌ **Daphy Restaurant** [124 A4] **m** 078 8420632; ⊕ 12.00–24.00 daily. Set in a large open-sided thatch building that forms an extension to the Exotica Mall, this is now more of a bar than an eatery, though it does serve inexpensive brochettes, grilled chicken & chips. There's a TV & a decent sound system, occasionally supplemented by live music at weekends, but the toilets are rather grotty. The attached Orion Nightclub opens its doors at around 23.00 at w/ends, & keeps going throughout the night.

❌ **Green Garden** [124 C5] Set a few hundred metres out of town past Brothers Inn, this is a great spot for a drink at sunset, thanks to its hillside location, & it also serves tasty brochettes & other snacks.

❌ **Horeb Coffee Shop** [124 B4] Part of the African Hills Hotel, this serves really good fresh coffee for around Rfr1,000, as well as a selection of light snacks & sandwiches. Access to the hotel's Wi-Fi is an added bonus.

❌ **Magnificat Bar** [124 C5] **m** 078 864 2849. Also known as Bar Oasis du Plateau, this spacious garden bar behind the Kobil Filling Station serves excellent & reasonably priced grilled whole fish.

❌ **Restaurant Tranquilleté** [124 A3] This long-serving & popular local eatery consists of a cheerful courtyard, with assorted shapes & sizes of tables, energetic waitresses serving customers briskly, & a blackboard with the dishes of the day chalked on it. The food is simple (meat, fish or chicken with chips/salad, fresh fruit for dessert) but good, & cheap.

With its distinctive tall green stem topped by a luxuriant clump of thick, wide leaves, the banana (or plantain, known locally as *insina*) is an integral feature of the Rwandan landscape, occupying a full 35% of the country's cultivated land. Grown at a wide range of altitudes – from as low as 800m to above 2,000m – the banana thrives in Rwanda's characteristically moist climate, and is unquestionably the most important cash crop countrywide, accounting for 60–80% of the income of most subsistence-level households.

So it might come as a surprise to many visitors to learn that the banana is not indigenous to Rwanda – or anywhere else in Africa for that matter. One Ugandan legend has it that the first banana plant was brought to the region by Kintu, whose shrine lies on a hill called Magonga (almost certainly a derivative of a local Ugandan name for the banana) alongside a tree said to have grown from the root of the plant he originally imported. If this legend is true, it would place the banana's arrival in east-central Africa in perhaps the 13–15th century, probably from the Ethiopian highlands. Most botanists argue, however, that the immense number of distinct varieties grown in the region could not have been cultivated within so short a period – a time span of at least 1,000 years would be required.

Only one species of banana, *Musa ensete*, is indigenous to Africa, and it doesn't bear edible fruit. The more familiar cultivated varieties have all been propagated from two wild Asian species, *M. acuminata* and *M. balbisiana* and hybrids thereof. Wild bananas are almost inedible and riddled with hard pits, and it is thought that the first edible variety was cultivated from a rare mutant of one of the above species about 10,000 years ago – making the banana one of the oldest cultivated plants in existence. Edible bananas were most likely cultivated in Egypt before the time of Christ, presumably having arrived there via Arabia or the Indian Ocean. The Greek sailor and explorer Cosmas Indicopleustes recorded that edible bananas grew around the port of Adulis, in present-day Eritrea, circa AD525 – describing them as 'moza, the wild-date of India'.

The route via which the banana reached modern-day Rwanda is open to conjecture. The most obvious point of origin is Ethiopia, the source of several southward migrations in the past two millennia. But it is intriguing that while the banana is known by a name approximating the generic Latin *Musa* throughout Asia, Arabia and northeast Africa – '*moz*' in Arabic and Persian, for instance, or '*mus*' or '*musa*' in various Ethiopian languages and Somali – no such linguistic resemblance occurs in East Africa, where it is known variously as '*ndizi*', '*gonja*', '*matoke*', '*insina*' et al. This peculiarity has been cited to support a hypothesis that the banana travelled between Asia and the East African coast either as a result of direct trade or else via Madagascar, and that it was entrenched there before regular trade was established with Arabia. A third possibility is that the banana reached east-central Africa via the Congolese Basin, possibly in association with the arrival of Bantu-speakers from West Africa.

However it arrived, the banana has certainly flourished there, forming the main subsistence crop for most people in the region – indeed, Rwanda's mean banana consumption of almost 2kg per person per week ranks among the highest in the world. Some 50 varieties are grown in the region, divided into four broad categories based on their primary use – most familiar are sweet bananas, eaten raw as a snack or dessert, while other more floury varieties are used especially for boiling (like potatoes), roasting, or distillation into banana beer or wine.

The banana's uses are not restricted to feeding bellies. The juice from the stem is traditionally regarded to have several medicinal applications, for instance as a cure for snakebite and for childish behaviour. Pulped or scraped sections from the stem also form very effective cloths for cleaning. The outer stem can be plaited to make a strong rope, while the cleaned central rib of the leaf is used to weave fish traps and other items of basketry. The leaf itself forms a useful makeshift umbrella, and was traditionally worn by young girls as an apron. The dried leaf is a popular bedding and roofing material, and is also used to manufacture the head pads on which Rwandan women generally carry their loads.

The banana as we know it is a cultigen – modified by humans to their own ends and totally dependent on them for its propagation. The domestic fruit is the result of a freak mutation that gives the cells an extra copy of each chromosome, preventing the normal development of seeds, thereby rendering the plant edible but also sterile. Every cultivated banana tree on the planet is effectively a clone, propagated by the planting of suckers or corms cut from 'parent' plants. This means that, unlike sexually reproductive crops, which experience new genetic configurations in every generation, the banana is unable to evolve mechanisms to fight off new diseases.

In early 2003, a report in the *New Scientist* warned that cultivated bananas are threatened with extinction within the next decade, due to their lack of defence against a pair of fungal diseases rampant in most of the world's banana-producing countries. These are *black sigatoka*, an airborne disease first identified in Fiji in 1963, and the soil-borne Panama Disease, also known as *Fusarium Wilt*. Black sigatoka can be kept at bay by regular spraying – every ten days or so – but it is swiftly developing resistance to all known fungicides, which in any case are not affordable to the average subsistence farmers. There is no known cure for Panama Disease.

So far as can be ascertained, Panama Disease does not affect any banana variety indigenous to Rwanda or neighbouring countries, but it has already resulted in the disappearance of several introduced varieties. Black sigatoka, by contrast, poses a threat to every banana variety in the world. It has been present throughout Uganda for some years, where a progressive reduction exceeding 50% has been experienced in the annual yield of the most seriously affected areas, and recent reports suggest it is rapidly spreading into parts of Rwanda and the DRC. In addition to reducing the yield of a single plant by up to 75%, black sigatoka can also cut its fruit-bearing life from more than 30 years to less than five.

International attempts to clone a banana tree resistant to both diseases have met with one limited success – agricultural researchers in Honduras have managed to produce one such variety, but it reputedly doesn't taste much like a banana. Another area of solution is genetic engineering – introducing a gene from a wild species to create a disease-resistant edible banana. Although ecologists are generally opposed to the genetic modification of crops, the domestic banana should perhaps be considered an exception, given its inability to spread its genes to related species – not to mention its pivotal importance to the subsistence economies of some of the world's poorest countries, Rwanda among them.

OTHER PRACTICALITIES

Banks and money There are no dedicated forex bureaux in town, nor is there any real call for them with Kigali being so close. However, if you do need to draw money against a VISA card, there is an ATM where you can do so outside the Ecobank [124 B4] on the main Huye Road opposite the market.

Internet The Alpha Cyber Café opposite the Fina Bank is a good central place to check internet. The only hotel/restaurant with free Wi-Fi is the African Hills and associated Horeb Coffee Shop.

Supermarkets There are also two supermarkets worth checking out: the **Alimentation le Sapin** opposite the bus station also doubles as a bakery selling tasty fresh bread, while the better-stocked **Centre St André Supermarket** opposite the market has an excellent selection of imported goods, including wine and spirits, as well a butchery and bakery.

Handicrafts In addition to Azizi Life (see below) there are two other good craft outlets in town. The better of the two is **Agaseke House** (⋀ *0252 562211;* m *078 3353766;* e *uwanastas@yahoo.fr*), a salmon-coloured building which lies on the right as you enter Muhanga from Kigali, opposite the prominent St André Cathedral. Adorned with a huge *agaseke* (a traditional Rwandan basket with its distinctive conical lid) painted on the side, this is the showroom for the 400 members of the Coopérative de Production d'Artisant d'Art du Rwanda (COPARWA) and sells a varied stock of good-quality basketwork, wood sculptures, mats, beadwork and other traditional artefacts. Also good, and more central, is the **Objets d'Art Craft Shop** next to the Job filling station on the main road.

WHAT TO SEE

Azizi Life [124 C2] (m *078 3049665/5781146;* e *info@azizilife.com; www.azizilife. com*) Situated just off the Kigali–Huye road alongside the Presbyterian Church, Azizi Life is a small local export business dedicated to supporting artisans by providing them with fair wages, market connections, and resources for developing their art, business, faith, and life as a whole. It works with about 25 different associations and cooperatives in the south of Rwanda, and has a variety of their handicrafts on sale in the on-site shop. It also now offers village visits designed to connect visitors with rural Rwanda, by joining in with local artisans and their families doing seasonal agricultural activities, sharing a midday meal, and learning to weave a simple object in sisal with expert tuition (see box *Village Visits* opposite). The full-day excursion costs US$70, and most of the fee directly benefits the cooperative members and their families, with 5% being set aside for community projects.

Kabgayi Cathedral & Museum The Kabgayi Mission, which lies a couple of hundred metres from the Huye road just 3km south of Muhanga (see *Centre St André* under *Where to stay*, page 127), was founded by Catholic missionaries in 1906, and it became the seat of the first Catholic bishop of Ruanda-Urundi, for which reason nearby Muhanga (then known as Gitarama) was once seriously considered as the colonial capital. Built in 1925, the massive Cathedral Basilica of Our Lady at Kabgayi, with its redbrick exterior, stained glass windows, and huge and tranquil interior, is the oldest and most historically important in the country, and worth a visit, especially now that the roof has been restored following a destructive earthquake in April 2008. During the colonial era, a hospital and various training schools were set up in Kabgayi – for midwives, artisans, printers, carpenters and blacksmiths, among others.

In the early stages of the genocide, Kabgayi, situated within walking distance of the Provisional Government headquarters at the then Gitarama, provided refuge to tens of thousands of civilians, many of whom died of disease or starvation. The full extent of the genocide killings at Kabgayi emerged in February 2009, when a report compiled by 18 Gacaca judges revealed that at least 64,000 people who

VILLAGE VISITS   *Camilla Gore*

Ever wanted to experience life in a welcoming rural village community for a day? Well now you can. **Azizi Life**, an initiative founded in 2007 to support independent artisan groups, now offers day visits to the rural communities they work with, allowing you to join in with all aspects of their life. The following account is my experience of a village visit to the Abarikumwe ('People who are together') Association in the village of Cyeza.

When our car arrived at Cyeza, a small village perched precariously on a hillside, we were warmly greeted by the women of the Abarikumwe Association. This group of women of various ages meet regularly to make handicrafts, namely earrings and bracelets out of the sisal plant, cultivate their fields and generally talk about daily life. We were welcomed into our host Yusta's home, and dressed for the field in fabric wraps. Then, hoes in hand, we walked down into the valley to a nearby cassava field to help the women to harvest the cassava. We joined in with the harvest and Jeannine, our translator, helped us to understand what to do. The women talked about their homes and their lives as they worked, and helped us with our hoeing technique! We tried to carry our harvest back to the house on our heads which was a great experience and the women helped us when our loads began to wobble.

Then we peeled the cassava roots together, again listening to tales of Rwandan village life as we did so. We fetched some water together from the village tap, and on our journey we passed through fields of coffee plants, banana trees, maize and bean crops, all with the stunning green hills of Muhanga District in the background. After finishing our work for the day, we were treated to a home-cooked lunch of fresh avocados, cassava, beans and rice, and we enjoyed the company of the women over lunch. The women laughed as we ate and with the help of our translator we shared stories about our homes.

After this hearty lunch, the women taught us how to make our own earrings and bracelets out of the sisal plant. Berthilde, my teacher, was very patient and guided me with her expert skill. We were shown the farm animals by our hosts' friendly children and then we danced outside in the sun. It was a real privilege to spend a day with these lively, vivacious and welcoming women and we learned so much about rural life in Rwanda from our experience. We felt as if we were part of the group as the women were so keen to involve us in everything they did. When I arrived back at the Azizi Life headquarters I felt tired but very content after such a wonderful day out in the Rwandan hills.

Azizi Life is based in Muhanga (see opposite for contacts), where it also has a handicrafts shop, and is busy developing other experience days such as beekeeping visits – call or check their website for the latest information.

sought refuge in the church grounds were killed there, with the probable complicity of local church leaders and Red Cross workers, who allegedly buried many victims alive. A genocide memorial stands alongside the hospital, where at least 6,000 victims are currently buried in a mass grave consisting of three concrete pits.

The Kabgayi Museum, tucked away in the Evêché (Archdeacon's residence) alongside the cathedral, is theoretically open from 08.00 to 17.00 Monday to Friday, though in practice you may need to ask around to locate the caretaker. Saturday and Sunday visits are also possible if booked in advance. A nominal entrance fee is charged. Within the very small interior are many historically and culturally interesting items such as:

- Ancient hand tools and weapons: knives, hoes, spears, arrows, etc
- Tools and implements connected with the iron industry
- Ancient examples of clothing: bark cloth etc
- Musical instruments
- Methods of transportation used for chiefs, high-born women and the sick
- Clay pots and pipes
- Baskets – ornamental and for domestic use
- The prestigious Milk Bar and jugs from the palace of the last queen mother
- Old indoor games such as *igisoro*, which are still popular in Rwanda and neighbouring countries

KAMAGERI'S ROCK   *Janice Booth*

A NEW VERSION OF AN ANCIENT TALE

It happened during the reign of Mwami Mibambwe II Sekarongoro II Gisanura, who ruled Rwanda almost four centuries ago. He was a fair and just ruler. Among other innovations, he required his chiefs to bring jars of milk from their own cows to the court – and these were then distributed to the poor and needy, three times a day: morning, noon and evening. Some chiefs grumbled at this, although they were careful to do so out of earshot of the Mwami; others admired his generosity, and sometimes brought small gifts of vegetables or meat in addition to the milk. Wise and observant as he was, he knew well which chiefs resented his laws, which had true kindness in their hearts and which tended to misuse or misdirect their powers.

One day, so the story goes, a man was convicted of stealing from the Mwami, which was considered a most serious crime. The Mwami called two of his chiefs to the royal court, selecting them carefully, and asked each of them to devise a suitable punishment.

The chief named Mikoranya thought for many days and then scratched a careful diagram on the ground; it represented a shaft of wood extending from a hut, on which the thief would be slowly tortured in full view of the populace. His cries would echo far and wide. The chief named Kamageri, on the other hand, remembered a large flat rock that lay close to his home place in Ruhango; he proposed to the Mwami that this rock should be heated until it was red hot, and the criminal should then be spread-eagled across it with his wrists and ankles securely tied, so that he roasted to a lingering death. The Mwami then asked the chiefs to demonstrate their ideas, so that he could decide which should be used, and eagerly they set to work.

After much hammering and hauling, the torture rack was in position. Mikoranya refused to pay his labourers, and two of them were whipped when

- Ancient military officers' costumes and pips
- A national drum captured from Ijwi Island (Kivu) in 1875, thereby effectively annexing it to Rwanda
- Information about traditional medicines, and tokens (*kwe*) formerly used as currency
- Modern clothing and historical photographs

RUHANGO

Straddling the Huye road about 25km south of Muhanga, and connected to it by regular public transport, the eponymous capital of Ruhango District is another nondescript but well-equipped and surprisingly substantial town. The 2002 census gave its population as 43,750, making it the twelfth largest in the country. It is of limited interest to tourists except on Friday mornings, when it hosts one of the largest markets in the country. Vendors trek in for the occasion from far afield, carrying their wares, and an astonishing range of merchandise is on sale, from livestock and vegetables to hi-fi equipment, household goods and swathes of brightly coloured cotton fabric. You could consider spending a Thursday night here and then watching activities unfold the next morning. Otherwise, the area is notable mainly for *Uratare rwa Kamageri* (Kamageri's Rock – see box below), which is signposted by the roadside ten minutes' walk south of the town centre, and

they complained, but grudgingly they finished the task. For a whole week Kamageri's rock was piled with brushwood fires which were kept burning day and night (some women came under cover of darkness to use the embers for cooking), although those tending the flames were burned and choked by smoke. At last the rock glowed crimson and the heat was unbearable from many yards away. Paths leading to the area were crammed with people – men come straight from tending their cattle, old women leaning heavily on canes, young women with babies on their backs, scampering children getting under everyone's feet – all excited to see the spectacle. The chiefs sent word to the Mwami, and he arrived with his retinue.

'Is everything ready?' he asked Kamageri and Mikoranya, and they nodded proudly, expecting praise and possibly some reward. The Mwami called forward his guards, to whom he had already explained what would happen. 'Take them,' he ordered. 'And subject them to the punishments they have devised! Let Kamageri roast on his rock and Mikoranya suffer his own torture. These were cruel men. They took pleasure from brutality. There is no place for such in my kingdom.' The guards seized the two chiefs and cast them to their fate; and from the watching crowd a great cheer rose into the sky, as the people acknowledged the wisdom and goodness of their ruler.

The rock can still be seen today, at Ruhango on the Muhanga–Huye road. Tourists stop to photograph it and guides recount various versions of the story. And on the blackest nights, when the moon is hidden by cloud and stars cannot pierce the thick velvet of the sky, you may still – if you lift your head to the wind and breathe as lightly as thistledown – smell the faint ashiness of smoke drifting from Kamageri's ancient fire.

for the Poterie Locale de Gatagara described under *What to see* below. Minibuses to/from Kigali cost Rfr1,600.

🏠 WHERE TO STAY AND EAT

🏠 **Hotel Pacis** (4 rooms) 📱 078 859 7483. This adequate new hotel has basic but clean dbl rooms with net & en-suite cold shower. *Rfr5,000 dbl.*

🏠 **Hotel Umuco** (12 rooms) 📱 078 8572352. Centrally located, & arranged around a pleasant courtyard, this sensibly priced hotel provides travellers with basic but clean accommodation close to the taxi park, as well as inexpensive meals

such as goat brochettes & chips or beef stew & rice. *Sgl using common shower Rfr4,000; Rfr6,000 dbl; meals Rfr800–1,000.*

🏠 **Restaurant-Bar Ituzi** (6 rooms) Situated right alongside the Umuco & probably only worth considering if the other options are full, this has basic sgls using a common shower only. The outdoor bar looks to be a pleasant spot for a drink or meal. *Overpriced at Rfr5,000 sgl.*

WHAT TO SEE

Poterie Locale de Gatagara (📱 *078 8656271;* ◷ *07.00–12.00 Mon–Sat, 14.00–17.00 Mon–Fri*) Marked by an inconspicuous blue signpost to the right of the Huye road about 10km south of Ruhango, this ceramic workshop lies alongside a locally well-known church centre for the handicapped, though the two organisations are apparently unaffiliated. Using foot-driven wooden treadle wheels, Gatagara produces much of the pottery you see for sale in craft shops in Kigali, but items can be bought more cheaply here at source, from a shop piled high with bowls, mugs, teacups, vases and other ceramic wares. Note that the wares produced at Gatagara are not overtly ethnic in style, but the quality is high. You can watch the Batwa potters throwing, baking and glazing the pottery, and see the clay in all its stages.

NYANZA

Sometimes known as Nyabisindu, the unassuming town of Nyanza lies about 20km south of Ruhango, along a surfaced feeder road that branches westward from the main Huye–Kigali road at Kubijega (literally, 'Place of Storage', in reference to a trio of nearby metal warehouses). With its wide dusty streets, waist-deep gullies caused by water erosion, and rather unfocussed layout, Nyanza has something of a Wild West feel, and until recently it boasted few tourist facilities. All the same, it's a reasonably substantial town (in fact, a population of 56,000 makes it the eighth largest in the country), and it seems destined to expand further following its surprise selection ahead of Huye as the capital of Southern Province in the administrative shake-up of 2006. Partly as a result of this, several new hotels have sprung up there in recent years.

The recent elevation of Nyanza to provincial capital is not without historical precedent. In 1899, Mwami Musinga Yuhi V, his sense of absolute authority undermined by the growing colonial presence in Rwanda, decided to break with the royal tradition of mobility that had led to his predecessor having had an estimated 50–60 residences scattered through the kingdom. The recently enthroned Musinga selected Nyanza Hill as the site of the first permanent royal capital, a role it would retain throughout both his reign and that of his son Rudahigwa Mutara III until the traditional monarchy was abolished in 1961. Today, the traditional palace built by Musinga and first house built by Mutara III have been restored to form the highly worthwhile Rukali Palace Museum, while the newer house built by Mutara III is now the Rwesero Art Museum – both well worth the minor diversion from the Huye road, whether you use private or public transport.

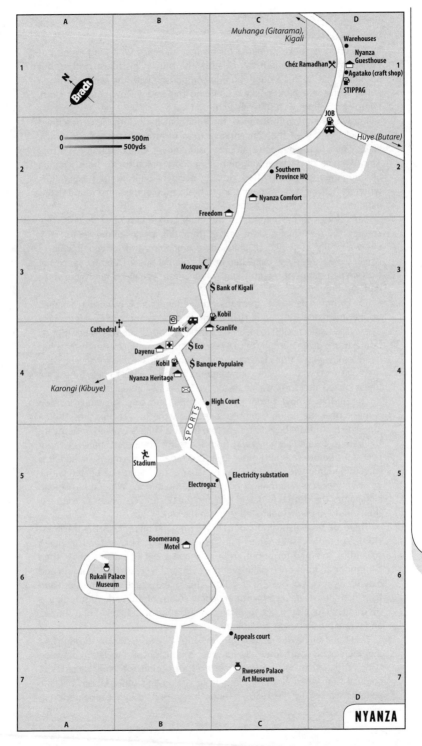

In 1862, when Speke prepared for his first audience with King Mutesa of Buganda (part of modern-day Uganda), he put on his finest clothes, but admitted that he 'cut a poor figure in comparison with the dressy Baganda [who] wore neat bark cloaks resembling the best yellow corduroy cloth, crimp and well set, as if stiffened with starch'.

Known as *impuzu* in Rwanda, the stiff, neat bark-cloth cloak described by Speke was then the conventional form of attire in this part of Africa. Exactly how and when the craft arose is unknown. One tradition has it that King Wamala of Bacwezi Kingdom (legendary precursor to both Rwanda and Buganda) discovered bark cloth by accident on a hunting expedition, when he hammered a piece of bark to break it up and instead found that it expanded laterally to form a durable material.

Bark cloth can be made from the inner bark lining of at least 20 tree species. The best-quality cloth derives from four species of the genus Ficus, known locally as *umutaba*, *umuhororo*, *umurama* and *umugombe*, all of which were extensively cultivated in pre-colonial times. Different species of tree yielded different textures and colours, from yellow to sandy brown to dark red-brown.

The common bark-cloth tree can be propagated simply by cutting a branch from a grown one and planting it in the ground – after about five years the new tree will be large enough to be used for making cloth. The bark will be stripped from any one given tree only once a year, when it is in full leaf. After the bark has been removed, the trunk is wrapped in green banana leaves for several days, then plastered with wet cow dung and dry banana leaves to help it heal. If a tree is looked after this way, it may survive 30 years of annual use.

The bark is removed from the tree in one long strip. A circular incision is made near the ground, another one below the lowest branches, then a long line is cut from base to top, before finally a knife is worked underneath the bark to ease it carefully away from the trunk. The peeled bark is left out overnight before the hard outer layer is scraped off, then it is soaked. It is then folded into two equal halves and laid out on a log to be beaten with a wooden mallet on alternating sides to become thinner. When it has spread sufficiently, the cloth is folded in four and the beating continues. The cloth is then unfolded before being left to dry in the sun.

There are several local variations in the preparation process, but the finest cloth reputedly results when the freshly stripped bark, instead of being soaked, is steamed for about an hour above a pot of boiling water, then beaten for an hour or so daily over the course of a week. The steaming and extended process of beating are said to improve the texture of the cloth and to enrich the natural red-brown or yellow colour of the bark. Although it is used mostly for clothing, bark cloth can also serve as a blanket or a shroud, and is rare but valued as bookbinding.

Oral tradition has it that the cloth was originally worn only by the king and members of his court. Ironically, however, this historical association between bark cloth and social prestige was reversed during the early decades of colonial rule, when clothing made from cotton and other fabrics became a status symbol. By the 1950s, bark cloth had practically disappeared from everyday use.

GETTING THERE AND AWAY Nyanza lies 2km west of Kubijega junction (⊕ S 02°20.749, E 029°46.001, 1,811m) on the main Kigali–Huye road, less than two hours' drive from Kigali and just 45 minutes' drive from Huye. A good surfaced road leads all the way to the hilltop museum [135 A6]. Direct minibus-taxis to/from Huye, Muhanga and Kigali leave from the town centre, adjacent to the market [135 B3], but it is also pretty easy to pick one up at Kubijega – minibus-taxis in either direction stop alongside the JOB filling station at the junction [135 D2].

WHERE TO STAY AND EAT
Moderate

Dayenu Hotel [135 B4] (42 rooms) m 078 4765204/8559330; e dayenuhotel@yahoo.com. This new 3-storey hotel in the town centre has good facilities including a garden bar, restaurant & swimming pool. The standard rooms are large & tiled with nets & TV, but they only have a ¾ bed. VIP rooms come with a proper double bed & a second sitting area with flatscreen TV. It is a decent set-up but indifferent value at *Rfr25,000/30,000 sgl/dbl; or Rfr50,000 VIP room.*

Nyanza Heritage Hotel [135 B4] (25 rooms) ✆0252 533295–7. Probably the best-value option in Nyanza, this central new hotel next to the Dayenu has a 1st-floor balcony restaurant serving mains in the Rfr3,000–4,000 range, while accommodation is in clean tiled rooms with private balcony, king-size bed with net, small writing desk, DSTV & en-suite hot shower. *Rfr20,000/30,000 sgl/dbl, or Rfr40,000 VIP dbl.*

Budget

Nyanza Comfort Hotel [135 C2] (8 rooms) ✆0252 533256; m 078 8896883. This pleasant & sensibly priced hotel is situated on the left side of the feeder road connecting halfway Kubijega junction & the town centre. The airy rooms all have dbl beds with netting, tiled bathrooms, ample cupboard space & a phone, while the balcony offers an attractive view over cultivated hills surrounding Nyanza. A garden bar serves brochettes, omelettes & the like. *Rfr12,000/16,000 sgl/dbl; Rfr20,000 for a twin with 2 dbl beds.*

Boomerang Motel [135 B6] (14 rooms) ✆0252 533396. This is the closest hotel to Nyanza's museums, situated about two-thirds of the way along the road running there from the town centre. The clean & brightly decorated rooms have ¾ beds, nets & hot showers, & a restaurant-bar serves typical local fare for around Rfr2,000 per main course. *It feels overpriced at Rfr10,000/15,000 sgl/dbl.*

Freedom Hotel [135 C2] (17 rooms) m 078 8510424. More or less opposite Nyanza Comfort, this adequate hotel has spacious but rather gloomy rooms with dbl beds, nets, tiled hot showers, & a decent garden bar. *Rfr12,000/15,000 sgl/dbl.*

WHAT TO SEE

Rukali Palace Museum [135 A6] (m *078 4577773; www.museum.gov.rw; entrance Rfr6,000 non-residents, Rfr5,000 foreign residents, Rfr3,000 children, in centry to Rwesero Art Museum, with a further photographic fee of Rfr2,000 & video fee of Rfr5,000 pp;* ☉ *08.00–17.00 daily except 1 Jan, 7 Apr, 1 May, 4 Jul, 25 Dec)* This is the top touristic reason for visiting Nyanza, situated on a hilltop about 2km southwest of the centre, and signposted (⊕ S 02°21.468, E 029°44.395, 1,805m). The traditional ancient palace of the Mwami has been reconstructed, together with some other buildings, 3–4km away from its original site, beside the newer Western-style palace built for Mwami Rudahigwa Mutara III in 1932. In olden times, Nyanza was the heart of Rwanda and seat of its monarchy, background to the oral tradition of battles and conquests, power struggles and royal intrigues. It is where the German colonisers came, at the end of the 19th century, to visit the Mwami – and contemporary reports tell of the great pomp and ceremony these visits occasioned, as well as the impressive size of the Mwami's court.

The capital of the kingdom was composed of a group of huts, an ephemeral town of some 2,000 inhabitants, well organised as far as the administration of the country and the comfort of the nobility were concerned… At his court the Mwami maintained the following retinue: the '*Ntore*', adolescent sons of chiefs and notables, who formed the corps de ballet; the '*Bakoma*', soothsayers, magicians and historians; the '*Abashashi*', keepers of the arsenal, the wardrobe and the furniture; the '*Abasisi*' and '*Abacurabgenge*', mimes, musicians and cooks; the '*Abanyabyumba*', palanquin bearers and night watchmen; the '*Nitalindwa*', huntsmen and runners; the '*Intumwa*', artisans working for the Mwami; and finally the hangmen, attentive servants of jurists, ever ready to respond to the brief order to fetch and kill.

Traveller's Guide to the Belgian Congo and Ruanda-Urundi,
Tourist Bureau for the Belgian Congo and Ruanda-Urundi, Brussels, 1951

The traditional palace has been carefully reconstructed and maintained, and contains the king's massive bed as well as various utensils. English- and French-speaking guides are available to relate the history and traditions of the royal court – there is even significance attached to some of the poles supporting the roof; for example, the one at the entrance to the king's bed is named 'do not speak of what happens here' and another conferred sanctuary on anyone touching it.

The newer palace is a typical colonial-era building with its spacious rooms and wide balcony. The *Travellers' Guide* above also states: 'In certain circumstances, and with the permission of the local authorities, he [the Mwami] may be visited at his palace which is built on modern lines, furnished in good taste and richly decorated with trophies in an oriental manner.' In more recent times, the rundown palace served for several years as the part-time home of Rwanda's National Ballet (the Intore dancers, see pages 29–30). Now fully restored, it reopened in May 2008 as a museum whose exhibits relate to the two rulers who lived here during the early to mid 20th century, as well as the more ancient history of the Rwanda Empire. Several original items of royal furniture decorate the interior, and the walls are adorned with monochrome photographs. Other displays depict the palace when it was in use, and chart the history of Rwanda from the 5th century onwards.

The museum can also arrange Intore dance performances by prior notice. The performances can start at anytime from 08.00 to 20.00 and last for about two hours. Between 08.00 and 16.00 on normal weekdays, the cost is Rfr50,000 for up to five people, then another Rfr10,000 for each additional one to five people. The price rises by Rfr20,000 from 16.00 to 18.00 and by another 25% after 18.00. An additional levy of 50% is charged on weekends and public holidays. The same photographic charges as the museum are applied. If that's too steep, a DVD of the same drum/dance troupe performing at the Festival Pan-African de la Danse (FESPAD) in 2008 can be viewed in the museum at no additional charge.

Rwesero Palace Art Museum [135 C7] (✆ 0252 553131; e *museumrwanda@ yahoo.fr; www.museum.gov.rw;* ⊕ *08.00–17.00 daily except 1 Jan, 7 Apr, 1 May, 4 Jul, 25 Dec; entrance inc in ticket for Rukali Palace Museum*) Prominently perched atop Rwesero Hill (✪ S 02°22.050, E 029°44.452, 1,834m) about 1km south of Rukali, this striking building was constructed for Mutara III Rudahigwa over 1957–59, but he died in July 1959 before he could take up residence. Later used as a Supreme Court and Appeals Court, the palace fell into disuse for several years before being renovated and reopening as an arts museum in 2006. It now hosts a combination of permanent and temporary displays, featuring a fascinating combination of traditional and contemporary Rwandan paintings and sculptures dating from the

Rosamond Halsey Carr

My introduction to the Mwami and his royal court was in 1956, when the Hollywood film *King Solomon's Mines* was shown to the king and queen and the royal courtiers. The movie, which was partially filmed on location in Ruanda and starred Stewart Granger and Deborah Kerr, contains some of the most authentic African dance sequences on film, including a dazzling depiction of the dance of the Intore.

The showing was arranged by the American consulate in Léopoldville and held in the royal city of Nyanza. Many of the European residents of Ruanda were invited, myself included. The Mwami and his queen, their courtiers, and the Tutsi nobles who took part in the film were all present. It was a mild, clear night, charged with an air of excitement and wonder. A large screen was erected in the middle of a wide dirt road. On one side of the screen, chairs had been set up for the invited guests. On the other side (the back side), a huge crowd of Banyaruanda sat with expectant faces waiting for the movie to begin.

The king and his entourage made a ceremonial entrance. One would be hard-pressed to find a more majestic figure than this giant of a monarch who could trace his family dynasty back more than four hundred years. Rudahigwa and his courtiers were dressed in traditional white robes with flowing togas knotted at their shoulders, and his queen, Rosalie Gicanda, was wrapped in billowing layers of pale pink…

The soundtrack for the film was in English and, as a result, the Africans were unable to understand the dialogue. Restlessness and murmurs of disappointment rippled through the crowd until the action sequences progressed to the familiar landscape of Ruanda. From that point on, the spectators provided their own soundtrack with cheers and improvised dialogue, as they followed the safari adventure across the desert to the royal city of Nyanza, shouting with glee each time they recognised friends – and in some instances themselves – on the big movie screen.

The city of Nyanza was almost entirely devoid of Western influence, as the Belgian administration had refrained from intruding upon the royal seat of the Tutsi monarchy. There were no hotels, and outside visitors were discouraged. When the movie ended, the Mwami and his entourage and most of the invited guests assembled at the one small restaurant in town for sandwiches and drinks.

From Land of a Thousand Hills: My Life in Rwanda *by Rosamond Halsey Carr with Ann Howard Halsey, Viking, 1999. See Appendix 2, page 309.*

The Road to Huye (Butare)   NYANZA

5

1950s onwards, though most postdate the genocide. In my estimation, this is one of the finest exhibitions of its type anywhere in Africa, and in many respects it is more interesting and rewarding than the nearby palace museum.

Nyabisindu National Dairy On the way to the palaces you'll pass this state-owned dairy, the largest in Rwanda, which was founded by the Belgian colonists in 1937 and is still going strong today. In theory you can just turn up and ask for a free tour, but in practice it's courteous to ask about this on your way out to the palaces and then have your tour (if convenient) on the way back.

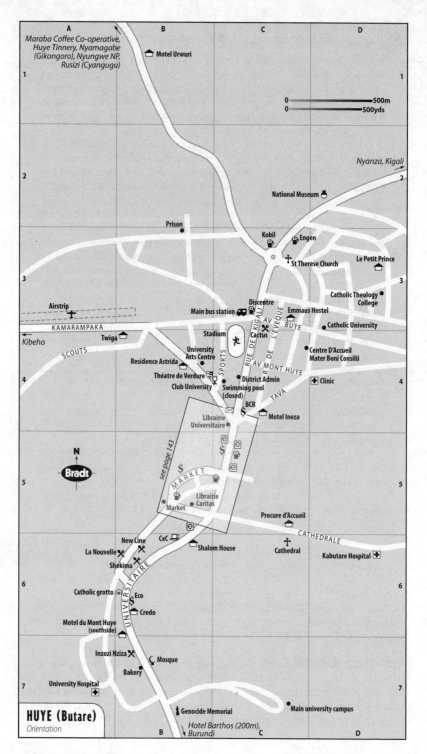

Maraba Coffee Co-operative,
Huye Tinnery, Nyamagabe
(Gikongoro), Nyungwe NP,
Rusizi (Cyangugu)

Motel Urwuri

0   500m
0   500yds

Nyanza, Kigali

National Museum

Prison

Kobil

Engen

St Therese Church

Le Petit Prince

Catholic Theology
College

Airstrip

Main bus station

Discentre

Emmaus Hostel

Catholic University

KAMARAMPAKA

Kibeho

Twiga

Stadium

Cactus

Centre D'Accueil
Mater Boni Consilii

SCOUTS

University
Arts Centre

Residence Astrida

Théatre de Verdure

Club University

District Admin

Swimming pool
(closed)

Clinic

BCR

Motel Ineza

Librairie
Universitaire

see page 143

N

Bradt

MARKET

Librairie
Caritas

Procure d'Accueil

Market

CATHEDRALE

New Line

CxC

La Nouvelle

Shalom House

Cathedral

Kabutare Hospital

Shekima

Catholic grotto

Eco

Credo

Motel du Mont Huye
(southside)

Inzozi Nziza

Mosque

Bakery

University Hospital

Genocide Memorial

Main university campus

HUYE (Butare)
Orientation

Hotel Barthos (200m),
Burundi

140

6

Huye (Butare)

Set at an altitude of 1,755m some 30km north of the border with Burundi, the pleasant, businesslike town of Huye (formerly Butare) is often referred to as the country's 'intellectual centre': the first secondary school in what is now Rwanda opened here in 1928, and it has been the site of the national university since 1963. Founded in the early colonial era, its name was originally Butare, but in 1935 it was renamed Astrida in tribute to Queen Astrid, the 29-year-old Swedish wife of Belgium's King Leopold III, who died in a car accident.

The town served as the administrative centre of the northern half of Ruanda-Urundi in the colonial era, when it was popular with Belgian settlers, and it was the second-largest town in the joint territory, after the capital Bujumbura (in modern-day Burundi). It reverted to the name Butare in 1962, and served as the administrative capital of the eponymous province prior to the administrative reorganisation of 2006, when it was renamed Huye (after Mount Huye, which rises to 2,278m about 10km west of town).

At the time of independence, it seemed almost inevitable that Huye would become the capital city of Rwanda. In the end, however, Kigali was favoured for its more central location. So while Kigali has mushroomed, Huye remains peaceful and compact – though it is still the third-largest town in Rwanda, with a population estimated at around 90,000 in 2012, and its neatly laid out centre still displays strong architectural evidence of its favoured status during the colonial era.

During term-time Huye has probably the country's greatest concentration of students, in relation to its size – not only at the university but also at technical and training schools and colleges. It's something of a religious centre, too, with its massive cathedral and other churches. Its most prominent tourist attraction is the National Museum of Rwanda, which lies on the northern outskirts of town alongside the Kigali Road, but the surrounding countryside also hosts several interesting cultural sites

GETTING THERE AND AWAY

Huye lies 136km south of Kigali (⊕ of Hotel Ibis S 02°35.993, E 29°44.508), a two-hour drive along good tarred roads. Most public minibus-taxis from Kigali will drop you either at the minibus station on the northern edge of town [143 C3] or opposite the town market by the Kobil petrol station [143 A6/7]. The fare from Kigali is Rfr2,500, while regular minibuses to/from Nyanza cost Rfr600. There are also direct minibuses to Huye from Rusizi/Cyangugu and Muhanga/Gitarama.

When you are ready to leave Huye, most minibus-taxis depart from the main taxi park opposite the stadium about 500m north of the town centre [143 C3]. There are also several private operators running services out of the town centre, one of the best being Volcano Express [143 C3] next to the Kobil filling station on the main road, which offers regular departures to Kigali and Nyanza (every 30 minutes from 06.00 to 19.00).

GETTING AROUND

The National Museum and the University are no more than about 5km apart, so everything is manageable on foot. If you need transport, however, plenty of motos can be found at the turning from the main street leading to the market [143 A6/7], and at other strategic points in the town centre.

SECURITY

For all its laid-back atmosphere, Huye is a busy modern town, so take normal precautions such as not carrying conspicuously expensive items. The larger street kids can be a bit pushy, but treat them understandingly and they're manageable. If you go out to eat at night it's wise to take a torch/flashlight, in case of a power cut.

WHERE TO STAY

UPMARKET

🏠 **Centre d'Accueil Mater Boni Consilii** [140 C4] (53 rooms) 0252 531329; m 078 3777626/8283903; e management@ mbcrwanda.com or mcentredaccueil@yahoo.fr; www.mbcrwanda.com. The newest & smartest hotel in town, just about nudging into the upmarket category, is owned & managed by the Abiszemariya Sisters; & profits are used to help take care of orphans, the handicapped, & other marginalised people. Situated 10 minutes' walk from the bus station & about twice that distance from the city centre, it has a good restaurant, high-speed WiFi, conference facilities, a chapel, & well tended en-suite rooms with hot showers & DSTV. *Singles are good value at Rfr25,000; & larger VIP doubles cost Rfr40,000/45,000 sgl/dbl occupancy.*
🏠 **Le Petit Prince Hotel** [140 D3] (25 rooms) 0252 531307; m 078 8358681;

e petitprincehotel@yahoo.fr; www. petitprincehotel.com. Set in large manicured gardens in the northern suburbs opposite the Catholic University, a few mins' walk from the National Museum, this private hotel isn't quite up to the standard of the Centre d'Accueil listed above, but it's still the next best pick. The smartest & most expensive rooms are mini-suites with dbl bed, lockable built-in cupboards, fridge, tiled bathroom with tub, satellite TV, phone & balcony. The cheapest rooms are smaller & some have rather awkward shapes, but still come with TV & en-suite showers. Rooms are very variable in price, size & layout, so it is worth asking to see one before you take it. Facilities include internet access, & a restaurant bar that stays open from 10.00 to 22.00. *Rfr22,000–30,000 dbl; Rfr35,000 mini-suite. All rates B&B.*

MODERATE

🏠 **Credo Hotel** [140 B6] (58 rooms) 0252 530505/530855; m 078 8504176; e credohotel@ yahoo.fr. Situated 500m from the town centre along the road to the university, this was once the smartest option around, & it is still the only hotel with a swimming pool Unfortunately it is also rather characterless, with dazzling labyrinthine corridors that make excessive use of bright white tiles. All rooms are en-suite, with impeccably clean WC & showers, & most also have a TV, phone

& balcony. There's a peaceful view across fields at the back, while facilities include a swimming pool, restaurant & outdoor poolside restaurant-bar. *Rfr15,000/25,000/30,000 sgl/dbl/twin B&B; Rfr40,000/50,000 suite.*
🏠 **Hotel Barthos** [140 B7] (26 rooms) m 078 8666802 or 073 0390191; e barthoshotel@yahoo.fr. Probably the pick in its range, this comfortable & friendly 4-storey hotel has an attractive façade with art deco influences, & lies out of town near

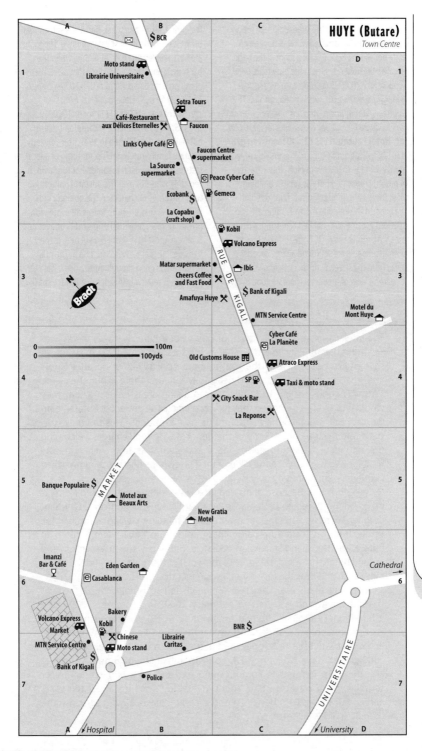

HUYE (Butare)
Town Centre

BCR

Moto stand

Librairie Universitaire

Sotra Tours

Café-Restaurant
aux Délices Eternelles — Faucon

Links Cyber Café

Faucon Centre
supermarket

La Source
supermarket

Peace Cyber Café

Ecobank

Gemeca

La Copabu
(craft shop)

Kobil

Volcano Express

Matar supermarket — Ibis

Cheers Coffee
and Fast Food

Bank of Kigali

Amafuya Huye

MTN Service Centre

Motel du
Mont Huye

RUE DE KIGALI

Cyber Café
La Planète

Old Customs House

Atraco Express

SP — Taxi & moto stand

City Snack Bar

La Reponse

N
Bradt

0 — 100m
0 — 100yds

MARKET

Banque Populaire

Motel aux
Beaux Arts

New Gratia
Motel

Imanzi
Bar & Café

Eden Garden

Casablanca

Bakery

Volcano Express
Market

Kobil

BNR

MTN Service Centre

Chinese

Librairie
Caritas

Moto stand

UNIVERSITAIRE

Bank of Kigali

Police

Cathedral

✓ Hospital

✓ University

the university campus. The large rooms are simply furnished with handcrafted wood, & have an en-suite hot shower & TV. Ask for a room at the back because the front side is near the busy road. *Good value at Rfr20,000/25,000 B&B for a tiled sgl/dbl with king-sized bed, net, writing desk, satellite TV & large en-suite bathroom. Also has smaller rooms at Rfr15,000/20,000 sgl/dbl, & dbl suites for Rfr30,000.*

⌂ **Hotel Faucon** [143 B2] (10 rooms) **m** 078 8301227; **e** faucon@yahoo.fr. Presumably of similar vintage to the nearby Ibis, this attractive & recently renovated hotel is set in a building with thick walls, high ceilings & faint colonial-era echoes! The en-suite rooms & suites are very spacious & come with dbl bed & netting, a sitting area with armchairs & TV, & en-suite bathroom with tub. Rooms are set round a large courtyard, away from the street, & the back windows have a peaceful view of greenery. There's a good main restaurant, also a bar/snack-bar, & the substantial b/fast is possibly the best value in town. The rooms are best avoided on Fri & Sat nights, when the bar transforms into a noisy disco that often keeps pumping until dawn. *Rfr15,000/20,000 sgl/dbl, or Rfr30,000 for a 2-bedroom apt, exc b/fast.*

⌂ **Hotel Ibis** [143 C3] (11 rooms) \0252 530335; **m** 078 8323000; **e** campionibis@ hotmail.com. Established in 1942, this centrally located, family-run hotel is something of a local institution, & whilst it is somewhat rundown, it certainly wins out over the upstart competition when it comes to character. The quaintly old-fashioned & cosy en-suite rooms all come with a private terrace, satellite TV, internet connection & phone, most have 1 dbl & 1 sgl bed, & the bedside lights are a welcome touch. The main restaurant is good though quite pricey. The more pleasant & relatively inexpensive terrace snack-

BUTARE AND THE GENOCIDE

The intellectual and cultural spirit of Huye – or Butare, as it was then – was so strong that initially it seemed that it could resist the madness of slaughter that erupted elsewhere in the country on 6 April 1994. For decades Hutus and Tutsis had lived and studied peacefully together there. When the killing started, people flocked to Butare from outlying areas believing that they would find safety – as indeed they did, for a while. The prefect of Butare, Jean-Baptiste Habyarimana (no relation to the late president), was the only Tutsi prefect in Rwanda at the time of the genocide. He took charge, welcoming the refugees, reassuring parishioners, and demonstrating such authority that, for two weeks while the killing raged elsewhere, relative calm prevailed in Butare, punctuated by only isolated instances of violence.

It couldn't last. Because of his defiance, Habyarimana was sacked from his post and murdered, to be replaced by a hardline military officer, Lieutenant Colonel Tharcisse Muvunyi, and an equally hardline civilian administrator. Under their orchestration, paramilitary units from Kigali were airlifted to Butare, and the killing started immediately. Ultimately, the massacres in and around Butare proved to be some of the worst of the genocide, and the death tally of 220,000 was the highest of any prefecture.

After the genocide, Tharcisse Muvunyi fled to Britain, where he was tracked down and arrested in February 2000. In September 2006, the International Criminal Tribunal for Rwanda (ICTR) sentenced him to 25 years' imprisonment. This ruling was annulled on appeal in August 2008 and retrial with regards to one count of the indictment commenced in June 2009. In February 2010 the ICTR found Tharcisse Muvunyi guilty of direct and public incitement to commit genocide, and he was given a 15-year sentence, with credit on time spent in custody since his arrest ten years earlier. In March 2012, he was granted early release, having served more than 80% of his jail term.

bar was closed for renovations in early 2012 but should reopen eventually. *Rfr15,000–35,000 depending on room size.*

⌂ **Shalom House** [140 B6] (8 rooms) m 078 3880153; e rusodilo@yahoo.fr. Run by the Anglican (EER) Diocese of Huye & situated on the south side of the town centre, this smart new

BUDGET

⌂ **Emmaus Hostel** [140 C3] (7 rooms) m 078 8865736/8748649; e emmaiscenter@yahoo.fr. Conveniently located on a quiet suburban road less than 5 mins' walk from the bus station, this agreeable church-run hostel is centred around a neat green courtyard & offers accommodation in a variety of clean spacious tiled en-suite rooms. *Great value at Rfr8,000/10,000/15,000 sgl/dbl/suite.*

⌂ **Motel du Mont Huye** [143 D3] (18 rooms) m 078 8504302. Arguably the best budget option, despite a recent price hike, is this centrally located but peaceful spot, which lies along a small side road away from the main street & its traffic. The clean, tiled, comfortable en-suite rooms with 1 or 2 ¾ beds all have hot water & a small balcony opening on to a central garden, & a more than adequate restaurant serves meals & snacks in the Rfr1,500–5,000 range. It's popular with NGOs, etc, so it's best to book in advance, though extra rooms are now available at an annexe on the university road about 100m past the Hotel Credo. *Fair value*

SHOESTRING

⌂ **Eden Garden Hotel** [143 B6] (13 rooms) ☎0252 530446; m 078 8409083. Also in the market area, this hotel, set around a central courtyard, offers adequate accommodation in plain, clean & rather gloomy rooms using shared facilities. *Rfr4,000 twin.*

⌂ **Motel aux Beaux Arts** [143 A5] (10 rooms) ☎0252 530037; m 078 8666802. The pick of a cluster of inexpensive hotels dotted around the market area, this comfortable & reasonably priced 2-storey place offers clean en-suite twin & dbl rooms. The restaurant no longer serves meals other than b/fast, but there are plenty of other options for eating out within a couple of hundred metres. *Great value at Rfr5,000/7,000 sgl/dbl.*

⌂ **Motel Ineza** [140 C4] (12 rooms) m 078 8953533; e motelineza@gmail.com. Situated along a side road opposite the post office on the north side of town, this popular & pleasant hotel

2-storey hostel has very large tiled rooms with lockable built-in cupboards, king-size or twin beds, nets, en-suite showers & access to a ground-floor lounge with TV/DVD. The rooms are among the best deals in this range, but there is no restaurant or bar (though it's not far to walk to the town centre). *Rfr20,000/25,000 sgl/dbl exc b/fast.*

at *Rfr10,000/18,000 sgl/twin; Rfr30,000 for a 2-bedroom apt at the annexe.*

⌂ **Residence Astrida** [140 B4] (5 rooms) m 078 0269145/5983006; e residence.astrida@gmail.com. This converted house lies in leafy gardens immediately north of the town centre opposite Théâtre de Verdure. The spacious clean rooms come with dbl beds, nets, writing desk & en-suite bathroom with shower & tub, & there is a common lounge with TV. *Good value at Rfr12,000/15,000 sgl/dbl bed only, rather less so at Rfr15,0000/20,000 inc b/fast.*

⌂ **Twiga Hotel** [140 B4] (40 rooms) m 078 8855032. In the northern suburbs close to the bus station, this place is decorated with garish sculptures of giraffes (*twiga* in Swahili), gorillas & other wildlife. There is a pleasant-looking garden bar & restaurant, & for rooms you have the choice of a small en-suite dbl with ¾ bed & hot shower or a larger mini-suite with dbl bed & TV. *Feels like poor value at Rfr10,000/15,000 dbl/mini-suite.*

has a friendly English-speaking owner-manager & a pretty secluded garden where you can sit out & eat, or just enjoy the peace & quiet. The en-suite rooms, though very clean & equipped with mosquito netting (a rarity here), are rather cramped, & the so-called dbls have a ¾ bed only, making it more suited to single travellers than to couples. It serves a variety of snacks & light meals, & it's very close to the town centre if you prefer to eat elsewhere. *Rfr5,000/6,000 sgl/dbl occupancy.*

⌂ **New Gratia Motel** [143 B5] (11 rooms) ☎0252 531044. Also situated close to the market, this is a reasonably comfortable set-up, with the basic but clean en-suite twins (adorned by a solitary net dangling pointlessly above the space between the 2 beds) set round a small, well-watered courtyard garden. *Not such good value at Rfr5,000/8,000/10,000 sgl/twin/dbl.*

WHERE TO EAT AND DRINK

Plenty of small restaurants round the market offer snacks and good-value *mélanges* of rice, vegetables and meat for around Rfr1,500–2,500, while most hotels also serve meals in the Rfr4,000–5,000 range. Several more formal restaurants are scattered around town, notably the following:

✕ **CxC Coffee Shop** [140 B6] m 078 6120712; ⏱ 07.00–17.30 Mon–Sat. With its minimalist interior dominated by a huge industrial coffee grinder, this friendly & funky little spot immediately south of the town centre is an outlet for Gata Keza coffee from the organic Kigufi Estate on Lake Kivu near Rubavu/Gisenyi. The delicious espresso & filter coffee are well worth the Rfr200 investment, though it is a shame no snacks or pastries are on offer to accompany them. You can also buy beans (or ask for them to be freshly ground in front of you) to take home at Rfr8,000/kg.

✕ **Cheers Coffee & Fast Food** [143 C3] ☏0252 531276; m 078 8474333; ⏱ 08.00–22.00 Mon–Sat; 12.00–21.00 Sun. This winning contemporary eatery is part of the Matar Supermarket, which stands directly opposite the Hotel Ibis. It is a good spot for b/fast, serving fresh coffee & a decent selection of freshly baked filled rolls, croissants, mini-pizzas & the like. It's also popular at lunch & to a lesser extent dinner, when a varied menu includes salads, sandwiches & a selection of grills & pasta dishes in the Rfr2,000–4,000 range.

✕ **Chinese Restaurant** [143 A7] m 078 8849793/8990203; ⏱ daily from 08.00 until the last customer leaves. Situated behind the Kobil filling station opposite the central market, this is arguably the best eatery in town, despite the rather scruffy exterior, serving a huge selection of Chinese fish, meat & vegetarian dishes in the Rfr4,000–5,000 range, as well as more typical grills (beef, chicken, rabbit & fish) at a similar price. You can eat indoors or on the balcony.

✕ **Hotel Faucon** [143 B2] m 078 8301227; ⏱ b/fast, lunch & dinner daily. Similar in character to the Ibis a few doors up, but a touch more downmarket, the terrace bar at the Faucon is another good spot for an evening drink, & the varied menu is cheaper, with most dishes in the Rfr3,000–4,000 range.

✕ **Hotel Ibis** [143 C3] ☏0252 530335; m 078 8323000; ⏱ b/fast, lunch & dinner daily. Assuming it's reopened after a recent closure for renovations, there's no more characterful or popular spot for an evening rendezvous than the terrace of the venerable Hotel Ibis, with its mix 'n' match of contemporary & period décor, & attached indoor bar. It serves the usual range of grills, mostly for around Rfr4,000–5,000, though brochettes & burgers are cheaper. There is also draft beer on tap & a pizza menu.

✕ **Inzozi Nziza** [140 B7] m 078 8738350; www.bluemarbledreams.org; ⏱ 07.00–22.00 daily. Translating as 'Sweet Dreams', this new ice-cream & coffee shop, on the university road opposite the Hotel Credo, is the only place in town to serve locally developed soft-serve ice cream, made freshly with local ingredients, at around Rfr500–1,200 depending on what toppings are added. It also serves fresh coffee roasted on the premises, fresh fruit juice, milkshakes, sandwiches & light snacks. Proceeds support a cooperative of more than 100 women from the drumming group Ingoma Nshya.

NIGHTLIFE

There's not a huge amount. Plenty of small bars are dotted around the market area, the most attractive being the **Imanzi Bar & Café** [143 A6] (m *078 8481276*), with its large-screen TV that often draws crowds for key football matches. Otherwise the terrace bars and the Hotel Faucon [143 B2] (and, assuming it has reopened, Hotel Ibis [143 C3]) remain popular places to while away the evening in the open air as the life of the town goes by. The Faucon has a popular disco on Friday and Saturday nights.

SHOPPING

There are two **bookshops**: the Librairie Universitaire [143 B1] at the northern end of the main street has a fair range of books and student stationery, as well as some dusty but original handicrafts. Librairie Caritas [143 B7] at the other end of the main street has a few more touristy books and items of stationery, as well as some international magazines and games.

For **self-caterers**, the central market [143 A6/7] is a good place to buy local produce such as fruit and vegetables, and there's a good bakery nearby, alongside the Chinese Restaurant [143 A7]. For imported foods as well as freshly baked bread and other goodies, there's the excellent Matar Supermarket [143 C3], directly opposite the Hôtel Ibis. Also on the main road, other good supermarkets include the Faucon Centre [143 B2] and La Source [143 B2].

For **handicrafts**, there's an excellent shop on between Matar and La Source supermarkets, selling products made by the Coopérative des Producteurs Artisanaux de Huye [143 B2] (*COPABU;* ✎ *0252 530762;* e *copabu@yahoo.fr; www.copabu.co.rw*). The items have set prices, but a little gentle bargaining will do no harm, particularly if you're buying more than one. The co-op was set up in 1997 with 47 members, working in banana-leaf products, wood-carving and reed baskets. Three years later it had 954 members (99 individuals and 35 associations) of which 66% were women, and it continued to grow. Handicrafts in the Huye area have been well organised, with the help of German aid.

OTHER PRACTICALITIES

COMMUNICATIONS The **post office** [143 B1] is at the northern end of the main street. An **internet café** is attached, and there are also several private internet cafés dotted around town, most offering reasonably fast services – try Cyber Café la Planète a few doors down from the Hotel Ibis [143 C3], or Links Cyber Café opposite the Faucon [143 B2]. There are MTN service centres near the market [143 A7] and on the main road near the Hotel Ibis.

MONEY The **Banque Commerciale du Rwanda** [143 B1] opposite the post office and the **Bank of Kigali** [143 C4] midway down the main street offer normal services, as do various other banks, but there are no private forex bureaux, so you are generally better off changing money in Kigali or (if you're heading that way) Rusizi/Cyangugu.

WHAT TO SEE AND DO

NATIONAL UNIVERSITY OF RWANDA [140 C7] (✎ *0252 530122;* e *info@nur.ac.rw; www.nur.ac.rw.*) Although not really a tourist 'sight', the National University is by far Huye's most important institution. Created in 1963, with only 51 students and 16 lecturers when it opened, the university had 8,221 students and 425 lecturers by 2005. It lost many of its students and personnel during the genocide and suffered considerable damage, but managed to reopen in 1995. It is now a vibrant and forward-looking institution, comprising faculties of agronomy, law, arts and human sciences, medicine, science and technology, economics, social sciences and management, and education, as well as schools of journalism and communication and modern languages. You may run across visiting professors in any of the town's hotels and guesthouses. There is a decent cafeteria serving a buffet for around

Rfr1,000, and over the weekend the main auditorium sometimes shows music and Premier League football in the evenings.

Out by the university is the **Ruhande Arboretum**, started in 1934. Its objective at the outset was to study the behaviour of imported and indigenous species, to determine what silvicultural methods were most suitable, to evaluate the trees' productivity and timber quality, and to develop the best of them. Now, it is of interest for the range and variety of its species – and it's a peaceful, shady place.

The university campus is the best place in Huye/Butare to look for **vervet monkeys**. The security policemen at the arboretum gate will usually allow in visitors who ask to see the monkeys, and will point you towards the football field straight ahead, which is where a troop of around 50–100 monkeys often hang out, usually in the surrounding trees, though obviously their presence cannot be guaranteed.

If you have an interest in the arts, you might want to check out whether any student productions are running at the **Théatre de Verdure** [140 B4] (*0252 530215; e cua_centre@yahoo.com*), part of the Centre Universitaire des Arts, which lies along a back road behind the post office.

THE NATIONAL MUSEUM OF RWANDA [140 D2] (*0252 530207; www.museum. gov.rw; entrance Rfr6,000 non-residents, Rfr5,000 foreign residents, Rfr3,000 children foreign students/pupils, Rfr1,000 Rwandan adults, Rfr500 Rwandan students/pupils, with a further photographic fee of Rfr2,000 per camera & video fee of Rfr5,000 pp; ⊕ 09.00–17.00 daily except 1 Jan, 7 Apr, 1 May, 4 Jul)* If you're in Huye, do allow time to visit this beautifully presented collection of exhibits on Rwandan history and culture. Opened in 1988, and presented to Rwanda as a gift from Belgium's King Baudouin I, it is situated on more than 20 hectares of land containing indigenous vegetation and a traditional craft training centre as well as the main 2,500m² museum building, whose seven spacious rooms illustrate the country and its people from earliest times until the present day. At the reception desk, various pamphlets and books are on sale. Until recently, no descriptions or background material were available in English, but most displays are now labelled in English as well as Kinyarwanda.

Room 1 (the entrance hall) has space for temporary displays as well as numerous shelves of traditional handicrafts for sale. **Room 2** presents a comprehensive view of Rwanda's geological and geographical background and the development of its terrain and population. In **Room 3** the occupations of its early inhabitants (hunter-gathering, farming and stock-raising) are illustrated, together with the later development of tools and methods of transport. The social importance of cattle is explained and there are even detailed instructions for the brewing of traditional banana beer (see box on page 153). **Room 4** displays a variety of handicrafts and the making of traditional household items: pottery, mats, baskets, leatherwork and the wooden shields of the Intore dancers. **Room 5** illustrates traditional styles and methods of architecture – and a full-scale royal hut has been reconstructed. In **Room 6** traditional games and sports are displayed and more space is given to the costumes and equipment of the Intore dancers. Finally, **Room 7** contains exhibits relating to traditional customs and beliefs, history, culture, poetry, oral tradition and the supernatural.

If you don't fancy the walk from town (about 1.5km from the centre), then a taxi to the museum will cost around Rfr1,500, more if you ask it to wait. If you're coming by minibus-taxi from Kigali you can ask to be dropped off there; and, if you want to go straight back to Kigali afterwards, you could try flagging down a minibus that has come from Huye – if it has spare seats inside, it will probably stop.

Or to be sure of getting one you can walk to the minibus-taxi stand, which is less than 1km away.

OTHER POINTS OF INTEREST The huge, red-brick, Roman Catholic **cathedral** [140 C6], built in memory of Belgium's Princess Astrid in the late 1930s, is the largest in the country and worth a visit. Its interior is fairly plain, but the atmosphere is tranquil and the size impressive. A service there can be a moving experience, especially if you arrive during mass, or choir rehearsals, and catch the Acapella choir of 30+ Rwandans in sing. It's possible to take a turning to the right a short distance east of the Motel Ineza and then to cross twisty tracks through the green and cultivated valley until you reach the cathedral, but ask for directions and advice.

There is some attractive architecture in the city centre, and the tranquil, tree-lined residential streets away from the centre are good territory for strolling. Major colonial landmarks along the main road through the centre of town include the **Old Customs House** [143 C4] (now a financial training centre) opposite the SP filling station, whose architecture would suggest it was built in the 1930s, and the handsome little **Librairie Universitaire** [143 B1], which was erected as a doctor's surgery in the 1950s and later served as a bank. A clear heritage of Belgian colonisation (in Belgium even the motorways are lit) is the generous amount of street lighting around the town.

Spectacular displays of **traditional dance** (*Intore*) take place in the town and the museum, and can be arranged on request (and for a fee); ask at the museum (see opposite) about this.

EXCURSIONS FROM HUYE

HUYE TINNERY (m *078 8640923*; e *info@rwanda-tin.com; www.rwanda-tin.com;* ⊕ *07.00–16.30 Mon–Fri, 07.00–12.00 Sat*) Established by a Benedictine monk who did his internship in Europe and managed by the affable Antoine Bizimana, this interesting tinnery is located about 5km northwest of Huye on the Nyamagabe/Gikongoro road (look for the signpost on the right reading 'Les Etains de l'Etainerie y'i Huye', and don't be put off by the fact the building looks closed from the road side). It uses Rwandan tin made from 99.8% pewter to produce an attractive range of products ranging from gorilla and giraffe statuettes to household utensils reminiscent of the Carrol Boyes range, but cheaper. Visitors are welcome to watch the artisans at all stages in the process, from making the moulds to pouring, burnishing and welding. Products are sold at the tinnery's on-site shop, as well as through various hotel boutique shops in Kigali.

KIBEHO Before the genocide, Kibeho hit the headlines because of the visions of the Virgin Mary allegedly seen there by young girls from 1981 onwards, starting with that of teenager Alphonsine Mumureke in November 1981. The phenomena were reported both nationally and internationally, and the small, remote community became a centre of pilgrimage and faith, as believers travelled from all over Rwanda and further afield to witness the miracles. During the genocide Kibeho suffered appallingly: hospital, primary school, college and church were all attacked. The church was badly burned while still sheltering survivors; a genocide memorial site stands beside it.

You pick up the Kibeho road by driving through the minibus park just north of Huye. Minibuses also make the trip, but not very frequently. It's a beautiful drive through a mixture of wooded valleys and farmland, on an unmade road. There's not a great deal to see at Kibeho, but developments are planned in order to attract tourists. If you want to spend the night, clean, comfortable, safe and inexpensive accommodation and decent meals are available by prior arrangement at the **Regina Pacis Hospitality House** (\ *0252 530242;* e *benebikira@yahoo.fr; www.paraclete.org/ benebikira/hospitality*), run by the Benebikira Sisters of Rwanda, a charitable order dedicated to creating sustainable revenue-generating projects for local communities.

MARABA COFFEE CO-OPERATIVE The fertile slopes around Mount Huye, west of the town, lie at the heart of Maraba coffee-growing country (see box overleaf), and also form one of the most scenic parts of Rwanda, all rolling green hills swathed in coffee shrubs and other lush vegetation. There's no formal tourist industry in the area, but it's easy enough to explore in a private vehicle or by bicycle – possibly even on foot – either as a day excursion from Huye, or *en route* from there to Nyungwe or Rusizi/Cyangugu.

The best place to start is the **Cyarumbo Coffee Washing Station**, which can be reached by following the main road west towards Rusizi/Cyangugu for 12km

MURAMBI GENOCIDE MEMORIAL   *Phil Vernon*

Arriving at Murambi Hill, one is first struck by the breathtaking beauty of its location. The site of a partially completed technical school in Nyamagabe District in southern Rwanda, it is a tidy array of unfinished classrooms, dormitories and washrooms situated on the grassy crest of a red dirt ridge that falls away on both sides to lush green bottom lands, beyond which rise the steeply cultivated and densely populated hills that hold this place in a close, but in no way comfortable, embrace.

Despite its beauty, however, Murambi was the site of a horrific massacre of Tutsi men, women and children during the 1994 genocide. It is where up to 50,000 Tutsi from all over the region were sent in the early days of the genocide, ostensibly for their safety, only to have their water and the flow of food shut off by the authorities. Local militias sent in to kill the Tutsi were met by fierce resistance and forced to turn back. But the *interahamwe* returned on the early morning of 21 April, together with the army, to massacre the refugees with guns, grenades, clubs, hoes and machetes. Only a dozen Tutsi are known to have survived.

Murambi, with its history as a killing site, and its unique compelling displays of preserved bodies, is arguably the most important site in Rwanda for confronting the truth of the genocide. The addition of an exhibition locating Murambi's story within that of the 1994 genocide against the Tutsi provides both a national and a local context for understanding what happened here.

After the massacre, the authorities used bulldozers to dig mass graves; upon later exhumation hundreds of the buried bodies were found mummified by the heat of decomposition. These bodies, preserved with lime, can now be viewed on white-painted racks in the dormitory blocks. The humanity of individual corpses – their torment still visible in the frozen cry of a child, the chopped skull and severed leg tendons, the missing limbs – is the grim legacy of Murambi.

On 26 May 2011, Murambi Genocide Memorial became the second commemorative site in Rwanda (the other being the Kigali Genocide Memorial) to offer visitors a museum-quality experience, with the official opening of a new exhibition created by Aegis Trust under the auspices of the National Commission for the Fight Against Genocide (CNLG).

to Maraba trading centre, then continuing for another few hundred metres across a bridge, where the washing station is clearly signposted to the left. A 1.5km dirt track leads to the station, which was founded in July 2001 with the assistance of USAID and other charities. Here, you can watch co-operative members dry the coffee beans, then wash them, before removing the pod and any bad beans.

Back on the road from Huye to Rusizi, 1km past the turn-off to Cyarumbo, you might want to stop at the **National Speciality Coffee Quality Laboratory & Training Centre** (known locally as 'the Laboratory'), which stands on the right. Another 500m past this, a good dirt road to the right reaches the tiny trading centre of Simbi after 2km, then continues deeper into the hills to the shambas where the coffee is grown – a wonderfully scenic area with great potential for hiking and cycling.

NYAMAGABE (GIKONGORO) This modestly sized town, administrative capital of Nyamagabe District, whose name was changed from Gikongoro to Nyamagabe in 2006, sprawls uneventfully along a green ridge on the Rusizi/Cyangugu Road almost 30km west of Huye. There's not a lot to see around

The Murambi exhibition comprises 350m² of exhibit space, complete with floor-to-ceiling displays of archival photos, interpretive text in Kinyarwanda, English and French, video installations, and an interactive GPS display of killing sites. The testimonies of survivors, of those who risked their own lives to shelter those targeted, and of the perpetrators themselves, provide a window into the stark emotions and inner struggles of Rwandans coming to terms with the genocide.

Incorporating recent scholarship and archival material, the Murambi exhibition traces the history of the genocide from colonial times – the cycles of anti-Tutsi violence and discrimination ushered in with independence, the escalation of propaganda and attacks against Tutsi by successive Hutu regimes – revealing how plans for extermination were prepared and carried out by the authorities at all levels, by the army and militia during the genocide, and what was done – and not done – to stop it.

Following the broad narrative of the genocide are exhibits that focus specifically on the events at Murambi. With chilling clarity, the story of what unfolded during the night of April 21, 1994, is told in the words of those few who survived. Visitors then pass through rooms of family photos mounted larger-than-life upon the walls – the smiling faces seeming to refuse the brutal fact of their slaughter – where glass-covered burial crypts, designed but not yet completed at the time of writing, will hold preserved bodies: adults in one chamber, and children in another.

'There are those who feel that only reburial can offer dignity for the dead, but some survivors ask what dignity there is in being forgotten,' reports Freddy Mutanguha, Country Director of Aegis Trust: 'They fear that unless the ultimate evidence is there to see, the genocide could be denied and perhaps one day happen again.'

A final room displays the important stories of people who risked death and suffered themselves to rescue Tutsi and to preserve human life.

The exhibition ends with a challenge to visitors: Now that you have heard the story of Murambi, what is in your heart, and what are you moved to do? Visitors are invited to write on slips of coloured paper and to post them on a bulletin board for others to read.

here except for a few shops and some beautiful, dramatically hilly landscapes. But if the area appeals and you feel like some steepish strolling, there's decent accommodation at the newish three-storey **Golden Monkey Hotel** (*23 rooms;* m *078 848 4849;* e *goldenmonkeyhotel@yahoo.com*), which lies alongside the main road and charges Rfr27,000 for a smart twin or double room with netting, tiled floors, lockable built-in cupboards and en-suite hot shower and toilet.

About 2km north of Nyamagabe, **Murambi Genocide Memorial** (see boxed text on pages 150–1) is one of Rwanda's starkest. More than 1,800 bodies, of the

MARABA BOURBON GOURMET COFFEE   *Janice Booth*

Rwanda's Maraba Bourbon coffee is one of the country's success stories. Beans being grown at Maraba, near Huye, have excelled in international taste tests – in a US study they were classed as second best worldwide – and are being marketed actively in the UK and US. Maraba is a very special type of Arabica coffee from Bourbon coffee trees, characterised by a smooth, full-bodied flavour with no astringency or after-taste.

The coffee plantation is run by the Abahuzamugambi Co-operative, set up in 2001, many of whose members are women widowed in the genocide who were struggling to support their families. The income from the Maraba coffee hasenabled them to pay school fees, improve their homes and acquire livestock. In 2005 the Co-operative won the prestigious City of Göteborg International Environmental Prize. International support from USAID, ACDI/VOCA, PEARL, the UK's Comic Relief, Union Coffee Roasters of London and others provided for new washing stations and improved equipment, and the area has acquired a new clinic, bank and market as well as schools and other ancillary shops and services. From an initial 200 members in 2001 there are now around 1,200; including their families and children, up to 6,000 people are directly or indirectly benefiting. In the UK, Sainsbury's has promoted Maraba coffee during Comic Relief campaigns and has also sold a speciality beer containing it. In the US, Maraba Bourbon is available from Starbucks as well as from speciality stores.Among other online sources, in the UK it's available from www.unionroasted.com (Union Coffee Roasters), where its flavour is described somewhat fancifully as 'red apple, white grape, candied orange & complex floral aromatics finishing with silky milk chocolate'.

Traditionally, Arabica coffee had always been Rwanda's principal export, but quality and quantity declined seriously after the genocide when production fell to about half its previous level. Now it's back on an upward curve, and other plantations around Rwanda are achieving similar success with different brands. The country as a whole has over 8 million coffee trees on some 33,000 hectares of land; other good coffee growing areas are Akagera, Virunga, and around lakes Kivu and Muhazi. Another brand doing very well on the international market is Rwanda Blue Bourbon from the Kivu area, also used by Starbucks and drunk as far afield as Japan.

You'll find Maraba Bourbon in Rwanda's restaurants, hotels and supermarkets, along with other Rwandan coffees and tea, and at prices far lower than in international stores. Watch out for it – whether in the UK, the US or Rwanda – and enjoy!

THE PREPARATION OF BANANA BEER   *(Free translation by Janice Booth)*

- When the bunches of fruit are ready, cut them.
- Cover the bunches with banana leaves and leave them in the courtyard to ripen for two to three days.
- Clean out the pit in which the fruit ripened.
- Lay banana branches across the top of the pit.
- Place the bananas on top of the branches.
- Wrap the bananas in fresh banana leaves and then scatter a layer of earth on top.
- Put leaves in the ditch under the bananas and set the leaves alight. Leave for three days.
- Peel the fruit, then crush it, then mix a little water into the pulp.
- Press the pulp and filter the juice.
- Grind up a small amount of sorghum.
- Pour the juice into a large jar and add the sorghum to it.
- Leave to ferment for three days.
- The beer is ready to drink.

27,000-odd exhumed from mass graves here, have been placed on display to the public in the old technical school. They people the bare rooms, mingling horror with poignancy, as a mute but chillingly eloquent reminder that such events must never, ever, be allowed to recur.

- Intercultural exchange   • Red rocks backpacker camping
- Gorilla trekking   • Volunteering in community projects
- Traditional dance lesssons

Email: amahorotours@gmail.com
Web: www.amahoro-tours.com
Tel: +250 788 655 223 or +250 788 687 448

CONSERVE THROUGH ECO-TOURISM

Wildlife Tours Rwanda

(Rwandan-owned company) organizes nature-based tours, community-based tours, volunteer tours and project tours which are all experiential, educational and encompass major components of ecotourism, responsible tourism and pro-poor tourism.

PO Box 601, Kigali (opp. Banque Populaire du Kimironko)
Tel: +250 78 852 7049/+250 78 835 7052
Email: info@wildlifetours-rwanda.com   Web: www.wildlifetours-rwanda.com

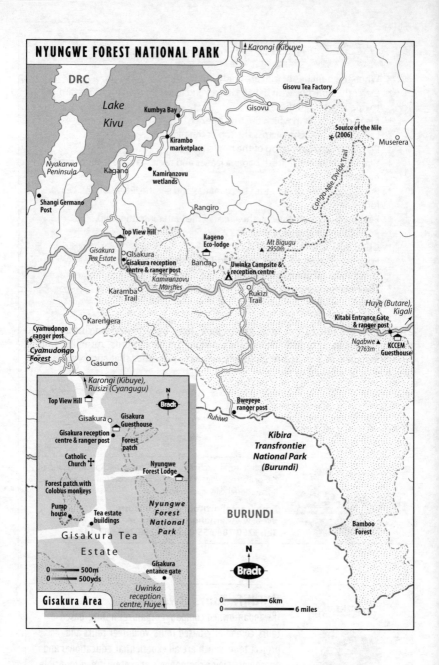

NYUNGWE FOREST NATIONAL PARK

Karongi (Kibuye)

DRC

Lake
Kivu

Gisovu Tea Factory

Kumbya Bay

Gisovu

Kirambo
marketplace

Source of the Nile
(2006)

Muserera

Nyakarwa
Peninsula

Kagano

Kamiranzovu
wetlands

Rangiro

Shangi Germano
Post

Top View Hill

Kageno
Eco-lodge

Mt Bigugu
2950m

Gisakura
Tea Estate

Gisakura

Gisakura reception
centre & ranger post

Banda

Uwinka Campsite &
reception centre

Kamiranzovu
Marshes

Huye (Butare),
Kigali

Karamba
Trail

Karengera

Rukizi
Trail

Kitabi Entrance Gate
& ranger post

Cyamudongo
ranger post

Ngabwe
2763m

KCCEM
Guesthouse

Cyamudongo
Forest

Gasumo

Bweyeye
ranger post

Ruhwa

Kibira
Transfrontier
National Park
(Burundi)

Gisakura Area

Karongi (Kibuye),
Rusizi (Cyangugu)

N

Brandt

Top View Hill

Gisakura

Gisakura
Guesthouse

Gisakura reception
centre & ranger post

Forest
patch

Catholic
Church

Nyungwe
Forest Lodge

Forest patch with
Colobus monkeys

Pump
house

Tea estate
buildings

Nyungwe
Forest
National
Park

Gisakura Tea
Estate

0 — 500m
0 — 500yds

Gisakura
entance gate

Uwinka
reception
centre, Huye

BURUNDI

N

Brandt

0 — 6km
0 — 6 miles

Bamboo
Forest

7

Nyungwe Forest National Park

The largest remaining tract of montane rainforest in eastern Africa, Nyungwe extends for 1,015km² over the mountainous southwest of Rwanda, forming a contiguous forest block with Burundi's 370km² Kibira National Park. The park is the most important catchment area in Rwanda, supplying water to 70% of the country, and its central ridge divides Africa's two largest drainage systems, the Nile and the Congo – indeed, a spring on the slopes of the 2,950m Mount Bigugu is now regarded to be the most remote source of the world's longest river (see *Ascend the Nile* box page 171).

As with other forests along the Albertine Rift (the part of the Rift Valley that follows the Congolese border with Uganda, Rwanda, Burundi and northwest Tanzania), Nyungwe is a remarkably rich centre of biodiversity. More than 1,050 plant species have been recorded, including 200 orchids and 250 Albertine Rift Endemics (AREs), along with at least 120 butterfly species. The vertebrate fauna includes 85 mammal, 310 bird, 32 amphibian and 38 reptile species, of which about 15% are AREs.

Statistics aside, Nyungwe is simply magnificent. The forest takes on a liberatingly primal presence even before you enter it. One moment the road is winding through a characteristic rural Rwandan landscape of rolling tea plantations and artificially terraced hills, the next a dense tangle of trees rises imperiously from the fringing cultivation. For a full 50km, the road clings improbably to steep forested slopes, offering grandstand views over densely swathed hills that tumble like monstrous green waves towards the distant Burundi border. One normally thinks of the rainforest as an intimate and confining environment, and Nyungwe's dank interior certainly possesses those qualities. But as viewed from the main road, Nyungwe is also a gloriously expansive sight.

For most visitors, primates are the main attraction. All 13 species are represented, including a chimpanzee population estimated at 500–1,000, which can usually be tracked at short notice, but several other monkeys are readily seen, including the acrobatic Ruwenzori colobus, and the localised L'Hoest's monkey. Nyungwe is also highly alluring to birders, botanists and keen walkers, with its 130km network of walking trails, and is it is the site of the region's only suspended canopy walk,

Bisected by the surfaced trunk road between Huye and Rusizi/Cyangugu, Nyungwe is unusually accessible by car. Despite that, it features on relatively few tourist itineraries. Partly, this is because the forest trails require more stamina than their counterparts in Volcanoes National Park, without the enticement of mountain gorillas to justify the effort. Another factor was the lack of any genuine tourist-class accommodation prior to the opening of Nyungwe Forest Lodge in 2010.

Furthermore, in keeping with the RDB's aim of attracting high-cost low-volume tourism, Nyungwe makes few concessions to independent or budget travel. Fees for guided activities are high, unguided exploration is forbidden, accommodation is costly, and getting around without private transport is tricky. Indeed, Nyungwe is probably not worth visiting on a daily budget of much less than US$150 per person – and even then, your options will be restricted if you are dependent on public transport.

ORIENTATION

Nyungwe is a large park, and facilities and attractions are widely spaced out along the 50km stretch of the surfaced Huye–Rusizi road that bisects it. As a result, exploration tends to entail lots of driving to-and-fro for those with private transport, and can be problematic for those without.

Coming from Huye, Kitabi Entrance Gate, site of the park headquarters and a reception/booking office, lies on the park's eastern boundary. Also here is the Kitabi College of Conservation & Environmental Management (KCCEM), and an associated guesthouse offering the most affordable accommodation in or around the park. Kitabi is the base for the little-used Ngabwe Trail, but it is somewhat remote from Nyungwe's key attractions, making it a frustrating base without your own vehicle.

About 45 minutes' drive further west, the park's most ambitious tourist development is the recently renovated Uwinka Reception Centre, which lies alongside the main road and is well signposted 90km from Huye and 54km from Rusizi/Cyangugu. This is the starting point for several trails, including the new canopy walkway, and it is also very close to some good sites for general birdwatching and primate viewing. The only campsite is found here, too, but there's no other accommodation nearby.

The main cluster of facilities lies 18km west of Uwinka, immediately outside the park boundary, close to the Gisakura Tea Estate. Nyungwe Forest Lodge, Gisakura Guesthouse and Nyungwe Top View Hill Hotel all lie close to the 2km stretch of road running from Gisakura Tea Estate to the eponymous village. Two activities can easily be undertaken from Gisakura without a private vehicle: the superb Isumo (Waterfall) Trail, and a visit to the monkey-rich relict forest patch in the nearby tea estate.

Trails and activities can be booked at any of the three reception centres: Kitabi, Uwinka or Gisakura (the latter lies right next to Gisakura Guesthouse). However, in most cases, the trailheads lie somewhere alongside the 50km road between Kitabi and Gisakura, which makes them difficult of access without a private vehicle. This is especially the case for chimp tracking, which usually entails a 05.30 rendezvous at Gisakura Reception Centre, then at least one hour's drive to the starting point.

PARK FEES

An entrance fee is no longer charged, but fixed fees apply to all activities, and many independent travellers find them prohibitively high. The somewhat Byzantine fee structure also comes across as the brainchild of somebody with way too much time on their hands, and a limited understanding of what a typical tourist might want to do over the course a few days' stay.

Different fees apply to five categories of adult visitor: non-residents (NR), resident foreigners (RF), residents of other East African Community countries (EACr), nationals of other East African Community countries (EACn), Rwandan citizens. Lower student/children fees are charged to foreign residents (FRc), East

ACTIVITY FEES

Activity	Days	NR ($)	RF ($)	RFc ($)	EACr ($)	EACn ($)	EACc ($)	RC (Rfr)	RCc (Rfr)
Nature walks up to 5km	1	40	30	20	35	25	15	3,000	1,5000
	2–3	60	45	30	50	40	25	4,000	2,000
	4–7	80	60	40	65	55	35	5,000	2,500
Nature walks of 5–10km	1	50	40	25	40	30	20	4,000	2,000
	2–3	70	55	40	60	55	35	5,000	2,500
	4–7	90	70	50	80	75	45	6,000	6,000
Chimp tracking	1	90	80	45	75	55	45	5,000	2,500
	2–3	110	95	60	100	80	60	7,000	3,500
	4–7	130	110	75	120	100	75	10,000	5,000
Other primate tracking	1	70	45	40	50	40	30	3,000	1,500
	2–3	90	60	50	80	55	45	4,000	2,000
	4–7	110	75	70	90	70	60	5,000	2,500
Birding walks	1	70	45	40	50	40	30	3,000	1,500
	2–3	90	60	50	80	55	45	4,000	2,000
	4–7	110	75	70	90	70	60	5,000	2,500
Canopy Walkway	1	60	50					5,000	
Congo-Nile Divide Trail	3–4	120	90	65	110	95	60	20,000	10,000

African Community residents (AECc) and Rwandans (RCc), but no such discount appears to apply to non-resident children and students.

Discounted fees are charged to those who spend more than one day in the park, provided that they keep doing the same activity (or one placed in the same category) day after day. Somewhat anomalously, for instance, a non-resident could track chimps on seven successive mornings for a total fee of US$130, or spend a full week birding with a specialist guide for US$110, yet if they had only one day in the park and divided it between a morning chimp walk and an afternoon birding session, the fees would add up to US$160.

In addition to paying activity fees, it is customary to tip your guide and trackers. The table above sums up the various activity fees.

NATURAL HISTORY

Nyungwe is a true rainforest, typically receiving in excess of 2,000mm of precipitation annually. It is also one of the oldest forests in Africa, which is one reason why it boasts such a high level of biodiversity. Scientific opinion is that Nyungwe, along with the other forests of the Albertine Rift, was largely unaffected by the drying up of lowland areas during the last ice age, and thus became a refuge for forest plants and animals which have subsequently recolonised areas such as the Congo Basin. Nyungwe's faunal and floral diversity is a function not only of its antiquity, but also of the wide variation in elevation (between 1,600m and 2,950m above sea level), since many forest plants and animals live within very specific altitudinal bands.

Most of Rwanda's forest inhabitants have a wide distribution in the DRC and/or West Africa, while a smaller proportion consists of eastern species that might as easily be observed in forested habitats in Kenya, Tanzania and in some instances Ethiopia. A significant number, however, are Albertine Rift Endemics (AREs): in other words their range is more or less confined to montane habitats associated with the Rift Valley escarpment running between Lake Albert and the north of Lake Tanganyika. The most celebrated of these regional endemics is of course the mountain gorilla, confined to the Virunga and Bwindi Mountains near the eastern Rift Valley escarpment. Other primates endemic to the Albertine Rift include several taxa of smaller primates, for instance the golden monkey and Ruwenzori colobus, while eight endemic butterflies are regarded as flagship species for the many hundreds of invertebrate taxa that occur nowhere else.

Of the remarkable tally of 37 range-restricted bird species listed as AREs, roughly half are considered to be of global conservation concern. All 37 of these species have been recorded in the DRC, and nine are endemic to that country, since their range is confined to the western escarpment forests. More than 20 AREs are resident in each of Uganda, Rwanda and Burundi, while two extend their range southward into western Tanzania.

All but two of the 29 endemics that occur on the eastern escarpment have been recorded in Rwanda's Nyungwe Forest. Inaccessible to tourists at the time of writing, the Itombwe Mountains, which rise from the Congolese shore of northern Lake Tanganyika, support the largest contiguous block of montane forest in East Africa. This range is also regarded as the most important site for montane forest birds in the region, with a checklist of 565 species including 31 AREs, three of which are known from nowhere else in the world. The most elusive of these birds is the enigmatic Congo bay owl, first collected in 1952, and yet to be seen again, though its presence is suspected in Nyungwe based on unidentified owl calls recorded in 1990 by Dowsett and Dowsett-Lemaire.

Several forest-dwelling AREs share stronger affinities with extant or extinct Asian genera than they do with any other living African species, affirming the great age of these forests, which are thought to have flourished during prehistoric climatic changes that caused temporary deforestation in lower-lying areas such as the Congo Basin. The Congo bay owl, African green broadbill and Grauer's cuckoo-shrike, for instance, might all be classed as living fossils – isolated relics of a migrant Asian stock superseded elsewhere in Africa by indigenous genera evolved from a common ancestor.

Among the mammalian AREs, the dwarf otter-shrew of the Ruwenzori is one of three highly localised African mainland species belonging to a family of aquatic insectivores that flourished some 50 million years ago and is elsewhere survived only by the related tenrecs of Madagascar. A relict horseshoe bat species restricted to the Ruwenzori and Lake Kivu is anatomically closer to extant Asian forms of horseshoe bat and to ancient migrant stock than it is to any of the 20-odd more modern and widespread African horseshoe bat species, while a shrew specimen collected only once in the Itombwe Mountains is probably the most primitive and ancient of all 150 described African species.

Vast though it may be, Nyungwe today is but a fragment of what was once an uninterrupted forest belt covering the length of the Albertine Rift. The fragmentation of this forest started some 2,000 years ago, at the dawn of the Iron Age, when the first patches were cut down to make way for agriculture – it is thought, for instance, that the isolation of Uganda's Bwindi Forest from similar habitats on the Virunga Mountains occurred as recently as 500 years ago.

It is over the past 100 years that the forests of the Albertine Rift have suffered most heavily. The Gishwati Forest in northwest Rwanda, for instance, extended over an area comparable to Nyungwe's in the 1930s, but by 1989 it had been reduced to two separate blocks comprising 280km², and it now covers little more than 6km². Nyungwe has fared well by comparison. It was first protected in 1933 as the 1,140km² Forêt Naturelle de Nyungwe, which was reduced in area by about 15% between 1958 and 1979, thanks to encroachment by local subsistence farmers, who also harvested it as a source of honey, bush meat, firewood and alluvial gold (an estimated 3,000 gold panners worked the Nyungwe watershed in the mid 1950s).

Nyungwe's extent has remained reasonably stable since 1984, when a coordinated forest protection plan was implemented under the Wildlife Conservation Society. This in turn led to the establishment of research projects by the likes of Amy Vedder (Angola colobus) and Beth Kaplin (L'Hoest's and blue monkeys), the creation of a vast network of tourist trails in the late 1980s, and the first reasonably comprehensive biodiversity survey as undertaken by Robert Dowsett and Françoise Dowsett-Lemaire in 1990. The tragic events of 1994 had little long-term effect on Nyungwe, which was formally accorded national park status in 2004.

FLORA The forest contains at least 200 tree species. The upper canopy in some areas reaches 50–60m in height, dominated by slow-growing hardwoods such as *Entandrophragma excelsum* (African mahogany), *Syzygium parvifolium* (waterberry), *Podocarpus milanjianus* (Mulanje cedar), *Newtonia buchananii* (forest newtonia) and *Albizia gummifera* (smooth-barked albizia). A much larger variety of trees makes up the mid-storey canopy, of which one of the most conspicuous is *Dichaetanthera corymbosa*, whose bright purple blooms break up the rich green textures of the forest.

Of the smaller trees, one of the most striking is the giant tree-fern *Cyathea mannania*, which grows to 5m tall, and is seen in large numbers along the ravines of the Isumo (Waterfall) Trail. Also very distinctive are the 2–3m-tall giant lobelias, more normally associated with montane moorland than forest, but common in Nyungwe, particularly along the roadside. Bamboo plants, a large type of grass, are dominant at higher altitudes in the rather inaccessible southeast of the forest, where their shoots are favoured by the rare and elusive owl-faced monkey. Nyungwe also harbours a huge variety of small flowering plants, including around 200 varieties of orchid and the wild begonia.

Within Nyungwe lie several swampy areas whose biology is quite distinct from that of the surrounding forest. The largest of these is the 13km² Kamiranzovu Marsh, sweeping views of which are offered along the main road between the campsite and the guesthouse – and which can also now be explored on the guided Kamiranzovu Marsh Trail. Formerly a favoured haunt of elephants, this open area is also rich in epiphytic orchids and harbours localised animals such as the Congo clawless otter and Grauer's rush warbler. The higher-altitude Uwasenkoko Marsh, bisected by the main road towards Huye/Butare, is dominated by the Ethiopian hagenia and protects a community of heather-like plants sharing unexpected affinities with the Nyika Plateau in distant Malawi.

You'll hear them before you see them: from somewhere deep in the forest, an excited hooting, just one voice at first, then several, rising in volume and tempo and pitch to a frenzied unified crescendo, before stopping abruptly or fading away. Jane Goodall called it the 'pant-hoot' call, a kind of bonding ritual that allows any chimpanzees within earshot of each other to identify exactly who is around at any given moment, through the individual's unique vocal stylisation. To the human listener, this eruptive crescendo is one of the most spine-chilling and exciting sounds of the rainforest, and a strong indicator that visual contact with man's closest genetic relative is imminent.

It is, in large part, our close evolutionary kinship with chimpanzees that makes these sociable black-coated apes of the forest so enduringly fascinating. Humans, chimpanzees and bonobos (also known as pygmy chimpanzees) share more than 95% of their genetic code, and the three species are far more closely related to each other than they are to any other living creature, even gorillas. Superficial differences notwithstanding, the similarities between humans and chimps are consistently striking, not only in the skeletal structure and skull, but also in relation to the nervous system, the immune system, and in many behavioural aspects – bonobos, for instance, are the only animals other than humans to copulate in the missionary position.

Unlike most other primates, chimpanzees don't live in troops; instead they form extended communities of up to 100 individuals, which roam the forest in small socially mobile subgroups that often revolve around a few close family members such as brothers or a mother and daughter. Male chimps normally spend their entire life within the community into which they were born, whereas females are likely to migrate into a neighbouring community at some point after reaching adolescence. A high-ranking male will occasionally attempt to monopolise a female in oestrus, but the more normal state of sexual affairs in chimp society is non-hierarchical promiscuity. A young female in oestrus will generally mate with any male that takes her fancy, while older females tend to form close bonds with a few specific males, sometimes allowing themselves to be monopolised by a favoured suitor for a period, but never pairing off exclusively in the long term.

Within each community, one alpha male is normally recognised – though coalitions between two males, often a dominant and a submissive sibling, have often been recorded. The role of the alpha male, not fully understood, is evidently quite benevolent – chairman of the board rather than crusty tyrant. This is probably influenced by the alpha male's relatively limited reproductive advantages over his potential rivals, most of whom he will have known for his entire life. Other males in the community are generally supportive rather than competitive towards the alpha male, except for when a rival consciously contests the alpha position, which is far from being an everyday occurrence. One male in Tanzania's Mahale Mountains maintained an alpha status within his community for more than 15 years between 1979 and 1995!

Prior to the 1960s, it was always assumed that chimps were strict vegetarians. This notion was rocked when Jane Goodall, during her pioneering chimpanzee study in Tanzania's Gombe Stream, witnessed them hunting down a red colobus monkey, something that has since been discovered to be common behaviour, particularly during the dry season when other food sources are depleted. Over subsequent years, an average of 20 kills has been recorded in Gombe annually, with red colobus being the prey on more than half of these occasions, though young bushbuck, young bushpig and even infant chimps have also been victimised and eaten. The normal modus operandi is for four or five adult chimps to slowly encircle a colobus troop, then for another chimp to act as a decoy, creating deliberate confusion in the hope that it will drive the monkeys into the trap, or cause a mother to drop her baby.

Although chimp communities appear by-and-large to be stable and peaceful entities, intensive warfare has been known to erupt once each within the habituated communities of Mahale and Gombe. In Mahale, one of the two communities originally habituated by researchers in 1967 had exterminated the other by 1982. A similar thing happened in Gombe Stream in the 1970s, when the Kasekela community as originally habituated by Goodall divided into two discrete communities. The Kasekela and breakaway Kahama community co-existed alongside each other for some years. Then in 1974, Goodall returned to Gombe Stream after a break to discover that the Kasekela males were methodically persecuting their former community mates, isolating the Kahama males one by one, and tearing into them until they were dead or terminally wounded. By 1977, the Kahama community had vanished entirely.

Chimpanzees are essentially inhabitants of the western rainforest, but their range does extend into the extreme west of Tanzania, Rwanda and Uganda, whose combined population of perhaps 7,000 individuals is assigned to the race *P. t. schweinfurthii*. The Rwandan chimp population of fewer than 1,000 individuals is now largely confined to Nyungwe National Park (including a small community in the Cyamudongo Forest), but a small population still survives in more northerly and badly degraded Gishwati Forest. Although East Africa's chimps represent less than 3% of the global population, much of what is known about wild chimpanzee society and behaviour stems from the region, in particular the ongoing research projects initiated in Tanzania's Gombe Stream and Mahale Mountain National Parks back in the 1960s.

An interesting pattern that emerged from the parallel research projects in these two reserves, situated little more than 100km apart along the shore of Lake Tanganyika, is a variety of social and behavioural differences between their chimp populations. Of the plant species common to both national parks, for instance, as many as 40% of those utilised as a food source by chimps in the one reserve are not eaten by chimps in the other. In Gombe Stream, chimps appear to regard the palmnut as something of a delicacy, but while the same plants grow profusely in Mahale, the chimps there have yet to be recorded eating them. Likewise, the 'termite-fishing' behaviour first recorded by Jane Goodall at Gombe Stream in the 1960s has a parallel in Mahale, where the chimps are often seen 'fishing' for carpenter ants in the trees. But the Mahale chimps have never been recorded fishing for termites, while the Gombe chimps are not known to fish for carpenter ants. Mahale's chimps routinely groom each other with one hand while holding their other hands together above their heads – once again, behaviour that has never been noted at Gombe. More than any structural similarity, more even than any single quirk of chimpanzee behaviour, it is such striking cultural differences – the influence of nurture over nature if you like – that bring home our close genetic kinship with chimpanzees.

7

MAMMALS The most prominent mammals in Nyungwe are primates, of which 13 species are present, including the common chimpanzee (see box on pages 160–1) and eight types of monkey (see below). In total, however, an estimated 86 different mammal species have been recorded in Nyungwe, including several rare forest inhabitants.

Of the so-called 'Big Five', elephant, buffalo and leopard were all common in pre-colonial times. Buffalo and elephant are now extinct. The last buffalo was shot in 1976. By contrast, between six and 20 elephants still lived in the forest as recently as 1990, but no spoor have been seen since November 1999, when the corpse of what was presumably Nyungwe's last elephant was found by rangers, cause of death unknown. Leopard, by contrast, are still present in small numbers, and regularly seen by local villagers, but as a tourist you'd be very lucky to encounter one.

A number of smaller predators occur in Nyungwe, including golden cat, wild cat, serval cat, side-striped jackal, three types of mongoose, Congo clawless otter, common and servaline genet, and common and palm civet. Most of these are highly secretive nocturnal creatures which are infrequently observed.

The largest antelope found in Nyungwe is the bushbuck. Three types of duiker also occur in the forest: black-fronted, yellow-backed and an endemic race of Weyns's duiker. Formerly common, all the forest's antelope species have suffered from intensive poaching as bush meat. Other large mammals include giant forest hog, bushpig, several types of squirrel (including the monkey-sized giant forest squirrel), Derby's anomalure (a large squirrel-like creature whose underarm flaps enable it to glide between trees) and the tree hyrax (a rarely seen guinea-pig-like animal whose blood-curdling nocturnal screeching is one of the characteristic sounds of the African forest).

Monkeys The primate species recorded in Nyungwe represent about 20–25% of the total number in Africa, a phenomenal figure which in East Africa is comparable only to Uganda's Kibale Forest. Furthermore, several of these primates are listed as vulnerable or endangered on the IUCN red list, and Nyungwe is almost certainly the main stronghold for at least two of them.

Disregarding the chimpanzee (see box on pages 160–1), the most celebrated of Nyungwe's primates is the **Ruwenzori colobus** *Colobus angolensis ruwenzori*, a race of the more widespread Angola colobus restricted to the Albertine Rift. The Ruwenzori colobus is a highly arboreal and acrobatic leaf-eater, easily distinguished from any other primate found in Nyungwe by its contrasting black overall colour and snow-white whiskers, shoulders and tail tip. Although all colobus monkeys are very sociable, the ones in Nyungwe are unique in so far as they typically move in troops of several hundred animals. A semi-habituated troop of 350, resident in the forest around the campsite, is thought to be the largest troop of arboreal primates anywhere in Africa – elsewhere in the world, only the Chinese golden monkey moves in groups of a comparable number.

Most of the other monkeys in Nyungwe are guenons, the collective name for the taxonomically confusing Cercopithecus genus. Most guenons are arboreal forest-dwelling omnivores, noted for their colourful coats and the male's bright red or blue genitals. The most striking of Nyungwe's guenons is **L'Hoest's monkey** *Cercopithecus l'hoesti*, a large and unusually terrestrial monkey, whose cryptic grey and red coat is offset by a bold white 'beard' which renders it unmistakable. As with the Ruwenzori colobus, L'Hoest's monkey, also known as mountain monkey, is more or less confined to the Albertine Rift, and is very scarce elsewhere in its restricted range. In Nyungwe, it is the most frequently encountered monkey, with troops of 5–15 animals often seen along the roadside, within the forest, and even in the campsite.

Likely to be encountered along the road, around the campsite, and in the grounds of Nyungwe Forest Lodge, the **silver monkey** *C. doggetti*, formerly considered to be a race of blue monkey *C. mitis*, is similar in build and general appearance to L'Hoest's monkey, but it is plainer grey in colour with a conspicuous white line along the brow, and it lacks the diagnostic white beard. The silver monkey typically lives in small family parties, though solitary males are also often encountered in Nyungwe. Some sources list the closely related golden monkey *C. kandti* for Nyungwe, but this appears to be an error – though it is not impossible that a small population of this ARE inhabits the remote bamboo forests close to the Burundi border.

These southerly bamboo forests definitely provide refuge to the rare and secretive **owl-faced monkey** *C. hamlyni*, another ARE whose modern range is restricted to a handful of montane forests. This thickset, plain grey, pug-faced monkey was first recorded in the Nshili sector of Nyungwe as recently as 1992, and it remains the least-known of the reserve's monkeys – the 1999 WCS survey was unable to locate a single individual despite searching around Nshili for three days, but locals still see them occasionally, most often when they emerge from the depths of the bamboo forest to raid crops on the surrounding fields.

Another guenon whose status within Nyungwe is uncertain is the **red-tailed monkey** *C. ascanius*, a small and highly active arboreal monkey most easily distinguished by its bright white nose. Generally associated with low-elevation forest, the red-faced monkey now faces extinction within Nyungwe owing to much of its habitat having been cleared for cultivation over recent decades. The solitary individual that hangs out with a colobus troop on the tea estate is presumably unlikely ever to find a breeding partner, though we have been told that a small but viable population of red-tailed monkeys survives on the fringes of the forest reserve near Banda.

Dent's monkey *C. denti*, formerly considered to be a race of mona monkey *C. Mona*, is widespread within Nyungwe, and occurs at all elevations. It is distinguished from other monkeys in the forest by its contrasting black back and white belly, blue-white forehead, and yellowish ear tufts. It often moves with other guenons, and is mostly likely to be seen in the forest patch in the Gisakura Tea Estate or at Karamba, along the road to Uwinka not far from the Gisakura Guesthouse. Some sources incorrectly list the **crowned monkey** *C. pogonias* for Nyungwe, but this is a West African lowland species, considered by some to be a race of mona monkey.

Unlikely to be seen within the forest proper, the **vervet monkey** *C. aethiops* is a grizzled grey guenon of savanna and open woodland, with a distinctive black face mask. Probably the most numerous monkey in the world, the vervet is occasionally encountered on the forest verge and around the Gisakura Guesthouse, where it is often quite tame and regularly raids crops.

Another savanna monkey occasionally seen along the road through Nyungwe is the **olive baboon** *Papio anubis*, a predominantly terrestrial primate which lives in large troops. After the chimpanzee, this is by far the largest and stockiest of the forest's primates, with a uniform dark olive coat and the canine snout and large teeth characteristic of all baboons. The olive baboon is very aggressive and, like the vervet monkey, it frequently raids crops.

Intermediate in size between the olive baboon and the various guenons, the **grey-cheeked mangabey** *Cercocebus albigena* is an arboreal monkey of the forest interior. Rather more spindly than any guenon, the grey-cheeked mangabey has a uniform dark-brown coat and grey-brown cape, and is renowned for its loud gobbling call. It lives in small troops, typically around ten animals, and is localised in Nyungwe because of its preference for lower altitudes.

Other primates In addition to chimpanzees and monkeys, Nyungwe harbours four types of prosimian, small nocturnal primates more closely related to the lemurs of Madagascar than to any other primates of the African mainland. These are three species of **bushbaby** or galago (a group of tiny, hyperactive wide-eyed insectivores) and the sloth-like **potto**. All are very unlikely to be encountered by tourists.

BIRDS Nyungwe is probably the single most important birdwatching destination in Rwanda, with 310 bird species recorded, of which the majority are forest specialists, This includes 27 Albertine Rift Endemics, of which three (Albertine owlet, red-collared babbler and Rockefeller's sunbird) are unrecorded elsewhere on the eastern side of the Albertine Rift. Birdwatching in Nyungwe can be rather frustrating, since the vegetation is thick and many birds tend to stick to the canopy, but almost everything you do see ranks as a good sighting.

You don't have to be an ardent birdwatcher to appreciate some of Nyungwe's birds. Most people, for instance, will do a double-take when they first spot a great blue turaco, a chicken-sized bird with garish blue, green and yellow feathers, often seen gliding between the trees along the main road. Another real gem is the paradise

CHAMELEONS

Common and widespread in Rwanda, but not easily seen unless they are actively searched for, chameleons are arguably the most intriguing of African reptiles. True chameleons of the family Chamaeleontidae are confined to the Old World, with the most important centre of speciation being the island of Madagascar, to which about half of the world's 130 described species are endemic. Another two species of chameleon occur in each of Asia and Europe, while the remainder are distributed across mainland Africa, with at least eight species recorded from Rwanda, most of which are forest species associated with Nyungwe National Park.

Chameleons are best known for their capacity to change colour, a trait that is often exaggerated in popular literature, and which is generally influenced by mood more than the colour of the background. Some chameleons are more adept at changing colour than others, the most variable being the common chameleon *Chamaeleo chamaeleon* of the Mediterranean region, with more than 100 colour and pattern variations recorded. Many African chameleons are typically green in colour but will gradually take on a browner hue when they descend from the foliage in more exposed terrain, for instance while crossing a road. Several change colour and pattern far more dramatically when they feel threatened or are confronted by a rival of the same species. Different chameleon species also vary greatly in size, with the largest being Oustalet's chameleon of Madagascar, known to reach a length of almost 80cm.

A remarkable physiological feature common to all true chameleons is their protuberant round eyes, which offer a potential 180° vision on both sides and are able to swivel around independently of each other. Only when one of them isolates a suitably juicy-looking insect will the two eyes focus in the same direction as the chameleon stalks slowly forward until it is close enough to use the other unique weapon in its armoury. This is its sticky-tipped tongue, which flycatcher, a long-tailed blue, orange and (sometimes) white bird often seen around the guesthouse. Other birds impress with their bizarre appearance – the gigantic forest hornbills, for instance, whose wailing vocalisations are almost as comical as their ungainly bills and heavy-winged flight. And, when tracking through the forest undergrowth, watch out for the red-throated alethe, a very localised bird with a distinctive blue-white eyebrow. The alethe habitually follows colobus troops to eat the insects they disturb, and based on our experience it sees humans as merely another large mammal, often perching within a few inches!

The priorities of more serious birdwatchers will depend to some extent on their experience elsewhere in Africa. It is difficult to imagine, for instance, that a first-time visitor to the continent will get as excited about a drab Chubb's cisticola as they will when they first see a paradise flycatcher or green pigeon. For somebody coming from southern Africa, at least half of what they see will be new to them, with a total of about 60 relatively widespread East African forest specials headed by the likes of great blue turaco, Ross's turaco, red-breasted sparrowhawk and white-headed wood-hoopoe.

From an East African perspective, however, it is the Albertine Rift Endemics that are the most alluring. Depending on your level of expertise, you could reasonably hope to tick off half of these over a few days in the forest. Of the 27 avian AREs found in Nyungwe National Park, the following are reasonably common: handsome francolin, Ruwenzori turaco, red-faced woodland warbler, collared

is typically about the same length as its body and remains coiled up within its mouth most of the time, to be unleashed in a sudden, blink-and-you'll-miss-it lunge to zap a selected item of prey. In addition to their unique eyes and tongues, many chameleons are adorned with an array of facial casques, flaps, horns and crests that enhance their already somewhat fearsome prehistoric appearance.

In Rwanda, you're most likely to come across a chameleon by chance when it is crossing a road, in which case it should be easy to take a closer look at it, since most chameleons move painfully slowly and deliberately. Chameleons are also often seen on night game drives, when their ghostly nocturnal colouring shows up clearly under a spotlight – as well as making it pretty clear why these strange creatures are regarded with both fear and awe in many local African cultures. More actively, you could ask your guide if they know where to find a chameleon – a few individuals will be resident in most lodge grounds.

The flap-necked chameleon *Chamaeleo delepis* is probably the most regularly observed species of savanna and woodland habitats in East Africa. Often seen crossing roads, the flap-necked chameleon is generally around 15cm long and bright green in colour with few distinctive markings, but individuals might be up to 30cm in length and will turn tan or brown under the right conditions.

Characteristic of East African montane forests, the horned chameleons form a closely allied species cluster of some taxonomic uncertainty. They are typically darker than the savanna chameleons and, significantly, the males of all taxa within this cluster are distinguished by up to three nasal horns that project forward from their face. In Rwanda, the cluster is represented by the Ruwenzori three-horned chameleon *C. Johnstoni*, a range-restricted ARE that can grow up to 30cm long and is reasonably common in Nyungwe National Park, where it supplements a diet of insects with more substantial fare such as small lizards.

apalis, mountain masked apalis, yellow-eyed black flycatcher, Ruwenzori batis, stripe-breasted tit, regal sunbird, blue-headed sunbird, purple-breasted sunbird, dusky crimsonwing and strange weaver. Also common but rather more localized, Grauer's rush warbler and red-collared mountain babbler are respectively confined to Kamiranzovu Swamp and Mount Bigugu. The nocturnal Ruwenzori nightjar and secretive creeper-loving Grauer's warbler are both common but difficult to observe. Short-tailed warbler, Shelley's crimsonwing, red-throated alethe, Kungwe apalis, Archer's robin-chat, Kivu ground thrush, dwarf honeyguide and Albertine owlet are uncommon, and Rockefeller's sunbird is very rare.

The guides at Nyungwe are improving and some are excellent, but others have only limited knowledge. For this reason, you will be highly dependent on a field guide, and without a great amount of advance research you are bound to struggle to identify every bird that you glimpse. Given the above, relict forest patches and the road verge are often more productive than the forest interior, since you'll get clearer views of what you do see.

OTHER CREATURES While monkeys and to a lesser extent birds tend to attract the most attention, Nyungwe's fauna also includes a large number of smaller animals. With only 12 species recorded, snakes are relatively poorly represented, due to the chilly climate – probably good news for most visitors – but colourful lizards are often seen on the rocks, and at least five species of chameleon occur in the forest. Nyungwe also harbours more than 100 different types of colourful butterfly, including 40 regional endemics. Look out, too, for the outsized beetles and bugs that are characteristic of all tropical forests. Equally remarkable, but only to be admired at a distance of a metre or so, are the vast columns of army ants that move across the forest trails – step on one of these columns, and you'll know all about it, as these guys can bite!

FURTHER INFORMATION A basic fact-sheet about the forest is available from the RDB tourist office in Kigali (see page 86). An excellent booklet entitled *Nyungwe National Park* is sold for around Rfr7,000 at RDB offices countrywide (including Uwinka). Two very useful websites about the park are also worth consulting. The more practical of these is USAID's www.nyungwepark.com, which has plenty of detail aimed at tourists but looked in need of some updating at the time this edition was researched. More academic in tone is www.nyungwe.org, maintained by the Antioch University of New England. Similar content can be found on the RDB website www.rwandatourism.com.

The combination of a good East African field guide and the recently published *Birds of Rwanda: An Atlas and Handbook* (see *Further reading* page 310) should be all that birdwatchers need in order to come to terms with the forest's avifauna. A more esoteric publication, of interest primarily to researchers, is the WCS Working Paper *Biodiversity Surveys of the Nyungwe Forest Reserve in Southwest Rwanda* (Plumptre, Andrew, 2002), which can be downloaded from www.nyungwepark.com.

GETTING THERE AND AWAY

Unless you have private transport, the easiest way to visit the park is as part of an organised tour or in a 4x4 with driver hired in Kigali. Either option is quite costly and we would advise a minimum of two nights, better three, to get the most from a visit. The drive takes about 4–5 hours from Kigali, 2–3 hours from Huye/Butare, and less than one hour from Rusizi/Cyangugu.

It is also possible to get to the forest using the regular minibuses that connect Huye to Rusizi, dropping off either at Uwinka or Gisakura depending on whether you plan to camp or stay at one of the lodges, However, it must be emphasised that exploring the park is difficult without private transport. Furthermore, when you decide to leave, most public transport will be full when it comes past; so depending on where you are headed, you may need to ask the people at reception to phone through to a minibus company in Huye or Rusizi to arrange for a seat to be reserved for you (at full fare).

There has long been talk that the section of the main road between Huye and Rusizi that passes through Nyungwe will be closed to non-touristic traffic – including all public transport – as and when the road between Karongi and Rusizi is surfaced, but there are no signs that such a move is imminent.

WHERE TO STAY AND EAT

LUXURY

Nyungwe Forest Lodge (24 rooms)
(South Africa) +27 (0)41 509 3000; e reservations@nyungweforestlodge.com; www. nyungweforestlodge.com; ✆ S 02°26.877, E 029°05.205. Built & managed by the Shamwari Group, one of the most respected safari operators in South Africa, this new lodge is so far ahead of the pack that few would question our rating it the top lodge or hotel in Rwanda. It has a fantastic setting within the Gisakura Tea Estate, right on the forested park boundary, where patches of relict forest support a semi-resident troop of silver monkeys along with some prodigious birdlife, & you might well also hear the thrilling pant-hoot call of chimpanzees. The large airy dining & sitting area combines clean modern lines with attractive ethnic décor & tall windows offering views across neat rows of tea bushes to the forest

gallery. Accommodation is in spacious state-of-the-art wooden chalets with king-size beds, air-con/heater, flatscreen satellite TV, bathroom with a welcome hot tub & shower, & a balcony only metres from the forest edge. The set menu lunches & dinners are mostly excellent, & service is good too (though breakfasts let the standards down slightly) & other facilities include a stunning heated infinity pool staring into the forest, a good spa, a gift boutique, & free Wi-Fi in the main building. Packed breakfasts & lunches can be arranged for those on activities in the forest. The lodge is situated about 2km from the main Rusizi road, along a dirt road signposted to the right (coming from Huye) between the junction to Gisakura Tea Estate & the Gisakura Guesthouse. *US$225/440 sgl/dbl or US$640 for a 2-bedroom suite, all rates FB*

UPMARKET

Kageno Eco-lodge (2 rooms) (US) 1 212 227 0509; e info@kageno.org; www.kageno.org. Set on the hillside above Banda village, about an hour's drive north of the main road between Huye & Rusizi, this lodge will form part of a community project that has already constructed a health

centre, pharmacy & fresh source of clean water for 5,000 people in the village (see website for more details). It was originally expected to open in 2010, but limited progress so far makes it unclear whether it will open during the lifespan of this edition.

MODERATE

Nyungwe Top View Hill Hotel (12 rooms)
m 078 7109335; e reservations@nyungwehotel. com; www.nyungwehotel.com. This welcome & well-managed new addition to Nyungwe's hostelries bridges the price & quality gap between the plush Nyungwe Forest Lodge & the budget options listed on pages 168–70. Situated about

1km from Gisakura village along a steep dirt track (4x4 required), it is set on an isolated hilltop with stunning panoramic views eastward over the forest & west to Lake Kivu. Accommodation is in stone chalets with a king-size bed, en-suite bathroom with hot combination shower/tub, large sitting room with fireplace, & a balcony with lake or forest view. The common area is a striking circular 2-storey building with a wide balcony on the 1st floor & a tall thatched roof in traditional style. The décor is a touch bare &

lets it down slightly, but that's a small quibble at the price. *US$100/150 sgl/dbl B&B, with 3-course lunches & dinners at US$15 each.*

BUDGET

🏠 **Gisakura Guesthouse** (12 rooms) m 078 8675051; e ghnyungwe@yahoo.com; www. gisakuraguesthouse.com; ✆ S 02°26.281, E 029°05.548, 1,931m. Once the only place to stay

at Nyungwe, this former government guesthouse, now privately managed, stands 2km outside the forest close to the Gisakura Tea Estate. Although it lies 18km from Uwinka, it has a convenient

THE NILE RIVER

The Nile is the world's longest river, flowing for more than 6,650km (4,130 miles) from its most remote headwaters in Burundi and Rwanda to the delta formed as it enters the Mediterranean in Egypt. Its vast drainage basin occupies more than 10% of the African mainland and includes portions of nine countries: Tanzania, Burundi, Rwanda, the DRC, Kenya, Uganda, Ethiopia, Sudan and Egypt. While passing through southern Sudan, the Nile also feeds the 5.5 million hectare Sudd or Bar-el-Jebel, the world's most expansive wetland system.

A feature of the Nile Basin is a marked decrease in precipitation as it runs further northward. In the East African lakes region and Ethiopian Highlands, mean annual rainfall figures are typically in excess of 1,000mm. Rainfall in south and central Sudan varies from 250–500mm annually, except in the Sudd (900mm), while in the deserts north of Khartoum the annual rainfall is little more than 100mm, dropping to 25mm in the south of Egypt, then increasing to around 200mm closer to the Mediterranean.

The Nile has served as the lifeblood of Egyptian agriculture for millennia, carrying not only water, but also silt, from the fertile tropics into the sandy expanses of the Sahara. Indeed, it is widely believed that the very first agricultural societies arose on the floodplain of the Egyptian Nile, and so, certainly, did the earliest and most enduring of all human civilisations. The antiquity of the name Nile, which simply means river valley, is reflected in the ancient Greek (Nelios), Semetic (Nahal) and Latin (Nilus).

Over the past 50 years, several hydroelectric dams have been built along the Nile, notably the Aswan Dam in Egypt and the Owen Falls Dam in Uganda. The Aswan Dam doesn't merely provide hydroelectric power, it also supplies water for various irrigation schemes, and protects crops downriver from destruction by heavy flooding. Built in 1963, the dam wall rises 110m above the River and is almost 4km long, producing up to 2,100 megawatts and forming the 450km-long Lake Nasser. The construction of the Aswan Dam enforced the resettlement of 90,000 Nubians, whilst the Temple of Abu Simbel, built 3,200 ago for the Pharaoh Rameses II, had to be relocated 65m higher.

The waterway plays a major role in transportation, especially in parts of the Sudan between May and November, when transportation of goods and people is not possible by road due to the floods. Like other rivers and lakes, the Nile provides a variety of fish as food. And its importance for conservation is difficult to overstate. The Sudd alone supports more than half the global populations of Nile lechwe and shoebill (more than 6,000), together with astonishing numbers of other water-associated birds – aerial surveys undertaken between 1979 and 1982 counted an estimated 1.7 million glossy ibis, 370,000 marabou stork, 350,000 open-billed stork, 175,000 cattle egret and 150,000 spur-winged goose.

location for the excellent Isumo Trail & for visits to the colobus troop on the Gisakura Tea Estate. It is also located next to the office where chimp tracking is booked (though you will need private transport to get to the starting point for the actual tracking). Vervet monkeys occasionally pass through the guesthouse grounds, & a fair variety of birds are present in the small patch of forest in front of the guesthouse. It serves good meals for Rfr5,500 & a selection of wine, beers & sodas. The one large flaw is that it seems chronically overpriced for what you get: a bone-bare guesthouse room using communal showers & toilets. However, given the lack of any comparably convenient alternative, it is the best option for travellers without private transport, assuming they can live with the price. *Rfr23,600 sgl, Rfr35,400 dbl or twin, Rfr47,200 triple, all rates B&B.*

The Nile has two major sources, often referred to as the White and Blue Nile, which flow respectively from Lake Victoria near Jinja and from Lake Tana in Ethiopia. The stretch of the White Nile that flows through southern Uganda is today known as the Victoria Nile (it was formerly called Kiira locally). From Jinja, it runs northward through the swampy Lake Kyoga, before veering west to descend into the Rift Valley over Murchison Falls and empty into Lake Albert. The Albert Nile flows from the northern tip of Lake Albert to enter the Sudan at Nimule, passing through the Sudd before it merges with the Blue Nile at the Sudanese capital of Khartoum, more than 3,000km from Lake Victoria.

The discovery of the source of the Blue Nile on Lake Tana is often accredited to the 18th-century Scots explorer James Bruce. In fact, its approximate (if not exact) location was almost certainly known to the ancients. The Old Testament mentions that the Ghion (Nile) 'compasseth the whole land of Ethiopia', evidently in reference to the arcing course followed by the river along the approximate southern boundary of Ethiopia's ancient Axumite Empire. There are, too, strong similarities in the design of the papyrus 'tankwa' used on Lake Tana to this day and the papyrus boats depicted in Ancient Egyptian paintings. Furthermore, the main river feeding Lake Tana rises at a spring known locally as Abay Minch (literally 'Nile Fountain'), a site held sacred by Ethiopian Christians, whose links with the Egyptian Coptic Church date to the 4th century ad. Bruce's claim is further undermined by the Portuguese stone bridge, built circa 1620, which crosses the Nile a few hundred metres downstream of the Blue Nile Falls and only 30km from the Lake Tana outlet.

By contrast, the source of the White Nile was for centuries one of the world's great unsolved mysteries. The Roman Emperor Nero once sent an expedition south from Khartoum to search for it, but it was forced to turn back at the edge of the Sudd. In 1862, Speke correctly identified Ripon Falls as the source of the Nile, a theory confirmed by Stanley in 1875. Only as recently as 1937, however, did the German explorer Burkhart Waldecker locate the most remote of the Nile's headwaters in Burundi: a hillside spring known as Kasumo which forms the source of the Ruvyironza River, a tributary of the 690km long Kagera, the most important river to flow into Lake Victoria. Remarkably, however, the absolute location of the most remote source of the Nile still remains up for grabs in the early 21st century – as you can see in the box *Ascend the Nile* overleaf.

Based partially on text kindly supplied by Laura Sserunjogi, of the Source of the Nile Gardens in Jinja, Uganda.

KCCEM Guesthouse (20 rooms) m 078 4152527/8501583; e kctckitabi@yahoo.com. The Kitabi College of Conservation & Environmental Management, set alongside the new Kitabi Gate on the eastern park boundary, about 45 minutes drive from Uwinka & twice as far from Gisakura, operates a reasonably priced guesthouse & canteen. There are 4 bungalows, each with 5 small but clean bedrooms & 2 shared bathrooms with toilet & hot shower, & pretty views over a valley covered in tea plantations & forest. Reservations are not usually required, but it sometimes hosts training & other events that use all of the rooms, so it is advisable to call ahead. The canteen charges Rfr2,500 for lunch or dinner & Rfr1,500 for b/fast. *Rooms Rfr7,000/10,000/14,000 sgl/dbl/twin; 5-room bungalow Rfr60,000.*

Å Uwinka Campsite m 078 8436763; ⊕ S 02°28.696, E 029°12.007, 2,442m. Set in the heart of the forest, yet only a couple of hundred metres from the main road, the campsite here has a perfect (albeit rather chilly) location on a high ridge, with individual sites scattered over a wide area of forest. It's also the most convenient base for hikes, particularly if you have no vehicle, as the trailhead for the coloured Uwinka Trails, for tracking the 350-strong troop of colobus, & for the new Canopy Walk. The campsite also offers good monkey viewing, with L'Hoest's & silver monkeys the most regular visitors, & a variety of forest birds is present. The main road adjacent to the campsite is also worth exploring, for the great views & variety of birds. Drinks are available at reasonable prices, but there is no restaurant, so pack food – as well as sufficient warm clothing to offset the chilly night temperatures at high altitude. *As for rates, are you sitting comfortably? It's US$30 pp per night for foreign non-residents, US$25 for foreign residents of other EAC countries, US$20 for foreign residents of Rwanda, or US$15 for residents of other EAC countries. These rates apply only to those who undertake at least one paid activity, otherwise it's US$50 pp per night for foreign non-residents, US$30 for foreign residents of Rwanda or other EAC countries, US$25 for residents of other EAC countries. Rwandan citizens pay Rfr5.000 either way. Discounts are offered to children, except for foreign non-residents who pay full price.*

TRAILS AND ACTIVITIES

A varied selection of walking possibilities and other excursions is available within Nyungwe. Visitors with a private vehicle, sufficient interest, and deep pockets could easily keep themselves busy for a week without significantly retracing their steps. The options for travellers without private transport are more limited, and depend greatly on which accommodation option they choose. All forest trails are steep and often very slippery, so dress accordingly. Jeans, a thick shirt and good hiking shoes are ideal outfit. A waterproof jacket will be useful too, especially during the rainy season.

Uwinka Reception Centre is the trailhead for the Canopy Walkway and several other trails, and is a good site for primate and bird watching. There are also some good walking options out of Gisakura Reception Centre (alongside Gisakura Guesthouse) while one trail runs within walking distance of the Kitabi Reception Centre. All reception centres are open 07.00–17.00 daily. Chimp tracking is best booked ahead, through either your tour operator or the RDB head office (☎ 252 580388; e reservation@ rwandatourism.com). Other activities can be arranged on the spot.

Unguided exploration of the park is forbidden, and a fee is charged for all activities (see table page 157). All activities leave at fixed times. Most leave at 09.00, but in theory there are further departures for medium-length hikes at 13.00 and for shorter hikes at 11.00, 13.00 and 15.00. Exceptions are dedicated birding excursions, which usually leave at 06.00 or 14.00 to coincide with the most productive birding hours, and the Canopy Walkway Trail, which leaves at 08.00, 10.00, 13.00 and 15.00. In practice, don't bank on doing any activities in the afternoon, as it often rains, and the guides tend to be reluctant to take activities after lunch.

The trails and activities below are covered from east to west, starting with the Ngabwe Trail near Kitabi entrance gate on the road from Huye and ending with chimpanzee tracking, which normally takes place in the Cyamudongo Forest, a western annex to the main national park.

NGABWE TRAIL (4.7km, 3 hours, moderate) Set on the slopes of Ngabwe near the park's eastern boundary, this new circular trail is the only straightforward option

ASCEND THE NILE

On 19 September 2005, three men set out to make a complete ascent of the Nile from the sea to the source.

Known as the Ascend the Nile Expedition, Neil McGrigor, Cam McLeay and Garth McIntyre took to the water in Rashid in Egypt and travelled in tiny inflatable boats ('Zap Cats'), just 4m long and with outboard engines, for the entire length of the river, over 6,700km. Their journey took them through five challenging countries: Egypt, Sudan, Uganda, Tanzania and finally Rwanda.

The expedition was self-sufficient but did receive some support from Fortnum & Mason, the famous store based in London's Piccadilly, which had previously supplied Stanley's 1875 expedition with goodies such as thick-cut marmalade, humbugs and sardines. Hampers were delivered to the team throughout their journey.

They faced enormous difficulties on the way, not least ascending the many river rapids, facing crocodiles head on and avoiding numerous pods of hippos. The weather ranged from searing heat to continuous rain, while the river changed from a wide blue delta in Egypt to a muddy puddle at its source in Rwanda.

Apprehension and frustration turned to real fear and sorrow when, in November 2005, the men came under attack from rebels in Uganda. A close friend of the team was killed and the remaining members were injured. But the team decided to continue to their goal.

On 3 March 2006 they resumed, crossing Lake Victoria and reaching the border of Tanzania and Rwanda. It was this part of the journey that offered unexpected challenges: larger-than-predicted rapids, cold nights and achingly slow progress on foot through the Nyungwe Forest as the team edged ever closer to the Nile's new source that they were so determined to find.

Finally, on 31 March 2006, they reached their goal at the headwater of the Rukarara River, a tributary of the Akagera which in turn drains into Lake Victoria. With their patient guides, the team planted a flag to mark the spot on the slopes of Mount Bigugu and the celebrations began. News of the expedition and its findings made its way across the world, reaching as far as China and Russia.

Using research and modern navigation equipment, they have been able to demonstrate that they discovered another, longer source than that pinpointed by Dr Kandt in 1898. Kandt had not had the benefit of either the maps drawn by the Belgians in 1937 or the Global Positioning System from which the team had re-measured the entire length of the Nile – which turns out to be some 107km longer than previously recorded! It's possible to walk to the source; see under *Trails and activities*, opposite.

The co-ordinates of the new longest source, deep in Rwanda's Nyungwe Forest, are: Latitude S 02°16'055.962"; Longitude E 29°19'052.470"; Elevation 2,428m/7,966ft. For more on the expedition, see www.ascendthenile.com.

7

open to people staying at the KCCEM Guesthouse without their own transport, since the trailhead lies about 200m down a side road on the left of the main road only 3km past Kitabi Entrance Gate. The trail passes through a wide variety of vegetation zones over a relatively short distance, including patches of mature forest rich in strangler figs, as well as shrubbier heath communities, and there is a spectacular camping/picnic site with a toilet and benches at the summit. L'Hoest's, silver and colobus monkeys are common here, while mangabey, chimpanzee and black-fronted duiker are seen occasionally. The trail, which can be extended to an 8-hour walk through Kitabi Tea Plantation, ends 1.2km closer to the gate than where it starts.

BIGUGU TRAIL (6.7km in either direction, 6 hours, difficult) Aimed squarely at the 'because it's there' fraternity, the steep and slippery 7km trail leads to the 2,950m Bigugu Peak, which is the highest point in Nyungwe National Park. Suitable only for reasonably fit walkers, the trail starts about 4km from Uwinka along the Huye/Butare Road (the trailhead is clearly marked). Birders come here to see the localised red-collared mountain babbler, but the area also boasts some wonderful wildflowers, ranging from red-hot pokers and orchids to giant lobelias.

BIRDING AND MANGABEY TRACKING ON THE RANGIRO ROAD The dirt road to Rangiro, which leaves the main tar road about 1km east of Uwinka, is regarded as the best excursion for dedicated birdwatchers. This is because the road passes through both high- and low-elevation forest within a relatively short distance, and affords good views into the canopy in several places. The road is also the only reliable place to see grey-cheeked mangabey, since a habituated troop lives in a forest patch 5–10km past the junction with the main road. The troop is usually monitored by researchers on Monday and Friday, the best days to visit. L'Hoest's, silver and colobus monkeys are also often seen in this area. A 4x4 vehicle is essential to explore this area, and a visit will generally be charged as a specialist birding or primate activity.

UWINKA TRAILS AND CANOPY WALK Uwinka Reception Centre forms the trailhead for the park's most extensive network of trails, as well as being the site of a worthwhile Interpretation Centre and new Canopy Walkway developed by USAID. The Uwinka Trails are a relict of the earliest attempt to develop tourism at Nyungwe in the late 1980s, and until recently each of the six routes was designated by a colour. However, a new set of names was recently adopted, and both are provided in the table opposite. The footpaths are all well maintained and clearly marked, but don't underestimate the steepness of the slopes or – after rain – the muddy conditions, which can be fairly tough going at this high altitude.

The most popular hike at Uwinka is now the short Igishigishigi Trail, site of a canopy walkway – similar to the famous one in Ghana's Kakum National Park – that opened in October 2010. Suspended between higher slopes and giant trees about 1km from Uwinka, the metallic walkway is almost 200m long, with a maximum height of around 40 metres, and it offers superb bird's-eye views into and over a steep stream bed lined with tall trees and ferns. It can feel quite unstable, especially in windy weather, and may be unsuitable to those with a poor head for heights

The slopes below Uwinka pass through the territory of a habituated troop of 300-plus colobus monkeys, and these might easily be seen on any of the trails. However, if you want to seek the colobus actively on the Uwinka Trails, you will need to pay extra for a dedicated primate visit. In addition to colobus, you can

New name	Old name	Length & grading	Meaning
Imbaraga trail	Red trail	9.8km, 6hrs, difficult	Imbaraga means strength, reflecting how difficult the trail is
Umuyove trail	Pink trail	5.5km, 3.5hrs, moderate	Umuyove is a mahogany, many large specimens of which are seen on this trail
Umugote trail	Blue trail	3.6km, 3hrs, moderate	Umugote is a Syzygium tree, which is common on this trail
Igishigishigi Trail	Green trail	2.4km, 1.5hrs, easy	Igishigishigi means a tree fern, a common plant along this trail, which also leads to the Canopy Walkway
Buhoro Trail	Grey trail	2km, 1.5hrs, easy	Buhoro means slow, and this short trail is an easy slow walk
Irebero trail	Yellow trail	3.6km, 3hrs, moderate	Irebero means a viewpoint, and there are some magnificent ones on this trail

reasonably expect to see some primates along any of the trails, as well as a good variety of forest birds, though the latter requires patience and regular stops where there are open views into the canopy. The Umugote Trail is regarded as especially good for primates and birds, while the Imbaraga Trail passes four waterfalls and also sometimes offers a seasonal opportunity to see chimpanzees.

Dedicated birdwatchers, rather than following the trails deep into the forest, are advised to explore the main road close to Uwinka, which offers some great views into the canopy and the likelihood of a greater variety of birds than from anywhere within the forest. Birding here will be charged as a birding activity rather than a standard trail, so make sure you ask for a specialist bird guide. About 500m east of Uwinka, the road offers some stunning views over the forested valleys, and passes a stand of giant lobelias.

KAMIRANZOVU MARSH TRAIL (6km, 3 hours, moderate) This botanically exciting trail leads from the forested main road downhill to the relatively low-lying Kamiranzovu Marsh, which is the park's largest wetland habitat, set within a caldera-like depression. It was the favoured haunt of Nyungwe's elephants before they became extinct, and it remains fabulously rich in orchids, particularly during the rainy season, and localised swamp-associated birds such as Grauer's rush warbler and Albertine owlet (the latter is most likely to be seen on a nocturnal visit, with a guide who has a recording of its call).

KARAMBA BIRDING TRAIL (4km, 3 hours, easy) One of the easiest walks in Nyungwe, and the best trail for birdwatching, this circular trail ascends through a relatively flat and open area to a 360° viewpoint. The absence of big trees is largely because of human disturbance, first as a gold mine and market, then as a quarry for road-building material, and most recently as an army camp. The footpath is on quartzite rock, so it's less muddy than other trails at Nyungwe, but it forms a stream after rain. About 500m into the walk, there is a large hole offering a perfect cutaway view of all rainforest strata. Plants here include white *Satyrium* orchids and giant tree ferns normally seen in moist, rainforest valleys. At the viewpoint is a bench where you can look out for birds and monkeys. Karamba area is the best part of Nyungwe for Dent's monkey, and the large troop that lives here sometimes keeps company with red-tailed monkeys.

GISAKURA TEA ESTATE Arguably the most rewarding activity in Nyungwe for those with limited time, funds and/or mobility – even if it will be charged as a primate or birding excursion – is a relict forest patch situated in the Gisakura Tea Estate only 20 minutes' walk from the Gisakura Reception Centre and Guesthouse. The forest here supports a very habituated troop of around 40–50 Ruwenzori colobus monkey, and the relatively small territory makes them easy to locate and to photograph.

The forest patch in the tea estate also seems to serve as a refuge for lone males of various other primate species, possibly individuals that were rejected by their original troop and now hang around with the colobus troop. Over the course of researching five editions of this guide we have always seen at least one and sometimes three other monkey species in the forest patch (most often red-tailed monkey but also sometimes silver, Dent's and red-tailed/Dent's hybrids).

Particularly in the early morning, the forest here is an excellent birdwatching site, since it lies in a ravine and is encircled by a road, making it easy to see deep into the canopy. Most of what you see are forest fringe or woodland species (as opposed to forest interior birds), but numerically this proved to be the most rewarding spot in Nyungwe, with some 40 species identified in an hour, notably black-throated apalis, paradise and white-tailed crested flycatcher, Chubb's cisticola, montane oriole, green pigeon, olive-green cameroptera, three types of sunbird, two greenbuls and two species of crimsonwing.

ISUMO (WATERFALL) TRAIL (10.6km, 4 hours, moderate) This superb trail starts at the Gisakura Reception Centre, making it the favoured option for people staying at the Gisakura Guesthouse without private transport (though for those with a car, the length can be reduced by driving the first 3km to the forest edge). The first part of the trail – in essence following the road to the car park – passes through rolling tea plantations dotted with relict forest patches, which are worth scanning closely for silver and other monkeys, as well as birds. The trail then descends into the forest proper, following flat contour paths through a succession of tree-fern-covered ravines, and crossing several streams, before a sharp descent to the base of a pretty but small waterfall. Monkeys are often seen along the way (the Angola colobus seems to be particularly common) and the steep slopes allow good views into the canopy. This trail can be very rewarding for true forest interior birds, with a good chance of spotting AREs such as Ruwenzori turaco and yellow-eyed black flycatcher.

CHIMP TRACKING (CYAMUDONGO/BANDA) Covering an area of about 6km², Cyamudongo is an isolated patch of montane forest situated about an hour's drive southwest of Gisakura via the Shagasha Tea Estate. Protected as an isolated annexe to Nyungwe National Park, Cyamudongo harbours a community of around 25 chimpanzees that are now the most usual goal of daily chimp-tracking excursions out of Gisakura. Chimp tracking here is altogether more hit-and-miss than gorilla tracking in the Virungas, partly because these smaller and less sedentary apes are usually found either feeding high in the trees or moving swiftly along the ground. Nevertheless, the success rate of chimp tracking at Cyamudongo is now pretty high (most visitors will at least get a glimpse) and if you find them in the right location, they can be quite relaxed viewing subjects.

At some times of year, depending on seasonal movements, trackers will not be taken to Cyamudongo but to the village of Banda, reached by a dirt road running south of Uwinka. Usually this happens when fruiting trees lure another habituated community to within a kilometre of Banda. For those without a vehicle (or when the Banda Road is impassable, as may be the case after heavy rain), it is also possible to track the chimps from Uwinka, but be prepared for a very tough hike on steep slippery slopes!

Whichever venue is used, chimp tracking is limited to one daily group of eight participants (who must be aged 16 or older). These days it is often heavily subscribed by tour groups, especially in the high season, so it is advisable to book well in advance. If you arrive without a reservation, it is still possible to go if there are places available, but you will need to arrange it the day before. For the best chance of locating chimps quickly, you need to be at the forest edge as early as possible, so trackers usually convene at around 05.30 at Gisakura Reception Centre, from where it is about one hour's drive to Cyamudongo or Banda.

CONGO-NILE DIVIDE TRAIL (42.2km, 3–4 days, difficult) Not to be confused with the Congo-Nile Trail that runs along the Lake Kivu shore (see page 204), the Congo-Nile Divide Trail is the only multi-day trek in Nyungwe. Cut in 2007, it follows the spectacular ridge that forms the continental divide between the Congo and Nile watersheds. It's a challenging but rewarding wilderness hike, and includes a visit to a sedge marsh identified as the source of the White Nile by Richard Kandt a century before *Ascend the Nile* identified a more remote source in 2006. There are stunning views most of the way, switchback ascents to several tall peaks, and the trail passes through a cross-section of the park's main habitats, including bracken fields, primary and secondary forest, bamboo forest, ericaceous shrub, marsh and open fields swathed in wildflowers. The park authorities recommend traversing from north to south, starting at a trailhead near Musarara about three hours north of Gisakura on a rough dirt road, and three overnight stops is ideal, though fit hikers could cut it back to two. The trail ends on the main road between Huye and Rusizi, 7km west of Uwinka.

SOURCE OF THE NILE It is possible to visit the newly identified Source of the Nile (see box *Ascend the Nile* on page 171) near Gisovu Tea Factory by advance arrangement with the RDB. It is an easy walk, taking 45–60 minutes in either direction from the trailhead, but the drive there from Gisakura or Kitabi takes 3–4 hours in either direction on rough dirt roads. The trailhead is more quickly reached from Karongi, a 60-minute drive following the Rusizi/Cyangugu Road southward then taking the signposted turn-off for Gisovu Tea Factory, but you will need to ring through to Uwinka to arrange for a guide to meet you there.

MUZIMU TRAIL (5.2km, 3.5 hours, moderate) This remote trail lies in the northeast of the park, and the trailhead lies two hours' drive from Gisakura. It passes through an area dominated by open heath-like vegetation and tangled scrub, and is particularly rewarding for wildflowers and non-forest birds. It is notable for offering several 360° panoramic views over the park, with Lake Kivu shimmering below, and – on a clear day – the volcanic peaks of the Virungas on the distant horizon.

8

Lake Kivu

Running along the Congolese border for 90km, the 2,370km² Lake Kivu is one of a string of 'inland seas' that submerge much of the Albertine Rift floor as it runs southward from the Sudan to Zambia. It is very a beautiful lake, hemmed in by steeply terraced escarpments containing several peaks of 2,800m or higher, including the smoking outline of volcanic Nyiragongo in the far north, and it has long served as a popular weekend getaway for residents of this otherwise landlocked country.

Kivu has a smaller surface area than the two most expansive Albertine Rift lakes, the more southerly Tanganyika and more northerly Albert. Nevertheless, a maximum depth of 480m and total water content of 333km³ places it among the world's 20 deepest and 20 most voluminous freshwater bodies. In addition, the 285km² Idjwi Island, which falls entirely within Congolese territory, is the second largest inland island in Africa and tenth largest in the world.

A shallower and larger incarnation of Kivu probably formed about two million years ago as a result of the same tectonic activity that created the Albertine Rift and other associated lakes. Back then, Kivu would have been contiguous with the lower-lying Lake Edward on the Uganda-DRC border, and it was thus part of the Nile watershed (as Lake Edward still is today). About 20,000 years ago, however, a natural dam created by lava from the Virungas isolated Lake Kivu from Lake Edward. As a result, Kivu's surface rose to its present-day altitude of 1,470m, the Rusizi River – which had formerly drained out of Lake Tanganyika into the southern tip of Kivu – reversed its flow, and the lake became part of the Congo Watershed.

Kivu supports an impoverished fauna by comparison with other large Rift Valley lakes, as a result of an unusually high level of volcanic activity. The geological record suggests that the release of methane trapped below the lake's surface has resulted in regular mass extinctions every few thousand years. As a result, fewer than 30 fish species are known from the lake and, while this does include 16 endemics, it pales by comparison with the many hundreds of species recorded from Lakes Victoria and Tanganyika. High methane levels probably also explain the complete absence of hippo and croc, and are also cited by those who claim that the lake has no Bilharzia (a claim contradicted by certain anecdotal reports from expatriates).

Kivu's attractively irregular shoreline, with its verdant slopes and sandy beaches, is served by three main resort towns. The most northerly of these, Rubavu/Gisenyi, has the best tourist facilities, partly because of its proximity to Volcanoes National Park. Karongi/Kibuye, further south and with the advantage of being far closer to Kigali, also has a few decent lakeshore hotels. At the southern end of the lake, overlooking the exit point of the Rusizi River, Rusizi/Cyangugu can easily be visited in conjunction with Nyungwe National Park and Huye/Butare, but lacks any accommodation approaching international standards. (For details of town name changes – Rubavu, Karongi, Rusizi etc – see pages 38–9.)

RUSIZI (CYANGUGU)

The most southerly of Rwanda's Lake Kivu ports, Rusizi (formerly Cyangugu, pronounced 'Shangugu') is also the most amorphous, sprawling along a 5km road through the green hills that run down to the lake shore. A district capital, it consists of discrete upper and lower towns whose combined population of 75,000 makes it the seventh-largest settlement in the country.

The upper town, Kamembe, which stands some 150m above the lakeshore at an altitude of 1,620m, is a lively business centre, and the site of the main taxi stand, market, banks and supermarkets, as well as a clutch of local guesthouses and restaurants. It has also seen plenty of new developments in recent years, in the form of recently built high-rises and other such buildings under construction, giving it the feel of a genuine small town rather than the incidental market centre it was a few years back. Nevertheless, aside from the marvellous views of the lake, and a couple of flaking colonial-era buildings, Kamembe is all energy and no character, with little to distinguish it from any other African town of comparable size.

LIMNIC ERUPTIONS

Shortly before midnight on 15 August 1984, villagers living around Cameroon's Lake Monoun recall being awoken by an explosive noise emanating from within the lake. Come dawn the next morning, 37 residents of a nearby low-lying valley lay mysteriously dead, their skin damaged and discoloured, the surrounding air overhung with the remnants of a pungent smoky cloud; bizarre circumstances that gave rise to any number of macabre and implausible theories: a vicious terrorist attack, a chemical weapon test gone horribly wrong, the malicious work of an angry lake spirit...

The truth was somewhat more prosaic, yet no less frightening. And even before scientific investigators were able to release their tentative findings, it happened again, only 100km further northwest, when an acrid cloud of gas erupted from beneath the surface of a 200m-deep crater lake called Nyos on 22 August 1986. Within the space of hours, 1,750 local villagers living in the surrounding valleys had suffocated to death, together with thousands of animals, with the furthest casualty occurring a full 27km from the lakeshore.

In March 1987, a UNESCO Conference was held at Yaounde to discuss the previously unknown phenomenon, unique to very deep lakes, which investigators called a *limnic eruption*. What seemed to have happened, in simplistic terms, is that carbon dioxide of volcanic origin seeps continuously into the lower strata of a deep lake, where its high solubility allows it to accumulate in volumes up to five times heavier than normal water, becoming increasingly volatile as it approaches saturation point – the carbonated pressure at the bottom of the lake might be three times greater than that of a sparkling wine or soda! By now, the time bomb is ticking. All it takes is a seemingly innocuous external trigger – a light landslide, a heavy storm, an otherwise inconsequential subterranean volcanic activity – to upset the lake's stratification. Then, suddenly, a cloud of noxious carbon dioxide will belch out from the lake surface, diffusing into lower-lying areas and effectively suffocating all oxygen-dependent creatures in its path until finally it dissipates.

Over the next few years, a French research team travelled around Africa trying to establish whether any other very deep lakes might be at similar risk to Monoun and Nyos. And as it turned out, the only contender for this unwanted distinction

Far more intriguing, the lower town – Rusizi/Cyangugu proper – consists of little more than one pot-hole-scored main road, yet within its abrupt confines it does have a decidedly built-up feel, suggesting it must once have been more grand and prosperous than it is today. Overhung with an aura of tropical ennui, and overlooking the Rusizi River as it flows out of the lake, this small urban enclave possesses a vaguely cinematic quality, like some semi-abandoned West African riverside trade backwater dotted with several forex bureaux and market stalls. The river, spanned by a solitary narrow bridge, not only forms the border between Rwanda and the DRC, but separates Rusizi from the much larger Congolese settlement of Bukavu, which sprawls across the hills of the lakeshore opposite.

During the genocide, what was then the prefecture of Cyangugu was the site of the second most extensive extermination of Tutsis (after Karongi/Kibuye). It is estimated that 85–90% of Tutsis here died before the French set up their 'safe zone', and many communities were wiped out completely. More recently, on 4 February 2008, the town was hard hit by an earthquake that measured 6.1 on the Richter Scale and was felt throughout the great lakes region. Several houses

is Kivu, whose lower strata, below around 260m, are infused with 60km3 of dissolved methane gas and 300 km3 of carbon dioxide, a mix potentially made doubly unstable by the high level of volcanic activity around the northern lakeshore. Indeed, it seems more than likely that the periodic faunal extinctions punctuating Kivu's fossil record can be attributed to prehistoric limnic eruptions, and experts regard another such incident as inevitable – though there is no immediate risk, since the water pressure is currently twice the gas pressure, and it might not happen for hundreds or thousands of years!

At the time of writing, the Cameroonian lakes are in the process of being 'degassed' – a procedure that involves laying a pipe to the lowest strata of the lake and pumping the pressurised water so that it shoots out from the lake surface in a spectacular 50m-high fountain to release the carbon dioxide safely into the atmosphere. Some fear that the degassing process might itself trigger another disaster, others reckon that it is simply not happening fast enough, but so far things have gone smoothly enough, and the two lakes are also being monitored by the joint Cameroonian-Japanese SATREPS IRGM Project, which runs from 2011 to 2016.

As for Kivu, experts believe that the best way to minimise the risk of future disaster is to extract the lake's practically inexhaustible reserves of methane as a source of fuel and energy for local and possibly international consumption. Prior to 2004, this took place only on a very small scale to fuel the Bralirwa Brewery near Rubavu/Gisenyi, a project that is still in operation today. However, following several trial extractions elsewhere on the lake, the Rwandan government has now committed to the large-scale extraction of methane for conversion to electricity at a new plant to be built outside Karongi/Kibuye as part of the US$325 million KivuWatt Project, which was formally awarded to the international company ContourGlobal in March 2009. This plant is still under construction, but it is expected to produce 25MW of electricity by 2012. It is hoped that eventually the lake will produce up to 700MW of electricity, leaving a large surplus for sale to neighbouring countries.

For further information about methane extraction at Lake Kivu, check out the website www.lakekivu.org.

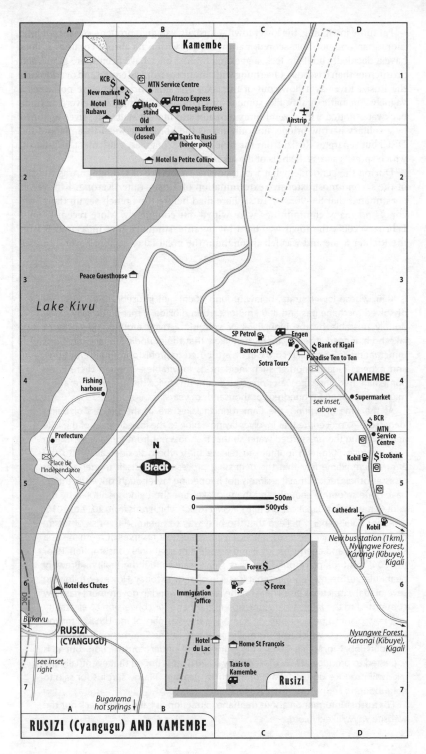

Kamembe

KCB
New market
Motel Rubavu
FINA
Moto stand
Old market (closed)
MTN Service Centre
Atraco Express
Omega Express
Taxis to Rusizi (border post)
Motel la Petite Colline

Airstrip

Lake Kivu

Peace Guesthouse

SP Petrol
Engen
Bancor SA
Sotra Tours
Bank of Kigali
Paradise Ten to Ten

KAMEMBE

see inset, above

Supermarket

Fishing harbour

BCR
MTN Service Centre
Kobil
Ecobank

Prefecture

Place de l'Indépendance

N

Bradt

0 ——— 500m
0 ——— 500yds

Cathedral
Kobil

*New bus station (1km),
Nyungwe Forest,
Karongi (Kibuye),
Kigali*

DRC

Hotel des Chutes

Bukavu

RUSIZI (CYANGUGU)

see inset, right

Forex
SP
Forex
Immigration office

Hotel du Lac
Home St François

Taxis to Kamembe

Rusizi

*Nyungwe Forest,
Karongi (Kibuye),
Kigali*

*Bugarama
hot springs ↓*

RUSIZI (Cyangugu) AND KAMEMBE

collapsed, and 30 people were killed when a church roof collapsed at Shangi, about 5km north of Kamembe.

Unless you are thinking of crossing into the DRC and Bakavu, Rusizi has to be classed as something of a dead end in travel terms. It is, however, the closest town to Nyungwe, and might therefore make an attractive alternative base for budget self-drive visitors to this national park. The lakeshore setting is lovely, too, and the atmospheric old town forms a good base from which to explore more off-the-beaten-track destinations such as the Bugarama hot springs and islands of Gihaya and Nkombo.

GETTING THERE AND AWAY

By air Rwandair Express (see advertisement on page 64) runs daily flights between Kigali and Kamembe.

By road The road from Huye/Butare to Rusizi is surfaced in its entirety but some parts west of Nyamagabe/Gikongoro are in relatively poor condition. Regular minibus-taxis connect Kigali and Huye to the main minibus stand in Kamembe [180 B1]. The fare from Kigali is around Rfr5,000 and from Huye around Rfr3,500, though this fluctuates with the current fuel price.

A steady stream of minibus-taxis run back and forth between Kamembe and the border post at Rusizi, at a cost equivalent to US$0.25 for the 5km trip. The Peace Guesthouse [180 B3] and Hotel des Chutes [180 A6] both lie within 50m of the taxi route, as does the main harbour and port.

Direct transport between Kamembe and Karongi/Kibuye is restricted to one bus daily. This costs around Rfr2,700, takes 5–6 hours, and leaves the bus park between 07.00 and 07.30 (sit on the left for the best views of the lake). Be warned that there are no minibus-taxis from the border post to Kamembe at this time in the morning.

GPS reading for Rusizi/Cyangugu (Hotel du Lac) is ✪ S 02°29.390, E 028°53.596, 1,473m and for Kamembe (Ten to Ten Hotel) ✪ S 02°28.410, E 028°54.513, 1,613m.

By boat Public lake transport may restart one day. Meanwhile, Cotralaki in Karongi/Kibuye (see page 193) has boats for hire linking Rusizi to Karongi and thence to Rubavu/Gisenyi. In Rusizi, the Hotel des Chutes [180 A6] can sometimes arrange lake transport.

 WHERE TO STAY Where the other two main lakeshore resorts in Rwanda have experienced a mushrooming of accommodation at all budgets, Rusizi still has a limited choice of mostly rather rundown hotels whose main point of interest to travellers would be as a relatively cheap base from which to visit Nyungwe Forest National Park. The Peace Guesthouse is the pick of the poor bunch in terms of quality, while the Home St François stands out as the best budget choice.

Moderate

Paradise Ten to Ten Hotel [180 C4] (28 rooms) m 078 3220806/3497202; e tentotenparadise2002@yahoo.com. Situated in the heart of Kamembe, a location that has little going for it aside from its proximity to the bus station, this modern 3-storey block is the smartest option available, despite a glaring deficit of character. The large tiled en-suite rooms, though a little frayed at the edges, come with nets, TV, fan, private balcony & hot water. Other facilities include a good restaurant, a rooftop bar, room service & a massage & sauna, & a swimming pool is planned. The echoing passages might make you vulnerable to noise from other guests, & things can get very noisy on Fri/Sat when the nightclub continues until the early hours. *Rfr30,000 ordinary dbl, Rfr35,000 dbl with a lake view, Rfr40,000 suite.*

⌂ **Peace Guesthouse** [180 B3] (20 rooms) ✆0252 537799; m 078 8522727; e info@ peaceguesthouse.org; www.will.reid.dsl.pipex. com. Overlooking the lake about 1km from Kamembe along the scenic road towards Rusizi proper, this popular guesthouse was constructed by the Anglican Church in 1998 & offers a wide selection of accommodation, ranging from en-

suite bungalows to simple rooms using common hot showers. Several Rwandan VIPs – including the president – have stayed here, & overall it's an attractive option, even though the accommodation is a touch rundown & overpriced. Adequate meals are available in the restaurant, but no alcohol is served, & there are no longer internet facilities. *It seems pricey for what it is at Rfr9000/15,000 sgl/dbl using common shower; Rfr18,000/23,00 en-suite sgl/dbl; from Rfr47,200/51,920 sgl/dbl bungalow.*

Budget

⌂ **Hotel des Chutes** [180 A6] (17 rooms) m 078 4343191. Set on a rise about 500m back from the border post, this pleasant & good-value hotel has an attractive location overlooking the lake, & the shady balcony is fun for a drink or snack. Following recent renovations, the rooms are also now among the best on offer here, with clean tiled floors, comfortable beds & crisp, fresh linen, TV, netting, hot bath, & in some instances a lake-facing private balcony. The restaurant serves good meals & snacks. You may be able to fix lake transport to Karongi/Kibuye at reception. Although all rooms have double or twin beds, on last inspection the management got itself in such a homophobic knot that it insisted accommodation is strictly single occupancy for westerners, until we specifically asked about sharing with somebody of the opposite gender, which is fine. *Rfr12,000/15,000/20,000 en-suite twin/dbl/VIP.*

⌂ **Hotel du Lac** [180 C7] (20 rooms) m 078 8305118; e hotel.dulac@yahoo.fr. Formerly the smartest option in Rusizi, this wonderfully located hotel overlooks the river immediately south of

the border post with the DRC. Unfortunately, the rooms are a bit shabby & seem poor value by comparison with other hotels in this range. The hotel's best feature is the open-air riverfront bar & restaurant, which serves excellent brochettes & grilled chicken, as well as more substantial meals, if you don't mind a wait. There's also a large swimming pool but it always seems to be empty! *Rfr12,000 en-suite with ¾ bed, cold water & fan, Rfr15,000 en-suite with dbl bed, Rfr20,000 for a VIP dbl with TV.*

⌂ **Motel La Petite Colline** [180 B2] (10 rooms) ✆0252 537824; m 078 6177725/072 6332944. Situated in Kamembe more or less opposite the market, this locally styled motel has lots of character & the semi-outdoor bar with banana-leaf roof is full of inventive decorations alongside more traditional African art. There's a nice feel about the place, & it is very close to the bus station, but the en-suite rooms with two dbl each are very gloomy, & a little basic at the asking price. *Rfr00020,000 en-suite dbl.*

Shoestring

⌂ **Home St François** [180 C7] (50 rooms) m 078 4093490. Situated directly opposite the Hotel du Lac, this homely church-run lodge is possibly the most savoury option in Rusizi despite the low price – in fact it's as good a deal as you'll find anywhere in Rwanda. The rooms are spacious,

clean & secure, some with en-suite hot shower, others with access to a common hot bath. Meals are very cheap but nothing to shout about, so you are probably better off eating at the nearby Hotel du Lac or Hotel des Chutes. *Rfr6,000 sgl using shared showers; Rfr8,000/10,000 en-suite sgl/dbl.*

✘ **WHERE TO EAT AND DRINK** The nicest place to eat, at least in terms of riverside ambience, is the **Hotel du Lac** [180 C7], which has a pleasant riverside terrace and charges Rfr3,000–5,000 for à la carte dishes, including superb barbecued whole fish, peri-peri chicken and brochettes. Also recommended is the terrace restaurant at **Hotel des Chutes** [180 A6], which has a reasonable menu in a similar price range. Up in Kamembe the restaurant at the **Paradise Ten to Ten Hotel** [180 C4] is adequate but a bit boring, while the more atmospheric **La Petite Colline** [180 B2] serves a varied selection of steaks, fish, chicken, pasta dishes and pizzas in the Rfr3,000–5,000 range. All these places are attached to hotels and open for breakfast, lunch and dinner daily. There are also plenty of small places around the market area serving adequate food.

OTHER PRACTICALITIES

Internet There are several internet cafés dotted along the main road through Kamembe.

Money The banks provide the normal **foreign exchange** services at the usual snail's pace. There are now quite a number of forex bureaux dotted around the border post and market area, offering an instant service for cash, generally at better rates than the banks – but do keep your wits about you. The Bank of Kigali [180 D4] has Western Union. So far as we could ascertain, there are no ATMs that accept foreign Visa cards.

WHAT TO SEE AND DO Rusizi forms the obvious base from which to explore the far southwest of Rwanda, a region which sees very few tourists. The southwest boasts a couple of points of interest in the form of the Bugarama hot springs and islands of Gihaya and Nkombo, though you could argue that these landmarks provide a good pretext to explore a remote corner of Rwanda as much as they rank as worthwhile goals in their own right. With access to a private vehicle, this area could be explored as a day trip out of Rusizi. Using what limited public transport exists, you're definitely in for an adventure, and should be prepared for long waits at the roadside, or a lot of walking.

Note that some old travel guides refer to the **Rusizi Falls** (Les Chutes de Rusizi) on the Rusizi River along the border with the DRC. In reality, whatever waterfall may once have existed here is now submerged beneath the waters of the Mururu Dam, which was built in 1958 about 10km south of Rusizi as a source of hydroelectric power and also serves as an obscure border crossing into the DRC.

Bugarama hot springs Situated slightly less than 60km from Rusizi by road, the Bugarama hot springs lie at the base of a limestone quarry, 5km from the Cimerwa Cement Factory, in a lightly wooded area dotted by large sinkholes. The springs bubble up into a large green pool which, as viewed from the roadward side, is initially somewhat disappointing. You can, however, follow a path around the edge of the

---

KUMBYA PENINSULA

Situated 90 minutes' drive north of Rusizi on the stunning lakeshore road to Karongi, Kumbya is a spectacular 10-hectare peninsula that has been used as a retreat by Protestant missionaries in the Great Lakes region since the 1950s. As a result, it has been saved from deforestation, and it protects around 100 bird species, as well as otters and vervet monkeys. A few years back, plans were in place to develop the site as Kumbya Eden Retreat, an eco-friendly tourist facility comprising six safari-tents and some simple family No progress seems to have been made on this project, though you might want to check their blog (kumbyaedenretreat.blogspot.com, still active but last updated in 2009) for news.

pool, past a large sinkhole to your left, then leap over the outlet stream to the base of the cliff. Here you are right next to the main springs, which bubble into the pool like a freshly shaken and opened fizzy-drink bottle, and are sizzling hot to the touch.

In a private vehicle the springs can be reached in about 90 minutes from Rusizi, but they are rather more inaccessible using public transport. The first part of the trip involves following the partially surfaced road that connects Rusizi to Ruha (a border post with Burundi) for approximately 40km to the junction town of Bugarama. You need to turn left at this junction, along a dirt road that passes through Bugarama and a series of small villages, until after 11km you reach the strip of tar outside the Cimerwa Cement Factory. Here you must turn right, passing the factory gate. After another 5km, immediately past a signpost reading Secteur Nyamaranko, you'll see a hillside quarry and three-way fork to your left. Follow the leftmost fork for about 100m, then turn right on to a small dirt track, and after 100m or so you'll see the pool in front of you. If in doubt, ask for directions to the 'Amashyuza' (aka 'Amahyuza'). From here, it would be possible to continue on the **Cyamudongo Forest** sector of Nyungwe Forest National Park.

Using public transport, one (very slow) bus and several minibus-taxes cover the Ruha road daily, leaving from Kamembe rather than Rusizi proper, and taking up to two hours to reach Bugarama town. Bugarama itself isn't much to shout about – a hot, dusty small town ringed by plantations of plantains and pines – and there is no regular public transport along the 16km road between the town and the springs. However, finding a lift on a pick-up truck – at least as far as the cement factory – shouldn't present a major problem. From there, the 5km walk is along flat terrain, and shouldn't take longer than an hour in either direction.

Gihaya and Nkombo Islands
A short boat ride away from Rusizi, this pair of islands in Lake Kivu makes for a diverting half-day outing, and forms a good excuse to get out on to the lake, without really qualifying as essential excursion. Gihaya is the smaller island, best known as the site of a derelict mansion set in large shady lawns that locals variously claim was built as a holiday home for King Baudouin II of Belgium or for President Juvenal Habyarimana. The 20km-long Nkombo Island, which was badly hit by the 2008 earthquake, offers plenty of opportunity for exploration, but the main attraction seems to be a rather impressive fruit-bat colony near a jetty at the south end of the island. *En route*, the lake is very pretty, with sweeping views to the heavily settled Congolese shore around Bukavu, and there is plenty of birdlife to be seen, notably cormorants and pelicans, as well as the unusual local boats – comprising three dugouts bound together – called *amato*.

Motorboats taking 8–10 passengers are usually available at Rusizi fishing harbour [180 A4], and local dugouts with paddlers can also be arranged; just ask around. Either way, you're looking at around Rfr20,000 for the boat hire, but the trip is far quicker with a motor: around 20 minutes each way as opposed to one hour.

KARONGI (KIBUYE)

The capital of Western Province, Karongi – known as Kibuye prior to 2006 – is also the most conventionally pretty of Rwanda's three main lake ports, a modestly sized town (population 78,000) that sprawls attractively across a series of hills interwoven with the lagoon-like arms of the lake. Karongi is now the most quickly accessible lakeside town from Kigali, to which it is linked by a good surfaced road through Muhanga/Gitarama, but it hasn't yet caught on with foreign tourists the way Rubavu/Gisenyi has. Nevertheless, it now boasts a decent selection of accommodation at all levels, and it is a popular weekend beach retreat for families living elsewhere in Rwanda. Hills planted with pines and eucalyptus give the locale a pristine, almost Alpine appearance, in contrast to the atmosphere of fading tropical languor which to some extent afflicts the other ports. It's a green, peaceful and appealing place, whose sudden views of the lake sparkling amid overhanging trees are true picture-postcard material.

THE CREATION OF LAKE KIVU   *Janice Booth*

A NEW VERSION OF AN ANCIENT TALE Long, long ago, before the beginning of what we now remember, there was nothing but a dry, grassy plain covering the area where Lake Kivu lies today. It was a hard, hot place, whose people had to work ceaselessly to scrape a living from the land. One of these people was a man whose heart was kind; he helped his older neighbours to till their ground and to gather in their crops. His wife scolded him for this, saying: 'Why do you spend so much time filling their grain-stores when our own lies empty?' But Imana had seen his good deeds and was pleased, and wanted to reward the man, so he gave him a cow whose udders yielded milk, millet, beans and peas. Imana warned the man that he must not speak of his special cow to others, lest they envy him and try to steal it, so the man milked his cow in secret and carried home the produce to his wife who began to scold him a little less.

A day came when the man was called away to work at the Mwami's court. Anxiously, he asked Imana what he should do about his cow. Imana said that his wife might be told, and might milk it in the meantime, but that she must not pass on the secret of the cow to others.

With her husband away from home, the woman invited a young man to her house. He dined off the milk and the millet and the beans and the peas, and he wondered how her poor land could produce so much. He searched all round her homestead for an extra storeroom or piece of land but he found nothing, and the cow looked just like an ordinary cow. Insistently the young man questioned the woman, using all kinds of persuasion to discover her secret, and eventually she weakened. She milked the cow in front of him and he was so amazed that he ran to the neighbours, crying: 'Here is an animal that will feed us all – we need work on the land no more!'

Imana heard this, and he frowned deeply, and that night he prepared a punishment. Before going to bed, the woman went out into her field to empty her bladder as usual, thinking to take only a few moments. But the flow was unstoppable. On and on it went, flooding her house and her fields and the land around about. Deeper and deeper it became, until the woman herself was drowned in it and even the trees were covered. Her household utensils – her wooden bowl and her woven mat and the gourd which held her grain – floated away into the distance, broke into bits and became islands. And as the morning sun rose into the sky it lit the new and shining surface of Lake Kivu as it is today.

When the man returned from working at the Mwami's court he found a lake of sweet water lapping at the edge of his fields. The land had become soft and fertile. Fish swam in the lake, and waterbirds bobbed on the wavelets. Of the cow there was no sign, but she had left behind a big heap of millet and peas and beans which he then planted, and his crop and all those after it grew richly on the irrigated land.

And Imana smiled.

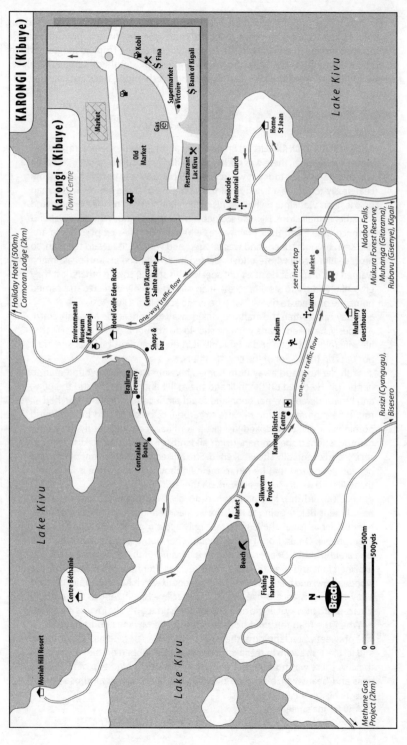

KARONGI (Kibuye)

Karongi (Kibuye)
Town Centre

Market

Old Market

Gas

Restaurant
Lac Kivu

Kobil

Fina

Supermarket
Victoire

Bank of Kigali

see inset, top

one-way traffic flow

Genocide
Memorial Church

Home
St Jean

Centre D'Accueil
Sainte Marie

Hotel Golfe Eden Rock

Environmental
Museum
of Karongi

Shops &
bar

Bralirwa
Brewery

Contralaki
Boats

Centre Béthanie

Moriah Hill Resort

*Holiday Hotel (500m),
Cormoran Lodge (2km)*

Market

Church

Mulberry
Guesthouse

Stadium

Karongi District
Centre

Silkworm
Project

Market

Beach

Fishing
harbour

one-way traffic flow

*Rusizi (Cyangugu),
Bisesero*

*Ndaba Falls,
Mukura Forest Reserve,
Muhanga (Gitarama),
Rubavu (Gisenye), Kigali*

*Methane Gas
Project (2km)*

Lake Kivu

N

Bradt

500m
500yds

It's hard to believe, amid today's sunlight and tranquillity, that the prefecture then known as Kibuye experienced the most comprehensive slaughter of Tutsis anywhere in Rwanda during the genocide. Previously there had been around 60,000 in the prefecture, an unusually high proportion of about 20%. When the French troops arrived afterwards they estimated that up to nine out of every ten had been killed. Whole communities were annihilated, leaving no witnesses to the crime. Near the sports stadium you will see just one of the mass graves, with a sign announcing: 'More than 10,000 people were inhumated here. Official ceremony was presided over by H E Pasteur Bizimungu, President of the Republic of Rwanda. April 26th 1995.' Now birds chirp on the surrounding wall and the laughter of children in the nearby primary school echoes across the enclosure. Here and throughout Rwanda, memories of the genocide remain acute but daily life carries on determinedly around them. As does tourism.

Looking ahead, Karongi is set to benefit not only from its recent elevation to provincial capital, but from two other recent government initiatives. The first is the methane extraction plant, which lies about 3km south of town (see box on pages 178–9), and started producing electricity in 2008, a move that has given the local economy a genuine shot in the arm. The second, less certain, development is the long-mooted construction of new surfaced roads south to Rusizi and north to Rubavu, the former part of a long-term plan to divert most incidental traffic away from the main road connecting Huye to Rusizi via Nyungwe National Park. A golf resort and marina is also planned a few kilometres out of town along the Kigali Road.

GETTING THERE AND AWAY

By road The main access is by an excellent road from Kigali via Muhanga/Gitarama, started by the Chinese in 1990. On some stretches it's a considerable feat of engineering, cutting through hillsides and teetering around steep valleys. The drive takes at least two hours in a private vehicle. Minibus-taxis are available from Nyabugogo bus station as well as from certain private operators in central Kigali and cost Rfr2,700 (or Rfr1,500 coming from Muhanga/Gitarama). GPS (Hotel Golf Eden Rock) is ⊕ S 02°03.559, E 029°20.893.

Travelling from elsewhere on the lakeshore, the drives are mostly on dirt roads, though this may change if the planned surfaced roads to Rusizi and Rubavu ever go ahead. For now, the trip from Rusizi or Nyungwe National Park takes up to five hours in a private vehicle (the junction of the Rusizi–Nyungwe Road and dirt road to Karongi is at ⊕ S 02°25.355, E 029°04.196) and the trip to Rubavu about three. Note that the trip to Rubavu involves following the Kigali road east for 17km as far as Rubengera (⊕ S 02°02.916, E 029°24.849), then turning left on to a clearly marked dirt road. There are two buses daily from Rubavu (around Rfr3,500). No minibus-taxis run regularly between Rusizi and Karongi, but there's one bus daily in either direction, leaving at 08.00 and taking about an hour longer than a private vehicle would.

When you arrive in Karongi by minibus-taxi, alight at the roundabout/crossroads at the entrance to the town if you want the Mulberry Guesthouse, Hotel Golf Eden Rock or the Home St Jean; continue to the final stop by the sports stadium for the Béthanie. There are sometimes some bicycle-taxis around if your bags are heavy. If you are driving, note that the main surfaced loop road around the sprawling town is one-way in an anti-clockwise direction.

By boat Public lake transport should eventually restart now that the situation with the DRC is calmer. In the meantime, a company called Cotralaki has about a dozen covered passenger boats for hire on the stretch of lakeshore near the Bralirwa depot. Carrying up to 15 people, these boats charge around Rfr120,000/200,000 one-way/return to/from Rusizi, a 5–6 hour trip, in either direction and Rfr100,000/120,000 one-way/return to/from Rubavu, which takes 2–3 hours one-way. The Hotel Centre Béthanie also has two boats for hire linking Karongi to Rusizi and Rubavu; these are a little faster than the Cotralaki boats but also significantly more costly.

WHERE TO STAY
Upmarket

Cormoran Lodge (7 rooms) m 072 8601515; e info@cormoranlodge.com; www.cormoranlodge.com. Situated on an isolated private beach about 3km out of town, this is the newest & most stylish lodge in the vicinity of Karongi, set in steeply sloping lawns that run down to the palm-lined lakeshore & jetty. Constructed mainly with wood, it offers accommodation in large en-suite rooms with king-size bed, walk-in nets, DSTV, Wi-Fi, hot water & private balcony with lake view. The restaurant is well-known for its pizzas, but it also serves a variety of meat & fish dishes in the Rfr5,000–7,000 range. Activities on offer include kayaking, waterskiing & boat trips to the isl&s. *US$135/180 sgl/dbl (non-residents) or US$75/110 (residents).*

Moriah Hill Resort (20 rooms) ☎ 568667; m 078 8512222/8307660; e info@moriah-hill.com; www.moriah-hill.com. The smartest hotel in Karongi prior to the opening of Cormoran Lodge, this remains a very pleasant option, boasting an isolated location further along the same peninsula as the Hotel Centre Béthanie. Spanning 4 storeys, the bright white main hotel building is somewhat intrusive, but it has been designed so that all rooms have large balconies with views across the lake to a nearby forested peninsula, & are perfectly positioned to catch the sunset. The rooms are large & comfortable, with dbl beds, satellite TV, fridge, seats & table, & a spacious modern bathroom with tub & shower. The restaurant, in a separate building, has plenty of indoor & outdoor seating, good service, an unusually imaginative menu, & very reasonable prices (most main courses falling in the Rfr4,000–5,000 range). There's a private swimming beach, a motorboat for hire, & kayaks available for free, as is Wi-Fi. *US$95/106 sgl/dbl B&B, US$125/134 sgl/dbl apartment, discounted by around 20% for residents.*

Moderate

Hotel Centre Béthanie (42 rooms) m 078 4957495/8413839; e bigltdbethany@hotmail.fr. This friendly Presbyterian lodge is definitely the best value in this range, with a beautiful lakeshore position on a wooded peninsula, though it seems a shame that most of that wood consists of eucalyptus, pine & other exotic trees. The brick chalet-style rooms are a bit cramped together, but very clean, & they come with hot showers, netting & a view of the lake. A decent restaurant overlooking the lake serves no alcohol but a good selection of main dishes in the Rfr4,000–5,000 range, & a selection of lighter meals & snacks for around Rfr2,000. Normally there is plenty of space but it can fill up if there's a religious gathering or seminar, so it's safer to book in advance. *Rfr15,000/21,000 twin/dbl; Rfr35,000/45,000 sgl/dbl suite exc b/fast.*

Hotel Golf Eden Rock (60 rooms) m 078 8590123/8719766; e golfedenhotel@yahoo.fr. Situated opposite the waterfront close to the post office, this large hotel has a great location, with excellent views over the lake, & pleasant en-suite rooms with a dbl bed, netting & polished floor. Ask for a room that leads on to the lower balcony. Facilities include an internet café & decent restaurant with indoor & outdoor seating. *Rfr16,000/20,000 dbl without/with lake view B&B.*

Holiday Hotel (28 rooms) m 078 3493388/8350535; e holidayhotel@yahoo.fr. Situated on the lakeshore about 1km north of the Golf Eden Rock, this hotel comprises a circular 3-storey building & a row of chalets set in uninspired gardens running down to the lakeshore. The rooms in the main building are poorly designed to accommodate a king-size bed, but they do have TV, large tiled en-suite bathroom with tub, & a small balcony. The semi-detached rooms in the chalets are also small & overall quite similar, but they seem less awkwardly laid out. Either way, it feels like poor value at *Rfr35,000 for a dbl with lake view or Rfr30,000 without.*

Budget

🏠 **Home St Jean** (26 rooms) ☎0252 568526;
m 078 4725107; e homesaintjean@yahoo.fr.
Arguably the best value option in Karongi, this
Catholic guesthouse is tucked away down a lane
to the right-hand side of the large hilltop church
that you see as you enter town. Its most attractive
feature is the tremendous hilltop views of the
lake, & access to a small swimming beach via a
steep footpath through neat gardens. A small
restaurant with DSTV serves brochettes, pizzas
& more substantial meals in the Rfr2,000–5,000
range, & it has a well stocked bar. The rooms are all
comfortable at the price, the nicest rooms being
the en-suites (with ¾ bed) in the new block facing
the lake. *Rfr8,000 twin using common shower;
Rfr10,000–15,000 en suite.*

Shoestring

🏠 **Centre d'Accueil Sainte Marie** (20 rooms)
m 078 8742303. Although it is a bit out of the
way unless you have private transport, this clean
little guesthouse run by Catholic Sisters is a pretty
good option for single travellers (no doubles are
available). *The cheapest rooms, using common
showers, cost Rfr3,500 & en-suite rooms cost
Rfr7,000–10,000 depending on size & facilities.*

🏠 **Mulberry Guesthouse** (10 rooms)
m 072 6326290/078 8410408. This is the
cheapest central option in Karongi, & seems quite
clean, pleasant & secure, set in a small green
compound close to the old market & bus station.
*Rfr4,000/5,000/6,000 en-suite sgl/dbl/twin with
cold water & net.*

🍴 **WHERE TO EAT AND DRINK** Most of the hotels listed above serve food. The pick
is undoubtedly the **Moriah Hill Resort**, which offers a good variety of mains at
affordable prices, but it isn't so convenient for people staying elsewhere (unless you
have a car). Elsewhere, the **Golf Eden Rock** serves a good selection of snacks and
meals in the Rfr3,000–5,000 range, but service is on the slow side, and nobody

seems overly concerned about serving the meal you actually order. The restaurant at the **Béthanie** is also good, with a standard menu, and a lot more efficient.

OTHER PRACTICALITIES The **post office** has international telephone and fax facilities. **Internet** facilities are limited, but there's Wi-Fi at the Moriah Hill (free if you stay or eat there) and internet access at Golf Eden Rock, as well as the more central Gas Internet. There is no forex bureau, nor any ATM where you can draw money against a Visa card.

WHAT TO SEE AND DO
Around town Karongi is such a relaxed, pleasant town that it's enjoyable just strolling and watching life unfold. There's a big **market** on Fridays, in an open area just beyond the hospital, when people come in from outlying villages and across the lake from Idjwi Island. The week-long market in the centre of town hasn't a huge range but is still worth a browse. A new development scheduled for completion in late 2012 is the **Environmental Museum of Karongi** (*www.museum.gov.rw*), which

---

BISESERO   *Janice Booth*

In the hills high above Karongi, often shrouded in mountain mist, Bisesero is a place of great sadness and great heroism. Of the estimated 800,000 or so people who lost their lives throughout the whole country during the genocide, more than 6% were slaughtered here in this one area; but the resistance they mounted against the killers – and maintained for almost three months – was the strongest and most courageous in all of Rwanda.

When the genocide began on 7 April 1994, Tutsis from the whole surrounding region converged on Bisesero for refuge, numbering around 50,000 at their height. Then the killers came, an assortment of military, trained *interahamwe* and villagers, heavily armed and equipped with vehicles. The people of Bisesero had machetes and other rudimentary weapons and managed to survive relatively well until mid-May, killing a number of their attackers and repulsing others. But it was bitterly cold in the hills and raining heavily, and they were short of food.

On 13 May the attackers returned in full force, including many militia and soldiers, and with weapons that the refugees in Bisesero could not match, although they did their best to group themselves effectively and fought fiercely hand-to-hand. The battle raged for eight hours and resumed the next day. By the end, around half of the refugees had died. The exhausted survivors had little choice but to hide in the forest and put up what sporadic resistance they could. The attacks continued relentlessly. By the time the French arrived at the end of June, only around 1,300 of the 50,000 were still alive. But – they had survived.

Set on a hillside about 30km from Karongi, Bisesero Genocide Memorial, maintained by the National Museum of Rwanda (*www.museum.gov.rw*), comprises nine small buildings, each of which represents one of the nine communes that formerly made up the province of Kibuye. Within these buildings are a chilling collection of human bones and skulls, along with other related documents. The site of the memorial is now called the 'Hill of Resistance' because of the heroic events that took place there. It's a sad, moving and evocative place, where the sense of history is very strong.

stands on the lakeshore close to the Hotel Golf Eden Rock, and will house a variety of natural and prehistoric artefacts from the region.

As the town map shows, you can do a **circular walk** along the main one-way road around Karongi. This offers some beautiful views across the lake and can be stretched to fill a couple of hours or so, depending on how often you stop to photograph, watch birds, or just enjoy the surroundings. Views are slightly better going clockwise rather than anticlockwise – with the added advantage that you'll be facing any oncoming traffic, so can take evasive action more quickly! Once you've passed the hospital on your way up to the Béthanie there's nowhere to get a drink until you're back down by the Golf Eden Rock, so you may want to carry some water.

Genocide memorial church As you enter Karongi from the east, you'll see a large church perched on a hill above the town. During the genocide, over 11,400 died there. Lindsey Hilsum caught the stark horror of it in an article in *Granta* issue 51:

> The church stands among trees on a promontory above the calm blue of Lake Kivu. The Tutsis were sheltering inside when a mob, drunk on banana beer, threw grenades through the doors and windows and then ran in to club and stab to death the people who remained alive. It took about three hours.

For some time the church remained empty and scarred. Then gradually work started – new mosaics were sketched out and then completed, and new stained glass filled the broken windows. New hangings adorned the altar. A memorial has been built outside by the relatives of those who died there and nearby. During the week it is generally empty, for anyone who wants to go to reflect peacefully on the past, but on Sundays now it is filled with worshippers and their singing wafts out across Lake Kivu. Sometimes commemorative services are held. A memorial of this kind is arguably more evocative and moving than the skulls of Nyamata or the corpses of Murambi. Here there is an echoing beauty, which is no bad accompaniment to thoughts of death. Try to find time for a few reflective minutes in this deeply memorable place.

Boat trips Apart from longer trips to Rusizi/Cyangugu and Rubavu/Gisenyi (see page 193) there are possibilities for trips on Lake Kivu and to nearby islands. The steep-sided Napoleon's Island, said to be shaped like its namesake's hat, supports quite a number of birds as well as a colony of thousands of fruit bats, which rise from the slopes like a massive chattering cloud when disturbed. By contrast, tiny Amahoro (Peace) Island is a popular chill-out spot with a restaurant, volleyball, swimming, camping (Rfr5,000 per person using your own tent or Rfr7,500 in standing tents), and a short walking trail around its rocky northern extension. The Hotel Centre Béthanie and Moriah Hill Resort (see under hotel listings on page 188) both have motorboats for hire, but it is cheaper to make arrangements at Cotralaki, near the Bralirwa Depot, which charges around Rfr20,000 per hour for groups of up to 15 people. Because the charge for motorised boats is per hour, you'll pay a lot more if the boat waits for you at one of the islands than if you are dropped and arrange to be collected later.

Chutes de Ndaba One of the largest waterfalls in Rwanda, Ndaba lies at an altitude of 2,150m about 26km from Karongi along the Muhanga/Gitarama Road (⊕ S 02°02.874, E 029°28.184). It is not easy to see, as the top of the waterfall lies just below the road, but there is a small signpost (on the right coming from Karongi) reading *Urutare Rwa Ndaba* (literally Ndaba Waterfall). In the rainy season it's an impressive 100m cascade, in the dry season a fairly unimpressive straggle. Either way, a rough footpath leads to the base of the waterfall, where you get a far better view than from along the road.

Mukura Forest Reserve This 12km² relict forest patch to the northeast of Karongi, formerly part of a continuous belt of forest connecting Nyungwe in the south to Gishwati in the south, remains one of the most extensive in Rwanda, despite having lost 50% of its area since it was gazetted in 1951. A true montane rainforest, it lies high on the Rift Valley wall, with an average altitude of 2,600m, and an annual precipitation of around 1,500mm, though much of the vegetation is badly degraded due to logging and encroachment. The most important component of the forest's fauna is its birdlife, which comprises more than 150 recorded species including 17 AREs, all of which it shares with Nyungwe. Although Mukura is not formally developed for tourism, it is accessible from the road connecting Karongi to Muhanga, heading north at Nyange on to a dirt road that leads close to the forest edge.

RUBAVU (GISENYI)

The largest port on the Rwandan shore of Lake Kivu, Rubavu (formerly Gisenyi) is an attractive resort town situated about 110km north of Karongi by road, and 60km west of the gorilla-tracking base of Musanze/Ruhengeri. It is the fifth-largest town in Rwanda, with a population estimated at 110,000, and it lies a mere 6km from the smaller lakeside village of Rubona, with its burgeoning concentration of bona fide beach resorts. This combination of good tourist facilities – arguably the best of any urban centre outside the capital – and a seductive tropical ambience make Rubavu the ideal place to chill out for a few days after tracking gorillas.

In 1907, the Duke of Mecklenburg wrote of the then Gisenyi:

> Kissenji possesses an excellent climate, for by virtue of its 1,500 metres above sea level all enervating heat is banished. The natural coolness prevalent in consequence makes a visit there a very agreeable experience. The man who has this place allotted to him for his sphere of activity draws a prize. In front are the swirling breakers of the most beautiful of all the Central African lakes, framed in by banks which fall back steeply from the rugged masses of rock; at the rear the stately summits of the eight Virunga volcanoes.

Split into an upper and a lower town, Rubavu today still has most of the attributes extolled by the Duke a century ago. This is particularly so for the lower town, which comprises a leafy and spaciously laid out conglomeration of banks, government offices, old colonial homesteads and upmarket hotels separated from the lakeshore by a neat park where children dive and swim, and courting couples walk hand-in-hand below shady trees. Indeed, with its red sandy beaches, mismatched architectural styles and shady palm-lined avenues, this part of Rubavu has the captivating ennui of a slightly down-at-heel tropical beach resort, except that the relatively high altitude means it has a more refreshing climate. How long this will last is an open question: whilst researching this edition in 2012, we noted that several of the more characterful old waterfront buildings have been knocked down, presumably to make way for larger modern developments.

Altogether more lively is the upper town, which consists of an undistinguished grid of busy roads centred around the central market but has some useful facilities for travellers, including the main bus station and several supermarkets, internet cafés, forex bureaux and banks. In clear weather, the northern skyline of the upper town is dominated by the distinctive volcanic outline of Nyiragongo, whose active crater often belches out smoke by day and glows ominously at night.

Rubavu offers little in the way of formal sightseeing, but its singular atmosphere makes it the sort of town that you could easily settle into and explore at random, whether your interest lies in the prolific birds that line the lakeshore, the fantastic old colonial buildings that dot the leafy suburban avenues, lazing around on the beach, or mixing in to the hustle and bustle of the market area. And once you have exhausted the town itself, there's always the 6km walk or minibus drive to **Rubona**, which now acts as a kind of satellite resort to Rubavu itself.

Further afield, the Congo-Nile Trail, which runs south along the lakeshore to Rusizi/Cyangugu, officially starts at Rubona, which is also the base for popular cycling trips pioneered by Rwandan Adventures (see page 198). Other day-tripping possibilities include the Imbabazi Orphanage, the Gishwati Forest, and the 'birding area' centred on Lakes Karago and Nyarakigugu on the Musanze/Ruhengeri road. More ambitiously, you could cross from Rubavu into the DRC to explore Goma and the magnificent Virunga National Park (see *Chapter 13*).

GETTING THERE AND AWAY All buses and minibus-taxis leave from the new bus station in the centre/north of the old town [195 E2]. The main port for Rubavu is at Rubona, about 6km south of town; the two are connected by regular minibuses. The GPS (Lake Kivu Serena Hotel) is ✪ S 01°42.077, E 029°15.605.

To/from Kigali and Musanze/Ruhengeri
Rubavu lies approximately 60km from Musanze by road, and 160km from Kigali. The road is sealed and mostly in good condition, though there are some pot-holed stretches. The direct drive from Kigali should take no longer than three hours. Regular minibus-taxis connect the three towns; the fare from Rubavu to Musanze is Rfr1,100 and to Kigali Rfr3,000. The most reliable service is Virunga Express (m *(Kigali) 078 8431960, (Musanze) 078 8510873, (Rubavu) 078 8597788); www.virungatravel.com/express.php*), which departs every 15 minutes between 06.00 and 17.00.

To/from Karongi/Kibuye and Rusizi/Cyangugu
To drive from Rubavu to Karongi, you first need to head out along the Musanze road for about 5km to Pfunda, before turning right at a poorly signposted junction on to the dirt road that leads to Rubengera on the surfaced road between Kigali and Karongi. It's a drive of about 110km in all, and the dirt stretch is in variable condition, so three to four hours should be allowed. Although the dirt road runs parallel to Lake Kivu, it offers disappointingly few glimpses of the lake, though this is compensated for by some spectacular mountain scenery and relic patches of Gishwati Forest (see pages 203–8). From Karongi, it's another 100km to Rusizi, a three-to-four-hour drive, mostly along dirt roads. It is rumoured that these lakeshore roads will be surfaced during the lifespan of this edition, which would cut the driving time in half.

Public transport between Rubavu and Karongi is relatively frequent; a few buses cover the route daily (Rfr2,000). At present they leave Rubavu at 06.00 and 14.00, but this could alter. Change vehicles at Karongi if you are heading on to Rusizi.

Boat transport on Lake Kivu lapsed while relations with the DRC were volatile, and there is no scheduled public transport between the lake ports, but Cotralaki in Karongi has boats for hire (see page 191). Another option, bookable through the RDB tourist office (195 F6, see page 198), is the Umunezero Boat, which charges

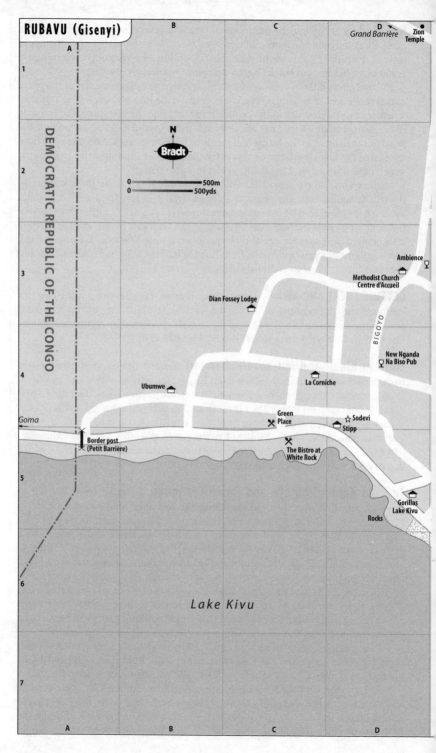

RUBAVU (Gisenyi)

A **B** **C** **D**

Grand Barrière

Zion Temple

N

Bradt

0 ——— 500m
0 ——— 500yds

DEMOCRATIC REPUBLIC OF THE CONGO

Ambience

Methodist Church
Centre d'Accueil

Dian Fossey Lodge

BIGOYO

New Nganda
Na Biso Pub

Ubumwe

La Corniche

Goma

Green
Place

Sodevi

Border post
(Petit Barrière)

Stipp

The Bistro at
White Rock

Gorillas
Lake Kivu

Rocks

Lake Kivu

A **B** **C** **D**

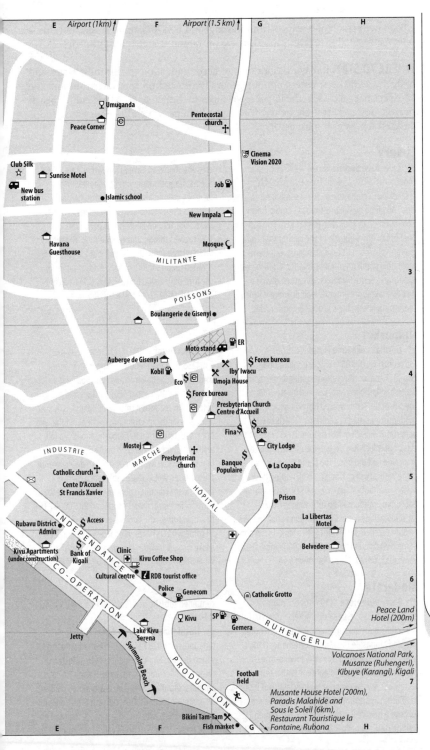

US$40 per person one-way to/from Karongi and US$70/from to Rusizi, but this is only really suitable to large groups, as the minimum charge is for five people.

WHERE TO STAY Rubavu has a range of accommodation to suit most tastes and budgets, with the smartest options generally situated on the waterfront and the cheaper ones set back in the upper town closer to the bus station. For genuine beach resorts, however, you are better heading to Rubona, which lies 6km away, and is covered separately on pages 199–202.

Luxury

🏠 Lake Kivu Serena Hotel [195 F6] (66 rooms) \0252 541111; m 078 8200430; e lakekivu@serena.co.rw; www.serenahotels. com. Acquired by the prestigious Kenyan-based Serena Group in 2007, the former Kivu Sun is the only urban hotel outside of the capital that truly conforms to international standards, & it forms a justifiably popular w/end retreat for Kigali-based expatriates & NGO workers. The green & well-wooded lakeshore grounds lead down to a sandy swimming beach; the spacious & comfortable en-suite rooms all have AC, mini-bar, safe, DSTV & en-suite bathroom with tub/shower. Other facilities include a sparkling swimming pool, a fitness centre with sauna & massage, a gift shop, well-trained English-speaking staff, free Wi-Fi access throughout the building, & a highly rated restaurant with indoor & outdoor tables & a varied menu serving grills, curries & salads in the Rfr4,000–6,000 bracket. Visa & MasterCard accepted. *US$172/232/358 sgl/dbl/suite B&B.*

Upmarket

🏠 Gorillas Lake Kivu Hotel [195 D5] (35 rooms) m 078 8531880; e gorillashotel@ rwanda1.com or reservation@gorillashotels.com; www.gorillashotels.com. Opened in late 2008 on the site of the sorely missed Hotel Regina, this modernistic upmarket addition to the Rubavu waterfront doesn't match the Serena in terms of class, but it feels like a reliable & efficient choice at around half the price. The bland but neat rooms come with a twin or king-size bed, writing desk, built-in wardrobes, flat-screen DSTV, & a small bathroom with combined tub/shower. Other facilities include a massive swimming pool, free Wi-Fi, & an excellent restaurant with a varied selection of main courses in the Rfr4,000–6,000 range. Decent value. *US$90/110/120 sgl/dbl/twin B&B.*

🏠 Stipp Hotel [194 D4] (26 rooms) m 078 8304335/6; e management@stipphotelrwanda. com; www.stipphotelrwanda.com Boasting a suburban location about 1km northwest of the Serena, this renovated colonial building lies in attractive landscaped grounds overlooking the lake, but is separated from the shore by a road & a tall wall. It is of similar standard to the Gorillas Hotel, but a lot smaller, with smart modern décor, a more personalised feel, & reasonable rates. There is a large, clean swimming pool, the restaurant serves a varied selection of meals for around Rfr5,000–7,000 per main course, the large carpeted en-suite rooms all come with DSTV, internet access & (in most cases) a lake view, & facilities include a gym, sauna & free Wi-Fi. *Rfr50,000/55,000/60,000 sgl/dbl/suite.*

Moderate

🏠 Belvedere Hote [195 H6] (22 rooms) m 078 8506555; e belvederehotel@yahoo.fr. This is a solidly built but unremarkable modern hotel situated alongside the Musanze/Ruhengeri road a few hundred metres from the town centre. It has pleasant landscaped gardens with a terrace restaurant & view over the town & lake, but it's not as alluring as staying on the lakeshore. The rooms all have a queen-size bed, netting, flat-screen TV, writing desk, free Wi-Fi & en-suite bathroom with combined tub/shower. *Rfr40,000/45,000/50,000 B&B sgl/dbl/suite.*

🏠 Hotel Dian Fossey Lodge [194 C3] (20 rooms) m 078 8517591; e hoteldianfossey@ yahoo.fr. This suburban lodge, set in a cluttered compound decorated with large Disney-on-acid animal sculptures, would be few people's choice on aesthetic grounds. Otherwise, it is an agreeable enough set-up, with friendly staff, & the tiled en-suite rooms represent good value for money in this range. *Rfr17,000 sgl with ¾ bed & net; Rfr25,000 dbl with queen-size bed, TV, tub & ample cupboard space; Rfr30,000 suite with king-size bed, sofa, TV & fridge.*

🏠 **Mostej Hotel** [195 F5] (20 rooms) ✆0252 540486; m 078 8350366; e mostej.hotel@yahoo. fr. Boasting an indifferent location alongside the main dirt road connecting the market area to the lakeshore, this solidly built & modern-looking hotel feels rather bland, functional & overpriced. All rooms are en-suite with hot shower & DSTV, but the cheaper rooms are quite cramped & have a ¾ bed, whereas more expensive rooms have a king-size bed, small balcony & large bathroom. *Rfr25,000/35,000 small sgl/dbl; Rfr30,000/40,000 large sgl/dbl; all rates B&B.*

Budget

🏠 **Centre d'Accueil St Francis Xavier** [195 E5] (20 rooms) m 072 8488576/078 448 8576. Situated on a back road between the town centre & waterfront, this new church-run hostel has clean twin rooms, each with two ¾ beds & en-suite hot shower. No food is available but it is close to several eateries. *Fair value at Rfr10,000/15,000 sgl/dbl occupancy.*

🏠 **La Corniche** [194 C4] (4 rooms) m 078 8322234. Set alongside a pleasant garden bar & restaurant a short walk north of the lakeshore, this is an adequate & homely lodge. Most rooms have 1 sgl & 1 dbl bed, & an en-suite hot bath or shower.

Shoestring

🏠 **Auberge de Gisenyi** [195 F4] m 078 8703456. Situated close to the market, this is a standard local guesthouse & bar/restaurant with small en-suite rooms (cold water, hot buckets by request). *Rfr7,000/8,000 sgl/dbl.*

🏠 **Methodist Church Centre d'Accueil** [194 D3] (8 rooms) m 078 8864161. Set in pleasant grounds to the north of the town centre, this good-value & friendly lodge used to be rather isolated but that has changed with the relocation of the bus station to just around the corner. The clean rooms come with a washbasin & shared hot shower/toilet, & there are also 3-bed dorms. Meals are prepared by request & there's a (very distant)

🏠 **Peace Land Hotel** [195 H6] (30 rooms) m 078 8511760/8346118; e peacelandhotel07@ yahoo.com; www.peacelandhotel07.com. This multi-storey hotel, set in the hills above Rubavu about 500m along the Musanze/Ruhengeri road, offers great views over the town & lake, especially from the rooftop restaurant/bar, but feels a bit remote from both. 5 types of tiled en-suite room are available, from ordinary sgls with ¾ bed & combined tub/shower to spacious VIP rooms with king-size bed, netting, TV, sitting area & balcony. The rooms are reasonable value, but most are accessed via a maze of tiled staircases & corridors that could be a nightmare to manoeuvre in rainy weather. A new block of suites was under construction in 2012. *From Rfr15,000/30,000/35,000 sgl/twin/dbl; all B&B.*

Some rooms are nicer than others so look before you commit. *Rfr15,000–30,000 dbl.*

🏠 **Sunrise Motel** [195 E2] (12 rooms) ✆0252 540779; m 078 8461676. Located right alongside the new bus station, this pleasant newish hotel has small but clean rooms with carpet, writing desk & en-suite hot shower & tub. It's one of the better deals in this range, but best avoided on Fri & Sat nights, when the adjoining Club Silk nightclub parties until the wee hours (the club is soundproofed but there's bound to be a lot of noise in the parking area). *Rfr15,000/17,000/20,000 sgl/ dbl/twin B&B.*

view of the lake. The downhill walk to the beach takes 10mins. *Rfr5,000/8,000 sgl/dbl; Rfr2,000 dorm bed.*

🏠 **Presbyterian Church Centre d'Accueil** [195 G4] (13 rooms) ✆0252 540397; m 078 5730113; e bigltd@hotmail.fr. This agreeable church-run lodge near the market has long been one of the best deals in this range, despite its distance (about a 10min walk) from the lake, with bright & fresh rooms set in spaciously laid-out grounds that also contain a basic but good-value restaurant. *Rfr8,000 en-suite dbl or twin with nets & hot water; Rfr12,000 trpl; Rfr2,000/3,000 for a bed in a 6-/8-berth dorm.*

✗ **WHERE TO EAT AND DRINK** Most of the smarter hotels have adequate to good restaurants. For top-notch continental cuisine, the new **Gorillas Lake Kivu Hotel** [194 D5] should be your first port of call, but it lacks the outdoor ambience of the almost-as-good **Lake Kivu Serena** [195 F6]. You can also eat well in the pretty gardens of the **Stipp Hotel** [194 D4]. There are plenty of budget eateries around the market area, of which the **Auberge de Gisenyi** [195 F4] is recommended. For dedicated clubbers, the **Sodevi Nightclub** [194 D4], set in a pretty garden bar, and **Club Silk** [195 E2] next to the Sunrise Motel are both active on Friday and Saturday nights.

✕ **Bar-Restaurant Bikini Tam-Tam** [195 G7] Situated alongside the Rubona Rd, this is a great spot for sundowners – indeed for a drink at any time of day – & the perfect lakefront position is only slightly undermined by the aromatic fish market next door. A limited selection of snacks & grills is available too.

✕ **Green Place** [194 C4] ◷ 12.00–23.00 daily. Situated opposite the White Rock, this agreeable palm-shaded garden bar serves inexpensive drinks & a limited selection of snacks, including brochettes & grilled chicken. The daytime vocal accompaniment of the garden's plentiful birdlife is replaced by the gentle sound of lapping water by night.

✕ **Kivu Coffee Shop** [195 F6] ◷ 08.00–18.00 daily. Situated next to the RDB tourist office, this small café serves excellent filter coffee for Rfr1,000, as well as a selection of inexpensive light meals & snacks.

✕ **La Corniche** [194 C4] m 078 8322234. Set in a pretty suburban garden, this place is notable for its expansive lunchtime buffets, which are great value for the hungry at Rfr2,800–3,500. It functions mainly as a garden bar in the evenings, but a limited selection of affordable snacks is available.

✕ **The Bistro at White Rock** [194 C5] m 078 3146082; ◷ 08.00–22.00 daily, with a downstairs nightclub on Wed & Sat only. This is the most attractive place to eat in Rubavu, centred on a large covered deck right above the lakeshore, but with indoor seating too, & a pool table & nightclub downstairs. The menu, though not extensive, includes snacks for around Rfr2,500, pizzas for Rfr4,000, a variety of full fish, meat & vegetarian meals at around Rfr3,500–6,000, & a tempting choice of desserts for Rfr2,000–3,500. The bar is well stocked but disproportionately pricey, so you may want to start or finish with a cheaper drink at the nearby Green Place.

OTHER PRACTICALITIES

Tourist information & gorilla tracking permits The Rwanda Development Board (RDB) tourist information and booking office [195 F6] (m *0252 540047;* ◷ *07.00–17.00 Mon–Fri, 07.00–14.00 Sat & Sun*) at the southeast end of Avenue de l'Indépendance, perhaps 200m from the entrance to the Serena Lake Kivu Hotel. This is the only place in Rwanda outside of Kigali and Kinigi where gorilla tracking permits can be booked; payments can be made in cash or by Visa card. The office can also supply information about travel elsewhere in the country, and stocks a variety of books, maps and handouts. It is also the place to book and make guide arrangements for the Congo-Nile Trail (unless you are cycling it with Rwandan Adventures, see below), and to arrange guides for other local attractions.

Tour operators

Green Hill Eco-Tours m 078 8219495; e rwandacongotours@gmail.com; www. greenhillsecotours.com. This new operator has been recommended for organised cross-border visits to Goma & Virunga National Park in the DRC, & also offers day excursions out of Rubavu to Batwa communities, Dancing Pots & other local attractions.

Rwandan Adventures m 072 2371414 or 078 6571414/5645478; e info@rwandan-adventures. com; www.rwandan-adventures.com. This dynamic, flexible & responsive new company is

operated by a British cycling enthusiast resident in Rubona. Its speciality is cycling tours that follow the Congo Nile Trail (see box, pages 206–7) in art or in full, & range from half a day to a week in duration. These can be either self-guided (US$30 pp/day for helmet & bicycle, including an emergency tool kit & essential spare parts), or guided (from US$50pp/day), with optional bicycle porter (US$30/day) in both cases. It also offers guided bicycle tours of Rubavu town, as well as walking tours to the likes of Gishwati Forest & the Kinunu Coffee Estate – see its website for an ever-expanding full list of activities. And if you have any other specialist interest in the Rubavu area, from birding or botany to hiking or caving, this would be an excellent first contact.

Foreign exchange Most of the banks marked on the map will change US dollars cash, but you'll get better rates and more efficient service at any of several forex bureaux dotted around the market area [195 F/G4]. The Bank of Kigali [195 E6] also has Western Union. The central EcoBank has an ATM where cash can be drawn with an international Visa card.

Internet Facilities are widespread: several cyber cafés can be found in the market area, and the one directly above the EcoBank [195 F4] has fast and inexpensive access. The Serena [195 F6] and Gorillas hotels [194 D5] both have Wi-Fi, which you should be allowed to use for the price of a meal or drink.

Shopping The **Boulangerie de Gisenyi** [195 F3] opposite the market is a very well stocked supermarket with a good bakery. For **handicrafts**, the shop run by the COPROVERA cooperative on the main road running south from the market is worth a look. There is also a good craft shop sandwiched between the RDB office and Kivu Coffee Shop.

AROUND RUBAVU

Rubona Set on an attractive bay 6km from Rubavu, the bustling little satellite town of Rubona is the main harbour on the northern lakeshore and the site of the Brasseries et Limonaderies du Rwanda (Bralirwa), the country's largest brewery. It has emerged in recent years as an important and very likeable tourist focus, the well established Paradis Malahide having been joined by three other mid-priced lakeside resorts since the last edition of this book was published – making it an attractive retreat both for Kigali residents and for travellers seeking a restful few days by the lake.

Although it is mainly of interest for its beaches, Rubona is fun to stroll around. At times – usually in the early morning or late evening – hundreds of small fishing canoes dot the harbour, some boasting a distinctive catamaran-style design comprising three separate dugouts held together by poles. The fish in this bay have an unusual diet, as dregs from the brewing process at Bralirwa Brewery are thrown into the water regularly, but the fishermen mostly ply their trade further afield, and at night their lanterns can sometimes be seen distantly bobbing on the open water. Most of the lakeshore resorts have boats you can use to explore the lake, but it is also easy enough to arrange an outing in a local dugout.

About halfway along this road, near the village of Gitsamba, a signposted dirt road leads uphill for about 1km to the **Rubona Hill Scenic Viewpoint** (easily located by its twin satellite towers), which offers wonderful views over the lake to central Rubavu and the Congolese city of Goma, with Nyiragongo and some of the other Virungas providing a compelling backdrop.

Getting there and away Rubona is connected to Rubavu by two surfaced roads, but unfortunately the more appealing of these, following the lakeshore in its entirely, is closed to the public due to the presence of an important military installation. The main road between the two towns runs inland, following a scenic route that would make for a pleasant stroll in one or other direction. Regular minibus-taxis run along the Rubavu-Rubona road, charging Rfr300 one-way in either direction. A moto costs around Rfr1,000.

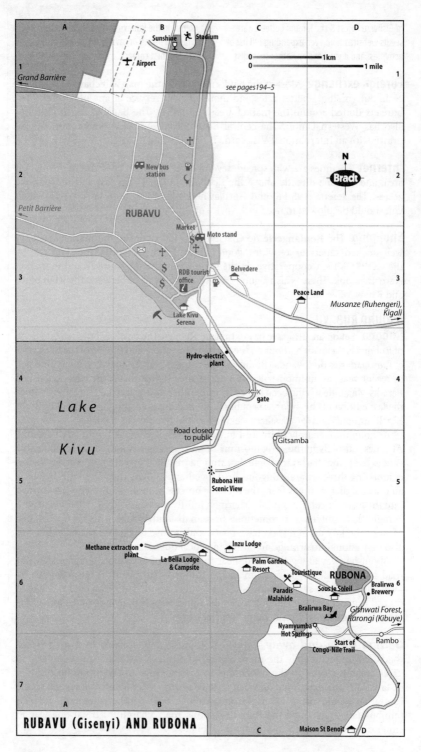

see pages 194–5

RUBAVU (Gisenyi) AND RUBONA

Where to stay There is now a good choice of midrange beach resorts in Rubona, but genuine budget accommodation is thin on the ground, and travellers seeking a cheap lakeside room are advised instead to head for the Maison St Benoît, which lies in Kigufi about 3km from Rubona traffic circle (see page 202).

Moderate

Inzu Lodge [200 C6] 072 5250101/078 4179203; e info@inzulodge.com; www.inzulodge. com. About halfway between Palm Garden & La Bella, but on the opposite side of the road to the lake, this scenic new lodge already functions as a restaurant serving brochettes, fish & traditional Rwandan fare, ranging in price from Rfr1,500 to Rfr6,000. By 2013, it should be offering accommodation in traditional huts (modelled on the royal dwelling at the Nyanza Museum), with furnishing made from natural materials, in the Rfr45,000–55,000 range. For the time being, camping costs Rfr10,000 pp, & includes access to a shower.

La Bella Lodge & Campsite [200 B6] (5 rooms) m 078 3373400/8510714; e labella@ labellalodge.com; www.labellalodge.com. This relaxed owner-managed resort has a secluded lakeshore setting 2km from the main traffic circle in Rubona, close to the junction for the methane extraction plant. The shady well-tended tropical gardens, dotted with lounger beds & thatched gazebos, are a delight. The restaurant is one of the best around, serving a varied selection of Rwandan & continental dishes for Rfr4,000–5,000. Comfortable en-suite rooms, set away from the public areas, have a king-size bed, en-suite hot tub, writing desk & private balcony facing the lake. It's a good spot for swimming & sunbathing, & there are plans to start operating night fishing trips with local fishermen, as well as to open a second lodge close to the Rubona Hill Scenic Viewpoint. *Rfr48,000 dbl B&B; Rfr12,000pp camping.*

Palm Garden Resort [200 C6] (12 rooms) m 078 8306830; e info@mercatorassistance. rw; www.yvke-beach-resort.com. Situated about 1.7km along the road from Rubona traffic circle

to La Bella Lodge, this attractive beach resort lies in pretty palm-shaded gardens that run down to a swimming beach. Facilities include internet, boats & bicycles for hire, & a chilled open-sided restaurant serving decent snacks & meals in the Rfr3,000–5,000 range. The standard rooms have a dbl bed with net & en-suite hot shower, but they are let down a little by the tacky décor & seem poor value compared with similarly priced options elsewhere in Rubona. By contrast, the pricier & larger bungalows – with a funky ethnic feel to the décor & great outdoor shower & toilet – are among the best rooms on offer in the Rubavu/Gisenyi area. *Rfr45,000 B&B dbl room; Rfr60,000 dbl bungalow.*

Paradis Malahide [200 C6] (10 rooms) m 078 8648650/8756204; e parmalahide@ yahoo.fr; www.paradisemalahide.com. Situated in Rubona, only 800m from the traffic circle, this long-serving & perennially popular beach resort has a rustically beautiful lakeshore setting, complete with secluded swimming beach. Accommodation is either in rooms with dbl beds, nets & en-suite hot shower, or in circular stone-&-thatch cottages with similar facilities. A terrace restaurant serves adequate meals in the Rfr4,000–5,000 range as well as cheaper snacks such as omelettes & brochettes, & there's a well stocked bar. The lodge is ideally sited to enjoy sunsets over the lake while kamikaze pied kingfishers dive into the water & local fishermen cruise past. Facilities include free canoeing & Wi-Fi, & there is also a motorboat for hire, if you want to explore the lakeshore or visit nearby Akeza Island to catch the sunset or enjoy candlelit dinners or a family picnic. Traditional dances are held here 2–3 nights per week. *Rfr45,000 dbl B&B. Camping Rfr15,000 per tent.*

Shoestring

Sous le Soleil [200 D6] (4 rooms) m 078 8490254. Situated in Rubona, between the brewery & Paradis Malahide, this has a nice

lakeshore location & the basic rooms with ¾ beds are about as cheap as it gets in this part of Rwanda. *Rfr5,000.*

 Where to eat All the hotels listed above serve good meals for up to Rfr5,000. The restaurant at the Palm Garden Resort probably wins out on ambience, but La

Lake Kivu RUBAVU (GISENYI)

8

Bella Lodge serves the most consistently good food, and if you don't fancy eating indoors, there are several gazebos in the lakeshore gardens. There is also one decent standalone restaurant in Rubona:

✖ Restaurant Touristique [200 C6] m 078 8689733; ☉ lunch & dinner daily. Set in attractive landscaped lakeshore gardens a few gates up from the Paradis Malahide, this pleasant al fresco restaurant, also known as Chez Maman Chakula, serves continental-style meat, rabbit & fish dishes in the Rfr4,000–7,000 range. It also offers a range of cheaper snacks & local dishes, & a bar.

Nyamyumba Hot Springs and Kigufi

A worthwhile short walk out of Rubona follows the lakeshore south via the Nyamyumba Hot Springs to the Kigufi Peninsula, site of the church-run Maison St Benoît, a lovely spot for a pot of tea or a chilled beer in secluded bird-rich gardens running down to the lake. The walk starts at the main traffic circle in Rubona (where the inland and lakeshore roads from Rubavu connect) and follows the third road running south past the prominent Bralirwa Brewery to your left. From here, it is perhaps 40 minutes in either direction to Kigufi, but you probably need to add 20 minutes or so for the diversion to the springs, and another 20–30 minutes for an uphill diversion through the village of Rambo.

Perhaps 500m past the brewery, you'll see the signposted motorable track that runs downhill for a few hundred metres to the Nyamyumba Hot Springs (✆ S 01°44.391, E 029°16.441), whose shallow searing waters run into the lake creating a bathing beach with the temperature of a sauna. Bathing in the hot water allegedly has a curative effect, relieving fatigue, curing skin rashes and mending simple fractures. More prosaically, in some places the springs are hot enough – and are used by the villagers – to boil potatoes and cassava. That aside, the springs are not much to look at, and visitors are likely to be mobbed by friendly children who come there to play and swim.

Less than 100m past the turn-off to the springs, you hit a junction where a signpost proclaims the official start of the Congo-Nile Trail. Here, the road to the left climbs through the village of Rambo to the main road connecting Pfundi to Karongi/Kibuye via the Gishwati Forest. If you feel like following this steep road for a short way, you'll be rewarded by some great views to the receding lake over the first kilometre or so. To head to Kigufi, however, you need to carry straight on at this junction, along the older and rougher lakeside road to Karongi/Kibuye, which brings you to La Maison St Benoît after 2km.

Where to stay

⌂ La Maison St Benoît (12 rooms) m 078 8409867/8504216; ✆ S 01°44.917, E 029°16.677. This little-known gem, run by friendly Catholic nuns, was originally constructed as the residence of Bishop of Rwanda in 1947, & was later home of the country's first African bishop Aloysius Bigirumwami, appointed in 1959. Today it is one of the best-value & most attractive places to stay in the Rubavu area, set in paradisiacal green lakeshore grounds that support plenty of colourful birds & also offer good swimming. Three kinds of en-suite room are available, all very clean with dbl bed & hot showers. It also serves b/fast (Rfr1,500), affordable lunches & dinners (Rfr3,000 each) & a selection of beers & soft drinks. *Rfr12,000–15,000 dbl; Rfr18,000 2-bedroom family unit (sleeping 4).*

Dancing Pots

This offers visitors the opportunity to interact with one of three forward-looking Batwa communities who now operate as potters outside Rubavu/Gisenyi. Hunter-gatherers by tradition, the historically marginalised Batwa comprise less than 0.5% of the population, and suffer from high levels of illiteracy, unemployment and landlessness. At Abatigayubuke outside Rubavu, however, the

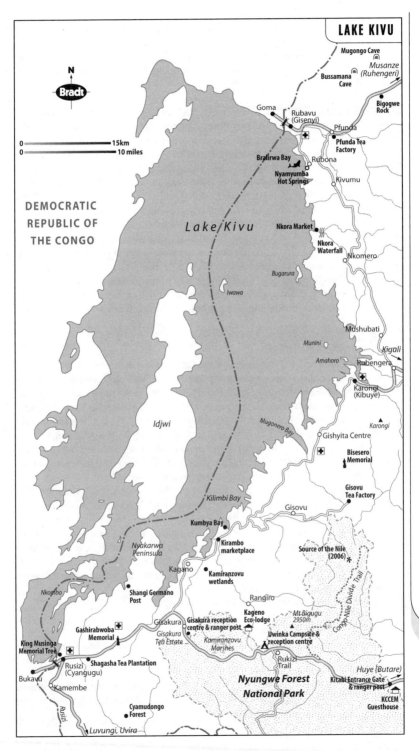

N

Bradt

DEMOCRATIC
REPUBLIC OF
THE CONGO

0 ────────── 15km
0 ────────── 10 miles

Lake Kivu

Mugongo Cave

Musanze (Ruhengeri)

Bussamana Cave

Bigogwe Rock

Goma

Rubavu (Gisenyi)

Pfunda

Pfunda Tea Factory

Bralirwa Bay

Rubona

Kivumu

Nyamyumba Hot Springs

Nkora Market

Nkora Waterfall

Nkomero

Bugarura

Iwawa

Mushubati

Munini

Kigali

Amahoro

Rubengera

Karongi (Kibuye)

Idjwi

Karongi

Mugonero Bay

Gishyita Centre

Bisesero Memorial

Gisovu Tea Factory

Kilimbi Bay

Gisovu

Kumbya Bay

Kirambo marketplace

Source of the Nile (2006)

Nyakarwa Peninsula

Kagano

Kamiranzovu wetlands

Rangiro

Kageno Eco-lodge

Mt Bigugu 2950m

Nkombo

Shangi Germano Post

Gisakura

Gisakura reception centre & ranger post

Uwinka Campsite & reception centre

Gashirabwoba Memorial

Gisakura Tea Estate

King Musinga Memorial Tree

Kamiranzovu Marshes

Rukizi Trail

Rusizi (Cyangugu)

Shagasha Tea Plantation

Bukavu

Kamembe

Cyamudongo Forest

Nyungwe Forest National Park

Huye (Butare)

Kitabi Entrance Gate & ranger post

KCCEM Guesthouse

Rusizi

Luvungi, Uvira

Batwa have harnessed traditional skills such as pottery and performing arts to make a living and become integrated into the greater community. A visit incorporates traditional dance performances, pottery and the opportunity to talk about the Batwa traditions and lifestyle. To arrange a Dancing Pots visit, the best contact is Green Hills Eco-Tours (see page 198).

Gishwati Forest Reserve In the early 20th century, Gishwati was Rwanda's second-largest tract of indigenous forest, extending over 1,000km² along the Albertine Rift escarpment from the base of the Virungas halfway down Lake Kivu. By 1989, when the last forest-dwelling Batwa hunter-gatherers were evicted from Gishwati, the forest comprised two main blocs that collectively covered less than a quarter of its former extent. Further deforestation occurred in the early 1990s to make way for exotic plantations and a dairy project, and again over 1998–99 to accommodate the land needs of returned refugees. By the turn of the millennium, all that remained of Gishwati was one disjunct 6km² stand of forest with a similar vegetation composition to Nyungwe. Forest biodiversity has been the most obvious victim of this 99% loss in Gishwati's original area, but it has also resulted in several fatal landslides, the drying up of streams fed by the watershed, decreased soil fertility, and flooding that destroyed hundreds of home in 2008.

A few years back, Gishwati seemed doomed to vanish entirely, and it was widely believed that its once prodigious populations of chimpanzee and golden monkey

THE CONGO NILE TRAIL

Officially launched in December 2011, the Congo-Nile Trail (not to be confused with the similarly named Congo-Nile Divide Trail in Nyungwe Forest) was developed by the RDB with two main goals: exposing active visitors to the thrilling scenery along the shores and escarpment hemming in Lake Kivu, and generating income for rural lakeshore communities. It is not a purpose-made hiking trail, but one constructed from existing roads and motorable tracks. Indeed, while the northern section, between Rubavu and Karongi/Kibuye, mostly follows a little-used old lakeshore road, the southern sector essentially comprises to the main road between Karongi and Rusizi, which is likely to be surfaced in the near future.

The ten-stage main trail runs roughly parallel to the eastern shore of Lake Kivu for 227km, and can be completed on foot in ten days, by bicycle in five days, and in a 4x4 over two to three days. Although the ten-stage trail is marketed as one entity, it is perfectly possible to do any single stage or sequence of stages in isolation from the others. In addition, for hikers with limited time, three different subtrails – Pfunda in the north near Rubavu, Gisovu a short distance south of Karongi, and Shangi in the south near Rusizi – can each be completed in 2 days on foot, or 1 day by bike.

The ten stages of the main trail are as follows:

Day One   Rubavu/Gisenyi to Rwinyoni, 8 hours
Day Two   Rwinyoni to Kinunu, 8.5 hours (arriving at 15.00, in time for an optional tour of Kinunu Coffee Estate)
Day Three   Kinunu to Musasa, 6 hours
Day Four   Musasa to Rubengera Junction, 7 hours (Rubengera lies on the surfaced road between Muhanga/Gitarama and Karongi/Kibuye, so it is advisable just to catch public transport from there to Karongi/Kibuye)

were either extinct or on the verge of it. Then, in late 2007, President Kagame and the Des-Moines-based Great Ape Trust (GAT) agreed to develop Gishwati Forest Reserve as a proposed 'national conservation park' to be managed by the Gishwati Area Conservation Program (GACP), directed and supported by the GAT. The aims of the GACP were not only to preserve the forest that remained, but also to extend its area with an ambitious reforestation project, with the eventual goal of creating a 50km forest corridor connecting it to Nyungwe National Park. Since then it has been established not only that the forest still supports a small chimpanzee community, but also that improved protection has allowed that population to increase from 13 to 20, an improvement of 50% in less than five years. The chimps are now habituated to people, and can be approached as closely as their counterparts at Nyungwe. Golden and L'Hoest's monkeys are also still quite common.

Gishwati is also an interesting destination for birders. Prior to the genocide, some 209 bird species had been recorded there, and, while some of these are probably now locally extinct, a survey undertaken in Oct–Nov 2009 recorded 101 species, 14 of which are Albertine Rift Endemics, including Ruwenzori turaco, strange weaver, handsome francolin, red-throated alethe, and four types of sunbird. Other alluring birds resident in Gishwati include black-billed turaco, Doherty's bush-shrike, white-headed wood-hoopoe and African hill-babbler.

Gishwati's status as a tourist attraction is uncertain at the time of writing. Based on announcements made by the RDB and the GAT in 2011, it seems likely that the

Day Five	Rest Day
Day Six	Karongi/Kibuye to Mugonero, 8 hours
Day Seven	Mugonero to Karengera, 6 hours
Day Eight	Karengera to Kibogora, 7.5 hours
Day Nine	Kibogora to Shangi, 8 hours
Day Ten	Shangi to Kamembe (Rusizi/Cyangugu), 8 hours

The best place to organise hikes is the RDB tourist office in Rubavu (see page 198), ideally with a day or two's notice. However, bicycle tours are better organised directly through the specialist operator Rwandan Adventures (see page 198). In both cases, itineraries can be tailored to suit your interests, available time, and fitness level. For keen hikers with a few days to spare, a good option would comprise the first four stages running from Rubavu to Rubengera (from where you could bus directly to Karongi or Kigali). A similar route is recommended to cyclists, who could complete it in two days, with the option of an organised boast transfer from Karongi back to Rubavu.

A fixed fee structure is in place for the Congo Nile Trail. The guide fee is US$30 per day for groups of up to five people, while (optional) porters cost US$20 per day, (optional) pack hire US$30 per day, and an (optional) back-up 4x4 US$100 per day. For accommodation, the guides can arrange either camping at US$5 per person per day, home stays at US$10 per person per day, or (where available) normal lodges and guesthouses at a similar price to the one quoted in this guidebook. Additional activities are overnight fishing (US$20 per person) or visits to coffee or tea estates (US$30 per person each).

forest will be upgraded to national park status during the lifespan of this edition, and almost certain that it will open up for tourist activities such as chimpanzee tracking, birdwatching and other forest walks. Indeed, several walking trails have already been cut through the forest, but the formal opening of these facilities has

CYCLING THE CONGO NILE TRAIL

By Tom Tofield of Rwandan Adventures (www.rwandan-adventures.com), which specialises in cycling tours through western Rwanda

The beautiful lake views and panoramic mountain scenery are a big part of what makes the Congo Nile Trail such an ideal destination for cycling. But the area also boasts a large network of unsurfaced roads, tracks and single-trails, many used almost exclusively by pedestrians and cyclists, creating a perfect adventure playground for biking. However, this undulating landscape – seemingly countless climbs of up to an hour each, rewarded by a corresponding downhill towards the lake – is not without challenges. And it forces us to take things easy, as a lot of energy is required to make it through the day.

When estimating how much time you need to pedal through each stage, base your first estimate on a riding time of 8km/hr, excluding pauses and photo breaks. It is also advisable to get up early and be riding off before 07.00, thus allowing some extra time to repair a puncture or to take a swim without the risk and stress of arriving after dark. Another challenge is making sure you have the right amount of water. Too much and the weight makes the climbs arduous, too little and you risk dehydration.

The trail can be travelled in either direction. In the dry season the winds come from the south, so those wanting the wind in their back should start in Kamembe and those who prefer the wind in their face should start in Gisenyi. Alternatively, for those with insufficient time to cover the whole trail, these towns and villages also make ideal starting points: N'Kora; Kinunu; Karongi/Kibuye; Nyamasheke; and Rusizi. They can all be reached by boat from Rubavu/Gisenyi or Kamembe, and Karongi/Kibuye can also be reached by road from Kigali.

Since Rwandan Adventures is based in Rubona, near Rubavu (also the closest lakeside port to Volcanoes National Park and its mountain gorillas), our trips normally start from there. And as we ride out of Rubona, the landscape is breathtaking. There are peninsulas and bays, *isambaza* fishing boats with their beams and telescopic poles, and the mountains and volcano on the other side of the lake. We ride through small villages and by fields, backing down to the lake from time to time.

Rwanda's coffee explosion is happening on the slopes next to the lake, while the longer-established tea plantations, in particular Pfunda and Gisovu, are on higher, cooler land with a greater rainfall. After a few hours riding through the coffee plantations and fields, we see a collection of small islands as we descend back down to the lake and to N'Kora, a unique lakeshore market town.

Predominantly Islamic, N'Kora developed after the creation of the eponymous coffee station. Today it has one of the largest beaches on Kivu's shores. In the 1960s, however, when the African rift lakes were at high-water, this beach did not exist! The market is on Fridays and Tuesdays, and people come from all over come – even paddling across the lake from the Congo – to sell and buy. Congolese coffee is bought and dried here, and we often see it laid out on sheets on the beach in the sun, with small children picking out the unwanted small stones.

been put on hold while the RDB take over the reins from the GAT, and it seems unlikely anything firm will be put in place before late 2012.

For the time being, informal day visits to Gishwati are possible. The main stand of forest lies about 40km from Rubavu, following the surfaced road from Musanze/

After an hour or two pedalling from N'Kora we arrive at Kinunu village centre, a good place to buy tasty brochettes and to stock up on bottled water. From here, it's a steep track – from where views encompass Nyiragongo, Karongi/Kibuye and Rubavu/Gisenyi – to the lakeside Kinunu Coffee Station, where rooms and meals are available. People in Kinunu are happy with the coffee explosion, as they have seen their standard of living increase in real terms. During the coffee harvesting periods, the station employs over 2,000 and operates 24 hours a day!

The section from Kinunu to Mushubati through Musasa is one of my favourite rides in Rwanda. It is challenging and rural, and the landscape is amazing. However, if you want to make Karongi/Kibuye in just one day, it's a tough 60 km ride, starting with a steep climb from the coffee station to the village centre, so you need to get going by 07:00 at the latest.

The passage across the river Koko can be very muddy, with slippery soils after rain. After the river crossing, there is a big climb towards Sure and Mushubati, where we join the main road from Rubavu to Rubengera junction, on the surfaced road between Muhanga/Gitarama and Karongi/Kibuye. From, it's a hilly 20km to Karongi/Kibuye, compensated for by some fantastic views over the islands as the sun sets behind the Congolese mountains west of the lake.

Many tours end in Karongi/Kibuye. But it is also possible to continue south along the main unsurfaced road to Rusizi/Cyangugu. Once again we follow the lake and there are more outstanding views as we ride through Gishyita and come to the paradisiacal L'Espérance Orphanage (see box, page 188) at Kigarama.

After spending some time at L'Espérance, we sometimes return to Karongi/Kibuye on the Gisovu subtrail. This is a big ride, and once again, you should head-off early. It climbs past the Bisesero Genocide Memorial into tea plantations on the edge of Nyungwe Forest, then returns to Karongi town with a descent of over 1,000m from Mount Karongi!

Alternatively, from L'Espérance the base-trail continues southward through the lakeside market town of Kirambo on to Nyamasheke, where there are some basic guesthouses and hotels. After a few kilometres, the dirt road connects with the surfaced road between Huye/Butare and Rusizi/Cyangugu. From here, the options are either to continue directly along the tarmac to Rusizi, or else, close by the Gashirabwoba memorial, to follow the longer historical lakeside Shangi subtrail there. From the intersection, it's also possible to continue on to Nyungwe (a full day's ride from Nyamasheke).

Rwanda's roads are fun to ride on, even though there are very few flat stretches, and the bumpy and sandy tracks really put the bikes – in particular brakes and gears – through their paces. Outside of the major cities, it is hard or impossible to find simple bike parts, or mechanics familiar with the likes of derailleurs and disc-brakes. So, for those travelling unguided, recommended bike tools and spare parts are as follows: spare inner tube; puncture repair kit; spare gear and brake cables; some oil and a rag; a multi-tool; tyre-levers; a pump; spare chain links and chain tool; and spare brake pads.

Janice Booth

As a young fashion illustrator in New York City, Rosamond Halsey boldly married a hunter-explorer, Kenneth Carr, and journeyed with him to the Congo in 1949. After their eventual divorce, Kenneth left; Rosamond stayed on. In 1955 she moved to northwest Rwanda to manage a flower plantation, Mugongo, and later bought it. For the next 50 years she witnessed the end of colonialism, celebrated Rwanda's independence and became one of Dian Fossey's closest friends. (In the film *Gorillas in the Mist*, she is played by Julie Harris.)

During periods of violence and upheaval, Mrs Carr always stayed fast in Mugongo while others fled. But when the genocide began in April 1994 the American Embassy finally insisted that she leave. After several months in the US, she learned that Sembagare, her friend and plantation manager of 50 years, had survived three attempts on his life. In August 1994, aged 82, she returned in a cargo plane, to find her home in ruins and 50 years' worth of possessions either stolen or destroyed. At Mugongo, she and Sembagare did the only thing that made sense to them: they converted an old pyrethrum drying-house and set up the Imbabazi Orphanage, to care for the genocide orphans.

In 1997 the orphanage was forced to move from Mugongo for security reasons and, after changing locations four times, settled in what was then Gisenyi until 2005, when it returned 'home' to Mugongo; the flower plantation and farm provided the orphanage with fresh vegetables and many Rwandan businesses – including the Lake Kivu Serena – with fresh flower

Ruhengeri out of town to Pfunda, then turning right on to the main dirt road towards Karongi/Kibuye. It can also be reached from Rubona by driving out past the Bralirwa Brewery towards Kigufi, and turning left (on to the Rambo Road) after about 600m. A useful contact for organised visits to the forest is Rwandan Adventures (see page 198), which can arrange day and overnight trips there with advance notice. For updates, contact the RDB tourist office in Rubavu, or check out our update website http://updates.bradtguides.com/rwanda.

THE MUSANZE (RUHENGERI) ROAD Several points of interest lie along or close to the road connecting Rubavu/Gisenyi to Musanze/Ruhengeri, as follows:

Pfunda Tea Estate (♦ *078 8625542; www.imporient.co.uk/about/pfunda-tea-estate*) Situated 9km from Rubavu along the Musanze Road, this Fairtrade certified estate is also a member of the Ethical Tea Partnership and Fairtrade, and in 2011 it became the first plantation in Rwanda to be certificated as having met the stringent criteria balancing ecological, economic and social considerations set by the Rainforest Alliance. It produces excellent tea, too, thanks to its location on the fertile volcanic soils of the Virunga foothills. Tourists are welcome, and visits can be set up either through the RDB office in Rubavu (see page 198), or through Rwandan Adventures (see page 198) as part of a full-day cycling excursion on the Pfunda sub-route of the Congo-Nile Trail.

Kiaka Cooperative (♦ *0252 540853;* **m** *078 8426429;* **e** *kiakacoop@yahoo.fr; www.kiaka.com;* ⊕ *10.00–16.00 daily*) Situated at Kanama, about 15km from Rubavu along the road to Musanze, this Atelier de Menuiserie (Carpentry Shop)

A novel fundraising scheme, 'Through the Eyes of Children' (www. rwandaproject.org), began in 2000: using disposable cameras, the children at the orphanage took photos of each other and their surroundings. At first the photos were developed locally, displayed on the orphanage walls and put into albums. A year later, the children were invited by the US Embassy to exhibit their work in Kigali, with all proceeds going towards their education. This led to international recognition and awards, and the cover of UNICEF's 2003 State of the World's Children report featured an Imbabazi child's photo of her friend. Since then, the project has been featured at about a dozen more exhibitions, mostly at universities and events in the USA.

Rosamond Carr died on 29 September 2006 at the age of 94 (she was officially Rwanda's oldest resident) and was buried at Mugongo. Friends (including many Rwandans) travelled from around the country to attend her funeral. She had lived in her peaceful, tree-shaded house by Rubavu's lake shore right up until her death, and continued to visit the orphanage several times a week to manage its affairs. Roz was also – flatteringly – a great fan of this guide, and was delighted when I visited her with a copy of the second edition to replace the first; she was 92 at the time. A contribution from her own book (see below) is on page 137.

Rosamond Halsey Carr is the author of Land of a Thousand Hills: My Life in Rwanda (written with her niece, Ann Howard Halsey); see *Further information*, page 313. She is also the subject of a short documentary film *A Mother's Love: Rosamond Carr & A Lifetime In Rwanda*.

showcases the highly regarded work of the Coopérative des Artisans de Kanama. The hefty furniture here is probably of greater interest to expatriates than tourists, but it also stocks a decent selection of basketwork, pottery, carvings and other handicrafts, and you can visit the workshop to watch the craftsmen in action.

Imbabazi Orphanage (m *078 4327058/078 2512682*; e *info@imbabazi.org; www.imbabazi.org, www.facebook.com/imbabazirwanda*) This positive and heart-warming project, founded by Rosamond Halsey Carr at her plantation in Mugongo in December 1994, originally sheltered some of the many orphans and displaced children left behind after the genocide. See box above. It still houses some 50 orphans, but they will complete their education soon, so the focus has changed. Now if you visit Imbabazi you can learn about Roz's life in Rwanda, her gardens, the orphanage and its current projects; and see where scenes from *Gorillas in the Mist* were filmed. You can stroll through English gardens with a vast variety of colourful flowers and birds, and beautiful views of Karisimbi, Mikeno and Nyiragongo volcanoes; and have tea there while watching a performance by Imbabazi's traditional dance troupe.

On the last Sunday of the month at 14.00, special Intore dance and cultural performances are held, followed by a tour of the orphanage and gardens, and afternoon tea: Rfr18,000 or US$30 per person, maximum 30 people. Lunch is available daily, in Roz's cottage or the garden, using local ingredients and produce from the farm (Rfr6,000 or US$10 per person, maximum 10 people) or bring your own picnic.

This is a new programme, so may change: check current details and prices on the website. Meals and visits can't be guaranteed unless booked at least three days in advance – see contact details above. To get to Imbabazi from Rubavu, follow the Musanze road out of town for about 20km to Kabari (aka Kabali) junction, then turn left on to a dirt road signposted to Mugongo. Imbabazi is signed and is on the right after 7km. It's a beautiful road, with spectacular views of two of the volcanoes and Lake Kivu.

Ibere rya Bigogwe [⊕ S 01°38.618, E 029°23.652]

Literally 'Breast Rock', this massive domed outcrop lies a few hundred metres south of the road from Musanze/ Ruhengeri and is clearly visible from the stretch between Kabari junction and the village of Mizingo. Undeveloped for tourism at the time of writing, it has enormous potential as a rock-climbing site – indeed, the main face is still studded with cables and pitons dating from pre-1994, when it was used as a commando training site – and it offers spectacular views over the surrounding farmland to Mount Karisimbi and Nyiragongo.

Lake Nyirakigugu [⊕ S 01°37.293, E 029°29.367]

Accorded official protection as of 2011, this small highland lake, situated at an altitude of 2,350m alongside the village of Jenda 35km from Rubavu, is one of the trio of 'Northern Lakes' (along with Karago and the relatively inaccessible Bihinga) earmarked for development as a formal birding route by the RDB. Historically, it is the most reliable site for several waterfowl with a localised distribution in Rwanda, among them the red-knobbed coot, little grebe, maccoa duck and southern pochard, but while the first two species remain common here, the other two have not been recorded for several years. Otherwise, the fringes support a fairly standard selection of ibises, herons, cormorants and small waders, and a pair of augur buzzard appears to nest in the cliffs rising to the east of the lake. The surrounding vegetation, dominated by exotic trees, is rather sterile in terms of birds and other animals. The lake lies only about 100m from the main road to Musanze Road, on the left coming from Rubavu, and it would be difficult to miss even if it were not clearly signposted (as the 'Home of Red-Knobbed Coot') about 2km before the junction town of Mukamiira.

Lake Karago

Larger than Nyirakigugu, this marsh-fringed lake – also part of the mooted Northern Lakes bird route – lies less than 2km south of Mukamiira. Once an important source of fish and freshwater to local communities, it also served for years as the site of the President of Rwanda's holiday home, but these days it is reputedly threatened by deforestation and terracing of the Gishwati watershed. Despite this, the birdlife is prodigious, with red-knobbed coot, pink-back-pelican and various ducks likely to be observed on the open water, while the swampy surround supports a selection of herons, ibises, wagtails, warblers and waders. To get there from Mukamiira on the main road between Rubavu and Musanze, follow the recently surfaced road running south to Ngororero and Muhanga/Gitarama for 1.2km, then stop at the signposted dirt track to your left. From here, you can follow an indistinct footpath downhill, then cross a small wooden bridge on to the lake floodplain, reaching the shore after about 10 minutes, depending on how muddy it is.

9

Musanze (Ruhengeri) and Surrounds

The fourth-largest town in Rwanda, with a population estimated at around 90,000, Musanze, formerly known as Ruhengeri, is also the closest town to Volcanoes National Park (see *Chapter 10*), and the most convenient urban base from which to track mountain gorillas. Despite this strategic importance, and its status as capital of Musanze District, it is an inherently unremarkable town, sprawling amorphously from the tight grid of roads that surround the lively central market.

Still, there is much to commend Musanze as a travel base. It boasts a more-than-adequate selection of lodges, a few eateries that rank as exceptional in a Rwandan context, and a friendly hassle-free mood. Set an altitude of 1,850m, it also has an agreeable temperate climate, and a stirring backdrop in the form of the distinctive volcanic outlines of the three most easterly mountains in the Virunga chain. The mountains and their gorillas are the main local attraction, but there are also some pleasant strolls around town, with the possibility of excursions further afield to Lakes Burera and Ruhondo.

GETTING THERE AND AWAY

The main taxi park [217 F7] is a patch of open ground at the edge of the compact town centre, a short distance south of the central market. However, superior express services to Rubavu/Gisenyi and Kigali operated by the likes of Virunga Express and Kigali Bus Service leave from in front of the respective company's office; they are clustered together on Avenue du 5 Juillet west of the central market [217 F2]. The GPS for the Hotel Muhabura is ✆ S 01°29.883, E 029°37.954.

TO/FROM KIGALI Kigali and Musanze are linked by a good 96km surfaced road, though the combination of outrageous bends and manic minibus drivers necessitates caution. Even so, you should cover the distance in under two hours.

Regular minibus-taxis connect Kigali (Nyabugogo bus station) and Musanze, leaving in either direction when they have a full complement of passengers. Tickets cost Rfr1,700 and the trip takes around two hours. The most reliable minibus service to Kigali is Virunga Express (m (Kigali) *078 8431960, (Musanze) 078 8510873, (Rubavu) 078 8597788); www.virungatravel.com/express.php*), which has departures every 15 minutes between 06.00 and 17.00. If they are full, try the Kigali Bus Service, which departs in both directions every 30 minutes between 06.00 and 17.30.

About 35km out of Kigali, on your left, you'll see a small but ornate cemetery, very different in style from those elsewhere in Rwanda. The graves there are those of Chinese workers who died during the building of this road and others in Rwanda – the excellent Kigali–Karongi road is also one of theirs.

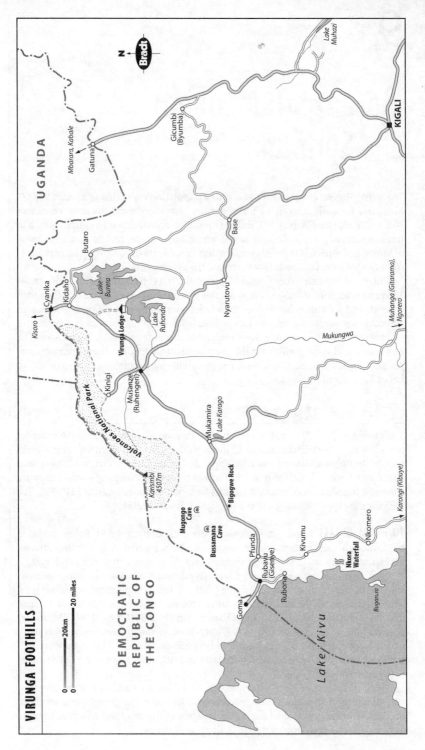

TO/FROM RUBAVU/GISENYI The 62km drive between Musanze and Rubavu follows a fairly good (and by Rwandan standards unusually straight) surfaced road, and should take no longer than an hour and a quarter. Minibus-taxis between the two towns leave regularly and cost around Rfr1,100. As with the Kigali trip, a reliable operator is Virunga Express, which departs hourly from 06.00 to 19.00.

Musanze to Muhanga via Ngororero

A newly surfaced road connects Musanze and Rubavu to Muhanga/Gitarama via Ngororero. It runs south from the Rubavu road at Mukamiira, 27km from Musanze, passes Lake Karago (see page 210) to the left about 1km later, then continues southwards towards Muhanga, winding high up into the hills and offering breathtaking views. It passes through hamlets and beside tea plantations, so there is human interest too, but the main attraction has to be the wonderfully panoramic landscape.

Situated at an altitude of 1,760m about halfway between Mukamiira and Muhanga, Ngororero is a small district capital surrounded by steep hills and notable mostly for the large multi-level market, which lies a few hundred metres downhill from the petrol station and is busiest on Wed and Sat. The former MRND Palace, where 14,500 Tutsis were burnt alive in 1994, is now a genocide memorial.

About 12km from Ngororero, the hilltop site known as Umukore wa Rwabugili (✪ S 01°52.380, E 029°35.204) might be of interest to history enthusiasts. It is here, on 30 May 1894, at what was then the temporary royal residence,that the powerful Mwami Kigeli IV (birth name Rwabugili) hosted the explorer Gustav Adolf von Götzen (who later became the Governor of German East Africa) at the first official meeting between a European and a Rwandan king. There is a sign marking the site, and a less than compelling reconstruction of the royal hut, but not much else to see, except for the views, which are quite spectacular from the 2,290m hilltop. To get there, follow the Muhanga road 2.3km south from Ngororero, then turn right, crossing a flimsy bridge after about 50m, and another after 2km, before climbing towards the village of Kageyo. The site lies about 600m past the village.

There is currently nowhere to stay in Ngororero, but a hotel is under construction and is likely to open – complete with swimming pool – during the lifespan of this edition.

TO/FROM UGANDA The border crossings between Uganda and Rwanda are covered more fully on page 38. Coming straight from Kampala, the most efficient option is to catch a bus or minibus heading directly to Kigali, where you can pick up a minibus-taxi to Musanze.

Coming from the west of Uganda, you will have to pass through Kabale. Prior to the recent surfacing of the road between Kabale and Kisoro, there was a strong case for taking the circuitous but smoother route between Kabale and Musanze via Kigali, crossing into Rwanda at the Katuna border post. These days, however, the quicker option from Kabale is to continue within Uganda along what is now a good surfaced 100km road to Kisoro and cross at the Cyanika border post. Kisoro and Musanze lie approximately 40km from each other along a mostly tarred road. On public transport, you'll have to change vehicles at the border, and can expect to pay around Rfr400–800 for each leg.

🏠 WHERE TO STAY

There is a good selection of moderate, budget or shoestring options in town. The few upmarket options are not of comparable class to the smarter lodges situated close to the Volcanoes National Park headquarters at Kinigi (see *Chapter 10*), or to the sumptuous Virunga Lodge near Lake Burera (covered later in the chapter), but they are also a lot less expensive.

UPMARKET

🏠 **Home Inn** [216 B4] (12 rooms) ✆0252 546333; m 078 4141000/8343127; e info@homeinnhotel.com; www.homeinnhotel.com. Set in a quiet back street southwest of the main road, this agreeable & friendly new hotel has large tiled en-suite rooms with flatscreen satellite TV, hot combination tub/shower, writing desk & rather overbearing décor. If you can get past the latter, it's decent value at *US$80/90 sgl/dbl with queen-size bed, or US$100 twin with two ¾ beds.*

🏠 **Hotel Gorillas Musanze** [216 C3] (24 rooms) ✆0252 546700; m 078 8425653; e reservation@gorillashotels.com; www.gorillashotels.com. Situated directly opposite the venerable Hotel Muhabura, this branch of the Gorillas Hotel chain (also represented in Kigali & Rubavu/Gisenyi) is easily the smartest option in town. Comfortable but somewhat lacking in character, it has good facilities including a restaurant & bar, & large en-suite rooms with tub or shower, satellite TV, free Wi-Fi & volcano views. *US$90/110 sgl/dbl.*

🏠 **La Palme Hôtel** [216 B3] (48 rooms) ✆0252 546428/9; e frontdesk@lapalmehotel.net; www.lapalmehotel.net. Rated highly by several local tour operators for its efficient service & reasonable prices, this well-managed but ambience-deficient hotel lies in small but green grounds at the northwest end of Av 5 Juillet, more or less opposite the landmark Hotel Muhabura. The carpeted

CLIMBING MOUNT KABUYE
Doug Teschner, updated by Philip Briggs

This 2,643m peak is a pleasant hike, all the more attractive because it can be done easily in a day from Kigali without having to leave before dawn – and you're still back in town before dark. Also, as it's so close to the main road, you can get there by public transport. The hike involves 1,000m of ascent and takes two to four hours to the top (a four-to-seven-hour round trip of about 12km) for most people.

The 'mountain' is visible to the east side of the main road, about an hour out of Kigali or 45 minutes out of Musanze. It stands out as a hill that is bigger than the rest. You may wish to obtain a topographic map (Gakenke, map number 9) from the Ministry of Public Works in Kigali, but it is not necessary as long as visibility is good enough to see the mountain (which it almost always is).

The junction village for Mount Kabuye is Gakenke, which straddles the main surfaced road 31km from Musanze and 63km from Kigali. Just north of this village, turn eastward into what appears to be a paved road signposted 'Hospital Nemba 1km'. The road becomes dirt within 100 metres and soon after you need to take the first switchback to the left through 'town', which leads to a soccer field on the right after about 1km. After another 300 metres, you pass the hospital to the right, then 400m further on a downhill fork to the right leads you to another football pitch with a small kiosk-like shop and a wooden footbridge across the river on the far side. The guy who owns the shop will probably offer to guard your car, but if in doubt you could always park in the hospital grounds.

Hikers should cross the wooden bridge and follow the road, climbing steadily to its end (about 2km). After 30 minutes, look for a little shack on the right which (if open) will sell you warm Fanta and you may even be able to arrange for a child to carry some to the top. This is a good way to keep hydrated and support the local economy.

Where the road ends at a pipe, there is an obvious steep section of trail. Above this, there are multiple trails and it is not always easy to pick the best one, but you rooms, which come with mini-bar, en-suite hot shower, balcony & satellite TV, are nothing special at the price, but the service & food are both very

good, & facilities include free Wi-Fi. *US$60 sgl with ¾ bed, US$80/90 sgl/dbl with king-size bed, US$100/110 sgl/dbl suite. All rates B&B.*

MIDRANGE

🏠 **Hotel Muhabura** [216 C3] (29 rooms) ☏ 0252 546296; m 078 8364774; e muhabura12@ yahoo.fr or info@hotelmuhabura.com; www. hotelmuhabura.com. The oldest tourist lodging in town, dating to Dian Fossey's time, this likeable old favourite lies in green grounds on the outskirts of town along Av 5 Juillet in the direction of Rubavu/Gisenyi. With its outmoded décor & wide balcony that comes across like a Congolese colonial time-warp, it is difficult to believe this was once the smartest hotel within staging distance of the Virungas. Still it is a very characterful & reasonably priced set-up, offering accommodation in spacious tiled en-suite rooms with king-size or twin bed, hot bath & shower,

& a small sitting room with TV. There is also a campground. A good bar & restaurant serves a wide selection of continental dishes inside or outdoors in the Rfr4,000–5,000 range. *Rooms cost Rfr24,000/30,000/36,000/45,000 sgl/dbl/twin/trpl B&B. Camping costs Rfr5,000 per tent.*

🏠 **Ishema Hotel** [217 E6] (42 rooms) ☏ 0252 546857; m 078 3641111/8558501; e ishema_ hotel@hotmail.com; www.ishemahotel.com. This former **Centre d'Accueil de l'Eglise Episcopale**, still run by the EER Church, lies in large well-tended grounds on Av du 5 Juillet near the junction with Rue de Pyrèthre, about 1km from the taxi park. Accommodation ranges from smart dbl rooms & suites with king-size or 2 ¾ beds, net, flat

can easily readjust on smaller trails if you lose the main one. The best route goes right at the top of the steep section and stays just to the right of the ridge, passing by the local water supply and eventually passing a school (prominently visible from below) in a big clearing. Above the school, the trail follows the right side of the ridge to a T-Junction. Turn left and enjoy the short flat stretch before turning right and heading steeply back up the very scenic ridge through farmlands and by houses with the mountain prominently visible above. If the sky is very clear, views of the volcanoes will appear off to the left.

After a while, the trail switches over to the left side of the ridge and soon reaches a flattish place on the ridge proper. Turn right after 50m for a scenic rest on rocks in a eucalyptus grove. You're about two-thirds of the way to the top. After your rest, continue up the steepening ridge toward the summit cone. A short steep section up a grassy patch leads to a rocky trail, which slabs off to the left and eventually swings around the peak to reach the pass on the left (north) side of the summit.

At the pass, leave the main trail by turning right on a smaller one. You're now 15 minutes from the top. Follow this vague path up the ridge, through new eucalyptus trees, to nearly the top. The precise but somewhat indistinct summit (visible *en route* from a prior false top) is reached by leaving the path for the final 20m. If it is very clear, you can see all the Virunga volcanoes and Lake Ruhondo to the north. Just down on the other side of the summit, there is a pine forest which offers shade on a sunny day.

As in all places in Rwanda, expect to be followed by a pack of children, although I have found that each time we go (I have done it five times), there are fewer, as they seem to be getting used to visitors.

Descend the same way, or pick another. The valley off to the right (looking down) is very beautiful, but it adds at least an hour to the descent.

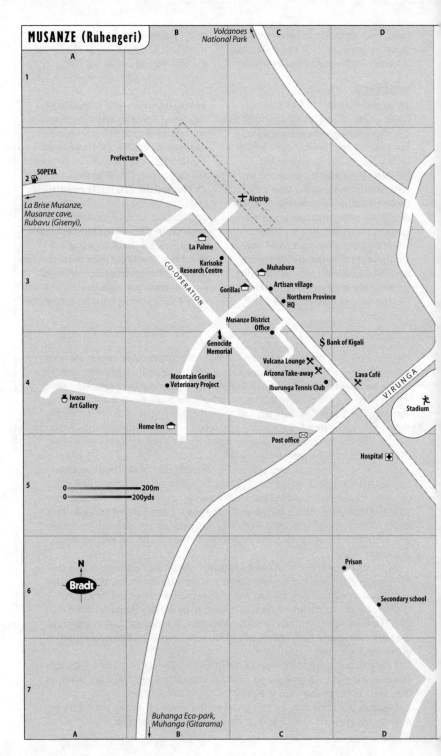

MUSANZE (Ruhengeri)

Volcanoes National Park

Prefecture

SOPEYA

La Brise Musanze,
Musanze cave,
Rubavu (Gisenyi),

Airstrip

La Palme

Karisoke Research Centre

CO-OPERATION

Muhabura

Artisan village

Gorillas

Northern Province HQ

Musanze District Office

Genocide Memorial

Bank of Kigali

Volcana Lounge

Arizona Take-away

Lava Café

Mountain Gorilla Veterinary Project

Iburunga Tennis Club

VIRUNGA

Iwacu Art Gallery

Stadium

Home Inn

Post office

Hospital

0 ————— 200m
0 ————— 200yds

N

Bradt

Prison

Secondary school

Buhanga Eco-park,
Muhanga (Gitarama)

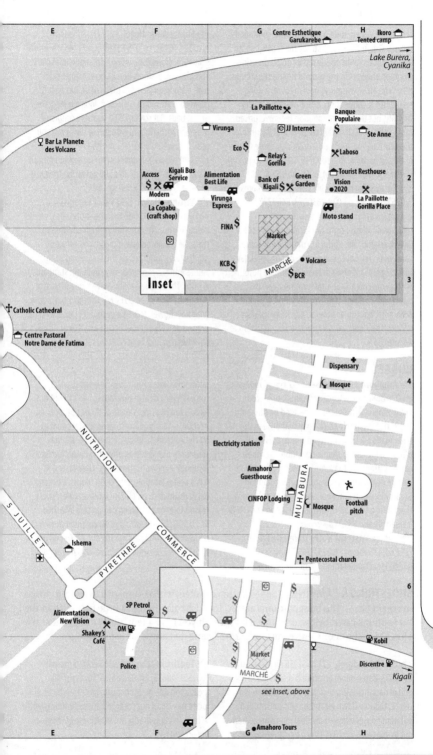

Inset

MARCHÉ

see inset, above

217

screen DSTV & en-suite bathroom with combined tub/shower in the new 2-storey main building, to more basic en-suite dbls & rather dour sgls using common showers in the ground floor outbuildings. It has the only swimming pool in town, a good restaurant & coffee shop, & the welcome is very friendly, but the accommodation feels overpriced. *Rfr45,000/50,000/70,000 en-suite sgl/dbl/suite in the new building. Rfr35,000/40,000 en-suite sgl/dbl in the old building. Rf10,000/15,000 using common facilities in the old buildings. All rates B&B.*

🏠 **Relay's Gorilla Hotel** [217 G2] (29 rooms) 📞0252 546280; m 078 8630073/8487777; e info@relaysgorillashotel.com; www.relaysgorillashotel.com. The location above the Silverback Top Link Nightclub might be of some concern on Fri, Sat & Sun nights, but on weekdays this is a pleasant enough lower midrange hotel, with a conveniently central location near the bus station, & large clean rooms with TV, phone & en-suite hot tub or shower. *Adequate value at US$20,000/30,000 sgl/dbl room or US$40,000 suite. All rates B&B.*

BUDGET

🏠 **Amahoro Guesthouse** [217 G5] (7 rooms) m 078 8687448; e amahorotours@gmail.com; www.amahoro-tours.com. Operated by Amahoro Tours, this small self-catering guesthouse in the back-roads north of the town centre bills itself as a 'home stay' rather than a guesthouse, & guests can be introduced to various aspects of Rwandan culture or shown how to prepare Rwandan food. Accommodation is in neat tiled twin or dbl rooms that share a bathroom, kitchen & lounge with TV & a small library. *US$25 per room.*

🏠 **Centre Pastoral Notre Dame de Fatima** [217 E4] (35 rooms) 📞0252 546780/4; m 078 8324033; e cpndefatima@yahoo.fr or info@

🏠 **Sainte Anne Hotel** [217 H2] (16 rooms) 📞0252 546461; m 078 8386971/8777455; e info@sainteannehotel.com; www.sainteannehotel.com. This pleasant 3-storey hotel, set on a quiet side road a block northeast of the market, has neat & clean en-suite rooms with tiled floor, a queen-size or 2 ¾ beds, flat screen DSTV, lockable cupboards, & a compact bathroom with tub or shower as you prefer. There's an internet café, Wi-Fi in all rooms, & a pleasant terrace & indoor restaurant serving African & Western dishes from Rfr3,500 upwards. *Adequate value at Rfr30,000/35,000 sgl/dbl.*

🏠 **Virunga Hotel** [217 F1] (23 rooms) m 078 8448958; e info@virungahotel.com; www.virungahotel.com. Another newish addition to the local accommodation scene, this efficient multi-storey hotel lies on the same road as the Sainte Anne, & is overall very similar in standard & price. The en-suite rooms have a queen-size or 2 ¾ beds, flat screen DSTV & a compact bathroom with hot shower. There's a decent restaurant on the ground floor, & internet access just a door down. *Overpriced at Rfr25,000/40,000 sgl/dbl/twin.*

fatimamusanze.com; www.fatimamusanze.com. The best deal in this range, by virtue of not having raised prices significantly since it opened in 2004, is this modern-looking hostel situated on the edge of the town centre opposite the stadium & alongside an affiliated Catholic church. Although a bit institutional for some tastes, it has a useful location, very clean rooms, a decent bar & restaurant, an on-site internet café, & very reasonable rates. A green campsite is attached. *Rfr10,000/12,000 sgl/dbl using common showers; Rfr15,000/17,000 en-suite sgl/dbl; Rfr30,000 apt with TV; Rfr5,000 dorm bed; Rfr3,000 pp camping.*

SHOESTRING & CAMPING The selection is limited, with several places having closed in recent years. The budget rooms at the Hotel Ishema, though a little pricier than the two options listed below, are quite a bit nicer. If you have a tent, you can pitch it at the Hotel Muhabura or Centre Pastoral Notre Dame de Fatima, as listed above.

🏠 **CINFOP Lodging** [217 G5] (56 rooms) m 078 8790603. Based out of an office & restaurant in the grid of back-roads immediately north of the town centre, this run-down establishment consists of 8 different houses whose individual rooms are rented out by the night. *Rfr10,000 for a musty en-suite dbl.*

🏠 **Tourist Resthouse** [217 H2] (6 rooms) 📞0252 546635; m 078 8520758. Centrally located on Rue de Muhabura, this friendly little lodge has clean but cramped en-suite rooms with ¾ bed, net & sporadic hot water. *Rfr8,000 sgl or dbl occupancy.*

As with hotels, there is plenty of choice when it comes to eating out in Musanze, with several excellent standalone eateries having opened since the last edition was published. The smarter hotels all serve extensive breakfast, lunch and dinner menus daily. The **Gorillas Hotel** [216 C3] is the pick if you want to splash out, serving high-quality French-influenced cuisine, with most main courses coming in at around Rfr5,000–6,000. Most of the other midrange hotels, including the La Palme [217 B3], Sainte Anne [217 H2] and Virunga [217 F1], have more than serviceable restaurants, with food in the Rfr4,000–5,000 range, but none really stands out. Far more alluring is the **Muhabura Hotel** [216 C3], where a selection of grills, stews and mild curries start at around Rfr4,000 for a heaped plate, and the semi-shaded balcony ranks as high on the ambience front as anywhere in town. Beers and other drinks are only slightly more expensive than at the local bars and restaurants in town. Dropping several rungs in both price and standard, the **Tourist Resthouse** [217 H2] also has an inviting menu, dominated by stews rather than grills.

✗ **Green Garden Café Resto-Bar** [217 H2] ⊕ 08.00–late daily Centrally located, with shady outdoor seating, this is a pleasant place for a cheap beer after dark, but also good for a lunchtime *mélange* buffet at the usual Rfr2,000–3,000.

✗ **La Paillotte Gorilla Place** [217 H2] m 078 5523561/072 2322066; e lapaillottegorillaplace@ hotmail.com; www.lapaillottegorillaplace.com; ⊕ 07.00–20.00 daily. Possibly our favourite eatery in Musanze, this clean, efficient, & friendly bakery & café – earthily decorated with basketwork & wood – produces excellent fresh bread & pastries right in front of customers' eyes. Centrally located, it also serves a great selection of s&wiches, pizzas, brochettes & other light meals for around Rfr2,000, along with fresh espresso & cappuccino, & the usual soft & alcoholic drinks.

✗ **Lava Café** [216 D4] m 078 3856246/ 8540060; ⊕ 07.00–21.00 daily. This modern eatery on the road out to the Hotel Muhabura has indoor & outdoor seating, free Wi-Fi & a flatscreen TV usually showing music videos. It produces a selection of fresh coffee in the Rfr1,000–1,200 range, as well as milkshakes, fresh juices & a selection of pastries. Also available is a meal of the day, plus sandwiches, salads, burgers & soups, mostly for around Rfr3,000.

✗ **Silverback Top Link** [217 G2] Set below Relay's Gorilla Hotel, & under the same management, this serves decent snacks by day, drinks in the evening, & it operates as a nightclub from 22.00 until late on Fri, Sat & Sun nights.

✗ **Volcana Lounge** [216 C4] m 078 5818501; ⊕ 11.00–late daily. Roughly opposite the Lava Café, this popular nightspot has a proper restaurant upstairs, & a sports bar, dance floor & pool table on the ground floor. Highly rated pizzas start at Rfr3,800 depending on your choice of toppings, & there's a selection of Italian & French-influenced mains & salads in the Rfr4,000–6,000 range.

TOURIST INFORMATION

The closest RDB offices are situated 12km out of town at the Volcanoes National Park headquarters in Kinigi (see pages 244–5) as well as in Rubavu/Gisenyi, 60km to the west. Gorilla tracking permits can usually be booked at both offices.

A useful online source of travel information is www.musanze.com, which hosts pretty detailed and up-to-date accommodation, restaurant and shopping listings.

TOUR OPERATORS In addition to the operator listed below, the Hotel Gorillas Musanze can arrange transport for gorilla tracking and other activities in the area.

Amahoro Tours [217 G7] \0252 546877; m 078 8655223/8687448; e amahorotours@gmail.

com; www.amahoro-tours.com; ⊕ 08.00–17.00 Mon–Fri, 09.00–12.00 Sat. Tucked away behind the market, this praiseworthy local operator can also arrange gorilla visits & all the normal tourist programmes, but it is mainly concerned with promoting community-based tourism. The main agent for home stays in the area, its itineraries also involve visitors in local activities such as canoeing, fishing, dancing, drumming, traditional medicine, beekeeping & local cuisine. It is a developing enterprise, so check the helpful website or email for the latest information. Note that the office is quite difficult to find; from the market, follow the road southwest towards the bus station, then turn left into the alley immediately after the Cooperative COODAF, & then left again at the end, & right into the next gate.

OTHER PRACTICALITIES

SHOPPING The central market [217 G7] can be enjoyable to explore, and it is surrounded by a variety of small stalls and businesses – tailors, cobblers, people ironing clothes with old coal-filled irons, and so on. The best place to buy local handicrafts is probably the COPABU Craft Shop [217 F2] on the main road a block or so from the market. Alimentation New Vision [217 E6] is a well stocked supermarket, as is the more central Alimentation Best Life [217 F2]. For fresh bread and pastries, you can't beat La Paillotte Gorilla Place [217 H2]. Even if you don't plan to buy, the Iwacu Art Gallery [216 A4] (m 078 3275904; e *fahanda2003@yahoo.com*) has an interesting collection of contemporary Rwandan paintings, though the standard is rather variable.

BANKING AND FOREIGN EXCHANGE There is an ATM where local currency can be drawn with an international visa card at the Ecobank [217 G2] north of the market.

| BAGENGE'S ROCK | *Janice Booth* |

A NEW VERSION OF AN ANCIENT TALE Ruganzu II Ndori was one of the greatest of Rwanda's warrior kings. One source puts his reign at 1510–43, another at 1600–24, so… who knows! His father, Ndahiro II, had catastrophically lost the Royal Drum, Rwoga, in battle, causing a time of great hardship for Rwanda: for 11 years the land was tortured by drought, sorghum withered in the ground, cows were barren and women conceived only sickly children. Considering the family cursed, the powerful *abiiru* (dynastic ritualists) banished Ruganzu from the kingdom – but after Ndahiro's death chiefs traced him and returned him to power.

Immediately rain began to fall on the parched land, sorghum grew fresh and sweet, cows produced rich milk and many calves, and woman became pregnant with fine, healthy sons. Ruganzu introduced the last of the Royal Drums, Karinga, to replace the lost Rwoga. He chose an adoptive Queen Mother from another clan; she was a poet and created a new form of dynastic poem. Ruganzu's conquests were many and much praised.

One day – so the ancient stories relate in various ways – the king and his entourage were visiting a part of Rwanda that today is just off to the right of the Kigali-Musanze road where it crosses the River Base. A sign to Nemba Hospital is nearby – as is a large rock known as 'Bagenge's Rock'.

Bagenge was the local chief in whose home the King was lodging for the night – and he had spent all that day in a state of great anxiety. The cause for his concern was the great rock, which was well known for moving about at night and relentlessly crushing anything that came within its path, whether mice, children, men, cattle or possibly even kings. Bagenge knew that death or injury to the King risked returning Rwanda to its previous state of drought and disaster.

Otherwise, the branch of the Bank of Kigali [216 C4] close to the Muhabura Hotel has foreign exchange facilities, as does the Banque Commerciale du Rwanda [217 G3] behind the market. The Bank of Kigali has Western Union too.

For travellers who arrive from Uganda, there are no private forex bureaux in town, so try to obtain some Rwandan francs when you cross the border. Otherwise, assuming that you have US dollars or euro cash, most of the hotels will sort you out at a rate fractionally lower than the street rate in Kigali, which is probably a safer bet than trying to change money on the street or in the market.

INTERNET There are a few **internet** cafés dotted around town, charging the usual affordable rates. One of the best for several years, with a really quick connection, is JJ Internet [217 G2], next to the Virunga Hotel. If you have your own laptop or phone, free Wi-Fi is available at the Lava Café for the price of a coffee or fruit juice.

SWIMMING There is a clean **swimming pool** at the Ishema Hotel [217 E6]; a nominal fee is charged to travellers staying at other hotels.

EXCURSIONS FROM MUSANZE

Most people who visit Musanze treat it purely as a base from which to track gorillas (see *Chapter 10*). But several local points of interest make for worthwhile day or overnight excursions, notably the little-visited Lakes Karago, Burera and Ruhondo. For visitors seeking upmarket accommodation, the Virunga Lodge at Lake Burera

He prepared a great feast, the greatest that the region had seen for some years, and the smell of the spit-roasted meats and pungent spices caused many a nearby villager's mouth to water. There was wine too, in great abundance, and banana beer; and after the feast dancers leaped and drummed and chanted in the firelight. Bagenge's aim was to entertain the King and his entourage until they fell deeply asleep, so that none would wander off and fall victim to the rock.

But kings sleep less than ordinary men. In the quiet of the night Ruganzu awoke. He wanted to feel air fresh upon his face and to plan new conquests in a silence unbroken by the snores of his attendants. He strolled off along the soft mud path and stood in the open, above the valley, looking upwards at the stars.

The ground shook, a shadow blotted out the starlight and the great rock lurched ominously towards the King. Ruganzu raised his staff threateningly and stood his ground. Disconcerted by such courage, the rock hesitated. Gently the King spoke (for he was wise, and knew that soft words hold the greatest power).

'Greetings, my subject. I hail you and I accept the offering you bring: the offering of your size and strength, to use for the good of my kingdom. Guard this village well. Protect the children who play in your shadow. Comfort the weary traveller who leans against you. Shelter the plants growing around your base. Remain in this spot for ever, the friend of all who live nearby. Perform this task well, my subject, and many centuries from now men will still remember you and tell this tale.'

As you will see, if you visit Bagenge's Rock today, it has indeed performed its task well and stayed peacefully in the same spot. All the same, if you wander the paths by night, keep your ears alert for the rumble of a sudden stealthy movement, because Rwanda is a Republic now and the power of kings is very much reduced ...

and a pair of lodges at Kinigi are far more alluring than anything on offer in Musanze itself.

BUHANGA ECO-PARK This undeveloped park lies 8km outside Musanze (⊕ S 01°34.061, E 029°38.169, 1,628m); just head out of town past the post office until you reach the Nyakinama College, turn right on to a poorly signposted and rough dirt track after another 500m, and you'll reach it after another 500m or so. Consisting of a small patch of forest dominated by spectacular dragon trees, this culturally significant site (see box *Ryangombe and the Buhanga Forest*, page 225) is of some interest to birdwatchers too. The exquisite and very seldom seen Angola pitta was recorded here in 2006 and 2008 (both times in May), a recent Nubian woodpecker sighting is the second for Rwanda, and rather more improbably we've heard unconfirmed reports of the green broadbill (an ARE known only from the Congo and one locality in Uganda).

A few years back, the park was reputedly under private development as a nature trail, with a bar and possibly a hotel. Instead, it has been made into an isolated annex of Volcanoes National Park, and foreign visitors must now pay a difficult-to-justify entrance fee of US\$40 at the RDB office in Kinigi before heading out here – if you arrive without a receipt you will be turned back.

MUSANZE CAVE AND NATURAL BRIDGE The impressive Musanze Cave lies in the grounds of a school about 2km from the town centre off the road to Rubavu/Gisenyi. The main cave, reportedly 2km long, has an entrance the size of a cathedral, and is home to an impressive bat colony. The large ditch out of which the cave opens is littered with pockmarked black volcanic rubble, and at the opposite end there is a natural bridge which was formed by a lava flow from one of the Virunga volcanoes.

Legend has it that Musanze Cave was created by a local king, and that it has been used as a refuge on several occasions in history. However intriguing it may be, it's advisable not to enter on your own. The cave was the site of a massacre during the genocide; local people consider it a tomb and don't take kindly to tourists scrambling about inside. Please respect this: either view from a distance or go with a local guide.

UBUSHOBOZI PROJECT   *Elizabeth Todd*

If you are looking for a fantastic off-the-beaten-path excursion in Musanze, the Ubushobozi Project (m *078 8583677;* e *info@ubushobozi.org; www. ubushobozi.org*) is a small, grassroots non-profit organisation devoted to educating and training at-risk and orphaned teenage girls. In a stable, social and caring environment, the girls are taught sewing (and have become highly competent), basic computer and business skills, life skills, and attend daily English class. They make beautiful bags (among other items), which are excellent souvenirs/gifts. Each is handmade and all proceeds go directly back into the project so not only are you getting a cool item, you're making a donation. The programme's director and house manager speaks great English, and has a million stories about Rwanda. If you want to see a programme up close and firsthand that's empowering and changing the course of young girls' lives while supporting the women and men of the local community, you won't be disappointed. We visited after gorilla trekking. It's a really nice and interesting way to spend an afternoon. It's most definitely a feel-good excursion.

To get to Musanze Cave from the town, follow Avenue du 5 Juillet past the Hotel Muhabura towards Rubavu/Gisenyi. Just short of 2km from the town centre, you'll see the large steel Entrepots Opravia Musanze to your left. Turn right directly opposite this building, following a curved dirt track which after about 100m leads to a football field and school. The cave lies in a ditch on the opposite side of the football field.

We've heard talk of developing Musanze Caves as a official tourist attraction, with proper guides and a formal entrance fee, but there is no indication this will go ahead in the immediate future.

LAKE BURERA AND RUGEZI BIRDING SITE The largest and most beautiful lake in the vicinity of Musanze, Burera (aka Bulera) is almost entirely neglected by travellers, despite being overlooked by one of Rwanda's top three tourist lodges. With a private vehicle, however, the dirt road that loops around its eastern shore makes for a superb day outing, while adventurous backpackers could happily spend several days exploring the lake using a combination of minibus-taxis, motos, boats, and foot power. As for budget accommodation, the area is dotted with small villages where it shouldn't be a problem to get permission to pitch a tent, and basic lodges now exist in Butaro, the largest town close to the lake, as well as Kirambo, 13km to its south.

With an eccentric shape defined by the incredibly steep hills that enclose it, Lake Burera is visually reminiscent of Uganda's popular Lake Bunyonyi – not too surprising when you realise that these two bodies of water lie no more than 20km apart as the crow flies. The slopes that fall towards the lake are densely terraced and intensively cultivated: very little natural vegetation remains among the fields of plantains, potatoes, beans and other crops, while the most common tree is the eucalyptus, a fast growing Australian exotic. The stunning and distinctive scenery around the lake is enhanced by the outlines of the Virunga Mountains, the closest of which towers 10km away on the western horizon.

Lake Burera lies at the northern end of the Rugezi Wetland, a vast highland marsh area that runs all the way south to Gicumbi/Byumba, where it is most easily accessed at Lake Nyagafunzo (see pages 261–2 for further details). However, the northern part of the wetlands is currently under development by the RDB as the Rugezi Birding Site, which now hosts three birding watchtowers along the 13km stretch of road running south of Butaro. Listed as a Ramsar Wetland and an Important Bird Area, this is a good place to see large water-associated birds such as herons and ibises, but the main attraction is Grauer's rush warbler, an Albertine Rift Endemic whose nondescript appearance is unlikely to enthuse anybody but the most dedicated of birdwatchers.

Getting there and around

By road For travellers with their own transport, the circuit around the lake is straightforward enough. The road is mostly in good shape, and likely to present no problems provided that your vehicle has reasonable clearance (a 4x4 would be advisable during the rainy season). The full round trip from Musanze covers about 120km, most of which is on dirt, and realistically takes a minimum of five hours to complete. Better, arguably, to leave after breakfast, carry a picnic lunch, and make a day of it, stopping along the way to enjoy the views and rustic villages.

To follow the circuit, head out of Musanze along the surfaced road towards Cyanika on the Ugandan border, passing the turn-off for Virunga Lodge to your right after 16km, then continuing for another 6km to Kidaho, where you need

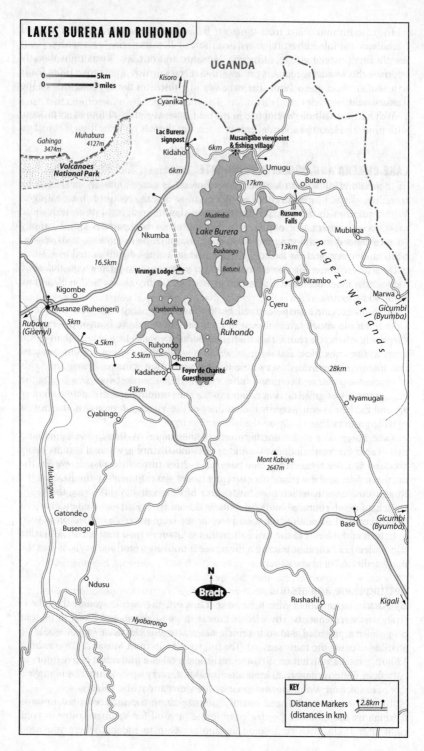

LAKES BURERA AND RUHONDO

UGANDA

0 ———— 5km
0 ———— 3 miles

Kisoro ↑

Cyanika

Lac Burera signpost

Musangabo viewpoint & fishing village

6km

Kidaho

Umugu

Butaro

6km

17km

Gahinga 3474m

Muhabura 4127m

Volcanoes National Park

Rusumo Falls

Mubinga

Nkumba

Mudimba

Lake Burera

13km

16.5km

Bushongo

Kirambo

Kigombe

Musanze (Ruhengeri)

Virunga Lodge

Batutsi

Cyeru

Marwa

Gicumbi (Byumba)

Icyabarihira

Rubavu (Gisenyi)

5km

Lake Ruhondo

4.5km

Ruhondo

5.5km

Remera

Kadahero

Foyer de Charité Guesthouse

28km

43km

Cyabingo

Mont Kabuye 2647m

Nyamugali

Mukungwa

Gatonde

Busengo

Base

Gicumbi (Byumba)

Ndusu

Rushashi

Kigali →

N

Bradt

Nyabarongo

KEY

Distance Markers (distances in km) ┃ 2.8km ┃

Rugezi Wetlands

to turn right into a dirt road signposted for Rugezi Birding Site. After about six relatively flat kilometres, the lake becomes visible to the right: on the shore you'll see a small fishing village, also called Kidaho, and dozens of small boats used to ferry locals around the lake. A few hundred metres further, a side road leads around the small Musangabo Peninsula, where a platform run by the Episcopal Church offers stunning views in all directions. The church operates a motorboat that can be hired for the two-hour round trip to the bridge between lakes Burera and Ruhondo (around Rfr15,000 per party).

RYANGOMBE AND THE BUHANGA FOREST   *Janice Booth*

A NEW VERSION OF AN ANCIENT TALE None could shoot an arrow so far and straight as Ryangombe, the greatest warrior and hunter of his time. None could run so fast or stalk so silently. The sun dimmed its rays in respect when he was taking aim and the rain paused as he pursued his quarry. He defended the forest against farmers who would fell trees to make space for their crops, and the branches murmured their thanks as he rested in their shade. Women competed for his favours, opponents feared him, storytellers throughout the realm extolled his exploits and his name was lauded far and wide. So powerful was Ryangombe that he challenged even the mighty King Ruganzu, who ruled Rwanda almost seven centuries ago.

Ryangombe's favourite hunting-ground was the Buhanga Forest, in the volcano foothills not far from what is now Musanze: a place of ancient trees, dark ravines and thrusting rocks, where sunlight throws patterns on the leafy floor and butterflies bask on mossy logs. Birds swoop and perch among the branches and small creatures scuttle in the undergrowth. In this forest is the sacred pool called Gihanga, empty in the rainy season but full to overflowing in the dry season, where Rwanda's early monarchs would come to bathe and drink the water.

It was on a dark, dark day here in the Buhanga Forest that Ryangombe faced his final opponent – no king or fellow warrior but a wild and angry buffalo, which burst upon him from the shelter of the trees. Its horns tore into his flesh and the forest floor was reddened by his blood. His companions, seeing their hero slain and wishing to be at his side in the higher world, taunted the buffalo until it gored them also and trampled their limbs with its hooves. The bodies of the young men lay beneath the great tree Umuvumu, still in the forest today, until Imana raised them to their final home on the slopes of Karisimbi. If you climb the mountain nowadays, you may – if your spirit is fair and you know how to listen with your heart – still hear their voices carried on the breeze as they talk and laugh together.

After Ryangombe's death, traditional healers from throughout the Great Lakes region would journey to the spot in Buhanga Forest where he fell. From the trees in that place they would take a branch back to their homelands, and use it as the base to build a shrine – Ingoro – from which to worship him and send prayers to their gods.

Sit quietly in Buhanga Forest today and you can sense its ancient history. Kings and healers and legendary heroes have walked its paths and felt its power. And – who knows – that sudden rustle that you hear behind you may even be the soft and stealthy footfall of Ryangombe as he stalks some ghostly prey.

For most people, Musanze does not come to mind as a place where one goes birding, but rather as a base for tracking the Mountain Gorillas. The area has a huge diversity of habitats with altitudes ranging from around 1,600m to the peaks of the Virungas at over 4,500m. The habitats include relic forest (Buhanga Forest), wetlands (Rugezi Swamps and areas along the Mukungwa and Mpenge rivers), eucalyptus plantations/stands, rocky areas (Kinigi) and freshwater lakes (including lakes Burera and Ruhondo).

Musanze town itself and most gardens of hotels and guesthouses there will surprise the keen birder with the number of species they contain, with **bronze, variable** and **scarlet-chested sunbirds** being fairly common. Lodge gardens in Kinigi will add **Ruwenzori double-collared sunbird** to this list. **White-eyed slaty flycatchers, African paradise-flycatchers** and **white-tailed blue-flycatchers** are often seen hawking for insects whilst the seed-eaters like **western citrils, yellow-fronted** and **brimstone canaries, common** and **black-crowned waxbills, bronze** and **black and white mannikins**, to name but a few, will undoubtedly make their appearance.

In the gardens, and even in the centre of town, the **red-billed fire-finches** will be around, occasionally with a **village indigobird**, for which the former is a host species. Look out as well for the lovely plumaged **cinnamon-breasted bee-eaters** and their aerial acrobatics, only beaten in complexity, low passes and speed by the **little swifts**. A garden in the middle of Musanze even hosted an **African pitta** for three days in 2006! At night (and in some places during the day), look out for the **spotted eagle-owl** and, easily identifiable during breeding season, **pennant-winged nightjars**.

Contesting the award as the loudest garden bird (other than **hadeda ibis**) will be the **white-browed robin-chat** and **grey-capped warbler** – the latter being more often heard than seen in its hiding places in thick hedges. In more wooded gardens there are **olive-** and **grey woodpeckers**, and the noisy but entertaining **spot-flanked barbets**. The **double-toothed barbet** can be seen in Buhanga Forest.

Birds of prey are well represented in the area with the ever-present **black kite** (look out during October to May for the migrant nominate race *Milvus migrans migrans*), but also the **African harrier-hawk, augur buzzard** (both white and dark morphs), **long-crested, Wahlberg's** and **martial eagle, lanner** & **peregrine falcon** and also the rather common (in Musanze) **hooded vulture**. Other sightings have included **gabar goshawk** and **European honey-buzzard**.

The largest centre near the eastern lake shore, Butaro is separated from Musangabo by a spectacular 17km stretch of road that hugs the cultivated contours about 100–200m above the lake shore. *En route*, the road passes through the small market village of Umugu. Butaro itself lies a couple of kilometres off the main road, along a side road to Gicumbi/Byumba, signposted for the Rugezi Birding Area. About 50m from this junction, the attractive Rusumo Falls (not to be confused with their namesake on the Tanzania border) used to tumble over a cliff to the fields next to the lake at the confluence of two rivers, one lateritic, the other black. The waterfall has been diverted to feed a small hydroelectric scheme so there is no longer anything much to see.

From the Butaro junction, you have three options: turn back, head southwest towards Gicumbi/Byumba via the Rugezi Wetlands, or head more directly south

Stands of eucalyptus trees also boast a huge variety of species, especially where they're not subject to much human activity. Species include **chinspot batis**, **spotted flycatcher** (October–May), **African stonechat** (also in cultivations), **brown-crowned tchagra**, and **yellow-bellied** and **fawn-breasted waxbills**, and there is even the chance of finding **narina trogon** (seen 1.5km from the centre of Musanze). **Klaas's diederik** and **red-chested cuckoos** are heard all the time during October to May.

Mpenge River and its associated wetland area is about 1km from the fuel station (Kobil) at the southern end of Musanze (also the location of a local market twice a week). Early mornings here can produce **black crake**, **cape** and **pied wagtails**, **white-browed** and **red-capped robin-chats**, and a variety of weavers. These include **baglafecht**, **slender-billed**, **northern brown-throated**, **yellow-backed (black-headed)** and **Holub's golden weavers**, which are all easily viewed and identified. The surrounding reed-beds and papyrus are easily accessible for viewing Palearctic warblers during the period from September/October to April/May.

The Rugezi Swamps are another location where the endangered **Grauer's swamp warbler** breeds and a host of reed-bed and papyrus specials can be found. This could also make up part of a journey around lakes Burera and/or Ruhondo, where flooded areas (such as the northern shore of Lake Burera) are the scene for jaw-dropping antics of **pied kingfishers**. **Yellow-billed storks**, **African spoonbills**, **little grebes**, **African jacanas**, **grey herons**, **intermediate-**, **cattle-** and **little egrets** frequent these areas as well. The **black saw-wings** are particularly obliging here and provide good viewing and photo opportunities.

The road to the southern part of Lake Ruhondo (turning off from the road to Kigali at the stone crushers) follows the Mukungwa River for part of the way, where **malachite kingfishers** can be observed from close proximity. The area is dominated by cultivated land but the irrigation 'ditches' often hide **hamerkop**, **African spoonbill**, **yellow-billed storks** and **sacred ibis**. **Fan-tailed widowbirds** are also seen close to the road. It is ideal for good sightings of swallows such as the **Angola**, **wire-tailed**, **mosque**, **barn** (October–May), and **lesser-striped** varieties.

A few days birding in and around Musanze can thus be very productive and result in a very respectable bird list which would include quite a few 'specials'.

Marcell Claassen (http://rwandabirdingguide.blogspot.com) is a birding guide who was based in Musanze/Ruhengeri until 2010.

to Base on the main road between Kigali and Musanze. If getting back to Musanze quickly is your main priority, then the best option is to return the way you came, a trip of around 40km (of which 30km is on dirt).

The dirt road from Butaro to towards Gicumbi is most likely to be of interest to birders wanting to check out the Rugezi Birding Area. Good vantages over the swamp can be obtained from the birding watchtowers at Mubinga, Marwa I, and Marwa II, which respectively lie 5km, 11km and 13km past Butaro, though you would need binoculars to see much birdlife properly. After passing the last of these watchtowers, it is around 40km to Gicumbi, or you could return to Musanze the way you came.

Alternatively, from the Butaro junction, you could carry on straight past the hydroelectric station to complete the lake circuit, an 85km trip of which 40km is on dirt, Be aware, however, that this road veers away from the lake, so the views are few and far between. Assuming that you do decide to sally forth, the next main settlement you will reach, after 13km, is Kirambo. Here, you can either turn left along a side road which leads to the village of Ruyange in a cultivated river valley at the southern tip of Lake Burera (a 20km round trip), or else continue straight ahead towards Base on the main Kigali–Musanze road. Base lies 28km past Kirambo, and is almost equidistant between Kigali and Musanze.

By public transport It is easy enough to get as far as Kidaho – any Cyanika-bound minibus-taxi can drop you there, though you will probably be expected to pay the full fare of around Rfr400 – from where a motorcycle-taxi to the Musangabo Peninsula will cost around Rfr500, Alternatively, there are now a few minibus taxis between Kidaho and Butaro daily, costing around Rfr1,100, but an early start is

THE NYABINGI CULT

Traditionally the most popular spirit among the Bakiga of southwest Uganda and neighbouring parts of Rwanda is that of a respected rainmaker called Nyabingi, who – possibly in the mid to late 18th century – was murdered by a rival medium at her home in Mukante in the Bufundi Hills of the Rwanda-Uganda border area. After the death of Nyabingi, legend has it, her attendants were visited by numerous ill or barren Bakiga villagers, who would make sacrifices to the late rainmaker's spirit, which would cure their ailment if it approved of the items offered. Over subsequent decades, the spirit possessed a succession of Bakiga mediums, mostly but not always women, who would be blessed with Nyabinga's powers of healing, rainmaking and curing infertility.

Several Nyabingi mediums incited local uprisings against colonialism. The first such rebel was Queen Muhumusa, of mysterious origin, but possibly a former wife of the late Rwandan King Rwabuguri Kigeri. In 1909, Muhumusa was imprisoned by the German authorities in Rwanda after threatening that her son Ndungutse would capture the throne and boot the colonists out of his kingdom. Upon her release in 1911, the Queen crossed the border into Uganda and settled at Ihanga Hill near Bubale, 12km from present-day Kabale on the Kisoro Road. She then announced that she had come in search of a cave wherein was secured a sacred drum which, she claimed, would call up a limitless stream of calves when beaten by her and her son. As the news of the magic drum spread though Kigezi, hundreds of young Bakiga men joined in the quest for its location, hoping for a share of the spoils, and Muhumusa received wide support from local chiefs.

The Christian Muganda chiefs installed by the British in southwest Uganda regarded the growing cult surrounding Muhumusa to be evil and insurrectionist, and refused to have anything to do with it. This angered Muhumusa, who attacked the home of one such chief, burning it to the ground, killing several people, and threatening to impale her victim on a sharpened pole, along with any other disrespectful chiefs she could capture. The colonial authorities responded to this affront by attacking Muhumusa's residence with 50 troops and a cannon. At least 40 of the medium's followers were killed on the spot and buried in a mass grave, and several more died of wounds after fleeing the battle site. Muhumusa was captured and imprisoned in Mbarara, where she remained until her death in 1945. The British authorities then proceeded to criminalise the Nyabingi cult through the Witchcraft Ordinance of 1912.

recommended if you want to be certain of getting back to Musanze the same day. No public transport appears to run from Butaro south towards Base or southwest towards Gicumbi/Byumba.

Lake Burera could also be explored more extensively by boat, but it is an option suitable only for those with a pioneering spirit. The obvious place to start a trip of this sort would be Musangabo, though boats are the main form of transport throughout the area, so it should be easy enough to hire a boat and paddler anywhere. There are at least four large islands in the southern half of the lake: Mudimba, Munanira, Bushongo and Batutsi. In theory, it should be possible to boat to the south of Lake Burera, hike across the narrow strip of hilly terrain that separates it from Lake Ruhondo, and then pick up another boat to the Foyer de Charité on the southern shore of that lake (see *Lake Ruhondo*, page 232). We've never heard of a traveller who attempted this, so drop us a line to let us know how it goes!

In order to help win over local converts, the earliest Christian missionaries to Rwanda and southwest Uganda used words associated with the Nyabingi cult in their sermons and descriptions of Christian rituals. The Virgin Mary was portrayed as a spiritual icon similar to but more powerful than Nyabingi, and many locals adopted the Mother of Jesus as a substitute for the traditional spirit associated with healing and fertility. By the 1930s, the Nyabingi cult, if not completely dead, had gone so far underground as to be undetectable – while it became increasingly common for locals to claim having seen the Virgin Mary at sites of worship formerly associated with Nyabingi.

At least one former Nyabingi shrine has more recently been adopted by a nominally Christian cult. The Nyabugoto Caves near the small town of Kunungu in southwest Uganda were in times past occupied by a renowned medium who regularly cured barren Bakiga women. In the late 1970s, it was reported that a local woman called Blandina Buzigye witnessed a large rock formation in this cave transform into the Virgin Mary before her eyes. It was in the same Ugandan cave, ten years later, that a former prostitute called Credonia Mwerinde founded a fertility cult that mutated into the doomsday movement whose entire membership was locked inside a blazing church by the leaders in a shocking massacre that attracted world headlines in March 2000.

Oddly enough, the term Nyabingi found its way across the Atlantic to Jamaica, where admirers of the rebellious Queen Muhumusa incorporated what are known as nyabinghi chants into their celebrations. Sometimes abbreviated to *bhingi*, the chants and dances were originally performed to invoke 'death to the black or white oppressors' but today they are purely ceremonial. Three differently pitched drums are used to create the nyabinghi beat, which – popularised in the late 1950s by the recording artist Count Ossie – has been a huge rhythmic influence on better-known secular Jamaican genres such as ska and reggae. Nyabinghi is also the name of a fundamentalist but strictly pacifist Rastafarian cult which regards the late Ethiopian emperor Haile Selassie as having been an earthly incarnation of God. Indeed, according to some Rastafarian cultists in Jamaica, the neglected Nyabingi spirit abandoned its home in the Rwanda-Uganda border area in 1937 and relocated to Ethiopia, where it took possession of Haile Selassie during the Italian Occupation. The present whereabouts of the spirit is unknown.

BATWA PYGMIES

We have always lived in the forest. Like my father and grandfathers, I lived from hunting and collecting in this mountain. Then the Bahutu came. They cut the forest to cultivate the land. They carried on cutting and planting until they had encircled our forest with their fields. Today, they come right up to our huts. Instead of forest, now we are surrounded by Irish potatoes!

> *Gahut Gahuliro, a Mutwa born 100 years earlier on the slopes of the Virungas, talking in 1999.*

The Batwa (singular Mutwa) pygmies are the most ancient inhabitants of interlacustrine Africa, and easily distinguished from other inhabitants of the region by their unusually short stature and paler, more bronzed complexion. Semi-nomadic by inclination, small egalitarian communities of Batwa kin traditionally live in impermanent encampments of flimsy leaf huts, set in a forest clearing, which they will up and leave when food becomes scarce locally, upon the death of a community member, or when the whim takes them. In times past, the Batwa wore only a drape of animal hide or bark cloth, and had little desire to accumulate possessions – a few cooking pots, some hunting gear, and that's about it.

The traditional Batwa lifestyle is based around hunting, undertaken as a team effort by the males of a community. In some areas, the favoured method involves part of the hunting party stringing a long net between a few trees, while the rest advance noisily to herd small game into the net to be speared. In other areas, poisoned arrows are favoured: the group will move silently along the forest floor looking for potential prey, shoot it from a distance, then wait until it drops and if necessary deliver the final blow with a spear.

Today, the Batwa population of Rwanda, Burundi, Uganda and the eastern DRC is around 100,000. Only 2,000 years ago, however, East and Southern Africa was populated almost solely by Batwa and related hunter-gatherers, whose lifestyle differed little from that of our earliest common human ancestors. Since then, agriculturist and pastoralist settlers, by persecution or assimilation, have reduced the region's hunter-gatherers to a few small and mostly degraded communities living in unwanted habitats such as rainforest interiors and deserts.

The initial incursions into Batwa territory were made when the first Bantu-speaking farmers settled on the forested montane escarpment of the Albertine Rift, some time before the 16th century, and set about clearing small tracts of forest for subsistence agriculture and pasture. This process of deforestation was greatly accelerated in the early 20th century. By the 1930s, the few substantial tracts of highland forest remaining in the region had all been gazetted as forest reserves by the colonial authorities. Although this move to protect the forests did ensure that what little remained of them would not be lost to agriculture, it was also detrimental to the legal status of the Batwa – true, they were still permitted to hunt and forage within the reserves, but, where formerly these forests had been recognised as Batwa communal land, they were now government property.

Fifty years later the Batwa faced the full ramifications of having thus lost all legal entitlement to their ancestral lands. In the 1970s and 1980s, Batwa communities resident in most of the region's conservation areas were evicted, a move backed by international donors who also insisted that hunting and other forest harvesting – traditional subsistence activities of the Batwa – should be criminalised. Adding insult to injury, while compensation was awarded to non-Batwa farmers who had settled within protected areas after they were gazetted and illegally cleared forest to make way for cultivation, the evicted Batwa were compensated only if they had destroyed part of the forest reserve in a similar manner.

In the early 1990s, Rwanda's last forest-dwelling Batwa were evicted from Gishwati to make way for a World Bank project intended to protect the natural forest. The World Bank later concluded that the project had failed, with more than half of the original forest having been cleared for pasture prior to 1994, and it admitted that the treatment of indigenous peoples had been 'highly unsatisfactory'.

Today, more than 40% of Batwa households in Rwanda are landless, and none has legal access to the forest on which their traditional livelihood depends. Indeed, most Batwa now eke out a marginal living from casual wage labour on other peoples' farms, porterage, simple craftwork (particularly pottery), and singing and dancing at festivals – many are in essence forced to live as beggars. Furthermore, with Batwa men no longer able to fulfil their traditional roles as hunters and providers, many have turned to alcohol and drug (or spousal) abuse, leading to the imminent collapse of Batwa cultural values.

Locally, the Batwa are viewed not with sympathy, but rather as objects of ridicule. The extent of local prejudice against them can be garnered from a set of interviews posted on the Ugandan website www.edrisa.org. The Batwa, report some of their Bakiga neighbours: 'smoke marijuana ... like alcohol ... make noise all night long ... eat too much food ... cannot grow their own food and crops ... depend on hunting and begging ... don't care about their children ... the man makes love to his wife while the children sleep on their side' – a collection of circumstantially induced half-truths and outright fallacies that make the Batwa come across as the debauched survivors of a dysfunctional hippie commune!

Prejudice against the Batwa is not confined to their immediate neighbours. The 1997 edition of Richard Nzita's otherwise commendable People and Cultures of Uganda contrives, in the space of two pages, to characterise the pygmoid peoples of Uganda as beggars, crop raiders and pottery thieves – even cannibals! Conservationists and the Western media, meanwhile, persistently stigmatise the Batwa as gorilla hunters and poachers – this despite the Batwa's strong taboo against killing or eating gorillas. Almost certainly, any gorilla hunting that may be undertaken by the Batwa today will have been instigated by outsiders.

The Batwa and their hunter-gatherer ancestors have inhabited the forests of the Albertine Rift for millennia. Their traditional lifestyle places no rigorous demands on the forest and could be cited as a model of the holy grail of modern conservationists: sustainable use of natural resources. They were not major participants in the deforestation of the region, but have certainly been the main human victims of this loss. And Batwa and gorillas cohabited the same forests for many millennia before their futures were both imperilled by identical external causes in the 20th century. As Jerome Lewis writes: 'They and their way of life are entitled to as much consideration and respect as other ways of life. There was and is nothing to be condemned in forest nomadism ... The Batwa ... used the environment without destroying or seriously damaging it. It is only through their long-term custody of the area that later comers have good land to use.'

Quotes from Lewis and Gahuliro come from Jerome Lewis's exemplary report Batwa Pygmies of the Great Lakes Region, *downloadable for a nominal fee at www. minorityrights.org/1056/reports/batwa-pygmies-of-the-great-lakes-region.html.*

On foot Keen walkers might also think about exploring the area over a few days. We've not heard of anybody doing this, so it would be uncharted territory, and would probably be practical only if you have a tent and are prepared to ask permission to camp at the many villages and homesteads you encounter. It could well be advisable to carry some food (though fish and potatoes should be easy to buy along the way). It is difficult to imagine that any serious security concerns are attached to hiking in this Uganda border area; you'll come across loads of local pedestrians for company, and travellers are still something of a novelty in this rural region.

The road to the east of the lake can effectively be viewed as an unusually wide hiking trail: it offers great views the whole way, is used by very few vehicles, and follows the contours for most of its length. The most beautiful stretch for hiking is the 44km between Musangabo and Butaro (which can also be covered by boat), and you would be forced to walk the 13km between Butaro and Kirambo. From Kirambo, there is a limited amount of public transport to Base, where it is easy to find a lift on to Musanze or Kigali.

Where to stay
Exclusive

🏠 **Virunga Lodge** (8 rooms) ☏ 0252 502452/ 576530 or (UK) 0870 8708480 or (US toll-free) 1 866 5992737; e salesrw@volcanoessafaris.com or salesuk@volcanoessafaris.com; www. volcanoessafaris.com; ⊕ S 01°26.694, E 029°44.517. Boasting one of the most stunning locations in Africa, this superb lodge lies on a 2,175m hilltop above lakes Burera & Ruhondo. In addition to stunning views over the lakes to its southeast, the panorama stretches northwest to embrace 4 of the Virunga Volcanoes, providing a magnificent overview of this wild volcanic landscape. If you're after organic bush chic rather than transatlantic luxury, this is one of the top 2 or 3 lodges anywhere in Rwanda, comprising 8 secluded & recently renovated stone-&-wood chalets that are both spacious & stylish, with hardwood floors, ample wood & bamboo in the décor, & private verandas offering superb views either to the volcanoes or to the lakes, depending which side you're on. All rooms have 2 dbl beds & a walk-in net, spacious net bathrooms with hot water, sensor lights at night, & a selection of current magazines for reading. This is an excellent base for gorilla tracking, with the one caveat being that the distance from Kinigi enforces an earlier start than other lodges (ideally at 06.00 – but the staff are used to this & organise early wake-up calls, showers & b/fast as a matter of course). The food is excellent, as the selection of complimentary wine is usually, & guests eat dinner at one large table. Other activities include a guided or unguided nature trail, village visits, & nightly Intore dancing. The lodge lies about 30mins' drive from Musanze, turning right off the Cyanika road after 16km at Nyaragondo junction (⊕ S 01°25.073, E 029°43.509). *US$500 pp inc all meals, alcoholic & non-alcoholic drinks, laundry, massage, activities around the lodge & all government taxes.*

Shoestring

🏠 **Burera Lake House** (17 rooms) m 078 8485751. The only guesthouse in Butaro, so far as we could ascertain, this unsignposted orange building next to the Bank of Kigali is nothing to write home about, but the basic rooms are sensibly priced. *Rfr3,000 sgl using common shower; Rfr7,000 en-suite dbl.*

🏠 **Paradise Motel** m 078 8478512; e harelimanaviateur@yahoo.fr. Situated in Kirambo, about 13km south of Butaro, this small newish establishment is very friendly & helpful, & it also serves meals, including outstanding rabbit & fried potatoes! *Rfr10,000 for an en-suite trpl with cold water only.*

LAKE RUHONDO Separated from Lake Burera by a 1km-wide strip of land (thought to be an ancient lava flow from Mount Sabinyo), Lake Ruhondo is, like its more northerly neighbour, an erratically shaped body of water whose shore follows the contours of the tall, steep hills that characterise this part of Rwanda. In common with Lake Burera, Ruhondo's shores are densely cultivated, and little natural vegetation remains, but it is nevertheless a very beautiful spot, offering dramatic views across the water to the volcanically formed cones of the Virunga Mountains looming on the horizon. Ruhondo is also an easy target for an overnight excursion, since good accommodation is available – though availability should be confirmed in advance.

The lake is most accessible from the southwest, where the Foyer de Charité guesthouse has a superb location on a hilltop overlooking the lake, with sweeping views across to the volcanoes in the northwest, and potentially stupendous sunsets. Several footpaths lead down the steep slopes below the mission to the lake shore, a knee-crunching descent and lung-wrenching ascent. At the lake, it is easy to negotiate a fee to take a pirogue to one of the islands, or to the hydro-electric plant on the opposite shore, where a small waterfall connects Lake Ruhondo with Lake Burera.

Getting around The best route to the Foyer de Charité starts on the main Kigali road about 5km south of Musanze. Coming from Musanze, you need to turn left along a dirt road signposted for Remera which initially leads through a marshy area dotted with traditional brickmaking urns, before following a cultivated river valley. After 2.8km, take a left fork, then almost 2km after that turn right to cross a bridge over the river. The road is flat until this point, but now it starts to ascend gently, with the lake becoming visible to the left about 2.5km past the bridge. Several footpaths lead from this viewpoint to the lake shore, an easier ascent than the one from the Foyer de Charité. Beyond the viewpoint, the road continues to climb for 3km to the village of Kadahero, where a left turn leads after about 200m to the mission.

This is all straightforward enough provided that you have a vehicle, ideally a 4x4, and that – if driving along the tar from Kigali – you don't inadvertently take an earlier road signposted for Remera (this road does lead to the mission, but it's longer and rougher). There is no public transport, however, and hitching might prove to be frustrating. One option would be to catch public transport towards Musanze as far as the turn-off to Remera, then to walk the final 10km to the mission (the last 6km would be steep going with a rucksack). The alternative is to hire a motorcycle-taxi from Musanze – the going rate is around Rfr2,000 one-way – and arrange to be collected at a specified time.

 **Where to stay**

Foyer de Charité (45 rooms) \0252 547024; m 078 8510659; e vdprw@yahoo.fr. Established as a religious retreat in 1968, this mission was renovated in 1995 after it had been damaged during the genocide. It remains first & foremost a religious retreat, but respectful lay visitors are usually permitted to stay provided that they make advance arrangements. Comfortable guest rooms with wash basins are available, as are communal solar-heated showers, inexpensive & filling meals, & cold beers & sodas. There is little in the way of formal entertainment (the beautiful singing at evening mass in the chapel might qualify I suppose), but it's a lovely place to relax for a couple of days, & there's plenty of room for exploration on the surrounding roads. It is essential to make contact in advance, as the mission closes to lay visitors for special religious events – which probably add up to around 100 days annually. *Room rates are negotiable, but expect to pay around Rfr10,000/15,000 sgl/dbl.*

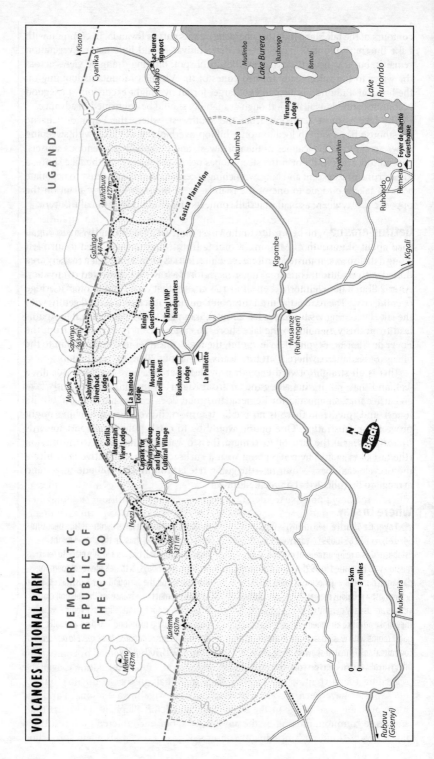

VOLCANOES NATIONAL PARK

UGANDA

Kisoro

Cyanika

Lac Burera signpost

Kidaho

Lake Burera

Mudimba

Bushongo

Batutsi

Virunga Lodge

Lake Ruhondo

Icyobarihira

Remera

Foyer de Charité Guesthouse

Ruhondo

Nkumba

Muhabura
4127m

Gasiza Plantation

Kigombe

Kigali

Gahinga
3474m

Kinigi VNP headquarters

Musanze (Ruhengeri)

Kinigi Guesthouse

Sabyinyo
3634m

Mountain Gorilla's Nest

Bushokoro Lodge

La Paillotte

Musule

La Bambou Lodge

Sabyinyo Silverback Lodge

Gorilla Mountain View Lodge

Carpark for Sabyinyo Group and Iby'Iwacu Cultural Village

N

Bradt

DEMOCRATIC REPUBLIC OF THE CONGO

Ngezi

Bisoke
3711m

Mikeno
4437m

Karisimbi
4507m

0   5km
0   3 miles

Mukamira

Rubavu (Gisenyi)

10

Volcanoes National Park

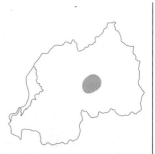

The 160km² Volcanoes National Park protects the Rwandan sector of the Virunga Mountains, a range of six extinct and three active volcanoes that straddle the Ugandan and Congolese borders and protect more than half the global population of the charismatic mountain gorilla. Sometimes referred to by its French name Parc des Volcans, it forms part of a contiguous 433km² transfrontier conservation unit that protects the upper slopes of the Virungas in their entirety, and also incorporates the southern portion of the Congolese Virunga National Park and Uganda's Mgahinga National Park. The three national parks function separately today, but prior to 1960 the Rwandan and Congolese sectors were jointly managed as the Albert National Park.

Volcanoes National Park is an immensely scenic and ecologically diverse destination. Indeed, this chain of steep free-standing mountains, spanning altitudes of 2,400m to 4,507m, and linked by fertile saddles formed by solidified lava flows, ranks among the most stirring and memorable of African landscapes. The tallest member of the chain, and the most westerly part of the national park, is Karisimbi (4,507m) on the border with the DRC. Moving eastwards, the other main peaks within the national park are Bisoke (aka Visoke) on the DRC border. Sabyinyo at the tripartite border with Uganda and the DRC, and Gahinga (aka Mgahinga) and Muhabura (aka Muhavura) on the Uganda border.

Tracking mountain gorillas is easily the most popular tourist activity in Volcanoes National Park. However, a wide variety of other hikes and activities are offered, making it possible to spend several days in the area without running out of things to do. The most popular activity after gorilla tracking is a visit to a habituated troop of the rare golden monkey, an Albertine Rift endemic whose modern range is more-or-less restricted to the Virungas. Also quite popular is the hike to Dian Fossey's former camp and grave on the forested slopes of Karisoke,. Fewer visitors embark on the more demanding day treks to the summits of Bisoke (famed for its beautiful crater lake) or Muhabura, and fewer still are up for the overnight hike to the highest point in the range, the summit of Karisimbi.

WILDLIFE

Gorillas and golden monkeys aside, primates are poorly represented by comparison with most other large forests in Rwanda and Uganda. Little information is available regarding the current status of other large mammals in the mountains, but 70-plus species have been recorded in neighbouring Mgahinga National Park, and most probably also occur in the larger Rwanda sector. Elephant and buffalo are still quite common, judging by the amount of spoor encountered on forest trails, but are very timid and infrequently observed. Also present are giant forest hog, bushpig, bushbuck, black-fronted duiker, spotted hyena, and several varieties of small predator. Recent extinctions, probably as a result of deforestation, include the massive yellow-backed duiker and leopard.

A bird checklist for Volcanoes National Park compiled in 1980 totalled 180 species. About 15 previously unrecorded species were noted during a 2004 biodiversity survey, but it is possible that several other forest specialists have vanished since 1980. A local speciality is the vulnerable swamp-dwelling Grauer's rush warbler, while at least 16 Albertine Rift endemics are present, including handsome francolin, Ruwenzori turaco, Ruwenzori double-collared sunbird, Ruwenzori batis, strange weaver, dusky crimson-wing, collared apalis, red-faced woodland warbler and Archer's ground robin.

HISTORY, CONSERVATION AND ECOTOURISM

The ecology of the Virungas remained practically unknown to western science until 1902, when the German explorer Oscar von Beringe ascended Mount Sabyinyo and became the first European to encounter – and to kill – a mountain gorilla (see box, page 10). Over the following two decades, at least 50 individual mountain gorillas were captured or killed in the Virungas, prompting the Belgian government to establish the Albert National Park by decree on 21 April 1925, protecting a triangle formed by the Karisimbi, Mikeno and Bisoke volcanoes.

At the time of its creation, this was the first national park in Africa to be known as such. The Institut du Parc National Albert was created by decree on 9 July 1929. A further decree on 12 November 1935 determined the final boundaries of the Albert National Park, then covering 809,000ha. About 8% of the park lay in what is now Rwanda and today constitutes the Volcanoes National Park, while the rest was in the Congo. At the time of independence, Rwanda's new leaders confirmed that they would maintain the park (the gorillas were already well known internationally), the pressing problem of overpopulation notwithstanding.

SCHALLER AND FOSSEY The gorilla population of the Virungas is thought to have been reasonably stable in 1960, when a census undertaken by George Schaller indicated that some 450 individuals lived in the range. By 1971–73, however, the population had plummeted to an estimated 250. This decline was caused by several factors, including the post-colonial division of the Albert National Park into its Rwandan and Congolese components, the ongoing fighting between the Hutu and Tutsi of Rwanda, and a grisly tourist trade in poached gorilla heads and hands – the latter used by some sad individuals as ashtrays! Most devastating of all perhaps was the irreversible loss of almost half of the gorillas' habitat between 1957 and 1968 to local farmers and a European-funded agricultural scheme.

George Schaller initiated the first study of mountain gorilla behaviour in the 1950s, and his pioneering work formed the starting point for the more recent and well-known behavioural study undertaken by the American primatologist Dian Fossey a decade later. Fossey arrived in Rwanda to study its mountain gorillas in 1967, supported by the eminent Kenyan palaeontologist Louis Leakey, who had earlier been responsible for placing Jane Goodall at Gombe Stream in Tanzania. She founded the Karisoke Research Centre high on the forested slopes of Mount Karisimbi, and for the next 18 years used it as the base for her ongoing studies of Volcanoes National Park's mountain gorillas.

It is largely thanks to Fossey's single-minded and somewhat paramilitary campaign to discourage poaching in Volcanoes National Park that this activity was curtailed while there were still some gorillas to save. For this, she would pay the ultimate price. Her brutal murder at the Karisoke Research Centre in December 1985, though officially unsolved, is widely thought to have been the work of one of the many poachers whom she antagonised in her efforts to save her gorillas. Three years after her death, Fossey's life work was exposed to a mass audience with the release of *Gorillas in the Mist*, a cinematic account of her life that was filmed on location in Volcanoes National Park. The film grossed more than US$60 million worldwide, was nominated for five Academy Awards, and generated unprecedented global interest in mountain gorillas and ecotourism in the Virungas.

GORILLA TOURISM 1979–94 In 1979, Amy Vedder and Bill Weber initiated the first gorilla tourism project in Rwanda's Volcanoes Park, integrating tourism, local education and anti-poaching measures with remarkable success. Initially, the project was aimed mainly at tourists in overland trucks, who paid a paltry – by today's standards – US$20 per person to track gorillas. Even so, gorilla tourism was raising up to ten million US dollars annually by the mid 1980s, making it Rwanda's third-highest earner of foreign revenue, and the industry was given a further boost with the release of the film *Gorillas in the Mist* in 1988.

By that time, Volcanoes National Park was the best organised and most popular gorilla sanctuary in Africa, and gorilla tourism was probably Rwanda's leading earner of tourist revenue. What's more, the mountain gorilla had practically become the national emblem of Rwanda, and it was officially recognised to be the country's most important renewable natural resource. To ordinary Rwandans, gorillas became a source of great national pride: living gorillas ultimately created far more work and money than poaching them had ever done. As a result, a census undertaken in 1989 indicated that the local mountain gorilla population had increased by almost 30% to 320 animals.

Gorilla tourism came to an abrupt halt in 1991, when the country erupted into the civil war that culminated in the 1994 genocide. In February 1992, the park headquarters were attacked, two park employees were killed, and the Karisoke Research Centre established by Fossey had to be evacuated. The park was closed to tourists and, although it reopened in June 1993, it had to be evacuated in April 1994 because of the genocide.

WAR AND THE GORILLAS The Rwandan civil war raised considerable concern about the survival of the gorillas, as land mines were planted there by various military factions, and the mountains provided an escape route to thousands of fleeing refugees. Remarkably, however, when researchers were finally able to return to the park, it was discovered that only four gorillas could not be accounted for. Two of those missing were old females who most probably died of natural causes; the other two might have been shot, but might just as easily have succumbed to disease. It is also encouraging to note that the war had no evident effect on breeding activity, a strong indication that it was less disruptive to the gorillas than had been feared.

But in this most volatile part of Africa little can be taken for granted. Just as Rwanda started to stabilise politically, the DRC descended into anarchy. For years, eastern Congolese officials, who lived far from the capital, received no formal salary and were forced to devise their own ways of securing a living, leading to a level of corruption second to none in the region. At least 16 gorillas were killed in three separate incidents in the DRC between 1995 and 1998, since when the Congolese part of the Virungas was effectively closed to tourists and researchers alike prior to re-opening in 2005.

Under the circumstances, it is remarkable to learn that a gorilla count undertaken in the Virungas in 2003 showed a continued increase to at least 380 individuals. No further killings were reported between 2003 and 2007, but then at least ten Congolese mountain gorillas were shot in four separate incidents in the space of a few months, culminating in the arrest of the alleged perpetrators in September of that year. The good news continued when the results of the latest census, announced in December 2010, placed the number of mountain gorillas in the Virungas at 480, the highest figure since the first formal census was undertaken 50 years earlier. A total of 36 groups were counted, of which 17 are normally resident in Rwanda.

PROS AND CONS OF GORILLA TOURISM Any concern about the fate of a few gorillas might seem misplaced in the context of a genocide that claimed a million human lives. But it is these self-same gorillas which have allowed Rwanda to rebuild the lucrative tourist industry that was shattered by the war. Gorilla tracking resumed

INTERNATIONAL CONSERVATION ORGANISATIONS

Mountain gorillas are the focus of several conservation organisations. The most important international organisations currently working in Rwanda are listed alphabetically with a summary of their activities:

DIAN FOSSEY GORILLA FUND INTERNATIONAL Founded in 1978, the Atlanta-based DFGFI funds and operates the Karisoke Research Centre (*www.gorillafund.org; select 'Karisoke Research Centre'*), originally established by Dr Dian Fossey in 1967. Although the original research centre was destroyed during the 1990s, it has been replaced by a new centre employing 80 staff in Musanze town. It continues to monitor three gorilla groups and to carry out daily anti-poaching patrols from a base outside the park. DFGFI aims to strengthen research and protection efforts through education, local capacity building, and support to a Geographic Information Systems unit based within the national university.

THE GORILLA ORGANIZATION (*www.gorillas.org*) Founded in 1992, this London-based organisation, an advocate of community-led conservation, manages several projects designed to integrate traditional conservation and research with economic development and education in Rwanda, Uganda, DR Congo, Cameroon and Gabon. These include:

- Beekeepers, who are supported to develop modern sustainable honey farms at the edge of, rather than inside, the park boundary.
- Fresh water in village schools using local engineering technology to provide water cisterns. Water collection is one of the main causes of encroachment in the gorilla habitat, and children living close to the forest often miss school to collect water for their families.
- Training in sustainable agriculture for farmers in areas adjacent to gorilla habitat.
- Tree planting to alleviate environmental degradation, since most fuel used in households comes from wood.
- Virunga Wildlife Clubs in schools, which organise field trips, tree planting and environment-week activities, and a Conservation Network that links local organisations in the Virunga region.

on a permanent basis in July 1999, and Volcanoes National Park has remained open ever since, a period during which the volume of permits sold annually has increased more than tenfold. Mostly, it's the gorillas that bring tourists to Rwanda, but once there they will usually spend money in other parts of the country, providing foreign revenue and creating employment beyond the immediate vicinity of Volcanoes National Park.

There are those who query the wisdom of habituating gorillas for tourist visits. One area of concern is health, with humans and gorillas being sufficiently close genetically for there to be a real risk of passing a viral or bacterial infection to a habituated gorilla, which might in turn infect other members of its group, potentially resulting in all their deaths should they have no resistance to the infection. Another concern is that habituating gorillas to humans increases their vulnerability to poachers, a theory backed up by the fact that most mountain gorillas poached since the mid-1990s belonged to habituated troops.

INTERNATIONAL GORILLA CONSERVATION PROGRAMME (*www.mountaingorillas.org*) IGCP is a joint initiative of three organisations: the African Wildlife Foundation, Fauna and Flora International and the World Wide Fund for Nature. Their goal is the sustainable conservation of the world's remaining mountain gorillas and their habitat. IGCP promotes communication and cooperation between protected-area authorities through regional meetings, training programmes, cross-border patrols and contact networks; and advises governments on environmental policy and legislation enforcement. It provides training and support for park staff, and has set up a Ranger-based Monitoring programme throughout the Virunga region.

MOUNTAIN GORILLA VETERINARY PROJECT (*gorilladoctors.org*) MGVP provides veterinary care to the mountain gorillas. The project's vets monitor the health of individual gorillas in both the research and tourist groups, and are able to intervene in emergency situations, such as a gorilla becoming trapped by a life-threatening snare. Since disease transmission from humans is a serious threat to the gorillas' survival, MGVP also monitors the health of government and project staff working in the park, and organises seminars addressing health and hygiene issues. The MGVP receives funding from the Morris Animal Foundation and is affiliated to the Maryland Zoo in Baltimore, USA.

WILDLIFE CONSERVATION SOCIETY (*www.wcs.org*) With strong historic links to the mountain gorillas, WCS's major programme in Rwanda is now the Nyungwe Forest Conservation Project, although it is still involved with the Volcanoes and Akagera National Parks. It also implements training programmes in monitoring and research with its partners, including the Rwanda Development Board (RDB); provides direct support to the management of parks and wildlife; and supports RDB in tackling immediate threats. In addition, the volcanoes fall within the WCS's **Albertine Rift Project** (*www.albertinerift.org*). The objective of this programme is to improve conservation by providing information for park managers, better management of these areas, and collaboration across national boundaries. Biological and socio-economic surveys are used to identify priority conservation areas and to plan measures to alleviate poverty in the communities that border them.

The birth of a child in Rwanda is a big event for the family and neighbourhood, and the naming of the child at the Kwita Izina ceremony is traditionally the chance to welcome him or her into the wider world. The baby is carried outside and shown to the public, and young children suggest names for this infant who has recently joined them. The parents then select one of the names. It's a lively gathering, accompanied by plenty of food, drink and, of course, dancing.

In the past few decades, the Kwita Izina naming tradition has also been applied to young mountain gorillas, with the park guides taking on the role of proposing the names – which are based on the behaviour, circumstances and background of the infants or their mother. This gorilla-naming ceremony was a low-key private affair up until 2004, but in June 2005 it was held publicly at the Mountain Gorilla's Nest Hotel in Kinigi, and the official naming of 23 gorillas was followed by a celebration party with traditional music and dancing.

So successful was the inaugural public ceremony that it has now become an annual event, held in mid to late June, when all gorillas born over the past 12 months are given a formal name to the accompaniment of traditional music and dance. In June 2012, 19 baby gorillas (including one set of twins) and one adult female were given names such as Gikundiro (the beautiful one) and Akabero (beautiful flower). Visitors are most welcome to attend these events, which are now held at a small area in Kinigi, close to the park headquarters. Kwita Izina raises valuable funds for the protection of the mountain gorillas; tour operators will fit it into your itinerary by request. As well as the naming, there is the opportunity to 'adopt' (sponsor) a gorilla and/ or to make general donations to the animals' welfare.

For more information, tickets and details of sponsorship contact RDB (details on page 86) or check www.rwandatourism.com.

Given the above, a reasonable response might be to query the wisdom of habituating gorillas in the first place. The problem facing conservationists is that gorillas cannot be conserved in a vacuum. At current prices, the Rwandan authorities can potentially earn US$48,000 daily in tracking permits alone, much of which is pumped back into the protection and management of the Volcanoes Park or distributed to local communities bordering the park. There are also the broader benefits of job creation through tourism in and around the Virungas. And even in terms of pure conservation, habituation has many positive effects, allowing researchers and rangers to monitor the gorillas on a daily basis, and to intervene when one of them is ill, injured or in a snare.

Put crudely, while tourism is probably integral to the survival of the mountain gorilla, the survival of the mountain gorilla is certainly integral to the growth of Rwanda's tourist industry. Ultimately, it's a symbiotic situation that motivates a far greater number of people to take an active interest in the fate of the gorillas than would be the case if gorilla tourism were to be curtailed.

GETTING THERE AND AWAY

Gorilla tracking and all other activities in Volcanoes National Park start at the RDB office/park headquarters in the sprawling village of Kinigi, which lies at an

COME EXPLORE
WITH PRIMATE

Primate Safaris, just as the name suggests, evokes dreams of mysterious jungles filled with rare flora and fauna and the world of free-living primates. The reality will not disappoint the traveller bored with mass tourism, seeking an exclusive, highly enlightening and enjoyable eco-tourism experience.

We select only the finest hotels and lodges in the cities and out in the bush. Each is carefully chosen to reflect not only our own high standards but also the spirit of the itinerary in which it is used.

Quality guides & transportation, with guaranteed window seats

Primate Safaris Ltd
98, Avenue de la Paix Kigali - Rwanda
Office line: +250 252 503428/9
Cellphone: +250 788300495 / 784300079
Email: info@primatesafaris.info, primatesafaris@rwanda1.com
Website: www.primatesafaris.info

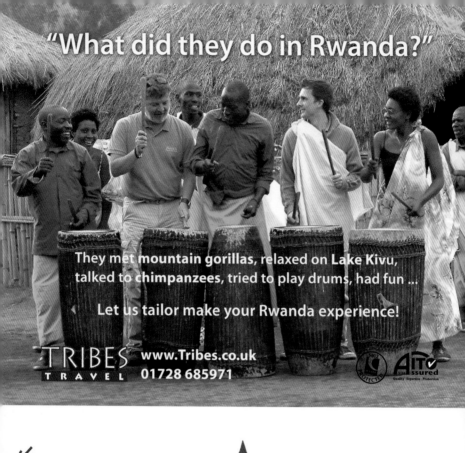

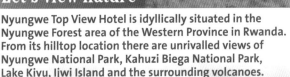

altitude of 2,200m on the eucalyptus-strewn Virunga footslopes (⊕ S 01°25.783, E 029°35.717). Kinigi lies 12km north of Musanze/Ruhengeri, along a recently surfaced road signposted to the left of the Cyanika Road about 300m past the Centre Pastoral Notre Dame de Fatima. All participants in gorilla tracking and other hikes must be at the park headquarters by 07.00, or they risk invalidating any permit bought in advance.

There is a fair amount of public transport to Kinigi. At least one minibus leaves from the bus station in Musanze every 30 minutes, charging Rfr400 per person, and taking 15–20 minutes to get there, but usually stopping a kilometre or two short of the park headquarters. A one-way taxi ride between Musanze and any of the hotels in and around Kinigi will cost around Rfr10,000, while a moto costs Rfr1,500–2,500.

Most visitors on organised trips stay at one of the midrange-to-upmarket lodges scattered in and around Kinigi on the night before they go gorilla tracking or do another hike, which eases the pressure to be at the headquarters by 07.00 on the morning of departure. By contrast, budget-conscious travellers tend to use Musanze as a base for gorilla tracking and other activities, though there are also now some genuinely affordable options close to the park headquarters.

Either way, there is no public transport from the park headquarters to any of the car parks from where one enters the forest to start tracking, and, while individuals may be able to beg a lift with another tourist group, this is not foolproof. Which means that even if you get as far as Musanze or Kinigi using public transport, you will need to arrange to rent a 4x4 with driver to get you to the trailhead. This costs around US$100 for transport in both direction, including waiting time, and it can be arranged a day in advance with Amahoro Tours in Musanze (see page 219), or through any hotel.

With a private vehicle, it is possible to drive to Kinigi from Rubavu/Gisenyi or Kigali on the day you track, though you would need a very early start to be at the assembly point by 07.00. Allow at least two hours from Kigali, or one hour from Rubavu. Virunga Lodge (see page 232), which overlooks Lake Burera 30–45 minutes' drive from Kinigi, is another popular upmarket base for gorilla tracking and other activities in the park.

🏠 WHERE TO STAY AND EAT

There is no accommodation within the national park and overnight camping is forbidden. However, several lodges catering to all budgets are situated within a few kilometres of Kinigi, and are all listed below. Many travellers on a restricted budget overnight in Musanze, and make their way to Kinigi early in the morning,), while those with limited time and a high tolerance for very early mornings sometimes base themselves further off at a hotel in Rubavu/Gisenyi.

EXCLUSIVE

🏠 **Sabyinyo Silverback Lodge** (8 rooms) 📞+254 20 2734000; m 078 5101759; e reservations@governorscamp.com; www. governorscamp.com. This is the swishiest lodge in the immediate vicinity of Kinigi, set on community land at an altitude of 2,515m on the footslopes of Mount Sabyinyo, only a 10min drive from the park headquarters. The land is owned by the Sacola Community Trust & leased to Governors' Camp, a long-serving & award-winning Kenyan luxury safari camp operator which built the lodge & also manages it. A community fee of US$58 pp per night is levied, & the community also receives a cut of the lodge's profits. Accommodation consists of 5 stone cottages, 2 suites & 1 4-bed family suite, all spread out across the grassy slopes.

The stylish & well-equipped rooms combine ethnically influenced decor with something of a country house feel, & come complete with log fire, mini-bar, tea/coffee-making facilities, mini-safe, direct radio contact with the main building (in lieu of a phone line), 24hr electricity, & a fabulously earthy bathroom with tub & shower. The restaurant & lounge area is in the main building & serves a different 3-course set menu daily. In addition to gorilla tracking, it offers birding expeditions, & trips to Musanze & lakes Kivu & Burera. The steep climb from the car park to the accommodation makes this lodge highly unsuited to disabled travellers, though it should be perfectly manageable to anybody fit & supple enough to track gorillas. Rates include full-board accommodation but exclude drinks, gorilla-tracking permits, transfers to/from Kigali & community fee. Visa is accepted. *From US$384/768 to US$849/1358 sgl/dbl, depending on season.*

UPMARKET

⌂ **Mountain Gorilla's Nest** (4 rooms) ☎0252 549016; m 078 3004914; e jeanluc.miravumba@ dubaiworldafrica.com; www.gorillanestlodge.com; ✪ S 01°26.365, E 029°34.729. Situated at an altitude of 2,295m between Kinigi & the Volcanoes National Park boundary, this well-established lodge lies in neat grounds enclosed by an intrusive circle of tall Antipodean eucalyptuses that block what would otherwise be a great view of the ragged-edged rim of Sabyinyo. Now part of the Mantis Collection, a highly regarded South African group of exclusive lodges, it suffered extensive fire damage in 2011 & was still only partially operational in mid-2012. At the time of writing, it effectively functions as a private lodge, serving only one party of up to 8 people at a time, with accommodation being in the stylishly refurbished 2-bedroom Jack Hanna Cottage (named after the US television presenter, who has strong links with the Dian Fossey Gorilla Fund) & 2 adjacent Ranch Rooms. Facilities include a lounge with flatscreen satellite TV, & rates are inclusive of all meals, which are prepared by the chef in the 5-star cottage's kitchen, & served in its dining room. *US$250/450 sgl/dbl in the cottage; US$200/350 sgl/dbl Ranch House, inc meals & selected beverages.*

⌂ **Mountain Gorilla View Lodge** (15 rooms with 10 more planned) m 078 8305708/9; e info@3bhotels.com; www.3bhotels.com. Built by the original owners of Gorilla's Nest, this newish lodge will eventually form part of a chain linking several major tourist attractions in Rwanda. Standing on the grassy, breezy saddle that connects Sabyinyo & Bisoke, it offers superb views to all 6 of the volcanoes in the Rwandan part of the Virungas. Accommodation is in large & attractive free-standing cottages with queen-size or twin beds, tea/coffee-making facilities, private balconies, fridge, mini-safe, log fire, a spacious bathroom with a hot shower, & generator power during key hours. The restaurant & bar is a massive thatched building with stone floors. *US$230/300/450 sgl/dbl/tpl FB.*

MODERATE

⌂ **Iby'Iwacu Cultural Village** m 078 8352009; e info@rwandaecotours.com; www. cbtrwanda.org. An interesting alternative to staying in a conventional lodge is the village stay offered by this cultural village bordering Volcanoes National Park (see pages 256–7). Accommodation is in traditional thatched mud houses, with en-suite long-drop & bathing area, surrounding a replica royal palace (similar to the one at Nyanza) big enough to accommodate more than 100 people. Fresh local food is eaten communally. *US$70 pp FB.*

⌂ **Kinigi Guest House** (11 rooms) ☎0252 547156; m 078 8433606/8461913; e kinigi2020@yahoo.fr; www.rwanda-kinigi- guesthouse.com. Situated in peaceful green gardens only 300m from the park headquarters, this likeably low-key lodge is run by the charity ASOFERWA (see box opposite) & its en-suite wooden chalets have an almost Swiss appearance. There are comfortable public areas, a good restaurant & bar, & the view of the volcanoes is superb. *Good value in this location at Rfr20,000/25,000 sgl/dbl; Rfr30,000 VIP dbl; Rfr5,000 per bed in a 4-berth dorm. All rates B&B.*

⌂ **Le Bambou Gorilla Lodge** (16 rooms) m 078 8307374/8586515; e info@ lebambougorillalodge.com; www. lebambougorillalodge.com. The newest lodge in the vicinity of Volcanoes National Park plugs the gap between the upmarket properties listed opposite & the more basic options below. Accommodation is in large stone cottages with firm king-size beds, en-suite hot shower, private balcony & a rather cluttered collection of furniture including a writing desk & wardrobe. As with other lodges in this area the setting of exotic eucalyptus trees is less than inspiring, but this is countered by the well-tended gardens. There is a slightly unfinished feel to the place, especially the sparsely furnished reception, bar & dining area, but this will hopefully improve with time. Food is good, & the staff very helpful & accommodating. There are also quite comfortable 'budget rooms', with common showers, in a separate block. *US$200/250 sgl/dbl FB, or US$40 pp B&B in the budget rooms.*

BUDGET

⌂ **Bushokoro Lodge** (4 rooms, more under construction) m 078 3697068. About 500m from La Paillotte, this basic new lodge has large clean tiled rooms with king-size beds & en-suite hot tub/shower. A mediocre restaurant & bar is attached. *Fair value at Rfr20,000 dbl.*

ASOFERWA

If you stay at the friendly Kinigi Guest House close to Rwanda's Volcanoes National Park (see opposite), you'll indirectly be helping the non-profit women's association ASOFERWA or Association de Solidarité des Femmes Rwandaises (*Kigali office:* ☎ *0252 586394;* e *asoferwa@rwanda1.com*), as profits from the Guest House are ploughed back into ASOFERWA's valuable programmes throughout Rwanda.

ASOFERWA was set up in August 1994 to help those left vulnerable and struggling as a result of the genocide, of whom many were women and children: widows, orphans, teenage mothers, traumatised women, victims of AIDS (through rape) and other forms of physical and moral violence, the old and handicapped, women in detention centres with their babies, and minors in re-education centres accused of genocide.

In meeting their multiple and urgent needs, ASOFERWA's first task was to provide shelter and other basic requirements for widows and for children being cared for by an older sibling. This was done within the framework of the 'Peace Villages' constructed throughout Rwanda under the national resettlement and rehousing programme. A village consisted of 100 to 150 houses and a population of 600 to 1,200. Widows rehoused under this scheme were asked, in return, to take in orphans and care for them, while ASOFERWA helped them to set up income-generating schemes (agriculture, handicrafts, livestock, small kiosks or boutiques).

The work quickly expanded and international funding agencies gave support. Women's groups were set up, schools and training centres opened, women and minors in prison supported, young people given practical skills, and a tannery, modern dairy farm and literacy training centre established. In one area a mobile medical team cared for the psycho-social needs of rape victims. The needs are still great, and the work is carried out country-wide; for example in 2012 ASOFERWA (among other activities) worked to improve conditions for 12 women's groups in the Muhanga/Gitarama area, comprising around 300 women.

Someone at the Guest House will gladly give you more information. And, if you have any clothing or other practical items that you don't need to take back home, you could ask at Reception whether they may be useful for the people involved in any of the projects.

🏠 **La Paillotte Gorilla Place** (6 rooms) m 078 5523561/072 2322066; e lapaillottegorillaplace@ hotmail.com; www.lapaillottegorillaplace.com. Affiliated to the eponymous bakery in Musanze, this is the most affordable option near the national park, about 3km from Kinigi at the junction of the roads from Musanze & Gorilla's Nest. Rooms, though a little rundown, are all en-suite, with a dbl bed, but vary greatly in size. The restaurant-bar has indoor & courtyard seating; it serves a good selection of tasty pizzas, sandwiches & meals in the Rfr2,500–4,000 range. *From Rfr10,000/15,000 for the smallest sgl/dbl to Rfr25,000 for a larger dbl with king-size bed.*

GORILLA TRACKING

Tracking mountain gorillas in the Virungas is a peerless wildlife experience, and one of Africa's indisputable travel highlights. It is difficult to describe the simple exhilaration attached to first setting eyes on a wild mountain gorilla. These are enormous animals: the silverbacks weigh about three times as much as the average man, and their bulk is exaggerated by a shaggily luxuriant coat. And yet despite their fearsome size and appearance, gorillas are remarkably peaceable creatures, certainly by comparison with most primates – gorilla tracking would be a considerably more dangerous pursuit if these gentle giants had the temperament of vervet monkeys, say, or baboons (or, for that matter, humans).

More impressive even than the gorillas' size and bearing is their unfathomable attitude to their daily human visitors, which differs greatly from that of any other wild animal. Anthropomorphic as it might sound, almost everybody who visits the gorillas experiences an almost mystical sense of recognition: we regularly had one of the gorillas break off from chomping on bamboo to study us, its soft brown eyes staring deeply into ours, as if seeking out some sort of connection.

Equally fascinating is the extent to which the gorillas try to interact with their visitors, often approaching them, and occasionally touching one of the guides in apparent recognition and greeting as they walk past. A photographic tripod raised considerable curiosity in several of the youngsters and a couple of the adults – one large female walked up to the tripod, stared ponderously into the lens, then wandered back off evidently satisfied. It is almost as if the gorillas recognise their daily visitors as a troop of fellow apes, but one too passive to pose any threat – often a youngster will put on a chest-beating display as it walks past tourists, safe in the knowledge that they'll accept its dominance: something it would never do to an adult gorilla. (It should be noted here that close contact with humans can expose gorillas to fatal diseases, for which reason the guides try to keep their tourists at least 5m away – but the reality is that there is little anybody can do to stop the gorillas from flouting rules of which they are unaware.)

The magical hour with the gorillas is relatively expensive and getting there can sometimes be hard work. The hike up to the mountain gorillas' preferred habitat of bamboo forest involves a combination of steep slopes, dense vegetation, slippery underfoot conditions after rain, and high altitude. For all that, the more accessible gorilla groups can be visited by reasonably fit adults of any age, and in 20 years of African travel we have yet to meet anybody who has gone gorilla tracking and regretted the financial or physical expense.

PERMITS Eight permits per day are issued for each of the eight habituated groups in the Volcanoes Park, making a daily total of 64 permits. At the time of writing, all these habituated groups stay within tracking range on a more-or-less permanent basis, but gorillas are not governed by international boundaries and it is always possible that groups which originated in Uganda or the DR Congo might cross there again. Trackers are not allocated a specific group in advance but the guides do generally make an effort to match people to a group based on their apparent fitness – Sabyinyo and usually Group Thirteen being the least demanding hikes and Susa the most challenging. The strictly enforced minimum age for tracking gorillas is 15.

In June 2012, the cost of a gorilla-tracking permit, including park entrance, increased from US$500 to US$750, a price that is likely to hold for the duration of this edition, though any changes will be posted at http://updates.bradtguides.com/rwanda as soon as we become aware of them. The permit is best bought in advance through the RDB office in Kigali or through a tour operator in Kigali or abroad. Depending on availability, permits can also be bought at short notice from the RDB office in Rubavu/Gisenyi. There is no guarantee a permit will be available on any given day: the likelihood is highest during the main rainy season of April and May, when trekking operates at well under full capacity, but you may need to wait for days or even weeks in the peak season of June to September, when booking 6–12 months ahead is strongly advised. In any event, the procedure regarding last minute bookings could always change, so you are strongly advised to check this beforehand with RDB in Kigali – see box *Booking a gorilla permit* on page 52. Either way, it is advisable for independent travellers to visit or ring the RDB office in Kinigi (m *078 8771633*) the afternoon before they intend to go tracking in order to confirm arrangements. Through June to September, when demand is high, permits for specific days can sell out well in advance, so be sure to book as far ahead as possible.

Trackers are required to check in at the park headquarters at Kinigi at 07.00, where they can enjoy a complimentary cup of tea or coffee (and if necessary make use of the last clean flush toilets they'll see for a few hours) before being allocated to one of the eight habituated groups. If you want to visit or to avoid any specific group, it helps to be there a little early so you have time to chat to the rangers. A briefing is held at around 07.30 after which you must drive to the appropriate trailhead, so the actual tracking generally starts at 08.15–08.30.

HABITUATED GROUPS The most difficult to reach of the permanent groups is the **Susa Group**, the one originally studied by Dian Fossey on the slopes of Mount Karisimbi. Until recently, it comprised more than 40 individuals, including four silverbacks, making it the second-largest group of mountain gorillas in the world (there is a larger research group). Following a split in 2010, it now contains about 30 members, still more than double the average group size of 12–15. A visit to the Susa Group is delightfully chaotic and totally unforgettable, with gorillas seemingly tumbling out of every bush and bamboo stand. The Susa Group is the first choice of most fit visitors, but it takes about an hour to drive from Kinigi to the starting point, and you should be prepared for a severe hike. The ascent from the car park to the forest boundary, though not as steep as it used to be from the new starting point, will also take the best part of an hour. On a good day, it will take no more than 20 minutes to reach the gorillas from the boundary; on a bad day you might be looking at two hours or more in either direction and it has been known to take as long as seven hours to locate the group in the dry season (the record from the previous day will give an indication of how deep in the gorillas are, as they generally don't move too far in one day).

At the other end of the severity scale is the trek to the **Sabyinyo Group**, whose permanent territory lies within the Volcanoes Park, on a lightly forested saddle between Mount Sabyinyo and Mount Gahinga. Depending on exactly where the gorillas are, the walk from the car park to the forest boundary is flat to gently sloping, and will typically take 20–30 minutes. Once you're in the forest, the gorillas might take anything from ten minutes to an hour to reach, but generally the slopes aren't too daunting, though they can be slippery after rain. The Sabyinyo Group consists of 11 individuals, with two silverbacks. Although it is less numerically impressive than the Susa Group, the Sabyinyo Group does seem more cohesive and one gets a clearer

MOUNTAIN GORILLAS: ECOLOGY AND TAXONOMY

The largest living primates, gorillas are widespread residents of the equatorial African rainforest, with a global population of perhaps 150,000–200,000 concentrated mainly in the Congo Basin. Until 2001, all gorillas were assigned to the species *Gorilla gorilla*, split into three races: the western lowland gorilla *G. g. gorilla* of the western Congo Basin, the eastern lowland gorilla *G. g. graueri* in the eastern Congo, and the mountain gorilla *G. g. beringei* living in highland forest on the eastern side of the Albertine Rift. The western race was formally described in 1847, but the eastern races were only described in the early 20th century – the mountain gorilla in 1903, a year after two individuals were shot on Mount Sabyinyo by Oscar von Beringe, and the eastern lowland gorilla in 1914.

The conventional taxonomic classification of gorillas has been challenged by recent advances in DNA testing and fresh morphological studies suggesting that the western and eastern gorilla populations, whose ranges lie more than 1,000km apart, diverged some two million years ago. For this reason, they are now treated as discrete species: *G. gorilla* (western) and *G. beringei* (eastern). One distinct western race – the Cross River gorilla *G. g. dielhi* of the Cameroon-Nigeria border region – fulfils the IUCN criteria for 'Critically Endangered', since it lives in five fragmented populations, only one of which is protected, with a combined total of fewer than 300 individuals. In 2000, the Cross River gorilla and mountain gorilla shared the unwanted distinction of being placed on a shortlist of the world's 25 most endangered primate taxa.

The status of the western gorilla is relatively secure, since it is far more numerous in the wild than its eastern counterpart, and has a more extensive range spanning half-a-dozen countries. In the 1980s, the western gorilla population was estimated at 100,000, but that figure was adjusted to 50,000 circa 2006, largely due to hunting for bush meat and the lethal Ebola virus (which had killed 5,000 gorillas in central Africa prior to 2006, according to a study published in *Science*. Encouragingly, however, a Wildlife Conservation Society survey undertaken over 2006/7 found more than 100,000 previously unreported gorillas in the Lake Tele region of the DR Congo.

The future of the eastern gorilla – still split into a lowland and a mountain race – is far less certain. In the mid 1990s, an estimated 17,000 eastern lowland gorillas remained in the wild, but is widely thought that the population has dropped to 5,000 or fewer since the outbreak of the ongoing Congolese civil war in the DRC. Rarer still, but more stable, is the mountain gorilla, which consists of at most 800 individuals confined to two ranges: the border-straddling Virunga Volcanoes and Bwindi National Park in Uganda.

The first study of mountain gorilla behaviour was undertaken in the 1950s by George Schaller, whose pioneering work formed the starting point for the more recent research initiated by Dian Fossey in the 1960s. Fossey's acclaimed book *Gorillas in the Mist* remains perhaps the best starting point for anybody who wants to know more about mountain gorilla behaviour.

The mountain gorilla is distinguished from its lowland counterparts by several adaptations to its high-altitude home, most visibly a longer and more luxuriant coat.

impression of the group structure and interaction. What's more, the dominant male Guhondo is the heaviest gorilla (of any race) ever measured, at 220kg.

Group Thirteen spends most of its time on the same saddle as the Sabyinyo Group. When it is in that area, it is normally as easy to reach as the Sabyinyo

It is on average bulkier than other races, with the heaviest individual gorilla on record (of any race) being the 220kg dominant silverback of Rwanda's Sabyinyo Group. Like other gorillas, it is a highly sociable creature, moving in defined troops of anything from five to 50 animals. A troop typically consists of a dominant silverback male (the male's back turns silver when he reaches sexual maturity at about 13 years old) and sometimes a subordinate silverback, as well as a harem of three or four mature females, and several young animals. Unusually for mammals, it is the male who forms the focal point of gorilla society; when a silverback dies, his troop normally disintegrates. A silverback will start to acquire his harem at about 15 years of age, most normally by attracting a young, sexually mature female from another troop. He may continue to lead a troop well into his 40s.

A female gorilla reaches sexual maturity at the age of eight, after which she will often move between different troops several times. Once a female has successfully given birth, however, she normally stays loyal to the same silverback until he dies, and she will even help to defend him against other males. (When a male takes over a troop, he generally kills all nursing infants to bring the mothers into oestrus more quickly, a strong motive for a female to help preserve the status quo.) A female gorilla has a gestation period similar to that of a human, and if she reaches old age she will typically have raised up to six offspring to sexual maturity. A female's status within a troop is based on the length of time she has been with a silverback: the alpha female is normally the longest-serving member of the harem.

The mountain gorilla is primarily vegetarian, with bamboo shoots being the favoured diet, though they are known to eat 58 different plant species in the Virungas. It may also eat insects, ants being a particularly popular protein supplement. A gorilla troop will spend most of its waking hours on the ground, but it will generally move into the trees at night, when each member of the troop builds itself a temporary nest. Gorillas are surprisingly sedentary creatures, typically moving less than 1km in a day, which makes tracking them on a day-to-day basis relatively easy for experienced guides. A troop will generally only move a long distance after a stressful incident, for instance an aggressive encounter with another troop. Gorillas are peaceable animals with few natural enemies and they often live for up to fifty years in the wild, but their long-term survival is critically threatened by poaching, deforestation and exposure to human-borne diseases.

It was previously thought that the Virunga and Bwindi gorilla populations were racially identical, not an unreasonable assumption given that a corridor of mid-altitude forest linked the two mountain ranges until about 500 years ago. But recent DNA tests indicate the Bwindi and Virunga gorillas show sufficient genetic differences to suggest that they have formed mutually isolated breeding populations for many millennia, in which case the 'mountain gorilla' should possibly be split into two discrete races, one – the Bwindi gorilla – endemic to Uganda, the other unique to the Virunga Mountains. Neither race numbers more than 500 in the wild, neither has ever bred successfully in captivity, and both meet several of the criteria for an IUCN classification of 'Critically Endangered'.

Group, but it does sometimes move deeper into the mountains and the hike can then be significantly longer. Group Thirteen's name dates to when it was first habituated, and numbered 13 gorillas, but today it numbers an impressive 26 individuals, including 13 adult females serviced by an ultra-promiscuous silverback, who acquired all the females from the Nyakagezi Group after it fled into Rwanda from Uganda following the arrival there of the Kwitonda Group from the DR Congo in 2006. Group Thirteen seems to be a favourite of many of the guides, probably because its silverback is more relaxed and approachable than those in other groups.

The **Amahoro Group**, numbering 17, and the more recently habituated **Umubano Group**, with 11 individuals, share an overlapping territory on the slopes

HOW TOUGH IS IT?

This is one of the most frequently asked questions about gorilla tracking in Rwanda. And it is also perhaps the most difficult to answer. So many variables are involved, and if they all conspire against you, you could be in for a genuinely exhausting outing (indeed, on rare occasions, the guides have had to carry tourists down). On the other hand, if everything falls in your favour, the excursion will be little more demanding than the proverbial stroll in the park.

The trek to see the gorillas has two distinct phases. The first is the hike from the closest car park to the forest and national park boundary, which usually takes 30–60 minutes depending on the speed of the party and the group they are visiting. The second is the trek into the forest in search of the gorillas, which will usually have been located by the advance trackers by the time tourists reach the forest edge. This might take anything from 10 minutes to two hours, but 20–30 minutes is typical, especially for those groups whose territory lies closer to the forest edge.

The first part of the trek is predictable, and it is usually quite flat and undemanding, unless you are going to the Susa Group, which involves a longer and steeper ascent. The second part is more difficult to predict, as it will depend on the exact location of the gorillas on the day, and on the steepness of the terrain *en route*. Other factors in determining how tough it will be include the density of vegetation (bending and crawling through the jungle can be tiring, especially if you have to dodge vicious nettles) and whether it has rained recently, in which case everything will be muddier and quite slippery underfoot.

At risk of stating the obvious, age and fitness levels are the key factors in how difficult the hike will feel. Susa Group aside, moderately fit people under the age of 40 seldom feel any significant strain, but a high proportion of trackers are in their 50s or 60s, in which case the hike might be somewhat tougher. As one reader of a previous edition wrote: 'We think you underestimate how strenuous the gorilla trip is. We are both 61 but fit and well, bicycling to work each day, and still we had to take regular breaks due to problems with breathing'. That said, while many older travellers do find the track quite demanding, it is very unusual that they are so daunted as to turn back.

An important factor in determining how difficult the hike will be is which group you are allocated. As a rule, the hike to the Susa Group is the most demanding (but also the most rewarding, with around 30 gorillas on show), while the Sabyinyo Group is the most reliably straightforward to reach. The hikes to Kwitonda, Hirwa and Group Thirteen are also usually quite undemanding, whereas the hikes to the Amahoro and Umubano Groups tend to be more difficult, but not as tough as the of Mount Bisoke. Both of these groups have one silverback and the hikes to reach them are typically intermediate in difficulty between those of Susa and Sabyinyo. As their names suggest, the Amahoro (literally 'Peace') and Umubano ('Live Together') groups have a quite harmonious relationship despite their territorial overlap, probably because there are strong familial links between them, with several individuals having brothers and sisters in the other group.

Three new groups have opened to tourism in recent years, partly because the increasing gorilla population encourages splits in older groups. The **Hirwa Group**, comprising nine individuals, was formed in 2006 by a silverback who had broken away from the Susa group about two years earlier, and it usually inhabits the foothills of Mount Sabyinyo on the Gahinga side. At about the same time, the

Susa Group. Unfortunately, these things aren't set in stone, and any group might be unusually demanding (or easy) to reach on a bad day. Furthermore, nobody can guarantee which group you will be allocated in advance. However, the guides at Kinigi do make a conscious attempt to match individuals to the most suitable group, especially if they are asked to. Generally, the party for the Susa Group consists of lean-looking under-30s, while the opposite holds true for the Sabyinyo party.

Two further factors are uneven underfoot conditions and high altitude. Most visitors to Africa live in towns and cities where roads and sidewalks are paved, and parks are serviced by neatly maintained footpaths, so they are unused to walking on the more irregular and seasonally slippery surfaces typical of the ascent paths and forest floor. It will help enormously in this regard to wear strong waterproof shoes or hiking boots with a good tread and solid ankle support. Furthermore, if you think you might struggle in these conditions, there is a lot to be said for avoiding the rainy seasons, in particular March–May, when conditions can be dauntingly muddy.

Don't underestimate the tiring effect of altitude. The trekking takes place at elevations of 2,500–3,000m above sea level, not high enough for altitude sickness to be a concern but sufficient to knock the breath out of anybody – no matter how fit – who has just flown in from a low altitude. For this reason, visitors who are spending a while in Rwanda might think seriously about leaving their gorilla tracking until they've been in the country a week or so, and are better acclimatised. Most of Rwanda lies at above 1,500m, and much of the country is higher – a couple of days at Nyungwe, which lies above 2,000m, would be good preparation for the Virungas. Likewise, if you are coming from elsewhere in Africa, try to plan your itinerary so that you spend your last pre-Rwanda days at medium to high altitude: for example, were you flying in from Kenya, a few days in Nairobi (2,300m) or even the Maasai Mara (1,600m) would be far better preparation than time at the coast.

Guides will generally offer you a walking stick at the start of the hike, and, even if you normally shun such props, it is worth taking up the offer to help support you on those slippery mountain paths. If you have luggage, hire a porter too. Once on the trail, take it easy, and don't be afraid to ask to stop for a few minutes whenever you feel tired. Drink plenty of water, and carry some quick calories – biscuits and chocolate can both be bought at supermarkets in Musanze. The good news is that most people who track gorillas find the hike to be far less demanding than they expect, and in 99% of cases, whatever exhaustion you might feel on the way up will vanish with the adrenalin charge that follows the first sighting of a silverback gorilla!

10

16-strong **Kwitonda Group** crossed into Uganda from the DR Congo, probably due to the Congolese civil war, and stayed in Mgahinga National Park for a while, forcing the smaller Uganda-based Nyakagezi Group to cross into Rwanda. The Kwitonda Group crossed into Rwanda in late 2006, and it now inhabits the lower slopes of Mount Muhabura, a relatively easy hike (comparable to that for the Sabyinyo Group). As a result of these territorial shifts, the Nyakagezi Group clashed several times with Group Thirteen, whose silverback poached all the Nyakagezi females before the rest of the (now all-male) group beat a retreat back to Uganda. Newer still is the **Karisimbi group**, whose 15 members are mostly former members of the split Susa Group, and who inhabit similarly territory on Mount Karisimbi.

WHAT TO WEAR AND TAKE Put on your sturdiest hiking boots or walking shoes, and thick trousers and a long-sleeved top as protection against vicious stinging nettles. It's often cold when you set out, so start off with a sweatshirt or jersey (which also help protect against nettles). The gorillas are thoroughly used to people, so it makes little difference whether you wear bright or muted colours. Whatever clothes you wear to go tracking are likely to get very dirty as you slip and slither in the mud, so if you have pre-muddied clothes you might as well wear them. When you're grabbing for handholds in thorny vegetation, a pair of old gardening gloves are helpful. If you feel safer with a walking-stick, you'll be offered a wooden one at the start of the ascent.

Carry as little as possible, ideally in a waterproof bag of some sort. During the rainy season, a poncho or raincoat might be a worthy addition to your daypack, while sunscreen, sunglasses and a hat are a good idea at any time of year. You may well feel like a snack during the long hike, and should certainly carry enough drinking water – at least one litre, more to visit the Susa Group. Bottled water is sold in Musanze. Especially during the rainy season, make sure your camera gear is well protected – if your bag isn't waterproof, seal your camera gear in a plastic bag (for further details about photographing gorillas see the box *Photographic tips* on pages 58–9).

Binoculars are not necessary to see the gorillas. In theory, birdwatchers might want to carry binoculars, though in practice only the most dedicated are likely to make use of them – the trek up to the gorillas is normally very directed, and walking up the steep slopes and through the thick vegetation tends to occupy one's eyes and mind.

If you are carrying much gear and food/water, it's advisable to hire one of the porters who hang about at the car park in the hope of work. This costs Rfr5,000 per porter. Locals have asked us to emphasise that it is not demeaning or exploitative to hire a porter to carry your daypack; on the contrary, tourists who refuse a porter for 'ethical reasons' are simply denying income to poor locals and making it harder for them to gain any benefit from tourism.

You may need to show your passport or some other form of identification when you check in; find out about this from RDB beforehand.

REGULATIONS AND PROTOCOL Tourists are permitted to spend no longer than one hour with the gorillas, and it is forbidden to eat, urinate or defecate in their presence. It is also forbidden to approach within less than 7m of the gorillas, a rule that is difficult to enforce with curious youngsters (and some adults) who often approach human visitors. Smoking is forbidden anywhere within the national park boundary ('it's unhealthy for the animals', according to one rather earnest guide, which seems to be taking concerns about passive smoking to stratospheric absurdity – more genuine justifications are litter, fire and annoying other tourists).

Gorillas are susceptible to many human diseases, and it has long been feared by researchers that one ill tourist might infect a gorilla, resulting in the possible death of the whole troop should they have no immunity to that disease. For this reason, you should not go gorilla tracking with a potentially airborne infection such as flu or a cold, and are asked to turn away from the gorillas should you need to sneeze.

To the best of our knowledge, no tourist has ever been seriously hurt by a habituated gorilla, but there is always a first time. An adult gorilla is much stronger than a person, and will act in accordance with its own social codes. Therefore it is vital that you listen to your guide at all times regarding correct protocol in the presence of gorillas.

GOLDEN MONKEY TRACKING

Although it's the gorillas that tend to hog the limelight, the little-known golden monkey *Cercopithecus kandti* (sometimes treated as a distinctive race of the more widespread blue monkey *C. mitis*) is also IUCN-listed as 'endangered', with a similarly restricted range within the Albertine Rift. As such, it's a rare treat for visitors to be able to view a newly habituated group of about 15 of these delightful creatures in the Volcanoes National Park. Visits can be arranged through any RDB office; they last for one hour and are for a maximum of six people. The cost is US$100 for non-residents and US$65 for foreign residents, including entry to the park. Booking is seldom necessary, but it would be advisable to do so in advance if you have to track on one specific day.

Endemic to the Albertine Rift, the golden monkey is characterised by a bright orange-gold body, cheeks and tail, contrasting with its black limbs, crown and tail-end. Once quite widespread in the forests of southwest Uganda and northwest Rwanda, it is now near-endemic to the Virunga volcanoes, though a small number still inhabit the degraded Gishwati Forest near Rubavu. Within its restricted range, however, it is the numerically dominant primate, and reasonably common – the number of individuals protected within Volcanoes National Park is a matter of conjecture, but a 2003 survey estimated a population of 3,000–4,000 in its smaller neighbour, Uganda's Mgahinga National Park.

In early 2002, the RDB approached the Dian Fossey Gorilla Fund International (DFGFI) to discuss the possibility of habituating the golden monkeys for purposes of tourism. The DFGFI welcomed the chance to learn more about this little-studied monkey and to help promote tourism in the park. First, two possible groups were selected for habituation – they are in areas of the park that would be suitable as part of a nature trail for tourists. Field assistants were then trained in habituation and data collection techniques, and work could begin.

The first few months were terribly frustrating. Dense vegetation (bamboo) made approaching the groups very difficult and the monkeys would flee at the first sight of humans. In time, the researchers were able to refine their techniques and determine at what time of day the monkeys were most active, which made them easier to locate. Gradually the monkeys came to accept the presence of the observers for longer and longer periods. Meanwhile the researchers were gathering more and more data about their diet, habitat use, social structure and behavioural ecology, all of which must be understood if the project is to succeed in the long term.

The first group was 'opened to the public' in summer 2003 and has delighted visitors. It's a very different experience from gorilla-viewing, where the huge creatures are entirely visible as they react and interact. The golden monkeys in their bamboo thicket are smaller, nimbler and can be harder to locate and follow,

10

though they are a lot more relaxed these days than they were a few years back, and the quality of sightings can be superb. The benefits of this project are mutual; for tourists, the pleasure of observing a rare species of monkey; for researchers, the satisfaction of learning more about a little-known species; and for the endangered golden monkeys, far less threat of extinction, as they are studied, protected and better understood.

THE VIRUNGAS

Straddling the borders of Uganda, Rwanda and the DRC, the Virungas are not a mountain range as such, but a chain of isolated freestanding volcanic cones strung along a fault line associated with the same geological process that formed the Rift Valley. Sometimes also referred to as the Birunga or Bufumbira Mountains, the chain comprises six inactive and three active volcanoes, all of which exceed 3,000m in altitude – the tallest being Karisimbi (4,507m), Mikeno (4,437m) and Muhabura (4,127m).

The names of the individual mountains in the Virunga chain reflect local perceptions. Sabyinyo translates as 'old man's teeth' in reference to the jagged rim of what is probably the most ancient and weathered of the eight volcanoes. Muhabura is 'the guide', and anecdotes collected by the first Europeans to visit the area suggest that its perfect cone, topped today by a small crater lake, still glowed at night as recently as the early 19th century. Gahinga is variously translated as meaning 'pile of stones' or 'the hoe', the former a reference to its relatively small size, the latter to the breach on its flank. Of the other volcanoes that lie partially within Rwanda, Karisimbi – which occasionally sports a small cap of snow, most often in the rainy season – is named for the colour of a cowry shell, while Bisoke simply means watering hole, in reference to the crater lake near its peak.

The vegetation zones of the Virungas correspond closely to those of other large East African mountains, although much of the Afro-montane forest below the 2,500m contour has been sacrificed to cultivation. Moist broad-leaved semi-deciduous forest dominates up until the 2,800m contour, whilst the slopes at altitudes of 2,800–3,200m, where an average annual rainfall of 2,000mm is typical, support bamboo forest interspersed with stands of tall hagenia woodland. At higher altitudes, the cover of Afro-alpine moorland, grassland and marsh is studded with giant lobelia, senecios and other outsized plants similar to those found on Kilimanjaro and the Ruwenzori. Above 3,600m, biodiversity levels are very low and the dominant vegetation consists of a fragile community of grasses, mosses and lichens. A total of 1,265 plant species identified across the range to date includes at least 120 that are endemic to the Albertine Rift.

The most famous denizen of the Virungas is the mountain gorilla, which inhabits all six of the extinct or dormant volcanoes, but not – for obvious reasons – the more active ones. The Virungas also form the main stronghold for the endangered golden monkey, possibly the last one now that their only other confirmed haunt, the more southerly Gishwati Forest, has been cleared to cover less than 1% of its original extent. Recent estimates based on dung surveys tentatively place the buffalo population at close to 1,000, while the total number of elephants might be anything from 20 to 100. Other typical highland forest species include yellow-backed duiker, bushbuck and giant forest hog. The mountains' avifauna is comparatively poorly known, as evidenced by sightings of 36 previously

Several non-primate-related hikes are now offered to visitors to Volcanoes National Park. Most of these are day hikes, attracting a uniform charge of US$100 for non-residents and US$65 for foreign residents, including park entrance, but the overnight ascent of Karisimbi is a two-day excursion costing US$175. The RDB will

unrecorded species during a cross-border biodiversity study undertaken in early 2004, bringing the total checklist for the Virungas to 294, including 20 Albertine Rift endemics.

Still in their geological infancy, none of the Virunga Mountains is more than two million years old and two of the cones remain highly active – indeed, they are together responsible for nearly 40% of documented eruptions in Africa. The most dramatic volcanic explosion of historical times was the 1977 eruption of the 3,465m Mount Nyiragongo in the DRC, about 20km north of the Lake Kivu port of Goma. During this eruption, a lava lake that had formed in the volcano's main crater back in 1894 drained in less than one hour, emitting streams of molten lava that flowed at a rate of up to 60km per hour, killing an estimated 2,000 people and terminating only 500m from Goma Airport.

In 1994, a new lake of lava started to accumulate within the main crater of Nyiragongo, leading to another highly destructive eruption on 17 January 2002. Lava flowed down the southern and eastern flanks of the volcano into Goma itself, killing at least 50 people. Goma was evacuated, and an estimated 450,000 people crossed into the nearby Rwandan towns of Rubavu and Musanze for temporary refuge. Three days later, when the first evacuees returned, it transpired that about a quarter of the town – including large parts of the commercial and residential centre – had been engulfed by the lava, leaving 12,000 families homeless. The lava lake in Nyiragongo's crater remains active, with a diameter of around 50m, and, although there has been no subsequent eruption, the crater rim still glows menacingly above the nocturnal skyline of Rubavu, and a new lava lake has started to form about 250 metres below the level of the 1994 one.

Only 15km northwest of Nyiragongo stands the 3,058m Mount Nyamuragira, which also erupted in January 2002. Nyamuragira vies with Ol Doinyo Lengai in Tanzania as probably the most active volcano on the African mainland, with more than 40 eruptions recorded since 1882. Only the 1912–13 incidence resulted in any known direct fatalities, though 17 people were killed and several pregnancies terminated as a result of ash-contaminated drinking water in the 2000 eruption. Nyamuragira most recently blew its top in January 2010 and November 2011, spewing lava hundreds of metres into the air, along with plumes of ash and sulphur dioxide that destroyed large tracts of cultivated land and forest.

It is perhaps worth noting that these temperamental Congolese volcanoes pose no threat to visitors to the mountain gorillas, as the relevant cones are all dormant or extinct. That might change one day: there is a tradition among the Bafumbira people that the fiery sprits inhabiting the crater of Nyamuragira will eventually relocate to Muhabura, reducing both the mountain and its surrounds to ash. Another Bafumbira custom has it that the crater lake atop Mount Muhabura is inhabited by a powerful snake spirit called Indyoka, which lives on a bed of gold and need only raise its head to bring rain to the surrounding countryside.

provide guides for all hikes, but trekkers should have suitable clothing and (if overnighting on Karisimbi) bring their own camping equipment. Hikes can be booked through the RDB office in Kigali, Rubavu or Kinigi. All hikes depart from the park headquarters at Kinigi at around 07.30 (check-in time 07.00), the same departure time as for gorilla tracking, which means that visitors can undertake

KARISIMBI CLIMB, JANUARY 2009   *Wil Resing*

4 January This was not my first visit to the Virungas. I had visited the Susa group back in 2002, the golden monkeys in 2004 and hiked Bisoke in 2006. But now my eyes were set on Karisimbi, at 4,507m the sixth-highest mountain in Africa, after Kilimanjaro, Mount Kenya, Ruwenzori, Mount Meru (Tanzania) and Ras Dashen in Ethiopia's Simien Mountains.

Before heading for Musanze, I visited RDB in Kigali twice for information. And twice I was told that I did not have to make an advance reservation for the Karisimbi hike, I must just pitch up at the RDB headquarters at Kinigi and pay. But once in Musanze, I called the park warden and he confirmed that normally you must book a Karisimbi trek a couple of days ahead so that they can make preparations.

Finally, I was told they would make an exception: I could leave the next morning. I did not have to be at Kinigi at 07.00, the normal reporting time, but at 08.30. Just before darkness fell, the sky cleared after an afternoon shower, and the magnificent volcanoes appeared – Muhabura, Gahinga, Sabyinyo, Bisoke and Karisimbi – though the summit of Rwanda's highest remained hidden in the clouds, as if it wanted to tell me: *I won't reveal myself to you entirely, you have to conquer me first.*

5 January At Kinigi, I paid them the standard fee for the two-day trek, plus US$10 to rent a tent, and I met my guide, who spoke perfect English and French. The drive from Kinigi to the trailhead was 16km and took 30 minutes. At 10.15 we arrived at the car park at Bisate, the same trailhead that is used for hikes to Bisoke and Dian Fossey's tomb. There we met the porters; one for me and one for the guide, at Rfr5,000 per day, not included in the price. I paid my porter after the trip. The guide paid for his own porter. Both guide and porters wore rubber boots: not a bad idea compared with my mountain shoes, as the trail is very muddy.

We set off at 10.20, starting at around 2,600m altitude. The guide carries a phone for communication with rangers/soldiers patrolling the park. At 10.30, we cross the stone wall that separates the park from the potato fields. Now we are in the jungle. Here, several armed soldiers join us, as protection against buffalo and elephants. We walk the same trail as for the Bisoke climb. With my binoculars I see a group of tourists approach the Amahoro group. There is a lot of fresh buffalo dung on the trail.

After an hour's gradual ascent, we reach a junction, with some benches, at the site where Dian Fossey reputedly rested *en route* to her camp. We go left. A light rain starts falling. We walk close to Dian Fossey's tomb and gorilla graveyard, but don't visit, which would involve paying extra. I put on my rain trousers, also good protection against the stinging nettles that hem in the narrow trail. The rain trousers become essential to combat the mud, which is everywhere – not so much a mountain hike as a swamp walk! We see a squirrel, and hear what the guide reckons to be a gorilla research group not normally visited by tourists.

only one activity per day within the park. Porters can be hired at a daily rate of Rfr5,000.

One popular hike is to **Dian Fossey's tomb** and the adjacent gorilla cemetery at the former Karisoke Research Camp. This trek involves a 30-minute drive from the park headquarters to the trailhead at the village of Bisate, which lies at 2,610m close to the

We cross different vegetation zones: bamboo and wild celery on the lower slopes, ideal food for gorillas. Then hagenia forest, with old-man's-beard moss on the branches. Then, above 3,000m, the marvellous giant groundsel and giant lobelia. At 15.50 we reach camp (3,700m), a similar altitude to Bisoke, which can be seen behind us. So today we climbed 1,100 metres in five and a half hours. I don't feel the effect of the altitude, but my legs are tired.

The staff pitch my tent. At 17.00 the sky clears and I finally see a glimpse of the top of Karisimbi, as well as Mikeno volcano in the Congo. I count how many we are now: one guide, two porters and seven soldiers, for just one *muzungu*! The wood is damp, so it's difficult to make a good fire and my porter uses the opening of his rubber boots to blow air into it. Around the fire we share the food we brought. At 20.00 I head to my tent for a deserved rest.

6 January Dawn at 05.30. I eat biscuits and drink water. Beautiful morning light. We leave at 06.10. The trail gets steeper, while the fog closes in. Sometimes I have to use my hands to crawl over the labyrinth of trees and branches above the muddy ground, which I would not like to fall into. On several occasions my porter has to give me a hand to pull me up. The terrain is more difficult than I had expected.

At about 4,000 metres we are above the tree line. The slope becomes more exposed and a cold wind blows. My guide already wears a hat and gloves; I put them on now too. The last couple of hundred metres we walk on volcanic scree (fortunately not loose, more like grey gravel). The wind gets harder and visibility drops to 25m. I see more and more junk and rubbish lying on the ground, and wonder where all this dirt comes from. Metal pipes, empty cans, etc. Suddenly I realise I don't climb any more. It is 08.45 and we are on the summit!

The rubbish is construction waste, left by the builders of the huge telecom mast at the summit. The Congolese border must be somewhere here, but the fog is so thick I don't have a clue where. There are two abandoned huts for the builders of the mast. One is open and we use it as a shelter. I put on all my warm clothes and take pictures outside, while my Rwandan companions, unused to this bitter cold, remain inside. The temperature is maybe 0°C, but the wind chill factor makes it feel much colder. My guide hugs and congratulates me: 'You are very strong, many people don't make it to the summit'.

At 09.15, we start the descent, arriving in camp at 11.00. The warm clothes can be taken off again. It is basically the same way down. *En route*, the sun starts shining, for the first time in two days. We spot a beautiful reedbuck and cross the stream where Dian Fossey was amazed to see gorillas looking at their own reflection in the water. At 15.10 we are at the car park, so today we hiked for about nine hours, including breaks: 800m up and 1,900m down. We pay the porters and get into the car. I turn around for a last quick look at Karisimbi, but Rwanda's roof has vanished in the clouds again. Did I really conquer her heart? Although she is invisible and far away once more, I know for sure she conquered mine.

forest boundary. From here, assuming you stop in the village (rather than continuing by car along the rutted road to the nearby car park), the 1.7km hike to the entry point into the forest, climbing steeply in parts to 2,820m, should take around 25 minutes. Once in the forest, a gently climbing path leads after 1km to the 2,970m clearing where Fossey used to take a break *en route* to her camp, and most hikers emulate her example. Depending on your fitness, and how often you stop to enjoy the scenery, this should take around 20–30 minutes, and it is then another 45–60 minutes to the camp itself, following a contour path that gains little in altitude. Fossey's old living quarters – which she nicknamed the mausoleum – are now in ruins, and several other landmarks in the camp are signposted. The hike offers a good opportunity to see birds and other creatures typical of the Virungas on the way.

Far more demanding is the day hike to the rim of the 3,711m **Mount Bisoke**, which is topped by a beautiful crater lake. It departs from Bisate, a trailhead it shares with the hike to Dian Fossey's tomb, and follows the same route as far as the resting point mentioned in the paragraph above, which you should reach in 45–60 minutes. It's only 2km from here to the rim, but the path is very steep (it gains about 650m in altitude from the resting place), so it normally takes at least 1.5 hours, and might take twice as long, depending on your fitness, how you respond to the altitude, and underfoot conditions (muddy at the best of times, and outright treacherous after heavy rain, when you'll be sinking to your knees in the bog with ever other step). However, the atmospheric vegetation of giant lobelias and hagenia woodland is fantastic, as is the view over the crater lake when you reach the rim. You reach the rim at 2,635m, so if bagging peaks is important to you, you might want to circle the crater rim to the highest peak. Note, however, that the crater lake is often obscured by clouds during the rainy season, so this is one walk best suited to drier times of year. The descent takes about 2 hours in normal conditions, but it might take a longer after rain, when you'd spend a lot of time sliding down on your butt! Allow for 6–8 hours in all, so bring food and plenty of water, and don't refuse the walking stick that will be offered to you at the parking lot. Porters are available at Bisate.

Recommended only to dedicated hikers, the overnight trek to **Karisimbi** (see box *Karisimbi Climb*, pages 254–5) is even more demanding, but as the highest peak in the range, it also offers the greatest vegetation diversity, rising through clumped bamboo and aromatic hagenia forest to the spectacularly otherworldly vegetation of the sub-alpine and Afro-Alpine zones, which are dominated by clumped moss and heather and stands of giant Senecio and lobelia. Be warned that you will be camping in near freezing conditions, so good camping gear and plenty of warm clothing are a prerequisite, and you'll need to be self sufficient when it comes to food and water. There are also plans to open up **Gahinga** and **Muhabura** to a day and overnight hike respectively.

IBY'IWACU CULTURAL VILLAGE

Situated next to the car park at the trailhead for the Sabyinyo Group and Group Thirteen, this award-winning venture was founded in 2004 by Edwin Sabuhoro of Rwanda Eco-Tours to help improve the livelihood of communities living around Volcanoes National Park, thereby reducing human pressure on the park's resources. The cultural village is essentially the public flagship for an ambitious project that provides legitimate employment in fields such as vegetable and mushroom farming, beekeeping and tourism to about 1,000 former and potential poachers.

Best arranged a day or so in advance, Iby'Iwacu offers a busy programme that lasts about two hours and slots in ideally after a morning's gorilla tracking. The

DEATH ON KARISIMBI

In February 1907 a German geologist named Kirchstein (who was later the first European to climb Bisoke) had a sad experience when descending Karisimbi with a group of porters.

We had safely traversed the first half of the moor when we were suddenly assailed by an extraordinarily violent shower of hail which came down from an almost bright sky, whilst a dense fog gathered at the same time. The temperature sank to zero, and then a snowstorm of such fury set in that, if I had not myself been a witness of it, I should have deemed it impossible in equatorial Africa. My carriers had scarcely perceived the snow when they threw away their loads, lay down on the ground, and with wails declared that the gods had decreed that they must die. It was in vain that I urged them to pursue the march … I fought my way, wading up to my knees in icy cold water, accompanied by my two Askari and a very few followers, through the storm and snow to the edge of the crater. Arrived there we contrived to erect a temporary camp in the shelter of the trees and made a fire. Time after time, accompanied only by the two Askari, I penetrated the pathless swamp, and so brought one hapless native after the other to the warm camp fire. I ordered my men to leave the loads where they were so long as they rescued the people. But even our own strength failed at last … and the closing darkness, too, made any further attempt at rescue hopeless…

Absolutely drenched through, without any tent, limbs shivering from emotion and cold, and wrapped in a blanket only – that is how we spend the sleepless night round the camp fire, only to have to resume our work of exhumation again with the first grey light of morning. Exhumation, not rescue, for what remained to be rescued was heartrendingly little. Very few of the luckless ones showed any trace of life. All the rest, twenty in number and nearly half my caravan, lay corpses in the snow. Frozen under a tropical sun!

From *In the Heart of Africa*,
by the Duke Adolphus Frederick of Mecklenburg (Cassell, 1910)

setting is a fantastic wood-and-thatch replica of a traditional Rwandan palace, second only in size to the restored palace at Nyanza Museum, and an ideal stage for traditional Intore dancers to share their drumming and dance routines. Also on offer are a short community walk, a church visit, a consultation with a traditional healer, shooting a bow and arrow with one of the local Batwa pygmies, and demonstrations of activities such as grinding millet and sorghum, making banana beer and harvesting potatoes and other crops.

Although Rwanda Eco-Tours plays a role in marketing and advising Iby'Iwacu, the cultural village is owned entirely by local communities, and the fee is split so that 40% goes directly to community members who perform and do other activities, while 60% goes to a village fund managed by a committee that channels it into various charitable efforts, from buying seeds for farmers to sponsoring schoolchildren and buying scholastic materials. Day visits cost US$35 per person, inclusive of all activities, which include a guided walk to visit village elders, women, children and various community projects. An overnight stay costs US$70 per person (see page 242). (For further details and bookings, contact m *078 8352009*; e *info@rwandaecotours.com*; *www.cbtrwanda.org*.)

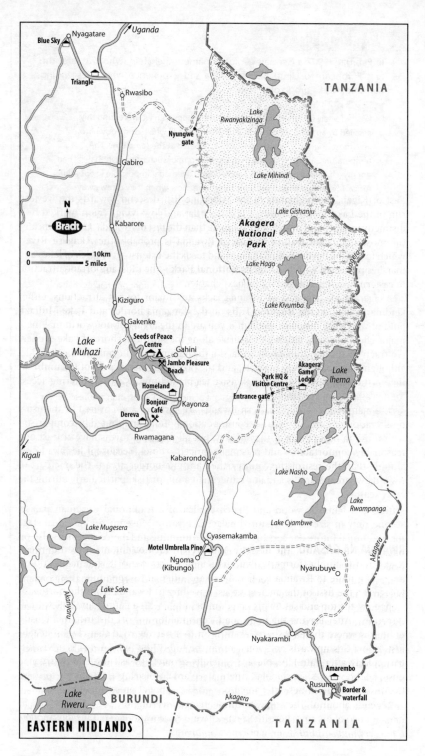

11

Eastern Rwanda

East of Kigali, the highlands of the Albertine Rift descend towards the western rim of the Lake Victoria Basin, a relatively flat and low-lying region marked by a distinctly warmer and more humid climate than the rest of Rwanda. Geographically, the most significant feature of eastern Rwanda is probably the **Akagera River**, which forms the border with Tanzania and feeds the extensive complex of lakes and marshes protected within **Akagera National Park** – the most important attraction in eastern Rwanda, covered in the next chapter.

Akagera aside, the east of Rwanda lacks any major tourist attractions. Other landmarks include the **Rusumo Falls** on the Tanzania border and **Lake Muhazi**, both of which are diverting enough if you are in the area, but not worth making a major effort to reach, although the drive along the northern shore of Lake Muhazi is attractive. The handful of towns that dot the region are uniformly on the dull side, although some have lively markets, and the breezy highland town of **Gicumbi** in the northeast is surrounded by extensive tea plantations, as well as offering access to the vast Rugezi Wetlands.

The main roads through eastern Rwanda are surfaced and covered by the usual proliferation of minibus-taxis. Accommodation options are limited by comparison with those in other parts of the country, but all the main towns have at least one reasonably comfortable – and reasonably priced – hotel. Because it lies at a lower altitude than the rest of the country, the Tanzania border area is the one part of Rwanda where malaria is a major rather than a minor risk, particularly during the rainy season.

THE GICUMBI (BYUMBA) ROAD

RWANDA NA GASABO The first substantial right turn off the main road between Kigali and Gicumbi (formerly Byumba), about 25km out of Kigali, takes you on a winding route to Rwanda Na Gasabo or the original Rwanda hill. This is where (allegedly) the first of the ancient kings, travelling to Rwanda from the northeast, stopped at the top and set up his kingdom. It's high, with a flat top and a view in all directions. After leaving the main road, continue for a short distance to a cluster of houses where there's a sharp left turn on to a narrow road that climbs steeply. Just follow this upwards and you'll reach the top of the hill. (A 4x4 is advisable, particularly after rain.) People are generally around, so ask directions if you're unsure. The view is spectacular. There are plans to develop this site for tourism (reconstructed dwellings, interpretation boards…) but at present it's peaceful.

Legends abound! The ancient King Gihanga (see box on page 270) is said to have left two of his cows here; their names were Rugira and Ingizi. One day another king went hunting and threw a branch after an animal; the tip sank into the ground and took root, becoming a species found nowhere else in Rwanda. The great trees planted as the gateway to his land are still standing, after many centuries. Then again, there was a magic earthenware pot in the court; it would fill with water of its own accord to signify that rain was on the way. Also one monarch had a very special group of royal drummers, whose drumming awakened him in the morning and sent him to sleep at night. And so on. You may well meet someone up there who will tell you other tales.

LAKE MUHAZI (NORTHWEST SHORE)

LAKE MUHAZI (NORTHWEST SHORE) About five minutes further up the Gicumbi road after the Gasabo turning, another right turn at ⊕ S 01°45.753, E 030°07.788, signposted for the village of Rwesero, leads to the northwest tip of Lake Muhazi. this western part of the lake was much studied by the Germans as they explored their new territory. Writing in 1907, a Doctor Mildbraed rather crossly commented:

> The west end of Lake Muhasi terminates in a papyrus swamp, and therefore promised rich spoils for zoological treasure-hunters. We were all the more keenly disillusioned to find the fauna far more meagre in character in this great water basin – the first we had explored in Africa – than we had been led to suppose in Germany. In spite of the luxurious vegetation at this part of the lake, the most diligent search was needed before we found a few sponges and polypi attached to some characeous plants.

About 25 minutes along this road (longer if you stop to look at birds and enjoy the lakeside views), you'll come to Rwesero. Here, the waterfront **Rwesero Beach Resort** has a bar/restaurant serving a varied selection of snacks and meals in the Rfr2,500–5,000 range. You can eat indoors or on a floating wooden deck suspended above the lake. There's also a picnic place, children's playground and campsite, and it is probably the better option for day trippers seeking a lakeside snack or drink. Both places have boats, so you can fish on the lake – or cross to the opposite bank and camp there. There's plenty of birdlife around too, including pied and malachite kingfishers and fish eagle, and otters are sometimes seen in the area.

Past Rwesero, a beautiful (but sometimes rough) road, offering a succession of tranquil watery views (and numerous birds), follows the northern bank of the 60km-long Lake Muhazi in an easterly direction to emerge near Gahini on the main surfaced road flanking Akagera National Park. Allow a half-day, including stops, to travel this full route – you can do it in less, but it's a shame to hurry and the road is sometimes quite rutted. It also crosses several small creeks on rough wooden 'bridges' so is best done in a 4x4 during the dry season. It may well become impassable in a couple of places when the lake rises: ask about this. Hitching could be difficult; transport comes in from either end but doesn't necessarily go right through

GICUMBI (BYUMBA)

GICUMBI (BYUMBA) The sprawling town of Gicumbi (formerly Byumba), which lies about 75km north of Kigali, some 3km off the main road to Kibale (Uganda), is the seventh largest in Rwanda (population estimated at 75,000) and the capital of Northern Province, It is the country's highest settlement of note, perched at an altitude of 2,220m above the Mulindi Valley, whose rich volcanic soils lie at the heart of a burgeoning tea industry that has assumed a growing economic importance in recent years and now creates employment for around 60,000 people. More than 10 million kilograms of tea is exported from Rwanda yearly, much of it to the UK and Pakistan, with annual earnings of US$60 million in 2011, a threefold increase since 2004. The only potential tourist attraction is Lake Nyagafunzo, which lies about 12km out of town in the heart of the bird-rich Rugezi Swamp.

There is plenty of transport from Kigali as well as from Gatuna, the border post with Uganda. The 42km road between Gicumbi and Base, notable for its spectacular views of the tea estates, is serviced by at least one bus daily, leaving Gicumbi in the early morning and returning from Base later in the day. There don't seem to be any minibus-taxis along this route, but hitching might be possible.

⌂ Where to stay

Moderate

⌂ **Hotel Urumuli** (27 rooms) ☎ 0252 564111; m 078 8346295/8796313; e hotelurumuli@ yahoo.com; www.hotelurumuli.com. This radically renovated stalwart is the smartest option on offer. Sgl, dbl & twin rooms with DSTV, phone & en-suite hot shower are available, & there's also a 2-bedroom suite. Facilities include an internet café & a decent bar-restaurant serving the usual Rwandan fare. The hotel lies at the top of the long main street, about 2km from the public taxi park, but is served by private minibuses. *Rfr25,000 sgl, Rfr40,000 dbl or twin; Rfr60,000 apartment*

Budget

⌂ **Hotel Ubwuzu** (6 rooms) m 078 8428353; e ubwuzultd@yahoo.fr. This friendly new guesthouse, operated by the same people who are trying to develop tourism at Lake Nyagafunzo, has a pretty hilltop location in gardens offering views to the Virunga Volcanoes in clear weather. The en-suite rooms are clean & bright, & a restaurant with indoor & outdoor tables serves good buffets in the Rfr1,500–2,500 range. To get there, follow the main road running southwest from the bus station towards the Urumuli Hotel for about 200m, then – almost immediately before the turn-off right to the Catholic Cathedral – take a left into a dirt road & follow its leftward curve for another 200m to the compound gate. *Rfr10,000/15,000 sgl/twin B&B.*

Around Gicumbi The only real tourist attraction is Lake Nyagafunzo in the Rugezi Swamp. But the neat green tea plantations that blanket the surrounding countryside are very pretty, and you could well spend a couple of days here just walking and enjoying the expansive views. The 45km dirt road connecting Gicumbi to Base, on the main road between Kigali and Musanze/Ruhengeri, is one of the most scenic in the country, though it's rather rough and requires at least two hours to cover.

Lake Nyagafunzo Situated at an elevation of around 2,050m about 12km west of Gicumbi, Nyagafunzo is one of the few substantial expanses of open water in the Rugezi Wetlands, an 80km^2 swamp that extends northward all the way to Lake Burera. Listed as a Ramsar Wetland and Important Bird Area, this headwater of the Nile came close to vanishing completely after a hole was blasted in the rocks that held in its water in 1979, order to feed a commercial sunflower scheme. During the course of the 1980s, the high rate of water drainage from the swamp caused large mammals such as the sitatunga antelope to become extinct, and it also had a negative impact on the water level of lakes Burera and Ruhondo, reducing their capacity to produce electricity. The hole in the rocks was eventually dammed, but as recently as 2000 the swamp was still only half its original area, and little or no papyrus remained. Since 2006, however, the concerted efforts of the Rwandan Environmental Management Authority (REMA) has helped regenerate the swamp close to its full former extent, and the northern part of the swamp is under development as the Rugezi Birding Area, by the RDB (see pages 232–3).

Set scenically among tall terraced slopes offering distant views to Mount Muhabura in clear weather, Lake Nyagafunzo is one of the most worthwhile sites in Rwanda for water-associated birds. The big draw for serious birders is the presence of Grauer's rush warbler, an Albertine Rift Endemic that might easily be confused with several more widespread warblers found in the area. But the reed-fringed lake also supports a wide variety of more striking birds, among them the spectacular grey crowned crane, great white pelican, African spoonbill, African marsh harrier, long-toed lapwing, and breeding colonies of black-crowned night heron and purple heron.

The lake is best explored by boat, which can be arranged through the Hotel Ubwuzu in Gicumbi. Guided tours inclusive of transport from Gicumbi, a boat trip and guide cost Rfr50,000 for parties of up to 4 people, and Rfr60,000 for 5–10 passengers. For those with their own transport, the charge is Rfr25,000 for up to six people, including the boat trip and guide, and Rfr35,000 for larger groups. The round day trip from Gicumbi would be fun on a bicycle, so you could ask the hotel management about renting one for the day. At the moment there is no accommodation on the lakeshore, but RDB-approved plans exist to start work on a private eco-lodge on the slopes above the launching point; check our update website for details.

To get there from Gicumbi, follow the surfaced road out towards the Catholic Cathedral for a few hundred metres, then after about 800m (⊕ S 01.34.449, E 030.03.463), shortly before you would reach the cathedral, turn left on to a good dirt road that leads after 6.5km to the junction for the village of Yaramba (⊕ S 01.23.710 S, E 030.03.234). Turn left here, keep going straight, and after another 5km you'll reach the lakeshore (⊕ S 01.34.466, E 029.59.171).

Coming from Musanze/Ruhengeri, it is also possible to reach Lake Nyagafunzo via Lake Burera, Butaro, and the north end of the Rugezi Wetland (see pages 223–32), passing the Mubinga, Marwa I, and Marwa II birding watchtowers, then continuing for another 30km to the junction for Yaramba.

THE NYAGATARE ROAD

RWAMAGANA Superficially just another unremarkable small Rwandan town, Rwamagana is in fact the capital of Southern Province, though it seems to have few of the associated trappings. This aside, it is unlikely to generate much excitement in passing travellers, especially as it lies only 60km from Kigali (no more than an hour's drive on a good surfaced road), and the limited accommodation seems overpriced for what it is. Regular minibus-taxis to Rwamagana leave Kigali from the Nyabugogo bus station and call at Remera bus station *en route*.

⌂ Where to stay and eat

⌂ **Centre D'Accueil Sainte Agnes** (20 rooms) m 078 2813656; e sainte_agnes@yahoo.fr. Situated right next door to the Dereva, this certainly looks the part with its neat exterior & pleasant dining area, but overall the plain en-suite rooms with hypothetical hot water seem overpriced. The restaurant is very good, though, & one of the few places outside Kigali to serve fajitas. *Rfr15,000/20,000 sgl/dbl occupancy for a room with a dbl bed, Rfr18,000/30,000 sgl/dbl occupancy of a twin.*

⌂ **Dereva Hotel** (60 rooms) ✆0252 567244; m 078 8322228; derevahotel@yahoo.com; ⊕ S 01°56.831, E 030°26.336, 1,534m. Set in large green grounds alongside the main road, the Dereva offers what are probably the most commodious lodgings in this part of Rwanda, though it does feel a bit overpriced. The attached restaurant serves large meals in the Rfr3,000–5,000 range; it's a great place to try the traditional groundnut stew called *igisafuriga*. *Rfr18,000/15,000/30,000 en-suite sgl/dbl/twin/ with nets & hot showers, Rfr15,000/25,000 for a similar room with DSTV, or Rfr20,000/30,000 for a suite-like apartment.*

In pre-colonial times, the Rugezi Wetland is where unmarried girls who became pregnant were customarily abandoned or drowned. One such victim was a teenage girl called Nyirantwari, who was reputedly raped and impregnated by a local chief in the 1880s, and then abandoned to die on an island in the heart of the swamp. She was rescued by a group of Batwa, however, and gave birth to a son, who grew up to become an important local chief known as Mutwa Basebya. In 1908, together with some powerful local Tutsi leaders, Mutwa Basebya led a rebellion against the German colonials, one that ultimately led to the subjugation of several semi-autonomous chieftaincies in the Gicumbi/Byumba area under central rule. Mutwa Basebya was captured and shot by the Germans in 1912, but several of his descendants still live in the Rugezi area.

KAYONZA This small, rather scruffy settlement is situated 78km from Kigali, at the junction (⊕ S 01°53.975, E 030°30.454) of the main north–south road connecting Kagitumba on the Uganda border to Rusumo on the Tanzania border. Kayonza is, if anything, even less remarkable than Rwamagana, though once again it serves as a possible base for exploring Lake Muhazi and Akagera National Park and is readily accessible from Kigali on public transport (minibuses leave from Nyabugogo bus station). Volunteers working in Kayonza reckon there is some good walking to be had by heading out of town in the general direction of Akagera National Park.

Where to stay

Eastland Motel (13 rooms) m 078 8673683; e eastlandmotel@yahoo.com; www. eastland-motel.com. Situated about 500m from the main junction along the Kigali Rd, this is the smartest place to stay in Kayonza, & it could serve as a useful & relatively affordable base for a day visit to Akagera National Park. It has clean, comfortable en-suite rooms with hot showers & writing desk, & a courtyard bar & restaurant serves chilled drinks & hot snacks & meals. *Rfr8,000/15,000/25,000 sgl/dbl/twin.*

LAKE MUHAZI (EASTERN SHORE) In common with most lakes in Rwanda, Muhazi is an erratically shaped body of water whose shores follow the contours of the surrounding hills. Roughly 60km long but nowhere more than 5km wide, Muhazi is a classic 'flooded valley' type of lake, its serpentine shape broken by numerous tendrils stretching northward or southward along former tributaries. It is a pretty spot, not as beautiful perhaps as the lakes around Musanze/Ruhengeri but – at least for travellers dependent on public transport – with the added virtue of easy accessibility. The birdlife here is highly rewarding, and the lake harbours an unusually dense population of spotted-necked otter, though no other large mammals are found in the area. The eastern tip of Lake Muhazi lies beside the surfaced Nyagatare road, about 8km north of Kayonza, opposite the turn-off to the small but attractive little town of Gahini, set high above the lake.

Where to stay and eat

Seeds of Peace Centre (25 rooms) m 078 8818018; e gahini@rwanda1.com; ⊕ S 01°50.502, E 030°28.496; 1,460m. Run by the Episcopal Church, this pretty lakeshore resort, opposite the turn-off to Gahini, is intermittently well organised for tourism, offering boating, swimming, birdwatching, a (booze-free) restaurant with fresh lake fish, camping, a picnic place & 2 reconstructed traditional dwellings. It also has rondawels, each with 2 bedrooms, bathroom, kitchen & lounge, & a new dbl-storey block with more conventional en-suite hotel rooms. Profits go back to the diocese for its work in the local community. *Rfr12,000/15,000 sgl/ dbl B&B, or Rfr20,000 for a 2-bedroom apartment.*

✗ Jambo Beach There's no accommodation at this resort, which lies a few hundred metres from Seeds of Peace along the road towards Rwamagana, but the restaurant is generally regarded to be superior, & it does serve beers & other alcoholic drinks. Camping space is available.

NYAGATARE This scattered but rapidly growing town of around 10,000 souls is the administrative centre of the sizeable but thinly populated Nyagatare District, which

---

KING OF THE ROCKS   *Janice Booth*

A NEW VERSION OF AN ANCIENT TALE The monarch Ruganzu II Ndori was so great and famous a king that the mountains, rocks and forests of Rwanda were proud when he passed among them. One day, one of the rocks boasted to an eagle flying overhead that the king and his entourage had walked across it that same morning.

'Krarrk!' croaked the eagle in mocking disbelief. 'With my keen eyes I can spot the smallest mouse as it slips into its hole or the thinnest snake coiled in the shadows. Yet I see no sign that the king has passed your way.'

The rock scratched its weather-beaten head and thought deeply. Then it devised a plan. The next time King Ruganzu approached, it softened itself slightly so that his footsteps left an impression on its surface. Now the eagles and the crows and the skimming bee-eaters could see clearly that the king had walked upon the rock.

Word got around, and other rocks soon adopted the same tactic. If you visit Rwanda today, you may still see various traces of Ruganzu's footprints. Then one of the more ambitious rocks thought: 'If I create a jug, and fill it with beer, the monarch can drink his fill when he passes and I will become the chief rock within his kingdom.'

Carefully it formed itself into a jug, and filled that jug with cool, refreshing banana beer, and the king and all his courtiers drank their fill. But then some other rocks nearby saw what was happening and were jealous; they quickly made bigger and better jugs, and filled some of them with sorghum beer too so that the monarch had a choice.

Today, if you visit the old district of Murambi, you can still see half-a-dozen of these jugs, and if you're very lucky you may even catch a fleeting, aromatic scent of ancient beer. The region is called Rubona rwa Nzoga (Rubona of the beer); and the local tradition is that whatever time a guest may arrive at a house, the hosts will always have a jug of beer ready and waiting to quench his thirst.

Of course rocks in several other parts of Rwanda eventually copied the idea and made their own jugs too ... but they never matched the quality or quantity of Murambi's beer, which remained the monarch's favourite throughout his reign.

Murambi was incorporated into Kayonza District in 2006. Minibus-taxis go to Kiramuruzi (between Gakenke and Kiziguro on the Akagera National Park map on page 274), from where Rubona rwa Nzoga is about 30 minutes' walk. But don't expect exact replica jugs ...

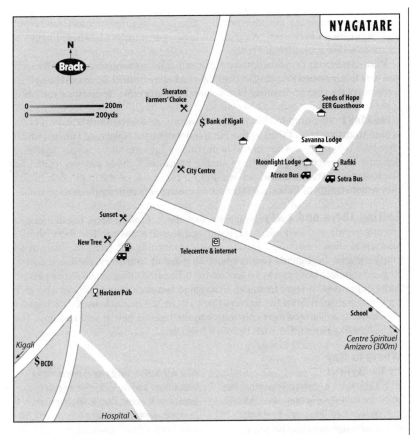

N

Bradt

0 ———— 200m
0 ———— 200yds

Sheraton
Farmers' Choice ✕

$ Bank of Kigali

Seeds of Hope
EER Guesthouse 🏠

Savanna Lodge 🏠

Moonlight Lodge 🏠   ♀ Rafiki

✕ City Centre   Atraco Bus 🚌   🚌 Sotra Bus

Sunset ✕✕

New Tree ✕   🅿
🚌   Telecentre & internet 🔵

♀ Horizon Pub

School ●

Kigali   Centre Spirituel
Amizero (300m)

$ BCDI

Hospital ↘

extends over the northeast of Rwanda to the borders with Uganda and Tanzania. Prior to 2006, Nyagatare was also the capital of the now-defunct Umutara Province, much of which lay within the north of Akagera National Park and the adjacent Mutara Wildlife Reserve before these areas were de-gazetted in 1997 to accommodate returned refugees. Set along the eastern bank of the forest-fringed Muvumba River, it lies at a relatively low altitude of 1,355m, making it hotter than most other parts of Rwanda, and it retains something of a dusty frontier feel, surrounded by rolling hills whose cover of scrubby acacias and cactus-like euphorbia trees is far more archetypically African than any other settled part of Rwanda.

It would be an act of febrile distortion to describe Nyagatare as any sort of travel magnet. All the same, if you are seeking a wholly un-touristy experience, you could do worse than spend a night or two here. The surrounding area is great walking country – ask for (and take note of) local permission and advice, fill up your water bottle and then just stroll off across fields, plains, hillsides… It's a wonderfully clear, open panorama (unlike in much of the rest of Rwanda with its jutting hills and intensive cultivation), fresh and gently green at moister times of year, parched and tinder dry just before the rainy season. For wildlife enthusiasts, local farmers claim that antelope and zebra often cross the border of Akagera to graze peacefully amongst their cattle, while the riparian woodland along the river as it passes the small town centre offers some potentially rewarding birdwatching. Also, in Nyagatare as in all of Rwanda, you can while time away pleasantly by people-watching and engaging in conversation – thanks to its proximity to Uganda and high population of returned refugees, this is one part of Rwanda where English is far more widely spoken than French.

With its relatively dry climate and infertile soil, this northeastern corner of Rwanda was very thinly settled prior to the gazetting of Akagera in 1935. It remains one of the few parts of the country dominated by pastoralism rather than agriculture: you won't travel far here without coming across herds of cattle – mostly the long-horned Ankole – plodding from clump to clump of bristly scrub. And as one might expect of an area so recently settled, there's a pioneering feel about the hamlets and villages, which were built (often with foreign funds) to provide for the returning refugees. Squatting defiantly on the empty plains, these are the houses of a child's pictures: plain and single-storied, with a small square window on either side of the front door. In fact they're dotted all over Rwanda, but the open landscapes here make them more visible.

Getting there and away Nyagatare lies about 175km from Kigali along a (mostly good) surfaced road via Rwamagana and Kayonza. The drive should take up to three hours in a private vehicle, branching left from the main road continuing to the Uganda border about 3km before you reach the town centre. Regular minibus-taxis run to Nyagatare from Kigali, costing Rfr2,000 per person. Most minibus-taxis leave from the Nyabugogo bus station, but you can also pick up direct transport from the Remera taxi park on the east side of Kigali. Regular public transport also connects Nyagatare to the Uganda border and Kayonza. The GPS (Blue Sky Hotel) is ⊕ S 01°17.340, E 030°19.655.

Where to stay

Blue Sky Hotel (30 rooms) ☏0252 563431; m 078 8301914; e b_skyhotel@yahoo.com. This prominent multi-storey hotel stands a block back from the main road. The cheaply fitted rooms feel a touch overpriced for what you get, but they are definitely the smartest option in town. In the evenings the bar is busy with local people & the restaurant serves a good-value buffet or à la carte menu. *Rfr10,000 sgl with ¾ bed & no TV; Rfr15,000/20,000 sgl/dbl with TV.*

Centre Spirituel Amizero (17 rooms) ☏0252 565051; m 078 8842765. Situated in nice gardens about 1km from the main road & taxi park, this out-of-town Presbyterian resthouse is the best overall value in Nyagatare, but it's not so convenient for those without a private vehicle. The en-suite brick-faced rooms have nets, TV & (usually) hot water, & an inexpensive restaurant serves b/fast for Rfr1,200 & lunch or dinner for Rfr2,400. *Rfr6,000/10,000 sgl/dbl; Rfr2,000 per dorm bed.*

Seeds of Hope EER Guesthouse (20 rooms) ☏0252 567422; m 078 8468295. Situated in large grounds just around the corner from the Blue Sky, this friendly but rather basic & rundown guesthouse, run by the Episcopal Church, offers the best value in the town centre. *Rfr3,000/6,000 en-suite sgl/twin; Rfr2,000/4,000 sgl/twin with shared bathroom; Rfr8,000 VIP room.*

Where to eat The best option is probably the **Blue Sky Hotel**, which serves heaped plates of meat or chicken with the starch of your choice for around Rfr2,500, and is open for breakfast, lunch and dinner. Otherwise, a good half-dozen eateries are scattered around town, serving the usual lunchtime *mélanges* of meat, rice and vegetables, including the **Sunset**, **New Tree** and winningly named **Sheraton Farmers' Choice Restaurant**.

THE RUSUMO ROAD

NGOMA (KIBUNGO) The largest town in the southeast of Rwanda (population 65,000), Ngoma (formerly Kibungo) sprawls westward from the main Rusumo

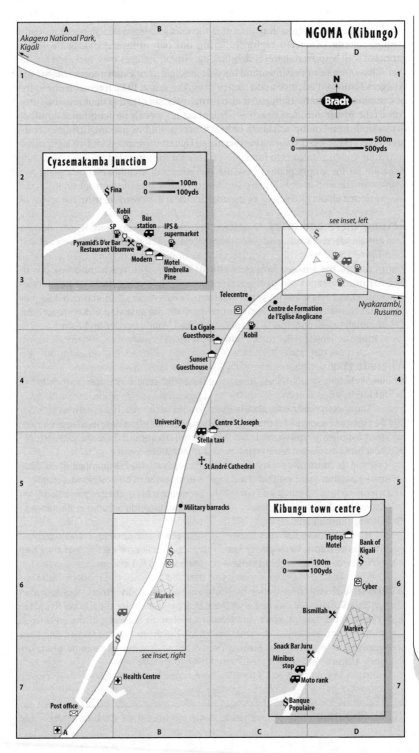

Akagera National Park,
Kigali

NGOMA (Kibungo)

Bradt

0 ——— 500m
0 ——— 500yds

Cyasemakamba Junction

0 ——— 100m
0 ——— 100yds

Fina

Kobil

SP

Bus
station

IPS &
supermarket

Pyramid's D'or Bar
Restaurant Ubumwe

Modern

Motel
Umbrella
Pine

see inset, left

Telecentre

Centre de Formation
de l'Eglise Anglicane

Nyakarambi,
Rusumo

La Cigale
Guesthouse

Kobil

Sunset
Guesthouse

University

Centre St Joseph

Stella taxi

St André Cathedral

Military barracks

Kibungu town centre

Tiptop
Motel

Bank of
Kigali

0 ——— 100m
0 ——— 100yds

Cyber

Market

Bismillah

Market

Snack Bar Juru

Minibus
stop

Moto rank

see inset, right

Banque
Populaire

Health Centre

Post office

Road about 25km south of Kayonza. It is the administrative centre of the recently created Ngoma District, a region suffering not only from the aftermath of the genocide, but also from several debilitating rainfall failures over recent years, so that it has often been dependent on outside food aid. It is a convenient base for the Akagera National Park if you don't fancy paying to stay at the upmarket game lodge or camping in the park itself, and it also forms a possible springboard for a half-day trip to the Rusumo Falls. Otherwise, Ngoma is no more distinguished than other towns in this part of Rwanda, with its main focal point being a small grid of scruffy roads lying 3km west of the altogether more dynamic junction suburb signposted

ANKOLE CATTLE

From mountain gorillas to elephants, Rwanda is blessed with its fair share of impressive wild beasts. But it is also a major stronghold for what is unquestionably the most imposing of Africa's domestic creatures: the remarkable long-horned Ankole breed of cattle associated with the pastoralist peoples of the Uganda and Rwanda border areas.

Sometimes referred to as the Cattle of Kings thanks to their association with the royal lineages of Uganda and Rwanda, Ankole cattle come in a variety of different colours, ranging from uniform rusty-yellow to blotched black-and-white, but always have a long head, short neck, deep dewlap and narrow chest; the male often sports a large thoracic hump. What most distinguishes Ankole cattle from any familiar breed, however, is their preposterous, monstrous horns, which grow out from either side of the head like inverted elephant tusks, and in exceptional instances can reach a length up to 2.5m – dimensions unseen on any Rwandan or Ugandan tusker since the commercial ivory poaching outbreak of the 1980s.

The ancestry of Ankole cattle has been traced back to Eurasia as early as 15000BC, but the precursors of the modern long-horned variety originate in Ethiopia, where the humpless Egyptian longhorn (as depicted on ancient Egyptian pictographs) and humped Asian zebu were crossed about 4,000 years ago to form a long-horned, humped breed known as the Ethiopian sanga. A number of credible oral traditions indicate that the sanga was introduced to northwest Uganda in medieval times, probably as part of the same wave of southward migration from Ethiopia associated with the foundation of the legendary Bacwezi Kingdom in Uganda circa AD1350.

Hardy, and capable of subsisting on limited water and poor grazing, these introduced cattle were ideally suited to local conditions, except that they had no immunity to tsetse-borne diseases, which forced the pastoralists who tended them to keep drifting southward. The outsized horns of the modern cattle are probably a result of selective breeding subsequent to their ancestors' arrival in southern Uganda about 500 years ago, at around the time the Ankole Kingdom was founded near modern-day Mbarara. Although the long horns were bred primarily for aesthetic reasons, the artificial process of breeding might have involved an element of natural selection. When threatened by large predators such as hyena or lion, it is customary for Ankole cattle to form a tight circle with horns facing outward, and it has also been noted how the calf often walks closely in front of its mother, protected by her horns.

Both in Uganda and Rwanda, pastoralists traditionally value cows less for their individual productivity than as status symbols: the wealth of a man would as Cyasemakamba but more often referred to as Rompway (from the French 'rond-point' for roundabout, although there is no traffic circle, just a triangle!).

Getting there and away The town lies 100km from Kigali along a good surfaced road, branching southward at the main traffic circle in Kayonza after 75km. The drive should take no more than two hours. Regular minibus-taxis between Kigali and Ngoma/Kibungo run throughout the day and cost Rfr2,000. There is also plenty of minibus-taxi transport on to Rusumo on the Tanzanian border. The main taxi park is at Cyasemakamba, more or less opposite the Umbrella Pine Hotel

be measured by the size and quality of his herd, and the worth of an individual cow by its horn size and, to a lesser extent, its coloration. In Rwanda, the noblest cow is the *inyambo*, which has an even deep blackish- or brownish-red hide, large lyre-shaped horns, and long hooves. Other long-horned cows of any coloration are called *ibigarama*, while stockier short-horned cows are referred to as *inkuku* – which may or may not be a pejorative derived from the widespread Bantu word for chicken!

Traditionally, the closely related pastoralist cultures of Rwanda and Uganda were as deeply bound up with a quasi-mystical relationship to cattle as the Maasai are today. Like Eskimos and their physical landscape, this abiding mental preoccupation is reflected in the 30 variations in hide coloration that are recognised linguistically by the Bahima of Ankole, along with at least a dozen peculiarities of horn shape and size. The Bahima day is traditionally divided up into 20 periods, of which all but one of the daylight phases is named after an associated cattle-related activity. And, like the Maasai, Rwandan and Ugandan pastoralists traditionally looked down on any lifestyle based around fishing or agriculture – and they also declined to hunt game for meat, with the exception of buffalo and eland, which were sufficiently bovine in appearance to make for acceptable eating.

In times past, the diet of the pastoralists of Uganda and Rwanda did not, as might be expected, centre on meat, but rather on blood tapped from the vein of a living cow, combined with the relatively meagre yield of milk from the small udders that characterise the Ankole breed. Slaughtering a fertile cow for meat was regarded as akin to cannibalism, but it was customary for infertile cows and surplus bullocks to be killed for meat on special occasions, while the flesh of any cow that died of natural causes would be eaten, or bartered for millet beer and other fresh produce. No part of the cow would go to waste: the hide would be used to make clothing, mats and drums, the dung to plaster huts and dried to light fires, while the horns could be customised as musical instruments.

Today, neither Rwanda nor Ankole is as defiantly traditionalist as, say, Ethiopia's Omo Valley or Maasailand, and most rural Bahima today supplement their herds of livestock by practising mixed agriculture of subsistence and cash crops. But the Ankole cattle and their extraordinary horns, particularly common in eastern Rwanda, pay living tribute to the region's ancestral bovine preoccupations. Meanwhile, on a more prosaic note, this hardy breed – first farmed in the USA in the 1960s, where they are most often called Watusi cattle, a name no longer used in Rwanda – is of growing interest to international stock farmers because its meat has the lowest cholesterol levels of any commercial breed.

11

A NEW VERSION OF AN ANCIENT TALE The great King Gihanga ruled a part of Rwanda in the early 12th century – or perhaps the late tenth. Some historians say that he was the first of the royal dynasty, others claim that many kings preceded him. That's the trouble with oral history – the facts are elusive, and who knows whether or not any of this story is true! Anyway, it's certain that Gihanga had many wives and many children.

One day, his favourite daughter Nyirarucyaba lost her temper with a wife who was not her mother, scratching at the woman's face and tearing her hair until she screamed in pain. To lose control was considered very shameful and all the courtiers had seen what happened, so the king had no choice. He banished Nyirarucyaba into the deep forest where only wild beasts live. She wept pitifully but he would not yield, although his heart was torn.

After many days alone, the girl heard a rustling in the leaves and a snapping of branches – and crouched to the ground in fear. But it was a young man who had, like her, been cast into exile. Now, together, they began to contact the animals around them. There was one that seemed friendly, despite its great size and ugly voice. By day it munched the forest grasses and by night they kept warm against its soft hide.

In time it gave birth to a young one, with wet matted skin and shaky legs, which nuzzled under its mother and sucked at her teats. They saw that it drank a white liquid and learnt that it was milk. Now they had food indeed! They shared the milk with the calf and grew strong and healthy. In time they bore children of their own and the cow had many more calves.

Meanwhile the king had fallen sick with an illness that robbed him of all strength and joy. Doctors could find no cure. Finally three of the court's wisest men, so old that their hair was white and thin upon their heads, recognised it as grief, and took it upon themselves to speak. They told him Nyirarucyaba was still alive – and at once he sprang from his couch and dispatched hunters to the forest to search for her. They found her beside a stream, her children at her side and many cattle grazing nearby. Her return to her delighted father was a time of great celebration at the court.

The cattle came too, with their rich supply of milk. The courtiers gained a taste for it, and grew fat and strong. There was great competition to own the calves, which the king presented to courtiers who had served him particularly well. Needless to say, the families of his three old advisers were given the pick of the herd. As the years and the generations passed, the people could no longer remember a time when the kingdom had been empty of cattle. And that is how it still is, in Rwanda today…

[267 B3]. The GPS for Cyasemakamba junction is ⊕ S 02°08.091, E 030°33.448 and for the town centre it's ⊕ S 02°09.283, E 030°32.778.

 ## Where to stay and eat

🏠**Centre de Formation de l'Eglise Anglicaine** [267 C3] (17 rooms plus dorm) m 078 4258882/8616797. Situated on the feeder road to Kibungo, just 50m from Cyasemakamba junction, the basic but clean rooms here are set around a maze of quiet grassy courtyards. Meals are provided to order; breakfast Rfr1,500–2,500 & mélange Rfr2,500 (or 4,000 for fish or chicken).

Rfr5,000/7,000 sgl/dbl with shared bathroom; from Rfr8,000/10,000 en suite sgl/dbl; Rfr2,000 bed in either of the cramped 32-bed single-sex dorm.

🏠 **Centre St Joseph** [267 C4] (35 rooms) 📞 0252 566303. Situated next to the eponymous church only 100m from the feeder road to Ngoma, this Catholic-run guesthouse has long been the best-value lodging in town. Rooms range from simple sgls using shared toilets & showers, to large en-suite mini-suites with dbl bed & sitting area, to full apartments, & they are all clean & well maintained. The restaurant has indoor & outdoor seating & it serves good, inexpensive local fare, as well as soft & alcoholic drinks. *Rfr53,000 sgl; Rfr10,000 dbl; Rfr15,000 suite.*

🏠 **La Cigale Guesthouse** [267 C4] (6 rooms) m 072 8505317/078 8505317. This new place alongside the road between the town centre & Cyasemakamba has very clean but sparsely furnished rooms with en-suite cold shower.

Unfortunately there is no restaurant. *Otherwise, good value at Rfr8,000/10,000 sgl/dbl.*

🏠 **Motel Umbrella Pine** [267 B3] (8 rooms) m 078 2525885/6491939. Situated in Cyasemakamba 200m south of the main traffic circle, this simple lodge has been a reliable bet for some years now, though it is starting to look its age, & suffers from dodgy plumbing & water shortages during the dry season – but the staff are so willing that it's worth a try. The restaurant serves inventive meals, & can rustle up a picnic if you need it for visiting Akagera. The hotel can be hard to spot, tucked away behind a petrol station on the right coming from Kigali. *Rfr10,000/15,000 for a dingy en-suite sgl/twin B&B.*

🏠 **Tiptop Motel** [267 D6] (5 rooms) 📞 0252 566471; m 078 8539604. The most central lodge, situated almost opposite the market, this has adequate but rather dingy en-suite rooms with dbl bed, net, writing desk & cold shower. A restaurant & bar is attached. *Adequate value at Rfr12,000 dbl.*

Other practicalities There is a post office [267 A7] and small bank [267 B6] on the main road, but no facilities for foreign exchange. The only internet café is in the double-storey mall between the Bank of Kigali and the central market [267 D6].

NYAKARAMBI If you are heading to Rusumo, it's definitely worth stopping at this large village, which straddles the road from Ngoma/Kibungo about 20km before the Rusumo border crossing. This part of Rwanda is noted for its distinctive **Imigongo** (cow-dung) 'paintings' – earthy, geometric designs which are mostly used to decorate the interiors of houses. In Nyakarambi, however, a couple of the houses have cow-dung paintings on their outer walls, and about 2km south of the town there's a craft co-operative. This is where most of the geometric paintings and pottery you see in Kigali originate from, but it's more fun (and cheaper) to buy them at source, especially as the people who run the co-operative aren't at all pushy. The sign outside reads 'Cooperative Kakira – Art "Imigongo"' and shows geometric patterns. A small brochure, sometimes available in the workshop, explains (in more or less these words) the origin of the form in the early 19th century:

In olden times, there was Kakira, son of Kimenyi, King of Gisaka in Ngoma province (southeastern Rwanda). Kakira invented the art of embellishing houses and making them more attractive. To decorate the inside walls, cow dung was used, in patterns with prominent ridges. Then the surfaces were painted, in red and white colours made from natural soil (white from kaolin, red from natural clay with ochre), or else in shining black made from the sap of the aloe plant – *ikakarubamba* – mixed with the ash of burned banana skins and fruits of the solanum aculeastrum plant. It was the art of mixing together the soil, fire, raw materials from the cow and medicinal art that is the source of this work.

Kakira's knowledge was disappearing, due to the increasing use of industrial materials (paint); and so a women's association was created to maintain Kakira's work. After the 1994 genocide, most of the women, now widows, restarted their work together. Since 2001, the association has benefited from better promotion. Previously the women made no more than 20 pieces a month; now it is much more as orders have increased. Today, the Kakira Association makes 'Imigongo' art: modelled and painted tiles, panels, tables and other objects.

Working hours are Monday–Saturday, 07.30–12.30 and 14.00–18.00. Kakira products can be ordered from the workshop or via a Fair Trade registered organisation in Huye/Butare called Rwanda Arts (\ *0252 530762;* e *info@rwanda-art.com; www.rwanda-art.com;* ✆ *S 02°16.165, E 030°41.812, 1,609m).*

RUSUMO FALLS The Rusumo border with Tanzania, 60km southeast of Ngoma/ Kibungo (✆ S 02°22.798, E 030°46.999, 1,320m), is also the site of Rwanda's most impressive waterfall. Rusumo Falls isn't particularly tall, and can't compete with the Victoria or Blue Nile Falls, but it is a voluminous rush of white water nevertheless, as the Akagera River surges below the bridge between the two border posts. The Rwandan officials don't appear to object to tourists wandering into No Man's Land and on to the bridge to goggle at the spectacle, though they may or may not ask to see a passport first. At present you can photograph the falls from the bridge, but nothing else in the immediate vicinity. It's best to ask permission anyway.

It's here at Rusumo that the German Count von Götzen, later to become Governor of German East Africa, entered Rwanda in 1894. He then travelled across the country to Lake Kivu, visiting the Mwami at Nyanza *en route*. Later, in 1916, when the Belgians were preparing to wrest the territory from the Germans, Belgian troops dug a trench and mounted artillery at the spot where one can see the falls today, in order to dislodge the German troops ensconced on the other bank who were guarding the only negotiable crossing. More recently, in 1994, Rusumo Bridge served as the funnel through which an estimated 500,000 Rwandans – half of them within one 24-hour period – fled from their home country to refugee camps around Ngala and elsewhere in northwest Tanzania. Journalists reporting on the exodus described standing on the bridge and counting the bloated bodies of genocide victims tumbling over the waterfall at a rate of one or two per minute.

Practicalities So far as travel practicalities go, the surfaced road between Ngoma/ Kibungo and Rusumo is in reasonable condition, and can be covered in an hour. Regular minibus-taxis service the route, and there are also direct minibuses to/from Kigali for around Rfr2,400. About 200m back from the Rusumo border, the basic **Amarembo Hotel** (m *078 3234911*) has a total of 11 double rooms at Rfr5,000, a decent restaurant serving a tasty buffet lunch and dinner, and a great balcony offering a view across the facing rooftops to the Akagera River and surrounding papyrus beds. It gets busy with cross-border traffic.

12

Akagera National Park

Named after the river that runs along its eastern boundary, Akagera National Park is Rwanda's counterpart to the famous savanna reserves of Kenya, Tanzania and the like. In contrast to the rest of the country, it is located in a relatively warm and low-lying area of undulating plains supporting a cover of dense, broad-leafed woodland interspersed with lighter acacia woodland and patches of rolling grassland studded evocatively with stands of the superficially cactus-like *Euphorbia candelabra* shrub. To the west of the plains lies a chain of low mountains, reaching elevations of between 1,600m and 1,800m. The eastern part of the park supports an extensive wetland: a complex of a dozen lakes linked by extensive papyrus swamps and winding water channels fed by the meandering Akagera (sometimes called Kagera) River.

In terms of game-viewing, it would be misleading to compare Akagera to East Africa's finest savanna reserves. The northern and western portions of the original 2,500km² park were degazetted in 1997 (along with the adjoining 300km² Mutara Wildlife Reserve) to accommodate returned refugees, reducing the protected area to 1,085km². Ongoing poaching has also impacted negatively on wildlife populations, and those lakes that remain within the national park were until recently often used to water domestic cattle – indeed, a few years back, long-horned Ankole cows were the most commonly seen large mammal in Akagera.

However, this seems set to change following the formation in 2010 of the Akagera Management Company (AMC) under the joint management of the RDB and the non-profit African Parks Network (APN), on a renewable 20-year basis. Since then, several new roads have been constructed in the park, work has started on an upmarket tented camp, and a 120km western boundary fence is being erected by a contractor with funds provided mostly by the RDB. A programme of reintroductions is also likely to be implemented during the lifespan of this edition.

Even as things stand, Akagera is emphatically worth visiting. For one thing, it ranks among the most scenic of Africa's savanna reserves, with its sumptuous forest-fringed lakes, tall mountains and constantly changing vegetation. On top of that, the birdlife is quite phenomenal – for specialist birders, the checklist of almost 500 species includes several good rarities, whilst for first-time African visitors, it's a great place to see eagles and other large raptors along with some truly impressive concentrations of water-associated birds.

Akagera also still retains a genuinely off-the-beaten-track character: this is one African game reserve where you can still drive for hours without passing another vehicle, never knowing what wildlife encounter might lie around the next corner. And contrary to some reports, there *is* plenty of wildlife around, with the likes of zebra, giraffe, hippo, baboon, warthog and half-a-dozen antelope species all reasonably visible, and less skittish than one might expect. In addition, the lakes

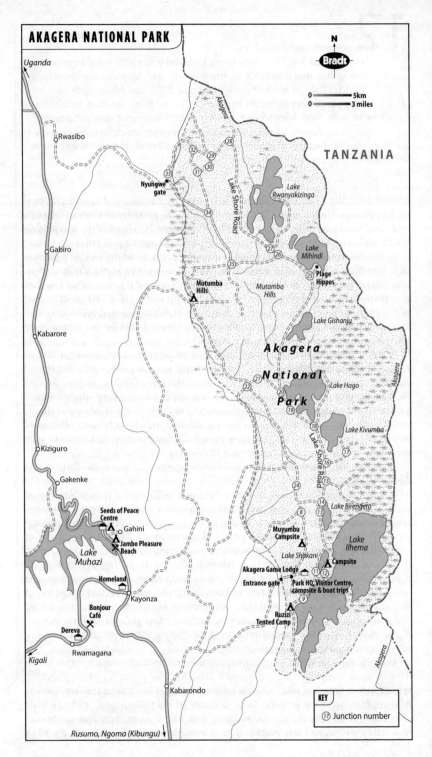

AKAGERA NATIONAL PARK

N

Bradt

0 — 5km
0 — 3 miles

Uganda

Rwasibo

TANZANIA

Akagera

32 29 28
33 31 30

Nyungwe gate

34

Lake Shore Road

Lake Rwanyakizinga

Gabiro

35 26 27

Lake Mihindi

25 **Plage Hippos**

Mutumba Hills

Mutamba Hills

Kabarore

Lake Gishanju

Akagera

National

22 21

Park

20
19

Lake Hago

Kiziguro

18

Lake Kivumba

17

Gakenke

16

15

24

14 Lake Birengero
13

8

Seeds of Peace Centre

Gahini

Jambo Pleasure Beach

Muyumbu Campsite

Lake Ilhema

Lake Muhazi

Lake Shakani

Homeland

Akagera Game Lodge

11 **Campsite**
12

Entrance gate

Park HQ, Visitor Centre, campsite & boat trips

Kayonza

9

Bonjour Café

Ruzizi Tented Camp

Dereva

Rwamagana

Kigali

Kabarondo

Akagera

Rusumo, Ngoma (Kibungu)

KEY

17 Junction number

support some of the highest concentrations of hippo you'll find anywhere in Africa, as well as numerous large crocodiles.

As for the coveted Big Five, buffalo are plentiful and easily seen, elephants are quite common but more difficult to track down, and leopards are present but secretive as ever. The last black rhino was seen in 2007, and while there have been plenty of rumoured lion sightings over recent years, none are truly reliable, and no spoor or calls have been documented of late. However, the AMC intends to reintroduce lions as soon as the new fence is complete, which may be as soon as 2013, and reintroduction of rhinos is also planned. All in all, the next few years look to herald exciting times for Akagera National Park.

NATURAL HISTORY

Akagera is notable for protecting an unusually wide diversity of habitats within a relatively small area. Prior to the civil war, it was regarded as one of the few African savanna reserves to form a self-sustaining ecological unit, meaning that its resident large mammals had no need to migrate seasonally outside of the park boundaries. Whether that is still the case today is an open question: roughly two-thirds of the original park was degazetted in 1997, and, while some of this discarded territory is still virgin bush, it is probably only a matter of time before it will all be settled, putting further pressure on Akagera's diminished wildlife populations.

The modern boundaries of the park protect an area of 1,120km², stretching along the Tanzania border for approximately 60km from north to south, and nowhere wider than 30km. The eastern third of the park consists of an extensive network of wetlands, fed by the Akagera River, and dominated by a series of small-to-medium-sized lakes. Lake Ihema, the most southerly of the lakes to lie within the revised park boundaries, is also the largest body of open water, covering about 100km². The lakes are connected by narrow channels of flowing water and large expanses of seasonal and perennial papyrus swamps. The eastern wetlands are undoubtedly the most important of the habitats protected within the park: not only do they provide a permanent source of drinking water for the large mammals, they also form an important waterbird sanctuary while harbouring a number of localised swamp dwellers.

Akagera's dominant terrestrial habitat is dense broad-leafed woodland, though pockets of acacia woodland also exist within the park, while some of the lake fringes support a thin belt of lush riparian woodland. Ecologically, the savanna is in several respects unique, a product of its isolation from similar habitats by the wetlands to the east and mountainous highlands of central Rwanda to the west. The flora shows strong affinities with the semi-arid zones of northern Uganda and Kenya, but the fauna is more typical of the Mara–Serengeti ecosystem east of Lake Victoria. Akagera's geographical isolation from similar habitats is emphasised by the natural absence of widespread plains animals such as rhino and giraffe, both of which have been introduced, and thrived in their adopted home (the absence of rhino today is due mainly to poaching). Much of the bush in Akagera is very dense, but there are also areas of light acacia woodland and open grassland, notably on the Mutumba Hills and to the northeast of Lake Rwanyakizinga.

MAMMALS While Akagera's considerable scenic qualities and superb birdlife are largely unaffected by the recent years of turmoil, the large mammal populations have suffered badly at the hands of poachers. Having said that, on every visit over the course of researching five editions of this book we've been pleasantly surprised at how much wildlife still remains. True, the populations of all large mammals are severely depleted in comparison with the pre-1994 levels, while a few high-profile species, if not already locally extinct, appear to be heading that way. But most large mammal species are still sufficiently numerous to form a viable breeding population.

Extirpated species include the **African wild dog**, probably a victim not of poaching but, in common with many other African reserves, of a canine plague which would have been introduced into the population through contact with domestic dogs. Of the larger predators, **spotted hyena** and **leopard** are still around, but infrequently observed (though you might well come across hyena spoor, particularly the characteristic white dung, and one female leopard was regularly seen in the vicinity of Akagera Game Lodge in 2011).

Prior to 1994, the park supported an estimated 250 **lion**, including a couple of prides that were uniquely adapted to foraging in the swamps, and others specialised in climbing trees. During the civil war, large numbers of lion were hunted out by the army to protect the presidential cattle herds; more recently they have been poisoned by cattle herders living outside the park. The situation today is open to conjecture. After a few years without any confirmed sightings, a female with three cubs was observed in the north of the park in the year 2000. More recent published estimates have placed the population at anywhere from 15 to 60 individuals, but local sources reckon it is unlikely any fully resident lions remain. Fortunately, the tenacity of this regal feline, combined with its tendency to wander long distances, makes it possible it could replenish naturally as a result of individuals crossing over from Tanzania. And reintroduction of a small number of lions is likely once the park's western boundaries are fenced.

Smaller predators are well represented. Most likely to be encountered by day are dwarf, banded and black-tailed **mongoose**, while at night there is a chance of coming across viverrids such as the lithe, heavily spotted and somewhat cat-like **genet**, and the bulkier black-masked **civet**. Also present, but rarely seen, are the handsome spotted **serval cat** and the dog-like **side-striped jackal**.

AKAGERA'S HISTORY

From 1920 onwards, the Belgian colonisers put conservation measures into practice through various legislative and administrative decrees. It was the decree of 26 November 1934 that created the Parc National de la Kagera, on about 250,000ha. The park included – which was extremely rare before 1960 – a Strict Natural Reserve and an adjoining area where certain human activities were tolerated. It came under the jurisdiction of the Institut des Parcs Nationaux du Congo Belge et du Ruanda-Urundi, which was also responsible for the three parks (Albert, Garamba and Upemba) in the Belgian Congo. (In fact 8% of the Albert Park was also in Rwanda; now representing the Volcanoes Park in the northwest.) Kagera was renamed Akagera after independence, when the new Republic's leaders announced their intention of maintaining the park (and the Volcanoes Park) despite population pressure. Akagera's borders were altered – a few thousand hectares were retroceded to local communities while almost 20,000ha of the lacustrine zone to the south were incorporated. In 1975, 26 elephants were transported, first by helicopter and then by truck, from Bugesera, which was to be developed for agriculture. In November 1984, Rwanda held an official celebration of the park's 50th anniversary.

One of the most common terrestrial mammals is the **buffalo** and, while the population is nowhere near the estimated 8,000 that roamed the park in the 1980s, it probably still stands at more than 1,000. **Hippo**, too, are present in impressive numbers: on some of the lakes there must be at least a dozen pods of up to 50 animals, and the total population probably exceeds 1,000. Small herds of **Burchell's zebra** are regularly encountered in open areas. The handsome **impala** is probably the most common and habitat-tolerant large mammal in the park, and of the park's 11 antelope species (see box *Antelope of Akagera* on pages 278–9), only the aquatic **sitatunga** is unlikely to be seen by visitors.

Also very common are three savanna primates: the dark, heavily built **olive baboon** (boldly resident around the safari lodge), the smaller and more agile **vervet monkey**, and the tiny wide-eyed **bushbaby** (the latter a nocturnal species likely to be seen only after dusk). The forest-dwelling **blue monkey** is probably now quite rare, due to habitat loss, but sightings are quite regular in the vicinity of Lakes Ihema and Birengero. It is unlikely that Africa's largest swine, the **giant forest hog**, still occurs in Akagera. The smaller **bushpig**, a secretive nocturnal species, is present but rarely encountered, while the diurnal **warthog** is very common and often seen trotting off in family parties, stiff tail held high.

Two large mammal species that don't occur naturally were introduced to the park prior to the civil war. The first of these is the **Maasai giraffe**, which was introduced from the Magadi region of southern Kenya in January 1986. The original herd of two males and four females produced its first offspring in 1988 and has since multiplied to a population of around 80, which tends to stick to patches of acacia woodland close to the park headquarters and safari lodge.

In 1957, Akagera became the recipient of Africa's first **black rhino** translocation, when a herd comprising five females and one male was flown across from the bordering Karagwe region of Tanzania, to be supplemented by another male a year later. The rhino prospered in the dense bush and by the early 1970s had colonised most of the park – one individual is known to have strayed south almost as far as the Rusumo Falls – and by the end of that decade the population comfortably exceeded 50. Then came the wholesale rhino poaching of the 1980s: by the end of that decade no more than a dozen individuals survived, and it was long thought that the remainder were shot in the civil war. An 11-year old female nicknamed Patricia, who died of natural causes in July 2006, was then thought to be the last of her kind in Akagera, but aerial footage of another rhino taken from a helicopter in 2007 provides scant hope that another straggler might still remain, Either way, it is likely that fresh rhino stock will eventually be translocated from South Africa.

Although the **African elephant** used to occur naturally in Akagera, the last recorded sighting of the original population was on the shores of Lake Mihindi in 1961. The present-day herd is descended from a group of 26 youngsters that was translocated to Akagera in 1975, part of an operation to clear all the elephants from the increasingly densely populated Bugesera Plains to the south of Kigali. Up to 100 adult elephants were shot in the process, while the young American filmmaker Lee Lyon was killed by one of the survivors upon its release into Akagera. By the late 1980s an estimated 45 individuals roamed Akagera and, although population growth was stunted by poaching during the civil war, the current population of around 80–100 is the largest the park has supported in 50 years.

BIRDS Akagera is the country's second most important ornithological site after Nyungwe, and these two bird-rich national parks complement each other to such an extent that very few species recorded in Rwanda aren't found in one or the other.

Before Akagera's area was reduced in 1997, the park checklist stood at around 550 species, but today it is thought to be around 480, of which as many as 100 are unrecorded in no other protected area in Rwanda. In addition to being the best place in Rwanda to see a good selection of savanna birds and raptors, Akagera is as rich in waterbirds as anywhere in East Africa, and one of the few places where papyrus endemics can be observed.

Among the more colourful and common of the savanna birds are the gorgeous lilac-breasted roller, black-headed gonolek (easily picked up by its jarring duets), little bee-eater, Heuglin's robin-chat, Meyer's parrot, spot-flanked barbet and double-toothed barbet. Less colourful, but very impressive, are the comical grey hornbill and noisy bare-faced go-away bird. The riparian woodland around the lakes hosts a number of specialised species, of which Ross's turaco, a bright-purple, jay-sized bird with a distinctive yellow mask, is the most striking.

A notable feature of Akagera's avifauna is the presence of species such as the crested barbet, white-headed black chat and Souza's shrike, all of which are

ANTELOPE OF AKAGERA

The 11 antelope species in Akagera range from the eland, the world's largest antelope, through to the diminutive common duiker. The most common, however, is the **impala** *Aepeceros melampus*, a slim handsome antelope which bears a superficial similarity to the gazelles, but belongs to a separate family. Chestnut in colour, the impala has diagnostic black and white stripes running down its rump and tail, and the male has large lyre-shaped horns. It is one of the most widespread antelope species in East and southern Africa, normally seen in large herds in woodland habitats, and common in the woodland around and between the lakes of Akagera.

The **Defassa waterbuck** *Kobus ellipsiprymnus defassa* is a large, shaggy brown antelope with a distinctive white rump. The male has large lyre-shaped horns, thicker than those of the impala. The waterbuck inhabits practically any type of woodland or grassland provided that it is close to water, and it is probably the most common large antelope after impala in the far south of Akagera.

Very common in the north of the park and in the Mutumba Hills, the **topi** or **tsessebe** *Damaliscus lunatus* is a large, slender dark-brown antelope with striking yellow lower legs. It has a rather ungainly appearance, reminiscent of the hartebeest and wildebeest, to which it is closely related, and is often seen using an anthill as a sentry point. Oddly, the herds of topi in northern Akagera seem to be far larger than those found in the Serengeti ecosystem.

Similar in size to a topi, but far more handsome, the **roan antelope** *Hippotragus equinus* has, as the Latin name suggests, a horse-like bearing. The uniform fawn-grey coat is offset by a pale belly, and it has short decurved horns and a light mane. After the civil war in the early 1990s, roan were very rare in Akagera: a 1998 estimate put their number at below 20, and the population today stands at around 40.

Much larger still is the **common** or **Cape eland** *Taurotragus oryx*, which attains a height of up to 1.75m and can weigh as much as 900kg. The common eland is light-brown in colour, with faint white vertical stripes, and a somewhat bovine appearance accentuated by the relatively short horns and large dewlap. In Akagera, small herds are most likely to be seen on the open grassland of the Mutumba Hills, where the population is thought to exceed 50.

associated with the *brachystegia* woodland of southern Tanzania and further south, but have colonised the mixed woodland of Akagera at the northernmost extent of their range. More noteworthy still is the red-faced barbet, a localised endemic of savannas between Lake Victoria and the Albertine Rift. It is quite often seen in the car park and gardens of Akagera Safari Lodge. A localised species associated with broken grassland in Akagera is the long-tailed cisticola.

Finally, the savanna of Akagera is one of the last places in Rwanda where a wide range of large raptors is resident: white-backed and Rüppell's griffon vultures soar high on the thermals, the beautiful bateleur eagle can be recognised by its wavering flight pattern and red wing markings, while brown snake eagles and hooded vultures are often seen perching on bare branches.

Most of the savanna birds are primarily of interest to the dedicated birder, but it is difficult to imagine that anybody would be unmoved by the immense concentrations of water-associated birds that can be found on the lakes. Pelicans are common, as is the garishly decorated crowned crane, the odd little open-bill stork

A trio of smaller antelope are also mainly confined to the Mutumba Hills. The largest of these is the **Bohor reedbuck** *Redunca redunca*, a light-fawn animal with moderately sized rounded horns; reedbucks are almost always seen in pairs, and in Akagera are rather skittish.

The smaller **oribi** *Ourebia ourebi* is a tan grassland antelope with short straight horns and a small but clearly visible circular black glandular patch below its ear. It is the commonest antelope on the Mutumba Hills, typically seen in parties of two or three, and has a distinctive sneezing alarm call.

The **klipspringer** *Oreotragus oreotragus* is a goat-like antelope, normally seen in pairs, and easily identified by its dark, bristly grey-yellow coat, slightly speckled appearance and unique habitat preference. Klipspringer means 'rock jumper' in Afrikaans and it is an apt name for an antelope which occurs exclusively in mountainous areas and rocky outcrops. It is often seen from the road between the entrance gate and Lake Ihema.

The only small antelope found in thicker bush is the **common duiker** *Sylvicapra grimmia*, an anomalous savanna representative of a family of 20-plus small hunchbacked antelopes associated with true forests. Generally grey in colour, the common duiker has a distinctive black tuft of hair sticking up between its small straight horns. It is common in all bush areas, though it tends to be very skittish.

A widespread resident of thick woodland and forest, the pretty **bushbuck** *Tragelaphus scriptus* is a medium-sized, rather deer-like antelope. The male is dark brown or chestnut, while the much smaller female is generally pale red-brown. The male has relatively small, straight horns, while both sexes have pale throat patches, white spots and sometimes stripes. The bushbuck tends to be secretive, but might be seen anywhere in Akagera except for open grassland.

Similar in appearance to the bushbuck, and a close relation, the semi-aquatic **sitatunga** *Tragelaphus spekei* is a widespread but infrequently observed inhabitant of west and central African swamps. The male, with a shoulder height of up to 125cm (much taller than a bushbuck) and a shaggy fawn coat, is unmistakable, while the smaller female might be mistaken for a bushbuck except for its more clearly defined stripes. The status of the sitatunga within Akagera is uncertain, but recent estimates place the population at around 150, largely restricted to inaccessible swampy areas.

and the much larger and singularly grotesque marabou stork. Herons and egrets are particularly visible and well-represented, ranging from the immense goliath heron to the secretive black-capped night heron, reed-dwelling purple heron and very localised rufous-bellied heron. The lakes also support a variety of smaller kingfishers and shorebirds, and a prodigious number of fish eagles, whose shrill duet ranks as one of the most evocative sounds of Africa.

On a more esoteric note, the papyrus swamps are an excellent place to look for a handful of birds restricted to this specific habitat: the stunning and highly vocal papyrus gonolek, as well as the more secretive and nondescript Caruthers's cisticola and white-winged warbler. Akagera is also one of the best places in Africa to see the shoebill, an enormous and unmistakable slate-grey swamp-dweller whose outsized bill is fixed in a permanent Cheshire-cat smirk (see box on pages 281–2). A useful birding report on Akagera can be sourced online at www.worldtwitch. com/rwanda_uganda_des.htm.

REPTILES The **Nile crocodile**, the world's largest reptile and a survivor from the age of the dinosaurs, is abundant in the lakes. Some of the largest wild specimens you'll encounter anywhere are to be found sunning themselves on the mud-banks of Akagera, their impressive mouths wide open until they slither menacingly into the water at the approach of human intruders. Not unlike a miniature crocodile in appearance, the **water monitor** is a type of lizard which often grows to be more than a metre long and is common around the lakes, tending to crash noisily into the bush or water when disturbed. Smaller lizards are to be seen all over, notably the colourful rock agama, and a variety of snakes are present but, as ever, very secretive.

DANGEROUS ANIMALS Although it is technically forbidden to leave your vehicle except at designated lookout points, the guides in Akagera seem to enforce this rule somewhat whimsically, so it is worth emphasising the folly of disembarking from your vehicle in the presence of elephant, buffalo or lion.

Hippo and crocodile are potentially dangerous, and claim far more human lives than any terrestrial African animal. For this reason, you should be reasonably cautious when you leave the car next to a lake, particularly at dusk or dawn or in overcast conditions, when hippos are most likely to come out of the water to graze. The danger with hippos is getting *between* them and the water; you have nothing to worry about when they are actually in the water. Special caution should be exercised if you camp next to a lake – don't wander too far from your site after dark, and take a good look around should you need to leave your tent during the night (if there are hippo close by, you'll almost certainly hear them chomping at the grass). Crocs are a real threat only if you are daft enough to wade into one of the lakes.

The most dangerous animal in Akagera is the malaria-carrying anopheles mosquito. Cover up after dark – long trousers and thick socks – and smear any exposed parts of your body with insect repellent. Many tents come with built-in mosquito netting. This will protect you when you sleep, provided that you don't hang a light at the entrance to your tent, which will ensure that a swarm of insects enter it with you. Incidentally, never leave any food in your tent: fruit might attract the attention of monkeys and elephants, while meat could arouse the interest of large predators.

Not so much a danger as a nuisance are tsetse flies, which are quite common in dense bush and can give a painful bite. Fortunately, the pain isn't enduring (though people who tend to react badly to insect bites might want to douse any tsetse bite in antihistamine cream) and there is no risk of contracting sleeping sickness during a short stay in Akagera. Insect repellents have little effect on these robust little creatures, but it's worth noting that they are attracted to dark clothing (especially blue).

FURTHER INFORMATION The RDB produces a free colour fold-out map and brochure for Akagera, but be warned that this doesn't show any of the new roads cut by the AMC, and it also retains the old obsolete junction numbering system. Far more accurate and up-to-date is the colour fold-out compiled by AMC and sold at the gate. This shows all new roads in the park, as well as the new junction numbers , which can help with navigation, even though not all junctions are actually numbered on the ground. Also for sale at the gate, the coffee-table book *Akagera: Land of Water, Grass and Fire* by Jean-Pierre Vande Weghe was first published in 1990 and has subsequently been reprinted but never updated. It presents an alluring picture of Akagera as it must once have been – historically fascinating, but likely to create false expectations of a visit to the park today, and ultimately a rather depressing testament to human destructivity.

GETTING THERE AND AWAY

The newly built reception centre to Akagera lies in the south of the park about 1km from Akagera Safari Lodge, and 6km past what is technically the entrance gate (marked by an the old arch that will soon be take down). It is reached via a 27km dirt road that branches east from the main surfaced road between Kigali and Rusumo at Kabarondo, about 15km north of Ngoma/Kibungo. This dirt road is in fair condition, and should be passable in any vehicle except perhaps after heavy rain, when 4x4 may be necessary (in any case, 4x4 is advisable for roads within the park, though any vehicle with good clearance should be OK in the dry season). In a private vehicle, the main gate is about two hours' drive from Kigali, or one hour from Ngoma/Kibungo or Rwamagana.

In the north of the park, an alternative entry point, Nyungwe Gate (not to be confused with the eponymous national park on the other side of the country), is accessible on a rough dirt track that branches east from the Kigali–Nyagatare road at the village of Kucyanyirangegene (sometimes referred to as Kizarakome) about 70km north of Rwamagana. This route requires a 4x4 and it may be impassable after rain. For those heading to Akagera Safari Lodge or Akagera Tented Camp, it is a far longer drive than the one via the main gate, but it does allow you to explore the park from north to south in one go. Driving without stops, bank on at least five hours from Kigali to the lodge via Nyungwe Gate, and allow the best part of a day to make a game drive of the section within the national park.

Reaching Akagera on public transport is problematic. Any minibus-taxi travelling between Kayonza and Ngoma can drop you at the junction, from where the only realistic option is a motorbike-taxi (assuming that you can find one). Inside the park, except within the grounds of the safari lodge, no walking is permitted with or without a guide. A three-hour game drive activity is offered by the park (see page 285), but you are still quite limited when it come to how much of the park you can explore without your own transport.

PARK FEES

Under the simplified 2012 fee structure, entrance costs US$30 per person per night for international visitors, US$20 per person for foreign residents of Rwanda and other states in the East African Community (EAC), and Rfr3,500 for nationals of

12

Rwanda and other EAC states, with a 50% reduction for under-12s in all cases. Unlike in some neighbouring countries, the fee is not calculated per 24-hour-period but per night – were you to arrive at 07.00 on one day and exit at 17.00 the next day, you are still charged for only one night. However, day visitors will pay the same entrance fee as people spending one night in the park. The only other fees

IN SEARCH OF KING WHALE-HEAD

Perhaps the most eagerly sought of all African birds, the shoebill is also one of the few that is likely to make an impression on those travellers who regard pursuing rare birds to be about as diverting as hanging about in windswept railway stations scribbling down train numbers. Three factors combine to give the shoebill its bizarre and somewhat prehistoric appearance. The first is its enormous proportions: an adult might stand more than 150cm (5ft) tall and typically weighs around 6kg. The second is its unique uniform slatey-grey coloration. Last but emphatically not least is its clog-shaped, hook-tipped bill – at 20cm long, and almost as wide, the largest among all living bird species. The bill is fixed in a permanent Cheshire-cat smirk that contrives to look at once sinister and somewhat inane, and when agitated the bird loudly claps together its upper and lower bill, rather like outsized castanets.

The first known allusions to the shoebill came from early European explorers to the Sudan, who wrote of a camel-sized flying creature known by the local Arabs as Abu Markub – Father of the Shoe. These reports were dismissed as pure fancy by Western biologists until 1851, when Gould came across a bizarre specimen amongst an avian collection shot on the Upper White Nile. Describing it as 'the most extraordinary bird I have seen', Gould placed his discovery in a monotypic family and named it *Balaeniceps Rex* – King Whale Head! Gould believed the strange bird to be most closely allied to pelicans, but it also shares some anatomic and behavioural characters with herons, and until recently it was widely thought to be an evolutionary offshoot of the stork family. Recent DNA studies support Gould's original theory, however, and the shoebill is now placed in a monotypic subfamily of the Pelecanidae.

The life cycle of the shoebill is no less remarkable than its appearance. One of the few birds with an age span of up to 50 years, it is generally monogamous, with pairs coming together during the breeding season (April to June) to construct a grassy nest of up to 3m wide on a mound of floating vegetation or a small island. Two eggs are laid, and the parents rotate incubation duties, in hot weather filling their bills with water to spray over the eggs to keep them cool. The chicks hatch after about a month, and will need to be fed by the parents for at least another two months until their beaks are fully developed. Usually only one nestling survives, probably as a result of sibling rivalry.

The shoebill is a true swamp specialist, but it avoids dense stands of papyrus and tall grass, which obstruct its take-off, preferring instead to forage from patches of low floating vegetation or along the edge of channels. It consumes up to half its weight in food daily, preying on whatever moderately sized aquatic creature might come its way, ranging from toads to baby crocodiles, though lungfish are especially favoured. Its method of hunting is exceptionally sedentary: the bird may stand semi-frozen for several hours before it lunges down with remarkable speed and power, heavy wings stretched backward, to grab an item of prey in its large, inescapable bill. Although it is generally a solitary hunter, the shoebill has applicable to self-drive visitors are a vehicle fee of Rfr4,000 and an optional guide fee of US$15 per party per half day.

Dedicated birdwatchers should take note that the 2012 tariff list rather bizarrely treats guided birding as a specific activity attracting a fee of US$80 per person per day over and above the standard entry fee. We have yet to encounter a guide at

occasionally been observed hunting co-operatively in small flocks, which splash about flapping their wings to drive a school of fish into a confined area.

Although the shoebill is elusive, this is less a function of scarcity than of the inaccessibility of its swampy haunts. Nevertheless, *BirdLife International* recently classified it as near-globally threatened, and it is classed as CITES Appendix 2, which means that trade in shoebills, or their capture for any harmful activity, is banned by international law. Estimates of the global population vary wildly. In the 1970s, only 1,500 were thought to persist in the wild, but this estimate has subsequently been revised to 10,000–15,000 individuals concentrated in five countries – Sudan, Uganda, Tanzania, Congo and Zambia. Small breeding populations also occur in Rwanda and Ethiopia, and vagrants have been recorded in Malawi and Kenya.

The most important shoebill stronghold is the Sudd Floodplain on the Sudanese Nile, where 6,400 individuals were counted during an aerial survey undertaken over 1979–82, followed by the inaccessible Moyowosi-Kigosi Swamp in western Tanzania, whose population was thought to amount to a few hundred prior to a 1990 survey that estimated it to be greater than 2,000. Ironically, although Uganda is the easiest place to see the shoebill in the wild, the national population probably amounts to fewer than 1,000 birds.

Outside of Uganda, Akagera National Park is potentially one of the most accessible shoebill haunts anywhere in Africa. In the 1980s, the local shoebill population was estimated at around 15–20 pairs, and there is no particular reason to think this has changed greatly in the interim – shoebills are not hunted as food, they pose no threat to cattle herders, and the inaccessible swamps they inhabit were largely unaffected by the 1997 reduction in Akagera's area. Certainly, at least one pair is resident in the papyrus beds fringing the eastern shore of Lake Birengero, and they are regularly seen by visitors, though lack of road access means you need decent binoculars to pick them out from the distant western shore. We have also had unverified reports of sightings on Lake Ihema. That aside, little effort has been made to establish the current status of shoebills in Akagera, or to make the bird's habitat accessible to tourists by boat.

The major threat to the survival of the shoebill is habitat destruction. The construction of several dams along the lower Nile means that the water levels of the Sudd are open to artificial manipulation. Elsewhere, swamp clearance and rice farming pose a localised threat to suitable wetland habitats. Lake Opeta, an important shoebill stronghold in eastern Uganda, has been earmarked as a source of irrigation for a new agricultural scheme. A lesser concern in some areas is that shoebills are hunted for food or illegal trade, while in others local fishermen often kill the shoebills in the belief that seeing one before a fishing expedition is a bad omen. As is so often the case, tourism can play a major role in preserving the shoebill and its habitat: a classic example being Uganda's Mabamba Swamp, where the local community has already seen financial benefits from ornithological visits from nearby Entebbe.

Akagera whose avian knowledge would justify that sort of outlay, and so far as we can ascertain, no additional fee would be charged for birding without a specialist guide.

 ## WHERE TO STAY

UPMARKET

🏠 **Ruzizi Tented Camp** (7 rooms) m 078 2166015; e akagera@african-parks.org; www. akagera.org. Scheduled to open in August 2012, this new tented camp is being built in a patch of lush riparian woodland on the shores of Lake Ihema about 15 minutes drive from the entrance gate. Accommodation will be in spacious furnished standing tents with ensuite hot showers, comparable in standard to upmarket tented camps in the likes of Kenya & Tanzania, & offering visitors a genuine bush alternative to the more motel-like Akagera Safari Lodge. *US$210/300 sgl/dbl for foreign visitors; US$170/240 residents, all rates include b/fast & dinner.*

MODERATE

🏠 **Akagera Game Lodge** (24 rooms) m 078 5201206; e akagera01@yahoo.de; ✪ S 01°52.314, E 030°42.911, 1,610m. Built in the 1970s, this motel-style lodge re-opened in 2003 & has switched hands several times since, so contact details are subject to regular change. It has a wonderful setting in wooded hilltop grounds that host a rich bird life & offer superb views over Lake Ihema into the hills of Tanzania. The angular monolithic architecture feels decidedly outmoded, & the décor is a touch faded, but the en-suite twin or dbl rooms are very comfortable. Facilities include a good & affordable à la carte restaurant, a swimming pool, conference facilities & tennis courts, & the overall level of service is impressive given the remote locale. Be aware that the baboons that loiter around the lodge grounds occasionally enter & raid rooms, so avoid leaving your door open, especially if you have any food inside. *Excellent value for money at US$80/100/150 B&B sgl/dbl/suite. Also 4-6 bed cottages from US$300.*

BUDGET Camping aside, there is no budget accommodation in the park itself, but it can easily be visited as a day trip from Rwamagana or Ngoma/Kibungo. The closest budget accommodation is in the junction town of Kabarondo, only 27km from the entrance gate.

🏠 **Best Lodge** (12 rooms) m 078 7005614. Situated about 100m from the bus station in Kabarondo, & on the opposite side of the main road, this is a very basic place offering en-suite rooms with ¾ bed & cold shower. *Rfr6,000 sgl.*

CAMPING For the self-sufficient, this is allowed at various locations in the park, and costs US$20 per person per night including firewood and water, irrespective of residence status.

ACTIVITIES

BOAT TRIPS Boat trips are available on Lake Ihema, and are worthwhile. Close encounters with outsized crocodiles and hippo are all but guaranteed, and you might also pass substantial seasonal breeding colonies of African darter, various cormorants, and open-bill stork. Other waterbirds are abundant: the delicate and colourful African jacana can be seen trotting on floating vegetation, fish eagles are posted in the trees at regular intervals, jewel-like malachite kingfishers hawk from the reeds, while pied kingfishers hover high above the water to swoop down on their fishy prey. Of greater interest to enthusiasts will be the possibility of marsh and papyrus specialists such as papyrus gonolek, white-winged warbler, blue-headed coucal and marsh flycatcher. Dedicated birders might also want to extend the standard one-hour trip to two hours, in order to visit a fantastic heronry where the likes of squacco heron, purple heron, striated heron, rufous-bellied heron and both types of night heron breed seasonally. Morning and afternoon boat trips cost US$30 per person per hour, while sunset trips cost US$40 per person per hour, with a minimum of two people. They are organised by the park management (m *078 2166015*); or ask at Akagera Safari Lodge, the park reception centre, or Ruzizi Tented Camp.

GAME DRIVES Between the normal opening hours of 06.00 and 18.00, visitors can do their own game drives in whatever vehicle they used to get to the park A 4x4 is pretty much mandatory, and guides are optionally available for US$15 per half-day. In addition, daytime game drives in the southern part of the park can be organised in the park's recently acquired game-viewing vehicle, but these should be booked in advance (m *078 2166015*) to avoid disappointment. The drives require a minimum of 4 people (maximum 7). The cost for a 3-hour trip is US$40 per person, in addition to entry fee, which includes vehicle, driver and a guide. Pick-up is from the park reception, or Akagera Safari Lodge, or Ruzizi Tented Camp.

Simplistically, the road network comprises two roughly parallel main roads that run northward from the main entrance gate. These are an eastern lowland route, which follows the lakes' western shores to the Kilala Plains in the far north, and a western highland route that passes through the so-called Giraffe Area and the Mutumba Hills *en route* to the northern Nyungwe Gate. The two main roads are connected by several shorter roads (mostly running east-west) that create a number of road loops of varying length running north from the main entrance gate, Akagera Game Lodge or Ruzizi Tented Camp.

All these loops are quite lengthy, however, so those with only an hour or two might prefer to stick to one of two short drives: the Giraffe Area west of the main entrance gate, or the network of roads running along the eastern shores of Lakes Ihema and Shakani. Another option is a full-day drive to the Mutumba Hills and far north, but there is no accommodation in this area so it is only recommended if you intend to enter or exit the park at Nyungwe Gate.

Giraffe Area This area of dense woodland can be explored along a 13km figure-8 loop road running west of the main entrance gate. As the name suggests, giraffe are frequently seen in the area, but the relatively open plains between junction 5 and 6 are also often good for zebra, buffalo and various open-country antelope. A dam and series of seasonal pools here can also be worthwhile for plovers, ducks and other water-associated birds. Birders might also want to divert to the **Muyumbu Campsite**, shaded by fruiting trees that often host various barbets along with green wood-hoopoe, Meyer's parrot and many smaller acacia-associated species. Note that the Giraffe Area isn't advisable after heavy rain, since it is in a valley that often gets waterlogged so it's easy to get stuck!

Lakes Ihema and Shakani Starting from the entrance gate, a hilly 5km road through very thick scrub (where oribi, klipspringer and buffalo are often seen) leads to **Lake Ihema**. Today, Defassa waterbuck are common residents around Ihema, as are impala, olive baboon, vervet monkey and buffalo (the latter with a reputation for aggression). You can get out of the car at the fishing camp and boat jetty, where you may see hippos and crocodiles, and are bound to encounter

12

the ghoulish looking marabou stork, various waterbirds, and the localised white-winged black chat that is resident.

Lake Ihema is a site of minor historical interest. It was here, on a humid and mosquito-plagued island near the eastern shore, that Henry Stanley, the first European to enter what is now Rwanda, set up camp on the night of 11 March 1876, only to turn back into what is now Tanzania the next day after being repulsed by the locals from the lake's western shore.

About 4km north of Lake Ihema, a road forks through more thick scrub to the small **Lake Shakani**, a scenic camping spot and home to large numbers of hippo. The bush here is rattling with birdlife (listen out for the jarring duet of the black-headed gonolek, a type of bush-shrike with a brilliant scarlet chest), and the rough

WEAVERS

Placed by some authorities in the same family as the closely related sparrows, the weavers of the family Ploceidae are a quintessential part of Africa's natural landscape, common and highly visible in virtually every habitat from rainforest to desert. The name of the family derives from the intricate and elaborate nests – typically but not always a roughly oval ball of dried grass, reeds and twigs – that are built by the dextrous males of most species.

It can be fascinating to watch a male weaver at work. First, a nest site is chosen, usually at the end of a thin hanging branch or frond, which is immediately stripped of leaves to protect against snakes. The weaver then flies back and forth to the site, carrying the building material blade by blade in its heavy beak, first using a few thick strands to hang a skeletal nest from the end of a branch, then gradually completing the structure by interweaving numerous thinner blades of grass into the main frame. Once completed, the nest is subjected to the attention of his chosen partner, who will tear it apart if the result is less than satisfactory, and so the process starts all over again.

All but 12 of the 113 described weaver species are resident on the African mainland or associated islands, with some 21 represented within Rwanda alone. All but five of the Rwandan species are placed in the genus Ploceus (true weavers), which is among the most characteristic of all African bird genera. Most of the Ploceus weavers are slightly larger than a sparrow, and display a strong sexual dimorphism. Females are with few exceptions drab buff or olive-brown birds, with some streaking on the back, and perhaps a hint of yellow on the belly.

Most male Ploceus weavers conform to the basic colour pattern of the 'masked weaver' – predominantly yellow, with streaky back and wings, and a distinct black facial mask, often bordered orange. Five Rwandan weaver species fit this masked weaver prototype more-or-less absolutely, and a similar number approximate it rather less exactly, for instance by having a chestnut-brown mask, or a full black head, or a black back, or being more chestnut than yellow on the belly. Identification of the masked weavers can be tricky without experience – useful clues are the exact shape of the mask, the presence and extent of the fringing orange, and the colour of the eye and the back.

The golden weavers, of which only one species is present in Rwanda, are also brilliant yellow and/or light orange with some light streaking on the back, but they lack a mask or any other strong distinguishing features. The handful of forest-associated Ploceus weavers, by contrast, tend to have quite different and very striking colour patterns; and, although sexually dimorphic, the female is often as track along the marshy western lake shore is a good place to pick up the likes of African jacana, long-toed lapwing, open-billed stork, squacco heron and common moorhen. Mammals are less numerous, but you might well see impala, bushbuck and other grazers on the floodplains.

Rwisirabo Loop This 35km loop is the shortest to connect the eastern lakeshore road to the western highland road, and it makes for an excellent morning game drive, taking around 3–5 hours, depending on how often you stop. Starting at **Lake Ihema**, and diverting to Lake Shakani (see opposite), you then continue for another 8km north to **Lake Birengero,** a shallow, muddy body of palm-fringed water that supports huge numbers of waterbirds, notably pelicans and storks. It is also home

boldly marked as the male. The most aberrant among these is Vieillot's black weaver, the males of which are totally black except for their eyes, while the black-billed weaver reverses the prototype by being all black with a yellow facemask.

Among the more conspicuous Ploceus species in Rwanda are the black-headed, Baglafecht, slender-billed, yellow-backed and Vieillot's black weavers – for the most part gregarious breeders forming single- or mixed-species colonies of hundreds, sometimes thousands, of pairs. The most extensive weaver colonies are often found in reed beds and waterside vegetation, such as can be seen around the lakes of Akagera. Few weavers have a distinctive song, but they compensate with a rowdy jumble of harsh swizzles, rattles and nasal notes that can reach deafening proportions near large colonies. One more cohesive song you will often hear seasonally around weaver colonies is a cyclic 'dee-dee-dee-Diederik', often accelerating to a hysterical crescendo when several birds call at once. This is the call of the Diederik cuckoo, a handsome green-and-white cuckoo that lays its eggs in weaver nests.

Oddly, while most East African Ploceus weavers are common, even abundant, in suitable habitats, seven highly localised species are listed as range-restricted, and four of these – one Kenyan, one Ugandan and two Tanzanian endemics – are regarded to be of global conservation concern. Of the other three, the strange weaver Ploceus alienus – black head, plain olive back, yellow belly with chestnut bib – is an Albertine Rift endemic restricted to a handful of sites in Rwanda and Uganda, notably Nyungwe National Park.

Most of the colonial weavers, perhaps relying on safety in numbers, build relatively plain nests with a roughly oval shape and an unadorned entrance hole. The nests of more solitary weavers are often more elaborate. Several weavers, for instance, protect their nests from egg-eating invaders by attaching tubular entrance tunnels to the base – in the case of the spectacled weaver, which inhabits riverine woodland in Akagera, this tunnel is sometimes twice as long as the nest itself. The Grosbeak weaver (a peculiar larger-than-average brown-and-white weaver of reed beds, distinguished by its outsized bill and placed in the monospecific genus Amblyospiza) constructs a large and distinctive domed nest, which is supported by a pair of reeds, and woven as precisely as the finest basketwork, with a neat raised entrance hole at the front. By contrast, the scruffiest nests are built by the various species of sparrow- and buffalo-weaver, relatively drab but highly gregarious dry-country birds which are poorly represented in Rwanda.

to at least one pair of shoebill, which can sometimes be seen by parking at one of the open areas on the western shore and scanning the papyrus beds opposite with binoculars.

At Junction 13, turn left on to a road that climbs northeast towards the Rwisirabo Ranger Post, where it's worth stopping to look for white-winged black chat and long-tailed cisticola. Then turn left again at Junction 23 to connect with the main highland road running back south to the Giraffe Area (described above). Before reaching this area of quite dense vegetation, you will pass through lightly vegetated slopes that offer lovely views to the lakes below, and are often good for grassland antelope such as topi and oribi, as well as giraffe and buffalo.

Kitabili Loop This is a longer variation of the Rwisirabo Loop, about 70km in total, or 5–8 hours, and probably as far as you'd want to go on a day drive out of Akagera Game Lodge or Ruzizi Tented Camp. It follows the same route as far as Lake Birengero, but instead of turning left at Junction 13, you continue straight ahead for about 15km to **Lake Hago,** which is generally regarded as the best lake for general game viewing. Partially encircled by a decent track, this lake is where elephant are most likely to be seen, as well as small herds of buffalo and zebra, and it must support several hundred hippo. Away from the lakeshore, the vegetation is mostly very dense, and animals are difficult to spot, though you can be reasonably confident of seeing baboons, vervet monkeys and impala. From here you continue north a short way to Junction 20, where you need to turn left along the road to Junction 21 at Kitabili, and keep bearing left at Junction 22. From here, you will follow the highland route back south to Rwisirabo and the Giraffe Area, mostly through open or lightly wooded grassland where topi, zebra and oribi are quite common.

The far north Game drive options north of Kitabili are restricted by the area's remoteness from the cluster of accommodation near the main entrance gate. This is a shame, because the game viewing is generally far better than in the south. However, you could realistically travel from the lodge as far north as the Mutumba Hills and back in a day. If you want to head further north than Mutumba, save it for your last day in the park, and plan on exiting through the Nyungwe Gate west of Lake Rwanyakizinga. Some tracks here are very indistinct, and should be attempted only in the company of a guide (who can be dropped at Nyungwe Gate). Note that if you take a guide from south to north, or vice versa, it is automatically charged as a full day, even if you do the trip in half a day.

The **Mutumba Hills** are one of the most rewarding parts of the park. From Kitabili, you first ascend through an area of park-like woodland whose large acacias are favoured by giraffe. Eventually the woodland gives way to open grassland where you can be certain of seeing the delicate oribi and reedbuck, as well as the larger topi. With luck, you'll also encounter eland, zebra, roan antelope, and (in the wet season) large herds of buffalo.

North of the Mutumba Hills, the vegetation is again very thick, and animals can be difficult to spot, though impala, buffalo and zebra all seem to be present in significant numbers. The papyrus beds around **Lakes Gishanju** and **Mihindi** form the most accessible marshy areas in the park, and are worth taking slowly by anybody who hopes to see papyrus-dwellers. The **Plage Hippos** (Hippo Beach) on Lake Mihindi was, oddly, about the one place in Akagera where we stopped next to open water and *didn't* see any hippos, but it's a pretty spot, and would make for an ideal picnic site.

Heading further north, **Lake Rwanyakizinga** is another favoured spot with elephants, and the Kilala Plains to the west of the lake are excellent for plains animals such as warthog, zebra and herds of 50-plus topi. This little-visited part of Akagera is the one area that might still support small numbers of lion.

NIGHT DRIVES Organised night drives in an open-topped game-viewing vehicle are the only way to explore the park after 18.00, offering the best chance of seeing some of the most sought-after species. Leopard and hyena are generally top of the wish list, and they are sometimes observed, but more common nocturnals include the agile bushbaby and oddball elephant-shrew, along with small predators such as genet, civet and various mongooses as well as owls and nightjars. Night drives last for about 2 to 2.5 hours and start in the late evening from 17.30. The cost is US$40 per person, with a minimum of 4 people.

BEHIND THE SCENES A new activity, aimed at educational groups but available to anybody, is the **Behind-the-Scenes Tour**. Since the formation of Akagera Management Company a significant amount of work has been done in Akagera National Park, much of it not visible to the tourist's eye. This illuminating tour includes a presentation on the park and recent conservation efforts, as well as providing an opportunity to meet the rangers and other staff integral to park management, and offers a tour around headquarters (the 'hub' of the park operations). It costs US$20 per person with a minimum of 4 people.

Akagera National Park   ACTIVITIES

12

13

Goma and Virunga National Park (DRC)

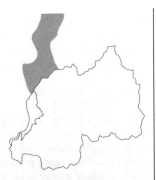

The second-largest country in Africa, the Democratic Republic of the Congo (DRC) extends over an area of 2,344,858km² running west from the Albertine Rift (where its long eastward border runs from northern Uganda via Rwanda and Burundi to southwest Tanzania) to the distant Atlantic coastline. Scarred by long years of poor governance and debilitating civil war, it is one of the continent's least visited countries, yet also one of its most intriguing.

The DRC is arguably the most biodiverse country in Africa, best known for the green swathes of rainforest associated with the vast Congo river basin, but also home to the western slopes of the immense Ruwenzori and Virunga Mountains, both of which are protected in Virunga National Park. And while political instability has left much of the DRC off-limits to visitors, Virunga National Park formally reopened in 2009, following the signature of a management agreement between the Institut Congolais pour la Conservation de la Nature (ICCN) and the Africa Conservation Fund (ACF), a dynamic British-based organisation funded mainly by the EU.

Of the 2,000-odd adventurers who visited Virunga National Park over the course of 2011, more than 80% did so as an excursion from Rwanda or Uganda. Partly this is because Virunga National Park offers cheaper gorilla tracking than either of its neighbours (not to mention a far better chance of obtaining a permit at short notice), as well as the opportunity to hike to the rim of Nyiragongo, an active volcano whose immense crater contains the world's largest lava lake. Partly it is simply because travel from elsewhere in the DRC is so logistically challenging. As a result, Virunga National Park seems likely to function as an extension of the travel circuit through Rwanda and Uganda for the foreseeable future. And so we have decided to include a chapter dedicated to the park, and the gateway town of Goma (bordering Rubavu/Gisenyi), in the 5th edition of this Bradt Guide to Rwanda.

THE CONGO IN BRIEF

Capital Kinshasa, more than 1,500km west of Goma as the crow flies
Population 72 million
International dialling code +243
Time zone GMT+2 in the east (the same as Rwanda)
Currency The Congolese franc currently trades at around Cfr900 to the US dollar (which means that Rfr1 equals roughly Cfr1.5). In practice, most items and services likely to be bought by tourists are priced and can be paid for in US Dollars, although small change is often given in local currency.
Language The official language is French. Other officially recognised national languages are KiSwahili, Lingala, Kikongo and Tshiluba.

Note: It is customary to refer to the DRC by its full name, or the acronym, in order to distinguish it from the similarly named Congo Republic (which lies on the northwest bank of the Congo River, more than 1,000km from Rwanda). Having clarified that, in the rest of this chapter we refer to it simply as the Congo.

ENTRANCE AND BORDER FORMALITIES

All visitors require a valid passport and visa to enter the Congo. This can be bought in advance at the Congolese embassy in your home country (or in a neighbouring country if your home country does not have an embassy), but this can be quite a complicated and costly process (the embassy in the UK, for instance, will require you to produce a letter of invitation certified by the Ministry of Foreign Affairs in the Kinshasa, and charges £60.00 – around US$100 – for a single entry visa valid for one month). It can also usually be bought on the spot at the border post between Rubavu/Gisenyi and Goma, but this costs a hefty US$280.

A better option than either of the above, assuming you are not exploring deeper into the Congo, is to buy a 14-day single-entry visa in advance through Virunga National Park's website (*www.visitvirunga.org/visa*) or an affiliated tour operator. This can be arranged only in conjunction with the purchase of a permit to track

BUKAVU AND KAHUZI-BIEGA

Travellers who arranged their visas through the *Visit Virunga* website should not attempt to cross into the Congo at any border post other than Goma (or Bunagana), since the email print out may not be accepted there. However, an interesting onward option from Goma would be to take a boat to Bukavu, which lies at the south end of Lake Kivu opposite Rusizi/Cyangugu. The visa arrangement might be extended to Bukavu in the near future, so, if you are thinking of entering that way, contact the Virunga National Park sales office for the latest info.

Several operators run boats that cover this trip in around 2.5 hours, one of the best being the Queen Ihusi and King Ihusi (m *099 4813235/4234071;* e *ihusiexpress@yahoo.fr*), both operated by the Ihusi Hotel (see *Where to stay* page 294). Tickets cost US$50 and at least one of the two boats sails every day, leaving Bukavu at 07.30 and Goma at 14.00.

There are plenty of hotels in Bukavu, ranging from the incongruously smart lakeshore Orchid Safari Club (*www.orchids-hotel.com; from US$125/175 B&B ensuite sgl/dbl*) and owner-managed Lodge Co-Co ⌢ *099 870 7344;* e *lodgecoco@kivu-online.com; www.lodgecoco.com; from US$120/150 sgl/dbl*), to the midrange Hotel Belvedere (*Av Patrice Lumumba; mob 099 7766460; US$25/35 sgl/dbl*) and Hotel Touriste (*Av Patrice Lumumba; mob 099 8669315; US$20/30 sgl/dbl*), to the altogether more basic Hotel Tanganyika (*Av Leopold; US$15 dbl*).

Bukavu also lies about 30km from the 6,000km² Kahuzi-Biega National Park, a UNESCO World Heritage Site named for the two extinct volcanoes that dominate its skyline, and best known as the only place where the eastern lowland gorilla can currently be tracked. A tracking permit (US$400) can be bought at the ICCN Office in Bukavu (m *099 7254296/3096120; reservationpnkb@gmail.com; http://kahuzibiega.wordpress.com; open 08.00– 16.00 Mon–Fri*).

gorillas in Virunga National Park, or to climb Nyiragongo. The visa currently costs US$50 (payable with a credit card or paypal), usually requires around one week to process, and will be delivered to your email address. All you need to do then is print it and present it at the Goma or Bunagana border post (it may not be accepted at other borders), and you should be able to cross between the counties in 15–30 minutes.

Note that if you plan to visit the Congo as a return trip out of Rwanda, and your nationality is among those that require a visa to enter Rwanda, then you will need to buy a multiple-entry Rwandan visa in advance.

SECURITY

The Congo remains volatile. In March 2012, Goma and the far south of Virunga National Park were considered reasonably safe, and visited by the author of this book. However, rebel activity forced the park to close to tourism in May 2012, and it seems unlikely to reopen before the end of 2012. For security updates, see www.visitvirunga.org or http://updates.bradtguides.com/rwanda. Even if things stabilise, it would be incautious to venture beyond Goma, Bukavu and those parts of Virunga National Park that are formally open to tourism.

Most government travel advisories explicitly warn against visiting the Congo. As of May 2012, for instance, the British FCO website warns 'against all travel to eastern and northeastern Democratic Republic of Congo (DRC). This includes entering DRC from Uganda, Burundi and Rwanda. The only exceptions to this are within the town of Bukavu and Goma, where we advise against all but essential travel.' Even if you chose to disregard such advice as overly cautious, be aware that a government warning of this sort will negate most travel insurance policies.

GOMA

Capital of the volatile province of Nord-Kivu, Goma lies on the north shore of Lake Kivu bordering the practically contiguous Rwandan port of Rubavu/Gisenyi. With a population currently estimated at anything from 400,000 to one million, Goma is much larger than Rubavu (or, for that matter, any Rwandan centre other than Kigali) and it has always enjoyed a reputation as a livelier and more colourful town, particularly when it comes to bar culture and nightlife. Goma is also the urban gateway for travellers heading to the nearby southern sector of Virunga National Park, home to the Congolese population of mountain gorillas and site of the spectacular volcano Nyiragongo, which dominates the town's northern skyline in clear weather.

Over the past two decades, Goma has been blighted by a succession of natural and political crises. In July 1994, Nord-Kivu Province received an influx of around one million refugees from Rwanda; this led to an acute food and water shortage, and a cholera outbreak that claimed thousands of lives. Natural disaster struck in January 2002, when Nyiragongo erupted, and a 1km-wide river of lava steamrolled the city centre, destroying more than 4,500 buildings and forcing most of the human population into temporary exile in and around Rubavu.

Goma has frequently been a focal point of the protracted Congolese Civil War, which was initiated by a coup in 1997 and has since reputedly claimed some five million civilian lives, more than any other conflict since World War II. The most recent fighting around Goma started on 25 October 2008, when the town and environs witnessed heavy battles between the UN-backed Congolese army and the Congrès National pour la Défense du Peuple (CNDP) rebel movement led by the Tutsi general Laurent Nkunda. Unknown thousands died in the conflict, and some 250,000 civilians were forced to flee their homes, leading to what the United Nations called 'a humanitarian crisis of catastrophic dimensions'. Despite several calls for ceasefires, the fighting continued intermittently until 22 January 2009 when Nkunda was arrested after crossing into Rwanda, where he remains under lock and key to this day.

Considering its turbulent recent past, Goma today has a surprisingly agreeable and vibrant atmosphere. Solidified flows of craggy black lava rock still lie beside some of the roads, but most of the town has been cleared and rebuilt (though one striking informal monument to the eruption, a group of planes trapped where they stood when the lava flowed through, can be seen at the airport on the left side of the road towards Nyiragongo and the national park). Furthermore, Goma has also been reasonably peaceful since the CNDP and the Congolese government signed a peace treaty on 23 March 2009 - and the lively nightlife curtailed by the civil war has resumed with vigour.

GETTING THERE AND AWAY Assuming you have a visa (see *Entrance and border formalities*, pages 292–3), getting to Goma from Rwanda could scarcely be more straightforward. The easiest place to cross is the so-called *petit barrière* near the Hotel Ubumwe at the west end of Rubavu's main lakeshore road . Coming from elsewhere in Rwanda, there are plentiful minibus-taxis to Rubavu, and a *moto* from the bus station to the border costs around Rfr300. Once you've crossed to Goma, several hotels lie within easy walking distance of the border post, or you can get a moto to the town centre.

 WHERE TO STAY There is no shortage of accommodation in Goma, though prices tend to be slightly higher than you'll be used to coming from Rwanda. A few reliable options are listed below, but there are plenty more to choose from, and further recommendations can be obtained from the Virunga National Park office on Blvd Kanya Muhanga.

Upmarket

🏠 **Ihusi Hotel** (75 rooms) [295 C7] 📞 081 3129560/3532300; e info@ihusi-hotel.net; www. ihusi-hotel.net. Boasting a pretty lakeshore location on Blvd Kanya Muhanga only 100m or so from the border post, this is about the smartest hotel in Goma, & a popular rendezvous for NGO workers & other foreigners. The large grounds offer great views over the lake, there is a good restaurant, & facilities include a swimming pool, tennis courts, gym, Wi-Fi, & satellite TV in all rooms. *The en-suite dbl rooms are mostly in the US$70–100 range, & there are also suites for US$150–200. All rates B&B.*

Moderate

🏠 **Hotel des Grands Lacs** (18 rooms) [295 B3] m 099 8899934; www.hoteldesgrandslacs.com. This faded colonial relict on Blvd Kanya Muhanga, a few doors down from the Virunga NP office, is stronger on character than facilities or cleanliness. Nevertheless the large en-suite rooms seem decent value at *US$30/40 sgl/dbl B&B.*

🏠 **Nyira Hotel** [295 E3] m 099 8011089; e nyirahotel@yahoo.fr. Located about 100m from Blvd Kanya Muhanga, around the corner from the Virunga NP office, this long-serving hotel has comfortable en-suite rooms with intermittent hot water & TV. It is a friendly place, with good food & seating in a green courtyard. It is also one of the few places in Goma to offer reliable free Wi-Fi. *US$50/60 sgl/dbl B&B.*

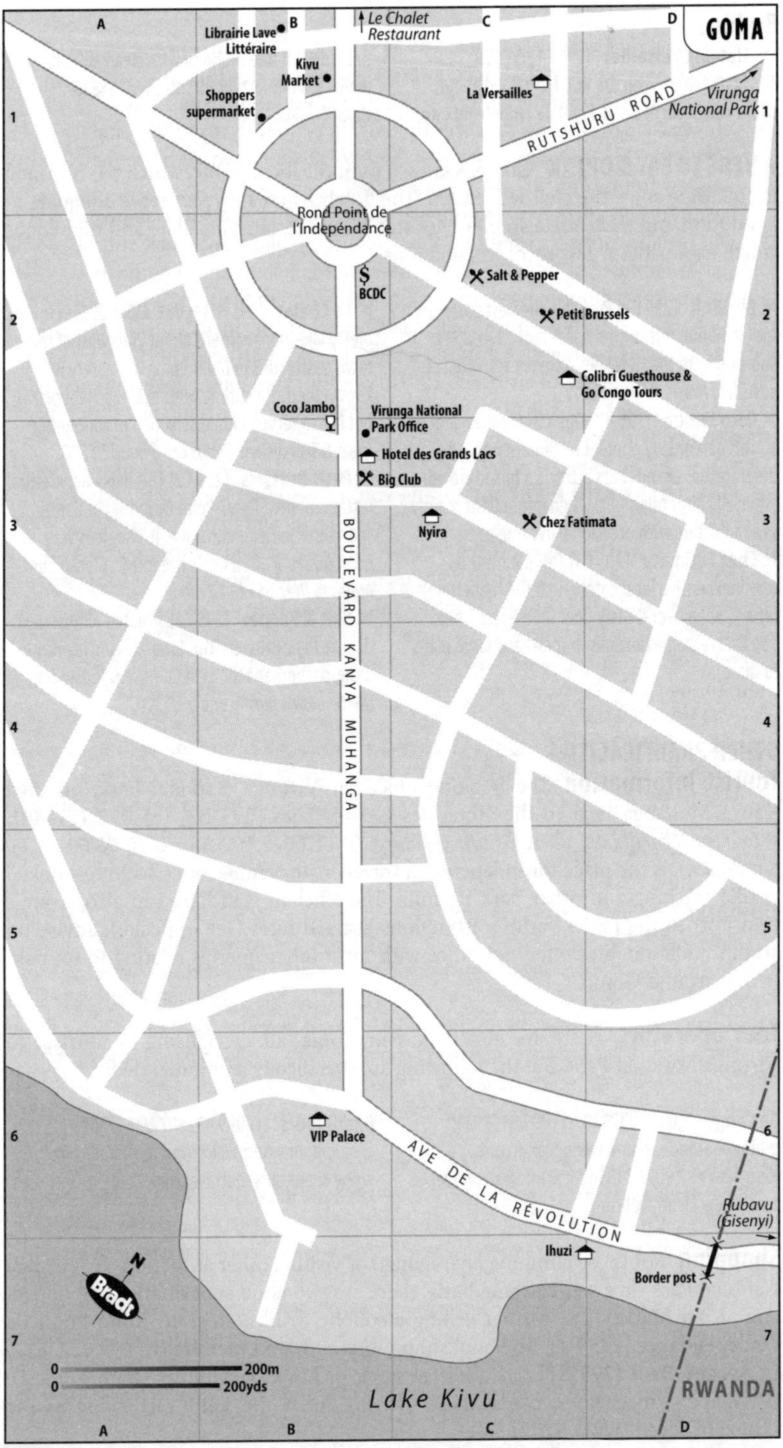

Le Chalet Restaurant

Librairie Lave Littéraire

Kivu Market

Shoppers supermarket

La Versailles

RUTSHURU ROAD

Virunga National Park

Rond Point de l'Indépéndance

BCDC

Salt & Pepper

Petit Brussels

Colibri Guesthouse & Go Congo Tours

Coco Jambo

Virunga National Park Office

Hotel des Grands Lacs

Big Club

Nyira

Chez Fatimata

BOULEVARD KANYA MUHANGA

VIP Palace

AVE DE LA RÉVOLUTION

Rubavu (Gisenyi)

Ihuzi

Border post

N

Bradt

0 — 200m
0 — 200yds

Lake Kivu

RWANDA

Budget

⌂ **Hotel la Versailles** [295 C1] m 099 7734710. Situated on the Rutshuru Road about 200m northeast of Rond-Point de l'Indépendance, this a decent budget hotel with clean en-suite rooms & a fair restaurant attached. *US$20/25 sgl/dbl.*

✗ **WHERE TO EAT & DRINK** Goma is known for its lively nightlife, which has resumed in full force since the civil war ended. The hotels listed above all serve adequate to good food, but there are also plenty of standalone restaurants, bars and nightclubs worth exploring. A few recommendations:

✗ **Big Club** [295 B3] Probably the best party spot in Goma, this central bar & nightclub, a few doors up from the Hotel des Grands Lacs, often hosts live music at w/ends.

✗ **Coco Jambo** [295 B3] Open 24/7, or as good as, this perennially popular restaurant opposite the Hotel des Grands Lacs attracts a mixed crowd, especially after midnight, when it functions mainly as a nightclub, with occasional live music.

✗ **Chez Fatimata** [295 C3] This pleasant & very inexpensive local eatery near the Nyira Hotel serves cheap beer & tasty goat brochettes (they don't serve single portions, but rather a large plate to share).

✗ **Le Chalet** [295 B1] ☎ 081 3150000. Set in pretty lakeshore gardens about 2km west of the town centre, this popular upmarket eatery is known for its lunchtime buffets & excellent pizzas, but it also serves a good selection of continental meat & fish dishes. *Mains are around US$10.*

✗ **Petit Brussels** [295 C2] This lively new central restaurant near Rond-Point de l'Indépendance specialises in Belgian cuisine. It also does very good pizzas & often hosts live music. Closed Sun. *Mains in the US$12–15 range.*

✗ **Salt & Pepper** [295 C2] Situated almost next door to Petit Brussels, this long-serving favourite produces perhaps the best Chinese & Indian food in town. *Mains mostly under US$10.*

OTHER PRACTICALITIES

Tourist information The booking office for Virunga National Park, on Blvd Kanya Muhanga next to the Hotel des Grands Lacs [295 B3] (m *099 1715401;* e *tourism@gorilla.cd; www.visitvirunga.org;* ⊕ *08.00–17.00 Mon–Fri, 08.00–12.00 Sat & Sun*), is the place for independent travellers to arrange or collect pre-booked gorilla-tracking and other park permits. The efficient staff here can also arrange transport to the park's various attractions at fixed rates (see opposite), advise on accommodation, and offer assistance with most other queries relating to tourism in and around Goma.

Tour operators There are quite a few in Goma, all specialising in tourism to Virunga National Park, but the following are specifically recommended:

Go Congo ☎ 081 1837010; m 099 8162331; e info@gocongo.com; www.gocongo.com
Kivu Travel ☎ 081 3135608; e info@kivutravel.com; www.kivutravel.com

Okapi Tours m 099 4328077/55473599; e okapitoursandtravelcompany@gmail.com; www.okapitoursandtravel.com

Shopping For those climbing Nyiragongo or visiting other attractions in Virunga National Park on a self-catering basis, there are two good supermarkets, Shoppers and Kivu Market, the former selling alcoholic drinks, close to Rond-Point de l'Indépendance [295 B1]. The bookshop Librairie Lave Littéraire (m *099 4133614*) in Avenue Beni [295 B1] has a useful stock of books (including Bradt guides!), newspapers, magazines, cards, maps etc. It's under the same ownership as the Ikirezi in Kigali (*www.ikirezi.biz*).

Banks and foreign exchange International Visa and MasterCard can be used to withdraw US dollars from about four ATMs dotted around Goma, including one at the Hotel Ihusi (Western Union) [295 C7], and the BIAC and BCDC near Rond-Point de l'Indépendance [295 B2]. Note that ATMs generally but not always dispense large bills (i.e. US$100 or US$50) so getting change can be a problem if you want to buy something small, though the Kivu Market and Shoppers supermarkets are used to accepting big notes, and some of the hotels can also change them. Money changers on the street will exchange US dollars for Congolese francs at the rate (currently) of 900; they can usually be located in front of Kivu Market [295 B1]. As in Rwanda, the Congolese are very strict about what bills they accept: anything printed before the year 2004 will be rejected, as will notes with any rips or tears on them.

VIRUNGA NATIONAL PARK

One of Africa's most biodiverse conservation areas, the 7,900km² Virunga National Park runs for more than 300km along the border with Rwanda and Uganda. It protects the entire Congolese portion of the Virunga Volcanoes, Ruwenzori Mountains and Lake Edward, and habitat range encompassing glacial peaks, Afromontane moorland, high-altitude forest, lowland rainforest, and open savanna. It is Africa's richest protected area in terms of avian diversity, with an astonishing 706 bird species recorded (more than in the whole of Rwanda), including several Congolese or Albertine Rift Endemics. A checklist of 208 mammal species contains 23 primates (including mountain gorilla, eastern lowland gorilla, and common chimpanzee) along with Congolese endemics such as the bizarre okapi (a striped, horse-sized relative of the giraffe) and typical savanna dwellers such as lion, elephant and buffalo.

Virunga National Park was established in 1925, and inscribed as an IUCN World Heritage Site in1979. In its original incarnation as the Albert National Park, it extended over just 200km², centred on the Virunga Mountains, but a series of boundary extensions over the next ten years meant it had more-or-less taken its modern shape by 1935. Since then, it has alternated between periods of conservation priority and high tourist volumes (notably during the late colonial era and over the 1970s and early 1980s) and periods of almost total neglect and abandonment. Happily, since 2010, after decades of being near-ungovernable, the park has enjoyed an upsurge in fortune, one that has seen the recent resumption of formal volcano climbs, and of gorilla and chimp tracking, as well as the opening of a new upmarket lodge and tented camp in 2011.

GETTING THERE AND AWAY Several local operators offer organised tours to Virunga National Park. These include the operators listed on the opposite page, as well as two Rwandan operators: Green Hill Eco-tours in Rubavu/Gisenyi (see page 198) and Amahoro Tours in Musanze/Ruhengeri (page 219). Alternatively, all accommodation, activities and transport within the park can be booked through the website www.visitvirunga.org or the park's booking office in Goma (see opposite).

Self-drive is possible, but the police have a reputation for hassling drivers of non-Congolese cars, so it is only recommended with an escort (this can be arranged with the park for free). People can use their own transport to reach park activities, but they need to inform the park when they make their booking so an escort can be arranged. The park advises against people driving themselves in non-park areas.

13

WHERE TO STAY AND EAT
Upmarket

 Mikeno Lodge (12 rooms) m 099
1280312/3926033; e mikenolodge@gorilla.cd;
www.mikenolodge.com; ✆ S 1°20.309,
E 29°21.794. Set at an altitude of 1,550m, this
superb new lodge opened alongside the park
headquarters at Rumangabo, about 90 mins' drive
from Goma, in Oct 2011. Unlike any upmarket
lodge in the Rwandan side of the Virungas, it is
set in the heart of the rainforest, an environment
teeming with monkeys & offering plenty of
opportunities to birders. Accommodation is in
large & stylishly decorated lava-block-&-thatch
cottages, each with a king-size or twin beds, cosy
sitting area with fireplace, en-suite hot shower &
tub, & secluded private balcony. The raised dining
& bar area has a large wooden balcony offering
good views into the forest canopy. *US$260/400 sgl/
dbl FB, but check the website for increases.*

Budget

 Bukima Tented Camp (6 tents) m 099
1715401; e tourism@gorilla.cd; www.visitvirunga.
org; ✆ S 1°22.784, E 29°26.004. Set at an altitude
of 2,130m among the cultivated fields immediately
bordering the National Park, this no-frills tented
camp is the ideal place to spend the night before
gorilla tracking, as it is also the starting point for
visits to the gorilla groups living around Bukima.
It has a magnificent setting, with Mount Karisimbi
& Mikeno – the two tallest Virunga volcanoes –
providing a dramatic backdrop & panoramic views
over the plains below Nyiragongo, which smoulders
on the horizon after dark. The tents are sheltered
by a thatch roof & each contains 2 sgl beds with
bedding. Meals & drinks are available, & there is
an ablution block with flush toilets & cold bucket
showers. Bring warm clothes, as it can get very chilly
at night. *US$60 pp FB; US$30 pp self-catering; US$15
pp in own tent.*

 Nyiragongo Huts (8 rooms) m 099
1715401; email: tourism@gorilla.cd; www.
visitvirunga.org. Perched at an altitude of 3,400m
immediately outside the rim of Nyiragongo
Crater, these basic huts each contain 2 beds with
waterproof mattresses but no bedding. A common
drop toilet lies about 50m from the block of
huts. There are no cooking facilities & no food is
provided. Use of the huts is included in the price of
the permit to visit Nyiragongo Volcano.

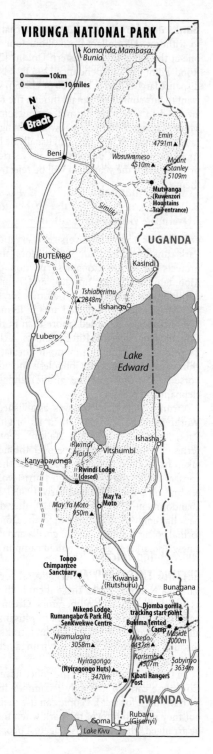

ACTIVITIES Gorilla and chimp tracking are both available in the park, as is a stunning but tough hike to the top of Nyiragongo Volcano, with its spectacular live lava lake. Permits for all activities can be booked online at www.visitvirunga.org/shop, along with transport from Goma and Congolese visas. Permits and transport can also be booked in person at the booking office in Goma (see page 296). Because the park only reopened properly in 2009, permits are still normally available at short notice, except during the peak gorilla tracking season (July–August), when the Congolese gorillas attract an overspill from Rwanda and Uganda. As the park becomes better known, however, it seems likely that advance booking will become necessary more often, especially with the price of gorilla-tracking in Rwanda rising to US$750 in June 2012.

Around Rumangabo Visitors to Mikeno Lodge, which stands adjacent to the park headquarters, will find the surrounding forest offers plenty of opportunity for free primate viewing and birdwatching, whether from the small network of roads that encircles Rumangabo, or from the short walking trail that connects to the lodge to the entrance gate. The most common primates here are the blue monkey, Ruwenzori colobus and olive baboon, all of which are frequently seen in the lodge grounds or close to the main administration building in the headquarters. Wild chimps are also seen in the forest from time to time.

Birdlife is varied, and includes a wide range of forest specialists, most conspicuously perhaps Sladen's Barbet (a Congo endemic), white-headed wood-hoopoe, cinnamon-chested bee-eater, yellow-whiskered greenbul and grey-green bush-shrike. Other attractive forest residents that often draw attention through their calls include black-billed turaco, Ross's turaco, black-and-white casqued hornbill, double-toothed barbet, yellow-billed barbet, narrow-tailed starling and Sharpe's starling.

Set in a jungle clearing five minutes' walk from the lodge, the **Senkwekwe Centre** is the only facility in the world for orphaned mountain gorillas. It is named after the silverback Senkwekwe, who was killed by gunmen, along with six other members of his group, on 22 July 2007. The 1ha enclosure is currently home to Senkwekwe's daughter Ndeze, a five-year-old female survivor of this massacre, and another female of the same age called Ndakasi. It also shelters two older gorillas, the eight-year-old male Kaboko, whose right arm was partially amputated as a result of a terrible snare wound, and a ten-year-old female Maisha, who was confiscated from poachers in 2004. The orphans can be watched from several viewing platforms, but tourists are forbidden to enter the enclosure.

Nyiragongo Volcano The most popular activity in Virunga National Park is the hike up the live volcano Nyiragongo, whose perfect cone rises above Goma and the Lake Kivu shore to an altitude of 3,468m. One of Africa's most active volcanoes, Nyiragongo was responsible for massive killer lava flows that devastated Goma in 2002, and the hike to the top passes the subsidiary cone formed by this most recent eruption. At the top, sheer windswept cliffs plummet into the nested main crater, which is at least 600m deep and has an average diameter of 1.2km. At the heart of this immense natural cauldron, a circular lake of live lava bubbles away like a massive casserole, its surface pattern ceaselessly mutating as blackened crusts of magma collide, crumble and melt, spewing bright red flumes of molten rock tens of metres into the air. It is a thrilling, mesmerising spectacle, especially towards dusk, when the glowing lava eerily illuminates a swirling red mist – no less so because the violent heat of the lake contrasts so strikingly with the chilly windy conditions experienced by observers on the crater rim, and with the more sedate view south over the nightlights of Goma on the Kivu shore.

The standard trip runs overnight, sleeping in one of the huts on the rim, which is highly recommended as the view of the lava lake is most spectacular at dusk and after dark. However, it is possible to hike there and back in a day, and a one-day trip can usually be organised upon request. Hikers should bring all the food and liquid they will need; there are no cooking facilities at the top, and you should bank on at least 3–4 litres of water per person. It can be very cold and windy at the top, so a sleeping bag is also necessary, as is a good rain jacket or windbreaker, hiking boots or sturdy walking shoes, plenty of warm clothes (ideally including gloves), and a change of clothes in case of rain. A torch and spare batteries are also essential. And once there, do step cautiously on the edge of the crater: in July 2007, a tourist died after falling into the crater whilst taking photographs.

The hike starts at Kibati Ranger Camp (✪ S 1°34.140 E 29°16.707), about 15km from Goma on the west side of the main road to Rumangabo, Mikeno Lodge and Bukima. It is only 6.3km from here to the rim, but it is a steep climb, starting at an altitude of 2,000m and gaining more than 1,400m, and the ascent takes around 4–6 hours, depending less on your individual fitness than on the overall fitness of the party (all hikers on any given day are expected to stick together for security reasons), as well as how acclimatised they are to high altitudes, and the duration of the customary breaks at each of the four 'posts' along the route.

The first 2.5km, from Kibati to Post One, follows a flattish trail that is generally easy underfoot through an area of montane forest, and takes around 40 minutes. The second stage to Post Two (2,533m) is steeper a 1.1km, 20–30 minute ascent of the scree-strewn southeastern slope of the dormant subsidiary cone created by the 2002 eruption. From here, it is slightly less than 1km to Post Three (2,762m), a 20–30- minute ascent along an old lava flow to the base of the main cone, which rises a daunting near-45° angle ahead. The toughest leg follows, gaining almost 500m over 1.3km, a 60–90-minute hike that brings you to Post Four (3,235m), site of a ruinous old mountain hut. En route, the trail passes some active steam vents (emanating from what is presumably a subterranean magma flow connecting the main crater to the subsidiary cone), as well as running through some stunning fields of giant lobelia, and offering views over the 2002 crater to Lake Kivu. From Post Four, the breathlessly steep scramble up the final 400m of loose rocks leading to the crater rim and cabana site should take 20–30 minutes.

Up to 16 overnight volcano permits are issued daily, corresponding to the number of beds in the eight double huts at the rim, and these cost US$200 for foreign adults, US$75 for foreign children, US$25 for Congolese adults or US$5 for Congolese children. Porters can be hired for US$12 a day (US$24 for the overnight trip) to carry up to 15kg of luggage each. In addition, you will need to pay for transport to/from Kibati, which can be arranged through the park website or booking office in Goma. This costs US$50 per group one-way from Goma or US$80 from Mikeno Lodge in a Hilux or Land Cruiser (carrying up to six people) or US$85 from Goma or US$165 from Mikeno Lodge in a MAN truck carrying up to 13. Transport can also be arranged through any tour operator in Goma. The hike usually starts at around 09.00 (which means you need to leave Goma or Mikeno Lodge about an hour earlier), and most hikers are back at the base by around 10.00 the next day. Note that even the most experienced hikers tend to suffer some leg stiffness after the steep ascent, so it is best saved for after other activities such as gorilla or chimpanzee tracking (which will also give you additional time to adjust to the altitude).

Gorilla tracking Virunga National Park offers a mountain-gorilla-tracking experience comparable in quality and in most other respects to that of neighbouring Rwanda. Six gorilla groups are habituated to tourist visits, with six permits being issued daily for larger groups, and four for smaller groups, creating a total availability of 30 permits daily. Ten of these permits apply to two gorilla groups based in the area around Djomba, which lies close to the Uganda border and is most normally visited as a day trip from the Ugandan town of Kisoro (so it falls outside the scope of a guidebook to Rwanda). The other 20 permits apply to four groups that are normally tracked from Bukima, which lies on the slopes of Mount Mikeno about 90 minutes' drive from Mikeno Lodge and twice that distance from Goma.

Gorilla-tracking permits for Virunga National Park cost US$400 (or US$150 for Congolese citizens), slightly cheaper than the US$500 charged in Uganda, and significantly less than the US$750 asked in Rwanda. The experience is broadly similar to tracking in Rwanda, with the same one-hour limit imposed on tourist visits, but the setting is a lot more remote and under-utilised – indeed, there are still days when nobody goes tracking at Bukima. In addition, there is the option of overnighting at the basic but affordable and magnificently located Bukima Tented Camp before you track, which really sets the tone for the adventure. That said, for independent or budget-minded travellers, the logistics of reaching Bukima are more complicated than getting to Kinigi (the base for tracking in Rwanda) and transport costs are higher. Transfers arranged through the park website or booking office cost US$145 per group one-way from Goma or US$45 from Mikeno Lodge in a Hilux or Land Cruiser (carrying up to six people); or US$290 from Goma or US$90 from Mikeno Lodge in a MAN truck carrying up to 13. Transfers can also be arranged through any tour operator in Goma.

Chimp tracking As of January 2012, up to 10 chimp-tracking permits are issued daily for Tongo, a 10km² block of medium-altitude forest isolated from other similar habitats by lava flows. Traversed by an 80km network of walking trails, Tongo is home to a community of around 35 chimpanzees first habituated by the Frankfurt Zoological Society (FZS) and opened to tourism in the late 1980s, only to close again in 1993 because of instability. The FZS relaunched the Tongo habituation programme in 2010, and the chimpanzees here are now very accustomed to visitors, so, while the quality and ease of sightings varies from one day to the next, the experience is comparable to tracking chimps at Nyungwe. Permits cost US$100 per person for foreigners and citizens alike. Additional costs are US$100 per party for the mandatory ranger escort and transport to Tongo, which can be arranged with through the park website or its booking office in Goma. This costs US$185 per group one-way from Goma or US$80 from Mikeno Lodge in a Hilux or Land Cruiser (carrying up to six people); or US$370 from Goma or US$160 from Mikeno Lodge in a MAN truck carrying up to 13. Tracking usually starts at 07.00 and tourists remain with the chimps for up to one hour.

Further afield The activities described above all take place in the far south of the National Park, but there are many undeveloped attractions further afield, their potential unrealised at the moment largely as a result of ongoing insecurity and/or lack of funding. However, several other attractions are likely to be developed over the course of this edition's lifespan, and in some cases new tented camps or lodges may be constructed. The closest such site to Mikeno Lodge is the Tongo Hippo Pools (near the eponymous forest), where around 100 hippos live in water so clear you can see them under the surface. Further north, the Rwindi Plains protect a lush savanna habitat similar to that of the Ishasha sector of Uganda's Queen Elizabeth National Park, while the Semliki Forest protects a lowland forest habitat hosting numerous bird species endemic to the Congo Basin, and habituated eastern lowland gorillas are present in the Tshiaberimu Forest east of Lake Edward. It is also in the Ruwenzori Mountains, the Congolese portion of which is technically open to tourists, though far less accessible than the Uganda side. For the latest on new tourist developments, check www.visitvirunga.org or visit our update website www. bradtguides.com/guidebook-updates.

Appendix 1

LANGUAGE

Words in Kinyarwanda are spelt phonetically here, to make their pronunciation easy. The letters 'r' and 'l' (and their sounds) are often interchanged, also sometimes 'b', 'v' and 'w'. When a word ends in 'e', pronounce it as the French 'é'. Pronounce 'i' as 'ee' rather than 'eye'.

English	French	Kinyarwanda
COURTESIES		
good day/hello	*bonjour*	*muraho*
good morning	*bonjour*	*mwaramutse*
good afternoon	*bonjour*	*mwiriwe*
good evening	*bonsoir*	*mwiriwe*
sir	*monsieur*	*bwana*
madam	*madame*	*mubyeyi*
how are you?	*ça va?*	*amakuru?*
I'm fine, thank you	*ça va bien, merci*	*nimeza*
please	*s'il vous plaît*	*mubishoboye*
thank you	*merci*	*murakoze*
excuse me	*excusez-moi*	*imbabazi*
goodbye (morning)	*au revoir*	*mwiliwe*
goodbye (afternoon)	*au revoir*	*mwirirwe*
goodbye (evening)	*au revoir*	*muramukeho*
goodbye (for ever)	*au revoir/adieu*	*murabeho*
BASIC WORDS		
yes	*oui*	*yego*
no	*non*	*oya*
that's right	*c'est ça*	*ni byo*
maybe	*peut-être*	*wenda*
good	*bon*	*ni byiza*
hot	*chaud*	*ubushyuhe*
cold	*froid*	*ubukonje*
and	*et*	*na*
QUESTIONS		
how?	*comment?*	*gute?*
how much?	*combien?*	*ni angahe?*
what's your name?	*quel est votre nom?*	*Witwa nde?*
when?	*quand?*	*ryari?*

English	French	Kinyarwanda
where?	où?	he he?
who?	qui?	nde?/bande?

FOOD/DRINK

Beans (kidney)	haricots	ibihyimbo
beer	bière	inzoga
butter	beurre	amavuta
bread	pain	umugati
coffee	café	ikawa
eggs	œufs	amagi
fish	poisson	amafi
meat	viande	inyama
milk	lait	amata
potatoes	pommes de terre	ibirayi
rice	riz	umuceri
salad	salade	salade
soup	potage	isupu
sugar	sucre	isukari
tea	thé	icyayi
tomatoes	tomates	inyanya
drinks	boissons	ibinyobwa
water	eau	amazi

SHOPPING

bank	banque	ibanki
bookshop	librairie	isomero
chemist	pharmacie	farumasi
shop	magasin	iduka
market	marché	isoko
battery	pile/batterie	bateri
film	filme	filime
map	carte	ikarita
money	argent	amafaranga
soap	savon	isabune
toothpaste	dentifrice	colgate

POST

post office	poste (PTT)	iposita
envelope	enveloppe	ibahasha
letter	lettre	urwandiko
paper	papier	urupapuro
postcard	carte postale	ifoto
stamp	timbre	tembure

GETTING AROUND

bus	bus	bisi
bus station	gare routière	mure gari
taxi	taxi	tagisi
car	voiture	imodoka
petrol station	station d'essence	steshen

English	French	Kinyarwanda
plane	*avion*	*indege*
far	*loin*	*kure*
near	*près*	*hafi*
to the right	*à droite*	*i buryo*
to the left	*à gauche*	*i bumoso*
straight ahead	*tout droit*	*imbere*
bridge	*pont*	*ikiraro*
hill	*colline*	*agasozi*
lake	*lac*	*ikiyaga*
mountain	*montagne*	*umusozi*
river	*fleuve*	*uruzi*
road	*route*	*umuhanda*
street	*rue*	*inzira*
town	*ville*	*umujyi*
valley	*vallée*	*umubande*
village	*village*	*umudugudu*
waterfall	*chute*	*isumo*

HOTEL

bed	*lit*	*igitanda*
room	*chambre*	*icyumba*
key	*clef/clé*	*urufunguzo*
shower	*douche*	*urwiyu hagiriro*
bath	*baignoire*	*urwogero*
toilet/WC	*toilette*	*umusarane*
hot water	*l'eau chaude*	*amazi ashushye*
cold water	*l'eau froide*	*amazi akonje*

MISCELLANEOUS

dentist	*dentiste*	*umuganga w'amenyo*
doctor	*médecin*	*umuganga*
embassy	*ambassade*	*ambasade*
tourist office	*bureau de tourisme*	*ibiro by ubukererarugendo*

TIME

minute	*minute*	*umunota*
hour	*heure*	*isaaha*
day	*jour*	*umunsi*
week	*semaine*	*icyumweru*
month	*mois*	*ukwezi*
year	*an/année*	*umwaka*
now	*maintenant*	*ubu/nonaha*
soon	*bientôt*	*mu kanya*
today	*aujourd'hui*	*uyu munsi*
yesterday	*hier*	*ejo hashize*
tomorrow	*demain*	*ejo hazaza*
this week	*cette semaine*	*iki cyumweru*
next week	*semaine prochaine*	*icyumweru gitaha*
morning	*matin*	*igitondo*
afternoon	*après-midi*	*ni munsi*

English	French	Kinyarwanda
evening	*soir*	*umugoroba*
night	*nuit*	*ijoro*
Monday	*lundi*	*kuwa mbere*
Tuesday	*mardi*	*kuwa kabiri*
Wednesday	*mercredi*	*kuwa gatatu*
Thursday	*jeudi*	*kuwa kane*
Friday	*vendredi*	*kuwa gatanu*
Saturday	*samedi*	*kuwa gatandatu*
Sunday	*dimanche*	*ku cyumweru*
January	*janvier*	*Mutarama*
February	*février*	*Gashyantare*
March	*mars*	*Werurwe*
April	*avril*	*Mata*
May	*mai*	*Gicuransi*
June	*juin*	*Kamena*
July	*juillet*	*Nyakanga*
August	*août*	*Kanama*
September	*septembre*	*Nzeli*
October	*octobre*	*Ukwakira*
November	*novembre*	*Ugushyingo*
December	*décembre*	*Ukuboza*

NUMBERS

1	*un/une*	*rimwe*
2	*deux*	*kabiri*
3	*trois*	*gatatu*
4	*quatre*	*kane*
5	*cinq*	*gatanu*
6	*six*	*gatandatu*
7	*sept*	*karindwi*
8	*huit*	*umunani*
9	*neuf*	*icyenda*
10	*dix*	*icumi*
100	*cent*	*ijana*
1,000	*mille*	*igihumbi*
2,000	*deux mille*	*ibihumbi bibiri*
3,000	*trois mille*	*ibihumbi bitatu*
4,000	*quatre mille*	*ibihumbi bikane*
5,000	*cinq mille*	*ibihumbi bitanu*
6,000	*six mille*	*ibihumbi bitandatu*
7,000	*sept mille*	*ibihumbi birindwi*
8,000	*huit mille*	*ibihumbi umunani*
9,000	*neuf mille*	*ibihumbi icyenda*

AFRICAN ENGLISH *Philip Briggs*

Although a high proportion of Rwandans were raised in Kenya, Uganda or Tanzania and so speak English as a second language, not all get the opportunity to use it regularly, and as a result they will not be as fluent as they could be. Furthermore, as is often the case in Africa and elsewhere, an individual's pronunciation of a second language often tends to retain the vocal inflections of their first language, or it falls somewhere between that and a more standard pronunciation. It is also the case that many people tend to structure sentences in a second language similar to how they would in their home tongue. As a result, most Rwandans, to a greater or lesser extent, speak English with Bantu inflections and grammar.

The above considerations aside, I would venture that African English – like American or Australian English – is over-due recognition as a distinct linguistic entity, possessed of a unique rhythm and pronunciation, as well as an idiomatic quality quite distinct from any form of English spoken elsewhere. And learning to communicate in this idiom is perhaps the most important linguistic skill that the visitor to any African country where English is spoken can acquire. If this sounds patronising, so be it. There are regional accents in the UK and US that I find far more difficult to follow than the English spoken in Africa, simply because I am more familiar with the latter. And precisely the same adjustment might be required were, for instance, an Australian to travel in the American south, a Geordie to wash up in my home town of Johannesburg, or vice versa.

The following points should prove useful when you speak English to Africans:

- Greet simply, using phrases likely to be understood locally: the ubiquitous sing-song 'How-are-you! – I am fine', or if that draws a blank try the pidgin Swahili 'Jambo!' It is important always to greet a stranger before you plough ahead and ask directions or any other question. Firstly, it is rude to do otherwise; secondly, most Westerners feel uncomfortable asking a stranger a straight question. If you have already greeted the person, you'll feel less need to preface a question with phrases like 'I'm terribly sorry' or 'Would you mind telling me' which will confuse someone who speaks limited English.
- Speak slowly and clearly. There is no need, as some travellers do, to take this too far, as if you are talking to a three-year-old. Speak naturally, but try not to rush or clip phrases.
- Phrase questions simply, with an ear towards Bantu inflections. 'This bus goes to Huye?' might be more easily understood than 'Could you tell me whether this bus is going to Huye?' and 'You have a room?' is better than 'Is there a vacant room?' If you are not understood, don't keep repeating the same question more loudly. Try a different and ideally simpler phrasing, giving consideration to whether any specific word(s) – in the last case, most likely 'vacant' – might particularly obstruct easy understanding.
- Listen to how people talk to you, and learn from it. Vowel sounds are often pronounced as in the local language (see Kinyarwanda pronunciation above), so that 'bin', for instance, might sound more like 'been'. Many words, too, will be pronounced with the customary Bantu stress on the second-last syllable.
- African languages generally contain few words with compound consonant sounds or ending in consonants. This can result in the clipping of soft consonant sounds such as 'r' (important as eem-POT-ant) or the insertion of a random vowel sound between running consonants (so that pen-pal becomes pen-I-pal and sounds almost indistinguishable from pineapple). It is commonplace, as well, to append a random vowel to the end of a word, in the process shifting the stress to what would ordinarily be the last syllable eg: pen-i-PAL-i.
- The 'l' and 'r' sounds are sometimes used interchangeably (hence Lake Burera/Bulera and Rue Karisimbi/Kalisimbi), which can sometimes cause confusion, in particular when your guide points out a lilac-breasted roller! The same is to a lesser extent true of 'b' and 'v' (Virunga versus Birunga), 'k' and 'ch' (the Rwandan capital, spelt Kigali, is more often pronounced 'Chigari') and, very occasionally, 'f' and 'p'.

- Some English words are in wide use. Other similar words are not. Some examples: a request for a 'lodging' or 'guesthouse', is more likely to be understood than one for 'accommodation', as is a request for a 'taxi' (or better 'special hire') over a 'taxi-cab' or 'cab', or for 'the balance' rather than 'change'.
- Avoid the use of dialect-specific expressions, slang and jargon! Few Africans will be familiar with terms such as 'feeling crook', 'pear-shaped' or 'user-friendly'.
- Avoid meaningless interjections. If somebody is struggling to follow you, appending a word such as 'mate' to every other phrase is only likely to further confuse them.
- We've all embarrassed ourselves at some point by mutilating the pronunciation of a word we've read but not heard. Likewise, guides working in national parks and other reserves often come up with innovative pronunciations for bird and mammal names they come across in field guides, and any word with an idiosyncratic spelling (eg: yacht, lamb, knot).
- Make sure the person you are talking to understands you. Try to avoid asking questions that can be answered with a yes or no. People may well agree with you simply to be polite or to avoid embarrassment.
- Keep calm. No-one is at their best when they arrive at a crowded bus station after an all-day bus ride. It is easy to be short tempered when someone cannot understand you. Be patient and polite; it's you who doesn't speak the language.
- Last but not least, do gauge the extent to which the above rules might apply to any given individual. It would be patently ridiculous to address a university lecturer or an experienced tour guide in broken English, equally inappropriate to babble away without making any allowances when talking to a villager who clearly has a limited English vocabulary. Generally, I start off talking normally to anybody I meet, and only start to refine my usage as and when it becomes clear it will aid communication.

Appendix 2

FURTHER INFORMATION

BOOKS
Historical background

Fegley, Randall (compiler) *Rwanda – World Bibliographical Series volume 154* Clio Press, 1993. This selective, annotated bibliography contains over 500 entries covering a wide range of subjects including Rwanda's history, geography, politics, literature, travellers' accounts, flora and fauna. Its preface and introduction give a condensed but useful (although somewhat dated) overview of Rwanda from early times until just before the genocide.

Kagame, Alexis *Un abrégé de l'ethno-histoire du Rwanda* and *Un abrégé de l'histoire du Rwanda de 1853 à 1972*, Editions Universitaires du Rwanda, Huye, 1972 and 1975. These works are now out of print (and there are no English translations) but the seriously interested should try to track down secondhand copies. Drawing on oral tradition, Kagame describes the country and its people from several centuries before the arrival of the Europeans (in the first book) through to the first decade of colonisation (in the second).

Reader, John *Africa: A Biography of the Continent* Hamish Hamilton, 1997. This award-winning book, available as a Penguin paperback, provides a compulsively readable introduction to Africa's past, from the formation of the continent to post-independence politics – the ideal starting point for anybody seeking to place their Rwandan experience in a broader African context.

Natural history

Briggs, Philip *East African Wildlife* Bradt, 2008. This is a handy and lavishly illustrated one-stop handbook to the fauna of East Africa, with detailed sections on the region's main habitats, varied mammals, birds, reptiles and insects. It's the ideal companion for first-time visitors whose interest in wildlife extends beyond the Big Five but who don't want to carry a library of reference books.

Field guides (mammals)

Dorst, J & Dandelot, P *Field Guide to the Larger Mammals of Africa* Collins, 1983 and Haltenorth, T & Diller, H *Field Guide to the Mammals of Africa including Madagascar* Collins, 1984. Formerly the standard field guides to the region, these books are still recommended in many travel guides. In my opinion, they have largely been superseded by subsequent publications, and now come across as very dated and badly structured – with mediocre illustrations to boot.

Estes, Richard *The Safari Companion* Green Books (UK), Russell Friedman Books (SA), Chelsea Green (USA). This unconventional book might succinctly be described as a field guide to mammal behaviour. It's probably a bit esoteric for most one-off visitors to Africa, but a must for anybody with a serious interest in wildlife.

Kingdon, Jonathan *The Kingdon Field Guide to African Mammals* Academic Press, 1997. This is my first choice: the most detailed, thorough and up to date of several field guides covering the mammals of the region. The author, a highly respected biologist, supplements detailed descriptions and good illustrations of all the continent's large mammals with an ecological overview of each species. Essential for anybody with a serious interest in mammal identification.

Stuart, Chris & Tilde *The Larger Mammals of Africa* Struik, 1997. This useful field guide doesn't quite match up to Kingdon's, but it's the best of the rest, and arguably more appropriate to readers with a relatively casual interest in African wildlife. It's also a lot cheaper and lighter!

Stuart, Chris & Tilde *Southern, Central and East African Mammals* Struik, 1995. This excellent mini-guide, compact enough to slip into a pocket, is remarkably thorough within its inherent space restrictions. Highly recommended for one-off safari-goers, but not so good on forest primates, which limits its usefulness in Rwanda.

Field guides & atlases (birds)

Stevenson, Terry & Fanshawe, John *Field Guide to the Birds of East Africa* T & A D Poyser, 2002. The best bird field guide, with useful field descriptions and accurate plates and distribution maps. It covers every species found in Rwanda as well as in Uganda, Kenya, Tanzania and Burundi. For serious birdwatchers, this is *the* book to take.

Vande Weghe, JP and GR *Birds of Rwanda: An Atlas and Handbook* (Rwanda Development Board, 2011). Available from the RDB office on Kigali, this is a must for anybody with a serious interest in Rwanda's birds, containing detailed modern and historical distribution details and maps for all 701 species recorded in the country. Other features include an overview of the country's natural history, and detailed descriptions and checklists for several key birding sites. Though not a field guide, it would be the perfect country-specific companion to the one listed above.

Van Perlo, Ber *Illustrated Checklist to the Birds of Eastern Africa* Collins, 1995. This is the next best thing to the above (and is cheaper and lighter), since it illustrates and provides a brief description of every species recorded in Uganda and Tanzania, along with a distribution map. I don't know of any bird found in Rwanda but not in Tanzania or Uganda, and I found that distribution details can normally be extrapolated from the maps of neighbouring countries. Be aware that the descriptive detail is succinct and many of the illustrations are misleading

Williams, J & Arlott, N *Field Guide to the Birds of East Africa* Collins, 1980. As with the older Collins mammal field guides, Williams' was for years the standard field guide to the region, and is still widely mentioned in travel literature. Unfortunately, it feels rather dated today: less than half the birds in the region are illustrated, several are not even described, and the bias is strongly towards common Kenyan birds.

Zimmerman et al *Birds of Kenya and Northern Tanzania* Russell Friedman Books, 1996. This monumentally handsome hardback tome is arguably the finest field guide to any African territory. The geographical limitations with regard to Rwanda are obvious, but its wealth of descriptive and ecological detail and superb illustrations make it an excellent secondary source. A lighter and cheaper but less detailed paperback version was published in 1999.

Others

Eckhart, Gene & Lanjouw, Annette *Mountain Gorillas: Biology, Conservation, and Coexistence* (Johns Hopkins University Press, 2008). Lovely pictures and authoritative but accessible text make this the perfect layperson's introduction to every aspect of the natural history and conservation of mountain gorilla.

Fossey, Dian *Gorillas in the Mist* Hodder & Stoughton, 1983. Enjoyable and massively informative, Fossey's landmark book is recommended without reservation to anybody going gorilla tracking in the Parc des Volcans.

Goodall, Jane *Through A Window* Houghton Mifflin, 1991. Subtitled *My Thirty Years with the Chimpanzees of Gombe*, this is one of several highly readable books by Jane Goodall about the longest ongoing study of wild primates in the world. Set in Tanzania, but obvious pre-trip reading for anybody intending to track chimps in Nyungwe.

Kingdon, Jonathan *Island Africa* Collins, 1990. This highly readable and award-winning tome about evolution in ecological 'islands' such as deserts and montane forests is recommended to anybody who wants to place the natural history of Nyungwe and the Virungas in a continental context.

Mowat, Farley *Woman in the Mists* Futura, 1987. An excellent biography of the controversial Dian Fossey, one which leans so heavily on her own journals that parts are almost autobiography.

Rouse, Andy (in partnership with World Primate Safaris) *Gorillas: Living on the Edge* Electric Squirrel Publishing, 2011. Over 100 beautiful, powerful and appealing images of Rwanda's gorillas by award-winning photographer Rouse, with a personal commentary adding depth and insight. A quarter of profits go towards supporting conservation projects in Rwanda.

Stuart, Chris & Tilde *Africa's Vanishing Wildlife* Southern Books, 1996. An informative and pictorially strong introduction to the endangered and vulnerable mammals of Africa, this book combines coffee-table production with impassioned and erudite text.

Weber, Bill & Vedder, Amy *In the Kingdom of Gorillas* Simon & Schuster, 2002. This superb and immensely readable account of the authors' pioneering conservation work in Volcanoes and Nyungwe National Parks featured as one of *BBC Wildlife*'s 'most influential books from the past 40 years of wildlife publishing' in 2003.

Background to the genocide

Barnett, Michael *Eyewitness to a Genocide: The United Nations and Rwanda* Cornell University, 2002. Tracing the history of the UN's involvement with Rwanda, Barnett argues that it did bear some moral responsibility for the genocide. A clear and factual study, also covering the warnings raised by the genocide and the question of whether it is possible to build wholly moral institutions.

Dallaire, Lt Gen Roméo *Shake Hands with the Devil: the failure of humanity in Rwanda* Arrow Books, 2004. Dallaire was force commander of the UN Assistance Mission for Rwanda at the time of the genocide. This angry, moving and deeply human book describes the impossible situation he faced, caught up in a nightmare of killing and terror and yet denied the men and the operational freedom he needed in order to quell it. We see the unfolding of the genocide, in all its aspects, from the perspective of probably the one man who, had he been better heeded and supported, could have lessened its effects.

Gourevitch, Philip *We wish to inform you that tomorrow we will be killed with our families* Picador, 1998. Subtitled 'Stories from Rwanda', this winner of the *Guardian* First Book Award is war reporting of the highest order. Blending starkly factual narrative with human anecdotes and observations, Gourevitch paints on a broad canvas and the picture he creates is unforgettable. He shows us 'little people' caught up in unstoppable horrors – and reaching great heights of heroism.

Keane, Fergal *Season of Blood – a Rwandan Journey* Penguin, 1995. Keane's prose is always impeccable. Here he blends factual narrative and analysis with spontaneous emotion in such a way that the reader is both moved and informed in a single phrase. As a BBC correspondent, he was travelling around Rwanda – among the killers and among the victims – as the genocide spread countrywide. His reports at the time brought home the extent of the human tragedy and their essence is preserved in this book, which won the 1995 Orwell Prize.

Kinzer, Stephen *A Thousand Hills: Rwanda's Rebirth and the Man Who Dreamed it* John Wiley & Sons 2008. This is one of the few books to deal with post-genocide Rwanda, focussing primarily on and quoting heavily from President Paul Kagame (who granted the author several exclusive interviews), and while it inevitably has the slightly partisan flavour endemic to authorised biographies, it also provides a worthwhile and insightful overview of Rwanda's recovery over the past 15 years.

Leave None to Tell the Story African Rights Watch, 1999. Another painfully comprehensive account, full of personal testimonies based on Rwandan government records, showing how ordinary administrative structures and practices were used as mechanisms of murder. It describes the opposition to and termination of the killing and how it was crushed, while survivors relate how they resisted and escaped. Using diplomatic and court documents, the survey shows what might have been the result had the international reaction been swifter and more determined.

Melvern, L R *A People Betrayed – the Role of the West in Rwanda's Genocide* Zed Books, 2000, revised 2nd edition 2009. Linda Melvern's investigative study of the international background to Rwanda's genocide contains a full account of how the tragedy unfolded. Documents held in Kigali, and previously unpublished accounts of secret UN Security council deliberations in New York, reveal a shocking sequence of events, and the failure of governments, organisations and individuals who could – had they opted to do so – have prevented the genocide. Described by Lt General Roméo Dallaire (see above) as 'the best overall account of the background to the genocide, and the failure to prevent it… She discovered so much that we did not know.

Melvern, L R *Conspiracy to Murder: the Rwandan Genocide* Verso 2004; extended paperback edition 2006. This powerful sequel to *A People Betrayed* (above) continues the investigation, drawing on a vast amount of new material including documents abandoned by the *génocidaires* when they fled Rwanda. It also features a confession by the interim prime minister, Jean Kambanda, who pled guilty in the International Criminal Tribunal for Rwanda to the crime of genocide, describing how Rwanda's full state apparatus was mobilised to carry out the killing.

Prunier, Gérard *The Rwanda Crisis – History of a Genocide* Hurst & Company, 1998. This painstakingly researched history of the Rwandan genocide, full of personal anecdotes and individual stories, describes with icy clarity the composition of the time bomb that began ticking long before its explosion in 1994. Prunier presents the genocide as part of a deadly logic, a plan hatched for political and economic motives, rather than the result of ancient hatred. He helps the reader to understand not only Rwanda's genocide but also the complexities of modern conflict in general.

Rusesabagina, Paul *An Ordinary Man: The True Story Behind Hotel Rwanda* Bloomsbury, 2007. This is a powerful and readable, but very controversial, autobiographic account of the genocide, written by the former manager of Hotel des Mille Collines, who claims to have sheltered more than a thousand refuges at the height of the killing.

Rwanda – Death, Despair and Defiance African Rights, London, 1995. This 1,200-page compilation by the UK-based organisation African Rights is a painfully thorough and detailed account of the genocide and its effect on Rwanda's people – the careful preparations, the identities of the killers and their accomplices, the massacres, the attacks on churches, schools and hospitals, and the aftermath. Victims tell their own stories and those of their families, and the horror and immensity of the slaughter are highlighted by the simplicity of their narratives. The impact is powerful, sometimes overwhelming. The index enables the reader to discover easily what happened in any particular area or village.

Sibomana, André *Hope for Rwanda* Pluto Press, 1999. In this very personal account, subtitled *Conversations with Laure Guilbert and Hervé Deguine*, the speaker describes the unfolding of the genocide, and his own experiences, with impressive fairness, clarity and lack of accusation. A touching and informative book by a remarkable man.

Miscellaneous

Crisafulli, Patricia & Redmond, Andrea *Rwanda, Inc.* (Palgrave MacMillan, 2012) Subtitled 'How a Devastated Nation Became an Economic Model for the Developing World', this soon-to-be-published titles promises to be an intriguing – and unusually upbeat – account of post-genocide Rwanda's achievements.

Halsey Carr, R & Howard Halsey, A *Land of a Thousand Hills* Viking, 1999. Rosamond Halsey Carr moved to Rwanda as a young bride in 1949 and stayed until her death in 2006. She watched the decline of colonialism, the problems of independence and the growing violence. When the genocide started she was evacuated by the American Embassy but returned four months later, and began turning an old pyrethrum drying-house on her flower plantation into a home for genocide orphans, which still functions today. This very readable and moving book chronicles the extraordinary life of an extraordinary woman, in the country she loved and made her home.

Lewis, Jerome & Knight, Judy *The Twa of Rwanda* World Rainforest Movement (UK), 1996. The Twa are the smallest 'ethnic' group in Rwanda. This report, published by the World Rainforest Movement in co-operation with the International Work Group for Indigenous Affairs (Denmark) and Survival International (France), traces their history, highlights their current impoverished situation, quotes their opinions about their past and future, and allows them to express their fears and aspirations. It also shows the dilemma faced by African governments as they try to build national unity while respecting cultural diversity.

Parkin, Gaile *Baking Cakes in Kigali* (Atlantic Books 2009) This bestselling novel tells the story of Angel Tungaraza, a philosophical baker from Tanzania who settles in Rwanda with her husband and five orphans after the genocide. It has drawn several comparisons to the popular Botswana-set series No.1 Ladies Detective Agency series.

Stassen, Jean-Philippe *Déogratias* Aire Libre, Dupuis (Belgium) 2000. If you can read at least some French, this 80-page *bande dessinée* (graphic novel) tells the story of a young Hutu who killed during the genocide and how this, together with drink, destroyed him. With skill and humanity, the creator succeeds in 'telling the untellable' and producing a powerful document.

A2

The best **map** available outside Rwanda is currently *Rwanda and Burundi*, scale 1:400,000, published in Canada by International Travel Maps (*www.itmb.com*). There is also *Tanzania, Rwanda and Burundi*, scale 1:1,500,000, published by Nelles Guides & Maps (*www.nelles-verlag.de*).

WEBSITES For up-to-the-minute news reports from Rwanda and elsewhere in Africa the most comprehensive site is probably **www.allafrica.com**. Follow links to Rwanda. The website of the Rwandan newspaper *The New Times* has a range of local news items not picked up elsewhere: **www.newtimes.co.rw**.

For regular updates and reader feedback covering all aspects of travel to Rwanda, visit **http://updates.bradtguides.com/rwanda**, overseen by Philip Briggs as an interactive update service for travellers, volunteers and service providers in Rwanda.

A good site for checking the latest currency exchange rate (not all include the Rwandan franc) is **www.xe.com**. Conditions in Rwanda – as elsewhere in Africa – may change, so as a precaution, before travelling, always check the Foreign Office website **www.fco.gov**.

uk/travel, or that of the US State Department: **www.travel.state.gov.** For up-to-date visa requirements (and online application) visit **www.migration.gov.rw**.

Four comprehensive websites on Rwanda are **www.rwandaembassy.org** (set up by the Rwandan Embassy in Washington, DC); the well organised **www.rwandagateway. org**; that of the Rwandan Embassy in London, **www.ambarwanda.org.uk**; and that of RDB (Rwanda Development Board), www.rdb.rw and **www.rwandatourism.com**. All have numerous links and between them cover a wide range of topics, including Rwanda's history, geography, economy, business potential and tourism. On the whole the essentials are up to date although some sections haven't been touched for a while at the time of writing. Another (self-explanatory) tourism site is **www.rwanda-golf.com**.

For more-or-less current phone numbers (and sometimes addresses) of hotels and other businesses in Rwanda, try **www.rwandaphonebook.com**.

The website of KIST (Kigali Institute of Science and Technology) reports interestingly on small-scale development and appropriate technology: **www.kist.ac.rw**. The site of the UN International Criminal Tribunal for Rwanda, **www.ictr.org**, has details of the current status of genocide criminals and trials. Human Rights Watch on **www.hrw.org** carries news of Rwanda, as does Amnesty International **www.amnesty.org**. For news relating to the genocide, visit the Aegis Trust's website **www.aegistrust.org**.

For specific out-of-print books on Rwanda (and any other subject under the sun), try the unmatchable **www.usedbooksearch.co.uk**. Other good sources of books, new and used, are **www.amazon.co.uk** and **www.amazon.com**.

Bradt Travel Guides

www.bradtguides.com

Africa

Access Africa: Safaris for People with Limited Mobility	£16.99
Africa Overland	£16.99
Algeria	£15.99
Angola	£18.99
Botswana	£16.99
Burkina Faso	£17.99
Cameroon	£15.99
Cape Verde	£15.99
Congo	£16.99
Eritrea	£15.99
Ethiopia	£17.99
Ethiopia Highlights	£15.99
Ghana	£15.99
Kenya Highlights	£15.99
Madagascar	£16.99
Madagascar Highlights	£15.99
Malawi	£15.99
Mali	£14.99
Mauritius, Rodrigues & Réunion	£16.99
Mozambique	£15.99
Namibia	£15.99
Nigeria	£17.99
North Africa: Roman Coast	£15.99
Rwanda	£16.99
São Tomé & Príncipe	£14.99
Seychelles	£16.99
Sierra Leone	£16.99
Somaliland	£15.99
South Africa Highlights	£15.99
Sudan	£16.99
Swaziland	£15.99
Tanzania	£17.99
Tanzania, Northern	£14.99
Uganda	£16.99
Zambia	£18.99
Zanzibar	£14.99
Zimbabwe	£15.99

The Americas and the Caribbean

Alaska	£15.99
Amazon Highlights	£15.99
Argentina	£16.99
Bahia	£14.99
Cayman Islands	£14.99
Chile Highlights	£15.99
Colombia	£17.99
Dominica	£15.99
Grenada, Carriacou & Petite Martinique	£15.99
Guyana	£15.99
Haiti	£16.99
Nova Scotia	£14.99
Panama	£14.99
Paraguay	£15.99
Peru Highlights	£15.99
Turks & Caicos Islands	£14.99
Uruguay	£15.99
USA by Rail	£15.99
Venezuela	£16.99
Yukon	£14.99

British Isles

Britain from the Rails	£14.99
Bus-Pass Britain	£15.99
Eccentric Britain	£15.99
Eccentric Cambridge	£9.99
Eccentric London	£14.99
Eccentric Oxford	£9.99
Sacred Britain	£16.99
Slow: Cornwall	£14.99
Slow: Cotswolds	£14.99
Slow: Devon & Exmoor	£14.99
Slow: Dorset	£14.99
Slow: Norfolk & Suffolk	£14.99
Slow: North Yorkshire	£14.99
Slow: Northumberland	£14.99
Slow: Sussex & South Downs National Park	£14.99

Europe

Abruzzo	£16.99
Albania	£16.99
Armenia	£15.99
Azores	£14.99
Baltic Cities	£14.99
Belarus	£15.99
Bosnia & Herzegovina	£15.99
Bratislava	£9.99
Budapest	£9.99
Croatia	£15.99
Cross-Channel France: Nord-Pas de Calais	£13.99
Cyprus see North Cyprus	
Dresden	£7.99
Estonia	£14.99
Faroe Islands	£15.99
Flanders	£15.99
Georgia	£15.99
Greece: The Peloponnese	£14.99
Hungary	£15.99
Iceland	£15.99
Istria	£13.99
Kosovo	£15.99
Lapland	£15.99
Lille	£9.99
Lithuania	£14.99
Luxembourg	£14.99
Macedonia	£16.99
Malta & Gozo	£12.99
Montenegro	£14.99
North Cyprus	£13.99
Serbia	£15.99
Slovakia	£14.99
Slovenia	£13.99
Spitsbergen	£16.99
Switzerland Without a Car	£14.99
Transylvania	£15.99
Ukraine	£15.99

Middle East, Asia and Australasia

Bangladesh	£17.99
Borneo	£17.99
Eastern Turkey	£16.99
Iran	£15.99
Iraq: Then & Now	£15.99
Israel	£15.99
Jordan	£16.99
Kazakhstan	£16.99
Kyrgyzstan	£16.99
Lake Baikal	£15.99
Lebanon	£15.99
Maldives	£15.99
Mongolia	£16.99
North Korea	£14.99
Oman	£15.99
Palestine	£15.99
Shangri-La: A Travel Guide to the Himalayan Dream	£14.99
Sri Lanka	£15.99
Syria	£15.99
Taiwan	£16.99
Tibet	£17.99
Yemen	£14.99

Wildlife

Antarctica: A Guide to the Wildlife	£15.99
Arctic: A Guide to Coastal Wildlife	£16.99
Australian Wildlife	£14.99
Central & Eastern European Wildlife	£15.99
Chinese Wildlife	£16.99
East African Wildlife	£19.99
Galápagos Wildlife	£16.99
Madagascar Wildlife	£16.99
New Zealand Wildlife	£14.99
North Atlantic Wildlife	£16.99
Pantanal Wildlife	£16.99
Peruvian Wildlife	£15.99
Southern African Wildlife	£19.99
Sri Lankan Wildlife	£15.99

Pictorials and other guides

100 Alien Invaders	£16.99
100 Animals to See Before They Die	£16.99
100 Bizarre Animals	£16.99
Eccentric Australia	£12.99
Northern Lights	£6.99
Swimming with Dolphins, Tracking Gorillas	£15.99
The Northwest Passage	£14.99
Tips on Tipping	£6.99
Total Solar Eclipse 2012 & 2013	£6.99
Wildlife & Conservation Volunteering: The Complete Guide	£13.99

Travel literature

A Glimpse of Eternal Snows	£11.99
A Tourist in the Arab Spring	£9.99
Connemara Mollie	£9.99
Fakirs, Feluccas and Femmes Fatales	£9.99
Madagascar: The Eighth Continent	£11.99
The Marsh Lions	£9.99
The Two-Year Mountain	£9.99
The Urban Circus	£9.99
Up the Creek	£9.99

Index

Page numbers in **bold** refer to major entries; those in *italics* indicate maps

INDEX OF ADVERTISERS